Boundaries, Communities and State-Making in West Africa

CW01024116

Border regions are often considered to be the neglected margins. In this book, Paul Nugent argues that through a comparison of the Senegambia and the trans-Volta (Ghana/Togo), we can see that the geographical margins have shaped notional centres at least as much as the reverse. Through a study of three centuries of history, this book demonstrates that states were forged through an extended process of converting a topography of settled states and slaving frontiers into colonial borders. It argues that post-colonial states and larger social contracts have been configured very differently as a consequence. It underscores the impact on regional dynamics and the phenomenon of peripheral urbanism. Nugent also addresses the manner in which a variegated sense of community has been forged amongst Mandinka, Jola, Ewe and Agotime populations who have both shaped and been shaped by the border. This is an exercise in reciprocal comparison and shuttles between scales, from the local and the particular to the national and the regional.

PAUL NUGENT is Professor of Comparative African History and is located in both the Centre of African Studies and the School of History, Classics and Archaeology at the University of Edinburgh. He has published extensively on borders, but also on Ghanaian politics, post-colonial African history and the history of South African wine. His books include *Africa since Independence: A Comparative History*, second edition (2012) and *Smugglers, Secessionists and Loyal Citizens on the Ghana–Togo Frontier: The Lie of the Borderlands since 1914* (2002). Nugent was the co-editor of the *Journal of Modern African Studies* (Cambridge University Press) from September 2012 until September 2017, alongside Leo Villalón, and has since joined the editorial board of this journal. He is also the founder and chair of the African Borderlands Research Network (ABORNE).

African Studies Series

The African Studies series, founded in 1968, is a prestigious series of monographs, general surveys, and textbooks on Africa covering history, political science, anthropology, economics, and ecological and environmental issues. The series seeks to publish work by senior scholars as well as the best new research.

Boundaries, Communities and State-Making in West Africa

The Centrality of the Margins

Paul Nugent

University of Edinburgh

CAMBRIDGE
UNIVERSITY PRESS

CAMBRIDGE
UNIVERSITY PRESS

University Printing House, Cambridge CB2 8BS, United Kingdom

One Liberty Plaza, 20th Floor, New York, NY 10006, USA

477 Williamstown Road, Port Melbourne, VIC 3207, Australia

314–321, 3rd Floor, Plot 3, Splendor Forum, Jasola District Centre,
New Delhi – 110025, India

79 Anson Road, #06–04/06, Singapore 079906

Cambridge University Press is part of the University of Cambridge.

It furthers the University's mission by disseminating knowledge in the pursuit of
education, learning, and research at the highest international levels of excellence.

www.cambridge.org
Information on this title: www.cambridge.org/9781107020689
DOI: 10.1017/9781139105828

First published 2019

Printed in the United Kingdom by TJ International Ltd, Padstow Cornwall

A catalogue record for this publication is available from the British Library.

Library of Congress Cataloging-in-Publication Data
Names: Nugent, Paul, 1962– author.
Title: Boundaries, communities, and state-making in West Africa : the centrality
    of the margins / Paul Nugent.
Other titles: African studies series.
Description: New York, NY : Cambridge University Press, 2019. | Series: African
    studies series
Identifiers: LCCN 2018061494 | ISBN 9781107020689 (hardback : alk. paper) |
    ISBN 9781107622500 (pbk. : alk. paper)
Subjects: LCSH: Africa, West–Politics and government. | Africa, West–History. |
    Borderlands–Africa, West. | Africa, West–Boundaries.
Classification: LCC DT475 .N84 2019 | DDC 320.96609–dc23
    LC record available at https://lccn.loc.gov/2018061494

ISBN 978-1-107-02068-9 Hardback
ISBN 978-1-107-62250-0 Paperback

For Kwally and Jasmine:
your turn!

Contents

Figures

Maps

Tables

Acknowledgements

It is chastening to have to confront the reality that this book has taken a decade and a half to see the light of day. Part of the reason is that the focus shifted with the passage of time, and another is that the manuscript suffered from competition with a very different project on the history of South African wine. At times, it has felt like a distinct burden. For a multiplicity of reasons, I am glad to finally wrap it up and send it on its way.

Not surprisingly, I have incurred innumerable debts. Some of these relate to funding bodies who funded different aspects of the research. It all began with a University of Edinburgh Development Trust grant back in 2000. That same year, I received a Nuffield Foundation small grant for a project on "Divided Border Communities of West Africa: A Comparison of the Senegal/Gambia and Ghana–Togo Borderlands". At about the same time, I received a grant from the Carnegie Trust for the Universities of Scotland for closely related research. And then in 2004 I was awarded a grant by the British Academy for another project entitled "Livelihoods and Identities in West African Boundary Communities: A Comparison of the Ghana–Togo and Senegal–Gambian Borderlands". These small, interconnected awards enabled me to conduct archival research in Banjul, Dakar, Accra and Lomé and to carry out fieldwork along both sets of borders. In subsequent years, as I became more engrossed in issues of state-making, I sustained elements of the research with internal grants from the University of Edinburgh and often from my own pocket. I owe the external funding agencies an apology for the length of time it has taken for the final results to emerge. But I also thank them for providing me with the building blocks for a project that now looks decidedly different to the research I initially applied to fund. It has also enabled me to think my way through to my next piece of substantial research. Since 2016, I have been leading an Advanced Grant project funded by the European Research Council (ERC), entitled *African Governance and Space: Transport Corridors, Border Towns and Port Cities in Transition (AFRIGOS)* (ADG-2014–670851). In the early phases of this project, I have been able to top up some of the research relating to border towns, some of which is reflected in Chapters 12 and 13.

I acknowledge the assistance of staff at various archives for their assistance over the years. I owe a particular debt to Gabriel Sanyang, then of the Gambian National Archives, whose assistance in the reading room was invaluable. The field research would have been impossible without the assistance of two individuals. The first is Yusupha Jassey, who was introduced to me by Gabriel when I had hit an obstacle in conducting fieldwork. Yusupha afforded me a deeper insight into the dynamics of Darsilami as a border town, but he also took me to numerous settlements in the Gambia and the Casamance where we conducted interviews and had less formal interactions. The second is Moses Agbovi of Agotime-Kpetoe who was introduced to me by my oldest friend in Ghana, Harry Asimah, back in 2001. Harry and Moses had served together in the People's Defence Committees, and later the Committees for the Defence of the Revolution. Much of their collaboration entailed border surveillance in Agotime and surrounding areas during the 1980s, and I learned much from my discussions with them. Over several years, Moses and myself conducted interviews in just about every Agotime settlement in Togo and Ghana. It was when I was returning for a fresh round of fieldwork in July 2004 that I learned that Moses had tragically been killed on the roadside a few days previously – and by the very school bus that he was scheduled to commission. I only wish Moses had lived to see the final product.

Also in Kpetoe, I have benefited from the insights of Nene Nuer Keteku III, the Konor of Agotime, and Nene Ahortor Makaku V. In recent years, Nene Dapaah VI has been particularly helpful in detailing how the different sections of Kpetoe relate to one another and in placing *Agbamevoza* in its historical context. I also thank lawyer Solomon Kwami Tetteh and Kofi Baku for talking me through the Adaklu-Agotime land case and providing access to key legal documents. Some of my most productive moments have unfolded while sitting under the tree (now alas no more!) at 'Buggie Hotel', watching motorcycles and taxis refuel while writing up fieldnotes and partaking of a cold Star. My long overdue thanks go to Buggie and Nelson. Further down, and on the other side of the road, Assih Batoubaha helped me to understand Agotime from the perspective of a Togolese *policier* stationed in Wodome. My second oldest friend in Ghana, by a matter of months, is Mohammed Abukari who has provided me with countless leads and introductions to people working in the Customs, Excise and Preventive Service (CEPS). His friendship, and that of Meri and the family, has meant a great deal to me over the years. In Accra, I would also like to acknowledge Mrs Emily Asiedu ('Auntie') who has afforded a home from home in Kokomlemle over many years, as well as the many researchers who have passed through its doors. Nana Soglo Allo IV, the current President of the Volta Region House of Chiefs, has been a good friend and matchless informant on chieftaincy matters for many years now.

A number of individuals have graciously shared material, dug stuff out of archives and generally offered insights that turned out to be helpful. I would especially like to thank Brigadier-General Stanley Alloh, Ernest Aubee, Nico Fru Awasom, Gareth Austin, Linn Axelsson, Daniel Bach, Alice Bellagamba, Thomas Biershenk, Lynne Brydon, Brenda Chalfin, Jos Damen, Ton Dietz, Maggie Dwyer, Setri Dzivenu, Edward Demba, Ulf Engel, Didier Fassin, Vincent Foucher, Nicoué Gayibor, Jan-Bart Gewald, Paolo Gaibazzi, Mariama Khan, Dennis Laumann, Benjamin Lawrance, Robin Law, Carola Lentz, Donna Maier, Xerxes Malki, Yves Marguerat, Andreas Mehler, Peter Skalnik, David Skinner, Kate Skinner, Silke Strickrodt, Isabella Soi, Dmitri van den Bersselaar, Meera Venkatachalam, Olivier Walther and the late Jan-Georg Deutsch. At the start of the project, I learned about Agotime weaving from Malika Kraamer who was finishing up her doctoral research when I arrived in Kpetoe and later shared a copy of her thesis. I owe a special debt to Ole Justesen who retrieved every reference to Agotime in the Danish records, which he was editing at that point, and pointed me in the direction of the important Thonning maps.

Since 2007, the African Borderlands Research Network (ABORNE) has afforded an incredibly fruitful forum for collaboration with respect to all things relating to borders. Much of what appears in the book has previously been aired in ABORNE workshops and on conference panels. I would like to especially thank fellow ABORNistas: Tony Asiwaju, David Coplan, Gregor Dobler, Pierre Engelbert, Amanda Hammar, Allen Howard, Thomas Hüsken, Georg Klute, Camille Lefebvre, Gillian Mathys, Bill Miles, Wafula Okumu, Tim Raeymaekers, Cristina Udelsmann Rodrigues, Olivier Walther, Wolfgang Zeller, Werner Zips and Manuela Zips-Mairitsch. More generally, I would like to thank fellow borderlands scholars and practitioners alike: Mohamadou Abdoul, Karine Bennafla, Hastings Donnan, Willie Eselebor, Gilbert Khadiagala, Kinza Jawara-N'Jai, Elaine Peña, Aboukakr Tandia and Chris Vaughan. I have finished up this book while embarking on a fresh intellectual quest with Wolfgang Zeller, Jose-Maria Muñoz, Sidy Cissokho, Hugh Lamarque and Isabella Soi. In Edinburgh and vaguely linked locations, I would like to acknowledge the continuing support of Ian Duffield, Ama Akuamoah, Gerhard Anders, Alan Barnard, Barbara Bompani, Sarah-Jane Cooper-Knock, Sara Dorman, Joost Fontein, Jamie Furniss, Emma Hunter, Steve Kerr, Kenneth King, Francesca Locatelli, Zoe Marks, Tom Molony and Tom Salter. Tom McCaskie, Fred Cooper and John Lonsdale deserve particular thanks for having supported my career over some years now.

Over 2015/16, I was fortunate enough to serve one year as a member of the Institute for Advanced Study (IAS), a truly unique haven of intellectual engagement located on the highly productive margins of Princeton. It was while I was at IAS that I rewrote large sections of the book (effectively for the third time) and finally found a framing that I was happy with. I would especially like to thank Didier Fassin for creating such a conducive academic environment and Donne Petito for all the administrative support. Kirsty Venanzi in the IAS library ensured that my table was constantly replenished with books on borders and on state-making in disparate regions of the world. I should also express my gratitude to other members of my cohort for their varied insights on the theme of "Borders and Boundaries", and especially the denizens of the braai: Duncan McCargo, Basile Ndjio, Tugba Basaran, Elena Gadjanova and Linda Bosniak. It was while doing justice to some well-marinated lamb chops that I first fell in with Laavy Kathiravelu, who was then a Fung Fellow at Princeton University. My time would not have been anywhere near as productive, and certainly not as enjoyable, were it not for the positive presence of Laavy. I was also extremely fortunate to have Raya Cohen and Luca Peliti as my highly sociable neighbours. I owe a special thanks to the unique Isabella Soi, my sometime research collaborator and co-author, who read many of the draft chapters when I was really toiling and counselled me as to whether I was making any sense. If I remain incomprehensible, it is at least partly Isabella's fault! I have also benefited from some very wise counsel from a couple of anonymous readers designated by Cambridge University Press. Finally, Maria Marsh at The Press has been endlessly understanding about slippages in the deadlines. I am relieved that I am finally able to honour our agreement.

Finally, I would like to acknowledge members of my extended family and oldest friends who, it has to be admitted, have displayed far more interest in the wine book than the current offering. But first things first. So thanks go also to Diddy and Marc Skinner, Tony Nugent and Daniela Vignazia, San Nugent, Mike Nugent and Mel Andrews, Aoife Nugent, Eliane Nugent Ngoué, Fiona de Beer and Rod Baker, David and Carol Taylor and Margaret Howie and Dale Whitfield. The book is dedicated to Kwally and Jasmine who have had to put up with my countless absences over the years. Hopefully, there will come a point in their lives when this won't seem so ... well, "boring"!

The following material is reproduced with permission from the publishers:

> Table 4.1 from Leigh Gardner, *Taxing Colonial Africa* (Oxford University Press, 2012), table 4.1, p. 64.
> Table 11.2 from Lucie Colvin Phillips, "The Senegambia Confederation", in Delgado and Jammeh (ed.), The *Political Economy of Senegal under Structural Adjustment* (Praeger, 1991), table 12.1, p. 181; and from Stephen Golub and Ahmadou Aly Mbaye, "National

trade policies and smuggling in Africa: the case of the Gambia and Senegal", *World Development* 37 (3) 2008, table 2, p. 602.
and Tables 11.5 and 12.1 from the Africapolis database (SWAC/ OECD)

The cover photograph of Nene Akoto Sah VII of Agotime-Kpetoe is reproduced with the kind permission of Philippe J. Kradolfer.

Abbreviations

ADC	Assistant District Commissioner (Gold Coast)
AEC	All-Ewe Conference (Gold Coast, British Togoland and French Togoland)
AFRC	Armed Forces Revolutionary Council (Ghana)
ANCT	Association des Chefs Traditionnels du Togo
AOF	l'Afrique Occidentale Française
ARPS	Aborigines Rights Protection Society (British West Africa)
BDS	Bloc Démocratique Sénégalais
CDRs	Committees for the Defence of the Revolution (Ghana)
CDW	Colonial Development and Welfare (Britain)
CEP	Commissioner of the Eastern Province (Gold Coast)
CEPS	Customs, Excise and Preventive Service (Ghana)
CFAO	Compagnie Française de l'Afrique de l'Ouest
CFDT	Compagnie Française de Développement des Fibres Textiles
CMB	Cocoa Marketing Board (Ghana)
CNF	Compagnie Niger-France
CNTS	Confédération Nationale des Travailleurs du Sénégal
CPP	Convention People's Party (CPP) (Gold Coast/Ghana)
CPS	Customs Preventive Service (Gold Coast)
CRAD	Centres Régionaux d'Assistance et Développement (Senegal)
CUT	Comité de l'Unité Togolaise (French Togoland/Togo)
DC	District Commissioner (Gold Coast)
DCE	District Chief Executive (Ghana)
ECOWAS	Economic Community of West African States
ERP	Economic Recovery Programme (Gambia)
FIDES	Fonds d'Investissement pour le Développement Economique et Social (France)
FPC	Food Production Corporation (Ghana)
GBA	Ghana Bar Association
GCU	Gambia Co-Operative Union
GES	Groupements Economiques du Sénégal

GNTC	Ghana National Trading Corporation (Ghana)
GOMB	Gambia Oilseeds Marketing Board
GPMB	Gambia Produce Marketing Board
GRA	Ghana Revenue Authority
GTP	Ghana Textile Printing Company
IMF	International Monetary Fund
JFM	June 4 Movement (Ghana)
JTP	Juapong Textiles (Ghana)
MFDC	Mouvement des Forces Démocratiques de Casamance
MOJA-G	Movement for Justice in Africa – the Gambia
NAP	New Agricultural Policy (Senegal)
NDC	National Democratic Congress (Ghana)
NIC	National Investigation Committee (Ghana)
NLC	National Liberation Council (Ghana)
NLM	National Liberation Movement (Gold Coast)
NORRIP	Northern Region Integrated Project (Ghana)
NPP	Northern People's Party (Gold Coast)
NPP	New Patriotic Party (Ghana)
NRC	National Redemption Council (Ghana)
NTC	National Trading Corporation (Gambia)
NUGS	National Union of Ghanaian Students
OCA	Office de la Commercialisation Agricole (Senegal)
OFY	Operation Feed Yourself (Ghana)
OMVG	Organisation Pour La Mise en Valeur du Fleuve Gambie
OMVS	Organisation Pour La Mise en Valeur du Fleuve Sénégal
ONCAD	Office National de Coopération et d'Assistance Pour le Développement (Senegal)
OTR	Office Togolais des Recettes
PAI	Parti Africain de l'Indépendance
PDCs	People's Defence Committees (Ghana)
PDS	Parti Démocratique Sénégalais
PNDC	Provisional National Defence Council
PP	Progress Party (Ghana)
PPP	People's Progressive Party (Gambia)
PS	Parti Socialiste
PTP	Parti Togolais du Progrès
RC	Regional Commissioner (Ghana)
RPT	Rassemblement du Peuple Togolaise
SCOA	Société Commerciale Ouest Africaine
SFC	State Farms Corporation (Ghana)
SFIO	Section Française de l'International Ouvrière
SGMC	State Gold Mining Corporation (Ghana)

SIP	Sociétés Indigènes de Prévoyance (Senegal)
SMC	Supreme Military Council (Ghana)
SODEFITEX	Société de Développement des Fibres Textiles (Senegal)
SONEPI	Société Nationale d'Etudes et de Promotion Industrielle (Senegal)
TC	Togoland Congress (British Togoland)
TOLIMO	Movement for the Liberation of Western Togoland
TU	Togoland Union (British Togoland)
TUC	Trade Union Congress (Ghana)
TVT	Trans-Volta Togoland (Gold Coast, British Togoland)
UAC	United Africa Company
UCPN	Union des Chefs et Populations du Nord-Togo
UGCC	United Gold Coast Convention
UGFC	United Ghana Farmers' Council
UN	United Nations
UNACOIS	Union Nationale des Commerçants et Industriels du Sénégal
UNHCR	United Nations High Commission for Refugees
UNIGES	Union des Groupements Economiques du Sénégal
UNIGOV	Union Government (Ghana)
UNTS	Union Nationale des Travailleurs Sénégalais
UP	United Party (Gambia, Ghana)
UPS	l'Union Progressiste Sénégalaise
URADEP	Upper Region Agricultural Development Project (Ghana)
VORADEP	Volta Region Agricultural Development Project (Ghana)
VRPT	Volta Region Public Tribunal (Ghana)
WAPCB	West African Produce Control Board
WDCs	Workers' Defence Committees (Ghana)

1 Centring the Margins

States, Borderlands and Communities

For all their apparent simplicity, maps make evocative statements about the way the world is – embellished, as they are with textual detail, colours, shading and the like. The maps of Africa that European merchants and explorers generated in previous centuries are so captivating to modern eyes precisely because they obviously distort size and shape – and famously fill in the empty spaces in inventive ways.[1] Contemporary cartography is less obviously idiosyncratic, but it harbours its own blind spots and pointed omissions – which becomes painfully obvious when actors are first confronted with the puzzling unfamiliarity of a map depicting a place they know intimately. As others have noted, maps are not innocent things, but have historically been associated with projects of state-making and enclosure in different parts of the world – including those bound up with empire.[2] The seductive power of maps resides in their normalizing character, which serves to close down alternative ways of seeing while authorizing particular modes of doing. In that sense, maps have been constitutive of power relations in their own right.

It follows that maps relate to the real world in a selective and differentiated manner. As James C. Scott indicates, the history of cadastral mapping in Europe was closely bound up with the desire to raise land-based taxes. This entailed striking a balance between the desire for uniformity and comparability, on the one side, and attention to local detail, on the other.[3] Given that most colonial states in Africa did not raise revenues from the land directly, they

---

[1] "So geographers, in Afric maps, With savage pictures fill their gaps, And o'er unhabitable downs, Place elephants for want of towns." from Jonathan Swift's, "On Poetry: A Rhapsody" (1733). For a collected volume that considers African maps in their historical context, see Jeffrey C. Stone (ed.), *Maps and Africa: Proceedings of a Colloquium at the University of Aberdeen, April 1993* (Aberdeen: Aberdeen University African Studies Group, 1994).

[2] Matthew H. Edney, *Mapping an Empire: The Geographical Construction of British India, 1765–1843* (Chicago and London: Chicago University Press, 1997); and James R. Akerman (ed.), *Decolonizing the Map: Cartography from Colony to Nation* (Chicago and London: Chicago University Press, 2017).

[3] James C. Scott, *Seeing Like a State: How Certain Schemes to Improve the Human Condition Have Failed* (New Haven: Yale University Press, 1999), pp. 44–7.

tended to generate maps that were attentive to other kinds of detail.[4] The German Karte Von Togo of 1905, which I will have cause to return to, contains remarkable levels of detail on communal boundaries, farming activity and tree cover, but it never set out to delineate actual farms.[5] This is one reason why (as we will see) its utility in deciding subsequent land cases was rather circumscribed. Colonial maps like this one paid close attention to the location of tracks, roads and rail links embedded within a landscape defined by mountains, forests, rivers and plains: in other words, a set of logistical challenges to be resolved. In the 1950s, state mapping acquired a renewed lease of life in the service of something now called 'development'. Two decades later, as Survey departments tumbled down the administrative hierarchy, they devoted what resources they could muster to tracking the shifting contours of internal administrative borders. Other cartographic work was put on hold, leaving administrators to work as best they could with archaic maps or none at all. Surprisingly perhaps, the mapping of border regions was left in abeyance, storing up multiple ambiguities for the future. At the time of writing, the Survey department in Accra still dispenses sheets from a national map that was produced in the early 1970s at a time when innumerable towns and villages in Ghana did not even exist or were little more than hamlets.[6]

Statistical series manifest a comparable trajectory. In West Africa, as we will see, counting population became a veritable obsession for colonial regimes that had every reason to be concerned about the implications of high levels of cross-border mobility for revenues and labour supplies alike. After independence, government agencies collected specific kinds of economic data – for example, figures for industrial output and urban food price indices – but in a manner that was often based on more or less informed estimation.[7] Population censuses became more episodic and were often distinctly unreliable when they did take place. It speaks volumes that in Africa's largest country, Nigeria, the size of the population has been a matter of guesswork in the absence of

---

[4] Settler colonies like Kenya did produce cadastral maps, but not for revenue reasons.

[5] The twelve sheets of the 1905 map (1:200,000), which is attributed to Paul Sprigade, is available online at the Basel Mission Archives online. The close detail came from the on-the-spot inspection of the German Commissioner, Dr Hans Grüner. See www.oldmapsonline.org/map/bmarchives/27825.

[6] "Ghana" (scale of 1:50,000), map produced jointly by the Government of Ghana and the Government of Canada under the Special Commonwealth African Assistance Programme. It appears to date from 1974.

[7] On Africa's statistical deficit and its consequences, see Morten Jerven, *Poor Numbers: How We Are Misled by African Development Statistics and What to Do About It* (Ithaca: Cornell University Press, 2013), and *Africa: Why Economists Get It Wrong* (London: Zed, 2015), ch. 4.

repeated and reliable census data. In a nutshell, we can discern a correlation between shifting state priorities, and capacities, and the propensity to make particular kinds of maps and to gather specific sorts of statistical data.

Although there is a close relationship between cartography and the exercise of state power, its techniques have been amenable to appropriation and its claims to authenticity have frequently been mimicked by societal actors. What is most revealing about land litigation across Africa is the proliferation of maps that parties have created for themselves, which often weigh more in the legal scales than the official ones. As a recent study by Julie MacArthur indicates, countermapping is nothing new.[8] Somewhere in between state cartography and countermapping lies the construction of mental maps, which typically do not have a didactic purpose and yet reveal an alternative spatial ordering. Mental maps differ from cartographic conventions in that they signal relationships of proximity that do not necessarily correspond to what is depicted on a physical map. Viewed from the geographical margins, which is the particular vantage point of this book, mental maps may include significant details that are entirely absent from state-centric cartography. This would include rotating markets and nodes within religious networks where, in each case, locations are related to each other in more or less stable patterns. When actors pursue their lives in accordance with these mental maps, they may challenge officially sanctioned versions of reality. State actors are conditioned to think in terms of a clearly bounded national space but are confronted by the realities of everyday connectivity, which persist even when the borders are officially closed. The manner in which official cartography ignores such connections – as reflected in roads that seem to trail off into blankness at the edges – has significant implications for even the best-intentioned interventions. For example, the advantages of tackling public health challenges from both sides of a given border might seem rather self-evident. And yet, it is actually rather rare for data to be collected, and to be mapped, across borders in Africa.

This is not primarily a book about maps, or indeed statistics, although they each receive their due in the pages that follow. But it *is* a study of the ways in

---

[8] Julie MacArthur, *Cartography and the Political Imagination: Mapping Community in Colonial Kenya* (Athens: Ohio University Press, 2016), pp. 15–23. Her account has some striking resonances with the account of how pueblos in Mexico at the end of the nineteenth century insisted on generating their own maps to establish communal boundaries, rather than trusting in official cartography. Raymond B. Craib, *Cartographic Mexico: A History of State Fixations and Fugitive Landscapes* (Durham and London: Duke University Press, 2004), pp. 81–7. See also the discussion of countermapping in David McDermott Hughes, *From Enslavement to Environmentalism: Politics on a Southern African Frontier* (Seattle: University of Washington Press, 2006), pp. 130–8.

which states have sought to regulate border spaces and, in turn, how the dynamics unfolding there have helped to shape institutions and governmental practices alike. The subfield of borderlands studies works with mental maps of a sort, given that it is generally concerned not just with the exercise of state authority, but also with the interplay between populations residing on either side of the line. This book was initially conceived of as a contribution to borderlands scholarship but coming from the angle of comparative history. In an earlier monograph on the Ghana/Togo border, I argued for the proactive role of local populations in shaping the borders that ostensibly divided them – by virtue of their investment in smuggling networks and their active enlistment of state agents in disputes over land.[9] I subsequently set out to test the broader applicability of these insights by means of a structured comparison of populations living astride the Ghana/Togo and the Gambia/Senegal (Casamance) borders – on which more later (see Maps 1.1 and 1.2). But as the research took shape, I became increasingly interested in following the impact of border dynamics at some distance from the physical line of separation. Being struck by the very different language and practice of governance in the four countries concerned, I began to consider the possibility that the underlying differences might be rooted in border dynamics. What began as a hunch acquired greater direction as I delved deeper into the archives and followed up leads in the field. At the same time, I became intrigued by the multiple connections between borderlands and other kinds of spaces. This led me into aspects of urban history and, in the process, forced me to rethink my own approach to the study of borders. The upshot was that the revisionist inclinations that drove the initial research agenda have culminated in an altogether more ambitious work – one that is as much about states and cities as it is about borderlands.

In this monograph, I maintain that the geographical margins have been productive in three respects: temporally, in that states were forged in the process of converting frontier zones into colonial borders; structurally, in that fiscal logics, which hinged on regulating border flows, fundamentally underpinned the morphology of colonial states and that of their post-colonial successors; and politically, in that the social contracts that were forged under colonial rule, and which were reconfigured after independence, hinged on the interchange between centres and the geographical margins. At the same time, I have remained loyal to aspects of the original borderlands agenda. I demonstrate that once colonial states became fully operational, they

---

[9] Paul Nugent, *Smugglers, Secessionists and Loyal Citizens on the Ghana–Togo Frontier: The Lie of the Borderlands since 1914* (Oxford and Athens: James Currey and Ohio University Press, 2002).

contributed to a context in which it was possible to rethink the meaning of community. I reveal how strikingly different patterns in the Senegambia and the trans-Volta were closely related to the ways in which states attempted to manage the circulation of commodities and the mobility of people across borders. Some aspects of my argument will seem more contentious than others, and in what follows I set out the parameters in greater detail.

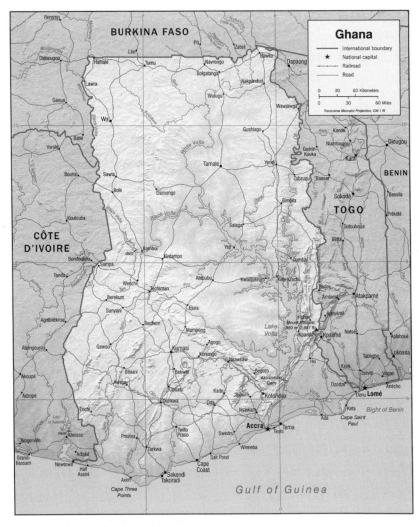

Map 1.1 Ghana and Togo.

Map 1.2 Senegal and Gambia.

The Question of the State: Again

Given the orientation of this book, there would be a strong case for *not* starting with the state. My reasons for doing so are that it makes my agenda that bit easier to convey. The intention is not to privilege 'the state', but rather to put it firmly in its place – in every sense thereof. It is customary to begin such a discussion with a health warning about the perils of reification.[10] In a formulation that has been repeated, or nodded at, by many others down the years, Ralph Miliband once observed "that the state is not a thing, that it does not, as such, exist".[11] The implication is that 'it' cannot be apprehended directly or accorded agency in its own right. The same could, of course, be said of most of what constitutes the core business of the humanities and social

[10] Gilbert M. Joseph and Daniel Nugent, "Popular culture and state formation in revolutionary Mexico", in Gilbert M. Joseph and Daniel Nugent (eds.), *Everyday Forms of State Formation: Revolution and the Negotiation of Rule in Modern Mexico* (Durham and London: Duke University Press, 1994).

[11] Ralph Miliband, *The State in Capitalist Society* (London: Weidenfeld and Nicolson, 1969), p. 49.

sciences, from kinship to gender. But this is, in a sense, the point that is being made. Historians, social scientists and political actors have all talked of 'the state' as if it *was* a discrete entity – or, to use Abrams' terms, something to be respected, smashed or studied.[12] This does, of course, raise the question of why scholars continue to refer to 'the state' in this way – whether that be a single thing or an assortment of things such as the 'failed state', the 'developmental state' or indeed the 'African state'. Part of the reason is that states – which "can accept no rival, no higher or even co-equal power"[13] – have laid claim to an exceptionalism that is generally denied to societal actors, and which has largely stuck. A Foucauldian reading, such as that favoured by Timothy Mitchell, considers the megalithic image of the state as a 'structural effect' of governance practices.[14] Although this begs many questions, it has the one great merit of interrogating in what sense the state really did come first. This is an issue that I take up in detail in the next chapters.

A discussion of borders is never very far from a consideration of state formation. The common presumption is that states define their borders. Indeed, the drawing of a boundary line, followed by its maintenance and surveillance, is considered to be the ultimate assertion of state sovereignty. The standard reference point is the Treaty of Westphalia of 1648 that brought the modern state system into being in Europe. This had been preceded by extended bouts of warfare that are credited with the fashioning of the modern state. Many influential interpretations emphasize the transformative effects of war-making, which stimulated improved techniques of fighting, but also sustained the imperative of building more predictable revenue streams.[15] As methods of revenue extraction improved, so the argument goes, the 'tax state' gave way to the properly 'fiscal state', of which Britain became the most developed, if not

[12] Philip Abrams, "Notes on the difficulty of studying the state (1977)", *Journal of Historical Sociology* 1 (1) 1 March 1988, p. 59. It is revealing that the same complaint is current decades later. See, for example, Douglas Howland and Luise White, "Introduction: sovereignty and the study of states", in Douglas Howland and Luise S. White (eds.), *The State of Sovereignty: Territories, Laws, Populations* (Bloomington: Indiana University Press, 2009), p. 2.

[13] Peter J. Steinberger, *The Idea of the State* (Cambridge: Cambridge University Press, 2009), p. 37.

[14] For Mitchell, trying to define the boundaries of the state is a fruitless exercise because the illusion of the state as something apart is one of effects "of detailed processes of spatial organization, temporal arrangement, functional specification and supervision and surveillance". Timothy Mitchell, "The limits of the state: beyond statist approaches and their critics", *American Political Science Review* 85 (1) 1991, p. 95; and "Society, economy and the state effect", in G. Steinmetz (ed.), *State/Culture: State-Formation after the Cultural Turn* (Ithaca: Cornell University Press, 1999).

[15] Charles Tilly, *Coercion, Capital and European States AD 990–1992* (Oxford: Blackwell, 1990), ch. 3; Richard Bonney (ed.) *The Rise of the Fiscal State in Europe, c.1200–1815* (Oxford: Oxford University Press, 1999). For the British case, see John Brewer, *The Sinews of Power: War, Money and the English State, 1688–1783* (London: Unwin Hyman, 1989).

the original, exemplar.[16] This was reflected in an institutional elaboration of the state (density) and its intrusion into all aspects of life (reach). But as European states maximized their revenues, it is said, they were forced to enter into bargains with sections of their own populations – initially landed elites and urban merchants – about who paid, how much and for what purposes.[17] As Martin Daunton indicates, whether there was compliance or opposition hinged critically on the nurturing of relations of trust. Tax systems functioned best when governments trusted citizens to pay, and when citizens could rely on each other to comply and on government to deploy the resultant revenue wisely.[18] As tax systems became more fully elaborated over the nineteenth century, the number of people who might be counted as fully-fledged – and hence taxable – citizens increased. Moreover, producing cadastral maps, enumerating populations and physically extracting revenues were themselves exacting processes that added to the administrative complexity of the state, at least where these were carried out with any degree of efficiency. But there was always a heavy element of contingency at work, as Tilly indicates:

Struggle over the means of war produced state structures that no one had planned to create, or even particularly desired. Because no ruler or ruling coalition had absolute power and because other classes outside the ruling coalition always held day-to-day control over a significant share of the resources rulers drew on for war, no state escaped the creation of some organisational burdens rulers would have preferred to avoid.[19]

Needless to say, this less-than-linear process was never part of the 'official transcript' of state-making – although it was often reflected in renditions of popular sovereignty.[20] Although European history has been written as a merry dance of war and taxes, it could equally well be retold as a history of boundaries and state-making. On the one hand, the imperative to wage war was largely driven by territorial imperatives that culminated in the conversion of contested frontier regions into fixed boundaries. On the other, the

---

[16] Martin Daunton, *Trusting Leviathan: The Politics of Taxation in Britain, 1799–1914* (Cambridge: Cambridge University Press, 2001).

[17] Margaret Levi, *Of Rule and Revenue* (Berkeley and London: University of California Press, 1988); Daunton, *Trusting Leviathan*, and *Just Taxes: The Politics of Taxation in Britain, 1914–1979* (Cambridge: Cambridge University Press, 2002). An instructive case is that of Risorgimento Italy, where Piedmont's struggle against Austria was reflected in higher levels of military expenditure than the other states and, correspondingly, higher levels of taxation. But in the context of parliamentary control of the budget, increased taxes on merchants were associated not only with greater military expenditure, but also with greater outlays on infrastructure that served military ends and those of commercial elites equally well. Mark Dincecco, Giovanni Federico and Andrea Vindigni, "Warfare, taxation and political change: evidence from the Italian Risorgimento", *Journal of Economic History* 71 (4) 2011.

[18] Daunton, *Trusting Leviathan*, pp. 10–13.   [19] Tilly, *Coercion*, p. 117.

[20] I am borrowing the 'official transcript' from James C. Scott, *Domination and the Arts of Resistance: Hidden Transcripts* (New Haven: Yale University Press, 1992).

development of elaborated tax systems required paying greater attention to where the writ of the state actually ran. As Peter Sahlins indicates in his study of the French–Spanish border, the state was actively made at the margins as much as it was a projection outwards from the political centre.[21] In addition, as Sahlins also demonstrates, the process of boundary-making was incremental, and hence state interventions were thoroughly intertwined with local dynamics. This is precisely the kind of case that I wish to advance in relation to the fashioning of colonial states in West Africa.

But before proceeding any further, I should be explicit about my own position on the question of states as an object of research. First of all, and at the most basic level, states may be seen as *ensembles of interlocking institutions* that demand compliance in the performance of functions that serve to constitute a political community. These institutions generally have a focal point, typically a capital city, and a series of notionally subordinate centres that are spatially and hierarchically arranged.[22] An example would be Asante, which, as Ivor Wilks has demonstrated in abundant detail, underwent a process of institutional elaboration in Kumasi in the later eighteenth century, at the same time as the provinces were more effectively bound to the centre through a system of 'great-roads' and a hierarchy of political offices.[23] States such as Asante paid close attention to revenue collection, which was fundamental to the maintenance of military dominance over their neighbours. Secondly, I follow much contemporary usage in referring to the *idea of the state* – or what is sometimes called the *state imaginary*.[24] This turns on certain shared expectations of what states are supposed to look like and how they are expected to behave – which is generally validated with reference to other states. States claim to exercise a right of command that notionally cascades downwards from the notional 'centre' and radiates outwards to the territorial margins, underlining the valence of both space and scale.[25] Inevitably, there is

---

[21] Peter Sahlins, "The nation in the village: state-building and communal struggles in the Catalan borderland during the eighteenth and nineteenth centuries", *The Journal of Modern History* 60 (2) 1988. See also his more expansive study, *Boundaries: The Making of France and Spain in the Pyrenees* (Berkeley and London: University of California Press, 1989).

[22] In some cases, as in Ethiopia for long periods, the capital could be mobile.

[23] Ivor Wilks, *Asante in the Nineteenth Century: The Structure and Evolution of a Political Order* (Cambridge: Cambridge University Press, 1975), chs. 1–2.

[24] Abrams, "Notes", p. 75. Thomas Blom Hansen and Finn Stepputat, "Introduction: state of imagination", in Thomas Blom Hansen and Finn Stepputat (eds.), *States of Imagination: Ethnographic Explorations of the Postcolonial State* (Durham and London: Duke University Press, 2001).

[25] Within critical geography, *space* and *scale* have been problematized as organizing concepts in large part because they are bound up with the state's own ordering logics that have been destabilized by processes of globalization. John Allen and Allan Cochrane, "Assemblages of state power: topographical shifts in the organization of government and politics", *Antipode* 42 (5) 2010; Neil Brenner, "The limits to scale? Methodological reflections on scalar

also a considerable amount of performativity attached to keeping up appearances, which tends to be especially pronounced at international borders – especially the most militarized ones – where it is considered necessary to create a discursive distance from the neighbouring entity.[26] The greatest challenge to state-builders comes from those who reject the terms of the state imaginary – either because they hold to an alternative idea of the state, as secessionists do, or because they can imagine belonging to a political community that lacks any such presumption of hierarchy, as with James C. Scott's highland anarchists.[27] While imposing the writ of the state by force is always an option, maintaining its mystique is fundamental to securing compliance from those who are governed – as well as from those who populate its institutions. But to focus exclusively on the *idea of the state* is to grasp only part of what is at stake. A third element, the *materiality of the state,* is every bit as fundamental to the overall package. In Scott's analysis, it is the instruments of calibration and extraction that are fundamental to the functioning of states everywhere. Scott's point is that pre-colonial states were not that different from colonial ones, or contemporary iterations of the post-colonial state, in that they all endeavoured to (forcibly) settle mobile populations, to render them 'legible' and thereby to extract revenue. He writes that:

Such coincidences of policy across several centuries, and in the modern period, across very different types of regime, is prima facie evidence that something fundamental about state-making is at work.[28]

And on the specific imperative of taxation, he observes that:

An efficient system of taxation requires, first and foremost, that the objects of taxation (people, land, trade) be made legible. Population rolls and cadastral maps of productive land are the key administrative tools of legibility.[29]

Maps, on this view, are all about establishing legibility. But modern states also leave so many other visible traces. Offices, files, uniforms and flags do not merely function as symbols, but actually help to make the claims to authority real. Offices are not merely spaces enclosed within physical walls but are

---

structuration", *Progress in Human Geography* 24 (4) 2001; Neil Brenner, *New State Spaces: Urban Governance and the Rescaling of Statehood* (Oxford: Oxford University Press, 2004). Here I have chosen to avoid throwing the baby out with the bathwater. Although I am mostly concerned with issues of space and processes of respacing, I have not entirely abandoned questions of scale.

[26] See Ravina Aggarwal, *Beyond Lines of Control: Performance and Politics on the Disputed Borders of Ladakh, India* (Durham: Duke University Press, 2004).

[27] Scott deals with the long-term – and ultimately doomed – efforts by stateless peoples in the mountainous regions of Asia to defend themselves against the advance of paddy states from the valleys below. James C. Scott, *The Art of Not Being Governed: An Anarchist History of Upland Southeast Asia* (New Haven and London: Yale University Press, 2009).

[28] Scott, *Art of Not Being Governed*, p. 79.   [29] Scott, *Art of Not Being Governed*, p. 91.

productive sites where state work is contracted. It is the material elements that enable the institutions to quite literally concretize the idea of the state – and, to return to our starting point, their visibility partly accounts for the illusion that the state is indeed a 'thing'.

Empire states raises additional challenges of interpretation that I cannot fully address in this book. In the eighteenth and nineteenth centuries, European empires wrestled with the very practical consideration of how to create a modicum of consistency in dealing with far-flung domains that exhibited radical differences of topography, demography and resource endowment. What emerged over time was a broad spectrum of imperial governance that stretched from zones of trade and influence, through self-governing territories (typically with a settler component) to substantive colonies where combinations of direct and indirect rule were operationalized.[30] Part of the contribution of imperial mapping resided in imparting an impression of coherence to a political patchwork arising out of an accretion of countless local compromises. The imperial state had the metropolitan capital at its epicentre where legislatures and executive authorities laid down the broad parameters of policy and monitored daily compliance by proconsuls in the field. For empire to function, however, there was also a need for institutions that could channel, process and act upon the flow of information between the metropole and the imperial margins. European states also invested heavily in the idea of empire in an effort to persuade domestic (and tax-sensitive) audiences of the necessity of the enterprise, to instil awe in populations who were on the receiving end, and to impress competitors about the superiority of their version of the civilizing mission.[31] The built environment of imperial capitals like Paris and London was intended to convey a sense of imperial grandeur that resided in being thoroughly global. The colonies had their own capitals that were scaled-down versions of the metropolitan centre and which exhibited their own claims to imperial greatness. Finally, the material existence of navies, armies and modern communications helped to draw the expanses of empire together into something vaguely coherent. While reproducing empire helped to shape European states in each of the respects I have identified above, what coalesced in the empire itself is less easy to capture because the political configurations

[30] The literature on this subject is too immense to document here. For a panoramic view, see Jane Burbank and Frederick Cooper, *Empires in World History: Power and the Politics of Difference* (Princeton: Princeton University Press, 2001), chs. 6, 10–11. On the evolution of the British empire, see John Darwin, *Unfinished Empire: The Global Expansion of Britain* (London: Penguin, 2013). A more extended argument is pursued in P.J. Cain and A.G. Hopkins, *British Imperialism 1688–2000*, 2nd edn. (Harlow and London: Pearson Education, 2002).

[31] For the French case, see Martin Thomas (ed.), *The French Colonial Mind, Volume 1: Mental Maps of Empire and Colonial Encounters* (Lincoln: University of Nebraska Press, 2012); and *The French Colonial Mind, Volume 2: Violence, Military Encounters and Colonialism* (Lincoln: University of Nebraska Press, 2012).

were never a simple reproduction from some European template. To be sure, the formal language of bureaucracy might be borrowed, but the context, the implementation and the underlying meaning was often markedly different. One might even conclude that the whole point about non-settler colonies is that they were not like the 'metropole'. In West Africa, where there were hardly any settlers to speak of, I argue that states bore the imprint of a process of coming into being that played out over more than a century. Not surprisingly, the final outcomes were distinct in each instance. Hence, while the Gold Coast and the Gambia may have shared a history of British rule, along with broadly similar cash crop economies, the states were constituted along quite different lines. Indeed, the Gold Coast was as distinct from the Gambia as it was from Senegal and Togo, two French territories whose governance patterns also diverged in significant respects.

A number of consequences follow from the discussion thus far. The first is that while 'the state' may provide a convenient shorthand, states only ever exist in the plural because the institutional and ideational permutations are potentially endless. No state looks very much like another because they are historically contingent constructions in which the institutional limits have come to be drawn in very different places.[32] Secondly, states presume some sense of territoriality because their writ needs be materialized in spaces that are formally bounded in some fashion. This is why processes of boundary-making and state formation travel so closely together. Thirdly, all states remain a constant work-in-progress. At critical junctures, to invoke the language of new institutionalism, there is often a recalibration in which some of the constituent elements are re-assembled. This is reflected spatially in the reality that states, and especially imperial ones, have often undergone cycles of expansion, contraction and a reconstitution at the margins. Finally, while imperial histories often reveal a great deal about the inner workings of state institutions in Europe itself, a history of state formation in a colonized region like West Africa requires much closer attention to processes unfolding there.

States, Frontiers and Borders: Beyond the Big Bang

Within African Studies, one of the most constructive developments of recent times has been a convergence between the concerns of historians and social anthropologists, working across disciplines that used to differ fundamentally on issues of temporality.[33] This development is clearly manifested, for

---

[32] Veena Das and Deborah Poole, "State and its margins: comparative ethnographies", in Veena Das and Deborah Pool (eds.), *Anthropology in the Margins of the State* (Santa Fe and Oxford: School of American Research Press and James Currey, 2004).

[33] Paul Nugent, "African Studies in Britain", in David Dabydeen, John Gilmore and Cecily Jones (eds.), *The Oxford Companion to Black British History* (Oxford: Oxford University Press, 2007).

example, in a literature that addresses the slave trade and related forms of slavery in a manner that unites the present with its troubled past.[34] As recent work on spirit shrines in the Senegambia and the trans-Volta amply demonstrates, we can pinpoint their emergence in history, but they also appear to exercise a contemporary agency that refashions linear time.[35] The manner in which the legacies of slavery impinge on the present is a recurring theme within this book as well. When it comes to the study of political formations, however, scholarship has tended to adopt a rather foreshortened timescale. If decolonization is not treated as the moment when the patterns were set, then the Partition of Africa is considered as the operative turning point. It is not uncommon to draw a straight line to the abrupt manner in which European rule was imposed over the last two decades of the nineteenth century and the travails of the present – including the installation of cultures of violence and habits of everyday authoritarianism.[36] At the same time, the arbitrary manner in which Europeans arrived at their colonial boundaries – which were defined by treaty, cursorily mapped and then demarcated without regard to the human landscape – is sometimes blamed for a fundamental deficit in state legitimacy.[37]

It is true that some political science has advocated taking a rather longer view of Africa's political trajectory. Hence Jean-François Bayart, while "[e]schewing the meanderings of dependency theory"[38], has argued for a much deeper history of extraversion that reshaped African societies and political systems centuries before the imposition of colonial rule. But his more extended treatment has more to say about societies than states in the sense that I have defined them.[39] Moreover, few political scientists have taken up Bayart's injunction to engage with the historicity of African social formations. Indeed, Mahmood Mamdani has rejected the agenda outright on the basis that it amounts to crediting Africans for fashioning the terms of their own

---

[34] See, for example, Alice Bellagamba, Sandra Greene and Martin A. Klein (eds.), *The Bitter Legacy: African Slavery Past and Present* (Princeton: Markus Wiener, 2013).

[35] Robert M. Baum, *Shrines of the Slave Trade: Diola Religion and Society in Precolonial Senegambia* (New York and Oxford: Oxford University Press, 1999); Judy Rosenthal, *Possession, Ecstasy and Law in Ewe Voodoo* (Charlottesville: University of Virginia Press, 1998); Meera Venkatachalam, *Slavery, Memory and Religion in Southeastern Ghana, c.1850 to the Present* (Cambridge: Cambridge University Press, 2015); and Alessandra Brivio, "Evoking the past through material culture: the Mami Tchamba shrine", in Bellagamba et al., *Bitter Legacy*.

[36] Crawford Young, *The African Colonial State in Comparative Perspective* (New Haven and London: Yale University Press, 1994), p. 283; Achille Mbembe, *On the Postcolony* (Berkeley, Los Angeles and London: University of California Press, 2001), ch. 1.

[37] A key proponent of this view is Pierre Englebert, *State Legitimacy and Development in Africa* (Boulder: Lynne Rienner, 2000), pp. 84–9.

[38] Jean-François Bayart, "Africa in the world: a history of extraversion", *African Affairs* 99 2000, p. 219.

[39] Jean-François Bayart, *The State in Africa: The Politics of the Belly* (London: Longman, 1993).

subjection.[40] For Mamdani, Africa's baleful legacy – the 'bifurcated state' – originated in the precise moment of the Scramble. Crawford Young's extended treatment of the colonial states comes to broadly comparable conclusions. With some sensitivity to history, he situates Africa within a comparative analysis of colonial state formation over a much longer temporal scale.[41] For Young, the end of the nineteenth century constituted a distinctive moment – clearly separated from what had gone before – in which African societies were confronted with "a colonial master equipped with doctrines of domination and capacities for the exercise of rule that went far beyond those available in earlier times and other places."[42] On this reading, colonial states in Africa assumed a rather different morphology by virtue of the coming together of racial ideologies, advances in modern science and insurgent technologies. The result was a system of domination in which African subjects were consciously differentiated from citizens in Europe, at the same time as the state form established "an important degree of autonomy from its metropolitan sovereign and a high order of autonomy from its subject society".[43] Although the latter formulation would seem to confirm that colonial states were fundamentally unlike their metropolitan progenitors, it is clear that Young also regards colonial states as exogenous to African history. Hence he concludes that: "[The] colonial system created the African states in most instances; only a handful have a more distant ancestry, and even fewer have decisive institutional continuities with the precolonial past."[44] Although it is true that existing states were not rescaled to fit colonial territory, my argument is that there was nevertheless an important pre-history to colonial states that helps to explain the subsequent variations.

Young's analysis resonates with a corpus of literature embodied in imperial history – most notably with respect to the consequences issuing from the lateness of colonization in Africa. However, most of these histories are not specifically concerned with Africa and often speak more to state-making processes in Europe. Insofar as imperial histories *are* concerned with Africa, they pose a rather different set of questions. That is, they wrestle with the reasons why there was a sudden shift from the 'imperialism of free trade' to outright colonization at the end of the nineteenth century. A well-worn debate turns on the relative weight to be accorded to expansionist impulses emanating from within the European 'metropoles' as against crises at the 'periphery' occasioned by the breakdown of older alliances.[45] P.J. Cain and A.G. Hopkins, who do pay considerable attention to Africa, make a fair point that peripheral

---

[40] Mahmood Mamdani, *Citizen and Subject: Contemporary Africa and the Legacy of Late Colonialism* (Princeton: Princeton University Press, 1996), pp. 10–11.

[41] Young, *African Colonial State*, ch. 3.   [42] Young, *African Colonial State*, p. 75.

[43] Young, *African Colonial State*, p. 76.   [44] Young, *African Colonial State*, p. 9.

[45] John Gallagher and Ronald Robinson, "The imperialism of free trade", *Economic History Review*, 2nd series, VI (1) 1953.

models do not rule out the significance of developments within the metropole.[46] But this cuts both ways: that is, it seems no less evident that the advocates for the various imperialist options – emanating from manufacturers, the City of London, journalists or religious bodies – were more likely to find a receptive ear in the light of circumstances as they unfolded on the ground. In this book, I am with Young in seeking to follow the genealogies of states in Africa. The difference is that I am more interested in exposing the temporal continuities and the relationship between the making of states and the shaping of space. As such, I feel no particular need to choose between metropolitan and peripheral interpretations of imperialism. Because I am concerned with processes unfolding within West Africa, the latter provide a more obvious fit, and yet one cannot understand the partition without reference to developments taking place within Europe and the wider world at the end of the nineteenth century. At the same time, whereas much of the literature on the partition itself is fixated on the minutiae of personalities and events, my concern is with identifying and explaining some of the larger patterns.

Borders represent the physical limits where the exercise of a given system of sovereignty terminates. Frontiers, by contrast, are zones of engagement that lie beyond any exercise of routinized rule. It follows that borders are intimately bound up with state practices whereas frontiers involve a multiplicity of possible actors. Frontiers proliferate when states break down, but states may also play a part in sustaining frontier dynamics. In West Africa, for example, it was common for states to uphold physical borders while raiding frontier regions for slaves – which bears a passing resemblance to the ways in which contemporary entrepreneurs thrive on a lack of regulation at the resource frontier.[47] While frontiers might appear to signal a lack – of state presence, of order, of certainty – they represent the work of human agency just as much as borders themselves do. This much is clear from Igor Kopytoff's influential formulation of 'the African frontier'.[48] Kopytoff drew on the American frontier thesis of Frederick Jackson Turner for the insight that cultures were made at the margins.[49] But whereas Turner imagined a rolling frontier of white settlement, Kopytoff posited a model in which African populations – "the disgruntled, the victimized, the exiled, the refugees, the losers in internecine

[46] Cain and Hopkins, *British Imperialism*, pp. 28–9.

[47] Anna Tsing, *Friction: An Ethnography of Global Connection* (Princeton: Princeton University Press, 2004), p. 27. The difference is that Tsing sees the frontier as derived from European models of conquest and shaped by capitalism.

[48] Igor Kopytoff, "The internal African frontier: the making of African political culture", in Igor Kopytoff (ed.), *The African Frontier: The Reproduction of Traditional African Societies* (Bloomington and Indianapolis: Indiana University Press, 1987).

[49] Frederick Jackson Turner, *The Frontier in American History* (New York: Henry Holt & Co., 1921).

struggles, the adventurous, and the ambitious"[50] – were constantly peeling away from existing political centres, and relocating to zones outside the control of existing states. These frontiersmen occupied 'interstitial' spaces, although at another point in the cycle they might be drawn back towards established centres of power. For Kopytoff, it was the recurrent cycle of fusion and fission that paradoxically reproduced elements of a common culture – most notably, a shared discourse of firstcomer and latecomer, which we will encounter in greater detail below.[51] Subsequent research has pointed to examples of rolling and interstitial frontiers. Carola Lentz's historical reconstruction of Dagara movement into areas previously occupied by Sissala peoples is illustrative of a rolling frontier amongst stateless societies.[52] Pastoralists across the Horn and in West Africa have been equally consummate frontiersmen during periods in their history.[53] But there are also countless examples of the interstitial frontier, not least in the trans-Volta and the Senegambia, which is closely bound up with the dynamics of the slave trade. The latter was conducive to the central-ization of power in states like Asante and Dahomey, but slave raiding also precipitated the flight of populations into more inaccessible zones – notably to areas of high elevation and coastal swamplands. In the trans-Volta, vulnerable populations retreated into the Togoland hills where successive waves of refugees gave rise to a veritable mosaic of peoples. In the lower Senegambia, including what is now Guinea-Bissau and the Casamance region of Senegal, there was a comparable retreat into the mangrove swamps. Here, the develop-ment of a highly productive system of wetland rice culture was associated not with state-making, as Scott has posited for South-East Asia, but rather with a stubborn attachment to statelessness.[54] As we will see in Chapter 2, some of

---

[50] Kopytoff, "Internal African frontier", p. 18. For a brief discussion of the models in question, see Benedikt Korf, Tobias Hagmann and Martin Doevenspeck, "Geographies of violence and sovereignty: the African Frontier revisited", in Benedikt Korf and Timothy Raeymaekers (eds.), *Violence on the Margins: States, Conflicts and Borderlands* (New York and Houndmills: Palgrave Macmillan, 2013), pp. 30–5.

[51] Kopytoff, "Internal African frontier", pp. 53–61.

[52] Carola Lentz, *Land. Mobility and Belonging in West Africa* (Bloomington and Indianapolis: Indiana University Press, 2013). Lentz's study is also fascinating because she indicates that where settlers entered into disputes over land, they proceeded to demarcate formal boundaries. A comparable account, which contrasts the frontier logics of the stateless Nuer with the more settled Anywaa, is Dereje Feyissa, "More than the state? The Anywaa's call for rigidification of the Ethio-Sudanese border", in Dereje Feyissa and Markus Virgil Hoehne (eds.), *Borders and Borderlands in the Horn of Africa* (Woodbridge and Rochester: James Currey, 2010).

[53] The frontier zones at the fringes of the Ethiopian empire have received especially detailed treatment. See Donald Donham, "Old Abyssinia and the new Ethiopian empire", in Donald Donham and Wendy James (eds.), *The Southern Marches of Imperial Ethiopia* (Oxford: James Currey, 2002); and John Markakis, *Ethiopia: The Last Two Frontiers* (London: James Cur-rey, 2011).

[54] Scott, *Art of Not Being Governed*; Peter Mark, *"Portuguese" Style and Luso-African Identity: Precolonial Senegambia, Sixteenth–Nineteenth Centuries* (Bloomington: Indiana University

the polities that became embroiled in raiding and dealing in slaves within frontier regions, such as Agotime, also mastered forms of military and political organization that were neither state-like nor stateless in any straightforward sense.

If the slave trade contributed to frontier dynamics, the gradual winding down of this trade in the early nineteenth century was associated with the weakening of West Africa's largest states, violent conflicts over relations of obligation and a proliferation of frontiers. European traders at the coast both responded to these changing dynamics and contributed directly to the process of respacing. Jeffrey Herbst's contention that African states were already characterized by a progressive weakening of control with distance from the capital underlines the point that the centres related differently to sections of their populations. But this is not the same thing as saying that states lacked a sense of territoriality.[55] Asante, which is cited by Herbst in support of his thesis, actually displayed a keen interest in maintaining its borders, where it taxed and regulated trade. To that end it posted Customs and officials to the margins rather than relying on the input of local rulers.[56] It was the increasing difficulty of protecting its territorial claims that signalled an important shift in the first decades of the nineteenth century. From the standpoint of African traders, states provided some guarantee of personal security in return for the taxes they demanded. But where there was no effective state presence, the viability of trade routes depended on the elaboration of relations of trust, cemented through commercial and marital alliances. These often operated over considerable distances and provided a broad measure of security – although, as we shall see, the practice of *panyarring*, or seizing people for unpaid debts, was a perennial source of discord. Where state demands became excessive, traders might be inclined to invest in networks embedded within frontier regions.

Whereas European merchants had hitherto been content to wait for trade to come to them, their growing interest in short-circuiting the trade routes brought them into direct conflict with the rulers of African states like Asante. Merchants in the port towns solicited metropolitan assistance, but European governments – mindful of the tax bargains they had struck with their own citizens – were reluctant to finance anything other than the most nominal commitments. The British, in particular, were narrowly focused on the naval campaign against the slave trade. In 1865, the authorities in London even contemplated withdrawing from the West African settlements altogether. Although complete retrenchment did not come to pass, there was a commitment

---

Press, 2002); and Walter Hawthorne, *Planting Rice and Harvesting Slaves: Transformations along the Guinea-Bissau Coast, 1400–1900* (Portsmouth: Heinemann, 2003).

[55] Jeffrey Herbst, *States and Power in Africa: Comparative Lessons in Authority and Control* (Princeton: Princeton University Press, 2000), p. 52.

[56] Wilks, *Asante in the Nineteenth Century*, pp. 55, 150, 434.

to scaling back and the merchants were enjoined to assume more of the responsibility. This part of the story is well known, but there was a new element in the equation that has received much less attention. From the first decades of the nineteenth century onwards, the port towns/cities attracted growing numbers of Africans, some of whom were re-captives, at the same time as becoming closely intertwined with neighbouring settlements. The earliest evidence of state-like functions was manifested in the mediation of commercial disputes in the coastal regions. In the nineteenth century, fledgling administrations came under pressure to assume greater responsibilities and this, in turn, required them to address the paucity of revenues. It was in an attempt to square the circle that coastal administrations and European merchants began to engage more directly with frontier regions. As an older literature emphasizes, the projection of influence beyond the coastal settlements was at odds with the expressed preferences of European governments, which could see very little advantage in costly African entanglements.[57] As inventive as the 'men on the spot' undoubtedly were in interpreting directives, their waywardness need to be viewed in the light of the emergence of a political community at the coast – one that happened to be numerically dominated by a combination of *métis* and local populations. As European merchants became frontiersmen of a kind, they wrestled with their own problem of trust. Striking up personal relationships and blood ties had historically provided one means of doing so,[58] but as the century progressed, merchants returned to seeking assistance from those whose authority derived from much further afield. At the end of the nineteenth century, European governments were prepared to contemplate the kinds of entanglement that they had hitherto studiously avoided. The context was the first Great Depression, which spurred protectionism in Europe and fed neuroses about being cut out of potentially valuable markets elsewhere. At the same time, as has often been noted, breakthroughs in medical science and military technology greatly reduced the barriers to intervention.

There is a common misconception that European statesmen sat around a table at the Berlin Conference in 1884/85 and drew lines on maps that carved up the continent on paper. As John Hargreaves and H.L. Wesseling have observed, and as Simon Katzenellenbogen has demonstrated in greater detail, this is based on a stubborn myth.[59] The object of the conference was actually to

---

[57] The classic statement on mid-Victorian reluctance to embrace empire is Ronald Robinson and John Gallagher, *Africa and the Victorians: The Official Mind of Imperialism* (London: Macmillan, 1961).

[58] For a historical reconstruction of such relations in the Senegambia, see George E. Brooks, *Landlords and Strangers: Ecology, Society and Trade in Western Africa 1000–1630* (Boulder: Westview Press, 1994).

[59] John D. Hargreaves, *Prelude to the Partition of West Africa* (London: Macmillan, 1963), p. 337; H.L. Wesseling, *Divide and Rule: The Partition of Africa 1880–1914* (Westport: Praeger, 1996), p. 126; and Simon Katzenellenbogen, "'It didn't happen at Berlin': politics, economics and ignorance in the setting of Africa's colonial boundaries", in Paul Nugent and A.I. Asiwaju

preserve African resources for the equal exploitation of all the European powers, and to make it more difficult to stake territorial claims without establishing effective occupation. However, the notional rules of the game became inoperative by virtue of a fundamental lack of trust on the part of the major parties. As the Scramble began in earnest, there was a mad dash to secure treaties as well as instances of military conquest. Chartered companies frequently acted in the name of a delegated authority, while attempting to ward off the perennial threat of bankruptcy.[60] Although they formally represented European states, they did not function *as* states in the accepted sense. In the parts of West Africa that I am concerned with, there was more of a phased transition from the frontier to the colonial border as French, British and Portuguese tried to extend their presence, while the Germans made up for lost time in the quest for treaties. Because there was an incentive to secure control over trade routes, it is striking that early colonial states were initially more visibly present at the margins than elsewhere. Hence, when representatives of the Independent Congo State and German East Africa sought to define a border at the western edge of the Rwandan kingdom, the two sides pragmatically erected posts facing each other – well before any formal administration had been established.[61] In general, the boundaries hardened at the same time as states themselves were in the process of being pieced together. This created a rather paradoxical situation in which the European states, in whose names the claims were being staked, were distant from the scene, while the actors on the ground were not in command of anything very state-like. Indeed, it was through the act of fashioning borders that new institutional practices arose. Whereas colonial armies were not so new, consisting as they did of ex-slaves and levies borrowed from allies, there was a qualitative shift associated with other bordering practices – especially in the work of Customs collectors, surveyors and mapmakers whose task was to impart greater fixity to some often rather wayward imperial cartography.[62]

Although it is certainly possible to point to examples of arbitrary decisions and fateful omissions,[63] in general the staking out of colonial territory

---

(eds.), *African Boundaries: Barriers, Conduits and Opportunities* (London: Frances Pinter, 1996), pp. 22–4.

[60] The British, who were the most ambivalent imperialists, had a particular penchant for using chartered companies to protect their interests. This included the Imperial British East Africa Company (IBEAC), the Royal Niger Company and the British South Africa Company (BSA).

[61] This is the distant origin of the twin cities of Goma/Gisenyi and Bukavu/Cyangugu that face each other across the DRC–Rwanda border today. Gillian Mathys, "People on the Move: Frontiers, Borders, Mobility and History on the Lake Kivu Region 19th–20th Century", PhD thesis, University of Ghent, 2014, p. 127.

[62] On the role of surveyors, see Jamie McGowan, "Uncovering the roles of African surveyors and draftsmen in mapping the Gold Coast", in Akerman, *Decolonizing the Map*.

[63] For example, when officials of the British Foreign Office took their eye off the ball, the Independent Congo State was able to extend its southern boundary with what is now Zambia. Katzenellenbogen, "It didn't happen at Berlin", p. 27.

followed a demonstrable spatial logic. On the one hand, where existing states controlled territory, European actors would appeal to treaties or conquest – in either case seeking to inherit the entire territory attached to the kingdoms in question. Hence the importance of defining the western margins of Rwanda for the Belgians and the Germans, the northern limits of the Sokoto Caliphate for the British and the French, and the geographical coverage of Borno for the Germans and the British.[64] There were so many disputes because it was a matter for debate where a given state started and ended. Tributaries might be considered either as part of a given state, on the principle that they were subordinate, or outside of it, on the basis that the whole point of paying tribute was to retain a degree of autonomy. The history of particular colonial borders indicates that the lines often needed to be adjusted several times over in order to take account of shifting interpretations of where power resided, or according to the lie of the land. On the other hand, in the interstitial zones between African states, the Europeans began by seeking to gain control over choke-points, such as river crossings and mountain passes, and then proceeded to convert these into territorial claims. In both cases, there was a carryover of the spatial logics that had become established over previous decades. In frontier regions, colonial officials had their work cut out trying to win over populations that had been on the receiving end of state violence. While frontiersmen often welcomed being liberated from the threat of raiding by powerful neighbours, they were not necessarily willing to accept the kind of demands – notably taxation and forced labour – that the Europeans sought to impose as they set about assembling state structures of their own. As a consequence, the relative ease of establishing a formal border was often the precursor to a struggle to convert stubborn frontiersmen into compliant colonial subjects. In the Senegambia especially, political cultures that had been forged over centuries proved an especially difficult nut to crack.

In Chapter 3, I will flesh out the argument in greater detail with specific reference to both the Senegambia and the trans-Volta. But at this point, I wish to underline my three fundamentals points. The first is that the partition was not a foundational moment when Europeans imposed an entirely new spatial reality upon the African landscape. Rather, the protagonists built more or less

---

[64] Mathys, *People on the Move*; D.J. Thom, *The Nigeria–Niger Boundary, 1890–1906: A Study of Ethnic Frontiers and a Colonial Boundary*, Africa Series, 23 (Athens: Ohio University, Center for International Studies, 2005); Camille Lefebvre, *Frontières de sable, frontières de papier: Histoire de territoires et de frontières, du jihad de Sokoto à la colonisation française du Niger, XIXe-XXe siècles* (Paris: Publications de la Sorbonne, 2015); and Vincent Hiribarren, *A History of Borno: Trans-Saharan African Empire to Failing Nigerian State* (London: C. Hurst, 2017). For another case where a colonial border mapped onto a pre-colonial boundary, see JoAnn McGregor, *Crossing the Zambezi: The Politics of Landscape on a Central African Frontier* (Oxford: James Currey, 2009).

consciously on the patterns that had been under development since earlier in the century. And secondly, it was in the act of fashioning boundaries that state repertoires emerged – extending some of the state-making processes that had begun in the coastal settlements. Both my temporal and spatial arguments point to a very different conceptualization of colonial state-making. I turn now to consider the manner in which colonial states were consolidated still in a dialectical interplay with the margins.

"This Is Not 'a State'!": Beyond Afro-Surrealism

The impression that the borderlands were marginal to colonial state formation is in itself a by-product of processes of respacing that unfolded over the first two decades of colonial rule. As regimes gradually found their feet, the material trappings of state-ness became more visible in the shape of administrative headquarters, with whitewashed buildings and flags, and roads linking one centre with the next. Because the central authorities generally preferred to have their district headquarters set back, border posts forfeited some of their former importance within fully-fledged administrative hierarchies. It also made a difference that most regimes were distinctly reticent about the construction of infrastructure that traversed borders, usually for fear of conferring an advantage on neighbouring colonies. Finally, prohibitive taxes often disrupted much of what had been funnelled along the trade routes in the past, and thereby reduced the perceived importance of the border posts as an instrument in revenue collection. In a sense, therefore, colonial state-making entailed a process of actively manufacturing the margins, turning historic relations inside out in the process.[65] However, as I will demonstrate, the borderlands remained fundamental to shaping the future trajectory of the colonial states.

Mamdani's formulation of the 'bifurcated' state draws a sharp distinction between the ways in which the colonial states sought to inscribe the right of Europeans to rule over Africans. In the cities, he claims, they were excluded through racialization, whereas in the rural areas they were tribalized under a system of 'decentralized despotism' that operated through administrative chieftaincies.[66] As I have already indicated, Mamdani attributes many of the continent's subsequent woes to this original sin. In this study, I am equally interested in urban and rural dynamics, but come to rather less categorical conclusions. In the case of Senegal, which receives a surprisingly modest treatment by Mamdani, the populations of the Four Communes of Dakar,

---

[65] This is broadly comparable to the making of the margins in Syria. See Benjamin Thomas White, *The Emergence of Minorities in the Middle East: The Politics of Community in French Mandate Syria* (Edinburgh: Edinburgh University Press, 2011).

[66] Mamdani, *Citizen and Subject*, p. 19.

Gorée, St. Louis and Rufisque enjoyed the formal status of French citizens that distinguished them from the subjects who were added on as the colony expanded towards the east and the south. Although the French authorities certainly endeavoured to make it more difficult for urban populations to access full citizenship, this manoeuvre was resisted with some success by the population of the Communes.[67] In the Gold Coast, Africans were not formally citizens, but coastal populations nevertheless regarded themselves as the coauthors of the colonial project dating back to the Bond of 1844 – according to which certain prerogatives were voluntarily ceded to the British. Given that it was traditional authorities who were signatories to the Bond, the distinction between urban and rural claimants was distinctly fuzzy right from the start. Moreover, while 'decentralized despotism' might serve as a shorthand for the imposition of chiefs upon the Jola of the Casamance, it hardly captures the reality that traditional authorities acted as the spokesmen for their communities in somewhere like the Gold Coast. Finally, while the eventual alliance with the Mouride brotherhood was reflected in a devolved authority in the central part of Senegal, it is far too simplistic to treat the marabouts as ciphers of the colonial state. The Mourides won special consideration by standing up to the French and attracted support by shielding Wolof peasants (many of whom were ex-slaves) from the full force of colonialism. These diverse patterns are not merely interesting in and of themselves but point to the quite different ways in which states were pieced together – which takes us back to the centrality of the margins. In each instance, I will argue, colonial states were conditioned by the imperative to regulate the flow of goods and the movement of people through border spaces.

The structure of taxation provides insights into the historical origins and inner workings of any state – and this is no less true of colonial variants. Because metropolitan governments expected the colonies to become financially self-sufficient with a minimum of delay, there was a pressing need to generate predictable revenue streams.[68] In the West African colonies, it was Customs duties that ensured the fiscal reproduction of colonial states. As we will see in Chapter 4, the most important were the duties that were collected on imported goods, which initially fell heavily on relative luxuries such as tobacco and alcohol, but increasingly on everyday items of consumption as well. In that sense, colonial states had an interest in feeding African consumer habits as much as the European firms did and understood that this was likely to turn on the increased income generated by cash crop production. This made

---

[67] Alice Conklin, *A Mission to Civilize: The Republican Idea of Empire in France and West Africa 1895–1930* (Stanford: Stanford University Press, 1997).

[68] Leigh A. Gardner, *Taxing Colonial Africa: The Political Economy of British Imperialism* (Oxford: Oxford University Press, 2012), pp. 3–4.

governments more responsive than they might otherwise have been to the demands for better roads in somewhere like the Gold Coast. Export duties were typically less crucial to colonial finances, which reflected the success with which European merchants lobbied against them. Direct taxes generally weighed lower in the scales than indirect taxes. Contrary to what Scott's reading might suggest, colonial states did not opt for maximum surveillance and optimal extraction, but typically followed the line of least resistance. Even where taxes on land existed, as they did in the Sokoto Caliphate, these were abandoned in favour of flat-rate assessments that were levied on the person or the household unit.[69] Colonial regimes had many different reasons for wanting to force Africans to pay head and yard taxes, including instilling habits of compliance. This contained an underlying threat of force but mediated by an appreciation that excessive zeal could precipitate the flight of population across borders.[70] In purely financial terms, head and yard taxes provided a relatively minor part of what kept colonial states financially afloat – although, as we will see, there were some marked variations.

Within such a fiscal structure, what mattered most was effectively taxing what entered and exited through the coastal ports. But colonial regimes needed to be sensitive to what their neighbours were doing for fear of forfeiting dutiable goods, and they had to pay close attention to commercial flows at the margins. Smuggling was one of the issues that most exercised colonial administrations and coloured their relationships with their neighbours. Of comparable importance was controlling mobility. The cash crop economies of the region depended to varying degrees on imported labour on a seasonal or a more permanent basis. Colonial governments sought to monitor physical movement through borders and to regulate the terms of access to land, while once again being sensitive to competing incentives next door. The promise of access to prized consumer goods and tax concessions were some of the enticements offered to potential migrants and settlers who generally proved extremely adept at seeking out the best deal. Given that consumer goods were also the main source of import revenues, well-managed border flows helped to create a satisfyingly virtuous circle. As I will indicate, however, the relative importance attached to regulating the flows of people and goods differed substantially in the Senegambia and the trans-Volta with enduring consequences.

In this study, I am not able to investigate the full range of colonial institutions. In Chapter 4, for example, I point to the very real demand for roads and schools, but I am only able to track the broad patterns of expenditure.

---

[69] Paul E. Lovejoy and Jan S. Hogendorn, *Slow Death for Slavery: The Course of Abolition in Northern Nigeria, 1897–1936* (Cambridge: Cambridge University Press, 1993), pp. 185–98.

[70] A.I. Asiwaju, "Migration as revolt: the example of the Ivory Coast and the Upper Volta before 1945", *Journal of African History* 17 (4) 1976, pp. 577–94.

However, I do subject three particular branches of the colonial administration to much closer scrutiny. The first is Customs, whose standing within colonial bureaucracies and physical presence at the borders was markedly different – especially as between the French West African Federation and the British colonies. The second is chieftaincy, which, as I have already indicated, was far more variegated than Mamdani's formulation allows for. In the Gold Coast, chiefs were not formally part of the colonial state, and, while the British authorities found ways to exert pressure upon incumbents, they retained a remarkable level of operational autonomy. In the other cases, traditional authorities were considered an integral part of the administration, but they related to it in distinct ways. In each case, the practical importance attached to chiefs was shaped by their role in levying taxes, managing the influx of migrants and settlers, and co-operating with Customs in the exercise of border surveillance. In that sense, 'decentralized despotism' misrepresents the extent to which traditional authorities were fully embedded within state structures. The third branch was the field administration, which answered to the central secretariat in the capital. District (and provincial) administrators worked closely with the chiefs, especially in matters pertaining to taxation and migration. But their involvement in other aspects of border management differed according to the presence of the Customs authorities.

In the immediate post-war period, greater resources were channelled into infrastructural expenditure in the colonies than ever before. This had consequences for the dimensions of bureaucracies as well as their ambitions towards maximizing geographical reach. Despite some deference to the benefits of co-operation, the tendency was to mould infrastructure to fit the contours of the existing borders. This predisposition did not change greatly after independence when developmental fetishism gained even greater traction. While mobility remained relatively unimpeded, governments often preferred to impose tighter controls over the flow of commodities that were considered of strategic importance – which is why Customs and territorial unions either failed to come to fruition or were killed off.[71] As has been well-documented, African states sought to finance their commitment to industrial development through increased duties on cash crops, the creaming off of marketing board surpluses and a degree of revenue diversification.[72] In the later chapters of this book, I will address the proliferation of parastatals and the role of new

---

[71] Although the French West African Federation had been wound up in the mid-1950s, there were attempts to revive it. The union between Senegal and Mali collapsed within a matter of months, amidst mutual recriminations, in 1960. The East African Community, which was founded in 1967, collapsed ten years later, partly because Uganda and Tanzania felt that Kenya was the real beneficiary.

[72] Robert Bates, *Markets and States in Tropical Africa: The Political Basis of Agricultural Policies* (Berkeley and London: University of California Press, 1981).

institutional actors such as the Armed Forces, each of which related to border dynamics in particular ways. But as before, I direct the focus to the changing nature of Customs work and the variable role of traditional authorities in border management.

The question of how best one might approach the study of post-colonial states is one that has not elicited a uniform answer. Patrick Chabal and Jean-Pascal Daloz have insisted that colonial states, unlike their European progenitors, were fundamentally weak and failed to emancipate themselves from African societies.[73] In the absence of genuinely autonomous institutions, they claim that African states today remain essentially an elaborate fiction barely concealing the realities of neo-patrimonialism:

> Hence the notion that politicians, bureaucrats or military chiefs should be the servants of the state simply does not make sense. Their political obligations are, first and foremost, to their kith and kin, their clients, their communities, their regions, even to their religion. All such patrons seek ideally to constitute themselves as 'Big Men', controlling as many networks as they can ... We are thus led to conclude that, in most African countries, the state is no more than a décor, a pseudo-Western façade masking the realities of deeply personalized political realities.[74]

This is disarmingly presented not as some African deficiency, but simply a statement of the world as it is.[75] But the yardstick for comparison is not any particular European state at any specific moment in history, but a reading off from Weber's ideal-types.[76] As critics of this approach have noted, one often learns more about what Africa is *not* than what 'it' is.[77] Moreover, African states are treated as essentially uniform, whereas (as I have indicated) it is the differences between them that are more striking. The blanket assertion that African states do not meet the criteria for 'stateness' arguably closes down the

---

[73] The authors part company with Bayart, ostensibly on the grounds of his imparting too much weight to the colonial moment, but their analysis of contemporary politics is remarkably similar. Patrick Chabal and Jean-Pascal Daloz, *Africa Works: Disorder as Political Instrument* (London, Oxford and Bloomington: International Africa Institute, James Currey and Indiana University Press, 1999), pp. 4–13.

[74] Chabal and Daloz, *Africa Works*, p. 15.

[75] Patrick Chabal, *Africa: The Politics of Suffering and Smiling* (London: Zed Press, 2008). For an even more explicit statement about the importance of cultural factors, see Stephen Ellis and Gerrie Ter Haar, *Worlds of Power: Religious Thought and Political Practice in Africa* (London: C. Hurst, 2004). In his later work, Chabal was rather more explicit at teasing out some of the cultural logics that have played themselves out in African politics – albeit in the most general terms.

[76] For a critique of the use of Weber, see Thomas Bierschenk and Jean-Pierre Olivier de Sardan, "Studying the dynamics of African bureaucracies: an introduction to states at work", in Thomas Bierschenk and Jean-Pierre Olivier de Sardan (eds.), *States at Work: Dynamics of African Bureaucracies* (Leiden and Boston: Brill, 2007), pp. 10–14.

[77] Two parallel critiques of the perceived tendency to define Africa in terms of what it is not are Mamdani, *Citizen and Subject*, p. 9; and Mbembe, *On the Postcolony*, p. 9.

most fruitful lines of enquiry. A more helpful way forward is surely to start from the presumption that states manifest themselves in very different guises, reflecting their distinct origins and divergent trajectories, and then to account for these in detail. To quote Hansen and Stepputat:

> Instead of talking about the state as an entity that always/already consists of certain features, functions and forms of governance, let us approach each actual state as a historically specific configuration of a range of languages of stateness: some practical, others symbolic and performative, that have been disseminated, translated, interpreted, and combined in widely different ways and sequences across the globe.[78]

Within anthropology, by contrast, the focus has tended to be directed to the ways in which government officials impart meaning to state practices. A substantial body of literature on the 'everyday state' in South Asia has its parallel in Africa where the focus is generally on the role of bureaucrats in fashioning 'practical norms'.[79] Rather than assuming that institutions are a mere façade, the most nuanced writing has looked at how public servants go about their daily business. This involves being creative in interpreting the rules, whether for the pursuit of graft or with the best of intentions. But what emerges is that the state is materialized through the interaction between those who exercise governmental functions and the ordinary people they interact with. In their analysis of the Indian case, C.J. Fuller and John Harriss argue strongly for the presumed existence of the state on both sides of that interface:

> Even if many petty officials do not spend much time on their offices, many others do, and nobody imagines that the endless cups of tea and coffee drunk in India's government buildings turn them into tea shops or homes. Furthermore, people in India also know that modern impersonal norms of secularised government and formally rational bureaucracy do or should apply in government offices and other locales of the state.[80]

This conclusion, which would hold equally well for most of Africa, conceals something of a paradox: while the ease of nurturing relationships of familiarity

---

[78] Hansen and Stepputat, "Introduction: state of imagination", p. 7.

[79] Taylor C. Sherman, William Gould and Sarah Ansari (eds.), *From Subjects to Citizens: Society and the State in India and Pakistan, 1947–1970* (Delhi and New York: Cambridge University Press, 2014). For a programmatic statement, see Bierschenk and Olivier de Sardan, "Studying the dynamics of African bureaucracies: an introduction to states at work", and Jean-Pierre Olivier de Sardan, "Practical norms: informal regulations within public bureaucracies (in Africa and beyond)", in Tom de Herdt and Jean-Pierre Olivier de Sardan (eds.), *Real Governance and Practical Norms in Sub-Saharan Africa: The Game of the Rules* (Abingdon and New York: Routledge, 2015). See also Giorgio Blundo and Pierre-Yves Le Meur (eds.), *The Governance of Daily Life in Africa: Ethnographic Explorations of Public and Collective Services* (Leiden and Boston: Brill, 2009) and Giorgio Blundo and Jean-Pierre Olivier de Sardan (eds.), *Everyday Corruption and the State: Citizens and Public Officials in Africa* (London: Zed Press, 2006).

[80] C.J. Fuller and John Harriss, "For an anthropology of the modern Indian state", in C.J. Fuller and Véronique Bénéï (eds.), *The Everyday State and Society in Modern India* (London: C. Hurst & Company, 2001), p. 23.

with officials would be regarded by Chabal and Daloz as evidence for a lack of a bureaucratic ethos, such daily interactions are also what keeps officials and citizens mutually invested in the idea of the state. What Hansen says of Mumbai applies equally well to Africa:

At the same time, it is also clear to most people that the state is something more permanent, more omnipresent and more central to their lives, something larger and more durable than the prevailing regime in power at any one time. The state is a name given to various practices and institutions of government, not only as an analytical concept but also as a locus of authority invoked and reproduced by an endless range of interventions — from validating documents and checking motor vehicles, to prohibiting substances or encouraging forms of behaviour that promote public health, and so on.[81]

Hence, it is through participation in the daily routines and rituals of governance that the idea of the state is converted into something other than a mere fiction, illusion or mask. While the anthropological literature has not addressed the issue of scale in a systematic fashion, a focus on the quotidian is important because it demonstrates how administrative conventions are internalized and reproduced over time. It is also reasonable to suppose that the same logics operate at different bureaucratic scales. That is, officials at the notional centre respond creatively to the pressures placed upon them by adapting and remaking procedures, much as those who are consigned to the peripheries do. Practical norms represent the sediment of so many daily interactions between officials employed at all levels of the administrative system – as well as between officials and ordinary citizens. If we accept this insight, the implication is that bureaucratic organograms do not always fully reflect the ways in which decisions are brought into effect.

A rather different approach is to focus on the ways in which state practices have been shaped by the engagement between institutions and special interests. I have already referred to the influence exerted by European import–export companies in the colonial period. In an influential book, Robert Bates has argued that most African governments after independence chose to tax agriculture heavily – through statutory marketing and price fixing, as well as systematic overvaluation of the currency in Anglophone countries – while at the same time subsidizing industrial production and urban consumption.[82] He offered two fundamental reasons for this. The first comes down to the social composition of the nationalist movements at the moment of decolonization. Bates posits that where the latter effectively mobilized rural constituencies, such as in Kenya and Côte d'Ivoire, there was a greater inclination to be responsive to agrarian interests. However, because nationalist movements

---

[81] Thomas Blom Hansen, "Governance and myths of the state in Mumbai", in Fuller and Bénéï (eds.), *Everyday State,* p. 34.
[82] Bates, *Markets and States.*

were dominated by urban dwellers in the majority of instances, policies came at the expense of the rural majority in a country like Ghana.[83] The second part of the explanation, which is more structural, is based on the premise that it was generally easier to aggregate and mobilize urban interests than rural ones. Because urban dwellers were more likely to protest than a scattered peasantry was, governments had a greater incentive to be attentive to their demands. The provision of state employment and cheap food, therefore, became a priority for African governments concerned with maintaining a firm grip on the levers of power.

The Bates thesis contrasts in significant ways with the more recent comparative analysis of Catherine Boone, despite the fact that she similarly invokes historical and structural elements.[84] Bates's account sets up an urban–rural distinction, but otherwise its spatial referents are quite unspecific. By contrast, Boone focuses on the evolution of distinctive relationships between the centre and particular regions in a three-way comparison between Ghana, Senegal and Côte d'Ivoire. Cities do not feature prominently in her analysis, and indeed it is blocs of rural support that are accorded the greatest weight.[85] Boone's is not an argument about the limited capacity of the state to project itself to all corners of its territory in the manner of Jeffrey Herbst.[86] Rather it is an interpretation of the institutional choices that governments make. Boone offers a nuanced account of how and why West African states engage with some regions and virtually ignore others, which, she argues, depends on the existence of organized interests, including traditional authorities, that compel the state to engage. What this would tend to indicate is that governance emerges out of the negotiations that take place at a subnational level. What Boone shares with Bates is a concern with how political coalitions are forged and reproduced over time, but within the confines of state boundaries. Here I seek to build on Boone's insights, but with some modifications. First of all, I deal with borderlands as particular kinds of spaces that are distinctive because they always have (at least) two sides to them. And secondly, I attribute many of the outcomes to the interplay between ordinary borderlanders, whose disposition may not be explicitly political, and state actors who are left to deal with the

---

[83] He cites Ghana and Zambia as cases where the nationalist movement was mostly urban. Robert H. Bates, *Essays on the Political Economy of Rural Africa* (Cambridge: Cambridge University Press, 1983), p. 113.

[84] Catherine Boone, *Political Topographies of the African State: Territorial Authority and Institutional Choice* (Cambridge: Cambridge University Press, 2003).

[85] The rural focus is also sustained in her more recent study of land. Catherine Boone, *Property and Political Order in Africa: Land Rights and the Structure of Politics* (Cambridge: Cambridge University Press, 2013).

[86] Herbst, *States and Power in Africa*.

contradictions in official policy. In that sense, I draw on some of the insights derived from the literature on everyday states as well.

States and Social Contracts

This brings me to the third of my claims: namely that the ways in which states have related to their populations more broadly has been mediated by border dynamics. I have consciously avoided the framing of 'neo-patrimonialism' – another derivative of Weber's categories via Eisenstadt – which has gained considerable traction within African Studies.[87] Despite the assertions of Chabal and Daloz, there is almost no empirical research that maps networks whose existence is typically assumed rather than demonstrated. 'Neo-patrimonialism' has mostly served as descriptive shorthand, signalling forms of personalized authority, rather than functioning as an analytical tool that might account for divergent outcomes.[88] How pervasive clientelist networks are is ultimately an empirical question, but it is only ever a fraction of the story. While African Presidents might favour a small circle of kinsmen and co-ethnics in key appointments, it is debatable whether there are networks that run deep and are well lubricated. The engagement of African leaders with the wider society has often taken place through the cultivation of images of strong/benign leadership and through offstage negotiations with interest groups that are often non-particularistic – such as market associations and religious bodies.[89] Finally, 'neo-patrimonialism' is a rather blunt instrument when it comes to accounting for change over time – especially when one is dealing with the kinds of extended temporalities that form part and parcel of this study.

---

[87] An early discussion of the concept was Jean-François Médard, "Patrimonialism, neo-patrimonialism and the study of the post-colonial state in Subsaharan Africa", in Henrik Secher Marcussen (ed.), *Improved Natural Resource Management – The Role of Formal Organisations and Informal Networks and Institutions* (Roskilde: IDS, 1996). For an illuminating synopsis of the way the term has travelled, see Daniel Bach, "Patrimonialism and neopatrimonialism: comparative receptions and transcriptions", in Daniel C. Bach and Mamadou Gazibo (eds.), *Neopatrimonialism in Africa and Beyond* (Abingdon and New York: Routledge, 2012).

[88] For a concise statement of what neo-patrimonialism covers, which tends to confirm its rather broad remit, see Michael Bratton and Nicolas van de Walle, *Democratic Experiments in Africa: Regime Transitions in Comparative Perspective* (Cambridge: Cambridge University Press, 1997), pp. 61–3. For a somewhat polemical critique, which nevertheless scores some decent points, see Zubairu Wai, "Neo-patrimonialism and the discourse of state failure in Africa", *Review of African Political Economy* 39 (131) 2012. For an attempt to instill greater rigour into the use of the concept, see Gero Erdmann and Ulf Engel, *Neopatrimonialism Revisited – Beyond a Catch-All Concept*, GIGA Working Papers, 16 February 2006. See also the contributions to Bach and Gazibo (eds.), *Neopatrimonialism.*

[89] For example, see Michael Schatzberg, *Political Legitimacy in Middle Africa: Father, Family Food* (Bloomington: Indiana University Press, 2001); and Andrew Apter, *Pan-African Nation: Oil and the Spectacle of Culture in Nigeria* (Chicago and London: Chicago University Press, 2005).

In this book, I work with a different concept – that of the social contract – which obviously comes with considerable historical baggage of its own.[90] Its utility lies in focusing on the ways in which a modicum of consent is manufactured even in the most authoritarian systems, including colonial settings. Practical governance emerges out of a constant process of negotiation, as states rub up against the populations they aspire to rule, leading to periods of consolidation and moments of recalibration. Because social contracts represent an accretion over time, the concept lends itself to thinking about the kinds of deeper historical trajectories that Bayart has directed our attention to.[91] It is also compatible with other heuristic concepts, of which the tax bargain is perhaps the most obvious. Tax bargains generally conform to one of two variants: they either involve using political leverage to deflect state attempts to raise revenue or, conversely, they involve paying higher taxes in return for the enjoyment of a privileged position and hence an opportunity to shape the agenda. In Bates's model of urban bias, the first is taken as the standard, whereas Boone's analysis would suggest that the second is often more relevant. As I will indicate, the most marginalized populations have often been the *least* highly taxed. In either event, the tax bargain is integral to the ways in which those who govern relate to those who are on the receiving end of governance practices. But the taxation-representation nexus does not exhaust the full range of interactions because what is offered or withheld is not necessarily something as tangible, or fungible, as a tax. Because states are typically deeply interested in the business of self-representation, much of what is up for active negotiation is pre-emptive, discursive and pitched in the future tense. Social contracts are therefore closely bound up with ideas of the state, but their practicalities are embodied in institutional realities. It would certainly be possible to craft a much more elaborate model, but for the purposes of this study I have chosen to distinguish between three forms of social contract – the *coercive*, the *productive* and the *permissive*.[92] Needless to say, in any given context there may be combinations of all three in operation. This is why I have

---

[90] My first foray in this discussion was published as Paul Nugent, "States and social contracts in Africa", *New Left Review* 63 May–June 2010. I deploy the concept much as Elizabeth Heath does in her comparative history, *Wine, Sugar and the Making of Modern France: Global Economic Crisis and the Racialization of French Citizenship, 1870–1910* (Cambridge: Cambridge University Press, 2014).

[91] Bayart, "Africa in the world", p. 224. Bayart maintains that a history of extraversion accounts for the emergence of a 'dialogic' relationship between ruler and ruled into the contemporary period. This builds on the insights of an earlier monograph in which he spelled out in much greater detail his model of the 'rhizome state' in which there is a mutual interpenetration between African states and societies. Bayart, *State in Africa*.

[92] The liberational contract, which is evident in those countries that underwent armed struggles for independence and/or secession is a fourth type. However, it is less relevant for the cases I am considering here.

chosen to refer to *composite* social contracts when dealing with specific instances. Moreover, the contracts may be spatially differentiated, such that what is offered to one region of the country may be denied to another. And finally, it stands to reason that social contracts are not necessarily benign – as a modern reading of Hobbes would confirm. All that is required is a common understanding between state authorities and populations over the terms of their engagement.

A coercive social contract is one in which populations are enjoined to obey the writ of state authorities in return for being spared from acts of violence. This variant is often deeply ambiguous because while it may be cast in the language of protection, it often contains a thinly veiled threat. In nineteenth-century West Africa, taxes and tributes were delivered to the rulers of Asante, Dahomey or the Wolof states of the Senegambia precisely in order to ward off the likelihood of being raided for slaves and booty. The nature of the obligation was what defined the precise relationship of populations to the states in question – as Ivor Wilks's discussion of the distinction between the capital, inner and outer provinces of greater Asante makes clear.[93] In Dahomey, subjects paid what were in effect head taxes, while others remitted tribute.[94] Those who did neither were considered to be on the frontier and were raided for slaves on a systematic basis. When early colonial regimes claimed to be ending violent enslavement, they were mostly addressing metropolitan audiences, but the offer of protection was made to Africans as well. However, as one Gambian Governor explicitly recognized, Africans consented grudgingly and conditionally:

So far as I have seen during a life time spent among the native tribes in and near to our settlements, they are just as much attached to their own forms of government, and just as desirous to hold positions of honor amongst themselves and enjoy the sweets of power as other human beings are. In no case have I known a tribe willing to come under the authority of or desirous of the protection of Her Majesty's Government except they felt that to accept Her Sovereignty or be under Her protection was the only means by which they could avert some greater evil which was imminent.[95]

It did not help that colonial regimes exercised their own command through the threat of violence. When officials burned granaries as a response to the failure to deliver taxes on time, this made a statement to the effect that accepting the authority of the state was the price to be paid for being left in peace. But

---

[93] Wilks, *Asante in the Nineteenth Century*, chs. 1–5.
[94] J. Cameron Monroe, *The Precolonial State in West Africa: Building Power in Dahomey* (Cambridge: Cambridge University Press, 2014), chs. 3–4. The Dahomeans treated the western margins, in particular, as raiding grounds.
[95] Sir S. Rowe to Sir H.T. Holland (16 November 1887), NAGB MP 1/1 "Correspondence Relating to the Territories of the River Gambia" (Colonial Office, section of Confidential Print Africa 248).

exactly who the real guarantors of 'peace' were was an issue that was actively debated during the early colonial period, as we will see in relation to Islamic conversion in the Senegambia. In independent Africa, one can point to many instances of coercive social contracts. The most famous instance is that surrounding the regime of Mobutu Sese Seko who invoked the logic of Thomas Hobbes's *Leviathan* by maintaining that he was all that stood between the Congolese people and anarchy. The implication was that while he offered an alternative to the kind of conflict that had erupted around the time of independence, he also reserved the right to inflict violence of his own if the population did not accept the offer on the table.

Secondly, the *productive* social contract is one where the legitimacy of the state rests on the delivery of certain social goods, or at least the performance of an enabling function. In fascinating detail, T.C. McCaskie has revealed how the annual ritual cycle in nineteenth-century Asante – which climaxed in a carnivalesque breakdown of order before normality was restored – was an exercise in forging hegemony by demonstrating the centrality of the monarchy to the well-being of the populace.[96] Equally, theocratic states such as the Sokoto Caliphate were based on the pledge to govern in accordance with the Koran and the teachings of the Prophet, and in that sense the claim to materialize the *umma*, or community of the faithful.[97] Colonial regimes were initially starved of resources, but by the 1920s they were staking their own claims to legitimacy on the basis of the provision of public goods such as roads and ensuring access to consumption. Retrenchment during the Great Depression, and the strictures of the war years, placed an acute strain on an incipient relationship because the understandings that had only recently been reached were openly violated.[98] This helps to explain the desire to make up for lost time after 1945 when Africa experienced its first taste of what we now call 'development'. The prospect of travelling along tarred roads and indulging in what used to be considered as household luxuries held considerable allure for a generation that had endured the strictures of the war. The nationalist movements tapped into these aspirations and commandeered states for their own lightly worked version of the productive contract. In Part IV of this book, I detail the ways in which the promise of state-led development was repeatedly repackaged in the four decades after the 1960s.

Finally, the *permissive social contract* is present where states fashion rules but refrain from implementing them in full. This is partly a matter of where the

---

[96] This study draws explicitly on Gramsci's writings. T.C. McCaskie, *State and Society in Pre-Colonial Asante* (Cambridge: Cambridge University Press, 1995).

[97] Murray Last, *The Sokoto Caliphate* (London: Longman, 1967); and Alhadji-Bouba Nouhou, *Islam et politique au Nigeria: Genèse et évolution de la chari'a* (Paris: Karthala, 2005), part 1.

[98] For a more detailed study of the impact of the Depression, see Moses Ochonu, *Colonial Meltdown: Northern Nigeria in the Great Depression* (Athens: Ohio University Press, 2009).

limits of the state are drawn. Where offices are essentially traded as prebends, the accumulation of private wealth through the exercise of public functions may be considered as an intrinsic part of the deal. Again, where states have not incorporated traditional authorities, their autonomy does not amount to evidence of a permissive contract. On the other hand, when forms of illegality are routinized and normalized, this may point to the existence of a permissive social contract in which the economic rents reside in the existence of a gap between the rules and the reality. Again, the best documented case is that of Mobutu's Zaire where the population was urged to *se débrouiller*, or to fend for themselves, by whatever means necessary. This was taken by everybody, including Mobutu himself, to mean a licence to pillage state resources. In this book, I will examine two cases, the Gambia and Togo, where state bureaucracies became so thoroughly entwined with the contraband trade that the permissive element was nothing less than foundational.

The all-important link to the margins lies in the wider implications of the various border flows that I have identified above. At a fundamental level, while the various social contracts were pitched in discourses of the nation, their viability depended on what was unfolding on the opposite side of an international border. As I have indicated, one of the limits to coercion during the colonial period was the prospect of losing population to flight. After independence, when controlling population mattered less, it was possible for one-party and military regimes to fall back on tactics of intimidation. But even the most repressive regimes generally sought to balance threats with permissive elements, of which the licence to smuggle was the most important. One of the distinctive features of a country like Togo was the curious mix between a climate of fear and extreme permissiveness in relation to trade, none of which was accidental. But crucially, the possibility of maintaining this balance hinged on the prospects for profitable cross-border trade – which was in turn bound up with the working through of productive social contracts in the neighbouring country. As I will demonstrate, the promise of accelerated and balanced development through the pursuit of state-led industrialization, and the respacing of agriculture, mostly culminated in failure in countries like Ghana and Senegal. One of the reasons was that contraband goods entering through ports in the neighbouring entrepôt states were considerably cheaper. This placed a severed strain on the relationship between regimes and their populations, and especially city dwellers who suffered the consequences of higher consumer prices. Hence, it often became necessary for governments to tolerate smuggling, hoarding and other illicit activities that they routinely blamed for the underlying malaise. It stands to reason that social contracts in the micro-states and those in the larger ones were configured differently and pulled in opposite directions. The relationship between them was also dynamic, such that a recalibration on one side of the border had a direct impact on the contracts on the other side. But even to conceive the relationship as inherently dynamic does not do complete justice to the complexity of the ways in which trade, mobility and politics intersected. The reason is that border flows served to reconfigure space itself. More than two decades ago, Janet MacGaffey produced a path-breaking account of the manner in which the implosion of Congo/Zaire's formal economy was accompanied by the development of a vast trans-national traffic in previous minerals, timber and just about every consumer good imaginable.[99] In West Africa, the shifting patterns of regional trade were almost as profound, but in addition they were associated with new forms of urbanism – which included not merely the growth of capital cities, but also the emergence of new urban hubs that connected borderlands and other urban spaces. All of this was unfolding at precisely the moment when Neil Brenner, Saskia Sassen and others point to a process of global restructuring that brought states, capital and cities together in novel combinations.[100] Although Africa is often treated as marginal to such global processes, it is clear that some of the same dynamics were operative – albeit with a twist. Since then, Structural Adjustment has redefined the institutional remit of states, while the opening up to China has produced a further restructuring of regional commerce in a manner that has threatened the favoured niche of the entrepôt states and weakened the associated social contracts.

Borderlands, Communities, Histories

Finally, I return to the central focus of the original project, namely the entangled histories of the borderlands and the various peoples who have come to populate them. At the end of the first decade of independence, there was a brief flurry of interest on the part of political geographers in the colonial origins of African borders and in particular territorial disputes.[101] A lull then ensued, punctuated only by A.I. Asiwaju's seminal historical study of partitioned Yorubaland.[102] It was really only in the mid-1980s that there was a revival of interest in African borders as an object of study. The new wave was partly informed by literatures on other parts of the world, and most especially

---

[99] Janet MacGaffey, *The Real Economy of Zaire: The Contribution of Smuggling and Other Unofficial Activities to National Wealth* (London and Philadelphia: James Currey and University of Pennsylvania Press, 1991), esp. p. 20.

[100] Brenner, *New State Spaces*; Saskia Sassen, *Territory: Authority, Rights: From Medieval to Global Assemblages* (Princeton: Princeton University Press, 2006).

[101] J.C. Anene, *The International Boundaries of Nigeria, 1885–1960* (London: Longman, 1970); A.C. McEwan, *The International Boundaries of East Africa* (Oxford: Clarendon Press, 1971); and Saadia Touval, *The Boundary Politics of Independent Africa* (Cambridge: Harvard University Press, 1971).

[102] A.I. Asiwaju, *Western Yorubaland under European Rule, 1889–1945: A Comparative Analysis of French and British Colonialism* (London: Longman, 1976).

the United States–Mexico border on which so much ink was then being spilled.[103] One volume that encapsulated an emerging trend was *Partitioned Africans*, in which the common thread was the experience of ethnic groups divided by Africa's international boundaries – for which Asiwaju helpfully attempted a comprehensive checklist.[104] Since then, the practice of studying two sides of a border has become the norm, even if researchers are sometimes less concerned with the physical border than its political and social effects.[105]

Since the publication of *Partitioned Africans*, the study of African borderlands has undergone a profound transformation. In particular, scholarship has complicated the narrative of ethnic groups arbitrarily divided by colonial borders. First of all, a number of studies have demonstrated that borders created as many opportunities as constraints, leading to an active investment of borderlanders in territorial arrangements.[106] Research that maps commercial networks and migratory flows also makes it difficult to regard the demography of the borderlands as a stable quantity.[107] At the point of partition, frontier regions were in flux and wholesale displacements of population continued thereafter. In more recent times, Africa's borderlands have been characterized by flight, refuge and migration, which problematizes any simple notion that the

[103] A classic study that inspired a generation of borderland scholars is Oscar J. Martínez, *Border People: Life and Society in the U.S.–Mexico Borderlands* (Tucson: University of Arizona Press, 1994).

[104] A.I. Asiwaju (ed.), *Partitioned Africans: Ethnic Relations Across Africa's International Boundaries 1884–1984* (London and Lagos: C. Hurst and University of Lagos Press, 1984).

[105] See, for example, William F.S. Miles, *Hausaland Divided: Colonialism and Independence in Nigeria and Niger* (Ithaca: Cornell University Press, 1994); Nugent, *Smugglers, Secessionists and Loyal Citizens;* and McGregor, *Crossing the Zambezi.* Somewhat different in focus is Hughes, *From Enslavement to Environmentalism.* For a more institutional focus, see Lauren M. MacLean, *Informal Institutions and Citizenship in Rural Africa: Risk and Reciprocity in Ghana and Côte d'Ivoire* (Cambridge: Cambridge University Press, 2010); and Denis Cogneau, Sandrine Mesplé-Somps and Gilles Spielvogel, "Development at the border: policies and national integration in Côte d'Ivoire and its neighbours", *World Bank Economic Review* 29 (1) 2015.

[106] This was highlighted in Paul Nugent and A.I. Asiwaju, "Introduction: The paradox of African boundaries", in Nugent and Asiwaju (eds.), *African Boundaries;* and Nugent, *Smugglers, Secessionists and Loyal Citizens.* See also Donna Flynn, "'We are the border': identity, exchange and the state along the Benin–Nigeria border", *American Ethnologist* 24 (2) 1997; Dereje Feyissa and Markus Virgil Hoehne (eds.), *Borders and Borderlands as Resources in the Horn of Africa* (Woodbridge and Rochester: James Currey, 2010); and Dereje Feyissa, *Playing Different Games: The Paradox of Anywaa and Nuer Identification Strategies in the Gambella Region, Ethiopia* (New York and Oxford: Berghahn, 2011).

[107] Olivier Walther, *Affaires des patrons: villes et commerce transfrontalier au Sahel* (Berne and Oxford: Peter Lang, 2008) and "Trade networks in West Africa: a social network approach", *Journal of Modern African Studies* 52 (2) 2014; and Tim Raeymaekers, *Violent Capitalism and Hybrid Identity in Eastern Congo: Power to the Margins* (Cambridge: Cambridge University Press, 2014).

border population is a fixed category.[108] This is particularly true of border cities and boom towns that have sucked in population from a wide area.[109] Finally, a more critical strain within anthropology and history has questioned 'ethnicity' and 'community' as categories on the basis that they assume an essential character that almost never exists in reality.[110] In a world of networks and flows, the tendency has been to privilege displacement and multi-locality as realities that can only be grasped through research conducted across a multiplicity of field sites.[111]

Rather than risk throwing the baby out with the bathwater, I have adopted the position that these terms are admissible provided one defines them clearly enough. By 'ethnicity', I understand a form of we-group identification that operates beyond the level of the face-to-face group and which does not necessarily depend on actual kinship, however much it may be invoked by actors. Ethnic identities may be expressed in overt forms, but they may equally be rather weakly articulated – and clearly the balance can also shift over time.

---

[108] Harri Englund, *From War to Peace on the Mozambique–Malawi Borderland* (London and Edinburgh: International Africa Institute and Edinburgh University Press, 2002); Judith Scheele, *Smugglers and Saints of the Sahara: Regional Connectivity in the Twentieth Century* (Cambridge: Cambridge University Press, 2012); James McDougall and Judith Scheele (eds.), *Saharan Frontiers: Space and Mobility in Northwest Africa* (Bloomington and Indianapolis: Indiana University Press, 2012).

[109] Karine Bennafla, *Le commerce frontalier en Afrique centrale: acteurs, espaces, pratiques* (Paris: Karthala, 2002); Gregor Dobler, "Oshikango: the dynamics of growth and regulation in a Namibian boom town", *Journal of Southern African Studies* 35 (1) 2009; and Isabella Soi and Paul Nugent, "Peripheral urbanism: border towns and twin towns in Africa", *Journal of Borderlands Studies*, 32 (4) 2017.

[110] There is a vast literature on this subject of ethnicity. For a synthesis, see Thomas Spear, "Neo-traditionalism and the limits of invention in British colonial Africa", *Journal of African History* 44 (1), 2003; Paul Nugent, "Putting the history back into ethnicity: enslavement, religion and cultural brokerage in the construction of Mandinka/Jola and Ewe/Agotime identities in West Africa", *Comparative Studies in Society and History* 50 (4) 2008; and Justin Willis, "Tradition, tribe and state in Kenya: The Mijikenda Union, 1945–1980", *Comparative Studies in Society and History* 55 (2) 2013. A rare attempt to compare the creation of ethnic categories in the colonial period is Alexander Keese, *Ethnicity and the Colonial State: Finding and Representing Group Identifications in a Coastal West African and Global Perspective (1850–1960)* (Leiden: Brill, 2016). 'Community' tends to be accepted for religious collectivities in a way that it is not for others. For example, see Sean Hanretta, *Islam and Social Change in French West Africa: History of an Emancipatory Community* (Cambridge: Cambridge University Press, 2010). Frederick Cooper has given further cause for reflection by demonstrating that the very term 'identity' carries an enormous weight of assumptions. The case he makes for breaking identity down and distinguishing identification from identity is a compelling one. Frederick Cooper, *Colonialism in Question: Theory, Knowledge, History* (Cambridge: Cambridge University Press, 2005), ch. 3.

[111] The literature on the migration is vast. For an account of early starters in the migratory process, see François Manchuelle, *Willing Migrants: Soninke Labor Diasporas, 1848–1960* (Oxford and Athens: James Currey and Ohio University Press, 1997). See also Paul Stoller, *Money Has No Smell: The Africanization of New York* (Chicago and London: Chicago University Press, 2002).

By 'community', I intend to convey a more localized kind of social organization that is embodied in particular spaces. These may be villages, towns and *quartiers* within cities, but they may also include centres of worship such as churches and mosques. A community may be very small, but it may also include members – for example adherents of a religious network – who have not encountered each other directly. It stands to reason that communities may encapsulate a multiplicity of ethnicities while ethnic groups may occupy communities that are differently configured and may be widely scattered. To bring this discussion back to borders, states make a difference because they are in the business of upholding the territorial lines that may cut across or reinforce ethnic and/or community boundaries – potentially altering the internal dynamics of each in the process. In this book, I seek to get to the bottom of why communities have come to be conceived in such different terms in the Senegambia and the trans-Volta and why ethnicity has had such variable salience in the two regions.

Sites of Study: Trans-Volta and the Senegambia

It remains to say something more about my specific choice of case studies and the structure of the book. When I was first looking for an appropriate intra-regional comparison, the Senegambia and the trans-Volta seemed like the obvious choices. In either instance a former British colony bordered onto a former French colony (even if French Togoland was technically a Mandated and later a United Nations Trust Territory). In addition, there was an intriguing asymmetry between a micro-colony and a much more substantial entity next door. This enabled me to weigh up the role of contraband in state-making processes. An added bonus resided in the fact that the micro-colony in the Senegambia was British (the Gambia) whereas in the trans-Volta it was briefly German and then French (Togoland). This enabled me to tease out how far different European predispositions – for example with respect to the powers of traditional authorities and taxation – made a significant difference to the final outcomes. The choice of localities where I could sharpen the focus still further was less straightforward because there were no exact equivalents. I eventually settled on two cases where the relative proximity of a coastal port – Bathurst/Banjul and Lomé respectively – and related populations living on two sides of a border, established a broadly comparable context. I was also keen to focus on cases where there was likely to be enough archival data to sustain a long-range historical comparison. As it turned out, the material was uneven, but for different points in time in either instance. This has resulted in some asymmetry within individual chapters, but across the piece I have been able to accord broadly similar weight to the two cases, and they have contributed in equal measure towards shaping the larger argument. The comparison is also a fully reciprocal one.[112]

In the trans-Volta, I elected to focus on the Agotime and their Ewe-speaking neighbours who surround them on all sides. Although the Ewe have been well served by recent historical literature,[113] almost nothing has been written about the Agotime, despite their prominent historical role in the nineteenth century. I have found myself trying to set the record straight at the same time as deploying the Agotime in the service of the wider comparison. Roughly two-thirds of Agotime today is located in Togo, although the main settlements are fairly evenly distributed on the two sides of the border: namely, Afegame, Kpetoe, Akpokope, Adedome, Agohokpo, Akuete, Bemla and Batome Junction (set hard against the border) in Ghana; and Zukpe, Nyitoe, Adzakpa, Lakwi, Agoudouvou, Kpodjahon, Amoussoukope (or Amoussoukodji), Adame, Akumase, Kodje, Letsukope, Vakpo, Wutegble and Batoumé inside Togo. As we will see, there is a long-running debate about whether Adame and Nyitoe should really be considered Agotime towns at all. In addition, there are a number of additional settlements such as Wodome, Sarakope, Bè, Abenyirase, and several other villages that are made up of former captives and Ewe 'strangers' (see Chapter 2). Kpetoe is the largest town as befits the capital of the Agotime. It was never an administrative headquarters in colonial times, but the central state has always been present in the shape of police and Customs officially and occasionally the military. Today, Kpetoe hosts the CEPS Training Academy, the national facility for training officers of the Customs, Excise and Preventive Service (CEPS).[114] It has also become the capital of a recently created Agotime–Ziope District, which has brought with it the material trappings of District Assembly buildings, a fire station, the District Police headquarters and an improved market. The Agotime towns in Togo are divided between Agou (Agu) and Ave (Kévé) *préfectures*, but none of them serve as the headquarters of an administrative district.

---

[112] Gareth Austin, "Reciprocal comparison and African history: tackling conceptual Eurocentrism on the study of Africa's economic past", *African Studies Review* 50 (3) 2007.

[113] D.E.K. Amenumey, *The Ewe in Pre-Colonial Times* (Accra: Sedco, 1986); Sandra Greene, *Gender, Ethnicity and Social Change on the Upper Slave Coast: A History of the Anlo Ewe* (Portsmouth and London: Heinemann and James Currey, 1996); Sandra Greene, *Sacred Sites and the Colonial Encounter: A History of Meaning and Memory in Ghana* (Bloomington: Indiana University Press, 2002); Emmanuel Akyeampong, *Between the Sea and the Lagoon: An Eco-Social History of the Anlo of Southeastern Ghana, c.1850 to Recent Times* (Oxford: James Currey, 2002); and Nugent, *Smugglers, Secessionists and Loyal Citizens*. For the politics of Eweland, see D.E.K. Amenumey, *The Ewe Unification Movement: A Political History* (Accra: Ghana Universities Press, 1989) and Kate Skinner, *The Fruits of Freedom in Togoland: Literacy, Politics and Nationalism, 1914–2014* (Cambridge: Cambridge University Press, 2015).

[114] In 2017, the CEPS Academy was in the process of being converted into a Revenue University.

Much like in Dmitris Dalakoglou's account of the Albania–Greece highway, Agotime has historically been defined by its relationship to roads.[115] Kpetoe lay astride an older slave trading route, which was later re-inscribed as a German hammock-road linking Ho with Aflao – and by extension Lomé. Amoussoukope, which marks the eastern limits of Agotime, is situated on another former German road that links Lomé and the commercial centre of Kpalimé (see Map 1.3). A Kpetoe chief once joked with me that Agotime is known for only two things – kente and smuggling. Most of the goods that have been smuggled through Agotime since the 1920s have travelled along the Lomé–Kpalimé road before jumping sideways to continue along the Aflao–Ho road. Connecting these two north–south arteries is a veritable maze of rough roads – often little more than dirt tracks that have been etched into the landscape by frequent use – that criss-cross the landscape and which have served as the conduit for trade in local produce and contraband goods alike. The only recognized crossing point is at Batome Junction where the road enters Togo, passes through Batoumé village and strikes the Lomé–Kpalimé road at Assahoun. But on market days in Amoussoukope, most of the vehicles originating from Kpetoe avoid Batome Junction altogether and enter Togo using one of the dirt roads.

Over the course of the book, I have turned to Agotime as a ready source of examples, but I have also systematically charted its trajectory from the eighteenth century to the present, with the intention that if anybody were to join all the passages together – as readers from Agotime might well prefer to do – they would be presented with a coherent history of the polity and its people. This is a history that begins with the first settlement of Adangbe migrants around the Todzie River, and their close engagement with trade to and from the coast, including slaves, ivory and salt, from the eighteenth century (see Chapter 2). It continues with the Agotime experience of colonization and territorial partition after the First World War. I have paid particular attention to the ways in which the Agotime became deeply implicated in the contraband trade during the interwar years, and I follow successive mutations in this trade down to the 1990s. I devote considerable space to the period of the revolution in Ghana (Chapter 12) for which the Public Tribunal records offer a rich insight into the way in which the contraband trade was organized. In the final chapter, I come full circle with an analysis of the attempt by Agotime leaders to recapture a sense of their shared history and cultural inheritance in the face of the many differences that the border has instilled. This is reflected in history writing,[116]

---

[115] Dimitris Dalakoglou, *The Road: An Ethnography of (Im)mobility, Space and Cross-Border Infrastructure in the Balkans* (Manchester: Manchester University Press, 2017).

[116] An important contribution to local history is Nene Ahortor Makaku V, *A Brief History of the Lehs Vis-à-Vis the Agotimes* (Accra: the author, 2016).

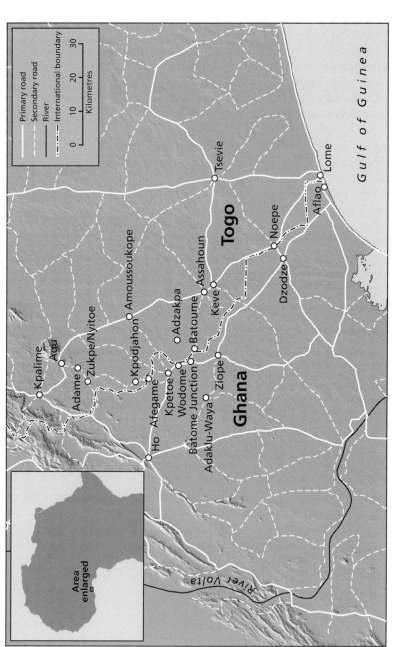

Map 1.3 Trans-Volta and partitioned Agotime.

but above all in the annual *Agbamevoza*, or kente festival. This study inevitably touches at many points on the relationship between the Agotime and neighbouring Ewe polities or *dukɔwo* (sing. *dukɔ*) – one that has been coloured by a history of slaving and contests over land. But at the same time, most Agotime openly acknowledge the extent to which they have borrowed from their Ewe neighbours – linguistically, culturally and demographically.

In the Senegambia, I am concerned with the south-western quadrant of the Gambia and the adjoining section of the Casamance in what is now Senegal (see Map 1.4). A distinction is sometimes made between Kombo proper and Fogny-Kombo. The former refers to a small kingdom that became a close neighbour of the British merchant community in Bathurst (later Banjul). In the nineteenth century, a protracted struggle for power between the kings of Kombo and Muslim reformers culminated in outright victory for the latter. Although the victors in the Soninke–Marabout wars conceived of Kombo as an Islamic state, ruled from its new capital of Gunjur, it never managed to consolidate itself and its leader, Fodé Sylla, was eventually defeated and exiled by the British. All of the former kingdom of Kombo was then folded into the Gambia, in effect superimposing colonial borders upon a pre-existing frontier zone. On the other side of the line, Fogny-Kombo is a misnomer and I have preferred to distinguish between Narang (in the forested area closest to Kombo) and Fogny-Jabangkunda to the west and to the south thereof. There were close connections between Kombo and many of the Mandinka settlements on the coastal seaboard, based on shared traditions of migration (see Chapter 2). But Fogny-Jabangkunda was politically distinct from the kingdom of Kombo in the period covered in this book. It was also home to people who traced their origins to the putative autochthons, the Bainunks, as well as to Jola who had been moving northwards over time. Although colonial ethnography made rigid distinctions between ethnic categories, oral traditions and family names both suggest a great deal of mixing between these various peoples. Further to the south, the Karoninka/Kalorn people of Karone were classified by the French as a sub-set of the Jola, a claim that has been hotly disputed in more recent times. In this book, I am mostly concerned with the southern section of Kombo, extending roughly from Brikama to the border. This includes settlements such as Kitti, Nyofelleh, Sifoe, Darsilami, Dimbaya and Kartong. In the Casamance, I deal with all of Narang – including villages such as Diébaly, Kujube, Makuda, Touba, Mahamouda, Donbondir and Daroussalaam – and all of Fogny-Jabangkunda, including Abéné, Kabadio and Kafountine. I deal in much less detail with Karone proper, although the migration of people from the islands is a large part of my story.

Together, Kombo, Narang and Fogny-Jabangkunda have been defined less by their relationship to roads than to bodies of water. The larger region is bracketed by the Gambia and the Casamance River systems and is

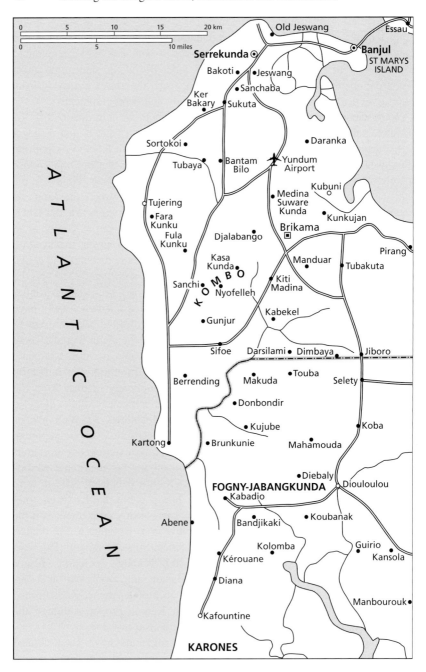

Map 1.4 The Gambia/Casamance border depicting Kombo, Narang and Fogny-Jabangkunda.

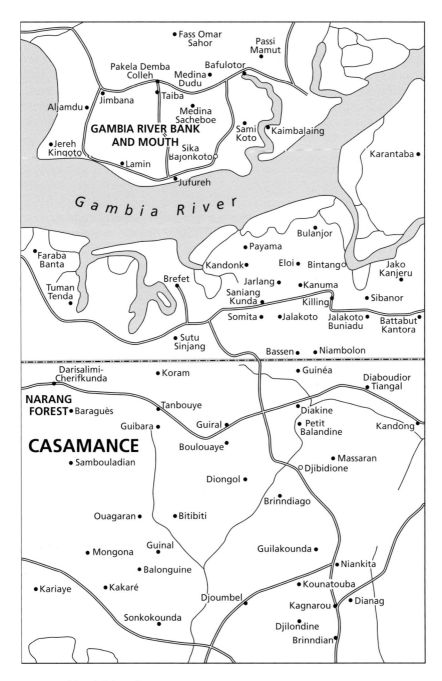

Map 1.4 (*cont.*)

characterized by a myriad of swamps and creeks. The British invested very little in roads, for the reason that they expected the Gambia River to carry most of the traffic of the colony. The French had a greater interest in infrastructure that might connect the two halves of their colony but invested relatively few resources in the Casamance. Although donkey carts have historically been crucial to cross-border trade, certainly before the irresistible rise of the motorbike, much of the contraband has been waterborne, with canoes connecting the Gambia, the Casamance and Guinea-Bissau.[117] Today, the most important arterial road is the one that runs from Serekunda, through Brikama to the border and then continues to the Senegalese administrative centre of Diouloulou, at which point the road divides – with one section continuing to Kafountine and the other proceeding to Bignona and Ziguinchor. Although large trucks and passenger vehicles follow this route, and subject themselves to Customs and Immigration formalities at Jiboro-Séléty, much of the contraband trade crosses the Allahein River to the west or passes through the many unofficial crossings. As we will see, the distinctive aspect of this border is its diverse settlement pattern, such that very few villages could be described as anything like ethnically homogeneous today. Although most settlements are made up of some combination of Mandinka, Jola and Karoninka people, Balanta, Manjago and Fula migrants are also well-represented. The most striking difference with Agotime is that even relatively recent arrivals have been able to stake claims to local citizenship.

The book speaks directly to historians, but it also aspires to engage with political scientists and anthropologists, while making a contribution to the renascent field of borderland studies.[118] The text is divided into four parts that are arranged chronologically and then assembled according to theme. In Part I, I address the deeper logics according to which frontiers were transformed into colonial boundaries over the course of the nineteenth century. Chapter 2 compares patterns of settlement in the Senegambia and the trans-Volta and probes the societal transformations that were wrought by involvement in the Atlantic slave trade. In Chapter 3, I develop the argument that African demands for public goods within the port cities helped stimulate the push to the frontier in the pursuit of taxable trade. I go on to account for the ways in which frontiers hardened into colonial boundaries at the end of the century. In Part II, I compare the architecture of the four colonial states and the points of contact with colonized populations. In Chapter 4, I elaborate upon the claim

---

[117] For an instructive comparison, see Eric Tagliacozzo, *Secret Trades, Porous Borders: Smuggling and States Along a Southeast Asian Frontier, 1865–1915* (New Haven and London: Yale University Press, 2005).

[118] The current state of the art is reflected in Thomas Wilson and Hastings Donnan (eds.), *The Blackwell Companion to Border Studies* (Chichester: Wiley-Blackwell, 2012).

that the fiscal imperatives that lay behind the partition were hardwired into colonial states, but according to quite distinct patterns. I compare the very different ways in which the authorities engaged with their populations through the taxation of consumption and the delivery of public goods. In Chapter 5, I address the differential success with which colonial regimes attempted to govern either through traditional authorities or with their co-operation. Chapter 6 pursues a detailed comparison of approaches to the regulation of the flow of goods and the mobility of populations – which were strikingly different in the Senegambia and the trans-Volta. I highlight the ways in which colonial regimes were often operating at cross-purposes with, and frequently undermining, one another in a conscious manner. In Chapter 7, I turn to some of the implications for the terms on which strangers could stake claims to land and local citizenship. Here, I also consider the different ways in which religion mediated the terms on which migrants could access each of these.

Part III is devoted to the decades on either side of independence when there was a momentary possibility of revisiting the positioning and practical meaning attributed to boundaries. In Chapter 8, I provide a brief overview of the way in which pro-Vichy and British administrations sought to instrumentalize borders during the Second World War, and the manner in which the discourse of 'development' became central to the attempt to rebuild legitimacy. This leads into Chapter 9, where I deal with the reasons why the ideal of a greater Senegambia foundered on the rocks of national independence. In the case of the trans-Volta, which is the subject of Chapter 10, I account for why there was a similar outcome despite the existence of a popular constituency for reunification of Eweland and/or the two Togolands.

Coming to Part IV, Chapters 11 and 12 pick up where Chapters 9 and 10 left off. Here, I contrast the efforts of governments in Senegal and Ghana to reconfigure social contracts through a respacing of development planning with the countervailing strategies of regimes in the Gambia and Togo, which gave full licence to the contraband trade through Banjul and Lomé. I demonstrate how an expansion of a regional contraband trade, in turn, gave rise to new manifestations of urbanism in which the relationships between centres and margins was altered in profound ways. In Chapter 13, I conclude with an account of more recent efforts to cement unity across borders through appeals to a shared history and common cultural attributes in each of the two sub-regions. A Conclusion identifies five transversal themes, ties together the threads and restates the broader argument.

A Note on Orthography

French and English sources have tended to use rather different spellings for place names, and since independence there have often been further modifications that reflect state naming practices. I have generally preferred the spelling that is appropriate to the context. Hence, I refer to *Agu* as a location in Togo, but when I allude to it in the context of Togolese administrative practices, I adopt the official spelling of *Agou*. I also refer to Batome Junction in Ghana, but to the Togolese village of Batoumé. Ethnonyms pose a different kind of problem. The term *Karoninka*, which is of Mandinka origin, has become contentious in the Senegambia, and there has been an attempt by activists to substitute *Kalorn*. Because Karoninka is the more widely used in the region, I have deployed it for most of the book. But in the context of a discussion of identity politics, I have also referred to the *Kalorn*. *Krepe* is a somewhat imprecise term that was current in the trans-Volta in the nineteenth century. It referred to northern Ewe peoples, but often folded in other peoples such as the Agotime. In the twentieth century, the term disappeared from usage.

Part I

From Frontiers to Boundaries

In the first section of this book, I am concerned with exposing the inner workings and spatial logics of societies in the Senegambia and the trans-Volta before the partition at the end of the nineteenth century. I also seek to understand the ways in which existing frontier regions were incorporated into boundary-making and how, in turn, the latter was integral to colonial state-making. I advance a case for viewing the relationship between boundaries and state-making in its West African context. Although I question the straightforward notion that institutions were transplanted from Europe to Africa, I also show how these processes were shaped by a longer engagement with the Atlantic world.

2 Configurations of Power in Comparative Perspective
Commerce, People and Belief to c.1880

As has been intimated in Chapter 1, a satisfactory account of state formation and boundary-making requires a deeper historical timeline than conventional chronologies allow for. I have two overarching aims in this chapter. The first is to excavate the deeper histories of the societies that form the basis of my larger comparison, treating these as dynamic entities that were forged within the context of a volatile frontier equation.[1] In either case, it is important that the colonial partition took place against the backdrop of considerable levels of violence during the last three decades of the nineteenth century. Secondly, the chapter sets out to advance an argument, contra James C. Scott, that there was no straightforward choice between belonging to a state and statelessness.[2] The political entities that emerged in the Senegambia and trans-Volta point to a range of intermediate possibilities, some of which I will consider below. The utility of this exercise resides in identifying conceptions of the political that subsequently informed reactions to colonial state-making.

The interpretations that are offered here are necessarily somewhat speculative because of the uneven quality of the data. The Agotime have fallen between the historiographical cracks to a surprising degree. Although contemporary sources of the eighteenth and nineteenth century – specifically Danish ones – routinely referred to Agotime, usually in the company of Akwamu and Anlo, this polity has never been the subject of academic study in its own right. Part of the reason may be that historians of the trans-Volta region have been more interested in Ewe polities or *dukɔwo* (*dukɔ* sing.) than with what are today regarded as 'minorities' like the Agotime.[3] On the other hand, research

---

[1] This chapter builds on Paul Nugent, "Putting the history back into ethnicity: enslavement, religion and cultural brokerage in the construction of Mandinka/Jola and Ewe/Agotime identities in West Africa", *Comparative Studies in Society and History* 50 (4) 2008.

[2] James C. Scott, *The Art of Not Being Governed: An Anarchist History of Upland Southeast Asia* (New Haven and London: Yale University Press, 2009), p. 79.

[3] D.E.K. Amenumey has done more than anyone to create Ewe history as a focus of study, although the Agotime are also mentioned in his research. See his short study, *The Ewe in Pre-Colonial Times* (Accra: Sedco, 1986). On the Anlo-Ewe, see Sandra Greene, *Gender, Ethnicity and Social Change on the Upper Slave Coast: A History of the Anlo Ewe* (Portsmouth and London: Heinemann and James Currey, 1996), and her sequel, *Sacred Sites and the Colonial*

on the Adangbe has mostly focused on the Ga and the Krobo of modern Ghana, rather than with the diaspora that is scattered across what is now the Volta Region of Ghana and southern Togo.[4] When it comes to ordering and structuring historical information, borders have had a profound impact down to the present. The partition of the Agotime between what is now Ghana and Togo has served to reduce their visibility in both countries. In sum, the Agotime have not merely been divided into two unequal halves but have suffered from the fracturing of knowledge that is embodied in maps, statistics and administrative archives. What I endeavour to do here is to piece together disparate fragments derived from contemporary European sources, oral traditions, early colonial reflections and local histories. As I will indicate in the final chapter, local actors are actively involved in a process of 're-membering' a polity that was dismembered after the First World War.

In the case of the Mandinka and the Jola, the data is fuller in some respects, but it is also uneven. What has been written about the Mandinka relates mostly to those located on the north bank of the Gambia or further to the east, extending down into what is now Guinea-Bissau.[5] The Mandinka of the western quadrant of the Casamance/Gambia border zone are less visible in the academic literature. This is true even of Kombo, which certainly impinged on the consciousness of European traders operating along the Gambia River. In the case of the Jola, there is a rich historical and ethnographic literature, but much of it relates to the regions bordering the Casamance River in the south.[6] Because the Jola are famously diverse, it is necessary to avoid the temptation

---

Encounter: A History of Meaning and Memory in Ghana (Bloomington: Indiana University Press, 2002).

[4] The one noteworthy exception is the research of Robert Sprigge. See R.G.S. Sprigge, "Ewelands's Adangbe: an enquiry into an oral tradition", *Transactions of the Historical Society of Ghana* X 1969. There is a large literature on the Ga. The pioneer was Rev. Carl Reindorf, whose book, *The History of the Gold Coast and Asante, Based on Traditions and Historical Facts Comprising a Period of More than Three Centuries from About 1500 to 1860* (Accra: Ghana Universities Press, 1966 (1st edition 1889)), remains an important reference point for historians. The most recent study is John Parker, *Making the Town: Ga State and Society in Early Colonial Accra* (Portsmouth, Oxford and Cape Town: Heinemann, James Currey and David Philip, 2000). On the Krobo, see Louis Wilson, *The Krobo People of Ghana to 1892: A Political and Social History* (Athens: Ohio University, 1991).

[5] Donald Wright has done a great service with his detailed research on the Mandinka polity of Niumi on the north bank of the Gambia. This is distilled in Donald Wright, *The World and a Very Small Place: A History of Globalization in Niumi, the Gambia* (New York and London: M.E. Sharpe, 2004). On the western Mandinka more broadly, with a particular focus on Kabu, see Djibril Tamsir Niane, *Histoire des Mandingues de l'ouest: le royaume du Gabou* (Paris: Karthala, 1989). See also Al Haji Bakary Sidibé, *A Brief History of Kaabu and Fuladu (1300–1930): A Narrative Based on Some Oral Traditions of the Senegambia (West Africa)* (Torino: L'Harmattan Italia, 2004).

[6] On the history of the Jola, see Robert M. Baum, *Shrines of the Slave Trade: Diola Religion and Society in Precolonial Senegambia* (New York and Oxford: Oxford University Press, 1999); and Peter Mark, *A Cultural, Economic and Religious History of the Basse Casamance Since 1500*

to transplant insights from one setting to the next. This poses some problems for writing about those who lived on the frontiers of Kombo. These are sometimes depicted as being not 'typically Jola' or as 'mixed'.[7] Leaving aside the unrewarding question of whether 'pure' Jola ever existed, the salient question becomes one of where the boundaries of ethnicity and community were drawn. As with the Agotime case, I have endeavoured to piece together a range of materials – including oral traditions and contemporary written records – to reconstruct the history of a classic frontier zone.

Material and Spiritual Foundations of Power: Agotime and Ewe, Mandinka and Jola

Historians of West Africa before the twentieth century are faced with source material that needs to be treated with some caution. On the one hand, there is a tendency for European sources to refer to 'kingdoms', implying a measure of political centralization that is often questionable. I have generally preferred to allude to 'polities', leaving for closer consideration the ways in which power was configured, both spatially and institutionally. On the other hand, while oral traditions are often extremely rich, they are notoriously difficult to reconcile, in part because they are the basis upon which claims to territory and belonging are made. A single 'truth' does not simply emerge, however much triangulation the historian or anthropologist engages in. And yet at the same time these traditions are not normally based on outright fabrication because the point is to persuade others of their veracity. Historical truth is typically the outcome of contestation, which means that its contours can shift over time. The challenge is to decide which claims seem the most plausible while recognizing that these may not be the ones that are the most current. The traditions in question typically detail movements of population that are readily comprehensible within Kopytoff's model of the African frontier.[8] My modus operandi

---

(Stuttgart: Franz Steiner Verlag, 1985). Pioneering ethnography was carried out by Louis-Vincent Thomas, *Les Diola; essai d'analyse fonctionnelle sur une population de Basse-Casamance, Mémoires de l'Institut Français d'Afrique Noire* (Dakar: IFAN, 1958). Important work on Jola agriculture has been carried out by Paul Pélissier, *Les paysans du Sénégal: les civilisations agraires de Cayor à la Casamance* (Saint-Yrieix: author, 1966), and subsequently by Olga Linares in *Power, Prayer and Production: The Jola of Casamance, Senegal* (Cambridge: Cambridge University Press, 1992). The most recent contribution to the ethnography of the Jola is Ferdinand de Jong, *Masquerades of Modernity: Power and Secrecy in Casamance, Senegal* (Edinburgh: Edinburgh University Press for the International Africa Institute, 2007).

[7] A rare attempt to study the north-western Jola in their own right is that of Jonathan Vaughan Smith, "The Jolas of Senegambia, West Africa: Ethnolinguistic Identity and Change Across an International Border", PhD thesis, University of Oregon, 1993 (Ann Arbor: UMI Dissertation Services, 1993).

[8] Igor Kopytoff, "The internal African frontier: the making of African political culture", in Igor Kopytoff (ed.), *The African Frontier: The Reproduction of Traditional African Societies* (Bloomington

in what follows is to pay close attention to detail in each of the case studies, whilst leaving space for more explicit points of comparison to emerge. This account begins with the Agotime/Ewe case before proceeding to that of the Mandinka/Jola.

The Agotime in the Trans-Volta Vortex

> You see, before the Agotimes came here, there was this Ando people – Ando and Atsi people. But they [the Agotimes] forced them and drove them away. The greater part of them now settle at Sokode ... So we completely seized their land from them right down to Agu ... We took [over] all those people from Atikpui – before the white men came .... Nyitoe was not our town. We captured them also and they became Agotime. Likewise Atikpui, Nyive. They were our vassal states. But when the white man came in with their rule, we lost those people. And then when this amalgamation came after the border – when this part went under the British – we lost almost all the vassal states. And our power was completely reduced.[9]

In March 2001, I conducted an extended interview with the Konor, that is the senior chief, of Agotime, Nene Nuer Keteku III, at his second home in Ho, the capital of Volta Region in Ghana. At the time, Nene Keteku was on the verge of retiring from the Ghana Education Service for whom he had worked for some years in its Regional office. By virtue of his employment, he spent most of his days in Ho, returning to Kpetoe at weekends or when meetings needed to be convened to deliberate on Agotime matters.[10] Nene Keteku offered a sweeping historical interpretation of Agotime history, which stressed that this polity had once been a powerful regional player, but had then suffered a series of mishaps dating from the advent of European rule. While the people of Ho always seemed to land on their feet, the Agotime had a decidedly unlucky streak.[11] What particularly rankled was that Nene Keteku was considered a sub-chief of the Asogli Traditional

---

and Indianapolis: Indiana University Press, 1987). European traders were often incorporated on these very terms. For the Senegambia, see George E. Brooks, *Landlords and Strangers: Ecology, Society and Trade in Western Africa 1000–1630* (Boulder: Westview Press, 1994).

[9] Interview with Nene Nuer Keteku III, Konor of Agotime, at Ho (26 March 2001). Technically speaking he was not a paramount chief, but he was regarded as the head of all the Agotimes in Ghana and was recognized by most Togolese Agotimes at some level.

[10] This happened rather a lot at this time because Nene Keteku was under a great deal of pressure from his sub-chiefs, amidst rumours of a possible destoolment action. Asogli chieftaincy affairs notionally gave Nene Keteku another reason to be in Ho, but at the time of the interview he had ceased attending Asogli Traditional Council meetings as a matter of principle.

[11] It is generally believed that Ho only ever became the Regional capital because Hohoe, which would have been the more natural candidate, was doggedly anti-CPP (Convention People's Party) in the 1950s.

Area underneath the Ho paramount chief. This arrangement dated from the time of the contentious British amalgamation policy, which I have written about previously.[12] Given that most of the Agotime were located on the Togo side of the border, the bargaining power of the Konor was even more narrowly circumscribed.

During the interview, Nene Keteku claimed that greater Agotime had once covered Hodzo to the west, Atikpui and Nyive to the north; parts of Agu to the north-east; and Kévé, Dakpa, Takla, Ziope and Dzalele to the east and south-east. The broad thrust of these claims was reiterated in a draft of Agotime history that he had been preparing and which he handed to me in the shape of a roughly typed document.[13] Having conducted detailed research in the Volta Region before, I was very conscious of the fact that the history of the trans-Volta was one of small chiefdoms that were pretty much of equal weight. The claims of Peki to have presided over a Krepe kingdom in the nineteenth century turned out to have been highly implausible – even if the British sometimes found it convenient to back Peki pretensions. All of this initially made me sceptical of the claims that Nene Keteku was advancing. Insofar as there had been a regional power, it was surely Akwamu that had relocated its capital to the left bank of the Volta River after its defeat in the Akwapim hills around 1730 (the riverain location of 'Aquambu' is clearly indicated on the 1802 map by Thonning: see Map 2.1).[14] The Akwamu are known to have extracted a tribute from the Krepe (or northern Ewe) dukɔwo up until their defeat by a coalition of Ewe polities, led by Peki, in the early 1830s. Moreover, the Akwamu were clients of the Asante, to whom they remitted part of their tribute. The reality of Akwamu sub-imperialism in the trans-Volta did not seem to leave much space for the kind of claims being advanced by Nene Keteku.

Nevertheless, a closer examination of the sources suggests that Nene Keteku's reconstruction of Agotime history is not fanciful. One of the distinctive aspects of Akwamu statecraft was actually the paucity thereof: that is, it did not seek to govern very much in the way of territory after the 1730s and was seemingly

---

[12] In more recent times, the autonomy of formerly independent dukɔwo has been restored, but they have continued to be denied their own traditional councils. See Paul Nugent, *Smugglers, Secessionists and Loyal Citizens on the Ghana–Togo Frontier: The Lie of the Borderlands Since 1914* (Oxford and Athens: James Currey and Ohio University Press, 2002), ch. 4 and "An abandoned project? The nuances of chieftaincy, development and history in Ghana's Volta Region", *Journal of Legal Pluralism and Unofficial Law* 28 (37–38) 1996.

[13] Nene Nuer Keteku III, "Short History of the Agotimes" (undated), copy in my possession.

[14] Akwamu was once the pre-eminent kingdom, but after its defeat in 1730, it never regained its former glory. On the earlier kingdom, see Ivor Wilks, *Akwamu, 1640–1750: A Study of the Rise and Fall of a West African Empire* (Trondheim: Norwegian University of Science and Technology, 2001), especially ch. 2 on administration, and Ray A. Kea, "Administration and trade in the Akwamu empire, 1681–1730", in B.K. Swartz and Raymond E. Dumett (eds.), *West African Culture Dynamics* (Berlin: De Gruyter Mouton, 1980).

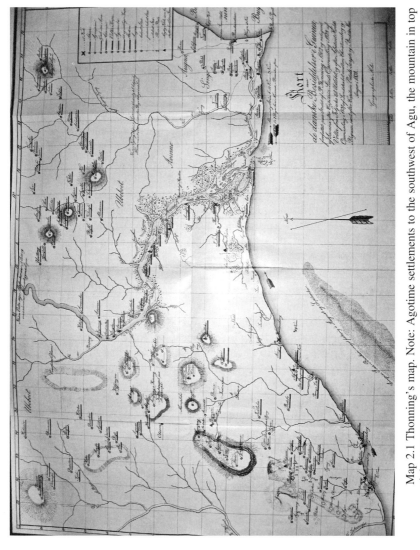

Map 2.1 Thonning's map. Note: Agotime settlements to the southwest of Agu, the mountain in top right corner.

content with extracting resources from its weaker neighbours, notably in the form of slaves. This left ample scope for relying upon the coercive force of other allied polities like Peki that were located further away from the Volta River. The Agotime seem to have consolidated their own position as the military allies of Akwamu, which would have strengthened their capacity to accumulate slaves of their own. This conforms to a pattern of political restructuring that took place right across the Slave Coast in the context of the slave trade.[15] Although it is exaggerated, there is some truth to the Agotime self-image as a people wedded to the pursuit of warfare: that is, as distinct from neighbouring Ewe peoples, such as the Ando and Adaklu, who were reputed to be consummate farmers, but easy prey. Crops produced by the Krepe – in particular maize, millet and cotton – featured prominently in the north–south trade.[16] Whereas the Krepe were sometimes treated in Danish sources as quintessential slaves, the Agotime were generally portrayed as suppliers rather than as victims. This is clear in spite of the fact that the commentaries sometimes elided the distinction between peoples who were enslaved and those who did the enslaving. In the following example, the Agotime were those who sold slaves, while the Nyive and the Takla would more often have been on the receiving end:

This seat [Fort Kongensteen], though it is situated inland 2 Miles [Danish miles] from the sea, is one of the best places on the Gold Coast as regards the slave trade, which is procured from Akotim [Agotime], Adakrue [Adaklu], Innive [Nyive], and Takra [Takla] Lands, and they are all brought hither in canoes in the *revier* from Malphy [Mlefi].[17]

---

[15] Robin Law's interpretation of the emergence of a Dahomean kingdom, using contemporary sources, is precisely that of a group of banditti who supplied slaves to Allada before consolidating and seizing control of the coastal ports in the 1720s. Robin Law, *The Slave Coast of West Africa, 1550–1750: The Impact of the Atlantic Slave Trade on an African Society* (Oxford: Oxford University Press, 1991), pp. 242, 261–5; Robin Law, "Dahomey and the slave trade: reflections on the historiography of the rise of Dahomey", *Journal of African History* 27 1986, pp. 253–4.

[16] Cotton was a significant item of trade and was despatched southwards towards Anlo and northwards towards Salaga. The Ho area was a significant supplier of yams, maize and palm oil to the coast. Peter Buhler, "The Volta Region of Ghana: Economic Change in Togoland, 1850–1914", PhD thesis, University of California, 1975, pp. 27, 92. Many of these foodstuffs were bought by the Danes, especially maize or what was called 'millie'. Hernaes estimates that the value of the millie trade in the second half of the eighteenth century exceeded that in slaves and ivory, although it was coming from all along the coast. In 1775, the Danes concentrated on Keta, rather than the Fante region, as the centre of this trade. The implication is that the trans-Volta became a more important supplier. The 'Crepees' were already mentioned by Rask in 1754 as one of the main suppliers of millet (or 'small millie'). Per Hernaes, *Slaves, Danes and African Coast Society: The Danish Slave Trade from West Africa and Afro-Danish Relations on the Eighteenth-Century Gold Coast* (Trondheim: University of Trondheim, Department of History, 1998), pp. 340, 346, 348. Raak has now been translated, as Selena Axelrod Winsnes (ed.), *Two Views from Christiansborg Castle: Volume I – A Brief and Truthful Description of a Journey to and from Guinea by Johannes Rask* (Accra: Sub-Saharan Publishers, 2008).

[17] I am extremely grateful to Ole Justesen for providing me with a translation of this document and for discussing its likely interpretation. The original of Andreas Riegelsen Biørn's, "*Account 1788 of the Danish Forts and Towns on the Gold Coast*", may be found at Archiv for Statistik,

Before returning to the question of what kind of polity Agotime had become by the nineteenth century, it is necessary to look more closely at the question of the origins of its constituent people. In fact, Agotime oral traditions are as much about mobility as they are about warfare and trade. All the traditions agree on the coastline east of Accra as the place from which the Agotime originated – and more specifically the area around Lekponguno between Old Ningo and the Songhor Lagoon (west of Ada).[18] Although the migration stories have to be taken with generous helpings of sea-salt, there is other evidence that broadly supports these claims. Linguistic evidence is perhaps the least conclusive, but it nevertheless needs to be added to the scales. Until the twentieth century, almost all Agotimes spoke a dialect of the Adangbe language. S.W. Koelle's *Polyglotta Africana*, which was published in 1854, made use of an informant from Agotime, one Tete, and described the language he spoke as 'Adampe'.[19] The map that accompanies the book places 'Adampe' not where Agotime is today, but west of the Volta – roughly where Ada is located. One assumes that Koelle, who was certainly a thorough researcher, regarded the Agotime as speaking the Ada language rather than being simply confused over the geography of the region. More persuasively, Danish sources bear out traditions of enforced migration away from the coastline near to Ada. There is always a possibility that some of the Adangbe living east of the Volta were leftovers from earlier migrations from the west.[20] However, the traditions of these groups do refer to specific episodes that led to their displacement in more proximate times.

When R.S. Rattray was collecting oral histories to firm up British claims to German territory in 1915, his Agotime informants stated categorically that "We are not Ewes – our race is the same as the Ses and we are also called Elles".[21] This is significant because the Danish trader, Isert, who published a series of letters dating from his time on the coast in 1788, noted that there had

Politik og Huusholdnings-Videnskaber, Heftskrift. Ed. by Frederik Thaarup, Kjøbenhavn, Bd. 3, 1797–1798, pp. 193–230. Takla is located near to Ho, but this could also be a reference to Takpla to the east of Agotime.

[18] "Lekpos or Lenden-kera Locality History in T.V.T", Ewe manuscript in my possession, dated 11 November 1954 (translation by Setri Dzivenu). This document makes the unusual claim that the Agotime were previously from Denkyira; see also Sprigge, "Eweland's Adangbe", p. 93.

[19] Entry in "Introductory Remarks" listed under 'Adampe' within "Dahomean or Slave Coast Languages" in Sigismund Wilhelm Koelle, *Polyglotta Africana* (Paul Hair and David Dalby, eds.) (Graz: Akademische Druk – U. Verlagsanstalt, 1963 (original edition 1854)), p. 4.

[20] On Ada traditions that claim a migration from the east, see C.O.C. Amate, *The Making of Ada* (Accra: Woeli, 1999), ch. 1. Similarly, on the Krobo versions of the Adangbe traditions, see Wilson, *Krobo People*.

[21] PRAAD (Ho) RAO 273, *Togoland: A History of the Tribal Divisions of the District of Misahuhe and of the Sub-Districts of Ho and Kpandu*. Rattray served briefly as District Political Officer in occupied Togoland before his appointment as a government anthropologist. He is most famous for his work on Ashanti and the Northern Territories.

once been a coastal settlement bearing the name of "Lai" [Le] situated halfway between Ningo and Ada.[22] It had attracted some English trade before it was attacked and its people were driven in either direction towards those very towns.[23] Apart from the port of Le, there was also a very old settlement called Ladoku/Ledoku. The 'kingdom of Ladoku', which appears on some European maps as 'Ladingcour', is also referred to in some Agotime traditions, although these conceivably draw on more recent sources.[24]

Andreas Biørn referred to the fate of the Les in a report, also dating from 1788, in which he observed that refugees from an Akwamu assault on the coast in 1679 were amongst the Adangbe peoples who turned up in Aflao.[25] His description, which has been closely interrogated by Sprigge,[26] reads as follows:

In the wars of the Akra, Aqvambue, Akim Kingdoms [in] 1679 almost all the Adampe Schay at Ningo, Prampram – Tessing [Teshie] – and Lay-Negroes fled hither, and divided themselves into 3 parties, viz.: Schay Negroes, who went up country, where they still are called Great and Little Schay, Tetetu, or all Adampe-Land; then Lay-Negroes, who settled down in high mountains approximately 20 Miles from the sea, which nowadays is called Augo [Agu], and consists of 19 towns situated on the mountains and a town in the valley; and finally the real Adampes, formerly situated at Lathe [Larteh] between Cobbo [Krobo] and Aqvapim [Akwapim], was ruled by 2 Princes, Offu and Debey, and settled down here at Aflahu [Aflao], and called it Verhue, where they lived until the year 1700, when the reigning Prince Affarry at Popo, though with the loss of his own life, repulsed them, whereupon they fled up country and settled down by a branch of Riowolta [Volta River], now called Akotim [Agotime].[27]

Sprigge observes that the first mention of refugees – those of Ningo, Prampram, Teshie and Le – does not correspond with the three groupings into which he subsequently divided them, namely the Shai, the Le of Agu and the Agotime. However, this may be a misreading of the source in question. If the

---

[22] See map from Ole Justesen (ed.), *Danish Sources for the History of Ghana, 1657–1754* (Copenhagen: Royal Danish Academy of Sciences, 2005), vol 2, p. 1009.

[23] Selena Axelrod Winsnes (ed.), *Letters on West Africa and the Slave Trade: Paul Erdman Isert's 'Journey to Guinea and the Caribbean Islands in Columbia' (1788)* (Accra: Sub-Saharan Publishers, 2007), p. 52. It was also referred to by Bosman as a slave port in the first years of the eighteenth century. William Bosman, *A New and Accurate Description of Guinea, Divided into the Gold, The Slave and the Ivory Coasts* (new edition by J.R. Willis) (London: Frank Cass, 1967 (original edition 1704)), p. 327. Also Sprigge, "Eweland's Adangbe", p. 94.

[24] Nene Keteku, "Short history", p. 1. The archaeological evidence suggests that Ladoku dates to the eleventh century. Wilson, *The Krobo People*, p. 34. It is probably a La settlement, with which the Les became associated.

[25] Sprigge, "Eweland's Adangbe", pp. 90, 95. The date of 1679 is possibly wrong because the documented attack dates to 1682. However, it seems that there may have been multiple attacks. Silke Strickrodt, *Afro-European Trade in the Atlantic World: The Western Slave Coast, c.1550–1885* (Woodbridge and Rochester: James Currey, 2015), p. 77.

[26] Sprigge, "Eweland's Adangbe", pp. 89–90.   [27] Biørn, "Account 1788", p. 212.

Shai category encapsulated the Ningo, Prampram and Teshie, then the Le might refer to all the rest. It is true that Biørn appears to equate the Le with the Agu exclusively, but it very likely included the Agotime as well. Biørn was possibly aware of the relationship between the people around Agu and the Agotime, but being unsure of his facts, chose to fudge his description.

Other evidence does lend some support to this re-reading of Biørn. First of all, the Agotime today claim a close connection with the people of Krobo, with whom they share *dipo* initiation rites and a closely related dialect of the Adangbe language. Biørn was probably correct, therefore, in tracing an earlier settlement of the Agotime to the vicinity of Krobo. Secondly, Agotime traditions themselves draw a historical connection between the Agu and the Agotime. Hence, Nene Keteku's written history claims that his people migrated eastwards into Fon country where they engaged in warfare, and that they were then split further into three groups: one founded Se-Godze (in present-day Togo), the second moved back to Anlo where they constituted the Wifeme clan, and the third settled at Kpele-Le (also in Togo).[28] Some of the latter group remained, but another section moved southwards and finally reached Agu where, it is claimed, they fought with the (presumably Ewe-speaking) people who were already established beneath the mountain. Thereafter, the Les sought a new place to settle, in some versions with the advice of the Agu,[29] which brought them to their present location. However, subsequent wars against the Agu supposedly led to the planting of permanent Agotime settlements at the foot of the mountain, whereas the Agu proper moved to higher ground. On this view, the Agotimes are related to some of the people in Agu as well as to all the settlements that carry the prefix or suffix of 'Se' or 'Le'.

This tradition is supported by documentary evidence that Robin Law has uncovered.[30] He notes that reports from the 1680s referred to considerable disruption created by Adangbe bandits operating as far east as Grand Popo. Their numbers were apparently swelled by the subsequent flight eastwards of other Adangbes from Ladoku – in other words, Les. After the founding of an Accra settlement at what became Little Popo (now Anecho), Law notes that the

[28] The traditions of the Wifeme clan in Anlo do in fact claim to have descended from someone (significantly enough) called Amega Le who married an Anlo woman, although they suggest he had come from an island on the Volta. Greene, *Gender, Ethnicity and Social Change*, p. 148. Ada traditions actually tell of a group of Ewe-speaking refugees having joined them from Kpele, having fled from there due to conflict. Some of them are said to have remained at Krobo, which was where they came to first. It is difficult to tell whether this tradition has any deeper significance. Amate, *Making of Ada*, pp. 15–17.

[29] "Lekpos or Lenden-kera Locality History in T.V.T.", Ewe manuscript in my possession, dated 11 November 1954.

[30] According to Robin Law, the Adangbes were also reputed to have brought with them the skills of salt-making. This would back up the claims of Nene Keteku. Law, *Slave Coast*, pp. 25, 243, 248–9.

latter came into conflict with the Adangbe in the Keta area (probably Aflao). In 1694, the Adangbe were victorious and proceeded to destroy the Popo capital of Glji. However, Ofori Bomboneen (or Foli Bebe) turned the tables the following year, and the Popos were able to enslave many of the enemy. In 1700, the Adangbe were expelled from the Keta region, and it seems likely that these were the very Les who made their way further north. 'Prince Affary' of Popo who Biørn credits with having driven the Agotime away from the coast in 1700 is evidently the same Ofori identified by Law. This interpretation of the evidence – which posits the Agotime and some settlements in Agu as one and the same people   provides the key to resolving the confusion in Biørn's account, which, after all, was written a century after the original flight of the Adangbe refugees from the coastal region. This may sound like a rather arcane point of detail, but it is fundamental to the case I am seeking to advance here. To sum up, therefore, it would seem that a section of Agotime derived from an Adangbe sub-group, the Le, who left the area around the Songhor lagoon to avoid perpetual warfare and moved eastwards along the coastline before being driven in a north-westerly direction, leaving a number of related pockets of population scattered amongst predominantly Ewe-speaking peoples.

There is broad agreement that when the Le reached their present location, they encountered the Adaklu, an Ewe group with links to Anlo, already *in situ*.[31] Crucially none of the Ewe sub-groups claim to be autochthonous, but rather to have migrated from the east. In the stylized versions of Ewe migrations that are current today, almost all the sub-groups claim to have come from Notsie, and before that from what is now Benin. Most are silent about who occupied the land before they arrived, although sometimes there are veiled references to indigenous peoples who were absorbed or driven away.[32] Adaklu traditions insist that the Agotime were received as strangers and that they agreed to allocate them a place to settle. The relationship between the two was notionally sealed by marriage ties. It is posited today that the intention may have been to use the settlers as a buffer and to secure the borders between Adaklu and her eastern neighbours.[33] The place that was chosen was where the fan-palm tree grew in abundance, from which derived the eventual ethnonym of *Agotime* – meaning literally 'amongst the fan palms'. *Agotime* is therefore an Ewe term, and it is probable that the people originally called themselves Le, Lekpo or Adampe (or all of these). However, over time the new monniker stuck. By the 1740s, the Danes were referring to Agotimes and, as late as 1802,

---

[31] Amongst other things, these oral traditions, backed up by Danish records, support D.E.K. Amenumey's claim that the Ewe *dukɔwo* were in their present location before the eighteenth century. Amenumey, *Ewe in Pre-Colonial Times*.

[32] Some of these notional autochthons are to be found amongst the Central Togo minorities in the Togo hills.

[33] Interview with Togbe Addo IV, Mama Ozakula and others, Adaklu-Waya, 14 September 2003.

the Danish maps of Thonning equate *Agotime* (or 'Akotim') with a particular town, that is Afegame (or Wenuam in the Adangbe language), as distinct from the related settlements of Kpetoe, Zukpe, Nyitoe and Adedome. On this map, 'Akotim' nestles in a bend of the Todzie River, where Afegame remains today, although it is situated on the left rather than the right bank. There is a second set of Agotime traditions that might help explain the latter anomaly. According to this version, when the Agotime requested land, the Adaklu, feeling that there were too many to accommodate, introduced them to the Hodzo who obliged. Since the Todzie River was notionally the boundary between the Adaklu and the Hodzo, the first Agotime settlement would have been located on the left bank. This version of the history then indicates that a section of the Agotime made a further request for land from Hodzo, and founded Zukpe by a river of that name, while another group crossed back and settled on Adaklu lands – apparently without seeking permission. This is supposedly the origin of Agotime settlements located on the right bank of the Todzie River.[34]

Whereas Adaklu (and Hodzo) traditions suggest that the Agotime were given an empty place to settle, their own versions present the facts somewhat differently. They generally accept that the Adaklu were there first but claim that they had to fight against people who were already on the land, including the Adaklu themselves. In the words of Nene Keteku's history: "The Lehs did not find the land empty on arrival. The Agu, Ando, Atsi and Adaklu occupied the North, South, East and Western parts of the plains and the Adaklus occupied the foot of the Adaklu scarp and beyond."[35] Indeed, the Agotime claim to have seized land from the Adaklu and speculate that their own name is a corruption of Ewe speech, translating roughly as "the Adas are pursuing them".[36] Deeply embedded in these linguistic trysts are highly loaded historical charters that have provided the focal point of disagreements in the twentieth century, as we will see.

As I have already intimated, the Agotime first made their appearance in the Danish records in the early decades of the eighteenth century. It seems that they were supplying slaves and ivory before this point and decided to embark on their own trading expeditions to the coast. A letter from a Danish factor at Keta in 1749 referred to Kwahu traders having arrived at Agotime in order to purchase slaves and ivory, and relayed the latter's demands for more trade

---

[34] Evidence of Tsadide Kofi, linguist to Togbui Gbogbi, divisional chief of Adaklu, in "Geze Anku and 7 others versus Togbe Mahumansro and nine others", in Ho District Native Court, 15 July 1959 (copy of court record in my possession), pp. 40–7.

[35] On an Adaklu interpretation, settling the strangers there might even have been a strategy for clearing these other groups from the land. In that sense, the Adaklu and Agotime interpretations may still be compatible. As we will see in Chapter 4, there was one attempt, in a court case of 1959, to assert that the Agotimes preceded the Adaklus, but this was exceptional.

[36] In Ewe: *Adawo kluwo denu.*

goods, including iron bars, knives and beads, to be able to exchange for them.[37] But the following year, it was reported that "Kettecu [Keteku], Caboceer in Agutim [Agotime]" had sent a message promising to settle some outstanding 'palavers' with Anloga and Keta in order that his people could bring their trade goods southwards – implying that there were contacts already in place. He promised to come with traders from four or five other towns and to bring more than thirty slaves and a supply of ivory with him.[38] A subsequent letter from 1751 reported that the 'Agotim Caboceer', presumably the same Keteku, had indeed sold a quantity of slaves and ivory at Klikor.[39] What this confirms is that the Agotime were not simply suppliers to the Akwamu and Anlo, who dominated the trade in slaves, ivory, dried fish, coastal salt and imported goods, but became significant players in their own right. Indeed, Kea posits that the three of them together dominated regional trade.[40]

According to Kea, the Agotime were suppliers of ivory to the Asante in the late eighteenth and early nineteenth centuries.[41] They were also involved in the salt trade in a northerly direction, and the Adangbe quarters in Atakpamé, which lay on a trading crossroads, were quite possibly populated by Agotime.[42] Their importance in the slave trade is also made explicit in one of Isert's own letters:

The trade of the inhabitants with the Europeans here is limited solely to slaves and ivory, but the latter is in fact very rarely available ... The vast majority of slaves come from the region of Krepee, most of them from a particular province name Achotim [Agotime] that lies three day's journey beyond Malfi [Mlefi]. It is not rare for an Achotim trader to bring 30 or 40 slaves for sale at one time, only he knows that there is an adequate supply of good wares for him at the fort. The traders travel to the fort in a number of canoes, going by way of Malfi, whose inhabitants escort them to the fort in return for payment. However it can come to pass that the Malfis fall into disagreement with the Achotims, who then take the route to Quitta [Keta].[43]

The correspondence of the 1750s relates to a period when internal conflict in Mlefi made it more expedient for the Agotime traders to revert to using the Keta route. Interestingly, Biørn observed that Mlefi had four towns that were

---

[37] Entry XI. 84 for 5 May 1749, in Ole Justesen (ed.), *Danish Sources for the History of Ghana, 1657–1754* (Copenhagen: Royal Danish Academy of Sciences, 2005), p. 766.

[38] Entry XL. 108, dated November 1750, in Justesen, *Danish Sources*, p. 798. Greene, *Gender, Ethnicity and Social Change*, p. 37.

[39] Entry XI 116, dated 3 February 1751, in Justesen, *Danish Sources*, p. 815.

[40] Ray Kea, "Akwamu–Anlo relations c.1750–1813", *Transactions of the Historical Society of Ghana* X 1969, pp. 58–9.

[41] Kea, "Akwamu–Anlo relations", p. 60.

[42] N'Buéké Adovi Goeh-Akue, "Atakpame, un carrefour seculaire d'echange multi-sectorel du XVIIIe au XXe siecle", in T. Gbeasor, *Espace, culture et developpement dans la region d'Atakpame* (Lomé: Presses de L.UB, 1999), p. 43.

[43] Winsnes, *Letters*, p. 111. Buhler notes that the route from Buem either passed down the Volta or via Kpandu, Kpalimé, Tové, Ho and Adaklu, and from there to either Kpong or Anlo. Although he does not mention Agotime, the latter was clearly important. Buhler, "Volta Region", p. 18.

subject to it, one of which was called *Laye* (Le), and these were made up of "Adampe Negroes [who] have moved hither because of disturbances and marriages and have [since] long ago been Ada-subjects".[44] This suggests that the Agotime may have cultivated kinship connections with some peoples in Mlefi, and also hints more generally at the manner in which Agotime traders may have cemented their commercial ties through marital alliances.

There was also a trade that was tied into ports further down the Slave Coast, such as Little Popo, Agbodrafo (Porto Seguro) and Whydah. Kea observes that Akwamu traders controlled the trade towards the borders of Dahomey, including salt, but the Agotime were certainly involved as well. Kea himself quotes Commandant Flindt at Fort Prindsensteen to this effect in 1807: "the Tubereku lake ... is a fish and salt storehouse ... for the populous nations [of] Asshianthe, Aquamboe and Agothim".[45] While this might be taken to mean that the Agotime were salt importers, they were definitely trading in this highly valued commodity. It may be no coincidence, therefore, that Biørn mentions that one of the four Adampe towns under Mlefi was populated by "Tubreku Negroes". Certainly, modern traditions attribute the participation of the Agotime in the trade to a much deeper historical association with salt-making in their original coastal homeland around the Songhor lagoon.[46] Despite the fact that relations between the Agotime and the Agu were often fraught, the two were connected by a trade route that connected up with another north–south route from Atakpamé to Agbodrafo.[47] The latter passed through Se-Godze, with which the Agotime claim a particular connection. A more southerly lateral connection between the north–south routes passed through Se-Dzogbedzi. Hence the Le, or Adangbe, peoples further south were very well positioned with respect to trade (Map 2.2), and it is tempting to hypothesize that historic connections may well have accounted for the success of Agotime traders – in the same way that they probably did in Mlefi further to the west. What we can say with some confidence is that trade from the area around Agotime extended to the principal ports of the Slave Coast. That is how the unfortunate Tete was placed on board a ship in what was referred to by Koelle as "Girefe the slave port of Dahome" – in other words Whydah.[48]

---

[44] Biørn, "Account", p. 217.

[45] Tubereku is known as Togbloku today. Peter Hopkins, *Peter Thonning and Denmark's Guinea Commission: A Study in Nineteenth Century Colonial Geography* (Leiden: Brill, 2013), p. 44.

[46] It is claimed that before they began their inward migration, the Agotimes were involved in the salt trade from the Songhor lagoon. Keteku, "Short History", pp. 1–2. The lagoon remains a major source of salt to this day.

[47] One report in 1819 noted that Agu had "an extensive trade with Agotime and other large towns in the interior". G.A. Robertson, *Notes on Africa*, quoted in Kea, "Akwamu-Anlo relations", p. 58.

[48] Koelle, *Polyglotta Africana*, p. 4. Girefe is the same as Glehue, another name for Whydah. I am grateful to Robin Law for confirming this point.

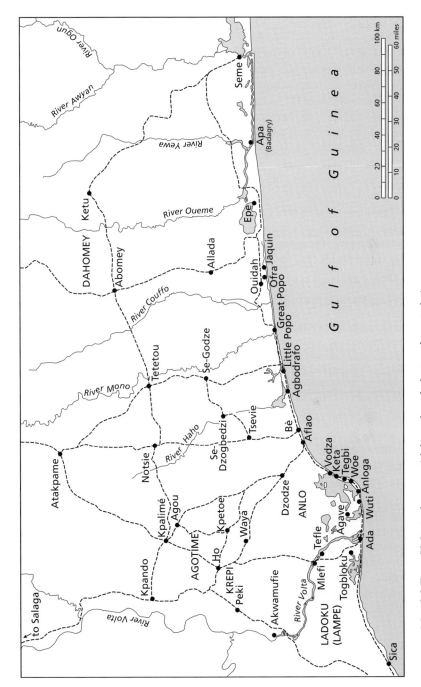

Map 2.2 Trans-Volta trade routes (eighteenth and nineteenth centuries).

The entire trading system was underpinned by lines of credit extended by Danish merchants at the forts. Amongst other things, this was used to keep the trade out of the hands of competitors like the English, the Dutch and the French. Credit did not just bind African traders to the Danes, but changed hands between Africans. Credit established relationships of debt and obligation, but also solidified relationships based on trust, which was essential in such a risky business as slave trading. The moral economy of debt was perhaps the most hotly debated of all topics in the late eighteenth and early nineteenth centuries. The act of *panyarring*, or seizing someone for unpaid debts, provoked innumerable disputes. Seen from the side of the creditor it might be the only recourse, whereas from the perspective of the debtor it could seem like a thinly veiled excuse for enslaving someone. The fact that the person who was *panyarred* was typically not the person who incurred the debt, but possibly a kinsman or someone from the wider community, was seemingly less controversial: there was a common understanding that debts were by their nature social things that could not be escaped. Isert described the situation at the coast:

When a creditor sees that by himself he cannot recover the debt, he brings a suit before the elders, and if this does not bring the rapid results, without asking, he seizes as many members of the debtor's family as are required by their market value to cover the debt. He then informs the debtor that he has *a pignaret* (seized) them and that the debt must be paid within a few days, or else his family, or the captives, will be sold. Indeed if the creditor lives in another town and people from the debtor's town come there, he takes them also, as compensation, whether they be relatives or acquaintance of the debtor or not. Such minor cases not infrequently give cause for serious wars between whole nations.[49]

The conflicts that ensued drew the Europeans into local politics, with the palaver becoming an institutionalized form of resolving disputes. If we are to look for the distant origins of colonial state formation, it lies precisely in the palaver as a form of mediation in which the Danes (and other Europeans) were sometimes the arbiters and sometimes amongst the litigants.[50] The fact that the first state-like practices concerned the protection of property rights – consisting of human chattel, money and commodities – is worth underlining because it indicated that warfare had a more indirect influence on state-making processes.[51] I will have more to say about the latter in Chapter 3.

One of the surviving pieces of Danish correspondence from 1754 deals with the subject of bad debts arising out of the extension of credit to Agotime

[49] Winsnes, *Letters*, pp. 178–9.
[50] On palaver involving the Danes, see Hernaes, *Slaves, Danes and African*, Part Two.
[51] I am grateful to Zoe Marks for helping me to clarify this distinction.

traders by one of the factors. A Danish employee had run up his own debts and claimed that he could not settle them because he had given out goods on credit to Agotime traders, some of whom had recently been killed in a battle with the Anlo. If Agotimes were to be *panyarred* for the debt, the likelihood was that the route to Ada would be closed and the West India and Guinea Company would end up incurring further losses.[52] The fact that debt was an endemic source of tension in the interior is illustrated again by the fate of the hapless Tete who ended up being Koelle's informant in Freetown. He was seized for a debt owed by another Kpetoe man to "Gadsa people" – that is those on the southern edge of Agu – confirming that the moral code outlined by Isert applied equally well in Krepe.[53] The transformative power of credit, whose lines extended to Europe in one direction and deep into the African interior in the other, has been demonstrated in great detail in Joseph Miller's magisterial study of Angola in the era of the slave trade.[54] The point can equally well be made for the so-called Slave Coast, of which Agotime was a part.

Where the Agotime were acquiring their slaves from is not entirely clear. It seems more than likely that some were extracted through relationships of indebtedness. That is, extending lines of credit could provide a means of entrapment, including the right to *panyar*. Others would have been enslaved as a direct result of warfare, although it seems likely that in low-intensity conflicts prisoners would normally be exchanged rather than sold on. The payment of tribute in slaves to stave off the threat of attack certainly provided a mechanism for transferring the ownership of captives from weaker to stronger parties. The Akwamu received much of their tribute in slaves, and it is likely that the Agotime received their share. But the Agotime surely received many of their slaves, and the ivory, by travelling to markets further inland. Quite how far they roamed is impossible to say on the basis of existing knowledge.

This brings me to the relationship between trading wealth and the configuration of political power. It is clear that the slave trade did not lead inexorably to political centralization – or, for that matter, to fragmentation. But it did help to create particular kinds of polities – always the minority of those that existed – that revolved around the mutual reinforcement of trade and militarism. These were entities in which power depended less on control of land, the taxation of subjects and forms of legitimacy centred on

---

[52] Letter from Governor Engman et al. to Directors of the Company, 7 October 1954, Document XII.40, in Justesen, *Danish Sources*, pp. 953–4.

[53] Koelle, *Polyglotta Africana*, p. 4.

[54] Joseph Miller, *Way of Death: Merchant Capitalism and the Angolan Slave Trade, 1730–1830* (London: James Currey, 1988), chs. 3, 4.

hereditary principles, than on the following combination: tributes extracted from neighbours through the threat of force; the recycling of trading profits in order to recruit followers; and the sealing of broader politico-commercial alliances through marriage and credit that helped to keep the trade routes open. The shorthand of 'wealth in people', which has been used to describe African political logics more generally, is applicable here, provided we remember that accumulating wealth and clients and controlling the instruments of violence were closely interlocking strategies.[55] Akwamu had certainly gone furthest down this route. Its rulers reproduced their polity by demanding taxes from traders seeking to cross the Volta at Asutsuare. They also exacted tribute from subject polities, which tended to take the form of slaves. When all else failed, the Akwamu simply raided weaker peoples. As Reindorf put it in a rather jaundiced description:

> It is shocking to the civilised world to hear of the deplorable and wretched condition to which the Krepes were reduced by the Akwamus, since they [the Akwamus] were driven by the Akras in 1734 to settle in the Krepe land ... Many towns were devastated by repeated attacks, kidnappings, extortions and the like; many parents were bereft of their children; while districts were depopulated, whole tribes were thinned out by yearly tribute or lawsuits ... In 1822–23, when Yaw Osekyere, an Asante general commissioned by Osei, assisted the Akwamus against the Krepes, they captured thousands of unoffending Krepes, so that a boy or girl of ten years old was sold for 25 strings of cowries, and an adult for one head and 25 strings.[56]

Akwamu provides an example of a polity built upon the foundations of a coercive social contract. Its minimalist institutional structures also provide some insight into Agotime, which pursued the same strategy on a smaller scale. As Nene Keteku puts it:

> Before the Germans came, the Agotimes were warriors. So any time there is conflict somewhere they will go and pick them to live with them, to go and fight for them. But what they do is that when they fight ... they share only booty and go away. They don't have any political administration with the people ...[57]

It is important that the Agotime were allied with Akwamu, from whom they clearly learned much about trade and fighting alike. The history written by Nene Keteku is of particular interest because it underlines a strategy of using military force to build the polity demographically. The document claims that as a result of the initial wars against Agu, some of the latter were taken as captives and survive today in the shape of the Agoe clan in Kpetoe. It goes on to

---

[55] Jane I. Guyer, "Wealth in people, wealth in things – introduction", *Journal of African History* 36 (1) 1995, pp. 83–90.
[56] Reindorf, *History*, p. 303.   [57] Interview with Nene Keteku, 26 March 2001.

observe that some subsequently escaped, precipitating a second war with Agu and their Ando allies, which culminated in a rare military defeat. But a third campaign was more successful and led to some Agotimes settling in the Agu area. A subsequent war against the Ando and Atsi apparently not only led to the displacement of many of the latter, but also to the settlement of war captives at Abenyirase and Wodome. Again, the village of Batoumé (Togo), which was originally settled to secure the border against the Ando, was later populated with slaves. The village of Nyitoe, whose status within Agotime is still rather ambiguous, was apparently an Adaklu-related settlement that was forced into a subordinate (but presumably protected) relationship.[58] The Danish map of 1802 situates Nyitoe at some distance from Zukpe whereas today they are effectively twin towns. It is not clear whether the people of Nyitoe relocated to Zukpe or the latter moved towards Nyitoe – or if the map is simply faulty. But it is more than likely that resettlement occurred in order to secure another border, this time with Agu.[59] Whatever the truth of the matter, the people of Nyitoe became Agotimes of a particular kind. This reading of the evidence suggests that the Agotime were certainly concerned with firming up boundaries with neighbouring polities, but according to military rather than administrative calculations. By the start of the colonial period, Agotime and Adaklu covered much the greatest area of the Krepe *dukɔwo* – as we can gauge from looking at the German Sprigade map in which only half of Agotime is depicted (see Map 2.3). The territory of the Adaklu was slightly larger, but was probably less densely populated than Agotime. There again, the Agotime were almost certainly less interested in land than trade routes, water supplies and defensible positions.

There is a consensus today that many of the peoples who came to make up Agotime were in fact descended from war captives – even if such a thing could never be uttered in public. Nene Keteku's history goes as far as to describe the Le as "a mixed race made up of the people they conquered".[60] It is also widely acknowledged that the Agotime made a particular point of incorporating women who produced Agotime children. However, there is an equally popular belief that those who have descended from slaves have been the most success-ful in the long run, whereas the 'pure Agotime' have been cursed by their violent history. Hence, Nene Keteku observed in a separate discussion that the

---

[58] This may not be the only town that had an Adaklu component. There are suggestions that Adaklus were also present in Akpokope.

[59] However, evidence given in court in 1959 by a native of Nyitoe claimed that they had moved towards Zukpe after the Ashanti wars. He also confirmed that the Nyitoe people originally came from Adaklu and settled on Hodzo land. Evidence of Daniel Agbodogli Todze Klu, native of Nyitoe, in "Geze Anku and seven others versus Togbe Mahumansro and nine others", pp. 26–9.

[60] Nene Keteku, "Short history", p. 5.

Map 2.3 Sprigade map: sheet for Misahöhe District (1905). Note: Agotime to the right above red line.

quarters of Kpetoe that were populated by captives had prospered, whereas those of the former slaving families were now in demographic decline.[61] This neatly inverts the earlier logic of the core clans taking captive women as wives and thereby expanding their numbers at the expense of 'captive clans'. In Batoumé, it is similarly claimed that the people of the village who have become the landowners are the former captives, while their former masters have regressed. In fact, the tribulations that are considered to have affected the entire Agotime polity since the coming of the Europeans might be seen as the same phenomenon playing itself out on a larger scale – embodying what one might call the 'curse of militarism'. These findings resonate very strikingly with other studies that have discovered memories of slavery deeply embedded in West African social structures, often taking the shape of spirit possession and cults.[62] In Agotime, the memory of slavery appears to live on within lineage politics more than in the spiritual realm, although this is not a feature that I have investigated in detail.

Danish records make clear that the Agotime were important players in the regional political game, which included, at different times, Akwamu, Anlo, Ada, Little Popo, Akyem, Kwahu and Asante. For most of the time, they were allied with Akwamu, which implied participating in a wider alliance with Peki and Anlo, the latter having absorbed its own Le minority. Around 1780, Biørn noted that the king of Akwamu, Darkon, had staged a series of attacks on Krepe groups, including "Adaffu" (a reference to Adaklu). Then in 1792, Darkon's successor is reported to have invaded "Innive" (Nyive), and seems to have made a military push as far as Agu.[63] Given the fact that the Akwamu enjoyed close commercial ties with the Agotime at this time, and that the Akwamu were attacking polities that were considered enemies of the Agotime, it is likely that there were two related processes at work. That is, the Akwamu were cementing their hold over Krepe, but in alliance with Agotime as the junior partner. These campaigns can also be understood in terms of the playing out of a regional power struggle. As early as the 1740s, Little Popo had been attempting to extend its power westwards along the coast, thereby competing with Anlo for control over the mouth of the Volta and threatening Akwamu's dominant position on the lower reaches of the river. In 1785, Agotimes were involved in a military coalition involving Anlo, Akwamu and Kwahu in an attempt to repel Little Popo's westward advance. The Popo enjoyed some

---

[61] Fieldwork diary, 31 March 2001.

[62] Rosalind Shaw, *Memories of the Slave Trade: Ritual and the Historical Imagination in Sierra Leone* (Chicago and London: University of Chicago Press, 2002); Judy Rosenthal, *Possession, Ecstasy and Law in Voodoo* (Charlottesville and London: University Press of Virginia, 1998); and Meera Venkatachalam, *Slavery, Memory and Religion in Southeastern Ghana c.1850 to the Present* (Cambridge: Cambridge University Press, 2015).

[63] Kea, "Akwamu–Anlo relations", pp. 34–5.

support amongst the Krepe *dukɔwo* of Agu, Ave and 'Tetete', and seemingly enjoyed a special relationship with the first of these, almost certainly rooted in trading connections. The members of the coalition were opponents of the Agotime, as well as being the scourge of the Anlo whose traders they pointedly attacked.[64] Hence, Kea plausibly construes the Akwamu attack on Nyive and Agu as, in effect, the opening of a second front in a regional power struggle. In 1792, Anlo suffered a disastrous defeat against the Popo, apparently because the Akwamu, and presumably the Agotime, were tied up with their campaigns in Nyive. Faced with the complete coastal dominance of the Popo, the Dutch and the Anlo together sent an embassy to Kumasi to seek Asante intervention.[65] Although the Asante army never materialized, the threat that they would wade in was apparently sufficient to discourage Little Popo from seeking to project its power beyond the Volta. From 1793 onwards, Asante imperial control was formally extended to both sides of the Volta. But this dominance was in reality exercised through an alliance with Akwamu, Anlo and Agotime, in which the first of these remitted part of the tribute to Kumasi.[66]

In the interview that I have quoted from, Nene Keteku referred to the Agotime fighting for others in expectation of receiving booty.[67] This is attested to in the written sources. Indeed, this particular role played by the Agotime placed them at the vortex of a spiral of events that eventually led to the unravelling of Akwamu – and hence Asante – hegemony east of the Volta in the third decade of the nineteenth century. The fullest account is Carl Reindorf's *History of the Gold Coast and Asante*, which was put together at the close of the century, and hence at some distance from the events themselves.[68] Reindorf notes that a quarrel between the Ewe settlements of Nyive and Atikpui led to the former requesting military assistance from Oku, "King of Agotime". Once the chief of Atikpui learned that the Agotime were going to become involved, he allegedly came to Oku seeking a way out, saying "I have been told that your assistance has been asked by the Nyives to fight against me, but if you, the old elephant, will engage in the fight, we are unable carry on against you and the Nyives."[69] Oku is reported to have consulted with the "chiefs and captains of the three Agotime towns" – presumably Afegame, Kpetoe and Zukpe – whose view was that they could not go back on their promise to assist Nyive. What is not stated is how much the Agotime were

---

[64] Kea, "Akwamu–Anlo relations", p. 43. Tetete may be a reference to Tetetu, which was an Adangbe settlement. Strickrodt, *Afro-European Trade*, p. 85.

[65] On Little Popo, see Strickrodt, *Afro-European Trade*, ch. 3.

[66] Kea, "Akwamu-Anlo relations", p. 47.

[67] Interestingly, the origins of Dahomey seem to have resided precisely in these kinds of mercenary operations. Law, "Dahomey and the slave trade", pp. 253–4.

[68] Keteku's rendition borrows freely from Reindorf's text in relation to the war.

[69] Reindorf, *History*, p. 297.

promised for taking up arms on the latter's behalf. Reindorf reports that when things were not going well, the Nyives fled the battlefield, leaving the Agotime to fight on and incur heavy casualties. Interestingly, he reports that when Oku himself suggested retreating, "Gbli, Chief Captain of the Army ... in reply swore that if he should retreat to Nyitoe, the king's name of an elephant must be changed to that of an antelope of the lowest species". In other words, there was the matter of Agotime military pride at stake. The battle therefore resumed, the Atikpui were defeated and, according to Reindorf, they were reduced to a tributary status.[70]

The Nyive were forced to pay compensation to the Agotime for their cowardice, which included giving a wife to the brother of Oku, called Nate Ngo. When the wife and children subsequently ran back to her people, the Agotime declared war on Nyive. The latter proceeded to enlist the support of a number of other *dukɔwo* who would have had their own reasons for joining the fight against Agotime. Reindorf lists Shia, Krunu, Kpaleve, Tove Atshave, Agu, Azavi, Assahun and Atigbe as the allies of Nyive. It is surely no accident that many of these shared borders with Agotime. Reindorf recounts that Nate Ngo, who seems to have become the new Agotime leader by this point, responded by sending a deputation to Accra to request military assistance from one Kwatei Kodzo. His Ga allies obliged by despatching a large force that was joined by the Akwamu, bringing the total army to some 5,000 soldiers.

However, there was to be no quick or conclusive victory. In the midst of a military stalemate, occasioned by a debilitating shortage of ammunition and food supplies, the Agotime-Ga-Akwamu coalition came apart at the seams. Reindorf details a rift between the Akwamu and the Ga over the ownership of war captives and the burden of maintaining the army in the field. The Akwamu king, Akoto, apparently took the view that the best reward lay in plundering freely on the way home. The difference of opinion culminated in a permanent rift between the Ga and the Akwamu, with fateful consequences for the latter because the campaign also precipitated a dispute between Akoto and the Peki chief, Kwadzo Dei, who had hitherto been a loyal ally. The latter now rebelled against his overlord and won the support of a large collection of Ewe *dukɔwo*, who had been on either side of the conflict that had only just ended. This included the Agotime who were apparently on close terms with Peki.[71] Having alienated his Ga allies, the Akwamu ruler was forced to turn to Anlo for assistance. After fierce fighting, the Akwamu and the Anlo were finally forced to retreat and concede defeat. When Rattray later drew up a list of those polities who accepted Peki claims to overlordship, the Agotime were amongst

---

[70] Reindorf, *History*, p. 298.
[71] See the list in C.W. Welman, *The Native States of the Gold Coast: History and Constitution* (London: Dawsons of Pall Mall, 1969 (part I on Peki first published in 1925)), p. 19.

those who demurred.[72] In fact, with Akwamu greatly weakened, it is more likely that Agotime leaders saw themselves as emerging as the effective power in the mid-Volta. In this regard, it is of interest to refer to an incident that occurred in 1843. The Danes had arrested a group of Akwamu who were caught trying to sell slaves in Akwapim. When the Anlo and the Akwamu laid siege to the Danish fort, the Governor was forced to request assistance from the Agotime – who he referred to as enemies of the Akwamu – some Krepe and the Ada to defeat the enemy.[73] Clearly, the Agotime remained a force to be reckoned with at this point.

Whereas a history of Agotime military engagement is relatively easy to chart, it is much more difficult to get to the bottom of how it actually functioned as a polity. I have already referred to evidence that war captives were incorporated and became Agotime over time. This is telling us something about the way in which a political community was forged. Although kinship established some claims to precedence, there were other ways in which affective bonds could be forged. In the case of a 'captive clan', they would presumably have been absorbed on the basis of their collective contribution to the aggrandizement of Agotime. But on the individual level, incorporation might involve a man attaching himself to a leader and winning favour through acts of bravery and loyalty. For women, the route to incorporation that is repeatedly alluded to is marriage, which one presumes was often less than consensual. The observation that many Agotimes were born by Ewe mothers in days gone by is a paradox that many people are well aware of today. The implication that the Agotime were not 'pure' Adangbe was also hinted at during two specific fieldwork interviews. Nene Keteku observed that part of the reason for a rift between the people of Afegame and those who left to found Kpetoe was over the use of war captives. Whereas those who led the breakaway from Afegame sought to build up their numbers, those who stayed put are said to have wanted to protect their integrity:

When we came to settle, we were all at Afegame. Then we have [had] to fight some tribes out of the place before we took over the whole land. But we settle[d] at Afegame for fear that these people can mobilize and come and attack. So we decided ... our forefathers, they decided to get married to those captured people. Do you understand me? So there were those intermarriages. That brought conflict amongst families at Afegame – because the Afegame people wanted to be distinct, but most of our people started marrying from the captured – the war captives.[74]

---

[72] PRAAD (Ho) RAO 273, *Togoland: A History of the Tribal Divisions of the District of Misahuhe and of the Sub-Districts of Ho and Kpandu*.

[73] Letter from Governor Edward Carstensen, dated 21 February 1843, in Tove Storsveen (ed.), *Closing the Books: Governor Edward Carstensen on Danish Guinea 1842–50* (Accra: Sub-Saharan Publishers, 2010).

[74] Interview with Nene Keteku, Kpetoe, 26 March 2001.

This is a very explicit statement to the effect that the Agotime were a composite of an Adangbe core and successive layers of incorporated captives. Further confirmation came in another interview in Nyitoe, whose ambiguous status has already been alluded to. Here the chief of the village suggested that there might be a deeper significance to the name *Agotime* itself – that is, it referred to all the people who came to reside in the vicinity of the fan palms rather than to any specific ethnic group.[75] By implication, Adangbes and Ewes could and did become Agotime.

It would appear that the split between Afegame and those who left to form Kpetoe and other satellite towns was played out in terms of competing conceptions of legitimacy. The Adangbe system was one in which there were priests rather than chiefs, that is until the widespread dissemination of an Akan model of government on both sides of the Volta. This seems to hold good for Agotime. Although modern traditions refer to a stool, it is sometimes admitted that this was actually a 'fetish', or an object bearing religious power. In fact, it is claimed that the Le brought both a male and a female fetish with them from Ledoku. Nene Keteku's own draft document implicitly accepts that the 'ancestral stool' of Nana Ntsrifoa (the 'salt giver') was not a stool at all, at least in the Akan sense.[76] Indeed he states that it was "worshipped as a god" and was controlled by a priest who was seldom seen in public. This amounts to a clear admission that the Agotime did not have anything approximating to a chief. This would help to explain why the supposed 'king lists' are so truncated and vague. What seems likely is that, as the Agotime became more involved in trading and warfare, an alternative model of leadership emerged that was based on martial prowess and commercial acumen. Success in both was always likely to depend on spiritual fortification, but the cults that the emergent leaders turned to often came from further afield – including Yewe, which originated from the Dahomey area.[77] It is easy to envisage a scenario in which the established priests of the Le were in danger not merely of being supplanted by emergent 'big men', but of being upstaged by newly imported religious shrines. Hence the split between Afegame and Kpetoe, which remains very apparent to this day, symbolized the fundamental transformations associated with the slave, salt, ivory and other forms of trade.

When Keteku was referred to by the Danes as a *caboceer* in the mid-eighteenth century, it is highly likely that he was amongst the first cohort of

---

[75] Interview with Togbe Kudiabor III, Agotime-Nyitoe (Togo), 19 August 2002. The Nyitoe traditions claim that the inhabitants migrated from Notsie and settled with the Adaklus for some time before moving on. This implies that they see themselves as not exactly Adaklus.

[76] Keteku, "Short history", p. 20.

[77] There were apparently two Yewe shrines in Kpetoe, but none in Afegame. Nene Ahortor Makaku V, *A Brief History of the Lehs vis-à-vis the Agotimes* (Accra: the author, 2016), p. 15.

'big men' whose reputation was self-made. 'King Oku', who is referred to in the history of the Atikpui–Nyive war, was almost certainly in the same mould, while Gbli would have represented the next cohort of leaders who might stake a rival claim to leadership in the event of a military setback. Trade conferred material wealth, which in turn made it possible to attract followers. Developing reliable coastal contacts was also essential in terms of securing a supply of arms and ammunition that enabled leaders to engage in the pursuit of warfare. The current chief of Batoumé confirmed that there had never been a paramount chief before colonial times and went on to observe that there had only been war leaders and men of wealth. Those who became rich were the ones that accumulated followers.[78] But it seems very likely that leadership in warfare and wealth accumulation were mutually reinforcing rather than competing routes to success. The kinship principle remained important to the extent that a war leader might become accepted as the political leader of all the Agotime and seek to pass this position down through his lineage group, but whenever a fresh crisis erupted, alternative leaders came to the fore, thereby disrupting neat lines of succession. What is clear was that it was Kpetoe that eventually provided the leaders, by virtue of being much the largest settlement.

Afegame had been the principal Agotime settlement, but it declined in tandem with the rise of Kpetoe. Nene Keteku's history claims that it was Nate Ngo that led the breakaway from Afegame along with his nephew Todje.[79] As we have seen, Nate Ngo is named by Reindorf as the leader of the Agotime in their war against Nyive, probably in the late 1820s. One of the present 'war chiefs', or *avafiawo*, in Kpetoe confirms the central role played by Todje who was the grandfather of their clan leader in the 1870s.[80] Given that Kpetoe already existed in 1802 and appears on the Danish map (Map 2.1), it seems likely that Kpetoe was founded some time in the last decades of the eighteenth century. The campaigns fought by Akwamu against Adaklu, Nyive and Agu in the 1780s and 1790s may in fact have led to the influx of a large number of war captives that brought the issue of the ownership of slaves to a head in Afegame. If so, the founding of Kpetoe could be considered an indirect consequence of the burgeoning Akwamu–Agotime military alliance. At some point, the Agotime adopted the Akan model, as did Peki, in which lesser war chiefs led the four military wings. This was almost certainly a direct borrowing from Akwamu practice.

The upheaval of the 1870s provides a clear illustration of how leaders were made – in real time, as it were. In 1869, an Asante invasion force led by Adu Bofo crossed the Volta and remained in the field for the next three years with reinforcements from Akwamu and Anlo. The campaign was ostensibly about

---

[78] Fieldwork diary, 23 August 2001.   [79] Keteku, "Short history", p. 6.
[80] Interview with Nene Todje-Agbo IV, Kpetoe, 7 September 2007.

restoring Asante hegemony, but was also bound up with a certain amount of personal interest on the part of Adu Bofo.[81] It was accompanied by widespread destruction of communities, enslavement and mass flight into the hills.[82] The brutality of the invasion was a reaction, in part, to the spirited resistance that greeted the Asante. The initial resistance was led by the Peki leader, Kwadzo De IV, and an Akyem Kotoku warlord by the name of Dompre. They fought on in the face of superior firepower, in the hope that the British might be persuaded to intervene on their side. However, as the war entered a second phase, following the execution of both protagonists, it was Ho and Agotime that provided the principal foci of resistance. Donna Maier has brought to light a German document, written some time after the events in question, which details the central role played by the Agotime. This provides a useful complement to the oral histories that tend to be short on specific details. It appears that the Agotime became involved in 1870 when Dompre, who had just lost a series of engagements, passed through en route to Accra. He was followed by Kwadzo De who was subsequently killed at Bator.[83] Nene Keteku's history tells of how the Adaklu allied themselves with the Asante and led the enemy straight to Kpetoe, where they were bolstered by Anlo reinforcements.[84] The document asserts that the chiefs of Ho, Sokode and Abutia had already taken refuge in Agotime by this point.[85] The written documents confirm that the Ho fighters, led by Motte Kofi, did indeed fall back upon Agotime. In the early stages of the war, the Agotime themselves were apparently fighting under the leadership of Akoto Sah I of Kpetoe who had previously distinguished himself in campaigns against the Agu. As the situation deteriorated, an offer was made to one 'Agbovi' (*a nom de guerre*) to lead the Agotime resistance. His contemporary successor (now deceased) claimed that part of the reason was that Agbovi was a direct descendant of Todje who had helped to found

---

[81] The war aims of the Asante are discussed in D.J.E. Maier, "Military acquisition of slaves in Asante", in David Henige and T.C. McCaskie (eds.), *West African Economic and Social History: Studies in Memory of Marion Johnson* (Madison: Wisconsin University African Studies Programme, 1990).

[82] A sanguinary account of the early part of the campaign when the missionaries, Ramseyer and Kühne, became captives of the Asante is recounted in the early chapters of F.A. Ramseyer and J. Kühne, *Four Years in Ashantee by the Missionaries Ramseyer and Kühne* (London: C. Nisbet, 1975). See also Lynne Brydon, "Constructing Avatime: questions of history and identity in a West African polity, c.1690s to the twentieth century", *Journal of African History* 49 (1) 2008, p. 28.

[83] Curiously, this event is not mentioned by Welman, although he mentions an oath that seemed to mark this event. 'Bato', or Bator, is located on the Volta near to Mepe.

[84] In Adaklu, the alliance with Asante became a matter of pride. In 1918, J.T. Furley was told that "The Ashantis, the Anglos [Anlo] and Adaklus were all one and fought together". Statement by headchief Bogbie Kodjoe of Adaklu Abuadie, PRAAD ADM 11/1620 "Togoland Secret and Confidential Papers" (1918–1924), Report of a meeting held at Adaklu-Abuadie on 8 February 1918, p. 35.

[85] Keteku, "Short history", p. 12.

Kpetoe.[86] His version of the history states that Agbovi ordered his men to set fire to the town when the enemy entered. In the ensuing confusion, many of the Asante and Anlo fighters were killed. The burning of settlements was subsequently adopted as a military strategy designed to deprive the Asante, who had fragile supply lines, of the resources they needed to maintain an army in the field.[87] But it equally deprived the Agotime and Ho allies of supplies, forcing them to live off other communities in a more or less predatory fashion.

The partial success with which the Agotime and their Ho allies wore down the Asante forces, together with the memories of specific heads that were claimed, has today been elevated to the status of a military victory. The historical record suggests that the Ho-Agotime alliance won few, if any, of the skirmishes. What we know from the work of Maier is that the Agotime and Ho forces had to fall back on Yokele, and after a major battle there in July 1870, had to retreat southwards to Agave, close to where the Agotime notionally originated. Although the Asante had won the main engagements, Maier nevertheless observes that the retreating army continued to be harried by the Agotime and Ho forces.[88] Possibly for that reason, the latter have continued to regard themselves as victorious: after all, the army of Adu Bofo was forced to return home without having brought them to heel. What happened in Agotime after the final withdrawal of the Asante and their allies is disputed between the descendants of Akoto Sah and Agbovi. The latter maintain that Agbovi I became the new leader, whereas the former claims that Akoto Sah remained the overall military leader, whilst permitting Agbovi to be elevated to the status of a war leader in his own right. This included the privilege of being carried in a palanquin.[89] One thing that both sides can agree upon is that there was no leader other than the *avafiawo* themselves – and their role was confined to leadership in times of war.

To sum up, then, how best might we characterize Agotime? First of all, it was clearly not a 'tribe' in the colonial sense. There was a residual sense of identity revolving around Le origins that linked the Agotime to other communities in what is now Togo and to others west of the Volta. These ties were renewed through marriage in the context of regional trade. But the very success of the Agotime political project rested on the permeability of its social

---

[86] Interview with Nene Todje-Agbo IV, Kpetoe, 7 September 2007.

[87] This may also have formed part of a scorched earth policy to deny supplies to the Asante. William Hudson Bryars, "The Evolution of British Imperial Policy on the Volta, 1857–1897: From Informal Opportunism to Formal Occupation", unpublished PhD thesis, University of Birmingham, 1994, p. 86.

[88] D.J.E. Maier, "The bird and tortoise syndrome: limitations imposed by populace and produce of the Asante–Ewe war of 1869–1871", paper presented at the African Studies Association Conference, Bloomington, 1981.

[89] Interviews with Nene Akoto Sah VII, Kpetoe, 5 September 2007; and Nene Todje-Agbo IV, Kpetoe, 7 September 2007.

boundaries, in which captives and clients could become accepted as Agotime. This is certainly not a unique case. The Krobo were an amalgam of successive waves of refugees, including Ewes, replicating the pattern in the Togoland hills where communities were similarly forged out of diverse fragments seeking sanctuary from endemic conflict. Again, the Anlo polity incorporated many new arrivals who brought spirit shrines with them and founded new clans. Agotime looks somewhat like Anlo, with which it indeed claims a direct connection through settlement. In both polities, slaves were integrated into the clan structure, constituting the reward of a strategy centred on warfare and trade. At the same time, refugees could be swallowed whole and become culturally Anlo or Agotime. The other reason why it makes little sense to read contemporary ethnic categories backwards into the eighteenth and nineteenth century is that there was never a clear line of cleavage. The Krepe may have been on the receiving end of Akwamu predation, but when they combined to fight in the early 1830s, it was as chiefdoms that had a common oppressor rather than as Ewe people per se. The Agotime sided with the Akwamu for most of the time, but later joined the Krepe revolt against them. On the other hand, the Anlo sided with the Akwamu, despite the fact that they are considered quintessentially Ewe today. Nor did the Asante invasion of the trans-Volta in 1869 produce a sense of common response, given that Adaklu and Taviefe were amongst those who sided with the invaders. When the Asante armies departed, those who had borne the brunt of the invasion unleashed their revenge. The Agotime, who had fought alongside the Ho, blamed the Adaklu for having sided with the Asante. But this was not a question of ethnicity: it was merely the latest episode in a longer struggle for dominance.

Secondly, Agotime was clearly not a state in the sense that was outlined in Chapter 1. Fundamentally, it lacked formal ensemble of institutions, an ideology of kingship and the material foundations of statehood. The big men who dominated Agotime politics accumulated personal wealth and used it to build up their personal followings. When the powers of a leader waned, others were primed to step into the breach. But Agotime was never simply a warlord band either. It occupied a specific locality and, as we have seen, there was some sense of territoriality that is reflected in a strategy of fixing boundaries through settlement. The constituent towns stood in relation to one another in a structured way that was based eventually on an Akan wing formation. In Kpetoe itself, clans occupied particular wards and competed amongst each other for influence, with a rather weak tendency to segmentation. It is also worth underlining that the Agotime system valued women for their reproductive role as much as it venerated men as fighters. Hence the underlying principles of kinship and precedence remained strong, despite the greater weight accorded to personal achievement. Agotime was a polity that was seemingly highly decentralized. If our reading of the sources is correct, there was a separation between those who exercised a spiritual influence – roughly speaking, priests – and those who led the Agotimes in the pursuit of war. Once Kpetoe was founded as a separate town, these dual centres of power were physically separated from one another, with the latter very much in the ascendant. There is no single term that neatly captures all of this complexity, which is symptomatic of the evolutionary assumptions built into most models of politics. The teleology that sees African segmentary societies as developing into chiefdoms that later congealed into states does not provide a viable framework for understanding political processes in the trans-Volta. The Agotime did not have kings or chiefs,[90] but they did have identifiable leaders who built their power on a combination of trading and warfare in a manner that was not unusual on the African end of the Atlantic trading system. Importantly, these Agotime military leaders wielded power and influence over neighbouring peoples, extracting tribute in return for a measure of protection. Although the orchestration of violence had the power to effect far-reaching change, it did not presume any one mode of social and political organization. This was equally true in the Senegambia, as we will now see.

Mandinka and Jola: Migration, Identity and Power

In this next section, I examine the Mandinka and Jola polities that were located in three adjoining areas, that are often described today as former kingdoms: namely, Kombo, Narang and Fogny-Jabangkunda.[91] The latter is not to be confused with Fogny proper, which lies further to the east. The first of these was a longstanding Mandinka polity located just south of the Gambia River and was routinely referred to by Europeans as the 'kingdom of Kombo'. It was the one the British had the most direct contact with by virtue of its proximity to Bathurst. Indeed, the future colonial capital was built on land purchased from Kombo. Immediately to the south lay Narang, which was a much smaller entity and may have constituted a frontier region under the loose control of Kombo. To the south of Kombo, across the Allahein River and west of what is now Diouloulou, lay Fogny-Jabangkunda, which was reputed to have existed as a separate polity before Kombo. The last two do not feature in European texts,

---

[90] Amongst the Krepe, where lineage-based forms of authority emerged, the terminology associated with chiefdoms is regarded as somewhat misleading by some. For a critique of the historicity of Ewe chiefdoms, see Michel Verdon, *The Abutia of West Africa: A Chiefdom That Never Was* (Berlin, New York and Amsterdam: Mouton, 1983).

[91] To further confuse matters, the term Fogny-Kombo is also encountered. It refers to southern edge of Kombo, which I consider as part of Fogny-Jabangkunda. This usage is quite common. Informants at Abéné, for example, referred to themselves as being part of what was once Fogny-Jabangkunda. Interview Braimah Jasseh (elder), Malang Jabang (elder), Amadou Jabang (*alkalo*), Abéné (Casamance) 14 February 2004. When the French referred to 'Kombo', they seem to have meant Fogny- Jabangkunda.

Map 2.4 Francis Moore's travels, 1738.

which tend to be fixated with peoples living along the Gambia River. This is an optic that, as we will see, played directly into the processes of colonial state formation. Francis Moore's map from the 1730s depicts Kombo, but beyond its boundaries, which are drawn fairly close to the coast, all that is written is 'Floops', or in modern parlance Jola (see Map 2.4).[92] This is despite the fact that there were Mandinka towns of some antiquity south of the Allahein River.

In the case I have just dealt with, it is noteworthy that neither the Agotime nor their Ewe neighbours claimed to be autochthonous. Mandinka and Jola traditions similarly acknowledge that there were peoples living in the areas they presently inhabit at the moment of their arrival. There are multiple local

[92] Francis Moore, *Travels into the Inland Parts of Africa* (London: E. Cave, 1738).

terms for these putative autochthons, but the first European visitors referred to them collectively as Bainunks/Bagnun – which is rendered as Bainunka in Mandinka. When the Portuguese arrived around the middle of the fifteenth century, they encountered Mandinka populations already living at the mouth of the Gambia River.[93] But the Portuguese also commented extensively on the importance of Bainunk traders who linked the Casamance and the Gambia river systems, and sometimes forged 'kingdoms' of their own, including the eponymous Casa Mansa.[94] However, references to the Bainunks become thinner and more ambiguous as time progresses, while the Jola (or Floups) begin to enter the Portuguese record on a more sustained basis.[95] Hence Peter Mark observes that whereas Alvares d'Almada (writing in 1594) only identified a Bainunk-speaking people called the Jabundos in Buluf, Lemos Coelho (in 1669) referred explicitly to 'Felupos'.[96] Other sources indicate that the increasing presence of the Jola in Fogny proper created bouts of conflict with the Bainunks towards the end of the seventeenth century.[97] By the time Moore travelled along the Gambia River in 1730, it appeared that Bainunks were on the way to becoming something else. On the lower end of the river, Moore identified three small kingdoms on the south bank that are featured on the accompanying map (Map 2.2): Kombo, Fogny (or 'Fonia') and Kiang ('Caen'). In the case of Fogny, Moore commented that "inland it is very large, and governed by two Emperors, who are of a Banyoon [Bainunk] Race, which is a sort of Floops, and have each their distinct Districts".[98] This passage is significant because it suggests that the Bainunk ruling houses had not been entirely displaced, but that they had also begun to merge into the 'Floop' population. For the same reason, it is possible that the 'Floops' that Moore located on the southern border of Kombo were Bainunks rather than what we would now call Jolas. In the case of Kiang, Moore observed that it was governed by Mandinkas, as was Kombo, but he referred to 'Banyoons' at the trading town of Geregia.[99] Because the latter had long been an important

---

[93] Wright, *The World*, p. 71.

[94] Casa Mansa was apparently subordinate to Kabu, see Baum, *Shrines*, p. 65

[95] Robert Baum observes that the Portuguese referred to the Bainunks or Cassangas as occupying much of the Casamance at the start of the sixteenth century, but also noted the existence of Floups (a term for what we now call Jola) who seem to have been more recent arrivals. Baum, *Shrines*, p. 63.

[96] He also referred to 'Usol', which appears to be a reference to the village of Thionk-Essil. This would have been a Bainunk settlement before becoming Jola. Mark, *Cultural, Economic, and Religious*, pp. 18, 26–7. The term Floup is a source of some confusion because at times it has been taken to refer to a particular sub-group, while at other times it has been used for all those we today call Jola.

[97] De la Courbe's text of 1685 cited by Mark, *Cultural, Economic and Religious*, p. 25.

[98] Moore, *Travels*, p. 24.   [99] Moore, *Travels*, p. 52.

crossroads linking Gambia and Casamance River trade routes, and because the Bainunk were reputed to be accomplished traders, this makes perfect sense.[100]

Today, the Bainunk survive only in very small pockets, such as at Yundum in the Gambia, at Niamone in Buluf and around Ziguinchor on the south bank of the Casamance River.[101] In the light of the present demographic realities, it might appear as if the Bainunk have been pretty much erased from the map in a pre-colonial version of ethnic cleansing.[102] The notion of a violent displacement is in fact posited by Mandinka and Jola traditions that pointedly refer to bouts of conflict with the Bainunks. Hence, in Kabadio there is a tradition that tells of how the future Mansa Dambeld (or Dambeli) – the notional leader of the Jabang clan – left Kabu because he realized that he could never become a king there.[103] On the course of his travels, he encountered a diviner who told him that when he reached the sea he would be able to establish a kingdom of his own there. He entered the Casamance from the south-east and came to a location that seemed to correspond with the land that had been prophesied. But the area was already occupied by Bainunks who gave him a hostile reception. The latter were more numerous and Mansa Dambeld was defeated in the ensuing battle. From his refuge at Katana, it is said, he sent a request for reinforcements from Kabu. This brought the Jassey and Sanneh clans to the region who helped Mansa Dambeld to prevail. This tradition recalls that Mansa Dambeld chased the Bainunk into Kombo and scattered them with enduring consequences for the latter:

Before Mansa Dambeld came to this land here, by then the Bainunkas were here. But when he came he wanted to settle first, but the Bainunkas were resisting. That is, they did not want him to settle here. So he had to fight with them. So because of the fight with them, that caused the Bainunkas to flee. So when they flee to any other area, people always fight with them because people were very hostile against them – against the Bainunkas. So that is why they are all scattered now, and that is why you hardly see a Bainunka tribe now.[104]

In the region south of the Allahein, Mansa Dambeld supposedly founded the new kingdom of Fogny-Jabankunda (literally 'Fogny of the Jabangs') with its

---

[100] The trading networks of the Bainunk have been examined by George Brooks, *Eurafricans in West Africa: Commerce, Social Status, Gender and Religious Observance from the Sixteenth to the Eighteenth Century* (Oxford and Athens: James Currey and Ohio University Press, 2003), pp. 44–9. Alvares d'Almada referred to the Bainunk trade at Geregia in his account, dating from around 1570. Mark, *Cultural Economic and Religious*, pp. 14–15.

[101] Mark, *Cultural, Economic and Religious*, p. 19. Linares estimates there are some 30 Bainunk settlements around Bignona and Ziguinchor, *Power, Prayer and Production*, p. 85.

[102] Christian Roche even goes as far as to use the term genocide. Christian Roche, *Histoire de la Casamance: conquête et résistance, 1850–1920* (Paris: Karthala, 1985), p. 23.

[103] Interview with Alkalo Landing Jabang et al., Kabadio (Casamance), 21 July 2005. Kabu or Gabou is in modern Guinea-Bissau.

[104] Interview with Alkalo Landing Jabang and others, Kabadio, 19 February 2004.

capital at Kabadio.[105] After some time, those who remained in Kombo informed Dambeld that they wanted to establish their own kingdom in the area that had been cleared of the Bainunks. A hunter who was also a diviner at the court in Kabadio foretold that when these migrants came to a forest where an antelope had been partly devoured by a leopard, that was where they should settle. This site became the settlement of Brikama, which was henceforth the capital of Kombo. The traditions of Sifoe support this version, merely adding the detail that the younger brother of the future *mansa* remained at Sifoe, while the elder one proceeded to Brikama.[106] Such traditions clearly have a contemporary political edge. The Kabadio version may be read as a statement to the effect that the town stood in the same relation to Brikama as Kabu did to it: that is, as the senior brother. Equally, the Sifoe version establishes the former as existing prior to Brikama and thus asserts a kind of parity.

Within the Kabadio tradition, which posits a violent displacement of the Bainunk, is buried the seeds of an alternative interpretation of the history. It makes clear that there were many Bainunk captives who were incorporated. It recalls that Mansa Dambeld gave them the name of Jabang, which he himself had adopted – his earlier name in Kabu being Trawali – to which the captives responded by demanding that if they were to share his name then they should not be treated as slaves. In other words, if they were to be assimilated, it had to be on the basis of equality. This interpretation explicitly acknowledges that captive Bainunks became Mandinka – which bears more than a passing resemblance to stories about incorporation of Ewe captives into Agotime lineages. While these stories are suggestive, it is likely that the incorporation of Bainunks had as much to do with slavery as the struggle for territory. The Mandinka certainly sold some slaves to the Europeans, and it seems likely that the Bainunk were amongst the victims around Kombo, as indeed they were further to the east. The sale of slaves would have gone together with selective incorporation, as happened in Agotime. It is easy enough to envisage enslavement as part of a strategy of demographic expansion in which Bainunk – and for that matter Jola – captives became Mandinka. Apart from slavery, it is likely that Kombo established a tributary relationship over remaining Bainunk settlements, extending into Fogny-Jabankunda and Narang. Over time, this may have led to a process of absorption, in which Bainunka communities began to associate themselves with Mandinka traditions and ways of conceiving of the

---

[105] However, it is also claimed that the original capital was located near to Diana and that Fogny-Jabangkunda was actually named after one Mansa Kasseh Jabang, a Bainunk ruler. Interview with Alhaji Demba Jabang, Kartong (Gambia), 4 June 2004.

[106] Interview with Alhaji Malanding Demba, Alkalo of Sifoe, 4 June 2004. Also Interview with Arfang Ansu Jatta, Sifoe, National Centre of Arts and Culture, Banjul [NCAC] Interview No.734. 5 January 1981. I am grateful to Paolo Gaibazzi for his help in securing copies of these transcripts.

political realm. This would almost certainly have been a highly uneven process, in which Mandinka identities would have been superimposed upon those that already existed – even as the Mandinka themselves borrowed aspects of their cultural practice from the Bainunk. This process is better conceived of, therefore, as a partial melding of communities rather than the physical elimination of one group by the other. The latter nevertheless remained important as a founding charter based on conquest.

To what extent can such an interpretation be supported by the evidence? The traditions of Sifoe recount that Mansa Dambeld in Kabadio gave wives to the Kombo settlers to establish an affective bond between them.[107] However, the status of Dambeld is open to more than one interpretation. It is usually maintained that he was a Mandinka from Kabu, which is crucial because he was the putative founder of the Jabang line that provides the chief in many villages and towns in the Gambia and the Casamance today. But the figure of Dambeld could also stand for a Bainunk leader who offered land to Mandinka settlers and intermarried with them. On this view, the Mandinkization of the Bainunka ruler stands for what happened to the Bainunk as a whole. That is, as they became more closely associated with the Mandinka – marriage may stand here for other kinds of contacts – they merged into their ranks. There is a Bainunk tradition that lends some support to this alternative interpretation. It tells of a Bainunk king, Banjuku Biayi, who was killed by his own people, just before which he issued a curse to the effect that the Bainunks would forever be the subjects of others: in effect, they would become deracinated. This has become a stock explanation for why the Bainunks have almost ceased to exist in Kombo and surrounding areas. Interestingly, some renditions even speculate that Mansa Dambeld might in fact have been a Bainunk. In Brikama traditions, for example, it is Mansa Dambeld who obstructs the Mandinka settlers and has to be defeated with reinforcements from Kabu. He is decapitated, clearing the way for the Bojang to cross the Allahein River and, following the intercession of a diviner, to found the town of Brikama.[108] But some contemporary readings of history further subvert this interpretation, pointing out that Bojang itself is not a Mande name, but actually a Bainunk one. Again, Jabang is said to be a corruption of 'Jambang', which is a Bainunk name.[109] Moreover, 'Brikama' is itself a Bainunk place name and not a Mandinka one. Finally, in the course of interviews more than one informant ventured the opinion that while his own people considered themselves Mandinka today, his ancestors were in all likelihood Bainunk. This kind of observation does not cause any particular discomfort because many informants make a point of remarking on

---

[107] NCAC Interview No. 734: Sifoe, Arfang Ansu Jatta.
[108] NCAC Interview No. 217: Brikama (first page missing).
[109] Interview with Alhaji Demba Jabang, alkalo of Kartong (Gambia), 4 June 2004.

the capacity of the Mandinka to absorb other peoples. But it points to an ongoing debate about identities, typically expressed through lineage and place of origin, that would seem to predate the colonial period by some way.

In fact, there are traditions that suggest that the Mandinka did not merely absorb the Bainunk, but the Kalorn as well. Today, the homeland of the Kalorn people – or the Karoninka, as they are called in Mandinka – lies south of Kafountine on the peninsula and islands of Bliss and Karone. Many Karoninkas insist that they are the original inhabitants of Kombo, and this enjoys some support from the traditions of Mandinka settlements. Interestingly, those of Brikama maintain that Mansa Dambeld was actually a Jola, which in this case is probably a reference to the Kalorn rather than a Fogny-Jola group.[110] Other traditions refer to a woman from Karone called Wulending who was living in Kombo before the Mandinka arrived.[111] In some accounts she is presented as a 'queen' who has been forced to leave Karone, but in the Brikama version she is presented as a poor woman living in a cave who is offered the choice between death or marrying the *mansa*, and opts for the latter. This establishes a convenient familial link between the Mandinka and the Karoninka. In fact, many informants ventured the opinion that the Karoninkas are not a kind of Jola, but rather a branch of the Mandinka that became cut off from the others – either when the latter moved north to Kombo or (less logically) when the Karoninkas relocated southwards.[112] This clashes with the rendition of Brikama history above, but it clarifies that at some level the Mandinka see themselves as sharing a bond with the peoples of Karone. The 'Floops' bordering Kombo, who appear on the map produced by Francis Moore, may therefore have been Kalorn/Karoninka as well as Bainunk.

By this point, what should be clear is that the traditions of people in Kombo, Fogny-Jabangkunda and Narang do not point to a neat separation between autochthons and incomers, but rather to an intermingling of peoples – despite the fact that the categories of Mandinka, Bainunk and Floup/Jola have persisted. This was neatly expressed to Winifred Galloway in the following terms: "When you say a Kombo Mandinka you mean a Jola; and when you say a Kombo Jola you mean a Mandinka. They are all mixed up together. Any Kombo Mandinka who says he is a 'pure' Mandinka is lying."[113] This is

---

[110] NCAC Interview No. 217: Brikama (first page missing). The Karlorn used to be classified as a Jola sub-group, but this is now contested by Kalorn activists, as I will demonstrate in Chapter 13.

[111] NCAC No. 213 C, Interview with Nyanko Baro, Gunjur, 14 August 1973.

[112] The claim that the Karoninkas are actually Mandinkas was made by no fewer than three alkalos during interviews. Interviews with Alhaji Demba Jabang, alkalo of Kartong (Gambia), 4 June 2004; Alhaji Malanding Demba, Alkalo of Sifoe (Gambia), 6 April 2004; and with Alkalo Landing Jabang et al., Kabadio, 21 July 2005.

[113] A conversation with Mbalefele Janneh, Bakau (2977), quoted in Winifred Galloway, "A Listing of Some Kaabu States and Associated Areas: Signposts Towards State-by-State

enough to make any self-respecting historian wary of taking oral traditions too seriously. Donald Wright, who has spent much of his career seeking to make sense of Mandinka stories of migration, ended up concluding that perhaps there were no population movements on any significant scale.[114] The context was one in which diffusionist interpretations of African history – in the mould of the infamous 'Bantu migrations' – had gone distinctly out of fashion. According to Wright's revised opinion, people could become culturally Mandinka without actually having migrated from elsewhere, as certainly happens today. But this argument surely presupposes a critical mass of Mandinka for cultural dominance to have been effective. It might be plausible to argue that Mandinka traders exercised an influence beyond their numbers, but one thing we know about the Bainunk was that they were consummate traders themselves. On balance, while it is credible that many Bainunk and Karoninka communities became Mandinka, it does seem likely that there were also real Mandinka movements of population – most probably from the direction of Kabu and Pakao rather than Mali itself. Where Mandinka power was weakest, a greater salience was probably attached to other layers of identification. Hence, while a Mandinka identity crystallized in Kombo proper, in the frontier regions of Narang and Fogny-Jabangkunda peoples were more likely to conceive of themselves as being primarily 'Floup' or Bainunk.

Beyond Kombo, it is not the Mandinka that hold the key to the virtual disappearance of the Bainunks, but rather the Jola. Unlike Mandinka traditions that claim migrations from particular places at specific moments in time, Jola traditions posit a steady drift northwards. Over time, Mark suggests, the Jola gained the demographic upper hand in Fogny and Buluf and absorbed the local Bainunk populations.[115] This would explain why Jola religious practice, for example, contains traces that are identified with the Bainunk.[116] One of the reasons for the demographic success of the Jola may have been that wetland rice cultivation permitted higher yields per unit of land. Under conditions of endemic insecurity, it was important for cultivators to farm in relative proximity to the safety of their villages, which conferred a premium on a more

---

Research in Kaabu", paper delivered at International Kaabu Colloquium, Dakar, 19–24 May 1980, p. 23. I am grateful to Paolo Gaibazzi for tracking this paper down in the Gambia.

[114] His readings of the evidence pointed to migration from the Kabu kingdom in what is now Guinea-Bissau from the fourteenth century onwards. Donald Wright, *The Early History of Niumi: Settlement and Foundation of a Mandinka State on the Gambia River* (Athens: Ohio University Center for International Studies, 1977). However, within a decade, he had become much more sceptical. See Donald Wright, "Beyond migration and conquest: oral traditions and Mandinka ethnicity in Senegambia", *History in Africa* 12, 1985, pp. 335–48. However, the essentials of the earlier interpretation are repeated in Wright, *The World*, pp. 74–5. See also Assan Sarr, *Islam, Power and Dependency in the Gambia River Basin: The Politics of Land Control, 1790–1940* (Rochester: Rochester University Press, 2016), ch. 1.

[115] Mark, *Cultural Economic and Religious*, p. 30.   [116] Baum, *Shrines*, p. 66–8.

intensive form of agriculture. Whereas James C. Scott has noted the correlation between paddy rice cultivation and state formation in the lowlands of South-East Asia, and between land extensive shifting cultivation and statelessness in the highlands, paddy rice was actually associated with statelessness and adaption to the slave trade across the Senegambia.[117] The common factor is that wetland rice farming made it possible to achieve higher than normal population densities in both regions of the world.

A process of steady assimilation also helps to account for the existence of Bainunk names amongst populations that consider themselves Jola today – names such as Diatta, Sambou or Koli.[118] In Fogny, the boundary between Mandinka and Jola seems to have been less permeable than in Kombo, and this may relate to greater slaving activity in that area. The picture that Francis Moore painted of Fogny in the 1730s was one of two sets of communities that stood in an antagonistic relationship to one another:

On the South-side of this River, over against James Fort, in the Empire of Fonia, and but a little Way inland are a Sort of People call's Floops, who are in a manner wild: they border close to the Mandingoes and are bitter Enemies to each other. Their Country is of a vast Extent, but they have no King among them, each of their Towns being fortified with Sticks drove all round and filled up with Clay: They are independent of each other, and under the Government of no one Chief; notwithstanding which, they unite so firmly that all the force of the Mundingoes (tho' so very numerous) cannot get the better of them.[119]

This passage stands in some tension with his earlier assertion that Fogny was under the control of 'Banyoon emperors'. But the point is presumably that while the latter claimed to govern territory, there were a large number of Jola settlements that were to all intents and purposes independent of each other as well as their notional overlords.[120] The passage also makes clear that the reason for the antagonism was that the Jola felt vulnerable to Mandinka raiding. George Brooks observes that Bintang was an important market on the Vintang creek that was visited by Mandinka traders. Further down the river, the port of Tankular ('Tankrewall' in Moore's account) was another trading town where slaves were brought for sale from further afield by Mandinka traders.[121] Many of the slaves that were traded along the river would have been Jola, while those who supplied them would have been Mandinka.

---

[117] Scott, *Art of Not Being Governed*, p. 74 and ch. 3 more generally.
[118] Mark, *Cultural, Economic and Religious History*, p. 19.   [119] Moore, *Travels*, pp. 35–6.
[120] Labat's almost contemporaneous account suggested that the king of Fogny had difficulty extracting tribute from the Jola. Mark, *Cultural, Economic and Religious*, pp. 25–6.
[121] Brooks, *Eurafricans*, p. 231.

Not surprisingly, therefore, the relationship between Mandinka and Jola was characterized by a considerable amount of mistrust. The Jola built fortifications in order to thwart raiding parties, although the purpose might also have been to provide a defence against hostile Jola neighbours. From Robert Baum's carefully constructed history of Esulalu, to the south of the Casamance River, it is clear that some Jola were involved in kidnapping and selling slaves. Indeed, he traces the emergence of new Jola shrines to this clandestine trade in slaves.[122] Mark similarly provides evidence of Jola slaving activity in Buluf. Indeed, the Jola must have been involved in slaving because the iron with which they tipped their long hoes that were so effective in wetland rice farming was imported.[123] But it was the Mandinka, with their networks of regional trade, who most came to be associated with acts of violent enslavement. The European stereotype was that the Mandinka were born traders, whereas the Jola were inward-looking and avoided contact with the whites. While the latter statement is perhaps true, they were certainly implicated in a wider system of inter-regional commerce. It seems likely that Mandinka traders were their points of contact with the external market, despite the fact that 'Mandinka' and 'Floup' came to assume connotations of mutual antipathy.

This touches on a fascinating aspect of the history of ethnonyms. When Francis Moore referred to 'wild Floops', he was almost certainly reproducing a Mandinka stereotype rather than something that was developed within an autonomous field of European discourse. But when Moore himself went on to paint a picture of a people with an underlying integrity, he was again surely drawing on a more nuanced Mandinka view that traders were the most likely to have put together. Hence Moore wrote that:

These Floops have the Character never to forgive, or let the least Injury go unrevenged; but then, to make amends, the least good Office done to them is always repaid by them with a grateful Acknowledgement.[124]

The term 'Floup' gradually gave way to that of 'Jola', surviving only in the name of one of its sub-groups. One version of the etymology of *Jola*, which became current in the nineteenth century, was precisely that of the 'people who pay back', in the literal and figurative senses.[125] The dictum that Moore

---

[122] Baum, *Shrines*, ch. 5.

[123] But whether the Jola kept slaves themselves is less clear. Mark suggests that they did in Fogny. Mark, *Cultural, Economic and Religious*, p. 27. Roche, *Histoire de la Casamance*, p. 35, sees the Jola as being distinctive in not holding slaves.

[124] Moore, *Travels*, p. 36.

[125] There is a lack of consensus on the etymological origins of the name Jola. The anthropologist Louis-Vincent Thomas took 'Di-ola' in the language of the Jola themselves to mean 'all the visible living'. Thomas, *Les Diola*. Mark, *A Cultural, Economic and Religious History*, p. 7 suggests that the name is rather of Wolof origin, but without providing any further explanation. But it is also widely believed that the name comes from Mandinka, meaning 'someone who

reproduces seems, therefore, to have been in usage for at least a century before finally giving rise to the ethnonym. This is an excellent example of an ethnic label under construction. Unlike 'Agotime', which refers to a place, 'Jola' is an allusion to shared cultural attributes.

At this point, I turn briefly to the question of how power was constituted in Mandinka and Jola societies. As I have already indicated, the language of kingdoms and kingships is rather misleading with respect to Kombo, Fogny-Jabangkunda and Narang. In the Mandinka polities, power was monopolized by ruling families that claimed to have been the first to establish themselves in particular localities when they arrived from Kabu and Pakao. This created a notional hierarchy of settlements based on who arrived first, but such claims to precedence were rather undercut by the notion that those who hived off did so with the intention of carving out separate kingdoms. Galloway suggests a tripartite division of Kombo: that is Kombo Santo (centred on Brikama), Kombo Dambeli (Fogny-Jabangkunda) and Kombo Afeet (centred on Busumbala). The Bojangs ruled the second and the Jattas the third. As regards the first, Galloway simply notes that "It was at first a kingdom ruled by the Jaabangs [sic], but soon became a series of independent villages, which it remained up to the colonial period."[126] The oral traditions suggest a close relationship between the rulers of Brikama and Busumbala, with the latter allegedly being founded by the nephew of the founding *mansa* in Brikama. Over time, there seems to have been a political convergence, with successive kings of the Kombo being drawn from the Bojang and Jatta families, each of which retained its own capital. The idealized pattern was that the succession passed from one family to the other and back again in the collateral line. When there was no brother to a former *mansa* within the eligible family, the office supposedly passed to his sons.[127] Hence Kombo was necessarily a polity that was held together through a structural tension between Brikama and Busumbala based on similarity rather than perceived difference. We know very little about Fogny-Jabangkunda and Narang, but what Galloway says is probably an accurate description. From the Kombo perspective, these may be seen as frontier regions that came under the influence of Kombo when the latter was strong but were otherwise independent.

In Kombo, rulers asserted the right to tax populations by virtue of their claims to the ownership of the land. A new study by Assan Sarr emphasizes the cardinal importance of control over land, and the people who worked it, to the

---

pays back'. Smith, "The Jolas of Senegambia", p. 157. This is the version I have repeatedly encountered in the field.

[126] Galloway, "A Listing", p. 22.

[127] Charlotte A. Quinn, *Mandingo Kingdoms of the Senegambia: Traditionalism, Islam and European Expansion* (London and Evanston: Longman, 1972), pp. 42–3.

maintenance of the Mandinka 'aristocracy'.[128] In addition, all forms of trade were subjected to levies.[129] It is not possible to gauge the relative importance of these sources of income, but it is likely that the taxes on trade were far more important in financial terms. The perceived centrality of commerce comes out clearly in one of the more fascinating Brikama traditions. The story begins with one Ma-Jabang leaving Fogny-Jabangkunda to go in search of palm trees to tap and striking up a friendship with one Ma-Sane (Sanneh) and one Suleyman at Sika in Niumi. The palm-wine tapper encounters a *jinn* (or evil spirit) assuming the form of a white man who asks him to exchange a gourd full of palm-wine for a key. Ma-Jabang turns down the offer, fearing the consequences, but informs his friends. Suleyman, who is evidently a Muslim advises against having anything to do with the *jinn*, but Ma-Sane asks his friend to be taken to the place where it made its appearance. Ma-Sane proceeds to make the swap, and when they return to the village, he builds a house. After some delay, three sailing boats arrive loaded with trade goods that are so plentiful that they cannot all fit into the single house, thereby requiring him to engage in further construction. From that point onwards, European traders become constant visitors to Ma-Sane, and his settlement becomes the focal point for all the trade in Kombo, Fogny and Niumi. The story then goes that Ma-Sane begins to abuse his position, demanding that the people of Kombo work on his fields before he will sell goods to them. The disaffected *Mansa* of Kombo encounters a man from Futa – presumably a marabout – who promises to turn Banjul into a centre of trade in return for two slaves. He writes on pieces of paper (presumably in Arabic), and these are then buried at specific points on the island, to which European traders are inexorably drawn. Each of the trading communities that became important much later is mentioned by name in the passage:

They left Ali Kodel's place [presumably a Lebanese trader] and went to Companyi (C.F.A.O); then they went to Maurel Freres, and then they went to Maurel and Proms. That was where their last juju was buried. The blessing and prosperity of the juju was what brought in all the others (traders).[130]

The notion that European traders were enticed towards Bathurst through the exercise of magic provides a rather interesting inversion of the conventional view that it was Europeans who forced Africans into making concessions there. The denouement in the narrative is predictable enough. The trade of Ma-Sane in Niumi collapses, while that of Bathurst prospers to the benefit of the *Mansa* of Kombo. Behind this myth-history, there is clearly a significant point. The presence of European traders brought material rewards in the shape

---

[128] Sarr, *Islam, Power and Dependency,* p. 82.   [129] Quinn, *Mandingo Kingdoms,* pp. 40–1.
[130] NCAC Interview No. 217: Brikama (first page missing), p. 31.

of duties that the kings of Niumi had been charging since long before Bathurst was founded on Kombo soil.

The rulers of Kombo certainly taxed commerce and developed something corresponding to an administration, but of a rather decentralized kind. Each *mansa* accumulated a band of slaves and loyal followers ('the king's men') who enforced his orders and collected the taxes. Because the kingship rotated, there was a strong element of contingency built into the structure of decision-making. By the early nineteenth century, the *mansa's* retainers were reputed to behave in a rapacious manner and with variable levels of accountability to their master. Kombo was a state, therefore, but of a rather decentralized kind. South of the Allahein, as we have seen, it seems likely that the towns were effectively independent of one another. But interestingly, a sense of bounded political space remained. Fogny-Jabangkunda was conceived of as the territory located between the Allahein River in the north and the Diouloulou marigot in the east, although its southern boundary was more sketchy. Narang was notionally bounded in the north by the forest and in the south by the Diouloulou *marigot*, thereby making it the neighbour of Kombo, Fogny-Jabangkunda and Fogny proper.

At one level, *mansas* were secular rulers, who governed in association with their councillors. However, Mande rulers were also considered to exercise power through their superior knowledge of the spiritual universe. For non-Muslims (or Soninke), the natural world was inhabited by spiritual forces that had the capacity to influence the affairs of men in important ways. There were particular spirits that were associated with forests, which is surely why the hunter who prophesied the founding of Kombo identified a wooded area. It is also the reason why the initiation of men into secret societies – the perform-ance of which was necessary for the holding of any office – took place in the forest. The *mansas* derived much of their power by manipulating the spirits that dwelt in particular sacred groves. One of these groves survives today in Narang, which used to be a more heavily wooded area than it is today.[131] Just outside the village of Kujube, which has been relocated away from the forested area, there is the sacred grove of Mansa Kalamar (see below) who is remem-bered as a Soninke of unusual spiritual prowess. The grove cannot be entered by Muslims, and informants tell of particular individuals who died on the spot when they were unwise enough to disobey the injunction to stay clear of it.[132] Farmers today maintain a *cordon sanitaire* between their fields and the grove for the same reason. Near the grove, there also used to be a large tree that

---

[131] It is said that the meaning of the name Narang is 'a way through' or 'route', which suggests that the forest was also seen as a physical barrier. Interview with Ibraima Dogolo Koli, Coubanac (Casamance), 23 July 2005.

[132] Fieldwork diary, 21 July 2005.

served as an oracle, although this has now ceased to exist. As is clear from Kabu itself, every *mansa* was considered to be both a magician and a ruler. Hence it is probable that the influence of Narang resided more in the importance of its shrines (or *jalang*) than in the exercise of any significant political authority.[133]

In most Jola societies, the largest political unit was the village, although there are references to Floup kingdoms in sixteenth-century Portuguese sources.[134] To that extent, Jola society was even more decentralized than that of the Ewe who did have chiefs of a kind. Each Jola village was comprised of separate wards (*kalol*) and family compounds (*fank*). Within the wards, power would have resided in the hands of senior men. Collective decisions within a village therefore emerged out of the interaction between elders from the constituent wards. In addition, each ward was responsible for its own shrines (*boekine*) that mediated (directly or more indirectly) between people and the creator of everything, *Emit* or *Emitai*. Although the latter is conventionally regarded as an instance of a 'withdrawn God', Baum maintains that the *boekine* performed an operative link: "While it was rare to pray directly to Emitai, most prayers addressed to the spirit shrines were relayed to Emitai."[135] Particular shrines were consulted for specific purposes, but some shrines emerged that served an entire village. The *oeyi* (sometimes written as *ai*), which Baum interprets as 'priest king', was considered to be the overarching spiritual authority – although Mark observes that the position did not exist in every Jola community.[136] The *oeyi* was usually associated with bringing rain and was responsible for the performance of rites that ensured the fertility of the fields. Crucially, he also mediated in land disputes. But the *oeyi* was not a chief in the conventional sense. He did not control the individual shrines and was really a mediator between the human and spiritual domains rather than the commander of men. Hence in his reconstruction of Esulalu history, Baum observes that the autochthons who preceded the Jola came to fill the position of *oeyi*, while a stigma remained attached to them.[137] Much like spirit mediums in southern Africa, the *oeyi* was expected to shun material goods and, in contemporary times, Linares observes that the incumbent is expected to live in poverty.[138]

---

[133] Another such forested enclave is to be found at Birassou, near to Diana. In his account of Soninke religion in Kabu, Niane writes of the *dialan* (or *jalang*), which were spirits thought to inhabit trees, animals, boulders, snakes and so on, and which often inhabited sacred forests. Niane, *Histoire des Mandingues de l'ouest*. This would be comparable to the spirits associated with the Todzie river in Agotime. The difference is that in Agotime, the priest in Afegame does not appear to have derived his influence from control of local spirits, but rather from control of the religious objects imported into the area.

[134] Baum, *Shrines*, p. 65.   [135] Baum, *Shrines*, p. 41.

[136] Mark, *Cultural, Economic and Religious*, p. 77.   [137] Baum, *Shrines*, pp. 91–2.

[138] Linares, *Power, Prayer and Production*, p. 41.

Europeans, like their Mandinka informers, came to regard the Jola as anarchic, but this belied a sophisticated level of social organization. Rice farming, which was only possible through the construction of dykes that could be used to desalinate fields, depended crucially upon a strong element of village co-operation – as did collective stockades that served a defensive purpose.[139] When it came to fighting, which the Jola were famously good at, they also demonstrated a capacity to work together. As Moore observed, they held their own against their ostensibly stronger Mandinka neighbours in Fogny. Although Jola villages often stood in an antagonistic relationship to one another, there are documented instances where they joined forces to repel a common Mandinka threat. In the Jola case, therefore, it is best to think of a plurality of sites of power, in which the lines seldom converged. Age, wealth and gender conferred a greater say in community affairs, but Jola communities remained remarkably democratic in their ethos and internal functioning. Whereas endemic conflict led to a separation of religious and military functions, Jola communities responded to insecurity by adding new shrines, but – and this is the crucial point – not new offices. Whereas it is reasonable to think of Kombo as a rather loosely organized kingdom, with some of the trappings of a state – built around a hybrid between productive and coercive social contracts – the Jola of Fogny seem, in Scott's terms, to have actively rejected the idea of the state.

I turn now to events in the nineteenth century that brought about a seismic shift within Mandinka societies and created an overtly hostile relationship between Mandinka and Jola populations. Islam was already well established by the time Richard Jobson travelled down the Gambia in the early seventeenth century.[140] He referred specifically to marabouts, or "Marybucks", although at that time Islam was still a religion that was associated with Mandinka traders. Over time, *mansas* sought to incorporate some of the repertoire that was associated with Muslims, in particular the spiritual fortification that was afforded by amulets. This was consistent with the conception of the *mansa* as a consummate magician. But as Islam sank deeper roots, a conceptual opposition between Marabout and Soninke took shape. The *mansas* were Soninke rulers who acknowledged the spiritual powers of the marabouts but sought to incorporate them into a wider pantheon of spiritual forces. This placed them at odds with reformist marabouts who associated their sacred

---

[139] On changing construction styles, with a view to minimizing the risks of being attacked, see Peter Mark, *'Portuguese' Style and Luso-African Identity: Precolonial Senegambia, Sixteenth–Nineteenth Centuries* (Bloomington and Indianapolis: Indiana University Press, 2002), especially ch. 6.

[140] Richard Jobson, *The Golden Trade or a Discovery of the River Gambra and the Golden Trade of the Aethiopians* (first edition 1623, revised edition by Walter Rodney) (London: Dawsons, 1968).

groves with the activities of *jinns*. Moreover, the manner in which the *mansas'* retainers preyed off subject populations, and their own penchant for alcohol consumption, brought about an increasingly strained relationship. In 1862, Governor D'Arcy of the Gambia described the great schism with a distinctly Orientalist flourish:

> The Mandingoes are Mahomedans but divided ... into two sections, Marabouts and Soninkes. The former tell their beads, are careful in their public devotions, abstain from drink, are industrious but crafty and sensual besides being given to slave dealing. The latter, on the other hand, are lawless and dissipated, plundering when they can from the European trade or from the industrious Marabout – warlike drones in fact.[141]

The Muslim critique of regimes across the wider Senegambia region achieved a resonance in the Mandinka polities on both sides of the Gambia River. An important point of reference was the short-lived polity headed by Ma Ba Diakhou in Rip/Baddibu (1861–67).[142] As in other parts of the Senegambia, Muslim reformers initially attempted to establish separate villages and to resist the 'unjust' demands that the *mansas* imposed. As the numbers of converts reached critical mass, mutual disdain escalated into open conflict between the two sides, in which the Europeans increasingly found themselves holding the balance of power.

The Soninke–Marabout struggle took a number of decades to play itself out in Kombo, but the eventual outcome was a total victory for the Muslims, unlike in Kajoor and Bawol. From their small post at Bathurst, the British contingent endeavoured to remain neutral, and sought to prohibit the sale of arms to the combatants – although smuggling activity could not easily be controlled. They also endeavoured to broker peace agreements at moments of crisis, but these seldom lasted for very long. In the end, the British were forced to accept the inevitability of a Muslim victory, an outcome that was considered tolerable as long as the incoming leaders respected earlier treaties and protected British commercial interests. By 1850, the marabouts had established their dominance in important towns in Kombo, with Sabaji (Sukuta), Gunjur and Brefet becoming the foci of militancy.[143] In 1853, the British settlement came to an agreement with the embattled ruler of Kombo, Suling Jatta, that they should be permitted to annex part of his territory in return for helping to deal with the Muslim rebellion elsewhere within the kingdom. This controversial deal, which handed over Sabaji to British control, soon drew the latter into

---

[141] Governor D'Arcy quoted in Martin Klein, *Islam and Imperialism: Sine-Saloum, 1847–1914* (Edinburgh: Edinburgh University Press, 1968), pp. 69–70. This description is reproduced almost word for word, without attribution, in J.M. Gray, *A History of the Gambia* (Cambridge: Cambridge University Press, 1940), p. 329.

[142] On Ma Ba, see Klein, *Islam and Imperialism*, ch. 4. Fodé Kaba was born in Wuli and spent time in Niumi. After suffering a military setback in Fuladu at the hands of Alfa Molo, he concentrated his military campaigns on Fogny from 1878 onwards.

[143] Gray, *History of the Gambia*, p. 389.

a full-scale war with the Muslims who were led by a Moor who – interestingly enough – had previously joined the fight against the French in Algeria in 1847.[144] After a temporary setback, Sabaji was taken in 1855 and the resistance was suppressed with French assistance. Suling Jatta had been killed at an early point in the fighting, and after his successor also died mysteriously, the Soninke side was weakened by internal dynastic politicking. Fighting between Muslims and Soninkes continued on and off during the 1860s, but by 1873 the whole of Kombo had fallen into Muslim hands with the exception of the dual capitals of Busumbala and Brikama. When the latter fell the following year, the king was left in a completely untenable position.

By this point, one Fodé Sylla had emerged as the leader of the maraboutic cause in Kombo.[145] In 1874, he came to an agreement with the British whereby a neutral zone would be established between an emergent colonial territory and his domains. The final act in the drama followed in June 1875 when the second capital of Busumbala was captured by Fodé Sylla's forces. *Mansa* Tomani Bojang was forced to seek refuge in British territory. Having lost his kingdom, he was offered the option of relocating with his followers to the 'Ceded Mile' on the north bank of the Gambia. Instead, he accepted the inevitable and came to terms with Fodé Sylla. As Gray neatly puts it:

At length on 29 September 1875 the last of a dynasty, which had ruled Kombo for two centuries or more, assented to a peace on the most humiliating terms. He agreed to shave his head, become a Marabout, adopt a Mohammedan name, lay down his arms and destroy his stockade. In return for which Fodi Silla agreed to give him and his people lands, which they might cultivate in peace.[146]

The symbolism embodied in the final sentence is profound because, in effect, the new Muslim 'Amir' claimed to be the owner of the land, while the former king was reduced to the role of supplicant. In this way, a new social contract was built on the ruins of the old ruling houses. Although most Kombo Muslims have regarded this outcome as victory for those fighting a just cause, it is not the case that Fodé Sylla was the uncontested leader of the Muslim side.[147] Moreover, a rendition of this history in Brikama makes the point that there were many Muslims present before the overthrow, implying that the Tures of Gunjur had staged a virtual coup d'état.

---

[144] The individual who allegedly fought with Abd-el-Kader in Algeria was called Omar. Gray, *History of the Gambia*, p. 391.

[145] Fodé Sylla was born into a Fula family at Gunjur. A full biography is contained in David Skinner, "Islam in Kombo: the spiritual and militant jihad of Fode Ibrahim Ture", *Islamic Africa* 3 (1) 2012. In colonial records, he was often referred to as Mandinka, as in ANS 13G 67 "Politique Musulmane: activité des marabouts (1906–1917)" (File 5), "De l'influence religieuse des cheikhs Maures du Senegal", 31 May 1915 (Paul Marty).

[146] Gray, *History of the Gambia*, p. 455.

[147] I owe this observation to David Skinner who is writing a more detailed account.

Fodé Sylla, who now governed an ostensibly Muslim Kombo from his seat at Gunjur, sought to consolidate his polity and to root out the remaining pockets of opposition to his rule. It was the latter that furnished an excuse for embarking on military operations in Narang and Fogny-Jabankjunda, where lesser *mansa*s still existed. Significantly perhaps, the flight of Soninke refugees appears to have been towards settlements with older connections based on memories of migration.[148] Meanwhile, Fodé Kaba had relocated across the Gambia River in 1875 and established his own embryonic Muslim polity straddling Jarra, Kiang and Fogny. Like Fodé Sylla, his pursuit of warfare was justified on the basis of the imperative of mopping up the remaining bases of Soninke resistance. Their common approach to the relationship between politics and religion was quite unlike that of Ahmadu Bamba. The latter followed in a venerable line of religious scholars in West Africa who regarded the exercise of power as being at odds with the spiritual quest of a devout Muslim.[149] By contrast, the two Fodés (like Ma Ba) regarded rule by non-Muslims as a threat to the forging of an Islamic community that needed to be tackled head on. Creating an Islamic state, and forcing people to accept the Muslim religion as the only true faith, implied that religion, politics and the pursuit of warfare were intimately bound up with one another. In other words, the *idea of the state* was absolutely fundamental, but its *material* foundations were rooted in an economy of plunder. As Fodé Kaba is reported to have expressed it:

I beg to say I have nothing to do with groundnuts, as, where I am, I am only a stranger. Ever since I knew myself to be a man, my occupation has been a warrior; and I make it my duty to fight the Soninkis [sic] who profess no religion whatever.[150]

But in each case, the campaign quickly degenerated into raiding against Jola communities. Because the Jola were considered idolatrous, they were also regarded as fair game.

Whereas Fodé Kaba has enjoyed a favourable press amongst Muslims in the Gambia and the Casamance, who credit him with having advanced the cause of conversion, attitudes towards Fodé Sylla have been more mixed.[151] Ture family traditions emphasize that Fodé Sylla was entirely sincere, but many

---

[148] Skinner's reading of Mandinka traditions suggests that this might have been because Soninke refugees in villages like Makuda and Diébaly posed an active threat to Sylla's fledgling polity. "Islam in Kombo", p. 19. A British report from 1894 does explicitly refer to people who had taken refuge from Fode Sylla in Selety, Diébaly and Makuda. NAGB ARP 33/1 "Reports on Kombo, Foni and Kiang", Sitwell's report on Kombo for 1895–96.

[149] On the Suwarian tradition, see Ivor Wilks "'Mallams don't fight with the heathen': a note on Suwarian attitudes to jihad", *Ghana Studies* 5 2002.

[150] Quoted by Gray, *History of the Gambia*, p. 452.

[151] Fay Leary asserts that Fodé Kaba came to enjoy the status of a 'folk hero'. Fay Leary, "Islam, politics and colonialism: a political history of Islam in the Casamance region of Senegal (1850–1914)", unpublished PhD thesis, Northwestern University, 1970, p. 123.

others contend that his forces engaged in raiding for slaves in a thoroughly cynical manner. He sold Jola slaves towards Fuladu and in return acquired the horses and guns that he needed to sustain the cycle of plunder. In that sense, the two Fodés were actually more similar than they were different: each indulged in slave raiding and each rewarded his followers with the resulting booty. They did little to institutionalize Islamic polities, and it is questionable how successful the enforced conversions really were. In the case of Fodé Sylla, a moral ambiguity is reflected in local accounts that I have collected. In some places, it is claimed that he used Karoninka fighters,[152] and in the village of Jiboro Kuta it is recalled that he specifically recruited Bainunks because of their supposedly superior physical strength.[153] In Kabadio, he is reported to have struck an alliance with the *mansa* that was sealed through marriage. This eventually led to the conversion of the *mansa*, if not his people. In Kabadio itself, the arrangement is remembered in less consenting terms:

Kombo [Sylla]'s fight was on two things: that is converting people on Islam and also conquering the people, so he would become their king. In fact, when he came to Kabadio here, when he conquered this area and the people were under his command, the first thing he did was he demanded a wife. He told the people he must be given a wife, by force. Likewise, the other story is . . . that is the other villages like the Jola said . . . he used to wait until after the harvesting period that is when he started waging the war . . . and steal the rice that people kept in their stores. And the animals too – he used to capture a lot and kill a lot and give them to his warriors . . . The negative story you have in the other Jola towns, that is the same thing he did here.[154]

Hence the Mandinkas of Kabadio have retained a rather jaundiced view of their supposed liberator. In Jola communities, Fodé Sylla is remembered very simply as a slave raider whose claims to be fighting a holy war belied a more cynical agenda. Crucially, this negative image is shared by Jola Muslims and non-Muslims alike.

For the defenders of Fodé Sylla, by contrast, it remains important to remember that he banned the consumption of alcohol, posted *talibés* in the areas he conquered, founded mosques and targeted Soninke religious practice.[155] These are taken as incontrovertible evidence of his commitment to the pursuit of religious orthodoxy. But it is interesting that in Narang, which is

---

[152] Circumstantial evidence in support is that after the defeat of Fodé Sylla, many of his fighters headed for Karone. ANS 1F8 "Délimitation de la Gambie", Commandant Canard, Kafountine, to the Governor (11 March 1894). Seasonal migration from Karone to Kombo might explain how the Karoninkas became involved with Sylla's cause.

[153] Interview with assistant Alkalo Bakary Diatta, Jiboro-Kuta (Gambia), 17 July 2005.

[154] Interview with Alkalo Jerreh Dembeh and others, Kabadio (Casamance), 19 February 2004.

[155] Sylla defended a particular raid against the Jola village of Jinaki on the basis that he never attacked Muslims, but only the drinkers of palm-wine – alcohol having become the key marker of identity. Roche, *Histoire de la Casamance*, p. 219. According to Leary, Sylla placed a ban on palm-wine tapping in the areas that came under his control. Leary, "Islam", p. 112.

entirely Muslim today, local traditions recall that when Fodé Sylla came up against Mansa Kalamar of Kujube, he singularly failed. It is said that Sylla's forces initially tried a frontal assault and were driven away by bees, which is the standard trope in Mandinka societies for Soninke spiritual potency. He then tried subterfuge, which similarly failed because Mansa Kalamar was privy to other-worldly knowledge. The story then goes that Sylla accepted that he could not take Kujube by force or stealth. Instead, he provided a cow as a peace offering. After feasting, part of the carcass was buried and Sylla prayed. He is said to have predicted that the people of Kujube would voluntarily convert to Islam within six generations. The fact that this happened in an even shorter time period is not credited to Fodé Sylla, as we will see. On the contrary, this story may be read as a clear statement to the effect that Fodé Sylla did not have divine endorsement – otherwise he would surely have defeated Mansa Kalamar on the field of battle. Moreover, he had been forced to admit that violent means to conversion did not work. There is no evidence that the softer approach was successful because Kujube remained amongst those villages that continued to resist Fodé Sylla until the end. A French official who visited the village in 1894 observed that it was well protected by a stockade and thick forest, and inhabited by people who remained as implacably hostile to Fodé Sylla as ever.[156]

Conclusion

What lessons emerge out of such a detailed exercise in comparative history? The first point to highlight is the importance of the Atlantic trade in shaping the contours of these various societies. Although Agotime was located some way from the coastline, it was moulded by its active involvement in trade. The trade in slaves, ivory and salt was particularly important in terms of enabling the Agotime to consolidate their military position – initially in alliance with Akwamu and later in opposition to it – and to branch out in both a demographic and a spatial sense. It is perhaps relevant that Agotime was founded on an open plain astride the key trade routes and that it enjoyed historic connections with other nodes including other Adangbe settlements. Many of the peoples who were the victims of slave raiding took refuge in the Togoland hills where a bewildering assortment of peoples speaking mutually unintelligible languages holed up. In some respects, this pattern resonates with Scott's depiction of the highland/lowland dichotomy in South-East Asia. The manner in which wealth and power were accumulated in Agotime was transformed by the dynamics of slavery, but this never amounted to the creation of a

---

[156] ANS 13G 372 "Casamance: Correspondance du Résident 1892–1894", A. Farque, l'administrateur supérieur, Sedhiou, to Directeur des Affaires Politiques, St. Louis (26 February 1894).

state.[157] Although the traditions of Kombo, Fogny-Jabangkunda and Narang
ostensibly make much less of trade, there can be no doubt that all the societies
between the Gambia and Casamance rivers were firmly locked into Atlantic
commerce. The Mandinka polities near the mouth of the Gambia, like Niumi
and Kombo, practised slavery and clearly derived much of their income from
taxes on trading activity. The Jola were often on the receiving end of raids,
but the combination of stockaded villages constructed in the midst of the
marigots, together with the cultivation of wetland rice, permitted relatively
high population densities to be maintained. Whereas the Agotime grew their
numbers through stealing people, one might say the Jola did the same through
intensive agriculture coupled with carefully crafted defensive strategies.

A second observation is that inter-group boundaries assumed complex and
variable forms that altered in tandem with the elaboration of this trade. The
Agotime, as I have already noted, sold many of their weaker neighbours as
slaves, which in part accounts for the difficult relations they had with a number
of the Krepe polities. However, their social boundaries were also highly
permeable. Agotime-ness was something that could be entered into, and there
are many accounts today of Ewes having been absorbed in relatively recent
memory. The hugely complex relationship between Mandinka, Bainunk and
Kalorn categories in the Senegambia is arguably an instance of the same
phenomenon. The Mandinka were able to incorporate populations that pre-
dated their arrival, without entirely sublimating older modes of identification.
The imputation that many Mandinkas were actually Bainunk or Karoninka –
including the Bojang and the Jabang ruling families in Kombo and Fogny-
Jabangkunda respectively – subverts the simple narrative of Mandinka and
Jola migrations. Far more than in the trans-Volta, the boundary between
Mandinka and Jola seems to have become a fairly impermeable one, characterized by a mutual antagonism that struck European commentators forcefully
and underpinned by mutual stereotypes that later administrators unwittingly
reproduced.

Thirdly, within all these societies there was a complex relationship between
the exercise of political and of spiritual power. The Agotime would have had
priests rather than chiefs until the militarization of Agotime led to the emergence of separate *avafiawo* whose leadership claims arose out of their capacity
to mobilize followers. No doubt charisma was important, but above all the
right to lead was achieved through the simple proof of military success. The
spiritual fortification that these 'big men' sought from outside Agotime led to a
further distancing from the original shrines based in Afegame. The structural
antagonism between Afegame and Kpetoe therefore stands for competing

---

[157] Scott, *Art of Not Being Governed.*

conceptions of legitimacy that emerged in the context of the slave trade. In the case of Kombo, the *mansas* looked like 'kings' to the Europeans, but the polity was relatively decentralized. The kingship rotated between ruling families located in the towns of Brikama and Busumbala, which was a structural opposition based on likeness. The claim to rule rested on a combination of conquest and being the first to settle, but it seems to have become increasingly coercive over time. At least that was what Muslim critics alleged as they attempted to launch their hegemonic counter-project. After the success of the jihadist cause in Kombo, the claim to rule rested on authority exercised within the parameters of an Islamic state. The idea of the state was based on the *umma*, or a community of the faithful, residing under the authority of a spiritual leadership. For Muslim reformers, this was a sublime embodiment of the productive social contract, replacing the coercive (and often magical) practices of the Soninke rulers. However, the violence was now projected outwards towards the margins of Kombo. The Islamic state was imperfectly materialized by Fodé Sylla and Fodé Kaba whose pursuit of militarism brought booty and captives but was not really conducive to effective state-making. In that respect, the patterns were not so unlike those in Agotime. South of the Allahein River, the Mandinka settlements were probably autonomous from one another for most of the time. A *mansa* was unlike the *avafia* in Agotime in the sense that he devolved responsibility to a separate war leader at times of crisis, and also because he was thought to command spiritual power in his own person. Amongst the Jola – and this would presumably go for the Kalorn as well – there was a priest who was in some senses the most important person in the village community, but without exercising secular authority. The influence of the priest was a function of his mediation between the spiritual realm and the concerns of the living for the maintenance of fertility, rainfall and inter-communal harmony. Because there was no ruler, but a multiplicity of actors, well-ordered communities managed to reproduce themselves in the absence of state forms. These contrasting permutations relate to quite different under-standings of the sources of power and corresponding modes of legitimation.

Finally, in each case there were conceptions of territoriality that certainly counted for something. In the Jola example, the village was the operative unit, but as a result of migration, communities retained memories of their connect-edness. Hence Baum refers to Jola settlers carrying soil from their former settlements when they relocated, thereby establishing a direct link between shrines – and hence also between localities.[158] Amongst the Mandinka, two

---

[158] Baum, *Shrines*, p. 73. The portability of shrines is something that comes through strongly in Lentz's discussion of earth shrines. The difference is that in her case the objects (stones) would typically be taken from the earth shrine that notionally owned the land rather than from the migrants' original home. Lentz, *Land, Mobility and Belonging*, ch. 2.

different principles coexisted. One was the connectivity that arose out of blood ties, which is why oral traditions place such store by who married whom and who settled where first. The other is a principle of territoriality that does not necessarily coincide completely with political boundaries. Hence Fogny-Jabangkunda seems to have survived as an idea long after it ceased to exist as a political entity: it was inscribed in a landscape defined by rivers and *marigots*. Equally Narang was imagined with reference to its boundedness by forests and *marigots*. The traditions of migration themselves make a point of underlining crossings (in the case of bodies of water) and entrances (in the case of forests), both representing human appropriations of a natural landscape. The Agotime similarly conceived of the landscape in terms of rivers and mountains, which helped to situate and define them in relation to their Agu and Adaklu neighbours. Although they did not fashion any mechanism for policing boundaries, the Agotime and their neighbours did seek to stake out territory by planting villages at the margins. In that sense, the Agotime certainly thought they knew where their territory began and ended. The notion that boundaries are a European import therefore needs to be treated with some caution – a finding that resonates with the recent work of Carola Lentz. While states need boundaries, the concept of a boundary is common to societies that were not constituted as states. The boundaries that the Europeans imposed performed another function, and they were often situated in different places, but they frequently played off pre-existing notions of territoriality – as we will see.

3   Port Cities, Frontiers and Boundaries
Spatial Lineages of the Colonial State

> No very urgent necessity existed for entering into so many treaties or
> arrangements with the authorities of the adjacent countries . . . You will have
> the goodness to bear in mind that His Majesty's Government are unwilling to
> sanction arrangements involving the cession of territory to this country; for,
> not to mention the political objections which attach to measures of this
> description, it is impossible to overlook the inconvenience, which must
> manifestly ensue from contracting obligations of alliance with small bodies of
> people, whose extreme weakness would be perpetually urging them to claim
> our interference on their behalf, so that we should eventually find our
> influence with them much less than if we had merely kept up a friendly
> intercourse with them without promising them anything.[1]

This rap over the knuckles, which was administered more than once by
political leaders in London, holds a double significance for what follows. At
one level, it represents an exchange between an embodiment of the British
state, namely the Minister of War and the Colonies, and his Governor in Sierra
Leone – in a matter pertaining to the subordinate settlement of the Gambia. In
that sense, it represents the history of a European state 'at work'. But at another
level, its content touches directly on the issue of what representatives of
the Crown believed they ought to be doing in West Africa. In line with the
argument pursued in Ronald Robinson and Jack Gallagher's *Africa and the
Victorians*, the unequivocal message was that Britain had no interest in raising
expectations of military assistance amongst its local allies, far less in acquiring
territorial commitments.[2] Putting it bluntly, as British politicians were often
wont to do, colonial possessions cost money and brought unwelcome and
messy entanglements. As such, this despatch provides a useful starting point
for an attempt to reconstruct the processes of colonial state-making in the

---

[1] Viscount Goderich, Secretary of State for War and the Colonies, to Sir Neil Campbell, Governor
of the West African Territories, 25 August 1827, quoted in J.M. Gray, *A History of the Gambia*
(Cambridge: Cambridge University Press, 1940), p. 340.
[2] Ronald Robinson and John Gallagher, with Alice Denny, *Africa and the Victorians: The Official
Mind of Imperialism*, 2nd edn. (London: Macmillan, 1981).

Senegambia and along the Gold Coast, in which the proliferation of unanticipated entanglements was nothing less than foundational.

In this chapter, I begin by embarking on two pieces of historical revisionism
that will enable us to make better sense of complex processes of state- and
boundary-making spanning almost a century. Firstly, as we take into account
the broad spectrum of actors and interests that played a part in shaping the
agenda, it is necessary to liberate earlier historiography from its subordination
to narratives of the nation. An initial focus on the agency of African and *métis*
leaders in the coastal settlements came to be seen as anachronistic by the mid-
1960s because they seemed altogether too politically docile and in awe of
imperial visions.[3] If the criterion is the role of elites in hastening national
independence, the critique certainly has some force, even if it remains profoundly teleological. But when the focus is redirected to a longer history of
discourses of entitlement – in this case, the right to enjoy public goods in
return for paying modest taxes – then their contributions cannot so easily be
dismissed. The West African coastal cities were always a fragile link in the
colonial system, because it was here that the right to command was routinely
challenged, and often in ways that directly contradicted the official version of
how the state itself had come into being.

The second slice of revisionism lies in treating port cities and frontier
regions as closely interconnected, both as imperial imaginaries and as geopol-
itical realities. The re-discovery of the connectivity between port cities on
either side of the Atlantic basin, the Indian Ocean and on both shores of the
Mediterranean, is welcome precisely because the parcelling of history into
discrete regional packages makes little intrinsic sense.[4] But West African port
cities only ever existed because they also served as entry points into the
African interior: the importation of goods from Europe, the Americas and
Asia – such as tobacco, spirits, textiles and iron – and the reverse flow of
slaves, gold, gum, rubber and palm-oil, created a two-way dynamic.[5] While
the port city was evidently founded on commerce, the frontier was altogether

---

[3] In the Nigerian context, E.A. Ayandele even went as far as to dub them 'deluded hybrids. E.A.
Ayandele, *The Educated Elite in the Nigerian Society* (Ibadan: Ibadan University Press, 1974).
For a more sympathetic view, see Akintola Wyse, *The Krio of Sierra Leone: An Interpretive
History* (London: C. Hurst, 1989).

[4] On the connectedness of Atlantic port cities, see Miguel Suárez Bosa (ed.), *Atlantic Ports and
the First Globalisation c.1850–1930* (Houndmills and New York: Palgrave Macmillan, 2014).
For an excellent study of the connections between Tunis and the ports of southern Europe, see
Julia Clancy-Smith, *Mediterraneans: North Africa and Europe in an Age of Migration
c.1800–1900* (Berkeley, Los Angeles and London: University of California Press, 2011).

[5] For case studies, see Robin Law, *Ouidah: The Social History of a West African Slaving Port
1727–1892* (Oxford and Athens: James Currey and Ohio University Press, 2004), and Kristin
Mann, *Slavery and the Birth of an African City: Lagos 1760–1900* (Bloomington: Indiana
University Press, 2007).

more elusive and constantly shifting. Roughly speaking there were three zones beyond the coastal ports that concerned Europeans in the nineteenth century: firstly, there were the small areas that Europeans laid direct claim to, like 'British Kombo' in the Senegambia; secondly, there were those where Europeans enjoyed trading privileges and wielded a measure of political influence over a wider area, but stopping short of ultimate control; and thirdly, there were large zones where commerce was transacted, but where European influence was strictly limited and which were often not governed by African states either.[6] The second of these, or what one might call *the proximate frontier*, was often a source of irritation for European merchants who were at odds with African rulers insisting on their right to tax and regulate trade. The third zone, or what I call *the further frontier*, held its allure because typically enough information was available to indicate that there was profitable business to be transacted, but insufficient to dampen the ambitions of the 'men on the spot'. In the early nineteenth century, the further frontier of the Senegambia was what is now eastern Senegal, whereas the proximate frontier was located along the banks of the Gambia and Senegal rivers and immediately inland from the trading ports. Most of what is the Casamance region of Senegal today constituted a further frontier zone, even for the Portuguese. In the Gold Coast, the proximate frontier became virtually synonymous with the southern fringes of the Asante kingdom, while the trans-Volta represented a further frontier as the grip of the latter over its tributaries weakened. While the proximate frontier zones have been central to histories of colonization in Africa, and especially the Gold Coast, the importance of the further frontier has tended to remain obscure. The aim here is to posit a different way of thinking about the construction of colonial space that accords the further frontier regions their rightful place in history.

The Pre-History of Colonial States

Where should we even begin an account of the origins of the colonial state? An obvious place to start is in Europe itself. Hence Crawford Young has observed that "[b]oth colonialism and resistance to it yielded diffusion of a notion of stateness whose lineage lay in the European core".[7] This is another way of saying that the idea of the colonial state had its origins in the metropole and was driven onwards by the will to empire – whether this was informed by the

---

[6] Those areas that were governed by existing states, but where direct European contact was limited, made up the rest. These become relevant to this account during the Scramble itself.

[7] Crawford Young, *The African Colonial State in Comparative Perspective* (New Haven and London: Yale University Press, 1994), p. 16. This observation is not made with specific reference to Africa.

rise of nationalism, often framed in terms of a competitive jingoism,[8] or the interests of industrial, finance or gentlemanly capital.[9] The attempt to impose a monopoly on the use of force, to define territorial boundaries, to create a routinized system of administration, to construct an infrastructure conducive to the export of cash crops and minerals – all of these could be seen as impelled by metropolitan imperatives. Indeed, it would be hard to deny that a certain idea of the state *was* derived from Europe, although it might well have remained just that. Once colonial rule was firmly implanted, there was indeed an effort to materialize this vision in the shape of nested bureaucracies and spaces of governance such as administrative buildings, Customs facilities and prisons.[10] But the point is that there was no straight line from one to the other. As late as the 1920s, colonial states were characterized by forms of personal rule as much as by bureaucratic routines and often struggled to make their writ run. The state was materialized through a decidedly non-linear process of trial and error.

If we are to look for turning points in the relationship between Europeans and Africans, the first came with the British withdrawal from the slave trade in 1807 and subsequent attempts both to persuade other European nations to follow suit and to pressurize Africans into signing agreements embracing 'legitimate commerce'.[11] This was important, firstly, because it led to a renewed willingness to consider limited territorial commitments, along with basic budgetary provisions. The port of Freetown was chosen as the location where slaves who had been intercepted on the high seas would be liberated. But in addition, successive British governments deferred to the abolitionist insistence that the supply lines needed to be cut, by military action if necessary. The fact that many slaves had historically been traded from the Sahel down the Gambia River made it imperative to control its entrance to the Atlantic. Hence, the decision to occupy St. Mary's island – what became Bathurst – in 1816 was taken with a view to imposing a blockade.[12] Throughout West Africa, the existence of a permanent British naval squadron, and the

---

[8] See John M. Mackenzie, *Propaganda and Empire: The Manipulation of British Public Opinion, 1880–1960* (Manchester: Manchester University Press, 1986).

[9] P.J. Cain and A.G. Hopkins, *British Imperialism 1688–2000*, 2nd edn. (Harlow and London: Pearson Education, 2002).

[10] For a comparable analysis of these bordering processes on the Dutch–British frontier in South-East Asia, see Eric Tagliacozzo, *Secret Trades, Porous Borders: Smuggling and States along a Southeast Asian Frontier, 1865–1915* (New Haven and London: Yale University Press), ch. 4.

[11] A.G. Hopkins, "The 'New International Economic Order' in the nineteenth century", in Robin Law (ed.), *From Slave Trade to 'Legitimate Commerce': The Commercial Transition in Nineteenth-Century West Africa* (Cambridge: Cambridge University Press, 1995). Of course, the Danes ended their role in the slave trade before the British.

[12] The weak link was Albreda, a French port on the Gambia, through which slaves continued to pass for some time.

introduction of a smaller French naval presence, enabled the Europeans to call on naval support in the event of a crisis. A further consequence was that the liberation of slaves in Freetown was followed by significant resettlements of population. While some ex-slaves gravitated towards their former homelands, many others settled in the Senegambia and along the Upper Guinea Coast. A fairly large number were despatched to Bathurst as indentured workers whose labour helped the town to cement its foundations in both a literal and a figurative sense. In the short run, ex-slaves provided military manpower, labour for construction and even a buffer against hostile neighbours, but over time they also became the resident majority in Bathurst. By 1826, the town contained a population of 1,800 inhabitants, of whom a mere 30 were Europeans.[13] There was also an expressed desire to attract British merchants to the island, from where they might provide a positive stimulus to legitimate trade in the interior.[14] When Britain returned the French islands of Gorée and Saint-Louis, which had been seized during the Napoleonic wars, British merchants, their *signares* wives and *métis* associates physically relocated to Bathurst and used it as a base camp for trading operations into the interior as well as towards Portendick on the Mauritanian coastline.[15] In the case of the Volta River valley, which was similarly a conduit for the slave trade, the British were operating in a very different environment. For a start, it was the Danes who regarded the trans-Volta as a rough sphere of trading influence. Secondly, the sand bars at the mouth of the Volta made it impractical to sail upstream, while the broken coastline east of the river provided multiple outlets for those who wished to continue what the British considered a clandestine trade. The campaign therefore tended to be prosecuted along the coastline and on the high seas rather than in the interior.

Although the assault on the clandestine slave trade provided the rationale for a token European presence at the coast, there were strict limits to what the British or the French citizenry was prepared to pay for, and these became more stringent as the nineteenth century wore on. In the British case, formal responsibility for the coastal settlements shuttled back and forth between London and the West African merchants in a game of administrative pass-the-parcel.[16] In the French case, metropolitan control was more of a constant,

[13] Gray, *History of the Gambia*, p. 306.   [14] Gray, *History of the Gambia*, p. 302.
[15] Florence K. Olamara Mahoney, "Government and Opinion in the Gambia, 1816–1901", unpublished PhD thesis, London University, 1963, chs. 2–3.
[16] Hence it was the Company of Merchants Trading to Africa who controlled the forts along the Gold Coast until 1821 when they were placed under government control due to concerns expressed about the persistence of the slave trade. The Gold Coast forts were then transferred back to the merchant community, exercising a form of devolved sovereignty, in 1828. In 1843, following a Parliamentary Select Committee, the Crown resumed control and seven years later the Gold Coast forts were separated from Sierra Leone. In 1865, a Select Committee

but administrators were constrained. The West African port settlements were not governed by modern bureaucracies, given that private merchants routinely alternated between wearing official and commercial hats. In Gorée and St. Louis, where the citizens elected their own mayors, this was formalized. Moreover, the coastal settlements were always decidedly flaccid in the fiscal department. Before the mid-nineteenth century, Europeans were not in a position to tax Africans, and indeed they were themselves forced to pay African rulers a rent for the land on which they constructed their establishments, as well as paying regular duties for the right to trade.[17] A skeletal administration and a token military force needed to be paid for out of the duties levied on European trading operations.[18] The dependency of the local administration was also reflected in the military sphere. Although metropolitan naval support could be invoked in the event of a serious crisis, most military action involved local militias and sailing craft that belonged to the merchants themselves.

It is entirely conceivable that the British and the French would have continued to cling unconvincingly to their islands and forts, or even that they would have abandoned the coast altogether in the manner of the Dutch and the Danes.[19] The fact that they proceeded to extend their spheres of influence, and then to claim actual territory, is therefore a development that needs to be explained. Much has to do with the downstream effects of the growing demand within the port cities for the provision of what we would now call public goods – beginning with dispute settlement, but proliferating into new areas as time went on. The merchant community had a deeply rooted sense of its own entitlement, given its contribution to revenues. Depending on the context, its demands might be framed in terms of the rights of Frenchmen or Englishmen,

recommended steadily withdrawing from all the possessions except Sierra Leone, but re-grouping them under Sierra Leone in the interim. These doubts receded and in 1872, the Dutch ceded the castle at Elmina and their other forts to Britain. Finally, in 1874, Britain annexed the so-called protected states, thereby creating a separate Crown Colony. David Kimble, *A Political History of Ghana, 1850–1928* (Oxford: Clarendon Press, 1963), pp. 193–9.

[17] The duties demanded by African rulers were part of the accepted business of the slave trade. For example, ships seeking to pass up the Gambia River had to provide gifts to the *mansa* of Niumi on the north bank, and only if these were considered satisfactory would they be permitted to proceed. Donald Wright, *The World and a Very Small Place: A History of Globalization in Niumi, the Gambia*, 2nd edn. (Armonk, NY and London: M.E. Sharpe, 2004), p. 108. In 1816, the British agreed to pay a rent of about £75 (300 bars) per annum to the king of Niumi for the reoccupation of James Island, which never resumed its former importance. More importantly, an agreement was made with the king of Kombo to permit the fresh occupation of St. Mary's Island in return for an annual rent. Gray, *History of the Gambia*, pp. 300–1. Likewise, the Dutch always made an annual payment to Asante for the occupation of Elmina castle. Larry Yarak, *Asante and the Dutch, 1744–1873* (Oxford: Clarendon Press, 1990).

[18] Bathurst was initially sustained by duties on imported goods. Gray, *History of the Gambia*, p. 306.

[19] The Danes and the Dutch vacated their forts on the Gold Coast in 1850 and 1872 respectively.

but more commonly this was a discourse framed in a local setting. Crucially, the script of the merchants was also susceptible to borrowing by others living in the coastal settlements. At least until the mid-nineteenth century, the European settlements typically consisted of a mixed trading community – both European and *métis* – a small African military complement, often made up of convicts and liberated slaves, and a handful of officials bearing titles. In her seminal doctoral thesis, which sadly remains unpublished, Florence Mahoney underlined the close 'consanguinity' between the European merchants and their 'mulatto' agents in Bathurst. The Europeans occupied many of the highest public offices, such as Superintendent of Police or Magistrate, but many positions were filled by leading sections of the *métis* population, who were descended from the same family lines, as well as from Portuguese progenitors.[20]

The *métis* were increasingly inclined to argue that they too made a vital contribution to the commercial prosperity of the port settlements, while African populations could either insist on their ownership over local spaces or, if they were descended from liberated slaves, they could maintain that by paying local rates or by contributing their labour they too had acquired rights. In Bathurst, the relationship with the British became a complicated one. By the 1860s, Africans were demanding a greater voice and more equitable treatment.[21] One complaint was that because the merchants served as magistrates, they dispensed a highly partial form of justice. Another was that the African population did not receive its fair share of resources, despite its increasing financial contribution. On the French islands of Gorée and St. Louis, where there had long been a history of *métissage*, a similar dynamic was apparent. Here the *habitants* had dominated much of the trade from the interior by virtue of their ownership both of trading vessels and the *laptots*, or slave sailors, that were essential for trading and military expeditions alike. The arrival of new trading houses from Bordeaux and elsewhere challenged their privileged position. Although the French trading houses exploited the language of free trade to demand equal access to interior markets, the authorities were also beholden to the *habitants*. As James Searing indicates, the French authorities sought to perform a balancing act, granting the commercial houses greater access to the valuable gum trade on the Senegal River, while underwriting the privileged relationship between the *habitants* and Moor traders.[22]

---

[20] Mahoney, "Government and Opinion", pp. 62–7.

[21] To some extent, however, their unity was fragile, given a rivalry between those who considered themselves indigenous and others who had come from Freetown. Arnold Hughes and David Perfect, *A Political History of the Gambia, 1816–1994* (Rochester: University of Rochester Press, 2006). The first African was appointed to the Legislative Council in 1883, pp. 73–7.

[22] James Searing, *West African Slavery and Atlantic Commerce: The Senegal River Valley, 1700–1860* (Cambridge: Cambridge University Press, 1993).

In the second half of the nineteenth century, there was mounting pressure within the port settlements for the authorities to multiply the functions they performed. As populations expanded, practical issues of urban management became more pressing. This included the identification and clearing of land for housing, which was at a premium on the islands. In Bathurst, which had grown in an entirely unplanned fashion, an effort was to lay out a grid of streets suitable for a colonial city.[23] The authorities sought to erect defences against seasonal flooding, conjure up a dependable water supply and see to the construction of public buildings – in addition to the routine maintenance of the forts and castles.[24] In due course, schools and basic medical facilities were added to the lengthening list of public goods that were considered legitimate expectations. The salient question then was who would pay for them. The merchants were sensitive to increases in spending that might lead to higher levels of duty, a consideration that often placed them at odds with more ambitious officials. As Alain Sinou observes, administrators like Louis Faidherbe wished to create the appearance of a modern city in somewhere like Saint-Louis, but the financial subventions from the metropolitan government were inadequate and the merchants were critical of plans that seemed overly grandiose.[25]

The same was true of Bathurst where merchants complained about the financial drain imposed by official salaries. In the Gambia, the question of fixing priorities frequently pitted sections of the urban population against each other. The merchants were sensitive to increases in indirect taxes and applied pressure in an attempt to shift some of the burden onto African populations. In the Gambia, where revenues derived from a small parliamentary grant and import duties, the Colonial Office initially insisted on an exemption for the French merchants based at Albreda on the north bank.[26] This anomaly enabled cheap American goods (especially rum and tobacco), which were landed free of duties at Gorée, to be distributed along the river by African traders to the detriment of British commerce.[27] The local administration was sympathetic to the repeated complaints of the merchant community, and lobbied the British government for the right to take action, not least because this 'contraband' trade had a disastrous effect on its own revenues. Under the Anglo-French

---

[23] Gray, *History of the Gambia*, p. 321.
[24] An extremely detailed account of the same processes is provided by Odile Goerg, *Pouvoir colonial, municipalités et espaces urbains: Conakry-Freetown des années 1880 a 1914*, Volume 1 and 2 (Paris and Montreal: l'Harmattan, 1997), especially chs. 18–19.
[25] Alain Sinou, *Comptoirs et villes coloniales du Sénégal: Saint-Louis, Gorée, Dakar* (Paris: Karthala, 1993), pp. 216–18.
[26] The French had occupied Albreda in 1817. Hughes and Perfect, *Political History*, p. 35.
[27] However, some merchants with agents in Gorée began to channel their own trade through Albreda. Mahoney, "Government and Opinion", p. 92.

Convention of 1857, the French relinquished their foothold at Albreda in return for free access to trade along the river. The net effect was that French merchants shifted much of their business to Bathurst, over the protest of the resident merchant community. The former now became liable to pay Customs duties, which was a small victory in the struggle to build reliable revenue streams.[28] However, French merchants were able to increase their share of the river trade by paying cash for groundnuts, whereas the British depended on a system of extending goods on credit. Because importation of the French dollar was itself not taxed, while the demand for British imported goods declined, the net result was not just bankruptcy for many British firms, but also a precipitous fall in government revenue.[29] This made it imperative to diversify the tax base. The means to hand included the introduction of a new range of duties, including an export duty on groundnuts, which French merchants would now have to pay, as well as an import duty on kola nuts that fell heavily on the liberated slaves who held a virtual monopoly on imports from Sierra Leone. A Rates Ordinance had already been introduced in 1850, which introduced a form of direct taxation that fell disproportionately on the urban African population. In addition, this period witnessed the first attempts to introduce direct taxes on the neighbouring mainland. In 1862, a Kombo Land Revenue Ordinance introduced a tax on land and dwellings in British Kombo and legalized compulsory labour in road building.[30] The clear beneficiaries of these reforms were the merchants themselves. As Mahoney indicates, African opposition to the taxes, and more particularly to the way the revenue was spent, quickly manifested itself.[31] A petition for repeal of the Rates Ordinance was signed by 375 African inhabitants of Bathurst in 1862 on the basis that they saw little benefit from the monies that were raised.[32] A recurrent grievance was that poor drainage led to periodic flooding of the parts of the island inhabited by the African population – which had been greatly compounded in 1849 by the collapse of the sea defences.[33] Despite the new taxes, and mounting evidence of state-like activity, revenue constraints remained as pronounced as ever at the close of the 1860s.

In Bathurst, the African population managed to exert some influence on the larger imperial chessboard. In the 1860s, Faidherbe had proposed making an offer for the Gambia in return for some concession elsewhere in West Africa, but in Paris it was felt that there was nothing that could be offered in return that would not be too valuable – or not valuable enough – to tempt the

---

[28] Hughes and Perfect, *Political History*, p. 63.
[29] Mahoney, "Government and Opinion", p. 238.
[30] J.M. Gray, *A History of the Gambia* (Cambridge: Cambridge University Press, 1940), p. 482.
[31] Mahoney, "Government and Opinion", pp. 239–44.
[32] Mahoney, "Government and Opinion", pp. 244–5.
[33] Mahoney, "Government and Opinion", p. 206.

British.[34] Then in 1870, a more concrete proposal was mooted that involved exchanging the Gambia for the Mellacourie region (now part of Guinea), which was considered important for the consolidation of Sierra Leone in the coastal south-west. This proposal was opposed by the merchants in Bathurst, including the French trading houses, but what is also significant is that Africans despatched three petitions, the largest of which contained 500 names, opposing the exchange.[35] As John Hargreaves commented:

> The people with the deepest interest in preventing the Gambia from becoming French were undoubtedly the African townspeople of Bathurst, whose livelihood depended on their education in the English tongue, and their acquaintance with British law or commercial practice.[36]

The African population acted as if it had a legitimate say in the matter, and ultimately the authorities had to take their opinion seriously. In 1871, the British government shelved the plan, citing local opposition as the principal reason. In 1874, the French government offered both the Mellacourie and Côte d'Ivoire in exchange for the Gambia, and once again the European merchants and the African population rallied to thwart the deal. The African population of Bathurst, and some 'headmen' from Kombo, raised three further petitions, and the proposal was seen off.[37]

On the Gold Coast, there were comparable dynamics at work. Here, Europeans had become involved in brokering peace treaties, settling personal disputes, including marriage and *panyarring* cases, and mediating in commercial affairs during the era of the slave trade. In the nineteenth century, these activities expanded incrementally. In particular, British and Danish officials began to assert a level of influence beyond the walls of the forts and castles to which they were notionally confined. This phenomenon, which caused some consternation in Europe, was partly a consequence of the men on the spot seeking to find a practical way to cut through the regular round of disputes. During the 1830s, George Maclean took matters in hand by sanctioning the creation of courts to handle cases well beyond any conceivable zone of British sovereignty. Although he was accused of unlawfully extending British control, and of riding roughshod over local sensibilities, his initiatives were ultimately vindicated by London. Interestingly, however, it was deemed necessary for Gold Coasters to formally consent to the arrangement. The defining moment came with the signing of the Bond of 1844 by a number of Fante chiefs who voluntarily relinquished certain rights of adjudication to British officials – a step

---

[34] John D. Hargreaves, *Prelude to the Partition of West Africa* (London: Macmillan, 1963), p. 126.
[35] Hughes and Perfect, *Political History*, p. 60.
[36] Hargeaves, *Prelude to the Partition*, p. 161.
[37] Hughes and Perfect, *Political History*, pp. 72–3.

which was subsequently legitimated through an Order-in-Council.[38] If there was a turning point in the history of colonialism in the Gold Coast, this was it because it became the basis for subsequent claims that the British were there by invitation; that Gold Coasters were the co-authors of the colonial project; and that the right of administrators to command was formally circumscribed. The colonial state, on this reading, had clearly defined limits from the word go. In 1903, J.E. Casely Hayford summarized the position as follows:

> ... I may broadly state that the relations between Great Britain and the Gold Coast originated in friendship, mutual trust and commercial alliance. It will be seen, therefore, that the people have a right to mould their institutions upon their own lines, Great Britain merely being a Protecting Power, and only properly concerned with their relations with the outside world. It will also be seen that at no time have the people divested themselves of their right to legislate for themselves.[39]

Predictably, the extension of governmental responsibilities further increased the pressure upon public finances in the Gold Coast. Given that the annual parliamentary grant already made up more than 70 per cent of revenues, there was pressure from London to raise more revenue on the spot. In the words of David Kimble:

> The Secretary of State, Lord Grey, was anxious to employ more magistrates, and to extend the provision of roads, schools, hospitals, and dispensaries beyond the strict limits of the forts. He thought that such services should be provided out of local resources, rather than by an increase in the parliamentary grant; and of the two possible alternatives, customs duties or direct taxation, Grey strongly inclined to the latter.[40]

The fact that neighbouring European forts were competing for the same trade, coupled with opposition from local merchants, rendered an increase in Customs duties potentially suicidal. The alternative that was resorted to in 1850 was a poll tax. This was to be paid not merely by the Fante and Ga populations in the immediate environs of the castles and forts, but also much further afield – as far, indeed, as the trans-Volta. The case for the tax was that the British authorities would be better equipped to provide public goods, including the delivery of justice, even in the absence of formal sovereignty. Because the British could not unilaterally impose the poll tax, it was necessary to secure the agreement of traditional rulers once again, to which end a succession of meetings was convened and the necessary signatures secured. In 1852, the actual collection began, but as Kimble demonstrates, the level of

---

[38] Kimble, *Political History*, pp. 194–5.
[39] J.E. Casely Hayford, *Gold Coast Native Institutions with Thoughts on a Healthy Imperial Policy for the Gold Coast and Ashanti* (London: Frank Cass, reprint edn. 1970), original 1903, p. 129.
[40] Kimble, *Political History*, p. 169.

resistance to the tax – precisely on the basis that the British were overstepping the bounds of their authority – was such that it had ultimately to be abandoned.[41] This was a fateful outcome because it put paid to the possibility of direct taxation in the southern Gold Coast for good, unlike in the Gambia where it remained central to official plans. The emergence of colonial states with quite different fiscal architectures had lasting institutional consequences, but it also had a long-term impact on discourses of citizenship that remain with us today.

The inability of the various administrations to extract more revenue through direct taxes contributed to a situation where the settlements struggled to balance their books. The solution was eventually found in a projection of trade and influence outwards towards the frontiers. On the one hand, it involved eliminating African taxes and restrictions on trade at the proximate frontier, and on the other, it led to more sustained efforts to control trade routes along the further frontier. As far as the proximate frontier is concerned, merchants routinely complained of unwarranted interference by African rulers with free trade. But as Mahoney demonstrates, African traders who acted as agents of the European firms were also demanding protection by the 1860s, both in letters to the press and in petitions to London.[42] In the Senegambia, merchants had established trading bases along the main rivers and had been accustomed to the authorities paying local rulers for the privilege. In the event of a dispute, they would seek support from the coastal administration, claiming for example that their goods had been unlawfully seized. When they had coercive resources at their command, the men on the spot would often feel morally impelled to intervene. Local officials, therefore, became embroiled in trade disputes, and sometimes used successful military action to extract treaties on the side. British governments were all in favour of treaties that underwrote a pledge to eradicate the slave trade but warned repeatedly against making more substantial commitments. Although intervention was justified using the language of free trade, there was also some appreciation that force had its part to play. Lord Palmerston expressed it thus in 1860: "It may be true in one sense that trade ought not to be enforced by cannon balls, but on the other hand trade cannot flourish without security, and that security may often be unattainable without the exhibition of physical force."[43]

As early as the first decades of the nineteenth century, Europeans sought to renege on the payment of annual rents and duties that they considered vexatious. Hence in 1826, following a standoff on the north bank of the

---

[41] Kimble, *Political History*, pp. 168–91.
[42] Mahoney, Government and Opinion", pp. 130–1.
[43] A Foreign Office minute by Lord Palmerston, 22 April 1860, quoted in Hargreaves, *Prelude to the Partition*, pp. 36–7.

Gambia, the British were able to impose fresh terms on Niumi. This included the cession of a section of territory, the Ceded Mile, and an end to the payment of trade tolls, although an annual retainer was intended to sweeten the pill. In 1832, following outright warfare, in which the British and the French joined forces, Niumi was forced to submit to humiliating terms that did not merely confirm the loss of territory, but also infringed on the sovereignty of its future rulers.[44] As Mahoney observes, the Gambian merchants – both British and 'mulatto' – regarded this outcome as setting a useful precedent, and they argued in favour of coercive force to prevent the kingdom of Wuli, which controlled the trade routes to the interior, from imposing its own unwelcome restrictions on trade.[45] In addition, they lobbied for the creation of a government fort in the upper reaches of the Gambia, along the lines of the French factories along the Senegal River, which would afford protection to the merchants and a riverain base for extended trading operations. Although the attempt seriously misfired during a punitive expedition in 1834, the merchant community and the coastal authorities had made their intentions clear.[46] In the Gold Coast, the refusal of the British to countenance Asante claims over the coastal strip conformed to the same pattern. In 1824, an initial round of fighting was resolved in favour of Asante, when Sir Charles MacCarthy was amongst the casualties. Two years later, however, the British and their local allies inflicted a significant defeat at the battle of Katamanso. Although the British government quickly retreated into its shell, a treaty was eventually signed in 1831 under which Asante formally relinquished its claims over the coastal states as well as the British forts. This was supposed to ensure the conditions under which trade could prosper in the absence of any British extension of sovereignty.

At the same time as merchants and administrators sought to recalibrate power relations at the proximate frontier, there was a more concerted effort to control the flow of trade at the further frontier. This inevitably came at the expense of African middlemen who had been able to channel goods to different ports according to the prevailing prices.[47] The objective was to direct trade towards the designated port city where it could be taxed. The rationale for a more proactive approach was that trade and agriculture was being hampered

---

[44] Wright, *World and a Very Small Place*, pp. 137–9.

[45] The trade routes from the interior converged at the towns of Yarbutenda and Fattatenda, which were located in the Wuli kingdom. Mahoney, "Government and Opinion", pp. 84, 100.

[46] Mahoney, "Government and Opinion", p. 104.

[47] In the period from the 1830s to the 1850s, the frontier zone that was contested as a sphere of influence by the British and the Danes covered Akwapim, Akyem and Krobo – while the trans-Volta represented the emergent further frontier towards the east. The details may be found in Ivor Wilks, *Asante in the Nineteenth Century* (Cambridge: Cambridge University Press, 1975), ch. 5.

by conditions of endemic insecurity in frontier regions. When European imperialists talked of 'pacification', historians are inclined to interpret this as a code for premeditated acts of conquest. However, the role of violence in nineteenth-century imperialism surely requires a more nuanced treatment. At a common-sense level, the fundamental difference between the slave trade and legitimate commerce was that the latter did indeed require minimal conditions of security for its actualization. If positive steps were taken to secure the conditions for free trade, so the thinking went, it would be possible to increase the total volume of commerce and to augment government revenues without needing to increase the absolute level of duty or to acquire physical territory. It was the push to the further frontier that would enable the fiscal circle to be squared. But there was, of course, a contradiction at the heart of this apparently perfect plan. Although many of the frontier zones floated in and out of the control of established states, new ones took shape as European intervention weakened their grip. This was especially clear in the Gold Coast where the British provided tacit support for the breakaway of the coastal polities from a tributary relationship to Asante and winked at secessionist tendencies in the provinces. Asante rulers naturally punished the first signs of dissidence for fear that the kingdom might otherwise unravel. The willingness of Asante to deploy military force to defend its realm contributed to a spiral of violence, especially along the Volta River whose significance in the north–south trade was enhanced as effective Asante power waned.[48] The patterns of violence merely confirmed the British in their belief that the old order was incompatible with free trade.[49]

In the Senegambia, the proximate frontier was initially riverain. In the north, the gum trade was the most important item of external commerce, although this was closely bound up with the grain trade that ran from south of the Senegal River into the desert.[50] In the early nineteenth century, the Senegal River valley was a zone of endemic instability as polities on the south bank were racked by internal disputes and were preyed upon by Moorish warriors from the desert. In the lower reaches of the river, Trarza raids greatly added to the political crisis in the kingdom of Waalo, which was the close neighbour of Saint Louis. The Trarza also pursued warfare against Futa Toro in the middle reaches of the Senegal in the early 1820s, thereby bringing the gum trade to an effective halt for a time. From the French perspective, it was essential to deal

---

[48] For an excellent synopsis, see the introduction by Per Hernaes to Tove Storsveen (ed.), *Closing the Books: Governor Edward Carstensen on Danish Guinea 1842–50* (Accra: Sub-Saharan Publishers, 2010).

[49] Asante refugees at the coast, who had fallen foul of the monarchy, confirmed them in this opinion. The dissidents included individuals who sought to evade barriers on the transmission of wealth. Wilks, *Asante in the Nineteenth Century*, ch. 15.

[50] Searing, *West African Slavery*, p. 188.

with the persistent threat, but it took two decades to neutralize it completely. After warfare between the Trarza and the French in 1833–5, a period of relative stability ensued. However, a second campaign was launched by Faidherbe in 1854–8, and on this occasion the Trarza were defeated. From this point onwards, the Moors were pinned back to the north bank of the Senegal River, which, Searing notes, subsequently hardened into a border between desert and savannah populations, and later still into a colonial boundary.[51] Under pressure from the Saint Louis merchants, Faidherbe went further and established military posts in the middle and upper Senegal River at crucial choke-points: that is, at Podor and Matam in Futa Toro and Bakel and Medina in the upper reaches of the river.[52] Searing observes that payments to the riverain states were now replaced by French market tolls, signalling a dramatic shift in the balance of power. The explicit intention was to ensure the dominance of French merchants in the Senegal River valley – which incidentally signalled the decline of the *habitants* – rather than to acquire colonial territory. Nevertheless, Al-Hajj Umar Tal, who was seeking to build his own Muslim polity in the upper Senegal valley, interpreted the French presence as evidence that they wished to establish their own dominion.[53] His defeat in 1857, following which he transported his own state-building project deeper into the Sahel, notionally secured the conditions for free trade in the absence of French rule.

In the mid-nineteenth century, an emerging trade in agricultural commodities closer to the coast tended to re-focus attention on sections of the proximate frontier that did not lie on the Senegal River. In the Senegambia, the gum boom proved short-lived when prices plummeted at the end of the 1850s. As Manchuelle has pointed out, this impelled Faidherbe to try to reduce the tax burden on gum exports by shifting some of the weight onto direct taxation. In 1861, a head tax was introduced for Saint Louis at 3 francs, and at 1.5 francs for other areas under French control, including those around the river forts.[54] Groundnuts had become the leading export from the Gambia in the 1840s, and in the second half of the century they became the most important export from Senegal as well, rising from 8,000 metric tonnes in 1859 to 22,142 in 1867.[55] Crucially, however, the epicentre of production was in Kajoor and Bawol, the kingdoms that lay close to the coastal ports. The French strategy was to seek to

---

[51] Searing, *West African Slavery*, p. 191.   [52] Searing, *West African Slavery*, p. 192.

[53] For the definitive account of the life of Umar, see David Robinson, *The Holy War of Umar Tal: The Western Sudan in the Mid-Nineteenth Century* (Oxford: Clarendon Press, 1985).

[54] François Manchuelle, *Willing Migrants: Soninke Labor Diasporas, 1848–1960* (Athens and London: James Currey and Ohio University Press, 1997), pp. 66–9.

[55] James F. Searing, *'God Alone is King': Islam and Emancipation in Senegal – The Wolof Kingdoms of Kajoor and Bawol, 1859–1914* (Portsmouth, Oxford and Cape Town: Heinemann, James Currey and David Philip, 2002), p. 58.

install friendly regimes there that would be amenable to the promotion of groundnut production. However, the political context was one of extremely complex dynastic disputes, overlaid by the growing restiveness of Muslim populations who complained of raiding at the hands of whichever *tyeddo* regime was in power. Marabouts sought to establish autonomous communities at the edges of these states, where they were raided by embattled rulers seeking to maintain a grip over their populations and their territory. The French position was in many ways contradictory because while it systematically undermined the old order, there was no great enthusiasm for facilitating the rise of Muslim successor states either.[56] This contributed to endemic instability and made the French the arbiters of the balance of power. In the case of the Gambia, as we have seen, the British were concerned about developments in Kombo, not least because it was located on their doorstep. The consolidation of a Muslim successor state under Fodé Sylla raised the prospect that an attempt would be made to tax and otherwise interfere with trade coming overland towards Bathurst. But it transpired that a far greater problem was posed by the armies of Fodé Sylla who pursued an economy of plunder against Soninke and Jola populations alike. This precipitated a flight of population from the very lands that the British hoped to render productive, and made everyday trading activities highly perilous. Moreover, the growth of a refugee population in Bathurst imposed a further call on the finite resources of the fledgling capital. Stabilizing the proximate frontier therefore became imperative for the maximization of trade and for securing the finances of Bathurst. Although the British and the French spoke of conditions of peace being the sine *qua non* for commercial activity, the reality was that the competition between them led them to strike political alliances that were at odds with the rhetoric of pacification. In the Gold Coast, the expansion of rubber and palm-oil exports in the southern regions created a somewhat similar dynamic. The British had an interest in steering trade towards their coastal forts. Following the Danish cession of its claims in 1850, the British thought of themselves as presiding over a sphere of influence extending to the east of the Volta. However, a recurrent cycle of conflict involving Akwamu, Anlo and the Krepe (Ewe) polities in the trans-Volta, compounded by the Asante invasion of 1868/69, threatened this plan. While the British decision to invade Asante in 1874 was intended to impart a lesson, a formal protectorate was declared over the coastal regions in the same year. East of the Volta, by contrast, the British attempted to broker agreements that

---

[56] This accounts in part for the downfall of two figures who sought to create alternative polities, namely Lat Dior in Kajoor and Ma Ba in Baddibu. Searing, *'God Alone is King'*, pp. 56–60; Martin Klein, *Islam and Imperialism in Senegal: Sine-Saloum, 1847–1914* (Edinburgh: Edinburgh University Press, 1968), pp. 90–1.

would permit the free circulation of commodities without an extension of their rule.

It is apparent, therefore, that the roots of colonial state-making lie in processes unfolding decades before the Berlin Conference of 1884–5. The skeletal administrations in the port cities had assumed increasing functions, largely in response to pressure from below, which was sustained in large part by increased revenues derived by funnelling taxable trade. Taxing African consumption through import duties created a forward momentum of its own. While the proximate frontiers came under closer control, there was normally a looser exercise of influence at the further frontier. All of this was to change in the context of the Scramble when it became imperative to stake substantive territorial claims. The reasons for abandoning a longstanding reticence about the acquisition of territory has much to do with the onset of the first Great Depression. As European states began to raise protective barriers against one another, fears were expressed about the loss of potential markets elsewhere. Being the economically dominant country, Britain had the most to gain from free trade, and was consequently the slowest to react. French statesmen, on the other hand, spoke openly about the importance of markets in West Africa and the ways in which railways could unlock the potential of the interior. In an illuminating analysis of debates surrounding differential tariffs for textiles, C.W. Newbury noted that while the merchants of Bordeaux and Marseilles opposed attempts to protect French manufacturing interests in Rouen and French India in 1875, they had come to accept the case for protectionism by 1884.[57] Significantly, the French advance across the Sahel began in 1879 – a few years before the crisis in Egypt, which carries so much of the burden of Robinson and Gallagher's interpretation.[58] Another consequence of the trade depression was that the prices for the principal export commodities – especially palm-oil and groundnuts – declined precipitously. This placed a renewed strain on public finances, given that administrations had become heavily reliant on Customs revenues. In addition, as A.G. Hopkins indicated many years ago, falling prices led to fresh disputes between European and African traders over debt and the terms of trade. In shrill tones, British merchants lobbied through their Chambers of Commerce for protection from what they claimed were illegitimate commercial practices.[59]

---

[57] C.W. Newbury, "The protectionist revival in French colonial trade: the case of Senegal", *Economic History Review* 21 (2) 1968, p. 345.

[58] Robinson and Gallagher, *Africa and the Victorians*.

[59] A.G. Hopkins, "Economic imperialism in West Africa: Lagos, 1880–92", *Economic History Review* 21 (3) 1968, p. 597.

It is in this context, the calculations of costs and benefits associated with acquiring colonies underwent a shift. On the one hand, the existing states had come to be seen as incapable of being reformed. In the words of A.G. Hopkins:

At this point, tropical Africa was judged no longer 'well kept' because Britain's grand plan for drawing the region into the new international economic order by way of 'legitimate' commerce was either foundering or heading for the rocks, and the region was no longer 'accessible', because the extension of the market through free trade, railways, commercial law and the adoption of modern currencies was being hampered or at least insufficiently assisted by African rulers who took their independence seriously. The problems of structural transformation, made critical by the downturn in the performance of the international economy during the last quarter of the century, appeared to a growing number of influential European interests to pose a choice between abandoning the 'great transformation' of the nineteenth century or impressing it on the continent by force.[60]

On the other hand, it was considered imperative to convert loose influence at the further frontier into something more tangible. European traders and officials who had traversed these zones, and had often mapped them, were often well-versed in local topography and politics alike. The imperative was therefore to secure possession of critical choke-points, especially along rivers and watersheds, through which trade typically passed. By connecting these points through road and rail, so the more ambitious version of the argument went, markets would be secured for the future, and existing trade would flow in the desired direction. The problem came when competitors entered the field and began to stake bold claims of their own. In the Senegambia, the French were the first out of the blocks, and managed both to confine the Portuguese to the coastal strip and to encircle the Gambia. The British were slow to respond in part because the expansion of groundnut exports came from the middle and lower river where they were already well-entrenched. But it meant that they lost the chance to exploit the resources of the larger Senegambia region, including the well-watered Casamance to the south. The sudden arrival of the Germans immediately to the east of the Gold Coast in 1884 elicited a similarly confused British response in the trans-Volta: while the men on the spot were keen to cement existing claims, there was less of an appetite in London for pegging the Germans back. When the Gold Coast authorities finally received the green light to defend their claims, it was too late, and the British were forced to concede much of Krepe, including the entirety of Agotime, to the Germans.

Across Africa, the Scramble was, as the very term suggests, a breathless affair. A motley array of adventurers and officials, bearing flags and notionally representing some metropolitan power or other, rushed to secure treaties of

---

[60] Hopkins, 'New international economic order', p. 257.

protection with Africans. In the French case, it was the Navy who secured vast tracts of the Sahel, as officers famously ignored orders in the quest for personal glory and in hope of post-facto vindication.[61] Where the Europeans staked claims based on the colonization of existing states, they tended to do so with reference to their presumed boundaries. In practice, this was contentious because in many cases provinces and tributaries had seceded at some point in the more or less distant past. But where Europeans were staking claims at the further frontier – and especially in the interstices between existing states – the treaties mattered less than the reality of who was in occupation of the choke-points. Where the British or the French had been engaged with frontier dynamics for some time, they held a distinct advantage over their rivals. But where the frontier was genuinely ungoverned space, there was a greater margin for manoeuvre. Not uncommonly, the actors in question ended up by staking claims to many of the very same places. After serious haggling, a border was usually delimited through a verbal agreement, a sketch-map and often some marker on the ground. Given the helter-skelter nature of the Scramble, the borders in many places were staked out well before most of the colonial territory had been filled in and before genuine administrative structures were in place. Crucially, therefore, colonial states did not really define their boundaries as conventional history textbooks would have one believe: in fact, boundaries and bureaucracies emerged simultaneously in an often inglorious moment of co-production in which surveyors played an instrumental role. Typically, there was an initial strategy both to tax and to channel trade towards the preferred coastal port and away from those of one's competitors. The formal demarcation, which was effected by substantive Boundary Commissions, usually took place much later. Having set out the logic of boundary-making in general terms, I turn now to consider the actual processes in greater detail, beginning south of the Gambia River, before returning to the trans-Volta.

Kombo and the Casamance: A Study in Colonial Boundary-Making

The Jolah are in comparison to their neighbours simple industrious folk. They have since the introduction of the Mohammedan element been the prey (between the Gambia and the sea), of the Marabouts of Combo. These are now represented by Fodey Silleh, the military adventurer who calls himself the Emir of Combo, and he oppresses the Jolas as he finds convenient. He kidnaps and robs them whenever he chooses. On the opposite border they are exposed to the attacks of another adventurer, Fodey Cabbah who, after having

---

[61] This is brought out in great detail in A.S. Kanya-Forstner, *The Conquest of the Western Sudan: A Study in French Military Imperialism* (Cambridge: Cambridge University Press, 1969).

> overrun most of Jarra and Kiang, has reached Fogni, and who has for some
> time carried his slave hunts to the eastern borders of the Jolah country . . .
> their only wish is to be allowed to live in peace on their own lands.[62]

This quotation provides a perfect illustration of changes in British perceptions
of the political dynamics in Kombo. Whereas moral judgements earlier in the
century would have been more nuanced, it was now taken as self-evident that
the marabouts were the principal threat to commerce and good order alike. At
the same time, the Jola were transformed into a virtuous peasantry in the
making – a 'simple industrious' people who wanted nothing more than to be
able to cultivate their lands in peace. This binary, which is rooted in older
accounts of the line of separation between Jola and Mandinka, repeats itself
with increasing regularity in the British and French colonial archives of the late
nineteenth century.

The relationship between Fodé Sylla and the Europeans was always destined to end in tears once his attempts to consolidate his hold over Kombo and
to extend his reach into Fogny-Jabangkunda and Narang ran up against the
decision by the British and the French to arrive at a boundary of their own.
Colonial administrators were impatient to begin the process of *mise en valeur*,
moving from coastal trade to the productive use of agricultural land which, in
their view, required the demarcation of fixed boundaries between one jurisdiction and the next. By contrast, Fodé Sylla and Fodé Kaba seemed intent on
perpetuating a strategy of plunder that the Europeans regarded as a throwback
to a bygone era. Fodé Sylla was the first casualty of the subsequent shakeout,
whereas Fodé Kaba played the Europeans off against each other with greater
diplomatic dexterity. But the net result was the same: that is, adjoining colonial
spaces that were emptied of the 'warrior marabouts' with a view to their being
refilled with hardworking peasants. In the process, existing frontier nodes were
converted into border towns and villages that helped to mark out one place as
French and the other as British.

Whereas the British government had resisted any suggestion that there
should be an extension of the enclave in the Gambia, there was a change of
mood in the 1880s in response to a perceived French campaign to force Britain
off this stretch of coastline. French competition with the Portuguese for control
of the Lower Casamance River in the mid-1880s culminated in an agreement
in 1886 (effective in 1887) that led to the formal partition of that region. The
boundary between Portuguese Guinea and French territory was drawn south of
the Casamance River, thereby locating the commercial centre of Ziguinchor

---

[62] NAGB MP1/1 "Papers Relating to the Gambia Colony and Protectorates", Sir Samuel Rowe,
Governor-in Chief, Bathurst, to Sir H.T. Holland (22 October 1887), *Correspondence Relating
to Territories on the Gambia River* (Colonial Office, 1887).

within French territory.[63] This outcome amounted to the final rolling back of the Portuguese from the Lower Casamance, where Portuguese and Luso-African traders had played a leading role in commerce since the earliest European contacts. Having defined their southern boundary to their own satisfaction, the French then sought to consolidate their hold over the rest of the territory between the Casamance and Gambia Rivers. This encroachment on what the British regarded as a rough sphere of influence – but in reality a classic frontier zone through which trade passed – produced a familiar sequence of responses: that is, heated competition to sign treaties with African rulers, followed by mutual recriminations between London and Paris, and winding up with a pragmatic division of the spoils.

At the start of 1888, the Gambian authorities and their French counterparts agreed that there should be a moratorium on staking fresh claims. But in September, the Administrator of the Gambia, G.T. Carter, fielded reports that French emissaries had been despatched to "Carrown [Karone] Country, Foniye" to secure agreements from local 'rulers' to come under the French flag. Amongst the towns listed were Diébaly, Kujube, Makuda (all in Narang) and Kafountine (in Fogny-Jabangkunda).[64] In these places, trade to and from Bathurst was considerable, but European influence was strictly limited. The French were reported to have sent a message directly to Fodé Sylla in an attempt to win him over. It is likely that they did not fully comprehend that this two-pronged strategy would be construed as deeply threatening by Fodé Sylla who already regarded the populations of these frontier settlements as hostile to his own ambitions. The following month, Fodé Sylla met with Carter in person and alleged that it was the people of Diébaly, Kujube and Koubanack who had requested the French flag in order to free themselves from 'allegiance' to himself. He also said that he had replied to the French that the towns in question were located within his domains and that they had recently betrayed him by siding with his former adversary, Birahim N'Diaye: "I advised the French to be very careful how they took words from the Naran [sic] people, for they were very deceitful".[65]

The French initiative brought Fodé Sylla closer to the Gambian authorities who accused their rivals of violating the status quo agreement. Sylla signalled

---

[63] For details of this treaty, see Ian Brownlie (ed.), *African Boundaries: A Legal and Diplomatic Encyclopaedia* (London and Berkeley: C. Hurst and University of California Press, 1979), pp. 351–3. See also Christian Roche, *Histoire de la Casamance: conquête et résistance, 1850–1920* (Paris: Karthala, 1985), pp. 199–212.

[64] NAGB MP1/1 "Papers Relating to the Gambia", J.H. Finden, Manager of British Kombo, to Administrator of the Gambia, G.T. Carter (29 September 1888).

[65] Reported in letter from G.T. Carter, Administrator of the Gambia, Bathurst, to Administrator in Chief, Sierra Leone (16 October 1888), *Correspondence Relating to Territories on the Gambia River.*

his willingness to sign a treaty with the British, on condition that the Muslim religion would not be interfered with. Carter speculated that he was more worried that his slave hunting might be infringed upon.[66] Be that as it may, Fodé Sylla was given the necessary reassurances and provided with a stipend, perpetuating the highly ambiguous practice of linking the exchange of money to the recognition of political claims. But whereas Sylla entered the British embrace in order to be free to continue his raiding into Narang and Fogny-Jabangkunda, Carter sold the deal to the British government on the opposite grounds. In his words:

The acquisition of Foreign Combo would release the industrious Jolas from their worst persecutors and open up a fine country which is far richer in natural resources than the small slice of Combo we now possess, and there can be little doubt unless we do acquire it that the French ere long will extend their boundaries almost to the doors of Bathurst.[67]

In the event, Fodé Sylla and the Gambian authorities were not able to prevent the French from consolidating their position. The French government responded to a formal British complaint about violation of the status quo agreement by alleging that Carter had himself hoisted a flag in Brefet, which he strenuously denied. In the final analysis, the British government was not prepared to escalate the dispute and it decided to come to terms. By April 1889, negotiations were underway to settle a number of West African claims, and a comprehensive agreement was signed in August of that same year (see Map 3.1). The 1889 agreement defined the length of the Gambia/Casamance border as follows:

To the south (left bank) the line, starting from the mouth of the San Pedro [Allahein] shall follow the left bank as far as 13°10' of north latitude. The frontier shall thence follow the parallel which, starting from this point, goes as far as Sandeng (end of the Vintang creek, English map). The line shall then trend upwards in the direction of the Gambia, following the meridian which passes through Sandeng to a distance of 10 kilom. from the river. The frontier shall then follow the left bank of the river at the same distance of 10 kilom. as far as, and including Yarbutenda.[68]

In the case of Kombo and Fogny, the boundary followed the Allahein River for a short distance before assuming the form of a straight line. The net effect was to deposit much of the area claimed by Fodé Sylla in the Casamance. Not surprisingly when the Gambian authorities sought to liaise over the demarcation of the border, they found the marabout in a truculent mood.

---

[66] Carter to Administrator in Chief, Sierra Leone (16 October 1888), *Correspondence Relating to Territories on the Gambia River.*

[67] Carter to Administrator in Chief (28 November 1888), *Correspondence Relating to Territories on the Gambia River.*

[68] Brownlie, *African Boundaries*, p. 215.

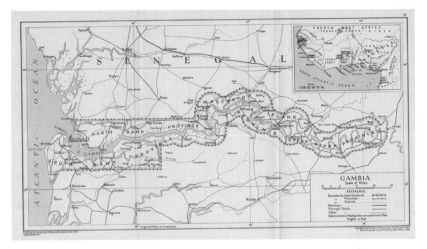

Map 3.1 Senegal and the Gambia. (War Office, London, 1948)

Much more than a paper treaty, the establishment of a Boundary Commission signalled the closure of the frontier and the formalization of colonial space. Whereas frontiers were inherently ambiguous zones of engagement, Boundary Commissions were expected to deliver certainties based on a modification of the paper agreements, where necessary through a reading of the landscape at close quarters. Because boundary pillars made explicit political statements, they often elicited equally vigorous reactions. In the early stages, the British conveyed the impression to Fodé Sylla that his rights would continue to be respected under the British flag. Carter sent a letter in advance of the commencement of the demarcation by a Joint Boundary Commission, reassuring him of its "pacific intent". He also promised that the Commissioners would pay Fodé Sylla a formal visit at Brikama, with the intention of bestowing gifts upon him "in accordance with the customs of the country".[69] The latter could be interpreted as a further acknowledgement of his moral claims. However, the demarcation quickly descended into a standoff. The Commissioners failed to make the promised courtesy visit and proceeded directly to the coast.[70] Having satisfied themselves that what people in Gunjur

[69] NAGB CO 54/9 "Correspondence Relating to Territories on the Gambia River", Carter, Administrator of the Gambia, to Lord Knutsford (8 January 1891), *Further Correspondence Relating to Territories on the Gambia River* (Colonial Office, 1892).
[70] The details in what follows are taken from ANS 1 F16 "Délimitation de la Gambie", report of Capitaine Pineau and members of the Mixed Commission to the Governor of Senegal (5 June 1891).

called the Allahein was in fact the San Pedro River mentioned in the treaty, they set to work. Before long, they were confronted by a party of armed men who insisted that they desist. Captain Kenney, the British Boundary Commissioner, reported that Fodé Sylla then arrived in person and objected to the entire exercise on the basis that the 1889 treaty provisions did not conform to his own borders and that he did not want the French to preside over any part of his territory.[71] Fodé Sylla was demanding in effect that the Franco-British boundary be pushed much further southwards to bring all of his lands under the British flag. As noted above, the assimilation of pre-existing frontiers to colonial boundaries was standard practice, but it depended on there being some manifestation of a state presence. The reality was that Fodé Sylla had chosen raiding over governing and had failed to impose his will on the local population who were ultimately his victims. It would have been well-nigh impossible to entertain his demand, but the Gambian authorities did what they could to humour him. While Kenney complained at the 'insolent' demeanour of Fodé Sylla, and the insinuation that he was in league with the French, the administrator conceded that earlier promises had not been honoured and that Sylla had some reason to feel affronted.

When Carter met in person with Fodé Sylla, the latter repeated the grounds for his opposition to the demarcation. He claimed that his border was positioned at a place called 'Alangha' (Atanha?) and requested that the Boundary Commissioners visit the site in person. Carter consented in order to appear flexible, but clearly he had no mandate to revisit the Franco-British agreement. The French Commissioner, Capitaine Pineau, was under the impression that Fodé Sylla had laid the field visit down as a precondition for withdrawing his objection to demarcation.[72] The party therefore travelled to a point some 12 kilometres south of Kafountine where they were shown a post that Sylla's official claimed marked his southern boundary. The Commissioners believed it had been freshly planted – apparently mimicking European conventions of boundary demarcation – and they were left in no doubt by the villages they passed through about what the local population thought of Fodé Sylla and his claims.[73] By any objective measure, these were in fact extremely tendentious. The main towns in Narang remained implacably opposed to Fodé Sylla, and although he enjoyed limited support in

---

[71] Captain Kenney to Carter, Administrator of the Gambia (18 December 1890), *Further Correspondence* (1892).

[72] ANS 1F16 "Délimitation de la Gambie", Report of Pineau (5 June 1891).

[73] Curiously, in 1913, the French administrator at Diouloulou reported that British officials had been to the site, after being informed of the exact location of Atanha. He was under the mistaken impression that the marker had been left by the Boundary Commission. ANS2 G13/57 "Résidence de Diouloulou, Rapports mensuels d'ensemble 1913", report for November 1913.

Fogny-Jagankunda, there was no sense in which he actually controlled the territory in question – far less administered it. The map accompanying the Boundary Commission report revealed a military camp at Jalong, but this was some way north of Kafountine. In no sense could it be considered an administrative headquarters. To all intents and purposes, the border that British and French negotiators had defined in Paris *was* the effective southern edge of the kingdom of Kombo. The area to the south had been a classic (further) frontier zone, outside the control of any genuine state for as long as anybody could remember. Map 3.2, which was produced by the Commission, depicts the borders as following the Allahein River to a border pillar (marked 'BP'). From that point, it tracked a straight line through what is depicted on the map as bamboo forest – signalling an unpopulated space. As so often happened, the British had moulded themselves to the boundaries of an existing state (Kombo), while the ungoverned frontier zone had passed to France. After their excursion, which left them decidedly sceptical, the Commissioners returned to the practical business of demarcating the boundary that had been defined in the Franco-British agreement. The crisis with Fodé Sylla had been momentarily defused, but the substantive issues remained unresolved.

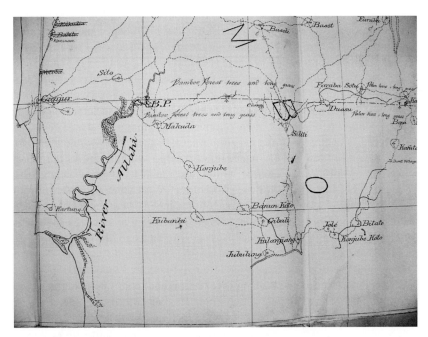

Map 3.2 1891 Boundary Commission map of Kombo.

Meanwhile, the survey team pushed eastwards, entering new regions and encountering fresh complications. Pineau observed that the Jola of Fogny had no dealings with Fodé Sylla but were in the position of being habitually raided – as was apparent from the many stockades. He described how Jola villagers fled on their approach, presumably interpreting the Commission as a military expedition – an understandable reaction because the theatrics were not that dissimilar. Initially considering the Jola as timorous creatures, the survey party soon found itself under threat of attack from a party of around a hundred men from the village of Guibanga. The Commissioners were instructed in no uncertain terms to turn back and were warned that if they ever returned, they would be greeted with gunfire. Unwisely, the Commissioners attempted to get the "savages to see reason", using the Mandinka chief of Bintang as their intermediary. In the light of recent history, it is difficult to conceive of a less sensitive course of action. The standoff was only resolved by bringing in military backup, and by recruiting the assistance of neighbouring Jola villagers who seemed to have their own scores to settle with Guibanga. The village was destroyed and, having imparted a lesson in colonial force, the Commissioners continued with their work. This case is of interest, however, because the attack on the survey party and the destruction of the temporary border posts by the people of Guibanga suggests that these Jola had some inkling that the act of marking out the terrain was a prelude to something altogether more permanent. Unlike Fodé Sylla, their complaint was not about where the boundary was being drawn: it was about the very presence of strangers in their midst.

The next area that the Boundary Commission entered was Kiang/Jarra where the raiding of Fodé Kaba posed a particular problem. His forces were reputedly well-armed and it was anticipated that he might seek to obstruct the survey party. At one point, with rumours of an imminent attack, many of the porters accompanying the expedition took to their heels, while members of the Gambian police detachment refused to go any further. As the Commission contemplated a tactical withdrawal, Jola deputations arrived and requested that the party advance in the direction of the fortified settlement at Sangadior that was occupied by one of the lieutenants of Fodé Kaba. When the Commissioners entered Sangadior, they were well received by the representative who claimed that it was the Jola who had started the rumour of an imminent attack for their own cynical reasons. Whether he had ever intended to obstruct the work of the Commission is unclear, but there is a strong likelihood that the Jola wanted to provoke a military confrontation that would lead the Europeans to attack Fodé Kaba. In fact, the British already harboured an extremely jaundiced opinion of the latter by this point. In October 1888, Carter had written accusing him in no uncertain terms of being the scourge of the Jarra and Kiang:

I must tell you frankly that your presence in Kiang and Jarra does not please me. The people rightly say that you are an interloper and have no right in the country, this is why you have many enemies; if you were not by trade a warrior, and did not capture slaves and rob industrious settlers, nobody would complain of you, but it cannot be denied that you are not a man of peace and, therefore, not a desirable neighbour. If you take my advice, you will remove from this country, otherwise it may turn out that you will be turned out forcibly. The French are your enemy and Musa Molloh is only waiting for an opportunity to join them; take care that you do not make an enemy of the English also.[74]

As a prediction, this was prescient, but Fodé Kaba bought some time by aligning himself with the French who, in turn, believed they could remould him to suit their purposes – thereby mirroring the British relationship with Fodé Sylla in reverse. In fact, the decision to proceed to Sangadior came after French reports that Fodé Kaba had agreed to co-operate with the demarcation exercise.

Although the Boundary Commission of 1891 completed its work without coming into open conflict with Fodé Sylla or Fodé Kaba, the fact remained that whereas the Europeans wanted to bring an end to raiding activity and to seal off properly defined colonial territory, these leaders had no interest in the fulfilment of either agenda. Continuing insecurity brought friction between British and French officials who complained about infringements made by their respective allies. In 1892, the British requested permission from the French to deal with Fodé Kaba who they accused of destabilizing populations on their side of the border. The French declined because they had decided to use him to cement their hold on their newly acquired territories. Indeed, they even bolstered his position by attacking Jola villages that refused to accept his authority. Hence in April of that year, a number of Jola villages were destroyed through joint military action.[75] But with some French officials expressing concerns about the predatory behaviour of Fodé Kaba, it was decided to place him on a tighter leash. Under a treaty of May 1893, he agreed to renounce any claims to Fogny in return for a stipend of 5,000 francs per annum that would be paid out of the resources that came from the French half of that district. It was expressly stipulated that he was to leave the Jolas in peace, an implied criticism that was sweetened by a clause to the effect that the French would also protect him from Jola counter-incursions.[76] In effect, Fodé Kaba was henceforth to be confined to the French section of Kiang. These arrangements were intended to prevent further cross-border incursions but were not greatly to the liking of the Gambian authorities who were sure they could detect the hidden hand of Fodé

---

[74] G.T. Carter, Administrator of the Gambia to Fodé Kaba (16 October 1888) in *Correspondence Relating to the Territories on the River Gambia* (1887).

[75] Diamaye and Guiro were destroyed, but Sindian put up effective resistance. Roche, *Histoire de la Casamance*, p. 146.

[76] Roche, *Histoire de la Casamance*, pp. 146–7.

Kaba in the daily challenges that confronted them. The moment of reckoning came in June 1900 when two British Commissioners, F.C. Sitwell and F.E. Silva, were killed while attempting to settle a land dispute between a Soninke village and a Muslim one in British Kiang. The perpetrators escaped across the colonial border and were granted refuge by Fodé Kaba. At this point, the French authorities decided that the latter had become an expendable nuisance and consented to a joint assault on his stronghold at Medina. As Carter had predicted, the final reckoning was effected by the troops of Musa Molo, a longstanding enemy of Fodé Kaba who remained in favour with the French. Outgunned and out-maneouvred, Fodé Kaba chose to go down fighting as honour demanded.

In the case of Fodé Sylla, the settlement of accounts came rather earlier. The French attempted to establish effective control over their side of the border, but for some time after the 1891 demarcation, raiding parties continued to foment turmoil in Narang. As we will see shortly, French efforts to neutralize the influence of Fodé Sylla only made things worse. But as they began to assert more of a grip on their side of the border, Fodé Sylla modified his methods. In the words of the Gambian administrator:

It is the practice of Fodi Sillah to lay in wait for and seize, as they pass through his country, harmless, helpless, heathen Jolahs, who come from the Casamance to work or trade in Bathurst. If they are on their way there he keeps them or sells them as slaves. If on their way back he robs them of all their hard-earned property and either sells them as slaves, or releases some of them on condition that they go back to Bathurst to bring him next season the proceeds of their labours to redeem their friends and relations detained in slavery. This, he informed me, at an interview I once had with him, he was justified in doing by his religion, which directs him to war against all heathens and as they are not British subjects he was cunning enough to know that I could not say anything further, as he was not breaking his treaty with the English. This long-continued, cruel and unjust persecution of these poor defenceless Jolahs, mostly women, calls for and justly meets with the greatest indignation amongst the merchants many of whom are French, who employ them to work in Bathurst, and they express surprise at the apathy of the English government in allowing such acts to be done by a Chief who gets a subsidy from the Government.[77]

The reference to Jola traders, and especially to women, is slightly surprising because previous correspondence had created the impression that virtually all commerce was in the hands of Mandinka traders. In building a case against Fodé Sylla, it was clearly convenient to be able to argue that the hardworking Jola wanted nothing more than to engage in peaceful trade with the British and that it was only the marabout that stood in the way. Although the report cannot

---

[77] NAGB CSO 1/120 "Draft Despatches to Secretary of State", R.B. Llewelyn, Administrator of the Gambia, to Marquess of Ripon (18 December 1893).

simply be taken at face value, it seems that there was a burgeoning trade between Bathurst and Jola settlements.

By 1893, R.B. Llewelyn was of the opinion that forceful means would be necessary to eliminate Fodé Sylla from the equation. In the letter just quoted, he made it clear that he had tried to offer Fodé Sylla a pension in return for retiring from the political scene but had been thwarted. The only alternative, in his view, was to issue a formal ultimatum backed up by the credible threat of force. In February 1894, the ultimatum was approved by the Executive Council and formally issued: Fodé Sylla was to be offered £150 for life (an increase on the original offer), but on condition that all his stockades were pulled down, all arms and ammunitions were handed over and the 'headmen' of all the towns came to Bathurst within a week "and agree with the Governor there that Foreign Combo shall be governed under English law, the same as British Combo now is, and the people will pay the same land tax."[78] In other words, an earlier promise that the British would interfere minimally inside the territory that was claimed by Fodé Sylla was rescinded. The inclusion of the clause concerning the land tax was more than a revenue matter, important as this was: it was also a statement to the effect that the rights of the *mansas* that had been inherited by Fodé Sylla were in turn to be transferred to the colonial power. Meanwhile reports reaching the Manager of British Kombo indicated that Fodé Sylla was silently preparing for war. The wooden stockades at Brikama and Busumbala were reinforced and his blacksmiths were alleged to be hard at work manufacturing ammunition.[79] The Gambian authorities also believed that Fodé Sylla enjoyed the covert backing of Fodé Kaba, although this rumour was considered unfounded by the French authorities.[80] On 21 February, Llewelyn reported that Fodé Sylla had rebuffed the ultimatum and so made requests for naval support to assist the West Indian Regiment and other local levies to embark on a military expedition.

The plan entailed a pincer movement against Gunjur, in which a land assault from the east would converge with a sea-borne attack from the west. The first of these went badly wrong when the British forces were repulsed with heavy casualties, prompting Fodé Sylla to boast that he would be eating at the Governor's table the next day.[81] He was also reported to have sacked a number of villages in British Kombo as his army closed in on Bathurst. However, the

---

[78] The final draft of the ultimatum is at NAGB CSO 23/4 "Expedition Against Foday Sillah (1893–94)."

[79] NAGB CSO 23/4 "Expedition Against Foday Sillah (1893–94)", Manager, British Kombo, to Administrator Bathurst (17 February 1894).

[80] ANS 1F8 "Rélations avec la Gambie", telegram from Governor of Gambia to Gouverneur du Sénégal (24 February 1894).

[81] ANS 1F8 "Relations avec la Gambie", Telegram from Adrien, CFAO, Dakar, to Gouverneur du Sénégal, St. Louis (1 March 1894).

arrival of reinforcements from Sierra Leone swung the advantage the other way, and Fodé Sylla was forced to retreat southwards. The French, who had long regarded the latter as a menace were monitoring events, and when his forces crossed into Narang, they were tipped off by the chief of Makuda, Fodé Moussa. A group of around 100 troops were detained there, while Fodé Sylla was intercepted at Burukugue. According to local traditions, he had been attempting to make good his escape across the *marigot* into Buluf. The baobab tree where he was supposedly captured still stands as a visual reminder of the last act in the Marabout-Soninke saga that had dominated the affairs of Kombo over the past fifty years. The French dealt surprisingly leniently with their prisoners. Fodé Sylla was exiled to northern Senegal and placed under the supervision of Demba War Sall in Kajoor.[82] The Governor specifically requested that an adequate sum of money be provided for his maintenance. Meanwhile, many of his soldiers in the Casamance were offered land at Bandjikaky in the hope that they too could be turned into peaceful cultivators.[83]

In the aftermath, the British and French authorities had to address the contrasting legacies of Fodé Sylla. The Gambian authorities had the simpler task. With the removal of Sylla from the equation, what was needed was to impress upon the population of Kombo that there was no chance of his ever being allowed to return. The display of force was also intended to convey the message that any future signs of resistance would be crushed. Gunjur had been bombarded from the sea and Brikama had been largely destroyed as well. The authorities enforced the dismantling of all the remaining stockades and insisted that the erstwhile supporters of Fodé Sylla make a formal act of submission. The 'headmen' of all the towns in Kombo were required to attend a meeting with the Governor and to engage in a public display, "taking off their caps [and] bowing their heads to the ground."[84] Towns that were considered uncooperative were physically destroyed, as happened at Mandina Ba in March 1894. The displaced populations were allowed to return later on, but in each case the towns were rebuilt from scratch according to British plans. The intention was presumably to make them less defensible, but also to impose a British sense of ordered space on a conquered landscape. Sitwell, the then Travelling Commissioner for the South Bank, wrote a report in April of 1894, accounting for the punishments that had been visited on particular towns and

[82] Demba War Sall, a royal slave, had become the trusted intermediary of the French as the ruling line in Kajoor was sidelined. Crucially, he was not in the maraboutic camp. James F. Searing, *'God Alone is King'*, pp. 61–3, *passim*.

[83] ANS 1F8 "Relations avec la Gambie", telegram from Administrateur Supérieure de la Casamance to Gouverneur, St. Louis (22 March 1894) and letter from Gouverneur to Ministre (9 April 1894).

[84] NAGB CSO 1/124 "Despatches from Colonial Office 1894", Report by Governor on palaver with Kombo chiefs (20 March 1894).

individuals, and mapping out a strategy for bringing the dissident elements in Kombo to heel. In his assessment, Fodé Sylla had not been supported by the local Mandinka population, but mostly by strangers who had entered Kombo. On this view, a return to normality might be anticipated relatively quickly, given the supposed tendency of the Mandinka to back the winning side. This rather optimistic assessment was convenient because the Gambian authorities wanted to draw a line under the affair as quickly as possible. Amongst other things, a return to normality was necessary for the resumption of food and cash crop production, the latter being crucial to the goal of achieving a measure of fiscal stability.[85] A particular concern was that the populations that had fled to Bathurst and other towns in British Kombo should return to the countryside to farm. Many of the refugees had, in fact, crossed over from the Casamance to escape raiding. Rather than returning them, the plan was to encourage as many as possible to take up farming on the Gambian side of the new border. Meanwhile, Aku traders from Bathurst were encouraged to tap rubber in the border zone, which for a time was the most important export from Kombo.[86] In the calculations of the British authorities, therefore, the border loomed very large indeed.

By contrast, the French were faced with a far more chaotic legacy. Much of the population had fled in the direction of Bathurst, while those that had remained had been unable to plant any crops. An infestation of grasshoppers only compounded the crisis. However, the distress was partly of French making. In the aftermath of the 1891 demarcation, when Fodé Sylla had made his opposition to the French explicit, his supporters had, if anything, intensified their raiding activity. The French had responded by installing their own strongman whose task was to bring about the submission of villages in Narang and Fogny-Jabankunda and to counteract the influence of Fodé Sylla. The chosen instrument was Mangone Seye, a Wolof from Kajoor who came complete with armed retainers and established his seat at Makuda, very close to the border. Because the nearest French administrator was at distant Carabane, Mangone was effectively given a free hand. He proceeded to 'govern' in the most predatory manner, insisting that nearby villagers work on his own fields. In January 1893, the French received a petition in Arabic, from Mandinka 'chiefs' in Makuda and Diébaly, alleging that Mangone was implicated in capturing people and selling them into slavery. Mangone responded to accusations of brutality by pointing out that most of the population was resisting his demands – as indeed they were. From Karone to Narang, there was concerted opposition to the attempts by Mangone to exercise his

---

[85] Expenditure had greatly exceeded revenue in 1893 and 1894, with the dramatic decline of Customs revenue being the primary cause in the latter year.
[86] As the name implies, the Aku were recaptives from Yorubaland who had been landed at Freetown, and then relocated to the Gambia.

devolved authority. When he retaliated, his clear expectation was that the
French would back him up. But it appears that an embattled Mangone had
also enlisted the support of Fodé Sylla's own soldiers. The gamekeeper had
turned poacher, and in November 1893 The French decided to remove Mangone from the scene.

In 1894, the administration was re-organized in such a way as to bring
French officers closer to the ground. Commandant Farque was appointed the
first *Administrateur Supérieur* at Sédhiou[87] and immediately embarked on a
tour of the border in order to assess the damage that had been done. In his
report, he described the scene that confronted him when he reached Diébaly:

Mangone Seye and Fodé Sylla have devastated everything: there remains neither rice
nor fowls; some porcupines drag themselves along with difficulty in the village, feeding
themselves as best they can, where there is nothing to give them. The village is still in
ruins. The mud walls of former huts have been burned by fire ... Only some huts have
been saved. The former rice granaries still exist, but they are completely empty. One
can just about see some rice [wrapped] in straw packets ... Moreover, grasshoppers
have become a veritable scourge for the Casamance. We still meet some thick clouds
[of grasshoppers] quite regularly. If you add another scourge which has been much
more terrible, Mangone Seye, you have a rough idea of the situation in Combo. It is
lamentable, and I have been genuinely affected by seeing the misery in which all those
unfortunate people live, in the midst of a country that is nevertheless very beautiful and
very fertile.[88]

Significantly, Farque was requested to mediate in the return of some fifty men,
women and children who had allegedly been taken away by Fodé Sylla. When
he came to the village of Bagnounkoto – evidently a longstanding Bainunk
settlement – he found it completely deserted. At Kujube, he found quite a large
population, but many of these were refugees from Makuda who had fled there
because of its impregnable defences. Makuda itself was occupied by a handful
of women and old people who had been sent there to cater to the needs of
villagers who had been ordered to work on the groundnut fields belonging to
Mangone. Farque was overtly critical of the former Commandant of Sédhiou,
who had apparently issued these orders on the basis that those compelled to
work were debtors. He was even more scathing about Laplène, the former
Commandant at Carabane who had been complicit in what was depicted as a
veritable reign of terror.

The immediate priority was to build trust, which was also a *sine qua non* for
the return of populations who had taken refuge in the Gambia. The decision to

---

[87] Farque henceforth had two deputies responsible for two newly created *cercles*, one based at
Sédhiou and the other at Carabane. Roche, *Histoire de la Casamance*, p. 230.
[88] ANS 13G 372 "Casamance: Correspondance du Résident 1892–1894", A. Farque, l'administrateur supérieur, Sedhiou, to Directeur des Affaires Politiques, St. Louis (26 February 1894).

impose the head tax, or *l'impôt*, did not make this an easy task. In areas where there was some tradition of paying tax, there was a greater likelihood of securing compliance, but the French met with stiff resistance across the Casamance. When the first *Commandant de Poste* at Diébaly, Lieutenant Moreau, attempted to extend his administrative reach to Bliss and Karone, he was greeted with open defiance.[89] The opposition was even greater in Buluf, necessitating successive military operations to compel villages to deliver their taxes. Indeed, as Christian Roche points out, Fogny had not really been properly subdued at the advent of the First World War.[90] The opposition the French encountered in imposing their will on the Jola and the Kalorn made it difficult to achieve the neat closure that they expected would follow the removal of Fodé Sylla and Fodé Kaba. With the latter out of the picture, French administrators imagined they would be greeted as liberators. Instead they were regarded as yet another unwanted intruder. I will pick up the theme of resistance to taxation and forced recruitment in Chapters 4 and 5. But I turn now to consider parallel processes in the trans-Volta.

The Dismembering of Agotime

Our second case is more complicated still, in that the trans-Volta was actually partitioned twice over. At the end of the nineteenth century, the northern Ewe, the central Togo minorities and the Agotime were placed within the boundaries of German Togo. However, following the Franco-British invasion of the colony in 1914, and its temporary division during the war years, the former German colony was formally split into two unequal halves in 1919. Although Ewe nationalists later bemoaned the fact that they were now divided three ways between the Gold Coast, British Togoland and French Togoland, the border that was eventually demarcated did not cut through many *dukɔwo*. By contrast, a line was driven through the middle of Agotime, depositing Kpetoe, Afegame, Adedome and some other settlements in British Togoland and the remainder in French territory. In what follows, I seek to elucidate why the borders were drawn, where they were and with what consequences.

The First Partition: The Remaking of the Trans-Volta c.1870–1914

In Chapter 2, we left our reconstruction of Agotime history at the point when the Asante forces withdrew from the trans-Volta. This was followed in 1874 by the British invasion of Kumasi, and the subsequent descent into political infighting within the kingdom, which contributed to the implosion

---

[89] Roche, *Histoire de la Casamance*, p. 274.   [90] Roche, *Histoire de la Casamance*, p. 294.

of Asante power east of the Volta. One of the side-effects was that much of the trade that had previously passed down the Volta River, where it could be taxed by Asante customs agents, now followed the land routes to the east. Agotime, and especially Kpetoe, found itself strategically positioned along these routes that terminated at various points along the coastline east of Keta, thereby evading the Gold Coast customs duties that the British sought to impose. A German report from 1884 noted that there was a significant trade in palm-oil and kernels between Agotime and Togo beach – what is Lomé today – which suggests that the Agotime had made their own adjustment to the ending of the slave trade.[91] Indeed it was the vibrancy of this trade that attracted the Germans and induced them to shift their capital from Anecho to Lomé in 1897. In the preceding decade, there was fierce competition between the British and Germans to corner trade and sign treaties that might then form the basis of a claim to territory. As in the case of the Gambia, the British government would really have preferred to settle for a loose exercise of influence east of the Volta. However, German competition ultimately forced Britain to take action in order to prevent a rival from monopolizing the trade and, crucially, cornering the revenues that came with it.

The Danes had been the dominant European presence in the commerce of the lower Volta, but in 1850, their government decided to cut its losses and cede its forts and interests to Britain – which were pretty nominal given that the Danes hardly travelled much beyond the Keta lagoon.[92] In the wake of the recommendations of the 1865 Parliamentary Select Committee, the principle that there should be no further additions to British territory was reinforced. The interpretation of the Danish cession in London was that rough spheres of influence had changed hands rather than territorial claims. However, W.H. Bryars has underlined that there was a much greater measure of interest within the Gold Coast administration for adopting a proactive policy.[93] One of the immediate consequences of the Asante defeat by the British was that those *dukɔwo*, including Agotime, that had fought against the invasion of the trans-Volta exacted their revenge on others, like the Taviefe and the Adaklu, who were accused of having aided and abetted the enemy. In the midst of the ongoing turmoil, the Gold Coast authorities sought to use their influence to

---

[91] Peter Sebald, *Togo 1884–1914: Eine Geschichte der deutschen 'Musterkolonie' auf der Grundlage amtlicher Quellen* (Berlin: Akademie-Verlag, 1988), p. 64.

[92] In the early nineteenth century, H.C. Monrad referred to a visit to a 'stone cliff' in Krepe that was an hour's march from the Volta, in a manner that suggested that such forays were unusual. Selena Axelrod Winsnes (ed.), *Two Views from Christiansborg Castle: Volume II – A Description of the Guinea Coast and its Inhabitants by H.C. Monrad* (Accra: Sub-Saharan Publishers, 2008).

[93] William Hudson Bryars, "The Evolution of British Imperial Policy on the Volta, 1857–1897: From Informal Opportunism to Formal Occupation", unpublished PhD thesis, University of Birmingham, 1994.

bring about a peace settlement.[94] Bryars observes that traders in Accra were supportive of any action that could be taken to remove obstacles to unfettered trade along the Volta, even if that meant having to shoulder somewhat higher taxes in the short term. In other words, there was a constituency for a forward policy that contrasted with official caution in London. When the Germans suddenly planted their feet on the coastline east in 1884, the Gold Coast authorities recognized that the exercise of influence without assuming political responsibility was no longer sustainable. However, the men on the spot had difficulty in persuading the Colonial Office, and even more so the Foreign Office, that the stakes were sufficiently high to risk offending the German government. As happened in the Senegambia, a de facto policy of drift enabled a European rival to consolidate its position, so that when the time finally came for a defence of British interests, it was too late to translate a notional sphere of influence into actual territory.

In 1869, the acting Administrator at Cape Coast, W.H. Simpson, had attempted to deter the Asante from invading the trans-Volta by asserting that the Akwamu, Krepe, Anlo and Agotime had considered themselves to be part of a British protectorate since the transfer of Danish interests. He had also insisted that Britain would not allow any other power to intervene on what it considered its own soil.[95] According to Alexander Keese, the Ada Manche had been actively lobbying on behalf of Agotime on the basis of the close affinity between them.[96] As Bryars indicates, Simpson was attempting to pursue a strategy that was completely at odds with the position of the British government. Not surprisingly, therefore, he was disowned by his political masters. Although the Gold Coast administration was subsequently allowed to provide some support for the Krepe polities to defend themselves, there was to be no military commitment to stem the Asante invasion. Nevertheless, there was a creeping imperialism that had its basis in the fiscal logics that were outlined in Chapter 2. The administration sought permission in 1871 to establish control over the strip of land between the Keta lagoon and the sea "to protect the trade of the River from Piracy and Smuggling."[97] The extension of Gold Coast Customs regulations to Keta and Dzelukope was a small victory for those who advocated a forward policy, but it merely had the effect of displacing traders still further to the east where they could avoid paying duties and still smuggle goods into British territory. In fact, the origins of Lomé lie

---

[94] Marion Johnson, "Ashanti east of the Volta", *Transactions of the Historical Society of Ghana* VIII 1965, p. 56.

[95] Bryars, "Evolution", p. 43.

[96] Alexander Keese, *Ethnicity and the Colonial State: Finding and Representing Group Identifications in a Coastal West African and Global Perspective (1850–1960)* (Leiden: Brill, 2016), p. 238.

[97] Quoted in Bryars, "Evolution", p. 132.

precisely in the success with which a motley array of traders were able to exploit the 1874 border to their own advantage. In the words of Philippe Gervais-Lambony:

> Therefore, Lomé was actually founded before the [German] protectorate was established. Indeed, when the British colony on the Gold Coast (currently Ghana) was established in 1874, a group of traders from different origins (German, Mina, Haoussa, Afro-Brazilian) wanting to escape customs controls and taxes came to settle on the site of Lomé – especially from 1879 onwards – because no colonial authority was to be found there. In Lomé, it was possible for traders to trade freely. They mainly exchanged palm oil, but were also involved in smuggling.[98]

The sudden German intrusion effectively expunged the duty-free zone and resolved one set of administrative problems for the British. But it also created a different set because the Germans were determined to ensure that the trans-Volta trade would find its way towards their own port at Lomé. If most of this commerce from the interior was siphoned off, the Gold Coast administration would end up assuming administrative burdens at a financial loss. This became a serious issue after the formal acquisition of Anlo in 1874, when government revenues were falling significantly behind expenditure.[99] The German factor therefore turned control of the Volta basin into an important focus of international rivalry, in which high imperialism and local concerns were thoroughly intertwined.

As German officials set about signing treaties with chiefs east of the Volta, the Gold Coast authorities felt the need to respond in kind (see Map 3.3). The attitude of the British government was initially as wary as ever, but there was gradual acceptance of the assessment of the men on the spot. Whereas Simpson had been severely criticized at the time, his claims were now called upon as evidence for the contention that Britain had regarded the trans-Volta as a de facto protectorate since the Danish cession. Evidence was also produced to show that the chiefs of the trans-Volta had participated in meetings and signed agreements in which they formally accepted their protected status. At the centre of these rivalries was Agotime, which was considered as the most important polity next to Peki. In 1886, the Agotime initially refused to accept an offer of German 'protection'.[100] This was taken as an encouraging sign, and in the hope of salvaging the situation before it was too late, the Commissioner of the Volta River District, C. Riby Williams, was despatched to secure British claims to the right bank of the Volta and to sign treaties with

---

[98] Philippe Gervais-Lambony, "Lomé", in Simon Bekker and Goran Therborn (eds.), *Capital Cities in Africa: Power and Powerlessness* (Cape Town: HSRC Press, 2012), p. 47.

[99] D.E.K. Amenumey, "The extension of British rule to Anlo (south-east Ghana), 1850–1890", *Journal of African History* IX (1) 1968, p. 105.

[100] Bryars, "Evolution", p. 300.

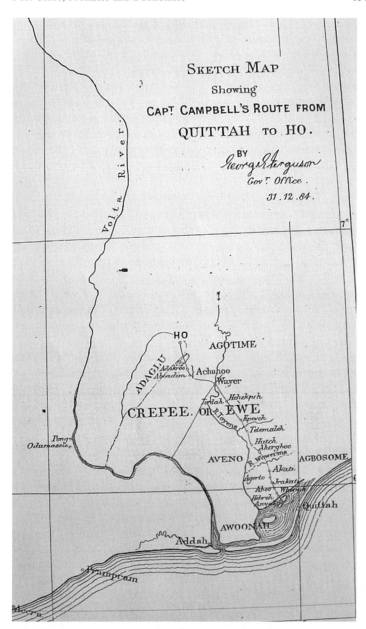

Map 3.3 Sketch-map of trans-Volta, including Agotime, in 1884.

the Krepe chiefs to the east. However, Williams was too late to prevent the Germans from announcing that they had successfully secured their own Agotime treaty. This appears to have been signed by Agbovi as the 'king' of Agotime, which implies that the latter retained his status as de facto leader after the Asante campaign.[101] This German coup was a source of considerable personal disappointment to Williams. Nevertheless, he did manage to persuade a number of other chiefs to gather at Peki to formally accept British 'protection'.[102] The Colonial Office position was that this merely confirmed what had already been known since the Danish cession of 1850. At this point, there was no real enthusiasm for contesting German claims to Agotime, Kévé or Tové.

In 1887, the British and German governments entered into an agreement that resolved "to leave within the British Protectorate the countries of Aquamoo and Crepee (Peki)". This is a good example of an attempt to co-opt the territorial limits of African states in the service of colonial boundary-making. But this became untenable when it transpired that there was only a patchwork of loosely organized polities in a fractured frontier zone. The wording of the agreement was the source of some misunderstanding because the Germans regarded it as limiting the British protectorate to Peki, whereas the British position was that they had acquired all of Krepe and had merely agreed to the inclusion of' Peki in the text to accommodate a slightly different German usage.[103] And so the politicking continued. In July 1888, a British official managed to secure a fresh declaration of 'fealty' from some sixty Krepe chiefs. At about the same time, C.E. Akers secured a statement from "the King and chiefs of Agotime" to the effect that they had never made any binding agreement with the Germans and declaring 'fealty' to Britain. Tellingly, it was not clear who the king was supposed to be in this case – two of the five signatories were Agbovi and Akoto, and both were listed as "Chiefs of Potoi [Kpetoe]".[104] Governor Branford Griffith was sorely tempted to resuscitate British claims to Agotime, using additional evidence that they had participated in a meeting in 1858, at which they had ostensibly consented to the poll tax. In 1889, the British government seemed willing to reopen the matter on the basis that the Agotime had previously accepted the leadership of the Peki 'king'.[105] For their part, the Germans countered that the British had only ever secured a claim to Peki

[101] Sebald, *Togo*, p. 67.   [102] Bryars, "Evolution", p. 301; Welman, *Native States*, p. 16.

[103] David Brown, "Anglo-German rivalry and Krepi politics, 1886–1894", *Transactions of the Historical Society of Ghana* XV ii 1974, p. 206.

[104] NAGB CSO 54/9 "Treaties", Declaration dated 3 July 1888 and signed by Agbovi, Akoto, Badabani (Zukpe), Kudiabo (Nyitoe) and Akakpo-Aley (Mawhi-Agotime).

[105] Slightly misleadingly, Knoll writes of the Peki ruler: "After he defeated the Taviefe people, even King Abovi [sic] of Agotime, who had signed a treaty of protection with the Germans,

itself, while adhering to the contention that the Agotime had already accepted the offer of German protection.[106] In the final analysis, the metropolitan governments decided to come to a settlement rather than escalate the dispute. Under the Heligoland Treaty of July 1890, which settled their claims globally, Germany received most of what it had been holding out for. While Peki itself passed to the Gold Coast, most of 'Krepe' – including Agotime, Adaklu and Ho – was transferred to Germany. As in the case of the Gambia/Casamance border, the majority of a historic frontier region passed to one colonial claimant, in this case the Germans. The Treaty defined the borderline as running from an agreed point on the coastline northwards to the parallel of 6°10' latitude and then westwards until it struck the left bank of the Aka River. From there an imaginary line followed the mid-channel of the Aka to the 6°20' parallel of north latitude, whence it tracked westwards to the right bank of the Dschawe and along the bank of that river to the confluence of the Dayi River and the Volta. The border then followed the left bank of the Volta River up to the so-called neutral zone in the north, which was itself partitioned in 1899.[107] This meant that the salient features of the border in the vicinity of Agotime were a straight-line boundary (east–west) that was drawn a few miles south of Batoumé, and a riverain boundary (north–south) that ceded the entire Volta River to the Gold Coast. These simple expedients made the positioning of the border more straightforward than might otherwise have been the case. Given that Peki claims to Krepe were pretty notional, the border did not divide any *dukɔwo*, although Adaklu and Ave farmland was deposited in the Gold Coast. This did not mean, however, that the partition was any less controversial. A number of chiefs had signed agreements with the British and had signalled their express desire not to come under the German flag – only to discover that they had in effect been traded.

German imperial statecraft in Togo provides a salutary lesson in how limited resources could be creatively marshalled in order to establish an effective administrative presence on the ground. The authorities in Lomé were faced with a very familiar conundrum: establishing greater administrative density required the raising of additional revenues, but this in turn hinged upon developing an effective system of resource extraction. Whereas many colonial

placed his land under Kwadjo-Deo's [sic] power". Arthur Knoll, *Togo Under Imperial Germany, 1884–1914: A Case-Study in Colonial Rule* (Stanford: Hoover Institution Press, 1978), p. 34. It is true that the Agotime chiefs signed an agreement accepting the leadership of Peki in July 1888, but this was a tactical move to remain within the British orbit. Welman, *Native States*, p. 19.

[106] The problem was that the Peki and Krepe were sometimes used interchangeably.

[107] The description of the boundary may be found at E. Herslet, *The Map of Africa by Treaty: Volume I* (London: Frank Cass reprint edn., 1967), p. 73.

rulers relied upon fairly crude forms of head taxation, the German response was more expansive. Their solution lay in expanding the production of cash crops, while finding a harmonious balance between direct and indirect taxes. An immediate concern was to ensure that the caravan trade from the north passed all the way down to Lomé rather than cutting through German territory and crossing the Volta into the Gold Coast. To this end, Customs agents were placed at strategic points, where they levied heavy duties on traders passing along an east–west axis. The Gold Coast authorities regarded this as discriminatory, and they responded in kind by preventing salt and kola from being traded into the German colony.[108] German efforts to pursue an autonomous Customs policy proved costly because higher duties than those in the Gold Coast provided ample scope for smuggling activity. In 1894, the Germans came to an agreement with the Gold Coast Government whereby they would maintain a common Customs zone within the Volta triangle, with a 4 per cent duty attaching to most imported goods alongside special rates for alcohol, tobacco and firearms. This dealt with the problem of contraband, but it also set limits on the revenue that the Togo government could raise. Hence, the agreement was rescinded by the Togo government in 1904, which was followed by an increase in the general level of duty from 4 to 11 per cent.

The context for this gamble was the decision to embark on very substantial investments in infrastructure. A network of roads and railways was planned that, it was hoped, would provide a greater stimulus to cash crop production and African consumption alike. In the process, the revenue from import and export duties could be expected to increase, which was vitally important because the colony was expected to become fully independent of imperial subventions.[109] In 1905, work on the Lomé–Anecho railway was completed, followed by the line from Lomé to Kpalimé (completed in 1907) and to Atakpamé (completed in 1911). Each of these lines was built with a view to stimulating the export of a particular crop: palm-oil and coconuts in the case of Anecho, cocoa in the case of Kpalimé and cotton around Atakpamé.[110] The Lomé–Kpalimé line was especially important because it partly compensated for the fact that the British had control of the entirety of the middle and upper reaches of the Volta River, furnishing a large, and partly navigable, waterway that linked the southern colony with the savannah. The gamble on railways paid off in a remarkably short period of time, as trade and revenues followed an upward trajectory, earning Togo the accolade of the *musterkolonie*. Between 1903 and 1912, exports increased from 3.6 million marks to 9.6 million marks, while imports increased from

---

[108] Knoll, *Togo*, pp. 52–4.   [109] Knoll, *Togo*, p. 62.   [110] Knoll, *Togo*, pp. 130–1.

6.1 million marks to 11.4 million marks.[111] Although this was a trade imbalance, it was one that favoured the metropole. By the eve of the First World War, a revenue of 4 million marks exceeded expenditure, which stood at 3.6 million marks, which signalled that the colony had ceased to rely on imperial subsidies.[112] Although Customs receipts increased significantly from 1 million marks in 1903 to 1.9 million marks in 1912, their contribution to total income in fact declined from 88.3 per cent to 53.7 per cent of the total. The reason was that direct taxes had assumed a heightened importance by this point. In the early years, the colony relied heavily on forced labour for public works. But in 1907, the administration introduced a levy on men of 12 days labour or a payment of 6 marks, with the possibility of combining them later on. The contribution of direct taxes increased rapidly from 57,000 marks in 1907 to 853,000 marks in 1912.[113] In addition, a whole raft of licences and fees was introduced, including trade, firearms and even dog licences. Although German taxes were distinctly unpopular, and led to some flight of population towards the Gold Coast, the German administration was successful in assembling a sound fiscal foundation for the state despite an unpromising start. A growing sense of confidence was reflected in the decision to invest not merely in connective infrastructure, but also in public buildings that pandered to a sense of imperial grandeur.[114] All of this came at a cost for the Africans who were required to provide the labour that, in a literal sense, materialized the idea of the German colonial state.

Agotime Partitioned, 1919–1939: Definition and Demarcation

Following the joint invasion of Togo in 1914, the territory was temporarily divided between the occupying powers. Britain took control of the western half, including Agotime, while France administered the east. In his brief tenure as an administrative officer, Captain R.S. Rattray set about evaluating whether a case could be made for the future integration of the region into the Gold Coast on the basis of the relatedness of the people.[115] He was particularly interested in gathering evidence to support the position that the *dukowo* of German Togo continued to accept their submission to Peki which, as we have seen, had formally become part of the Gold Coast. He listed Agotime as amongst the

---

[111] Knoll, *Togo*, table 1, p. 75.   [112] Knoll, *Togo*, p. 81.

[113] Knoll, *Togo*, p. 182, footnote 33.

[114] Yves Marguerat, *Lomé: une brève histoire de la capitale du Togo* (Lomé and Paris: Haho and Karthala, 1992).

[115] Rattray is more famous for his work on Asante and the Northern Territories when he was employed as Government Anthropologist. His brief involvement in southern Togoland has been largely forgotten.

divisions that emphatically rejected any such claims, although his overall assessment remained more or less in line with what he wanted to find. Rattray maintained that many *dukowo* had admitted a tributary status to Peki in the past, and had secreted British flags throughout the German period.[116] In 1918, the Secretary of Native Affairs of the Gold Coast, J.T. Furley, collected oral evidence from all the chiefs of any note in the British sector, the main purpose of which was to establish that the Germans had ruled with such brutality that they ought not to be permitted to return – leavened by evidence of enthusiastic support for British rule. He managed to secure a litany of complaints about harsh and arbitrary treatment, land seizures, forced labour and excessive taxation. At Agotime, he held a meeting with 'Headchief Jogbo', that is Matti Sorkpor, eight village chiefs and four sub-chiefs. The office of 'headchief' was a German creation because, as I have already indicated, there had never been any such position in the past. Matti Sorkpor obliged his visitor with a damning indictment of German rule, but his account differed from the other statements gathered by Furley, insofar as it dwelt much more on issues of trade: "Their treatment of us was not good. They flogged the people and taxed them. We worked for them for nothing. The Agotimes are traders and the Germans didn't allow us to travel to the Gold Coast. We weave cloths and trade mostly in cloths."[117] The only other chief who was quoted was Nene Mahumansro of Afegame, who produced a tattered British flag and claimed that the Germans had fought and killed many of their people when they had refused to give it up.

Whereas the Agotime had initially traded in ivory, slaves and salt, and had then gravitated to dealing in palm products, the reference to a regional trade in kente cloth is of particular interest. Some cotton had been traded out of Krepe, including Adaklu, in the nineteenth century, and had been used to make cloth. This led the Germans to encourage the production of approved varieties of cotton that would help the metropole to reduce its dependence on the United States. As early as 1890, an expert report judged a number of areas suitable for cotton plantations, including northern Agotime.[118] However, the breakthrough came with the agreement of Booker T. Washington to back an African–American expedition from the Tuskegee Institute. This led to the creation of a model farm at Tové-Dzigbe – just north of Adame and in close proximity to Kpalimé – and the dissemination of

---

[116] PRAAD (Ho) RAO C.273 "Togoland: A History of the Tribal Divisions of the District of Misahuhe and the sub-Districts of Ho and Kpandu", compiled by R. Sutherland Rattray, District Political Officer (undated).

[117] PRAAD ADM 11/1620 "Togoland Secret and Confidential Papers" (1918–1924), Report of a meeting held at Kpetoe on 7 February 1918, p. 34.

[118] Pierre Ali Napo, *Togo, Land of Tuskegee Institute's International Technical Assistance Experimentation: 1900–1909* (Accra: Onyase Press, 2002), p. 7. On this episode, see also Andrew Zimmerman, *Alabama in Africa: Booker T. Washington, the German Empire and the Globalization of the New South* (Princeton: Princeton University Press, 2010).

'American cotton' seed in 1900. Although the experimental plantations enjoyed mixed success, there was an increase in production across the Misahöhe District, including areas that bordered Agotime.[119] It was some of this cotton that was presumably used by by Agotime weavers to produce a more refined form of kente cloth. In the light of complaints about unfair German pricing for cotton, it seems likely that Agotime weavers, producing a high-quality product, were able to pay more for this crop.[120] As the statement quoted by Furley implied, they had also made money trading this cloth across the border into the Gold Coast, thereby creating a fresh commercial niche for the Agotime. The efforts of the German authorities to interfere with this trade culminated in many Agotime weavers relocating to the Eastern Province of the Colony where they combined kente weaving with labouring on cocoa farms – a tradition that continued through the post-war period. One informant from Amoussoukope recalled that there were many Agotimes living around Tafo and Kukurantumi, including her own father who left many valuable cloths to his children.[121]

Some of the complaints about German ill-treatment are verifiable. In one documented episode, the acting Commissioner, Lt. Smend, killed seventeen people in Afegame and another two in Nyitoe after his demands for labour were received with what he considered to be an impertinent response.[122] The incident came on the back of a petition from the people of Ho, which cited a long list of grievances against the hardships of German rule, including the routine use of forced labour.[123] Apart from the physical work on the roads, villages were expected to provide hammock-bearers on demand. Indeed, the village of Agotime-Bè was populated by people from the Lomé area who were sent there in order to provide carriers to bridge the extended no-man's land on the hammock-path between Adaklu and Kpetoe. In Zukpe, a version of what was presumably the same incident recalls that a German official had entered Afegame expecting to find people ready to work, instead of which he found them sitting around playing *oware*, a popular board game.[124] When he remonstrated with the villagers, he was bluntly – or as he would have had it, 'impertinently' – informed that labour in the Gold Coast was actually paid for. This confirms that the Agotime had more than a passing acquaintance with what went on in British territory and were actively comparing notes.

Although Agotime statements to the effect that they had always intended to come under British rule were filed for use in future negotiations, the subsequent

---

[119] Ali Napo, *Togo*, p. 28.
[120] The book by Ali Napo includes a photograph of a member of the Tuskegee team, John W. Robinson, against a backdrop of kente cloths. It is possible that these cloths were actually made in Agotime.
[121] Interview with Etu Adabra, Amoussoukope (Togo), 9 September 2003.
[122] Sebald, *Togo*, p. 214.   [123] Knoll, *Togo*, pp. 55–6.
[124] Interview with Nene Teh-Doku III, Zukpe (Togo), 27 August 2001.

passage of events led to a very different outcome. As the First World War drew to a close and the future of German Togo became an issue requiring resolution, it was apparent that it was not going to be a simple matter of absorbing the occupied territory into the Gold Coast. The internationalization of the debate about the fate of the German colonies led to an acceptance that the British and the French would have to settle for something less than a colonial relationship. But more crucially for our purposes, the French government bargained hard, insisting that they needed the port at Lomé in view of the inadequacy of the facilities at Cotonou. Going further, they argued that it was necessary to take possession of the three railway lines upon which the viability of the capital and the finances of the territory had come to depend. Once the British government conceded that the French had a convincing case for claiming Lomé and the railways, the other pieces fell into place. This was bound to have a profound impact upon Agotime because the railway passed near to the easterly town of Amoussoukope, which was historically an offshoot of Kpetoe. In 1917, Furley had expressed the opinion that the location of the railway meant that it might be necessary to position the boundary line west of Agotime, an assessment that was used by the Colonial Office in its "Memorandum on Togoland" of November 1918.[125] There was, however, a strong sentiment on the part of local officials that it would be unwise to concede Agotime in its entirety, or worse, to cut it in two.

Some account seems to have been taken of Agotime as a special case, as is reflected in the final negotiations between Britain and France. The Milner-Simon Agreement of 10 July 1919 awarded most of the German colony, including the railways and the greater part of Agotime, to France. The Todzie River constituted the boundary up to Kpetoe, but the line was then deflected to enable it (and two other villages) to be placed in British territory. The relevant passage reads:

Thence the River Damitsi to its confluence with Todschie (or Wuto). Thence the River Todschie to the boundary of the lands of the village of Botoe [Kpetoe], which it passes on the east so as to leave it wholly to Great Britain. Thence the road from Botoe to Batome to the western limits of the latter village; Then the line passes south of Batome so as to leave this village in its entirety to France; From south of Batome the boundary runs to the point of junction of the present boundary of the Gold Coast Colony (parallel 6°20' North) and the River Magbawi. Thence it follows, to the sea, the present frontier as laid down in the Anglo-German Convention of July 1st, 1890.[126]

While Kpetoe was placed in British territory, Batoumé, which had once been the slave village of Agbovi I, was deposited in French territory. In Agotime today, it is firmly believed that there were no consultations at all. As the written

---

[125] "Memorandum on Togoland", p. 9, Confidential Print No. 1065 (West Africa), enclosed in PRAAD (Accra) ADM 11/1620 "Togoland Secret and Confidential Papers" (1918–1924).

[126] A copy of the document is at Brownlie, *African Boundaries*, p. 256.

history of Nene Keteku tartly puts it: "The division of the land and the people was made without the consent of the Agotimes. They were not even informed."[127] The truth is, however, somewhat more complicated.

No sooner had the ink dried than doubts began to be expressed. In November, Furley himself submitted a detailed report on the problems that could be anticipated to issue from the partition of the German colony. Unusually, he treated the Agotime as a distinct 'tribe' that warranted a separate consideration from the Krepe, and whose interests needed to be protected. Furley admitted that he had previously advocated the cession of the entirety of Agotime to France but recalled that he had written his assessment before soliciting the preferences of the Agotime in 1918. He had now revised his opinion:

To include the whole of Agotime within British territory would therefore be an act of justice only. The only objection that could be made would be that [the] portion of the Eastern boundary of the tribe runs rather close to the railway, but this it is submitted should not outweigh other considerations. If it does the only alternative to splitting up the tribe is to cede the whole of it to France. But before this alternative to disintegration is decided on the wishes of the people themselves on this hard alternative for them should be ascertained. There is no doubt that they would strongly resent being put to such a choice and it is urged that the whole of this tribe should be allowed to remain under the British. The actual boundary in the East should be investigated by the Commissioner on the spot.[128]

The second-best option was for all the Agotime to be consigned to France, but even this was not straightforward because if the Todzie River defined the entire stretch of border, Afegame would remain British. Meanwhile, the Officer Commanding British Forces, Major F.W.F. Jackson launched his own campaign to persuade the British government of the need to reopen the negotiations, questioning the entire premise upon which French claims were based, namely the fundamental importance of Lomé. As the handover date loomed, the educated population of Lomé and Chambers of Commerce in Britain lobbied furiously against the Milner-Simon Agreement, but to no avail.[129] In October 1920, the French finally took possession of the territory that had been assigned to them a year before. The Agotime people were henceforth split unequally between British and French Togoland, with four towns located in the former territory and thirteen in the latter. The two Togolands were governed under League of Nations Mandates, but the two sets of administering authorities operated on a very long leash. The Permanent

[127] Nene Nuer Keteku III, "Short History of the Agotimes" (undated).
[128] NAK CO 724/1 "Division of Togoland", Notes by J.T. Furley, entitled "Togoland Boundary".
[129] I have dealt with these events in Paul Nugent, *Smugglers, Secessionists and Loyal Citizens on the Ghana–Togo Frontier: The Lie of the Borderlands Since 1914* (Oxford and Athens: James Currey and Ohio University Press, 2002), pp. 29–36.

Mandates Commission exhibited no particular interest in the fate of divided peoples like the Agotime, and it was in the interests of the mandatory powers not to make an issue of it.

The consequences for the Agotime were felt almost immediately because the Gold Coast authorities swiftly shifted the Customs frontier to the new international border. Given that there were no direct taxes in the Gold Coast, it was decided that the full raft of duties should apply, lest the colony end up subsidizing the costs of administering British Togoland. Hence Customs stations were opened at Kpetoe and Ziope in 1920, and also briefly at Afegame – and subsequently at Shia and Nyive. Henceforth officers were instructed to collect money on all dutiable goods.[130] The French reciprocated with a Customs frontier of their own, opening posts at Noepé, Ave-Dzolo and Batoumé.[131] More controversially, the French authorities re-imposed direct taxes, in the shape of *l'impôt*, which had fallen into abeyance during the British occupation. Meanwhile, because the borders had not yet been physically demarcated, there was ample scope for confusion as to whether particular areas fell within British or French territory. This became very obvious during a series of incidents, which merit closer consideration.

In November 1920, the French authorities filed a complaint that two Gold Coast Customs Preventive Service (CPS) men attached to the station at Kpetoe had entered the villages near Agotime-Adzakpa and helped themselves to four sheep and some chickens.[132] In June 1922, the French Governor again complained that members of the CPS had installed themselves four miles from Adzakpa, at a place called Bakakope, and had made illegal demands on the people of Kpodzahon. The latter village was located close to the left bank of the Todzie, just across from Afegame, and so was unquestionably inside French Togoland.[133] While the complaint was being investigated, Captain Braddick of the CPS relayed a complaint from Matti Sorkpor to the effect that the French were levying the head tax in his villages. It later transpired that the villages in question were in French territory,[134] a misunderstanding that pointed to different conceptions of political relationships. The headchief apparently assumed that any village that was an extension of Kpetoe was

---

[130] PRAAD (Accra) ADM 39/5/73 "District Record Book".
[131] NAK CO 724/1 "Division of Togoland", Ivor Lewis, Inspector, Customs Preventive Service, Aflao, to Comptroller of Customs, Accra (4 May 1921).
[132] ADM 39/5/81 "Customs Dues on Boundary between British and French Zone", Major F.W.F. Jackson, Officer Commanding British Forces, to Commissaire, Lomé (23 November 1920).
[133] PRAAD (Accra) ADM 39/5/81 "Customs Dues on Boundary between British and French Zone", translation of Governor of French Togoland, Lomé, to Governor of the Gold Coast (21 June 1922), and Administrateur en Chef, Lomé, to Jackson (16 November 1920).
[134] PRAAD (Accra) ADM 39/5/81 "Customs Dues on Boundary", Captain Mansfied, Record Officer, Ho to CEP (9 October 1922).

necessarily British, while the Europeans took the Milner-Simon definition as the point of reference.

The Record Officer (later renamed District Commissioner) reported that there had been genuine confusion as to the status of villages located around Batoumé and Ziope where the boundary was no more than an imaginary line. For that reason, Captain E.T. Mansfield and M. Coez, his opposite number, met together and agreed that particular villages should be considered as British or French until such time as a Boundary Commission could resolve the uncertainty.[135] But this did not greatly ease the transition in the short-term. Matters came to a head over the treatment meted out to one Laklitza who was arrested by the CPS in 1922 for smuggling and was then appre-hended for a second time as a repeat offender. The French denied that Laklitza was a hardened smuggler and claimed that he had actually been arrested 500 metres west of Batoumé. The status of the latter village was unambiguously French, but there remained the philosophical question of where a village began and ended. The French view was that he was still on Batoumé land, which meant that he was in French Togoland at the time of his arrest. The British took the contrary view. This local affair became the source of friction between the two Governors, with Auguste Bonnecarrère accusing the CPS of pursuing a personal vendetta and Gordon Guggisberg repeating the assertion that Laklitza was a recidivist deserving of firm punishment.[136] And yet what could not be resolved was the fundamental issue of whether the incident had occurred in British or French territory. Both sides appreciated that this and other disagreements could only be resolved if a Boundary Commission made a detailed inspection on the spot and established visible markers. At the same time, it was agreed that the CPS men and the douaniers needed to be properly educated as to the location of the border and to be reminded of the fact that they were not permitted to cross the line in hot pursuit.

Although there was a protracted discussion about possible exchanges of territory, the Agotime puzzle came to be regarded as insoluble from a very early juncture. At some point, Matti Sorkpor was asked for his views on the possible deployment of the Todzie River as the boundary. This small adjust-ment would have had the effect of placing Kpetoe in French territory, whereas Afegame would have remained British. Nene Mahumansro, the chief in Afegame, apparently advised Sorkpor that it would be better to remain in British territory, even if the logical implication was that he would remain cut

---

[135] PRAAD (Accra) ADM 39/5/81 "Customs Dues on Boundary", Mansfield, to CEP (9 October 1922).

[136] TNAL Klouto 2 APA/2, Guggisberg to Bonnecarrère (5 February 1924) and Bonnecarrère to Guggisberg (27 February 1924).

off from the majority of his people.[137] That apparently concluded the matter and the proposal was shelved. In 1926, a Joint Boundary Commission came into existence and over three seasons, between 1927 and 1929, Captain Lilley and M. Bauché physically demarcated the boundary and attempted to resolve the outstanding ambiguities. In Agotime, the Commissioners entered into the finest detail on the ground, but seemingly performed their work without any opposition or great controversy. Pillars 16 to 31 were located along the Agotime stretch of border, with a number of intermediate pillars interpolated in the vicinity of Batoumé for good measure. If one compares the demarcated border with the verbal definition in the 1919 agreement, two things are clear: first, that a fairly large section of land to the north-east of Kpetoe, including the village of Bemla, was added to British Togoland; and second, that a smaller wedge of land located west of Batoumé changed hands in the opposite direction.[138] The concrete pillars helped to clear up the ambiguity about where the border ran, but they did not create a line that made any more intrinsic sense (see Map 3.4). It was inevitably the case that many villagers owned farms on the wrong side of the line. Although there was an agreement that entitled Togolanders to relocate to one or other side of the border, this did not address the practical problem of people whose homes were on one side while their lands were on the other. It was no great help to suggest that they could relocate, because the nearest town on the opposite side might be even further from the farms in question. The inevitable consequence was that an Agotime who was transporting goods from farm to homestead could be accused of smuggling if he/she was carrying crops in what were defined as being in commercial quantities. Nevertheless, the demarcation did perform one useful function: once the work was complete there were no further instances where the authorities, or villagers, were confused as to the positioning of the boundary. These pillars still exist and serve as a point of reference for villagers to this day.

---

[137] PRAAD (Ho), DA/D288 "Agotime Native Affairs", Nene Mahumansro, Afegame, to District Commissioner, Ho (15 September 1928). This account is confirmed in British records. Entry for Agotime in PRAAD (Accra) ADM 39/5/73 "District Record Book".

[138] Pillar 17 was located on the Batomé-Ziope road, whence the border travelled in a straight line to pillar 18, situated on a path between Batomé and Agodeke; then in a straight line for 1,550 metres to pillar 19 which was situated 5 metres from the southern edge of the Batomé-Kpetoe road at a distance of 1,250 metres from Batoumé. Pillar 19 A was located on the junction of the Kpetoe-Batomé and the Kpetoe-Akpokope-Ziope roads. The border then followed the main road as far as pillar 21 when it was deflected eastwards to follow the Kporekpore river as far as pillar 22. The border then followed a straight line to pillar 21, before tracking west and eventually joining the River Todze at pillar 30. It then followed that River until its confluence with the River Dasi.

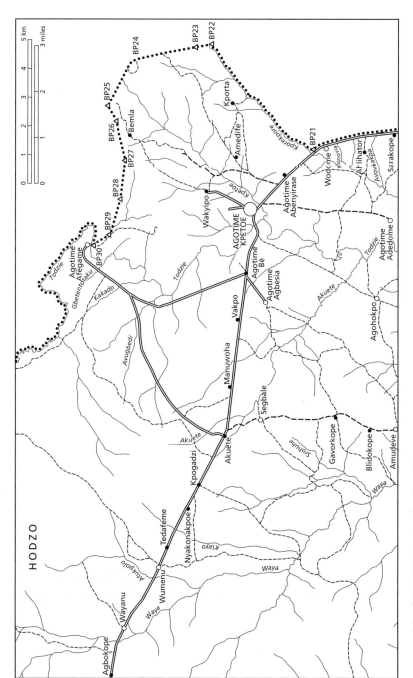

Map 3.4 (A,B) Agotime border pillars.

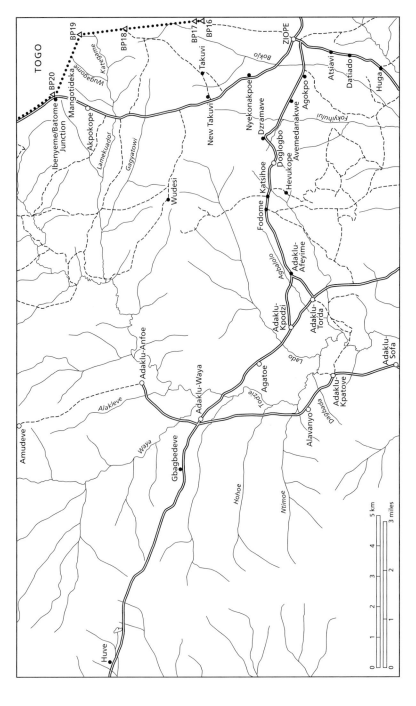

Map 3.4 (A,B) (cont.)

Conclusion

In 1906, the Deputy Governor of the Gambia, Francis Archer, produced a detailed handbook that was intended to offer both a history of the fledgling colony and a guide to its institutions and progress. It contained a detailed map that depicted the international borders with Senegal and identified the main towns and villages inside the Gambia and the routes connecting them. It also contained copious statistical information. Archer was keen to convey a strong sense of the Gambia having turned a corner after a period of struggling to become a viable concern. His data revealed that the 1890s had been a difficult decade, but that after 1897 there had been a steady increase in revenue, expenditure and export volumes. Archer observed that:

As the expenditure during the past few years shows an increase greater in proportion than the increase in the colony's revenue, it should in fairness be stated that more substantial works have been carried out since 1900 than, probably, in the whole previous history of the country. The condition of public buildings was deplorable; but these have now been out in proper repair.[139]

He went on to list a new female hospital and a post office, and improvements to the Customs warehouse and barracks for the military and police. After an overview of agriculture, health, education and communications, Archer concluded that:

Both colony and protectorate would seem to have emerged from the darkness of a troubled past into the dawn of a future which, it may reasonably be hoped, shall never be seriously overclouded.[140]

The Gambia handbook was evidently an attempt to sell a much-maligned colony, which the British government had at one point considered giving away without compensation.[141] But this should not obscure the more fundamental point that Archer was not merely detailing the shaping of a colony: he was also evidencing the materialization of the state itself in the form of bricks and mortar. As such, it can usefully stand for the historical processes that I have endeavoured to trace in this chapter.

There are three comparative points that I wish to extract from the welter of detail that has been presented in this chapter. The first is that the transformation of a nominal European presence into something altogether more substantial

---

[139] Francis Bisset Archer, *The Gambia Colony and Protectorate: An Official Handbook* (London: Frank Cass, 1967, new impression of 1906 1st edn.), p. 120.

[140] Archer, *Gambia Colony*, p. 138.

[141] During discussions over the Mellacourie exchange, it was suggested that it might be better to give the Gambia away rather than acquire an unwanted French possession in return. Hargreaves, *Prelude to the Partition*, p. 138.

arose less from imperial ambitions than the pressures exerted by local constituencies – European, Africa and *métis* – over the course of nearly a hundred
years. The expansion of the remit of the state to cover a lengthening range of
public goods stretched the resources of fledgling administrations to the limit.
As in the case of state formation in Europe, the pursuit of warfare was an
important part of the overall picture, but the difference is that it typically
resulted from the pressures exerted by European merchants who regarded
armed force as one of the public goods in question. In this case it was the
paymasters in London and Paris who typically sought to hold back. Militarism
was also limited by virtue of the fact that European merchants were reluctant to
pay the additional taxes to finance more ambitious military adventures.
A relationship between warfare and state-making did exist, therefore, but the
permutations were very different to historic patterns in Europe itself.

The second point is that a resolution to the issue of sustainability was sought
in a projection of commerce and political power to the margins. At the
proximate frontier, the objective was to dismantle the taxes and controls that
the rulers of African polities imposed upon trade, which generally required
some resort to force. At the further frontier, the object was to gain control over
trade routes and to redirect commerce towards the coastal ports. The African
polities that posed a threat to 'free trade' were met with force, but the relative
weakness of the Europeans before the second half of the nineteenth century
required them to rely more on alliance-building. Although the emergence of
new zones of agricultural production closer to the coast imparted a greater
significance to the proximate frontier – which was reflected in investments in
infrastructure such as railways – the further frontier remained important for the
control of taxable trade. Hence, the Scramble was very much about the
struggle to control the choke-points along regional trade routes.

Finally, when the partition did unfold, it was informed by deeper spatial
logics. African states like Asante or Kajoor and Bawol were typically swallowed whole. The historic frontier zones that had previously existed outside
the control of any state were more contested. In the Senegambia, the British
had every intention of absorbing Kombo. Although they also claimed Narang
and Fogny-Jabangkunda as a rough sphere of influence, they did not seek to
repel the French advance from the south. Moreover, they poured cold water on
Fodé Sylla's own claims to have ruled most of the area in question despite the
fact that these might have strengthened their negotiating hand. In the second
case, the positioning of the Gold Coast/Togo boundary along the Volta River
conferred most of a historic frontier zone upon the Germans. Peki, which was
treated as a minor state, was transferred in its entirety to Britain once its claims
to have presided over the rest of Krepe were shown to be implausible. Having
forfeited the Volta to Britain, the viability of the colonial project in German
Togo depended on an ability to funnel trade through Lomé. Although revising

Customs duties to take account of the border dynamic was a short-term expedient, the construction of the railways enabled the German regime to find a more permanent solution. The French perfectly understood that the viability of Togoland depended on the railway and the port at Lomé, both of which were embedded in the borderlands. This guaranteed the partition of Agotime in 1919, an act that became definitive once the chiefs in Afegame and Kpetoe set their faces against being transferred to France.

Part II

States and Taxes, Land and Mobility

The next three chapters deal with closely related aspects of state-making and governance in the borderlands. Chapter 4 affords a panoramic view of the former through a systematic comparison of the patterns of colonial taxation and expenditure in the Gambia, Senegal, the Gold Coast/British Togoland and French Togoland. By contrast, Chapter 5 offers a much more fine analysis of the challenges associated with the construction of administrative chieftaincies in the light of tax imperatives and the quite different political inheritances within historic frontier zones. Chapter 6 takes up the argument that colonial states were shaped differently through their engagement with the task of regulating the flow of people and goods across borders. Chapter 7 picks up the implications for the ways in which strangers were able to access land across borders and to claim membership of communities outside their home areas. It also deals with the role of land disputes in either easing access to local citizenship or reinforcing the binary opposition between landlord and stranger.

4   Constructing the Compound, Keeping the Gate
A Fiscal Anatomy of Colonial State-Making, c.1900–1940

Taxation is the chief occupation of the state. Nay more, it is the state.[1]
(Edmund Burke)

Having engaged with the simultaneous sedimentation of colonial states and their boundaries over the course of more than half a century, I turn now to consider some of the distinct attributes of the colonial states in question. In a formulation that has commanded widespread support, Fred Cooper depicts African colonial states as carrying out little more than "gatekeeping" functions.[2] In a more elaborated comparison between the British colonies in Africa, Ewout Frankema depicts the West African colonies as 'night watchmen' or 'minimalist' states whereas Kenya leaned more towards the 'extractive' mode.[3] This conveys something of the understated fashion in which states endeavoured to reproduce themselves – that is, through taxing tradable goods at the points of entry and exit. While endorsing this depiction in general, my intention here is to offer some further refinements emerging from a sustained comparison of fiscal processes in the four colonies. My contention is that what it meant to keep the gate differed significantly from one colony to the next; that the relationships between states and their subjects differed substantially as a consequence; and finally, what I call the *border equation* was integral to

---

[1] Quoted in Patrick K. O'Brien, "Fiscal exceptionalism: Great Britain and its European rivals from Civil War to triumph at Trafalgar and Waterloo", in Donald Winch and Patrick K. O'Brien, *The Political Economy of British Historical Experience, 1688–1914* (Oxford: Oxford University Press for British Academy, 2002), p. 263.

[2] "They had weak instruments for entering into the social and cultural realm over which they presided, but they stood astride the intersection of the colonial territory and the outside world." Frederick Cooper, *Africa Since 1940: The Past of the Present* (Cambridge: Cambridge University Press, 2002), p. 5. This formulation bears some resemblance to the 'extraversion' to which Bayart refers, but on a shorter time-scale. Jean-François Bayart, "Africa in the world: a history of extraversion", *African Affairs* 99 (395) 2000. For a history of colonial taxation, see Leigh A. Gardner, *Taxing Colonial Africa: The Political Economy of British Imperialism* (Oxford: Oxford University Press, 2012).

[3] Ewout Frankema, "Colonial taxation and government spending in British Africa, 1880–1940: maximizing revenue or minimizing effort?", *Explorations in Economic History* 48 (1) 2011, pp. 136–47.

shaping the outcomes. There are three indices to which I attach particular weight: the extent to which colonial regimes conceded a voice and/or degree of autonomy to African actors; the overall size and distribution of the tax burden; and the extent to which public goods were widely and evenly dispensed across the colonies. Having projected these elements onto a larger historical canvas, I will return to the local implications in the chapters that follow.

Fencing the Colonial Estate

In attempting to understand why colonial states assumed the shape and form they did, one should remain mindful of the pre-history of these states that was sketched in the previous chapter. The mercantile and urban roots of colonial states constituted part of their genetic code, whereas the inheritance from the erstwhile frontier regions was less immediately obvious but was in reality no less crucial. Here I wish to focus on three specific factors that fed into the making of states in rather different ways. The first is the predisposition of the various regimes, as modified in the light of realities on the ground. This is very apparent with respect to revenue gathering, which was evidently the platform on which all colonial states were constructed. Colonial proconsuls tended to express well-rehearsed positions on both the practical necessity and the intrinsic virtues associated with taxation. These were, in turn, based on distillations of European history. Fundamentally, the introduction of personal taxation was construed as an integral dimension of the civilizing mission itself. In the words of William Ponty, the Governor-General of l'Afrique Occidentale Française (l'AOF), in 1911:

For the native, taxation, far from being the sign of a humiliating servitude, is seen rather as proof that he is beginning to rise on the ladder of humanity, that he has entered on the path to civilization. To ask him to contribute to our common expenses is, so to speak, to elevate him in the social hierarchy.[4]

In other words, Europeans were actually doing Africans a favour by making them pay their way. The French formulation was very close to the position espoused by Frederick Lugard, the architect of Indirect Rule in West Africa. However, Lugard introduced a further refinement, which was that it was above all direct taxes that mattered:

The payment of direct taxes is in Africa, as elsewhere, an unwelcome concomitant of progress. It marks the recognition of the principle that each individual in proportion to his means has an obligation to the State, to which he owes security for life and property, and his increased wealth . . .[5]

---

[4] Quoted, in Alice Conklin, *A Mission to Civilize: The Republican Idea of Empire in France and West Africa 1895–1930* (Stanford: Stanford University Press, 1997), p. 144.
[5] F.D. Lugard, *The Dual Mandate in British Tropical Africa* (Edinburgh and London: Blackwood, 1926), pp. 232–3.

There was more than a crude revenue calculus at work here. Lugard recognized that indirect taxes might be more lucrative and easier to collect, but he considered direct taxes preferable because of their educative effects on the individual.

> The disadvantage of limiting taxation to this source [indirect tax] lies in the fact that, when a further stage of progress has been reached, it becomes difficult to inaugurate those direct contributions towards the cost of the Administration, which are recognised among all civilised nations as justly due from the individual, in proportion to his wealth, and the protection and benefit he receives from the State.[6]

Where direct taxes already existed, Lugard thought they should be improved upon and consolidated into a single payment, but where they did not, they needed to be introduced from scratch. In *The Dual Mandate in Tropical Africa*, Lugard argued specifically against taxes on "a man's hut or cultivated land, to neither of which has the State any right", and insisted instead on the advantage of moving towards some form of income tax.[7]

However, the extent to which taxes were fine-tuned varied in the light of practical exigencies. In Northern Nigeria itself, the attempt to introduce a graduated land tax proved unworkable, resulting eventually in the implementation of a flat-rate assessment.[8] In the Gambia, the British authorities opted early on for the very mode of taxation that Lugard found unpalatable – namely the yard tax – for essentially the same reason. By stark contrast, the retreat of the British from direct taxation in the Gold Coast came as result of having burned their fingers in the 1850s. Colonial regimes did not always learn quickly from their mistakes, but here we have an example of a setback being converted into a deeper insight into colonial governance: namely, that if indirect taxes delivered more revenue, it would be possible for the Gold Coast authorities to find common ground with their African subjects through the provision of a wider range of public goods like roads and schools. What one might regard as a Guggisbergian version of the taxation/governance nexus offered a counterweight in West Africa to the vision outlined by Lugard. This assumes additional significance in light of the fact that Indirect Rule had relatively few champions in the Gold Coast.

The second element is the weight of special interests that bore down upon the structures of decision-making. In a different setting, John Lonsdale and Bruce Berman have argued that the colonial state in Kenya was forged in the process of "coping with contradictions".[9] These contradictions typically took

---

[6] F.D. Lugard, "Memo No 5: Taxation", in *Instructions to Political and Other Officers on Subjects Chiefly Political Administrative* (London: Waterlow and Sons, 1906), p. 86.

[7] Lugard, *Dual Mandate*, p. 237.

[8] Paul E. Lovejoy and Jan S. Hogendorn, *Slow Death for Slavery: The Course of Abolition in Northern Nigeria, 1897–1936* (Cambridge: Cambridge University Press, 1993), pp. 185–98.

[9] John Lonsdale and Bruce Berman, "Coping with contradictions: the development of the colonial state in Kenya, 1895–1914", *Journal of African History* 20 1979, pp. 487–505. See also Bruce

the form of conflicting demands and pressures upon fledgling institutions, reflecting disparate visions of how the colony ought to be configured. The conception of the state as lying at the centre of a field of political forces is the staple of an older literature on the Gold Coast.[10] As I have indicated, the push to the frontier owed much to the aversion of merchants and urban populations to shouldering higher taxes. Once colonial territory had been properly staked out, the question of how the state would pay for itself became a pressing concern. In all of the colonies in question, European merchants represented a well-organized interest group. Unlike African and Lebanese traders, they could call on the active support of Chambers of Commerce in the metropole as well as local variants in the colonies. In Senegal, there were three large companies that held sway: the CFAO (Compagnie Française de l'Afrique de l'Ouest), the SCOA (Société Commerciale Ouest Africaine) and the Compagnie Niger-France (CNF). In addition, there were around ten other more specialized firms that were based in Bordeaux, including Maurel et Prom.[11] The merchants enjoyed a voice within the official structures, but also exploited informal access to the administration at both the local and federal levels. The lack of an export tax on groundnuts was the most obvious manifestation of their success in manipulating these channels of access.

In the Gold Coast, as Rhoda Howard has pointed out, mining companies and the import-export firms like John Holt and the United Africa Company (UAC) were granted formal representation on the Legislative Council, while Chambers of Commerce enjoyed direct access to the Colonial Office through the Joint West Africa Committee.[12] The latter ensured that merchants were in a position to shoot down unfriendly draft legislation and to influence directives emanating

---

Berman, *Control and Crisis in Colonial Kenya: The Dialectic of Domination* (London, Nairobi and Athens: James Currey, Heinemann Kenya and Ohio University Press, 1990), ch. 2.

[10] This literature was heavily inflected by the dependency paradigm but remains useful to this day. See especially Geoffrey Kay (ed.), *The Political Economy of Colonialism in Ghana: Documents and Statistics, 1900–1960* (Cambridge: Cambridge University Press, 1972); and Rhoda Howard, *Colonialism and Underdevelopment in Ghana* (London: Croom Helm, 1978), ch. 5. A more recent analysis of the limits to colonial state ambition is provided in Anne Phillips, *The Enigma of Colonialism: British Policy in West Africa* (London, Bloomington and Indianapolis: Indiana University Press, 1989). Much the same point is made in Gardner, *Taxing Colonial Africa*, p. 242.

[11] Catherine Boone, *Political Topographies of the African State: Territorial Authority and Institutional Choice* (Cambridge: Cambridge University Press, 2003), p. 44.

[12] In 1886, two European and two African unofficial members were appointed to the Legislative Council. One of the Europeans represented the merchants and the other the mining industry. In 1916, a third European unofficial member, representing banking and shipping interests, was added to provide a balance between the mining and merchant representatives who had serious differences. In 1926, the European representation was increased to five: one for a representative of local Chambers of Commerce, one for the Chamber of Mines and three to be appointed by the Governor, but with an anticipated division between banking, shipping and mining. Howard, *Colonialism and Underdevelopment*, pp. 149–50.

from the centre. In general, while indirect taxes were essential to the finances of all the colonial states, the merchants opposed taxes on agricultural exports and preferred import duties for the simple reason that these could be passed on to African consumers. Hence, a cocoa export duty was only introduced in the Gold Coast in 1916, and then in the face of considerable opposition from the merchants who insisted that nothing should be done to discourage African producers from maximizing their production.[13] But the merchants were not the only interests that had to be accommodated. In British West Africa, shipping and banking interests and mining companies came to constitute powerful lobbies in their own right.[14] In the Gold Coast, privileged access to decision-makers on the part of the mining companies helps explain why the sector was relatively lightly taxed, while mining equipment was often exempted from import duty.[15] Moreover, the perverse policy of creating gaps between sections of the trunk roads, in order to force cocoa onto the railways, was intended to defray the costs of a major infrastructural investment designed with the requirements of the mining industry in mind.[16] Mining and trading interests were often diametrically opposed to one another, and no more so when it came to the allocation of African labour. Whereas the mining companies demanded government support in channelling northern labour to their concessions, the merchants recognized that such direct intervention would affect the future of the cocoa sector.[17] Eventually, Guggisberg came down in favour of the primacy of peasant agriculture, and concluded that mining would have to play second fiddle to cocoa, which, he acknowledged, contributed far more to export earnings and government revenues alike.[18] Finally, in some colonies the missionaries were also a force to be reckoned with. In Senegal, Catholic missionaries enjoyed rather little influence outside the southern Casamance and Sine-Saloum, whereas in the Gold Coast the missionaries cemented a much stronger niche – in spite of the fact that most of the missionaries were drawn from other parts of Europe.

Finally, there were important differences in ways in which Africans were incorporated into decision-making processes. In British West Africa, Africans were (s)elected to serve on the Legislative Council from an early point. In the Gold Coast, Africans enjoyed parity with the European 'unofficials' between 1886 and 1916. In that year, they were allocated a plurality of appointed seats:

---

[13] The royalties on mining concessions stood at 5 per cent of profits. Howard, *Colonialism and Underdevelopment*, p. 159, 162.

[14] Howard, *Colonialism and Underdevelopment*, pp. 94–140.

[15] Howard, *Colonialism and Underdevelopment*, p. 159.

[16] Kay, *Political Economy*, pp. 20–25; Howard, *Colonialism and Underdevelopment*, p. 75.

[17] Phillips, *Enigma*, pp. 45–8; Howard, *Colonialism and Underdevelopment*, pp. 201–6; and Jeff Crisp, *The Story of an African Working Class: Ghanaian Miners' Struggles, 1870–1980* (London: James Currey, 1980), ch. 2.

[18] Phillips, *Enigma*, p. 47.

whereas the business interests held four, the chiefs and the intelligentsia received three each. This majority was further increased despite an enlargement in European representation to five in 1926. Under the new constitution, three elected seats were created for Cape Coast, Sekondi and Accra, and a further six were reserved for chiefs in the colony. Although urban elites in the Aborigines Rights Protection Society (ARPS) railed against this weighting in favour of the chiefs, they also shared a common interest in protecting 'native interests'.[19] In Senegal, Africans in the Four Communes of Dakar, Saint-Louis, Gorée and Rufisque were able to thwart French efforts to restrict citizenship entitlements after the First World War.[20] The elected General Council had hitherto advised the Governor, and until 1892 it had controlled the budget for the rest of Senegal. In 1920, the Communes and Protectorate were united under a Lieutenant-Governor, who was to be assisted by a Colonial Council made up of an equal number of French citizens and canton chiefs from the interior. The Council had limited legislative autonomy, but was empowered to deliberate on a range of issues, including taxation, and had the right to intervene with respect to those parts of the budget that were classed as 'non-essential'.[21] Finally, the creation of Councils of Notables in French Togoland similarly created a space in which a minority of Africans could participate in debating the patterns of taxation and spending in the Mandated territory. Whenever issues of taxation or social reform presented themselves, a diverse range of actors sought to influence policy interventions – typically claiming to be championing some version of the greater good. The shifting alliances spanned continents and frequently cut across colour lines. A much older literature about power relations in the colonies repays closer reading, because what it underlines is that colonial states were not simply engines of imperial domination: they were also the foci for lively debates about political morality and the very meaning of public goods in the colonial context.[22] Whether the particular issue was the unequal burden of taxation, curbs on liquor consumption, the need to encourage labour migration, or the freedom to promote religious preferences, institutional reflexes were conditioned through the active pursuit of politics.

---

[19] David Kimble, *A Political History of Ghana, 1850–1928* (Oxford: Clarendon Press, 1963), pp. 441–55. Ashanti and the Northern Territories were not brought into the Legislative Council until 1946.

[20] Conklin, *Mission to Civilize;* G. Wesley Johnson, *The Emergence of Black Politics in Senegal: The Struggle for Power in the Four Communes 1900–1920* (Stanford: Stanford University Press, 1971).

[21] Raymond Leslie Buell, *The Native Problem in Africa*, Vol. 1 (London: Frank Cass, 1965 reprint of 1928 edition), pp. 970–5.

[22] Cases in point would be Kimble, *Political History*, and Johnson, *Emergence*.

The third factor was the success with which colonial administrations were able to achieve a measure of administrative density. Where the bureaucracy was numerically thin and geographically dispersed, as was the case in the Gambia, it was less able to insulate itself from special interests. The level of functional differentiation between branches of the bureaucracy was equally important for the development of clusters of specialist knowledge. In the case of the Gold Coast, the Customs Department was often able to face down representations from the merchants and mining companies because of the concentration of expertise and experience within its ranks. In French Togoland, where manpower was at a premium, specialization was limited because government offices were often fused – and often in ways that were distinctly counter-intuitive. As Buell observed:

In Togo, personnel is reduced to a minimum. The Commandant of the Cercle of Lome has been obliged to act as the Procureur Général, the head of the judicial system of the territory. The Director of Political Affairs in the Secretariat has also been head of the Educational Service, while the direction of the education and veterinary services have been confided to one man.[23]

In the case of l'AOF, an additional factor in the equation was the reality of different bureaucratic scales that also embodied a spatial dimension. The federal government in Dakar reserved substantial powers to itself. The Governor-General nominated members of the civil service across the Federation, held direct responsibility for four technical departments – namely agriculture, posts and telegraphs, public works and sanitary services – and, crucially, exercised control over the Customs service.[24] The federal bureaucracy was also extensive enough to staff specialized offices, such as the Bureau of Muslim Affairs, which collected intelligence on Muslim activities across the l'AOF. The centralization of powers ensured that the federal administration retained considerable leverage over the individual colonies, including Senegal, which was governed from the geographical margins at Saint-Louis. In particular, the attribution of all Customs revenue to the Federation after 1905 minimized some of the scope for special pleading that was commonplace in colonial capitals.

Although open politicking took place in the port cities, there is a substantial literature that demonstrates the manner in which rural interests also exercised an influence on colonial decision-making. The tale of how the Senegalese administration shifted from suspicion of the Muslim brotherhoods towards

[23] Raymond Leslie Buell, *The Native Problem in Africa*, Vol. 2 (London: Frank Cass, 1965 reprint of 1928 edition), p. 290.
[24] Michael Crowder, *West Africa under Colonial Rule* (London: Hutchinson, 1968), p. 178.

striking formal alliances has been recounted in abundant detail.[25] For the Mourides, the alliance was one that permitted a degree of social autonomy to communities of believers in return for the remittance of taxes to the centre. The French administration displayed sensitivity to the concerns of the brotherhoods: for example with respect to the wider distribution of alcohol, which had historically provided an important source of government revenue in Senegal.[26] In the Gambia, the British cultivated their own trusted intermediaries, but there was nothing comparable to the formalized system that prevailed in Senegal.[27] In the Gold Coast, the British had been forced to make some practical concessions to the claim that the colonial state had been co-authored by the African population through the Bond of 1844. Certain chiefs, such as Nana Sir Ofori Atta I of Akyem-Abuakwa, were treated as valuable intermediaries and sat as members of the Legislative Council. Moreover, District Commissioners were not at liberty to treat the chiefs as lowly functionaries, as they did elsewhere. Although many chiefs who fell foul of the authorities were destooled, this required the backing of elders and chief-makers. Conversely, many successful destoolments were effected against chiefs who actually found favour with the authorities. In a manner somewhat akin to French treatment of the Mourides, therefore, the British tacitly accepted that chieftaincy represented a semi-autonomous sphere where the writ of the state did not fully run. This circumscription of state power had an additional consequence, namely that chiefs felt empowered to articulate their own demands for state intervention. Hence, during the great liquor debate of the 1920s, chiefs and missionaries in the Gold Coast joined forces against the trading houses in an attempt to restrict the importation of Dutch gin, alleging that the latter represented a threat to health, fertility and social order.

[25] James F. Searing, 'God Alone is King': Islam and Emancipation in Senegal – The Wolof Kingdoms of Kajoor and Bawol, 1859–1914 (Portsmouth, Oxford and Cape Town: Heinemann, James Currey and David Philip, 2002), ch. 7; David Robinson, Paths of Accommodation: Muslim Societies and French Colonial Authorities in Senegal and Mauritania, 1880–1920 (Oxford and Athens: James Currey and Ohio University Press, 2000); Cheikh Anta Babou, Fighting the Greater Jihad: Amadu Bamba and the Founding of the Muridiyya of Senegal, 1853–1913 (Athens: Ohio University Press, 2007), chs. 5–7. In the second decade of the twentieth century, Sociétés Indigènes de Prévoyance (SIPs) were set up to sell planting material and to rent tools to farmers. Catherine Boone, Merchant Capital and the Roots of State Power in Senegal, 1930–1985 (Cambridge: Cambridge University Press, 1992), pp. 42–3.

[26] At the turn of the century, Senegal was a major importer of French alcohol. Remarkably, Senegal was the third largest importer of bottled claret after Britain and the United States between 1900 and 1904. James Simpson, Creating Wine: The Emergence of a World Industry, 1840–1914 (Princeton and Oxford: Princeton University Press, 2011), p. 124.

[27] David E. Skinner, "The incorporation of Muslim elites into the colonial administrative systems of Sierra Leone, the Gambia and the Gold Coast", Journal of Muslim Minority Affairs 29 (1) March 2009, pp. 96–9.

In this short resumé, what I hope to have established is that – contra Patrick Chabal and Jean-Pascal Daloz[28] – there was in fact considerable variation in the extent to which colonial states were permeated by societal interests. In the Gold Coast, the state was functionally differentiated and relatively dense, but there were also powerful interest groups that jockeyed for influence. Mediating between these conflicting interests, while seeking to remain above the fray, was the everyday task of the central secretariat in Accra. Over the long run, however, these exchanges helped to fashion a sense of collective identity within the bureaucracy that enabled officials to make better sense of their role in relation to the society they sought to govern. Equally, the complex layering of the bureaucracy within l'AOF meant that federal institutions were able to achieve a measure of insulation from interests in the Senegal in spite of the fact that the colony provided the federal capital. In the Gambia and French Togoland, the bureaucratic complex was much more rudimentary, while the influence of the merchants was more obvious. But this was counter-balanced by the fact that in Bathurst most of the commercial establishments were actually French, while British firms like John Holt and the UAC were no less prominent in Lomé. Let us now turn to what difference these permutations made for the structure of taxation.

Distributing the Burden of Taxation

Of all the colonies under review, it is the most difficult to generate a reliable profile for Senegal because so much of the available data relates to the Federation as a whole. The exercise is further complicated because of the steady depreciation in the value of the franc in the decades after the First World War. However, the general patterns are easy enough to discern. Having insulated the metropolitan budget from the costs of running the empire, the second stage involved creating a budget for l'AOF that would be separate from that of the individual colonies.[29] One thing that is abundantly clear is that Senegal was the big loser when Customs revenues were reserved for the federal government in 1905. In the words of Leslie Buell, writing in the late 1920s:

In 1905, the Senegal budget had receipts amounting to five and a half million francs. But the establishment of the federal budget in 1905 took away the customs dues of Senegal and the other colonies, and at one stroke deprived Senegal of seventy-eight per

---

[28] This has been discussed in Chapter 1. Patrick Chabal and Jean-Pascal Daloz, *Africa Works: Disorder as Political Instrument* (London, Oxford and Bloomington: International Africa Institute, James Currey and Indiana University Press, 1999), pp. 11–12.

[29] For an in-depth fiscal history of l'AOF see N'Bueké Adovi Goeh-Akue, "Finances Publiques et Dynamique Sociale en Afrique Noire Sous Influence Française: Le Cas du Togo (1920–1980)", thèse pour le Doctorat d'Histoire et Civilisations, Université Paris VII-Jussieu, December 1992, Chapter 2.

cent of its revenues. In return, the federal government, according to Senegal spokesmen, assumed only thirty-nine per cent of the expenses which these sums had met.[30]

Because Dakar was the main port of entry for much of West Africa, the administration raised much of its Customs revenue there. However, many of the actual goods were destined for neighbouring colonies that would not otherwise have seen any of the revenue collected. Given that Senegal accounted for no less than half of all Customs duties collected in l'AOF in 1926, the consequences of not re-allocating the revenues would have been very serious for the other colonies.[31]

Part of the revenue that was collected at the federal level was initially redistributed to the individual colonies as budget subventions. But by the 1920s, the colonies – especially the wealthier ones such as Senegal and Côte d'Ivoire – were expected to cover their own recurrent expenditure and also to meet many of their infrastructural requirements. Federal expenditure was principally devoted to substantial public works that benefited more than one colony.[32] In addition, the French state ceased offering loans to the African colonies after 1913, which further tied the hands of the Lieutenant-Governors.[33] All of this meant that the Senegalese authorities became reliant upon raising direct taxes to meet their financial obligations. The head tax, or l'impôt personnel, was an annual obligation that fell upon men, women and children over a minimum age that differed from one colony to the next. In Senegal, the age was fixed at 10 years in 1921. The tax itself stood at 5 francs per capita by the outbreak of the First World War, but with the progressive depreciation of the franc – which lost four-fifths of its value between 1914 and 1926 – the nominal rate increased progressively.[34] In addition, there were taxes on firearms, licences, trading activity and government services. In the Casamance in 1914, for example, there were no fewer than seven categories of tax, including a tax on weights and measures, and another on transportation. Other revenue derived from a range of fines, such as one levied on stray cattle.[35] Moreover, there was an annual labour service requirement, or prestation, of four days that could be remitted in cash, as well as compulsory

---

[30] Buell, *Native Problem*, Vol. I, p. 933.
[31] The total Customs duties collected were 87.9 million francs, of which Senegal accounted for 42.3 million. Buell, *Native Problem*, Vol. I, p. 934.
[32] Buell, *Native Problem*, Vol. 1, p. 939.   [33] Buell, *Native Problem*, Vol. I, p. 936.
[34] Buell, *Native Problem*, Vol. I, p. 1035. The figure for depreciation of the franc comes from Catherine Coquery-Vidrovitch, "The colonial economy of the former French, Belgian and Portuguese zones 1914–35", in A. Adu Boahen (ed.), *General History of Africa VII: Africa Under Colonial Domination 1880–1935* (Paris and London: UNESCO and Heinemann, 1985), p. 366.
[35] "Rapport mensuel, Cercle de la Casamance 1914", section entitled 'Rendement des impôts' ANS 2G 14/51 "Casamance, Rapports mensuels d'ensemble 1914".

military service. However, the head tax was by far the greatest contributor to revenues at this time. Of the 888,812 francs raised in the Casamance in 1914, no less than 839,286 francs derived from the head tax.

Across l'AOF, the amount raised in federal taxes was initially lower than the amount collected in direct taxes. Hence in 1926, federal receipts stood at 235 million francs, while local budgets that were funded out of direct taxes added up to 284 million francs.[36] That same year, 190.5 million of federal revenue was accounted for by Customs duties, of which Senegal contributed 100.7 million – making the colony the largest contributor to the Customs receipts by some margin.[37] Over time, the relative balance shifted towards indirect taxes almost certainly because these were easier to collect in the context of expanding international trade.[38] By 1938, the contribution of direct taxes had fallen back to 31.0 per cent of total revenues across l'AOF, of which the greater part (around 25 per cent of the total) derived from the head tax.[39] This was still a considerably higher proportion than in Kenya, where direct taxes only made up 18.6 per cent and taxes specifically on Africans 14.1 per cent of revenues. Direct taxes were somewhat higher in Southern Rhodesia at 38.6 per cent of revenue, but only 11.7 per cent were derived from the African population.[40] Given that settler colonies were characterized by strong local pressures to squeeze Africans, the ability of the French to extract around a third of their revenue from direct taxes is certainly noteworthy. The individual tax burden in the settler colonies was probably higher than in l'AOF, although a meaningful comparison would need to take account of the differential access to income between cash crop and other zones.[41] However, to depict the colonial state in l'AOF as performing purely gatekeeping functions arguably underestimates the extractive 'achievements' of French administration.

---

[36] Buell, *Native Problem*, Vol. I, p. 935. Gardner provides a figure for Kenya of around 15 per cent, accounted for specifically by the hut and poll tax in 1937. In 1924, the figure was 27 per cent, having declined from a peak of 38 per cent in 1921. Gardner, *Taxing Colonial Africa*, pp. 96, 110–11.

[37] Gouvernement Général de l'Afrique Occidentale Française, *Bulletin Mensuel de l'Agence Economique de l'Afrique Occidentale Française*, No 77, May 1927, p. 100.

[38] Virginia Thompson and Richard Adloff, "French economic policy in tropical Africa", in Peter Duignan and L.H. Gann (eds.), *Colonialism in Africa, 1870–1960 – Volume 4: The Economics of Colonialism* (Cambridge: Cambridge University Press, 1975), p. 135.

[39] Lord Hailey, *An African Survey, Revised 1956* (London, New York and Toronto: Oxford University Press, 1957), p. 684.

[40] Hailey, *African Survey*, p. 685.

[41] Because of the travails of the franc and the substantial regional variations in wealth, it is difficult to generalize about the scale of the burden on ordinary families. Manchuelle estimates that direct taxes consumed about 11 per cent of total income from economic activity in the cercle of Nioro (Mali) in the early 1920s. François Manchuelle, *Willing Migrants: Soninke Labor Diasporas, 1848–1960* (Athens and London: James Currey and Ohio University Press, 1997), p. 157. Searing makes an estimate of about 10 per cent of gross cash income in Bawol around 1910/11. Searing, *'God Alone'*, p. 255.

Coquery-Vidrovitch's rule-of thumb – "25% from customs revenues and 25% from the head tax" – suggests a pretty close engagement with rural society in l'AOF in the interwar years.[42]

The French tax system was in many ways highly regressive. First of all, it was not simply the case that the metropolitan governments were unwilling to subsidize colonial expenditure. To some extent the colonies actually supported France. According to Buell:

In 1926, the Minister at Paris increased the military contribution of French West Africa to the home country from 1,800,000 to 7,500,000 francs. The federation expends another 3,500,000 francs in behalf of France upon such items as military pensions for native soldiers, and the reimbursement of the Mother Country for advances in regard to the Thiès-Niger railway. In addition, the budget of each colony supports military bureaus and other military services, at a total expense of 4,793,000 francs. The Dakar Government estimates that in 1926 the colonies expended another 1,913,000 francs on expenditure which would normally be borne by the home government.[43]

Buell calculated that l'AOF actually paid 19.4 million francs into the metropolitan budget in 1927.[44] A major source of these payments was the obligation to contribute to the military expenditure of the metropole, which was justified on the basis that colonial defence was a major call on French resources. Needless to say, some of the costs were incurred in deploying military force to compel Africans to pay their taxes in the first place – as we will see in relation to the Casamance in Chapter 5. Secondly, the opposition of the merchants to an export duty on groundnuts meant that import duties became the principal source of indirect taxes. Thirdly, the fact that nearly a quarter of all revenue derived from head taxes meant that the poorest regions and sections of the population contributed disproportionately. Conversely, the use of federal funds to cover infrastructural investments meant that the French merchants, and to some extent Lebanese traders, were the principal beneficiaries – alongside those Senegalese who could engage in the cultivation of cash crops. The swathes of the colony that were located away from the main lines of communication, including most of the Casamance, derived little benefit – although this has to be weighed against the ability of border populations to evade the full thrust of taxation.

Finally, because the citizens of the Four Communes were granted a political voice, they were also able to deflect most of the burden onto the rural populace. James Searing makes the point that only the heads of household and single employed adults in the Communes incurred the tax obligation of 5 francs before the First World War, while *l'impôt* fell upon multiple members of the

---

[42] Coquery-Vidrovitch, "Colonial economy", p. 368.
[43] Buell, *Native Problem*, Vol. I, p. 939.   [44] Buell, *Native Problem*, Vol. I, p. 930.

same household in the villages.[45] Buell also observed that while citizens received individual tax receipts, there was considerable scope for chiefly manipulation.[46] The inequitable distribution of the tax burden did not go unnoticed. Buell indicates that simmering discontent amongst the chiefly representatives on the Colonial Council culminated in an open rift in 1923, when they backed an official proposal to increase registration taxes in the urban centres.[47] Amidst mutual recriminations, the proposal was eventually withdrawn. If taxation is normally a pretty reliable indicator of where power lies, it is clear that in Senegal it resided with French merchant houses and the citizens of the Four Communes. In this there was a good measure of continuity with the nineteenth century.

The dynamic in French Togoland, which was never considered an integral part of the Federation, was significantly different. The Mandated territory remained financially autonomous, even during the 1930s when the Lieutenant-Governor of Dahomey – and subsequently the Governor-General – were formally placed in control of the territory.[48] The major priority for the French administration in 1920 was to render Togoland financially self-sufficient as quickly as possible. As a consequence, many of the direct taxes that had been allowed to lapse during the war years were re-introduced, while the authorities sought to maximize their return from Customs duties. Metropolitan subventions were acquired in the first few years – while the authorities managed the transition from the widespread use of sterling to recognition of the franc as the sole legal tender – but these peaked in 1923. Thereafter, French Togoland depended mostly on its own resources. Crucially, the Customs revenues that were collected in French Togoland were reserved for exclusive use within the territory, although a lengthy debate about harmonization of duties with neighbouring Dahomey led to the introduction of the same schedule of duties prevailing in the rest of the l'AOF in 1931.[49]

The French authorities aimed to maximize the advantages that came with geographical proximity to the Gold Coast. Although they failed to persuade the

---

[45] Searing, 'God Alone', p. 258. The privilege of being a citizen involved being spared from compulsory labour obligations, but not personal and property taxes. In the late 1920s, citizens paid a personal tax of 12 francs and 6 per cent tax on the rental value of urban property in the Communes. Buell, *Native Problem*, Vol. I, p. 1036, footnote 5.

[46] A lump sum was imposed on each village, on the basis of the last enumeration, which gave some scope to chiefs to vary the burden amongst their subjects who often did not receive receipts. Buell, *Native Problem*, Vol. I, p. 1036.

[47] Buell, *Native Problem*, Vol. I, pp. 976–9.

[48] In 1934, the Commissaire de la République was located in Dahomey, but was assisted by an *Administrateur Supérieur* in Lomé. The latter position remained when control passed to the Governor-General in Dakar. Robert Cornevin, *Histoire du Togo* (Paris: Editions Berger-Levrault, 1962), pp. 227–8.

[49] Cornevin, *Histoire*, p. 262. Dahomey itself was only brought into line in 1936.

British to dispense altogether with the Customs frontier between the Mandated territories, both sides recognized that British Togoland would depend on the Kpalimé railway and the Lomé port facilities for some time to come.[50] Because Lomé provided a valuable stream of Customs revenues, this enabled the French administration to display a more sanguine attitude towards direct taxation – which underlines the centrality of the border to institutional consolidation in Togoland. This was influenced in part also by the need to convince the Permanent Mandates Commission that taxes on Togolanders were not too onerous. The system of direct taxation was modelled on that of l'AOF, but the important difference was that *l'impôt* applied only to adult males in Togoland. There was also a range of other taxes – including one on bicycles and another on firearms – as well as levies covering health and hygiene, and various licences. The most significant innovation was the introduction of a four-tiered income-based tax in Lomé and Anecho, which hinted at a Senegalese-style distinction between urban citizens and rural subjects.[51]

In many respects, the state in French Togoland was created much more in the mould of a gatekeeper state. According to Buell, the real value of trade increased by more than half between the end of German rule and 1925. However, government revenues were only about 60 per cent of those in the period before the war. Part of the reason was that the authorities had decided not to pursue direct taxation very aggressively – certainly by comparison with their German predecessors. At 4.8 francs per capita, *l'impôt* represented about half of the current rate in l'AOF at the time when Buell was writing. Table 4.1, which is distilled from the data of N'Bueké Adovi Goeh-Akue, demonstrates that the contribution of all direct taxes was relatively high in the early years of the Mandate, peaking at 28.4 per cent of recurrent revenue in 1922, falling back in the relatively prosperous years of the mid-1920s and then rising again at the start of the Depression to around 25 per cent in 1930. In 1938, direct taxes receded to 19.9 per cent of total revenues, which was a considerably smaller percentage than in l'AOF where they amounted to 31 per cent.[52] Indirect taxes assumed a greater significance over time, but with a pronounced weighting towards import duties as befitted an *entrepôt* state in the making. In 1928, when the total raised in indirect tax was some 20.7 million francs, around 18.2 million thereof derived from import duties.[53] The rest was attributable to duties on agricultural exports, notably on cocoa, coffee and palm products. In effect, therefore, the finances of the territory depended

---

[50] Cornevin, *Histoire*, p. 262.   [51] Buell, *Native Problem*, Vol. II, pp. 318–19.

[52] Hailey, *African Survey*, p. 684.

[53] Report of French to League of Nations, 1934, quoted in Silivi d'Almeida-Ekué, *La révolte des Loméennes 24–25 January 1933* (Lomé: Les Nouvelles Editions Africaines du Togo, 1992), p. 29.

Table 4.1 *French Togoland, revenue and expenditure, 1922–1935 (millions francs)*

Year	Total revenue	Total recurrent revenue	Direct taxes	Direct tax as % of recurrent revenue	Indirect taxes	Indirect tax as % of recurrent revenue	Other receipts as recurrent revenue, incl. subvention
1920	2.19	2.19	0.08	3.65%	0.76	34.70%	1.35
1921	4.32	4.32	1.13	26.16%	1.71	39.58%	1.48
1922	4.26	4.26	1.21	28.40%	2.28	53.52%	0.77
1923	13.51	13.41	2.61	19.46%	5.86	43.70%	4.94
1924	17.67	15.47	3.04	19.65%	10.29	66.52%	2.14
1925	33.63	20.43	3.78	18.5%	14.03	75.84%	2.62
1926	37.90	28.10	5.33	18.96%	19.27	68.58%	3.50
1927	47.63	33.78	5.79	17.14%	21.70	64.24%	6.29
1928	49.70	32.89	7.44	22.62%	20.70	62.94%	4.75
1929	46.90	31.65	7.48	23.63%	22.15	69.98%	2.02
1930	48.84	31.79	8.40	26.42%	20.42	64.23%	2.97

Source: calculated from N'Bueké Adovi Goeh-Akue, "Finances Publiques et Dynamique Sociale en Afrique Noire Sous Influence Française: Le Cas du Togo (1920–1980)", thèse pour le Doctorat d'Histoire et Civilisations, Université Paris VII-Jussieu, December 1992, table A.3, p. 672.

overwhelmingly upon taxes on goods that were consumed in Togoland. However, increasing returns from import duties needs to be viewed in the light of a vigorous re-export trade across the Gold Coast border. Although it is impossible to estimate with accuracy, many of the commodities that were taxed at the port of entry ended up being sold on to consumers in British Togoland and the Gold Coast. The authorities in Lomé were well aware that a lively contraband trade existed, especially as the British regularly complained that the firms in Lomé turned a blind eye to the activities of their employees. This was especially true of spirits and tobacco, which were smuggled in prodigious quantities into British Togoland and the Gold Coast.[54] In effect, therefore, the ability to tax the population relatively lightly hinged on the immersion of French Togoland in a system of trade that was largely illicit. The French kept the gate at Lomé but chose to leave it wide open along the western boundary. The reason is easy enough to understand: the fiscal reproduction of the state itself depended upon the contraband trade.

---

[54] Paul Nugent, *Smugglers, Secessionists and Loyal Citizens on the Ghana-Togo Frontier: The Lie of the Borderlands Since 1914* (Oxford and Athens: James Currey and Ohio University Press, 2002), ch. 3.

The fiscal profile of the Gambia was comparable to that of French Togoland. Here too, the authorities set out with the intention of raising a significant part of the revenue through direct taxes, but eventually followed the line of least resistance. The British were keen to assert their rights based on conquest and insisted that they were taking over the right of extraction that has previously attached to the former rulers. As early as 1862, a Kombo Land Revenue Ordinance had imposed a tax on land and dwellings in British Kombo and legalized compulsory labour in road building.[55] In 1895 the yard tax was introduced in the newly acquired territory, which demanded less administrative effort. It was levied on the basis of 4s for a yard consisting of not more than four huts and an additional 1s for an additional hut occupied by a member of the family – or 2s. for a hut occupied by a stranger.[56] This basic formula remained in place, although Protectorate Ordinance No. 2 of 1935 increased the base rate to 5s and to 8s for a stranger dwelling.[57] In addition, a range of special licences was imposed on the ownership of dogs, canoes and trade – the latter of which was glossed as a continuation of the demands levied by chiefs on traders in the nineteenth century. The amount contributed by yard and stranger tax was by no means negligible, but it never amounted to more than a fraction of the revenue that derived from Customs duties. In 1913, total government revenue stood at £124,995, of which £97,691 (or 78.2 per cent) derived from Customs duties and £10,614 (8.49 per cent) from direct taxes in the Protectorate. Around half of that rather modest amount was derived from the yard tax. The amount collected through the yard and stranger tax declined in the 1920s but stabilized at around 5 per cent of revenues in the 1930s. This pales into insignificance with the 25 per cent raised across l'AOF, and even by comparison with French Togoland. Finally, given the opposition of the merchant houses to export taxes, it is telling that the revenue derived from the export duty on groundnuts was generally less important for public finances. The important exception was during the Depression when import duties plummeted and the groundnut duties briefly accounted for a third of revenues (see Table 4.2). However, this did not last and in 1935 the groundnut duty contributed only £22,358, or 9.1 per cent of total revenue.[58] Strikingly, this was far less than half of the £54,689 (22.3 per cent) derived from the import duty on the African-controlled import trade in kola nuts.

There was one significant difference in what motivated the authorities in the Gambia. Whereas in French Togoland the administration was sensitive to

---

[55] J.M. Gray, *A History of the Gambia* (Cambridge: Cambridge University Press, 1940), p. 482.

[56] Francis Bisset Archer, *The Gambia Colony and Protectorate: An Official Handbook*, new impression of 1906 1st edn. (London: Frank Cass, 1967), p. 122.

[57] Harry A. Gailey, *A History of the Gambia* (London: Routledge and Kegan Paul, 1964), p. 132.

[58] In 1938, it fell further to 8.6 per cent. Hailey, *African Survey*, p. 682.

Table 4.2 *Contribution of indirect taxes to Gambian government revenue (£000s)*

Year	Total revenue	Yard and stranger tax	Yard and stranger tax as % of revenue	Import duty	Import duty as % of revenue	Export duty on groundnuts	Export duty on groundnuts as % of revenue
1915	92.3	6.4	6.9%	33.5	36.3%	32.0	34.7%
1920	268.8	7.8	2.9%	174.5	64.9%	26.6	9.9%
1925	189.0	7.3	3.9%	65.4	34.6%	46.1	24.4%
1930	216.7	11.1	5.1%	65.6	30.2%	74.3	34.3%
1935	245.5	11.4	4.6%	151.7	61.8%	22.4	9.1%

Source: Gambia, Blue Books, various years.

criticism of the head tax, in the Gambia the primary consideration was competition for population, as we will see in the coming chapters. The British administration endeavoured to set the yard tax at a rate that would undercut *l'impôt* in Senegal and thus encourage settlers to relocate to their side of the border. The calculation was that a greater number of cultivators would translate into a larger volume of groundnuts produced. However, because the export tax was relatively small, it was actually the purchasing power that came with this particular cash crop that was the crucial factor. Although the price for groundnuts was often higher in Senegal, the fact that consumer goods were often more accessible in the wharf towns along the Gambia river meant that Senegalese farmers often preferred to cross the border with their crops in order to purchase valued items. The Gambian exchequer gained twice over: from the export duties levied on the groundnuts when they were despatched from Banjul and from the import duties levied on the goods as they entered the Gambia. The authorities in l'AOF were not a little vexed by the attendant loss of revenue, but ironically it was French firms who were the primary beneficiaries of this cross-border trade. There were, of course, other factors in the commercial equation: this included the prevailing exchange rates, which had an important bearing on the price of goods imported through Dakar, and the range and quality of consumer goods that could be sourced from France and Britain respectively. For example, British textiles were especially valued and conferred an advantage on Bathurst. The overall conclusion to be drawn is that, even more than in French Togoland, the very reproduction of the Gambian state came to hinge on keeping the gate open. Fully 70.9 per cent of Gambian government revenue in 1935 derived from Customs duties as against only 23.9 per cent in l'AOF. The fiscal profile was therefore radically different from that of Senegal. As in French Togoland, the fiscal balancing act turned on a

Table 4.3 *Contributions of indirect taxes to Gold Coast government revenue* (*£000s*)

Year	Total revenue	Import duties	Import duties as % of revenue	Export duties	Export duties as % of revenue	Other	Other as % of revenue
1900	383	281	73.4%	–	0	102	26.6%
1905	586	334	57.0%	–	0	252	43.0%
1910	1,007	611	66.2%	–	0	396	33.8%
1915	1,456	828	56.9%	–	0	628	43.1%
1920	3,722	1,711	46.0%	571	15.3%	1,440	38.7%
1925	4,116	2,165	52.6%	274	6.7%	1,677	40.7%
1930	2,671	1,427	53.4%	296	11.1%	948	35.5%
1935	3,268	1,858	56.9%	539	16.5%	871	26.6%
1940	3,869	1,208	31.2%	1,328	34.3%	1,333	34.5%

Source: G.B. Kay (ed.), The Political Economy of Colonialism in Ghana: A Collection of Documents and Statistics, 1900–1960 (Cambridge: Cambridge University Press, 1972), table 24a, pp. 348–57.

trade that was very largely illicit in nature. In either case, it is no exaggeration to conclude that the margins were what kept the centre in business.

In the Gold Coast, the crucial determinant of fiscal policy was the perceived aversion to direct taxation. Hence nothing comparable to the yard or head tax was even attempted in the twentieth century, with one exception. Guggisberg did broach the question of municipal rates in the mid-1920s, as part of a package in which elected Municipal Councils would provide the building blocks for representation in the central legislature. However, this provoked such a storm of protest that it was necessary to beat a hasty retreat once again.[59] The authorities therefore concentrated squarely on the revenues that accrued from Customs duties. As Table 4.3 reveals, import duties provided well over half of all government revenues over the first half of the twentieth century. In the relative boom years between 1925 and 1929, import duties averaged £2.1 million of which no less than £1.3 million was collected on imported alcohol – notably Dutch gin. This tidy little earner was placed in jeopardy at the end of the decade when the Gold Coast authorities bowed to pressure from the anti-liquor lobby to begin phasing out gin imports. The impact on revenues was potentially disastrous and the Customs Department backed the call from the merchants that the decision be rescinded.[60] The second greatest contributor to the exchequer, namely imported textiles and

[59] Kimble, *A Political History*, p. 447.
[60] Nugent, *Smugglers, Secessionists and Loyal Citizens*, pp. 82–7.

clothing, contributed a mere £291,000 on average. The defeat of the anti-liquor lobby underlined the institutional dominance of Customs within the Gold Coast administration, to a far greater extent than in other African colonies.

Export duties, which fell heavily on cocoa and to a lesser extent on minerals, only became operative in 1916, but thereafter accounted for a steadily increasing share of the total. However, the ability of the merchants to fight their corner was apparent at the start of the Great Depression. With the revenue from gin imports in jeopardy, attention focused on increasing the cocoa export duty. The Chambers of Commerce in Britain lobbied the Colonial Office through the Joint West Africa Committee, arguing that export duties were much less desirable than import duties.

It is doubtless within your knowledge that the West African Section of this Chamber, in conjunction with the West African Sections of the Liverpool and Manchester Chambers of Commerce – acting through the Joint West Africa Committee – has in years past consistently submitted to the Governments of the various British West African Colonies the view that export duties on produce are wrong in principle, discourage production, and are borne by only a limited portion of the population. The Joint West Africa Committee has submitted as an alternative that in all cases where further Revenue is required, the better method is to impose import duties on goods entering the Colony. Such duties are naturally spread over a larger proportion of the population than export duties on native produce.[61]

Ultimately, the merchants had their way because the contribution of import duties to government revenues actually increased in the 1930s, while export duties rose only marginally. The remainder of the revenues derived from a variety of sources, including railway receipts in the early decades, royalties and returns on investments and loans. The overall picture that emerges, therefore, is of a state that depended on taxing African consumption, but one that also became more assiduous at soliciting revenue from other sources, including the mining industry (Table 4.4). The result was the Gold Coast became significantly less dependent upon import duties than its counterpart in the Gambia and French Togoland, although the total contribution of Customs duties was of the same order. If this was a gatekeeper or 'night watchman' state – and clearly it was much more of the former than Senegal – it was one that also enjoyed some success in diversifying its revenue streams. But none of this should obscure the fundamental point that the fiscal reproduction of the state hinged on being able to regulate the flow of commodities through the ports and across the land borders. With Lomé just next door, the threat that an orgy of smuggling would undermine state finances lent further clout to the Customs Department and imparted a particular strategic significance to the eastern border.

---

[61] National Archives (UK), CO 96/693/14 "Customs Queries and Protests", W.J. Eales, Secretary, London Chamber of Commerce, to Secretary of State for Colonies (31 January 1930).

Table 4.4 *Revenue in the Gold Coast by five-year intervals, 1900–1930 (£000s)*

Year	Total revenue	Import duties	Export duties	Royalties	Railways
1900	383	281	–	1	130
1905	586	334	–	9	249
1910	1,007	611	–	18	556
1915	1,456	828	–	26	736
1920	3,722	1,711	571	23	1,106
1925	4,116	2,165	274	23	–
1930	2,671	1,427	296	72	–
1935	3,268	1,858	539	72	–
1940	3,869	1,208	1,328	122	–

Source: Kay (ed.), Political Economy of Colonialism, table 24a, pp. 348–57.

Tending the Colonial Estate

The picture that I have presented is incomplete without addressing the matter of expenditure. Inevitably, much of the expenditure was concentrated on infrastructure for ports, roads and railways that were deemed essential to rendering the various colonies viable. But over time, and to varying degrees, states placed a greater emphasis upon social expenditure. Apart from the very practical considerations shaping expenditure patterns, infrastructure also served to impart material substance to the state. Customs posts, barracks and hospitals provided visible evidence of colonial states 'at work', while roads, railways, bridges and wharfs drew these into a spatial arrangement and a scalar hierarchy. What mattered politically is that physical infrastructure linked villages to District and Regional/Provincial headquarters and the latter to the colonial capitals. Typically, the priority for government was linking nodes within designated colonial boundaries rather than building infrastructure that traversed them. This was most starkly apparent in the Senegambia where colonial infrastructure was moulded to a rather unusual map. In the process of creating administrative and commercial centres, other spaces were actively marginalized.

Once again, it is helpful to begin this comparative discussion with Senegal and its unique position within l'AOF. The first point to underline is that fiscal conservatism was a hallmark of French rule in the first half of the twentieth century. Buell calculated that while total revenue had increased between 1913 and 1926, the real value of receipts measured in gold was about the same. However, real expenditure had actually halved, which he attributed in part to falling salaries and reduced 'native labour' costs.[62] The implication is

---

[62] Buell, *Native Problem*, Vol. I, p. 935.

that the amount of money that was available for spending in colonies such as Senegal was limited – and almost certainly smaller than it had been before the war. During the Great Depression of the early 1930s, there was a further contraction. But what remains noteworthy is that the federal government maintained a consistent surplus of revenue over expenditure, which Buell estimated at nearly half of total federal expenditure in 1924.[63] One of the quirks of a system in which Customs revenue accrued to the federal government, whose spending was also concentrated in quite specific domains, was that there was an inherent bias towards expenditure on public works and administration. Most of the infrastructural spending was concentrated on roads and port facilities, with a view to facilitating the evacuation of cash crops from central Senegal.[64] As for the administration, the French employed more administrators per head of population than the British did, even if the balance was somewhat offset by lower salaries.[65] In Senegal, the density of the administration was relatively high. Within l'AOF, there were only more administrators per square kilometre in Guinea and Dahomey. On the other hand, the ratio of administrators to population was only more favourable in Côte d'Ivoire, Mauritania and Dahomey.[66] Social spending was a casualty because it was disproportionately funded from local budgets.[67] According to Buell, only 12.5 per cent of total expenditure in l'AOF – that is from the federal and local budgets counted together – was allocated to 'native welfare' in 1926. In British West Africa the average was 15.5 per cent, while for the Gold Coast it reached 17.9 per cent. When expenditure for Senegal alone is considered, 'native welfare' amounted to only 11.4 per cent.[68] The downstream consequences are readily apparent in the specific instance of education. In 1926, only around 35,000 students attended school across the whole of l'AOF (0.3 per cent of the total population), which was only 5,000 more than for the single colony of the Gold Coast.[69] Although Senegal performed much

---

[63] Buell, *Native Problem*, Vol I, p. 937.

[64] There were few significant additions to the rail network after the initial outlays.

[65] Michael Crowder estimated that in the 1930s, the ratio of administrators to ruled was 1:27,000 in l'AOF, but only 1:54,000 in Nigeria. Michael Crowder, "The white chiefs of tropical Africa", in L.H. Gann and Peter Duignan (eds.), *Colonialism in Africa, 1870–1960, II: The History and Politics of Colonialism, 1914–1960* (Cambridge, New York and London: Cambridge University Press, 1970), table 4, p. 329.
For a comparison, see A.H.M. Kirk-Greene, "The thin white line: the size of the British colonial service in Africa", *African Affairs* 79 (314) 1980, pp. 33–8.

[66] Buell, Vol. I, *Native Problem*, p. 984.

[67] Buell, *Native Problem*, Vol. I, pp. 941–2; Vol. II, pp. 208–9.

[68] Buell, *Native Problem*, Vol. II, pp. 208–9. Buell adopted a rather liberal definition of 'native welfare', including agriculture, forestry and veterinary services alongside medical and educational provision.

[69] Of the Senegalese total, 5,688 were pupils in mission schools. Buell, *Native Problem*, Vol. II, pp. 54, 64.

better than the average, there was little formal schooling outside of the Four Communes that was not specifically provided by the missionaries.

The pattern of expenditure clearly favoured urban areas. Although the Four Communes were required to levy additional rates to cover services, some heads of expenditure – including education, policing and European salaries – were transferred to the colonial budget.[70] Schooling and medical facilities were overwhelmingly concentrated in the Communes themselves, where they met the demands of the citizens. In addition, the running of Dakar was heavily subsidized by the rest of l'AOF, which was justified on the basis of the essential functions it performed. In Dakar, 29.5 per cent of total expenditure in 1926 was devoted to social services, which suggests that the needs of the European population, and to a lesser extent African citizens, were treated as the priority.[71] While rural populations paid most of the taxes, they received very few of the benefits in the shape of schools and medical facilities. The inputs from the agriculture, veterinary and forestry departments – which Buell included in 'native welfare' – cut both ways in that any services they performed for the African population have to be weighed against the coercive manner in which these were often delivered.

In French Togoland, where the structure of public finances was significantly different, the patterns of expenditure also varied from those in l'AOF. The French administration kept its administrative expenses to a minimum and financed most of its public works out of accumulated surpluses. The administration was permitted to bank these in a reserve fund that was used to finance public works, and in 1931 the territory was allowed to raise a loan to cover an extension of the railway to the north as well as items of social expenditure.[72] The structural weakness was that public finances were heavily dependent upon import duties that were acutely sensitive to the trade cycle. Nevertheless, while direct tax rates were much lower than in l'AOF, Buell observed that 27.7 per cent of expenditure was devoted to 'native welfare', which was more than double that in l'AOF.[73] Much like in neighbouring Dahomey, mission schools bore part of the burden, but considerable public resources were channelled into education. In 1926, 5.3 per cent of total expenditure, and 28.1 per cent of the tax levied directly upon the Togolese population, was dedicated to education. During the Depression years, the relative proportions increased and then settled at 5.9 per cent and 21.4 per cent respectively in 1935.[74] Expenditure on medicine and hygiene represented even greater commitments, consuming 20 per cent of the total budget and 74 per cent of the tax levied directly on Togolanders in 1935.[75] There was certainly a bias towards Lomé and the south

---

[70] Buell, *Native Problem*, Vol. I, p. 961.
[71] Buell observed that Dakar levied no taxes of its own. Buell, *Native Problem*, Vol. I, p. 962.
[72] Cornevin, *Histoire*, p. 246.   [73] Buell, *Native Problem*, Vol II, p. 291.
[74] Cornevin, *Histoire*, p. 246.   [75] Cornevin, *Histoire*, p. 269.

of the territory, but this was probably less extreme than in Senegal. This has a direct bearing on the two case studies that I am developing in detail. Whereas there was very little to see for colonial taxation in the Casamance, in the shape of roads or schools, the colonial state materialized itself in a more visible manner in southern French Togoland.

In the Gambia, fiscal caution was a reflex that was conditioned in part by strict orders from London and in part by lingering worries about the very viability of the colony. In the later nineteenth century, the authorities had struggled to balance revenue and expenditure, but after the colonial enclosure in the early 1890s, revenues had regularly exceeded expenditure – and often by substantial margins as a result of rising Customs receipts. In 1913, for example, total revenue came to £124,995, whereas expenditure amounted to a mere £67,405.[76] The Gambian authorities generally preferred to bank the surpluses and draw on the interest rather than engaging in significant outlays – except for making necessary improvements to port and wharf facilities. This reluctance to dig more deeply struck the authorities in Dakar as perverse despite their own conservatism. Given the French obsession with public works – for institutional reasons already indi-cated – the apparent inactivity of the Gambian authorities seemed to defeat the whole object of colonialism, namely *mise en valeur*. But the Gambian authorities were trapped within the logics of their own fiscal systems. In 1912, Henry Fenwick Reeve, who had served on the 1895 Boundary Commission, provoked some debate by publishing a book that in a handful of pages – sandwiched between sections dealing with history and topography – argued that the British could display more urgency in countering French designs on the Gambia.[77] In a reaction to what was held to reflect the views of many British officials, the French Consul in Bathurst – a merchant and by no means an Anglophobe – attempted to capture what he imagined to be a cardinal difference of colonial philosophy:

Contrary to the fact of the French character, [that is] inclined to criticize his national patrimony, the Englishman generally has only admiration for that which is English; he is extremely self-interested and does not make an expense of [in?] the public interest unless there is a certain profit. One can say that the Gambia is today much what she was before – no important work has been accomplished except for the digging of the Kayage barre . . . From the point of view of instruction, the Englishman does very little for the native who is nevertheless attached to him because he respects his customs and traditions. The French methods of colonization are very different from the English processes. It seems without doubt, however, that the French administration – and this is to the credit of our race – develops in his sphere of influence civilizing qualities,

---

[76] *Gambia Blue Books, 1914.*

[77] It is difficult to conceive of a less polemical text. The title pretty much says it all. See Henry Fenwick Reeve, *The Gambia, Its History Ancient, Medieval and Modern Together with Its Geographical, Geological and Ethnographic Condition and a Description of the Birds, Beasts and Fishes Found Therein* (New York: Negro Universities Press, 1969, reprint of 1912 original), pp. 106–10.

intelligent initiative and professional capacity superior to those that one witnesses in spheres placed beneath English administration.[78]

In a word, the British were habitually lethargic as well as overly self-regarding.

After the First World War, the British government was reluctant to do more than to hold out against French demands by appearing to be interested in the Gambia:

> I am to inform you that Mr. Churchill does not consider it necessary or desirable to make a further statement, as you suggest, to the effect that 'the Gambia will ever remain a part of the British Empire', but that you should proceed on that assumption and take all possible steps to develop the resources of the Colony. One means of effecting this would doubtless be a judicious programme of public works, but in considering how the funds are to be provided for this purpose you must of course bear in mind the possibility of a shrinkage in revenue . . .[79]

The inclination to play safe was accentuated by a serious deterioration in public finances (Table 4.5). The historic dominance of French commercial interests had led to a situation in which the franc was widely used as a unit of currency in the Gambia. As early as 1843, the French silver five-franc coin – known confusingly as the dollar – had been recognized as legal tender and was governed by a fixed exchange rate against the pound. But the falling international price of silver after 1870 created an escalating problem of overvaluation. When the franc was devalued in 1921, the net result was that the silver dollar lost much of its value in Senegal, while continuing to be governed by the official exchange rate in the Gambia. This created an overwhelming incentive for speculators to acquire coins in Senegal and then to offload them across the border.[80] Under pressure from the British government, the Gambian administration was compelled to demonetize the dollar and to insist on the exclusive use of alloy coins distributed by the West African Control Board (WACB), which had been extremely unpopular up until this point. There remained the question of who would pick up the tab for the losses incurred in effecting the transition, which amounted to £189,190 – a massive sum considering that total government revenue for 1921 amounted to only £183,210.[81] The British Treasury made it abundantly clear that it had no intention of doing so and the merchants, some of whom had been freely speculating in currency, were equally unresponsive. The upshot was that the Gambian administration was forced to cover the losses itself, helped in part by

[78] CAOM (Aix), "Affaires Politiques": 1AFFPOL/92, Agence Consulaire de France, Orcel, Bathurst, to Consul General de France, London (16 May 1912).

[79] CSO 4/10 "Gambia: Development and Relations with Neighbouring Territories of". Letter from Colonial Office to Captain Armitage, Governor of Gambia (14 December 1921).

[80] On this episode, see Kenneth Swindell and Alieu Jeng, *Migrants, Credit and Climate: The Gambian Groundnut Trade, 1834–1934* (Leiden: Brill, 2007), pp. 189–92; and Leigh Gardner, "The curious incident of the franc in the Gambia: exchange rate instability and imperial monetary systems in the 1920s", *Financial History Review* 22 (3) 2015.

[81] Swindell and Jeng, *Migrants*, p. 101, 192.

Table 4.5 *Gambian expenditure priorities (£000s)*

Year	Revenue	Expenditure	Pensions and gratuities as % of expenditure	Governor + Colonial Secretary + Protectorate as % of expenditure	Education as % of expenditure	Medical as % of expenditure	Public Works, recurrent and extraordinary spending as % of total expenditure
1915	92.3	89.0	3.0 / 3.4%	14.4 / 16.2%	1.8 / 2.0%	8.8 / 9.9%	26.9 / 30.2%
1920	268.8	171.2	5.9 / 3.5%	22.8 / 13.3%	1.7 / 1.0%	13.5 / 7.9%	35.9 / 21.0%
1925	189.1	271.8	8.3 / 3.1%	24.2 / 8.9%	2.6 / 1.0%	13.0 / 4.8%	85.4 / 31.4%
1930	235.2	253.2	12.0 / 4.7%	26.0 / 10.3%	8.7 / 3.4%	17.2 / 6.8%	65.6 / 25.9%
1935	245.5	194.7	17.8 / 9.1%	25.1 / 10.2%	5.0 / 2.6%	32.3 / 16.6%	35.0 / 17.8%
1937	286.1	343.3	17.3 / 5.0%	26.2 / 7.6%	5.0 / 1.5%	32.1 / 9.4%	69.3 / 20.2%

Source: Gambia, Blue Books, various years.

a WACB loan, while many ordinary Gambians were left holding defunct coinage. Kenneth Swindell and Alieu Jeng justifiably refer to the entire debacle as "a horrendous episode in the economic life of the Gambia".[82] It was also one that underlined the extent to which the Gambian state was at the mercy of cross-border commercial flows.

In 1922, the Gambian government raised £204,244 in revenue, but expenditure catapulted to £430,312 as a result of the currency crisis. This necessitated placing a cap on public spending at a time when the Gold Coast was making seminal strides. Some savings were made in administrative expenses at the level of the central secretariat and the provincial administration. Swindell and Jeng observe that the authorities responded to the initial shock by cancelling public works commitments in Bathurst, notably electrification, the drainage of the Half Die swamp and improvements to the harbour.[83] What they do not indicate is that there was a renewal of public works expenditure in the mid-1920s at a time when government finances remained in a parlous state. By contrast, the amount spent on education remained pitifully small at £2,600 in 1925, while expenditure on medical and health provision was cut back significantly. The onset of the Great Depression brought about a further contraction of revenues and corresponding curbs on social expenditure. Towards the end of the 1930s, expenditure outstripped revenue once more, which meant that economies continued to be made in the area of health and medical provision. Together these amounted to only 11 per cent of spending in 1937 as opposed to the 7.6 per cent that was absorbed by the political administration. This was, however, an improvement on 1925 when their combined total came to 5.8 per cent at a time when the political administration consumed 8.9 per cent of total expenditure. The reality was, however, that the Gambian state concentrated the majority of this expenditure on the Bathurst area, while there was little evidence of schooling and health provision upriver.

Finally, I come to the singular case of the Gold Coast/British Togoland, where the story was as different from that of the Gambia as it was from l'AOF. Here, relatively robust public finances in the early 1920s enabled Guggisberg to announce a Ten-Year Plan in which infrastructural spending and social investments figured equally prominently. The vision was ahead of its time, and it is worth remembering that it took place a full two decades before the discovery of 'development' in the 1940s. Although the onset of the Depression forced some of the more ambitious plans to be scrapped, most notably the railway extension to the north, a platform had been prepared for the second surge in the 1950s. In addition, the Guggisberg years left an important imprint on the state and public imaginaries alike in which the provision of public goods was considered essential for the maintenance of consent. In 1930, the combined totals on expenditure for education and health came to roughly

---

[82] Swindell and Jeng, *Migrants*, p. 193.   [83] Swindell and Jeng, *Migrants*, p. 194.

Table 4.6 *Gold Coast recurrent expenditure on community (A) and social services (B) in selected years*

Year	A1: Construction	A2: Scientific services	B1: Education	B2: Health	(i) Total of A and B	(ii) Total Recurrent expenditure
1920	401	43	56	223	723	1,845
	55.46% of (i)	5.95% of (i)	7.75% of (i)	30.84% of (i)	39.19% of (i)	100.00%
	21.73% of (ii)	2.33% of (ii)	3.04% of (ii)	12.09% of (ii)		
1930	486	81	304	369	1,240	2,707
	39.19% of (i)	6.53% of (i)	24.52% of (i)	29.76% of (i)	45.81% of (i)	100.00%
	17.95 of (ii)	2.99% of (ii)	11.23% of (ii)	13.63% of (ii)		
1934	311	47	220	284	862	2,183
	36.07% of (i)	5.45% of (i)	25.52% of (i)	32.95% of (i)	39.49% of (ii)	100.00%
	14.25% of (ii)	2.15% of (ii)	10.08% of (ii)	13.01% of (ii)		

Source: Kay (ed.), Political Economy of Colonialism in Ghana, table 27c, p. 370.

25 per cent of the budget (Table 4.6) – which was proportionately slightly lower than in French Togoland, but more than double the relative allocations in the Gambia. But in the Gold Coast, the colony generated proportionately far higher revenues and expenditure, which meant that the overall sums dedicated to health and medical expenditure were considerably greater. In the south, there were substantial improvements to the road network, which partly reflected the pressure coming from communities sprouting up along the cocoa frontier. This included British Togoland where the chiefs frequently lobbied the administration for all-weather roads.

Colonial Social Contracts

I will now wrap up this comparative analysis by considering the implications for the relationship between colonial states and the populations they sought to govern. In Senegal, and across l'AOF more broadly, there were relatively high rates of personal taxation, while the state provided remarkably few public goods outside of the Four Communes. The primary emphasis fell upon public works that were intended to facilitate agricultural exports. The distinctive feature of Senegal was that the social contracts that coalesced in the first three decades were spatially highly variegated. The colonial state, whose historical roots lay in the port cities, pieced together a productive social contract in dialogue with urban populations. An altogether different kind of productive social contract emerged in the groundnut basin where the alliance with the Mourides was contingent upon state intervention both to provide the necessary infrastructure and to make land available upon which groundnuts could be cultivated and model Muslim communities founded. Through the choices that were made, a series of centres and margins were created across Senegal with the northern, eastern and southern regions of Senegal being treated on a different footing to the groundnut basin and the Four Communes – whilst at the same time exhibiting their own specificities.[84] Hence a simple binary between citizen and subject – which ought to fit Senegal better than other cases – scarcely does justice to the complexities of the graded relationships that emerged between the colonial state and populations within the colony.[85] Border regions underwent a double marginalization – that is through exclusion from most public goods and through the creation of the borderlands as a specific site of territorial governance. As we will see in the next chapter,

---

[84] Much of this is captured in the historical sections of Catherine Boone, *Political Topographies of the African State: Territorial Authority and Institutional Choice* (Cambridge: Cambridge University Press, 2003), pp. 46–60, 282–98.

[85] Mahmood Mamdani, *Citizen and Subject: Contemporary Africa and the Legacy of Late Colonialism* (Princeton: Princeton University Press, 1996).

colonial rule in the Casamance was characterized by high levels of coercion and low levels of trust, moderated somewhat by the reality that populations could turn the borders to their own advantage. It is certainly striking that at precisely the moment when the French authorities and the Muslim brotherhoods were coming to terms, in large part over the latter's support for conscription during the First World War, the Casamance was being placed under renewed military occupation.

In French Togoland, which was spared the weight of the federal bureaucracy, the state was altogether leaner, while the balance between revenue and expenditure was quite different. The burden of personal taxation was about half that of Senegal, while social expenditure was also correspondingly higher. Whereas the north of Togo was largely left to its own devices, southern Togo was bound together through infrastructure, a common educational system and above all through commerce[86] – all of which reflected purposeful state intervention. In this case, a productive social contract was combined with permissive elements as the administration placed relatively few fetters on cross-border trade with the Gold Coast. However, the balance began to shift in the 1930s as a result of two developments. The first was the emergence of a critique of French rule amongst migrants to the Gold Coast who actively supported a return to German rule. The second was the decision to cut back on social spending and to extend the range of taxes during the Great Depression. These two developments were closely related, given that the critics were making explicit cross-border comparisons. Togolanders in Accra appropriated the argument that they encountered there – namely that the colonial state did not have the right to impose direct taxes – and applied it to the situation at home. Their sympathy for the Germans, on the other hand, arose from the belief that while the latter had levied taxes and introduced forced labour, they had also done much to build the colony. Given that the south was bound to Lomé by road and railway, the emerging discourse of the rights of Togolanders, which gestated in the border zone, enjoyed a much wider purchase. The French response to criticism was crucial in setting the tenor for future relations with the African population. Having created consultative structures in the shape of the *Conseils des Notables*, the authorities made the mistake of riding roughshod over them.[87] Togolanders were suddenly faced with the prospect of swingeing cuts in expenditure and increases in direct taxes whose legitimacy was already being questioned. When protests broke out in 1933, the administration responded with a military crackdown that

---

[86] Benjamin N. Lawrance, *Locality, Mobility and Nation: Periurban Colonialism in Togo's Eweland, 1900–1960* (Rochester: Rochester University Press, 2007), ch. 5.

[87] Government revenues fell on average at 2 per cent per year between 1928 and 1934. Goeh-Akue, "Finances Publiques", p. 93.

led to the loss of many lives and a further flight of population across the border.[88] Once the immediate crisis had passed, the French authorities attempted to repair the damage by increasing social expenditure, but they had forfeited much of their moral authority. In the minds of many Togolanders, French rule had come to rest on brute force more than consent.

In the Gambia, the financial crisis of the 1920s meant that expenditure was very limited, while the little money that was available was dedicated to improving basic economic infrastructure. However, the authorities in the Gambia did not make much of an effort to extract revenues directly from their colonial subjects primarily for fear of losing population to Senegal. Hence while the colonial state was far more lethargic than in French Togoland, it was also less abrasive during the hardships accompanying the Depression. In the Gambia, one can point to mild variants of the productive social contract in Bathurst, where much of the expenditure was concentrated. The urban population was critical of the failure of the administration to accomplish more. But in this case, there was no alternative model to point to – visible from across the border, as it were – that might have presented an attractive alternative. Furthermore, the population of Bathurst consistently expressed its opposition to any exchange of territory that might have integrated them into Senegal. In the rural areas, the colonial state provided very little in the way of public goods like roads or schools. But by facilitating access to farmland for 'strange farmers', and bolstering the authority of the *seyfolu* and *alkololu*, it did succeed in consolidating rural alliances. Alongside these elements, there was the reality that many traders made a living from selling groundnuts and imported goods across the borders with Senegal. The rather relaxed approach of the Gambian authorities to this trade was fundamental in interpolating a pronounced permissive element into the larger social contract.

Finally, in the case of the Gold Coast what stands out is the absence of personal taxation. Nevertheless, the cocoa boom of the 1920s, together with a diversification of revenue streams, generated a steady improvement in public finances. This enabled the government to augment its investments in infrastructure, while at the same time greatly increasing the resources that could be allocated to schooling and health provision. However, as in the case of French Togoland, there remained a pronounced spatial divide, with the Northern Territories being relegated to the status of an afterthought. In the rest of the Gold Coast, the productive element had become the dominant part of the composite social contract by the 1920s, building on an active negotiation with urban populations and the chiefs of the colony dating back to the nineteenth century – and which was later extended to Ashanti and the Mandated territory.

---

[88] See D'Almeida-Ekué, *La révolte*; and Benjamin N. Lawrance, *Locality*, chs. 3–4.

Table 4.7 *Buell's comparison of tax obligations, 1926 (decimal £)*

Colony	Hut/poll tax per capita	Customs duty per capita	Total tax per capita
French West Africa	0.084	0.026	0.110
Gold Coast	–	0.915	0.915
Nigeria	0.04	0.179	0.223
Sierra Leone	0.039	0.333	0.372
French Togoland	0.048	0.110	0.158
Kenya	0.194	0.274	0.468

Source: Raymond Lesley Buell, The Native Problem in Africa, Vol. I, p. 944.

Table 4.8 *Customs revenues as a proportion of total revenue (1925–1929 at 1913 prices)*

Colony	Total revenue (£)	Customs revenue (£)	Customs as % of total
Gambia	127,950	81,160	63
Sierra Leone	455,964	289,155	63
Gold Coast	2,221,226	1,464,274	66
Nigeria	3,834,141	1,883,744	49
Southern Rhodesia	1,209,686	349,230	29
Northern Rhodesia	276,900	79,307	29
Kenya	1,591,504	459,503	29
Uganda	821,741	239,034	29
Nyasaland	1,196,888	52,717	27

Source: Leigh A. Gardner, Taxing Colonial Africa (Oxford University Press, 2012), table 4.1, p. 64.

Buell's comparative data from 1926 suggests that overall tax rates were significantly higher than in l'AOF and in Kenya (Table 4.7). This should be read alongside Gardner's tabulation of Board of Trade Statistics for 1925–29 (Table 4.8), which reveal that the Gold Coast raised significantly more revenue than the other British colonies – with the exception of the much larger colony of Nigeria – with as much as 66 per cent of the total deriving from Customs duties. The Gold Coast nevertheless avoided significant controversy over its high levels of taxation – the cocoa holdups of 1930s being about the prices paid by buying firms – and in part this was because the taxes were hidden from view. But it was also because the Gold Coast state was oriented much more towards the provision of public goods that were actively solicited. During the Depression years, the overall budget for education and health reduced, but their share of total public expenditure actually increased.[89] The fact that social

---

[89] Frankema, "Colonial taxation", table 1, p. 148.

spending was broadly upheld is indicative of a common understanding about the core responsibilities of the state. During the interwar years, there was greater tension in the border regions, and especially along the border with French Togoland, because that was precisely where the most serious threat to public finances emanated from. Although the British authorities permitted inward migration, they endeavoured to maintain a strict Customs cordon, which led to periodic disagreements between the Customs Preventive Service and local populations – as will see in greater detail in Chapter 6. But for the most part, the social contract was based on a constant process of negotiation between state institutions and the peoples of the trans-Volta who actively demanded their own share of public goods.

Conclusion

In this chapter, I have demonstrated, firstly, that each of the colonial states was configured very differently, reflecting the varying levels of assiduity with the authorities' extracted revenues and the manner in which they set expenditure priorities. Although it is tempting to contrast the Gambia with Senegal, in many respects the Gambia and the Gold Coast were even further apart despite the fact that they were both British colonies. The differences between Senegal and French Togoland are also striking, which merely confirms the observation that the complexion of the colonial power was of secondary importance. Secondly, I have sought to nuance the observation that colonial states were purely and simply 'gatekeeper' or 'night watchmen' states. On the face of it, the Gold Coast was the most extreme case because it dispensed with personal taxation altogether and relied overwhelmingly upon Customs duties. However, the Gold Coast was also the most oriented towards the provision of public goods of all the colonies under consideration – and arguably of all the mainland African colonies. It may not have been a Mauritius or a New Zealand, which Frankema has deployed as the basis for comparison,[90] but it was unlike the other West African colonies. This was not because the authorities were any more benign. What mattered was the relentless pressure exerted by Africans, both in urban and rural areas, for roads, schools and social amenities, which were conceived of as rights rather than privileges. This, in turn, was rooted in a much older discourse about the foundations of British rule dating back to the Bond of 1844 – that is a state founded on conditional consent – and the bargaining that played out in the port cities in the nineteenth century. Eboe Hutchful rightly highlights the importance of subsequent constitutional reforms "giving rise to an increasingly vibrant civic realm and culture,

---

[90] Frankema, "Colonial taxation", pp. 142–3, 147.

and conferring on the colonial state a relatively responsive and benign veneer."[91] This pressure from below also induced the colonial authorities to force vested European interests to contribute more over time, whilst resisting the temptation to impose swingeing cuts in social expenditure during the Depression years. Classic tax bargains are about political recognition as much as revenue considerations, and the manner in which each of the colonial regimes juggled the various demands upon them had a profound impact on the shaping of social contracts in the long run.

Finally, I have demonstrated that the entire revenue–expenditure nexus, and hence the wider social contracts that were sustained by them, were shaped in important ways by border dynamics. Trans-boundary flows of people and goods had the potential to make or break the colonial project, or at the very least to force a reordering of priorities. Where administrators failed to impose their agenda, the credibility of the colonial project could be called into question – as happened on numerous occasions in Portuguese Guinea and in the Casamance. In the case of the Gold Coast, the protection of Customs revenues depended on maintaining active surveillance over the border with French Togoland, whereas in the latter case there was a countervailing premium on facilitating border flows. The control of smuggling was never a minor detail of colonial governance but was fundamental to the ways in which institutional priorities were arrived at and bureaucratic hierarchies were cemented. In l'AOF and in the Gold Coast, the Customs authorities sat at the top of the institutional tree. In the Senegambia, the border areas were also fundamental to the regulation of population flows. Attracting and retaining population was regarded as the key to maximizing groundnut production. But it was no less important for the aggregation of higher yard/head taxes and Customs duties, which derived from the consumption of imported goods. At the border, the operations of the state were manifested in the form of uniformed Customs officers and chiefs whose functions were largely complementary. In the following chapters, I probe border control in greater detail.

---

[91] Eboe Hutchful, "The fall and rise of the state in Ghana", in Abdi Ismail Samatar and Ahmed I. Samatar (eds.), *The African State: Reconsiderations* (Portsmouth: Heinemann, 2002), p. 104.

5   Being Seen Like a State
Frontier Logics, Colonial Administration and Traditional Authority in the Borderlands

---

In the Chapter 4, I pointed out that the colonial authorities needed to be mindful of the policies that were effected on the opposite side of a given border. Populations proved themselves highly adept at exploiting the points of divergence. In a seminal article on migration as revolt, A.I. Asiwaju drew attention to the multiple ways in which West Africans turned mobility to their advantage by escaping across colonial borders.[1] In this chapter and the next, I confirm the applicability of this insight to the Senegambia and the trans-Volta. But I also want to go beyond documenting forms of resistance. Practical governance arose out of the quotidian interplay between state actors and those who populated, moved through and traded within the borderlands. In the initial phases, European administrators felt the need to establish their physical presence through shows of force, but as they settled into more of a rhythm, they relied on the assistance of intermediaries and interlocuteurs of various kinds. Clerks and policemen played their part, but even more important were traditional authorities who were the daily point of contact with the people who were on the receiving end of colonial governance. Chiefs were variously called upon to collect taxes, monitor border flows and serve as the eyes and ears of the administration. Crafting structures of collaboration was a challenge at the best of times, but it was especially tricky at the margins because there was always an alternative model close at hand. Moreover, where borders were superimposed upon historical frontier regions, such as in the Casamance, an ingrained suspicion of state intentions meant that force needed to be deployed repeatedly. This consequence is that it was much more difficult to construct hegemony or to exact even the most basic habits of compliance. In this chapter, I will tease out the differences on two sides of a border as well as between the two sub-regions. I begin with an overview of the spatial predispositions of the colonial regimes, before turning to the Senegambia and the trans-Volta in greater detail.

---

[1] A.I. Asiwaju, "Migrations as revolt: the example of the Ivory Coast and Upper Volta Before 1945", *Journal of African History* 17 (4) 1976, pp. 577–94.

Seeing and Being Seen Like a State

In Chapter One, I alluded to James C. Scott's assertion that that there is an imperative for states to render their subjects legible in order to extract necessary revenues and to impose cherished conceptions of order and/or progress.[2] A somewhat similar view is expressed in Timothy Mitchell's account of nineteenth-century Egypt, where he refers to colonialism as a system of 'enframing' in which elaborate attempts to represent Egyptian society went together with a desire to minutely order and fix the colonized population in space.[3] If one takes the rhetoric of imperialism at its word, the 'civilizing mission' – or *la mission civilisatrice* – certainly did involve some notion of colonial officialdom reaching down into the smallest hamlet. However, the gap between the programmatic statements and the practice was enormous, and nowhere more so than in West Africa before the Second World War. Nevertheless, the visual metaphor of 'seeing like a state' remains a suggestive one because what was taken in depended very much on where the focus was directed. By foregrounding certain issues, colonial regimes opened up blind spots elsewhere that often had significant consequences.

The blindspots are starkly apparent in the Senegambia where the British and the French authorities struggled to make sense of the actions of their neighbours. The early colonial state in the Gambia had maintained a decidedly watery existence before the formal demarcation of the boundaries in the 1890s. Even after partition, the Gambia River remained the focal point of administrators and traders alike. Most of the commerce of the colony was conducted at wharf towns dotted along the river, from where groundnuts transited through the port at Bathurst and met consumer goods passing in the opposite direction. If Bathurst was imagined as the commercial centre, then the margins were conceived of in terms of distance from the capital: that is, along the river and away from its banks, a distance that in most cases did not exceed 10 kilometres. The building of roads was not initially considered a priority, and those that were constructed tended to shadow the contours of the river. This obsession with the river was the cause of considerable bemusement to the French. Whereas the groundnut basin of Senegal was connected to Dakar by rail, the Casamance was effectively cut off by the very existence of the Gambia. The solution was thought to reside in persuading the British to give up the Gambia, but successive attempts to revisit the issue stalled – largely on

---

[2] James C. Scott, *Seeing Like a State: How Certain Schemes to Improve the Human Condition Have Failed* (New Haven: Yale University Press, 1999), and *The Art of Not Being Governed: An Anarchist History of Upland Southeast Asia* (New Haven and London: Yale University Press, 2009).

[3] Timothy Mitchell, *Colonising Egypt* (Cambridge: Cambridge University Press, 1988).

account of popular resistance in Bathurst itself. Moreover, the refusal of the British to bridge the Gambia at its narrowest point, or to create an effective system of ferries, always struck the French as wantonly perverse. Although part of the reason was that the British authorities wanted to avoid the Gambia being turned into an economic dependency of Dakar, the lack of attention to north–south communications conformed to a deeply ingrained conception of colonial space that ran east–west. However, none of this misunderstanding was pre-ordained. The Gambian authorities might have tempered their obsession with the river and invested in roads and bridges as part of a strategy of turning Bathurst into a successful regional *entrepôt*, given that it was French commercial houses who dominated the trade anyway. Equally, the French might have concentrated on improving infrastructure in the Casamance that would have been conducive to the development of rice and groundnut exports by road and boat. Although some investments were made,[4] the Casamance remained one part of the Senegalese colonial estate that seemed to be stuck in the future tense. Although its agricultural potential was often remarked upon, and the apparent fertility of its agricultural land contrasted with the dessicated landscapes of northern Senegal, its development awaited final resolution of the Gambian puzzle.

Once the colonial boundaries were fixed, the task facing each of the regimes was to establish a visible presence in the borderlands. A common pattern in Africa was one in which government troops were stationed close to, or on, the border itself, frequently at the choke-points referred to in Chapter 3. A classic instance was Misahöhe, which was established as a German inland station in 1890. Perched at the top of the Togoland hills, it was expected to serve as a vantage point from which to survey British actions and to project German influence in the direction of the Volta River.[5] With formal colonization, the next step was the designation of a particular settlement as the administrative headquarters, with a European official and a police or military complement. In the case of Misahöhe, the post had around fifty troops (and fifty reservists), forty police and around twenty African administrators attached to it by 1913, although many were physically stationed in the commercial centre of Kpalimé.[6] The administrative post was usually set back for the reason that it

---

[4] Most of the attempts to promote development in the Casamance date to the post-war years. See, for example, Marina Diallo Co-Trung, *La Compagnie générale des oléagineux tropicaux en Casamance: autopsie d'une opération de mise en valeur coloniale (1948–1962)* (Paris: Karthala, 2000).

[5] Ametépé Yawovi Ahadji, "Le rôle de la station de Misahöhe dans l'integration de l'hinterland a la colonie allemande du Togo (1890–1914)", in Badjow Tcham and Thiou K. Tchamie (eds.), *L'integration de l'hinterland a la colonie du Togo: actes du colloque de Lomé (22–25 mars 1999)* (Lomé: Presses de l'UB: 2000), p. 110.

[6] Nicoué Lodjou Gayibor (ed.), *Le Togo sous domination coloniale (1884–1960)* (Lomé: Presses de l'UB, 1997), p. 28.

was considered unwise to position the headquarters too close to the line. In the normal course of events, the status of the border post was progressively downgraded as the administrative headquarters became more firmly established. One can see some of this logic at work in the case of Misahöhe itself. Although German, and later French, administrators retained their residences in the town, because of its elevation and hence its relative coolness, the administrative functions were transferred to Kpalimé after the partition of Togoland – when it was transformed into a rather remote border town.

The construction of a fabric of administration was sometimes expressed in terms of the spatial metaphor of the ink-stain. The basic idea is that the creation of each new administrative centre would create a radius of effective control around it. Hence, colonial proconsuls would begin by setting up a handful of administrative posts and then steadily interpolate a series of smaller sub-stations until the entire colony was converted into a saturated space of colonial governance. Although the image of the ink-stain is evocative, it is perhaps more helpful to think in terms of a series of nodes that were linked in a chain that led back to the capital. According to the bureaucratic manual, information would flow from node to node in a more or less predictable manner, and ideally in the form of paper. Hence, circulars from the centre would be received at the district headquarters, while monthly and/or quarterly reports would be sent from the districts to the provincial or colonial capitals. But within a district, it was not paper that travelled, but the administrator himself. The *tournée*, or the movement of an administrative officer through his district, was invested with an almost mystical significance.[7] In the Gambia, officials even bore the title of Travelling Commissioners, implying that they were almost permanently on the move. Crucially, the tour made the colonial presence visible, underlining the importance of *being seen* like a state. To a considerable extent, it was an exercise in theatre – and one might even say, in bluff. The tour also enabled the administrator to get to know his subjects as well as the terrain that he might use to outwit his agents. This was especially salient in border zones where mobile populations presented particular challenges. Finally, the *tournée* provided an opportunity to check the tax registers on site, and if necessary, to supervise collection, and more generally to spot trouble well in advance. For the French, the payment of taxes signified an act of submission, whereas refusal was considered tantamount to an act of rebellion. Equally any delay or display of recalcitrance was read as an ominous warning sign. Examining the tax registers was, therefore, an exercise in reading the entrails for clues as to the disposition of the colonized. Over time, the administrator would seek to establish a hierarchy of traditional authorities through whom directives could be passed down and day-to-day routines of

---

[7] See, for example, Trutz Von Trotha, *Koloniale Herrschaft: zur soziologischen Theorie der Staatsentstehung am Beispiel des 'Schutzgebietes Togo'* (Tübingen: Mohr, 1994), pp. 117–42.

governance maintained. But even when fixed systems of chiefly rule were established, and it became possible for the administrator to spend more time in the office, the *tournée* remained one of the rituals of governance.

The tour was subordinated to the world of paper by being written up in reports that were despatched to the centre. But the extent to which colonial regimes were properly bureaucratic remains questionable, at least before the 1930s. Although secretariats in the capitals collected information more systematically than before, District Commissioners and Commandants de Cercle functioned in a highly personalist manner. These were often obsessive and eccentric figures – occasionally verging on the pathological – and were typically highly opinionated.[8] In the early days, they often made and unmade chiefs, and enforced punishments in a manner that could be decidedly arbitrary. German Commissioners in Togo often functioned as a law unto themselves, but in the 1930s French and British officials could still be found who ran the show according to their own lights. Such was the case with Captain C.C. Lilley who was the undisputed authority in southern British Togoland in the 1920s and 1930s and whose name is immortalized in the 'Lilley-trees' that stand in designated village squares where public meetings are held to this day. The image of the steel frame of colonial administration therefore belied a reality of something altogether more contingent. The progression from the *tournée* to a regularized system of administration depended on establishing enough of an administrative presence at the local level, but also on the cultivation of a cadre of willing chiefly intermediaries. The differences between British and French chieftaincy policies is a well-trodden line of enquiry, not least in relation to borderland studies where the consistent finding is that traditional authorities enjoyed greater autonomy on the British side of the borderline.[9] But what is as striking from the case studies that follow is the differences within the British and French territories respectively.

Neither Traditional nor Authoritative: The Travails of Governance in the Senegambia

In the case of the Gambia, the British sought to capitalize on the congruence between the boundaries of Kombo and the colonial border. They also staked a

---

[8] For a recent study of the often atomized nature of colonial rule in the British colonies, with an emphasis on the administrators, see Christopher Prior, *Exporting Empire: Africa, Colonial Officials and the Construction of the British Imperial State* (Manchester: Manchester University Press, 2015).

[9] A.I. Asiwaju, *Western Yorubaland under European Rule, 1889–1945: A Comparative Analysis of French and British Colonialism* (London: Longman, 1976); and William F.S. Miles, *Hausaland Divided: Colonialism and Independence in Nigeria and Niger* (Ithaca: Cornell University Press, 1994).

claim to legitimacy on the basis of continuity with customary practice, even as they introduced fundamental changes to the way authority was actually constituted. During the public gathering at which he formally accepted the submission of the Kombo 'headmen', the Governor underlined the basis on which the British were claiming the right to govern and laid down what could be expected in future:

I then told them that as the king had conquered this country. I was now their Chief and they would be governed by English law and not the law of the Koran. I informed them that as their Chief I was entitled to receive 'Customs', but I could not tell them at that meeting what they would have to pay but possibly a land rent as their neighbours in British Combo did. This did not surprise them at all for they all know the law and practices in the Colony.[10]

He also informed his audience that the 'animist' Soninke who had been forced to flee would be allowed to return to Brikama and Busambala without recriminations. The responsibilities of 'Headchiefs' and 'Headmen', as they were initially referred to in the Gambia Protectorate Ordinance of 1902, were defined as the maintenance of peace, the prevention and detection of crime and the "enforcement within their Districts and sub-Districts of all sentences, judgements and orders of any native tribunal or any other court of law in the Colony". The chiefs were mandated to operate native tribunals that had some criminal as well as civil jurisdiction. The chiefs also had a crucial role to play in the collection of the 'hut and yard tax' that was introduced in 1895. The regular enumeration of huts and the collection of the taxes were a major logistical exercise that could not have been carried out without the mediation of the chiefs. Finally, a cadre of officials to carry out chiefly orders – known as 'Badge Messengers' – was also provided for under the 1902 Ordinance. This bore a passing resemblance to the older system of 'the king's men' that had prevailed under the Soninke regimes.

The choice confronting the authorities was between seeking to co-opt the families associated with Fodé Sylla or recreating Kombo more or less along the lines of the defunct kingship. The strategy that was eventually adopted fell somewhere in between these extremes. What had been known as 'Foreign' Kombo was not treated as a single entity but divided into four districts headed by a headchief or *seyfo* (pl. *seyfolu*) – namely Kombo North (with its capital at Sukuta), Kombo South (Gunjur), Kombo Central (Brikama) and Kombo East (Farabananta). Former 'British Kombo, that is the area purchased from the king of Kombo in the nineteenth century, constituted the fifth district of Kombo St. Mary, with its *seyfo* located at Bakau. Below the *seyfo*, the only

---

[10] NAGB CSO 1/124 "Despatches from Colonial Office 1894", Report by Governor on palaver with Kombo chiefs (20 March 1894).

other chiefly category that was recognized was that of the village chief, or *alkalo (pl. akalolu)*. The British sought to avoid perpetuating a feud with the population of Gunjur, which had been bombarded during the war with Fodé Sylla. The town was rebuilt in a slightly different location, and the Ture family periodically provided the *seyfo*, but the position was now shared with the Dabos who claimed to be the founders of the town.[11] Although Gunjur continued to be regarded as a nest of 'troublemaking' for some years, the situation gradually stabilized. By making Brikama the capital of Kombo Central, the authorities were recognizing the historical importance of that town. The Bojang line was restored in 1894, with the recognition of Fodi Musa Bojang. In 1918, Demba Bojang was appointed *seyfo* and remained in office until his death in 1938, thereby providing two decades of continuity. Indeed, the *seyfoship* has remained in the hands of the Bojangs to this day. In this way, the revolution of the nineteenth century was partially reversed – eased somewhat by the fact that the *seyfos* of Brikama were now Muslim rather than Soninke. Nevertheless, for the Bojangs this represented a moral victory over the Tures whose influence was henceforth confined to Kombo South.

But perhaps the best insight into British pragmatism derives from the case of Kombo North. The original expectation was that Busambala would serve as "the chief town in Combo and that all main roads will pass through and radiate from there in all directions."[12] The authorities began by tapping into the traditional structure, appointing Landing Jatta to the *seyfoship*. On his death, two other members of the Jatta family followed in very close succession, but were deposed because of their inability to command support. A later report, which forgot the early experiment, laid out the logic of abandoning the Jattas altogether in the following manner:

The appointment of a chief in this district is usually attended with some stir and heart-burnings. The families of the old kings of Kombo (who reside in this district) consider the appointment should lie with them, and another, that more than one person living in Sukuta thinks he has the right qualifications and has been born to fill the post. From the time the district was formed, Sukuta, the largest and most important town has always supplied the chiefs, and the people together with the residents of Brufut, another important town, would never have lived peacefully under a chief selected from one of the Soninki [sic] families of the old kings.[13]

---

[11] On the history of the Tures in Gunjur, see David Skinner, "Islam in Kombo: the spiritual and militant jihad of Fode Ibrahim Ture", *Islamic Africa* 3 (1) 2012.

[12] NAGB CSO 1/124 "CSO 1/124 Despatches from Colonial Office 1894", "Headings of principal orders given to the people of Combo at a palaver on the 19th March 1894".

[13] NAGB ARP 33/5 "Annual Report, Kombo and Fogni Province 1923–29", Annual Report for Kombo and Fogni, 1928, p. 10

Hence in 1897, the administration broke with tradition and appointed one Kabba Cham as *seyfo*. The latter was a trader and favourably described as a "clever man and a good Arabic scholar". Significantly, he carried out his duties from Sukuta rather than Busumbala, which was relegated from being the putative centre of all of Kombo to a small town devoid of any administrative importance. When Kabba Cham died in 1907, the *seyfoship* did not return to the Jattas, but was conferred on a cousin, Karranta Cham, and from there it passed to Fodi Madi Cham.[14] In 1918, on the death of the latter, no suitable candidate from the Cham family could be found, with the result that the Commissioner turned to one Mambuna Bojang. The latter was related to the Cham by marriage and was selected because he was "the most able man in Sukuta and the district".[15] Mambuna Bojang was, however, fiercely opposed by the Chams, and after an altercation over a legal judgement that led to the burning of a government building, he tendered his resignation. At this point, the *seyfoship* passed to Mamadi Cham, although in 1936 the Chams were bypassed once again when one Fansu Bojang succeeded. The contrasting trajectories between the the *seyfoship* in Kombo Central and Kombo North neatly illustrates the extent to which the Gambian authorities were driven by very pragmatic concerns rather than by Indirect Rule orthodoxies.

In Kombo, the British were able to build upon the foundations of Mandinka traditional authority. But in Fogny, they faced greater difficulties because there was no pre-existing form of centralized authority amongst the Jola. As the annual report for 1899 put it:

Fogni is so different to any other part of the country, there are no large towns, no headmen, each family has its own little stockade and farm, and many will not even take a message from another stockade owner and the majority fear to give one.[16]

The authorities began by attempting to work through Mandinka chiefs, but this was deeply resented.[17] Relations between Mandinka and Jola in Fogny remained hostile, as was reflected in clashes between the Mandinka and Jola sections of Karenai and elsewhere. There were also many reports of Mandinka traders being predated upon by Jola in the border zone. Hence the annual report for 1901 stated:

---

[14] NAGB ARP 33/4 "Annual Report Kombo 1908", Annual Report by Travelling Commissioner, Sangster, to Colonial Secretary (25 June 1908).
[15] NAGB ARP 33/5 "Annual Report", Annual Report Kombo/Fogni, 1928, pp. 11–12.
[16] ARP 33/1 "Reports on Kombo, Fogni and Kiang", Report for 1898–9 by Sitwell.
[17] The British adopted a similar expedient in southwestern Uganda, for example by using Baganda chiefs to rule Kiga populations who refused to accept chiefs appointed from amongst them. Derek Peterson, *Ethnic Patriotism and the East African Revival: A History of Dissent, c.1935–1972* (Cambridge: Cambridge University Press, 2012), pp. 52–60.

Crime in Fogni is excessive, the Jolahs they are continually committing murders & highway robberies. The hard part of a Commissioner's work in this District is his inability to make arrests, no Jolah will ever arrest another, & the Mandingos are afraid to; another point is that it is very hard indeed to get one Jolah to give evidence against another.[18]

Sitwell reported that his attempts to use the 'Headmen of the wharf towns' to collect taxes in kind had failed because the Mandinka chiefs were simply too scared to visit the Jola settlements.[19]

The Gambian authorities came to appreciate early on that the only policy that stood a chance of winning compliance was that of working through Jola chiefs, however alien the institution of chieftaincy might be. The *alkalos* in the Jola villages might not enjoy much innate respect, but this was considered unavoidable in the short run. When it came to the choice of *seyfo*, the British hoped to be able to cultivate Jola candidates for these offices in places where they were in a clear majority. In Fogny East, they recognized one Yannki Baji as the chief following the expedition against Fodé Kabba. In Fogny West, they struggled to find anyone until they briefly managed to install one Kekote Darrami, described by the Commissioner in 1906 as "A Jolah by birth and the only Jolah I have ever met who had any authority over his fellow countrymen".[20] But the report for 1907 noted that they had been unable to come up with a suitable successor when they lost his services:

As I have often stated before the great trouble in Fogni is that the Jolah people will not recognise head men, yet there are a few men who they deign to listen to a little & such men are few and far between. In the late Kekote Darrami Hd. Chief of Fogni West we lost a good man, & one I regret to say I have been unable to replace up to date. I have heard of men but it is no use to act in a hurry & present men to His Excellency who may turn out useless, but next tour I hope to find the right man. Kekota's son and boys make for messengers but are not old enough, nor have they power enough over the people to be head men.[21]

Subsequent annual reports indicate that the authorities believed they were making slow, but steady progress in Fogny. In 1898, Sitwell had depicted the Jola in disparaging terms: "The country itself is much the same as usual, drinking bouts among the Jolas with the usual drunken fights, which are bound to continue as long as there are palm trees in the country."[22] The following

---

[18] NAGB ARP 33/2 "Reports on Kombo, Foni and Kiang (1900–01 and 1906–07)", Report from the Travelling Commissioner, Sangster, 26 September 1901.

[19] NAGB ARP 33/1 "Reports on Kombo, Fogni and Kiang", Report for 1898–99 by C. Sitwell.

[20] NAGB ARP 33/3 "Travelling Commissioner's Report on the Kombo and Foni Province, 1902–6, 1908–21", Annual report by Sangster, dated July 1906.

[21] NAGB ARP 33/3 "Travelling Commissioner's Report", report by Sangster for 1903–04.

[22] NAGB ARP 33/1 "Reports on Kombo, Foni and Kiang", Sitwell to Acting Administrator of the Gambia (2 July 1898).

year in one of his last reports before he met his untimely death, Sitwell wrote quite simply that: "There is only one name for Jolah, 'Savage', and he must be treated as such; naturally it will take many years to work him up to the standard of other tribes."[23] However, a report from 1904 assumed a rather different tone:

Fogni has made great strides in the last few years and I am glad to say that I have been able to gain the confidence of the people and now they come to me with troubles and are very friendly. At first they would run into the bush rather than have any talk with a white man at all. They are a very good people and once they get to properly understand what is required of them, I guarantee that they will be more tractable and hardworking than the Mandingoes.[24]

Subsequent reports continued in the same, rather more positive, vein. By 1929, the Commissioner was able to report that "general progress" was proceeding "somewhat faster" in Fogny than in parts of Kombo and Kiang West and that many of the Jola customs that the British found offensive were disappearing.[25] By this point, the incidence of banditry had declined, the Jola were paying their yard taxes and evidence for conversion to Islam seemed to coincide nicely with a decline of 'excessive' palm-wine consumption. By this point, the Jola were being routinely depicted as hardworking and productive farmers who had acquired a taste for foreign goods. Although administrators continued to bemoan the dearth of good chiefly material amongst the Jola, the continuity of administrative boundaries and the recognition of the need to respect ethnic difference, gave rise to a system that worked tolerably well – and crucially at very little cost.

By contrast, the French encountered far greater challenges in creating a system of trusted intermediaries in Narang and Fogny-Jabangkunda. As we have seen, this had previously been a rather unstable frontier zone. Here the task was not so much one of unravelling the networks of allegiance to Fodé Sylla as building administrative structures on the rubble left by decades of spoliation. On the one hand, the region had been severely depopulated, as can be judged from a census of 'French Kombo' in 1906 (see Table 5.1). The lack of a resident population made it difficult to create a linked colonial space in the border zone. Although Bliss and Karone had been much less affected, their somewhat remote location presented additional problems of administrative penetration. A report from 1894 presented the matter thus:

[23] NAGB ARP 33/1 "Reports on Kombo, Foni and Kiang", Sitwell to Administrator (29 June 1899).
[24] NAGB ARP 33/2 "Report on the Kombo and Fogni Province 1906–1907", Reports by Sangster on Kombo, Foni and Kiang (1900–01 and 1906–07).
[25] NAGB ARP 33/5 "Annual Report, Kombo and Fogni Province 1923–29", Annual Report for Kombo and Foni for 1928, submitted in March 1929.

Table 5.1 *Population of villages in French Kombo (1906 enumeration)*

Village	Chief	No. compounds	No. of men	No. of women	No. of children	Total pop.
Diouloulou	Assoumane	NA	109	77	50	272
Diébaly	Birama Coli	2	22	19	23	64
Coulobor	Gualy Mané	1	10	19	17	40
Cabaddio [Kabadio]	Bakary Diabay	2	17	17	45	80
Coubanac	Lamine Badian	2	27	26	27	80
Condioubé [Kujube]	Lamine Diaban	1	39	52	78	169
Koulandian	Dirabo	2	21	19	32	67
Kabyline	Sei	7	53	30	157	287
Binking	Magnati	4	52	73	165	270
Balini	Samako	3	48	45	76	169
Dinaki [Jinaki]	Binimba	7	58	82	131	271
Kakané	Guilancon	5	30	32	65	127
Badiana	Diabouba	5	78	92	180	350
Belaye	Dialambaye	2	29	28	30	82

Source: ANS 13G 375 "Casamance: Documents provenant des Archives de Ziguinchor".

Bliss and Foukou are completely independent from the country of the Karones; as for Kafountine it forms part of a land which the indigenes call Fogny-Diabancounda and which comprises all the villages situated between Combo in the north and Karones in the south. All this part of the Casamance, dry and relatively spread out and lightly populated these days – the wars and pillage carried out for many years by the Mandingues [Mandinkas] under the direction of Fodé Sylla have chased away almost the entire Diola [Jola] and Baynounk population of old – the Karones represent virtually the only group that managed to resist thanks to its geographical position. It is this that explains in part the spirit of isolation of the population who don't leave their town or their marigots other than to go to Carabane or to the nearest escales in order to acquire tobacco and alcohol which they need.[26]

On the other hand, there was little in the way of traditional authorities who commanded respect beyond their own immediate settlements. In the Mandinka villages closest to the Gambia, the territorial reach of the *mansas* had been strictly limited, whereas in Bliss and Karone no system of chiefly authority existed. According to one official, the populations that were the easiest to govern were those who had previously been subjected to 'kingship', whereas the further one progressed into Fogny and towards Karone, the more ingrained opposition to state authority was manifest.[27]

---

[26] Report on Karones (pages missing), ANS 13G 372 "Casamance 1892–1894".

[27] ANS 13G 372 "Casamance 1892–1894", "Rapport de la situation actuelle et les ressources du Fogny Nord-Ouest (Diébaly)", from Lt. Moreau to Commandant le Poste de Sédhiou (5 September 1894).

The problem of the demographic deficit was not easily resolved. Lieutenant Moreau discretely sent messages to Jola who had taken refuge in the Bathurst area, encouraging them to return. Some 250 people were reported to have come back to Bitaké, Coulandian and Kujube, where the rubber trade was gathering momentum,[28] but French attempts to levy taxes soon led to a reverse flow back into the Gambia. Even Fodé Moussa of Makuda, who had been regarded by the French as an ally, was reported to have led members of his family across the border.[29] This provided a salutary reminder of the need to adjust the exercise of colonial authority to the realities of the border situation where populations enjoyed a range of options. The second problem, namely the lack of an indigenous hierarchy, was one that the French never really found an answer to. The expedient of imposing chiefs from above provided a constant source of opposition to French rule, not least because their primary function was to collect taxes. The collection in kind was presumably intended to take account of the fact that many Jola communities had limited access to cash, but if anything the toll on domestic consumption was seen an even more unwarranted attack on household subsistence. The issue of taxation became part of an ongoing struggle on the part of the French to establish their right to govern, as we will see below.

Whereas the Gambian administration settled into a fairly predictable pattern in the first years of the twentieth century, the same could hardly be said of the Casamance where so many alterations were made that it is difficult to identify a consistent plan of action prior to the Second World War.[30] The constant reshuffling of administrative units, together with the making and unmaking of chiefly hierarchies, provides an insight into the failure to implant viable institutions. More fundamentally, it reflected the stubborn failure of African realities to fit into the kind of tidy administrative grid that the French felt most comfortable with. In the Casamance, colonial governance never really progressed beyond the *tournée* in which power had to be physically witnessed in the shape of men in uniform for it to be accepted. Admittedly, the failure was not as total as in neighbouring Portuguese Guinea, but it was starkly apparent all the same.

In 1894, Sédhiou was elevated to the position of administrative headquarters, with separate *cercles* being created for Sédhiou and Carabane.[31]

---

[28] ANS 13G 372 "Casamance 1892–1894", undated draft of 1894 report on different parts of the Casamance by Farque.

[29] ANS 13 G372 "Casamance 1892–1894", Report on Karones (pages missing).

[30] For a more comprehensive treatment, see Phillippe Méguelle, *Chefferie coloniale et égalitarianisme diola: les difficultés de la politique indigène de la France en Basse-Casamance (Sénégal), 1828–1923* (Paris: L'Harmattan, 2012).

[31] Christian Roche, *Histoire de la Casamance: conquête et résistance, 1850–1920* (Paris: Karthala, 1985), p. 230.

This arrangement was intended to create a presence that could be more evenly spread across the Casamance, in the manner of the ink-stain. In the same year, and for the same administrative reasons, Commandant Farque founded separate administrative sub-posts at Diébaly and Bignona.[32] But as early as 1904, there was a further re-adjustment that led to the formation of a single *cercle* for the Casamance, headed by the *Administrateur Supérieur* at Sédhiou. The *cercle* was sub-divided into eight regions (later called *subdivisions*), each controlled by a resident, including one unit for Fogny (at Bignona) and another for Kombo (at Diébaly).[33] The latter post was subsequently relocated to Diouloulou, which had the considerable advantage, for traders and administrators alike, of being located on the *marigot*. In tandem with these changes, the French sought out chiefs who they hoped might exercise authority over a wider area. The choices they made were informed by the perceived virtues of particular personalities, which meant that they did not delve too deeply into the pre-existing landscape of power. Hence they recognized a 'priest' as the chief of Karone, despite the fact that spiritual authority had not previously been associated with the exercise of political power.[34] Conversely, whereas they might have built upon the political traditions of Kabadio and Kujube, their chiefs were not recognized as enjoying an influence beyond their respective villages. Over subsequent decades, canton chiefs were made and unmade according to short-term expedience. The same haphazard quality was apparent in Fogny, but with the additional complication that Mandinka chiefs were frequently imposed upon Jola communities. This policy, which was deeply unpopular in Fogny, was maintained until the First World War and contributed to the upheavals during those years.

In 1912, the *subdivision* of Diouloulou was brought under a civil administration, signalling that the Casamance authorities believed they were firmly in control of the north-west if nowhere else. But it became clear the following year that the level of compliance with French directives was patchy. While the situation along the Gambian border was deemed satisfactory, serious complications became evident south of Kafountine. The appointed chief in Esaloulou, Drame Diassi, was credited with successfully bringing in the tax from across Bliss, and as a reward the resident recommended that he be made a canton chief. But it was clear that Bliss remained in the balance, while in Karone tax was collected with the greatest difficulty.[35] The villages of Bankassouk and Couba were reported to be holding out, and the fear was expressed that unless

[32] Roche, *Histoire de la Casamance*, p. 273.
[33] Roche, *Histoire de la Casamance*, pp. 308–9. The French continued to use the term Kombo for an area that was not strictly speaking part of the former kingdom.
[34] Roche, *Histoire de la Casamance*, p. 274.
[35] ANS 2G 13/57 "Résidence de Diouloulou, Rapports mensuels d'ensemble 1913", Reports for July and August 1913.

direct action was taken against the latter, there would be further ripple effects across Karone – as indeed there were in 1915 when the villages of Itou and Hilol took up the banner of resistance to taxation.

With the onset of the First World War, the entire fabric of administration threatened to unravel. The dilution of the French presence on the ground may well have created the impression that they were too weak to respond or even that their days were numbered. Rumours to that effect were certainly rife. The stresses were very visible in Diouloulou where the lack of any French person-nel necessitated the appointment of a 24-year-old interpreter, Gorgui N'Diaye, as the acting resident. The latter had at his disposal a police detachment of only four men, a complement that occasionally fell lower.[36] The assessment of his performance by his superiors was highly positive, with particular commen-dation attaching to his successful enumeration of refractory villages for tax purposes. Hence in June 1916, at a time when the Kolda post was entirely unmanned, the following précis of the state of play was penned: "In the residencies of Diouloulou and of Oussouye, led by the lone interpreters of these posts, situation excellent: tax levied, nominative enumeration completed, no incidents."[37] In April 1917, Gorgui N'Diaye even managed to carry out a successful enumeration in Bliss and Karone. However, the subsequent passage of events caught the French entirely by surprise.

Some months earlier, a marabout from French Soudan (or possibly from Portuguese Guinea), by the name of Al-Haji Haidara, installed himself at Kujube where he declared himself a Chérif – and allegedly even the Mahdi.[38] A subsequent French report suggested that he had arrived in Kujube with only four followers, but had managed to recruit additional supporters from the Gambian side of the border.[39] On 24 June, he launched what may have been intended as a holy war, which began with an attack on the Customs post at Sélèty. The assailants killed the French officer in charge, decapitating the corpse, as well a cook and an African *douanier*. The insurgents then moved against Diouloulou itself. Fortunately for government employees there, a warning arrived in enough time for the attack to be repulsed. The affair was concluded very quickly thereafter with the arrest of Haidara and his followers as they fled across the border into the Gambia. What is interesting from our point of view is that the recently appointed administrator in Sédhiou, Benquey,

[36] ANS 2G 14/51 "Casamance, Rapports mensuels d'ensemble 1914", Report for August 1914. By the end of the year three of these had been recalled to Ziguinchor (report for December), although the complement of four was back in April 1915.

[37] Report for June 1916, ANS 2G 16/37 "Casamance, Rapports mensuels d'ensemble 1916".

[38] In Kujube, he is said to have been from Gabou in Guinea-Bissau. Interview with Tombon Ture and others, Kujube (Senegal) 18 February 2004.

[39] Benquey, l'Administrateur Supérieur to Lieutenant-Gouverneur, Saint-Louis (undated), ANS 13G 382 "Casamance Affaires Politiques".

regarded the population of Narang as fully complicit, whereas previous administrative reports had considered them the least troublesome of all. Benquey
deduced that the inhabitants of Séléty had aided the first assault, and that the
villagers of Diébaly and Coba had also played their part. These settlements
were completely destroyed in the pointed retribution that followed. Benquey
also believed that the people of Kujube were willing participants, given that
this village had provided a home for Al-Haji Haidara in the months leading up
to the attack. In Kujube today, it is recalled that there had actually been little
sympathy for the marabout, and that when the attack took place all the youth
were sent across the border for safety.[40] The thinking was that if the French
forces came across a village composed entirely of elderly people, Kujube
might be spared collective retribution. However, it is said that the French were
intent on exacting their revenge and apparently killed many residents.

In the aftermath of the Séléty affair, two factors were invoked to explain the
unexpected turn of events. The first was the limited competence of Gorgui
N'Diaye who, it was noted, had been given such responsibility because of the
local intelligence that he was presumed to be privy to.[41] In the event, it was
concluded, he had failed to detect a conspiracy unfolding beneath his nose. As
N'Diaye became the scapegoat, the praise that had been heaped upon him in
earlier reports was conveniently forgotten. More generally, the incident was
blamed on the dilution of the French presence, with the result that many
communities had been tempted to reassert their autonomy. Before the events
in question, a monthly report for the Casamance in 1916 had observed that
despite a pledge that the military complement at Bignona would not be
permitted to fall below 200, it had actually slipped to somewhere between
120 and 130 men under arms.[42] In the face of renewed Jola militancy, these
forces were considered entirely inadequate. If peaceable Narang could secretly
nurture armed insurgents, so the reasoning went, an armed rebellion in Karone
and in Fogny was a distinct possibility. Following a visit to Kabadio, Benquey
reported a complete disdain for French authority on the part of traders from
Karone who passed through in groups of 50–60 people en route to Bathurst.
The latter carried palm-oil in one direction and consumer goods in the other
and refused to pay any Customs duties. Moreover, Benquey complained, they
taunted and physically threatened the Customs men as they passed through. On
one occasion when the latter fired warning shots, the lack of any casualties was

---

[40] Interview with Tombon Ture, 18 February 2004.
[41] Gorgui N'Diaye was presumably a Wolof from central or northern Senegal, which made it
unlikely that he would be especially well attuned to local political currents. Presumably, the
authorities felt that being African was enough. ANS 2G 17/37 "Territoire de la Casamance:
Rapport Politique mensuel (1917)", "Situation politique du mois de Juillet 1917".
[42] ANS 2G 16/37 "Casamance, Rapports mensuels d'ensemble 1916", "Situation politique du
mois de Juillet 1916".

Table 5.2 *Official summary of police and military actions in Fogny,*
1897–1909

	Incidents	Tax raised
1897	Operations against Zankoran, and show of force against Kartiak, Kaniobo, Dianki, Basire, Thionk-Essyl, Suelle	1,500
1898	Thionk-Essyl, Kartiak, Mlomp burned	2,100
1899	–	7,820
1900	Several villages in Fogny Central reportedly hostile	10,370
1901	Display of force against Sindian	17,536
1902	–	17,327
1903	Villages of Kakoudie and Brinduega (?) bombarded	23,000
1904	Rebellion of Thionk-Essyl, Kartiak, Mlomp spreads to Dianki, Kaniobo, Bagaya	15,000
1905	Attack by villages of Basire, Dianki, Kartiak et al.	54,334
1906	Show of force by police in Fogny and Ziguinchor area	75,661
1907	Show of force by police. Posts established at Sindian, Bralandian, Kartiak. Post at Kartiak attacked by villages of Thionk-Essyl, Mlomp, Dianki and Kartiak	188,821
1908	-	202,277
1909	-	232,722

Source: ANS 13 G375 "Casamance: Documents provenant des Archives de Ziguinchor", "Notes sur le Fogny: Situation Politique – Impôt".

interpreted as evidence that the traders were impervious to French bullets. Sensing a brewing storm, Benquey blamed his predecessor, Richard Brunot, for not having meted out more object lessons in colonial discipline:

Since then [the incident just referred to], their insolence and audacity has grown. All these facts were known to my predecessor, but I don't know why no measure was taken to put an end to them. Meanwhile, there were almost 100 unoccupied tirailleurs at Bignona![43]

In Fogny/Buluf, the French did not even enjoy the interludes of relative tranquillity that had prevailed in Diouloulou subdivision. Although the French had expected to be welcomed by the Jola as liberators, the very first attempts to raise taxes met with a truculent response. In the years leading up to the First World War, military conscription was, if anything, an even greater source of friction. Table 5.2 gives a list, contained within an administrative report, of

---

[43] ANS 2G 17/37 "Territoire de la Casamance, "Rapport politique, Juillet 1917".

episodes of resistance in Fogny between 1897 and 1909. Although it can be seen that the collection of tax steadily improved, certain communities refused to accept the 'lessons' meted out to them. Hence the village of Kartiak is referred to in no fewer than five years as being in a state of rebellion, and was repeatedly found in league with the villages of Dianki, Thionk-Essyl and Mlomp. A cycle was established in which a display of military force would secure grudging compliance for a year or two, only for the pattern of opposition to repeat itself. The Casamance authorities found themselves caught on the horns of a dilemma. The costs of assigning significant numbers of police and/or *tirailleurs* to tax duties were considerable, and they nullified efforts at creating a regular civil administration, which had been a stated objective since the end of the previous century. But equally a failure to maintain an adequate display of force risked local standoffs in which the authorities would not necessarily have enough firepower to prevail: after all, the Jola remained very well armed. The fear was that the slightest sign of weakness would embolden neighbouring villages, thereby spreading the contagion of rebellion from one locality to the next.

Already by the end of 1916, the Governor-General in Dakar, Gabriel Angoulvant, had concluded that it would be necessary to revisit the colonial conquest with troops brought in from other parts of West Africa. This gave effect to a 'pacification' plan devised by Brunot, the *Administrateur Supérieur*, even if Von Vollenhoven (the incoming Governor-General) was inclined to agree that the latter was to blame for having allowed the situation to deteriorate in the first place.[44] In September 1917, Benquey re-stated the case for the military re-occupation of the Casamance, citing the Séléty incident as proof of a resurgent spirit of resistance:

> The situation in Fogny, although not assuming as acute a character, is no less bad. The population evades us completely and rare are those inhabitants who come to us to settle their differences. A number of villages have not handed over all their guns; others have not handed over any. Certain groups do not even conceal their hostility and one has the impression that the least incident could be the signal for very serious troubles. The Selety affair is a striking example of this spirit. If the post of Diouloulou had not been warned in time it would have been taken by the partisans of Al Hadji Haïdara and all the population of Combo would have joined him.[45]

Von Vollenhoven was persuaded by the alarming picture that Benquey presented, concluding that "We are not the masters in the Lower Casamance. We are only tolerated there." The Lieutenant-Governor of Senegal, who was altogether more cautious, nevertheless accepted the seriousness of the

---

[44] Roche, *Histoire de la Casamance*, p. 348.
[45] ANS 13G 384 "Casamance Affaires Politiques", Gouverneur Général Von Vollenhoven, to Lt. Gouverneur, Saint-Louis (17 November 1917).

situation, adding that it was not merely southern Buluf that posed a challenge, but also Bliss and Karone.[46] His answer to the puzzle of why the populations that had seemed the most tractable – namely those of Narang – had suddenly turned against France, lay in the nefarious influence of foreign marabouts who were spreading dangerous Islamist ideas. As in other West African theatres, Islamic conspiracies provided a convenient explanation for resistance that arguably had much more to do with the singular failure of the French to establish viable networks of collaboration. But the recognition that people and ideas could traverse the borders with consummate ease underlined the challenge to surveillance at the geographical margins.

In November 1917, the re-conquest began with yet another reorganization of the administration. The *cercle* of the Lower Casamance was now broken into three, creating the *cercle*s of Ziguinchor, Kamobeul and Bignona (including the subdivision of Diouloulou). As a military officer, Benquey was placed at the head of three military companies located at Sédhiou, Kamobeul and Bignona. Henceforth he was expected to combine military and civil functions, being answerable in the latter regard to the Lieutenant-Governor in Saint-Louis. Military officers were also placed at the head of the reconfigured *subdivisions*. The stated aim of the military occupation was to secure open (and safe) routes, the prompt payment of taxes, the delivery of colonial justice, the regrouping of some populations into villages and above all the disarmament of the Jola. Any resistance was to be dealt with firmly, and suspected leaders of the opposition could be detained. On the other hand, the Governor-General expressly forbade the pursuit of a scorched earth policy lest it bring about greater impoverishment.[47] In all likelihood, the real apprehension was that it might provoke a mass flight of population into the Gambia. Benquey proceeded to use all the military means at his disposal to enforce compliance with demands for taxation and conscription, and to secure the surrender of a very large quantity of guns. There were some complaints about the excessive use of force, which the Governor-General had difficulty in verifying because Benquey managed to restrict the flow of information.[48] The Lt.-Governor was his most persistent critic, partly out of irritation that Benquey made a point of keeping him in the dark. Although the show of force did bring the desired results in the short run, the weakness of the military option was that it did away with any pretence of a 'native policy'. In 1916, Ansoumane Diatta was recognized as the only canton chief across the whole of the Bignona *cercle*.

[46] ANS 13G 384 "Casamance", Levecque, Lt. Gouverneur, Saint-Louis to Gouverneur Général (1 September 1917).
[47] ANS 13G 385 "Casamance", Memorandum by Chef du Service des Affaires Civiles (7 February 1918).
[48] See the correspondence in ANS 13G 385 "Casamance".

This meant, in effect, that the military administrators dealt with a plethora of village chiefs whose status and local bargaining power was strictly minimal. French rule had regressed to the *tourneé*, but this time in full military attire.

In March 1918, following complaints about collective punishments, Angoulvant – now back in the office of Governor-General – signalled that it was possible to contemplate a return to some form of civil administration in the near future, but that this would have to be phased in such a way that compliant localities would be the first to benefit. But as late as April 1919, he was still insisting that it was too early to envisage a complete withdrawal of the troops.[49] After the War, there were renewed efforts to construct a system of civilian administration that would be held together by the sinews of French administrative posts and a hierarchy of traditional authorities carrying out important day-to-day responsibilities. The map of the Lower Casamance was now redrawn as three *cercles*: Ziguinchor (absorbing Kamobeul) south of the Casamance River, and Sédhiou and Bignona to the north thereof. The latter comprised two *subdivisions*, one centred on Bignona itself and the other on Diouloulou. The latter was, in turn, broken into four new cantons – Bliss and Karone, Kombo, Narang and Fogny-Jabangkunda – each with its own canton chief.

In 1923, the *Administrateur Supérieur* submitted a detailed report that provided an overview of past administrative policy that was as damning as it was insightful. He noted that very little cognisance had been taken of distinctions between, and relations amongst, the various Jola sub-groups, with the result that internal boundaries had been arbitrarily drawn. Moreover, the canton chiefs that had been recognized in the past had been selected according to criteria that made it difficult for them to build any local legitimacy. Many of them had been strangers from far afield, and these were often Mandinka who were only too happy to preside over Jola settlements. Furthermore, the chiefs had lived off the people because they were never properly remunerated. As a result, when the opportunity presented itself in 1915, many Jola communities had divested themselves of these unwanted chiefs. What was entirely lacking, in his view, was a proper system of 'native administration' or *commandemant indigène*, in which chiefs might serve as genuine intermediaries between the administrators and the people.[50] In putting forward proposals for a series of new canton chiefs, the administrator proposed that this should be backed up with a proper system of remuneration.

But despite the pledge to cultivate chiefs from amongst the local population, the list of nominees that the administrator proposed suggested that individual qualities remained the most important criterion. Judging from the names of the

---

[49] ANS 13G 385 "Casamance", telegram from Angoulvant to Lt. Gouverneur (4 Avril 1919).
[50] ANS 2G 23/70 "Territoires de la Casamance, Administrateur Supérieur: rapports d'ensemble semestriels 1923", Report for first trimester.

two nominees in Bignona subdivision, Tamba and Bojang, it does not appear that either was a Jola. In Diouloulou subdivision, the picture was equally mixed: the nominee for Bliss and Karone, one N'Faly Diaban, was probably a Mandinka. More understandably, Malick Sonko, the candidate for Kombo, would have been a Mandinka as well. However, the canton chief for Fogny-Jabangkunda, Lan Diadhiou, was in all likelihood a Jola, while Bourama Diatta of Narang was possibly one as well. These nominations for canton chiefs represented some progress, but the extent to which the French could be said to be working with the grain of local society still remained questionable.

In 1926, the administration made substantial changes to the administrative boundaries in a way that disrupted the system that had only very recently been put in place. Most importantly, the canton of Kombo was added to a part of Fogny to create a separate canton of Combo-Fogny under the chiefly oversight of Lan Diadhiou.[51] In Bignona subdivision, a special category of 'provincial chief' was subsequently created in an attempt to restore order in Kadiamoutaye (northern Fogny). The context was one in which there were renewed signs of restiveness amongst the Jolas of Fogny and the population of Bliss and Karone, which necessitated deployment of the *tirailleurs* once again. The administrator estimated that there were 15,000 guns in the *cercle* of Bignona alone, as the Jola re-armed themselves with imports from the Gambia.[52] In the face of renewed evidence of defiance, the French authorities reverted to type, repeating many of the same errors that had only recently been identified with great clarity. Hence Lamine Sonko, who was elevated to the position of provincial chief, was not even from Fogny, but was a stranger from Sine-Saloum.[53] Official reports once again bemoaned the lack of credible chiefs, and stated the need for a proper chieftaincy policy, but each successive reshuffling of the pack made this even less likely to transpire.[54]

In 1931, there was yet another reorganization of the administrative bound-aries, which led to Bliss and Karone being hived off to form part of the *subdivision* of Kamobeul within the *cercle* of Ziguinchor.[55] Kafountine was placed in the latter *cercle*, but the villages with which it had the closest connections remained in the *cercle* of Bignona. This reflected some confusion in French minds as to whether Kafountine was really a part of Karone or of

[51] Malick Sonko was made redundant. ANS 2G 26/66 "Territoire de la Casamance: rapport politiques général annuel (1926)", "Situation Politique et Etat Generale des Cercles (1926)".
[52] 2G 28/61 "Territoire de la Casamance: rapport général annuel 1928", Report on cercle of Bignona.
[53] ANS 2G 29/83 "Cercle de Bignona: rapport général annuel 1929", "Situation Politique et Etat Generale des Cercles (1929)".
[54] ANS 2G 29/91 "Territoire de la Casamance: rapport politique annuel 1929", Lt.-Gouverneur, St. Louis, to Administrateur Supérieur de la Casamance (1 Avril 1930).
[55] 2G 31/74 "Territoire de la Casamance: rapport annuel 1931".

Fogny-Jabangkunda. Strictly speaking, it had previously represented a kind of frontier settlement that was not part of Karone proper. Moreover, within the Bignona *cercle*, the *subdivision* headquarters was transferred from Diouloulou to Balandine and then briefly to Bignona itself in an attempt to reduce running costs during the Depression years. This threatened to bring about a significant contraction of the field administration. Hence, after some time the process was reversed and Diouloulou was reoccupied. In 1940, three villages, including Kafountine, were transferred from the subdivision of Bliss and Karone to Fogny-Combo.[56] This redressed the earlier anomaly, but it created a fresh separation between Kafountine and Karone that was only slightly less problematic. It was only a matter of time before Bliss and Karone and Fogny-Jabangkunda were reunited in the post-war period. Nothing very positive had resulted from this incessant tinkering. Unsurprisingly, the same ad hoc interventions were apparent in the making and unmaking of chiefs. In 1926, one Lonka Demba from Kafountine was made a chief in Karone, and in 1931 he was elevated to the position of canton chief. However, he was not held in any great esteem by the French administrators who accused him of being a heavy drinker and of being incapable of commanding the respect of his people. Hence in 1940, the Commandant de Cercle recommended that he be forced to step down in favour of a younger candidate, Joseph Diatta.[57]

The purpose of mapping out these fluctuations in such detail is to demonstrate that there was only a limited sense in which the demarcation of international boundaries was followed by the deepening of a bureaucratic presence. The ideal was one in which European officials manned a number of administrative posts – ideally distributed evenly across the colonial landscape – and relied on recognized chiefs to implement directives. If the system was functioning well, the administrator would need to do little more than maintain a periodic check on the chiefs and deal with special challenges as and when they arose. The taxes would flow in on time, an annual ritual that was supposed to renew the bond between the administrator and the chief and between the chief and his people. In the western part of the Gambia, this ideal was achieved to a reasonable extent. To be sure, the Commissioner continued to do a fair amount of travelling, but it was no longer necessary to be seen in person for the basis of his authority to be accepted. The British were helped in Kombo by the fact that they were able to tap into the pre-existing structures of the former kingdom whose effective borders coincided with those of the colonial boundary. But they also helped their cause by reconciling the old ruling houses with the Tures whose legitimacy hinged on descent from Fodé Sylla. In the Gambia, the chiefs carried out important practical functions, although they

[56] ANS 11D 1/151 "Casamance, Bignona: Renseignements Politiques et Militaires (1927–1954)", J.C. Haumant, Commandant de cercle de Ziguinchor to Gouverneur du Sénégal (13 Mars 1940).
[57] ANS 11D1/151 "Casamance", notes on Joseph Diatta.

enjoyed less inherent authority in Fogny than in Kombo, and to a large extent they did provide some kind of link to the European administration.

The French faced more of a challenge because they inherited a historical frontier zone where there had been no recent history of political centralization. The authorities locked themselves into a vicious cycle: believing that there was no traditional authority worthy of the name in the areas they had inherited, they resorted to arbitrary expedients. Although they hoped to win sympathy for having brought peace to a region wracked by conflict – invoking a version of the coercive social contract – the execution was decidedly clumsy. Amongst the Jola and the Karoninka, there was fierce opposition to the payment of taxes and a refusal to accept the legitimacy of colonial chiefs, especially when these turned out to be Mandinka who were associated with the abuses of the past. The fact that populations could acquire guns and seek refuge across the border meant that the French were repeatedly confronted with the practical limits to their power. Before the First World War, the administration was constantly moving from one area to the next to dampen the threat of resistance through a physical display of force. In the years leading up to the First World War, there was a widespread perception that their grip was slipping, and it was this that necessitated a complete military re-occupation of the Casamance in 1917. But even the crackdown did not have enduring effects. During the 1920s and 1930s, when civilian control was restored, the authorities repeatedly shuffled personnel and repositioned internal boundaries in the hope that they would come up with the winning formula. If anything, the opposite occurred: relentless change undermined attempts to forge a coherent 'native policy', prevented the sedimentation of a collective bureaucratic memory and, above all, advertised the weakness of the French position. The latter, in turn, fed a vicious circle because it emboldened Jola communities to reclaim their autonomy. Whereas the French eventually managed to find willing allies in northern Senegal, the Casamance came to assume the status of a problem case. Over the long run these patterns led to the emergence of something like a bifurcated state that assumed a very different form in the two halves of Senegal.

The Fracturing of Agotime

1. The chief should lead his people according to the realization of the European knowledge
2. He should be in unity with the Mission, and urge the children to attend school
3. He should love his people [more] than his belly.[58]

---

[58] PRAAD (Ho) DA/D288 "Agotime Native Affairs", "Laws of Reining [sic]" (undated).

I turn now to consider parallel attempts to create administrative order along successive sets of international borders that were drawn in the trans-Volta. As we have seen, the Gold Coast/Togo border assigned Peki to the British and the rest of Krepe to the Germans. In that sense, the Germans inherited a historical frontier zone, much as the French did in the Casamance. As in the case of Kombo, the colonial boundary largely mapped onto an older political topography with the Volta River defining different colonial spheres. The German colony of Togoland was divided into eight districts, of which Misahöhe was one of the largest and most economically important.[59] Unlike in the case of the Jola, the decentralized chieftaincies of the Ewe provided modest foundations on which administrative chieftaincies could be constructed. In Agotime, where there were big men rather than chiefs, colonial chieftaincy was probably experienced as more of a radical break. In the early years, the Commissioners spent the greater part of their time on tour. The need to ensure that taxes were collected and to extract forced labour for infrastructure projects frequently required the physical presence of the Commissioner, and not uncommonly a show of force. Once the last pockets of open resistance had been dealt with, and a solid cadre of chiefly intermediaries had been installed, a more sedentary form of administration took shape – albeit one that remained highly personalized. Whereas there was a fairly rapid turnover of officials in the Casamance, it is remarkable that Dr. Hans Grüner remained the Commissioner in Misahöhe between 1890 and 1912.[60] As a consequence, he was able to build up an intimate knowledge of each and every *dukɔ* that made up his district. Grüner had a particular interest in determining and physically demarcating the boundaries between the *dukɔwo* – which came to be immortalized in the Karte Von Togo of 1905. At one level, this was all about administrative tidiness, but it was not the purity of the cadastral survey that motivated Grüner so much as a pragmatic desire for agreed boundaries between chiefdoms based as far as possible on historical claims. The context was the expansion of cash crop cultivation and a proliferation of land disputes.

As in the Gambia, the German administration recognized two categories of chiefs, namely superior and village chiefs. The chiefs in Misahöhe District played a vitally important role in the collection of taxes, with 5 per cent of the

---

[59] Strictly speaking there were five Bezirksamtern and three Stationsbezirke, but Cornevin noted that the difference between them was hard to discern. The former referred to the more southerly districts that were considered more advanced, including Misahöhe. Robert Cornevin, *Histoire du Togo* (Paris: Editions Berger-Levrault, 1962), p. 171.

[60] Arthur Knoll, *Togo under Imperial Germany, 1884–1914: A Case-Study in Colonial Rule* (Stanford: Hoover Institution Press, 1978), p. 44. This seems to have been a pattern in Togo. Hans Von Doering was well-ensconced in Atakpame before being promoted as deputy Governor. M. Amegan, "Les administrateurs allemands de la circonscription d'Atakpame (1898–1914)", in T. Gbeasor, *Espace, culture et developpement dans la region d'Atakpame* (Lomé: Presses de L'UB, 1999), p. 67.

head taxes being retained by them. These were then sub-divided in such a way that the superior chief received a third and the village chief two-thirds of the proceeds. The chiefs also played a role in the policing of their communities and in the exercise of justice. The chiefs' courts had civil and a limited criminal jurisdiction, with the headchief's court exercising the right to impose fines of up to 100 marks, and half that for a village chief.[61] Knoll observes that most of the colonial chiefs were new men, rather than those who had signed the original treaties, because a premium was placed on "energy and obedience".[62] But over a time certain chiefly lines cemented their grip, which made for a system that resembled the Gambia more than it did the Casamance.

After the departure of the Germans, a rather nostalgic re-interpretation of German order took hold that is difficult to reconcile with the statements that were collected after 1914.[63] In Agotime, however, the German period is remembered as a litany of woes balanced by very few positives. What was especially keenly felt was the loss of the two things that the Agotime had excelled at: namely the pursuit of warfare and profitable trade. It appears as if dealing in slaves continued in a clandestine fashion because German officials felt it necessary to mount an expedition to stamp out the practice in Agotime.[64] As has been noted in Chapter 3, the authorities also interrupted a profitable trade in cotton into the Gold Coast. Whereas the Agotime had once prided themselves on their extended trade networks, these became greatly attenuated during the German period. On the face of it, the Agotime benefited from investments in infrastructure, even if it was they who provided much of the labour. Kpetoe was located on the established trade route from Ho, which was later transformed into a hammock-road that ran to the capital of Lomé. This positioning rendered Kpetoe even more attractive to Anlo traders, who had apparently been using the route for some time. Many of the latter chose to settle permanently in the town and became integrated into Agotime (as we will see in Chapter 6). Moreover, the Lomé–Kpalimé railway line skirted the eastern edge of Agotime close to Amoussoukope. The railhead provided a potential outlet for producers of agricultural commodities. Partly for this reason some people from Kpetoe relocated to be closer to the market there. But the Agotime had never been renowned for their farming prowess, and much of their land was considered as being sandy and of poor quality for food crop farming. One French official was later to distinguish between a relatively fertile zone in northern Agotime, around Nyitoe and Zukpe, and a poorer zone to the south, including Batoumé and Amoussoukope, which was largely

[61] Cornevin, *Histoire*, p. 175.   [62] Knoll, *Togo*, p. 48.
[63] Dennis Laumann, *Remembering the Germans in Ghana* (Berne: Peter Lang, 2016).
[64] Interview with Nene Akoto Sah VII, Kpetoe (Ghana), 5 September 2007.

uncultivated.[65] Finally, most of Agotime was unsuited to cocoa production, which had such a transformational impact on the areas to the north of Agotime, most notably around Kpalimé and Agu.

The loss of political influence is something that looms equally large in the Agotime imagination. A number of informants bemoaned the fact that Agotime tributaries were permitted by the Germans to break away. If the Agotime were perceived as recidivists, with a lingering attachment to slave dealing, this might help to account for an unwillingness to grant them a relatively privileged position within the emerging pecking order. At one point, Governor Von Puttkamer is reputed to have remarked, vis-à-vis some problems with chief Badabani of Zukpe "Please never forget that those wretches are all, without exception, rascals without use."[66] Unfortunately, the Karte Von Togo distributes Agotime across two discontinuous sheets. But it does depict Agotime as bordering onto Hodzo, Adaklu, Atikpui and Nyive to the south and west, Tové to the north[67], and Assahun,[68] Atigbe and Ave to the east, and Ahundo to the south-east. This represented a large swathe of territory running almost from the straight-line boundary with the Gold Coast to the margins of Kpalimé and Agu. The map depicted a number of *dukɔwo* who the Agotime claimed to have extracted tribute from in the past as separate entities. When J.T. Furley conducted interviews in 1918, the linguist to the chief of Atikpui indicated that he still fell under Agotime division, whereas Nyive and Atigbe constituted separate divisions to the north. To the south, the Kévé had been excised from Agotime, and its chief had been placed above the chiefs of Ave and Assahun (amongst others).[69] Hodzo was placed beneath Ho, while separate Adaklu and Waya divisions were recognized. In addition, Adame, which was depicted on the 1905 map as the northern limits of Agotime, seems to have been cut free altogether.[70]

[65] TNAL 2APA/31 "Rapports periodiques des Cercles: Cercle de Klouto", Rapport concernant la Tournee effectué par M. Goujon, Commandant le Cercle de Klouto dans la region de l'Agotime, Atigbe, Assahoun-Fiagbé, 21–30 Juin 1935", dated 13 July 1935, p. 8. This is borne out by the 1905 Karte Von Togo, Map E1, which clearly identified Agotime farms to the east of Zukpe and Nyitoe.

[66] Peter Sebald, *Togo 1884–1914: Eine Geschichte der deutschen 'Musterkolonie' auf der Grundlage amtlicher Quellen* (Berlin: Akademie-Verlag, 1988), p. 69.

[67] Tové is located just south of Kpalimé.

[68] This Assahun (Fiagbe) is not to be confused with the Ando town of the same name, which lies east of Batoumé.

[69] The statement by the Kpedze chief that he came under Agotime is clearly a typographical error and should have read 'Avatime', PRAAD ADM 11/1620 "Togoland Secret and Confidential Papers" (1918–1924), Report of a meeting held at Nyive on 5 February 1918, p. 25. Although Lawrence cites an informant stating that the people of Kévé used to be one with Kpetoe, and that their contacts were severed by the border, it would surely have been a tributary rather than an integral part of Agotime. Benjamin N. Lawrance, "'En proie à la fièvre du cacao': land and resource conflict on an Ewe frontier, 1922–1939", *African Economic History* 31, 2003, p. 156.

[70] The map produced by Furley places Adame outside of Agotime.

The Germans did not consider Kpetoe as possessing the importance of a town like Ho or Kpandu, as is evident from the absence of any official buildings dating from the period. Commissioners passed through Kpetoe rather than seeking to deploy it as a node within a wider network of administration. The Bremen and Catholic missions similarly concentrated their efforts else-where. Agotime was visited by the Bremen missionary, Bernhard Schlegel as early as 1858, but nothing came of it.[71] By the time of the Asante invasion there were four principal mission stations in the trans-Volta: those of Keta, Anyako, Ho and Adaklu-Waya.[72] After the Asante withdrawal, the Bremen missionaries returned to their former stations and began to make greater inroads. They were joined by the Catholic Steyler Mission, and fierce compe-tition between the two was reflected in interspersed Catholic and Protestant congregations across the southern half of the German colony. Ho regained its earlier significance for the Bremen mission, while Agu became another leading centre of Protestant mission activity from 1901. As with the political adminis-tration, neither mission considered Agotime as a centre of operations.[73] By contrast, while Adaklu-Waya was downgraded to a sub-station, it retained a residual importance.[74] The Catholics initially focused on the more northerly areas of Hohoe, Kpalimé and Kpandu, but in 1908 they diverted some of their attention to Ho and Assahun, followed by Agu-Tomegbe two years later.[75] These were all on the borders of Agotime and, with the exception of Ho, had hitherto been considered as either bitter rivals or tributaries. The uncomfortable reality was that Agotime fell behind its neighbours in the pace of conversion and in access to schooling. Although some Agotime children were sent to mission school in Agu, this was not a realistic option for the majority.

Finally, German rule wrought a transformation in the Agotime power structure. Whereas there had hitherto been a priest in Afegame and rival war chiefs (*avafiawo*) in Kpetoe, the Germans introduced the position of headchief for the first time. Quite how this came about remains somewhat unclear. It is generally agreed that a male fetish/stool was brought to Kpetoe at some point in the past, possibly for safe-keeping, while the female one remained in Afegame.[76] One version that is told by the Agbovi family is that the

---

[71] Hans Debrunner, *A Church between Colonial Powers: A Study of the Church in Togo* (London: Lutterworth Press, 1965), p. 78.

[72] Debrunner, *A Church*, pp. 79–84.

[73] It is surely significant that Debrunner's very thorough history of the church makes very few references to Agotime. In fact, there are only three references for the post-1874 period. There appear to be none at all in Werner Ustorf, *Bremen Missionaries in Togo and Ghana: 1847–1900* (Legon: Legon Theological Studies and Asempa, 2002).

[74] Debrunner, *A Church*, p. 109.   [75] Debrunner, *A Church*, p. 110.

[76] Fieldwork diary entry on discussions in Kpodjahon (Togo), 20 August 2001. The chief of Batoumé thought that the fetish/stool might have reached Kpetoe by stealth or force. Interview with Togbe Apaloo, Batoumé (Togo), 22 August 2001. In 1946, the Agotime Divisional

grandfather of Agbovi I had been sent to live with his uncle in Afegame, who was the custodian of the fetish.[77] When the latter died, the grandfather returned to Kpetoe with it, but after an accident resulting from violation of a taboo, it was lodged with a leper in Kpetoe who was kept in confinement.[78] By a cruel twist of colonial fate, it was the latter (or someone else in his family) that subsequently ended up being recognized as the headchief of Agotime. Quite how this might have happened is never satisfactorily explained, but one can easily imagine a literally minded German administrator demanding to know the keeper of the sacred objects and then recognizing that person as the chief. The Agbovi version also points out that Agbovi I was residing at the hamlet of Batoumé with his slaves and dependents, and hence would not have been as visible to the Germans.[79] However, there was also a belief that Agbovi was punished for being too independently minded, as J.T. Furley was informed in 1918:

The Germans came and asked Agbovi to give them our land. Agbovi refused because the land belonged to the English. The Chiefs of Agotime sent messengers to Accra to thank the English because they saved them from the Ashantis.[80]

Having been denied the position of headchief, Agbovi may well have decided to disengage from the administration. The Akoto family version simply recalls that the Germans appointed the person they found it convenient to lodge with as their chief.[81] But they are both agreed on one material point, namely that the Keteku family had never provided anything like a paramount chief in the past – although what they cannot explain away is the fact that the eighteenth-century *caboceer*, Keteku (sometimes rendered as Keteku I), is remembered as the first or second leader of the Agotime.

The contention that the headchiefship was a German creation was echoed for different reasons by the dominant families in Afegame. In November 1930, Nene Mahumansro of Afegame swore in an affidavit that he was the rightful headchief and that because Kpetoe was a subsidiary settlement it could never

---

Council ruled that "the Divisional stool of Agotime moved to Kpetoe before the Ashanti invasion on Ewe land". PRAAD (Ho) DA/D288 "Agotime", Agbo, Presiding Member of Agotime Divisional Council, Adedome, to District Commissioner, Ho (14 August 1946).

[77] Fieldwork diary 20 August 2001.

[78] A British official collected a version of the story in which one Ameganyi brought the 'stool' to Kpetoe from Afegame. PRAAD (Ho) DA/D288 "Agotime", undated handwritten notes, probably by H.C. Ellershaw.

[79] Fieldwork diary 20 August 2001.

[80] PRAAD ADM 11/1620 "Togoland Secret and Confidential Papers" (1918–1924), Report of a meeting held at Kpetoe on 7 February 1918, p. 34. As I indicated in Chapter 3, Agbovi had actually signed a treaty with the Germans. He was possibly playing it both ways. The point is that his loyalty was in question.

[81] Interview with Nene Akoto Sah VII, Kpetoe, 5 September 2007.

have filled that position in the past.[82] Two years later, he submitted his own version of the history of Agotime chieftaincy.[83] It made no reference to stolen fetishes and implied that there was an actual stool that had always resided with his family. It also insisted that there had been an unbroken line of chiefs based in Afegame. Mahumansro claimed that Sevor was actually the headchief when the Germans arrived, but that he had fallen foul of the authorities after his people had resisted attempts to force them to work on the roads. This is presumably a reference to the Smend affair (see Chapter 3). Mahumansro went on to allege that the Germans had recognized a chief in Kpetoe, called Kowu Dade, and that it was the latter who had put forward one Matti Sorkpor as the headchief. When Sevor was told to sign a 'chief's book' by Dr. Grüner, so the story goes, he did not realize that he was in fact endorsing Sorkpor as the new Agotime headchief. This account is superficially convincing, except for the fact that the Germans and the British alike had previously treated Agbovi as if he had been the 'king' of the Agotime. There had never been any suggestion that there was a chief in Afegame who was worthy of any great note, although a Union Jack exchanged hands earlier in the century. An enquiry by an Assistant District Commissioner (ADC) generated a list of sixteen former chiefs, "all acknowledged by other Agotime towns as Fiaga", which is of some interest. It began with Ameganyi and Keteku and listed Akoto Sah and Agbovi in more recent times.[84] But it did not tally with the list produced by Mahumansro, and Sevor was not even mentioned there. If the Afegame 'chiefs' were in fact priests rather than military-cum-political leaders, as I have argued in Chapter 2, this would not be too surprising. The British list also included the names of people from clans other than those of Agbovi and Akoto – most obviously Keteku – which is consistent with the interpretation that military leadership had been earned rather than being hereditary. The only real doubt remains over the status of Kowu Dade who appears in the British list as the headchief that preceded Matti Sorkpor. If he was indeed the Agotime headchief, it is unclear why he would have handed the reins to Matti Sorkpor, unless the German Commissioner had decided that he was not fit for office. Sorkpor was fairly young and probably had some prior connection with the Germans – Matti being a corruption of the name, 'Martin'. His recognition would therefore serve as an illustration of the German selection of chiefs on the basis of their capacity to act as interlocutors rather than being the repository of traditional legitimacy. Quite how this relates to custodianship of the fetish/ stool remains unclear. Agbovi family traditions clearly seek to elevate

[82] PRAAD (Ho) DA/D288 "Agotime" affidavit by Mahumansro in the Supreme Court of the Gold Coast Colony, Eastern Province, 10 November 1930.

[83] PRAAD (Accra) CSO 21/22/30 "Agotime History", "The preliminary history of Agotime".

[84] PRAAD (Ho) DA/D288 "Agotime", handwritten notes (undated).

themselves above those who came to provide the headchief, on the basis that they brought the Ntsrifoa fetish/stool to Kpetoe. By contrast, the family of Matti Sorkpor claimed that it had actually come with the founder of Kpetoe, namely Ameganyi. This remains the basis of the structural tension today between the occupant of the position of the Konor of Agotime and the *avafiawo* of Kpetoe, each of whom asserts a claim to precedence based on conflicting renditions of history. As we have seen, the attempt to impose chieftaincy on the Jola of the Casamance was met with a lack of interest and, when they were required to raise taxes, with actual resistance. Many Agotimes were clearly displeased by the elevation of a relative parvenu to the status of headchief. But at the time, there were certain risks associated with the position that might explain why there was seemingly no outright opposition at the time. The Agotime political system was one that revolved around big men who remained confident that they possessed legitimacy as opposed to a German chief who assumed the burden of implementing unpopular policies such as the raising of head taxes.

After the partition of Togoland in 1919, the former administrative units of the German period were broken in two in a manner that had decisive consequences for the Agotime. Matti Sorkpor continued to regard himself as headchief of all the Agotime regardless of the contours of the border. However, the fact remained that he was a colonially created chief, who lacked the legitimacy surrounding the heads of the Agbovi and Akoto families in Kpetoe. Moreover, whereas chiefs had been an instrument of the German colonial state, the Gold Coast political model became operative in British Togoland after 1919. This meant that chiefs existed outside the institutions of the colonial state, whereas in French Togoland there was greater continuity with the German system. The District Commissioners (DCs) could cajole, but they could not command the chiefs to act – and the same was true of the headchief in relation to his notional subjects. Logically, therefore, there was no question of the headchief projecting his power to settlements in French territory. The maintenance of cross-border jurisdictions was not a possibility that was entertained by either set of authorities in any event. As far as the French were concerned, it was important to disabuse the headchief in Kpetoe of any notion that he retained either interests or influence across the line. Officials kept their ears open but were satisfied that their Agotimes regarded themselves as effectively independent of the headchief in Kpetoe. If the chieftaincy had not been a German creation, the French might have had a much greater problem on their hands, but there was probably some support for a change that restored the balance between the historical Agotime settlements. For their part, the British were keen that Matti Sorkpor adjust to the realities of the situation of being chief over a handful of villages on their side of the border.

In British Togoland, where the political system was civilianized during the occupation, the system of administration revolved around the person of the DC who was answerable to the Commissioner of the Eastern Province (CEP) in the Gold Coast. Between 1921 and 1924, there were separate districts for Ho and Kpandu, but these were then merged into a single Ho District, with an ADC residing at Kpandu. In 1928, the District headquarters was moved to Kpandu, where it remained until 1945 when the *status quo ante* was restored. The individual DCs and their ADCs personified the British administration, but they had generally had enough critical mass, in terms of support staff, to maintain a reasonable level of continuity during periods of leave, sickness and retirement. During the occupation, direct taxation had been terminated, and the fact that it was not revived thereafter meant that some of the most time-consuming work for colonial officials and chiefs alike was dispensed with. *Contra* Scott, the authorities were left with no idea of how many people resided in any given community, being entirely dependent upon the infrequent national censuses for an update of the numbers. The chiefs were none the wiser because they were not required to enumerate the population either. Nevertheless, the workload for the DCs remained considerable because they needed to keep on top of the minutiae of local politics, to construct and maintain roads and – wearing a different hat – to sit as magistrates on behalf of the Supreme Court of the Gold Coast. Captain Lilley was obsessed with the first two parts of his job and performed his fair share of judicial work as well.[85] In local memories, the personalities of Grüner and Lilley have often fused into one, which provides a good indication of their visibility.

Elsewhere I have dealt in detail with the determination of the British administration, and more especially Lilley, to forge larger traditional units under the controversial 'amalgamation policy'.[86] Suffice it to recall that, as the British authorities saw it, the Germans had bequeathed a very fragmented administrative map. Instead of attempting to build up the political prestige of a select cadre of chiefs, it was claimed, they had made each *dukɔ* independent, with the consequence that there were no fewer than sixty-eight autonomous divisions in British southern Togoland. In 1929, a number of ground-rules were laid down that were supposed to determine whether or not an amalgamation of chiefdoms should be allowed to proceed: it needed to be voluntary; there had to be unanimity within a given division; any amalgamated states had to be of sufficient size and geographically practicable; an amalgamation was only to be recognized if 'native customs of a binding nature' had been performed; and finally, the head

---

[85] Lilley began his administrative career as the Acting District Political Officer in Kpandu in 1920 and became the substantive DC in 1926 – a position he held until his retirement in 1938.

[86] For a more detailed account of the amalgamation policy, see Paul Nugent, *Smugglers, Secessionists and Loyal Citizens on the Ghana–Togo Frontier: The Lie of the Borderlands since 1914* (Oxford and Athens: James Currey and Ohio University Press, 2002), ch.4. See also Benjamin Lawrance "Bankoe v Dome: traditions and petitions in the Ho-Asogli amalgamation, British Mandated Togoland, 1919–1939", *Journal of African History* 46 (2) 2005.

of a given state was to be regarded as first amongst equals, leaving divisional chiefs with a free hand with respect to their own affairs.[87]

In practice, Lilley twisted the arms of particular chiefs to persuade them to come underneath others he regarded as possessing the requisite level of influence, and at other times he quashed initiatives he did not approve of. The insistence on unanimity was diluted so that only a majority of sub-chiefs needed to approve of a proposed amalgamation for it to proceed. Over time, the heads of the amalgamated states came to be regarded as substantive paramount chiefs, which was formalized within the Native Administration Ordinance, despite earlier assurances that this would not happen.[88] Hence, the Togoland authorities ended up replicating the Gold Coast system despite the fact that the political map had always been more fragmented to the east of the Volta. By 1931, a total of forty-seven divisions had been folded into four states – namely Akpini, Awatime, Buem and Asogli. Many independent divisions continued to hold out, and they were vindicated when it was eventually admitted that the states that did exist did not really function as well as had been intended. Asogli, which had witnessed innumerable internal disputes, was held up as the best of a bad bunch.[89]

The amalgamation policy was bound to be controversial in Agotime where memories of former military glories were kept alive. Now that most of the Agotime were deposited on the French side of the border, the headchief was left with a small rump with which to jostle for a place in the chiefly pecking order. As far as Lilley was concerned, the dearth of 'subjects' disqualified Kpetoe from becoming the headquarters of an amalgamated state. With so much investment going into building up the Ho chief at the head of Asogli, it was inevitable that pressure would be placed on the Agotime chief to accept a lesser position. For local patriots, this was an anathema because Ho had been considered an equal in the past – most notably during the Asante war when they had fought alongside one another. Unfortunately for Lilley, internal political divisions made it extremely difficult to arrive at an easy consensus. As I have already indicated, Nene Mahumansro of Afegame claimed in 1930 that he was the rightful headchief. This signalled the start of a protracted dispute that Lilley and his colleagues were powerless to resolve. Although they had a solid grasp of who the protagonists were, their presumption that the Agotime had always been governed by chiefs misconstrued realities. Because

[87] PRAAD (Accra) ADM 39/1/545 "Amalgamation of Divisions in Togoland under British Mandate", "Memorandum on Amalgamation in British Togoland" (1944).

[88] PRAAD (Accra) ADM 39/1/545 "Amalgamation of Divisions", Memorandum (1944).

[89] PRAAD (Accra) ADM 39/1/545 "Amalgamation of Divisions", Memorandum (1944). See also PRAAD (Ho) DA/D78 "Handing over Notes", "Handing Over Report by Captain C.C. Lilley, O.B.E., District Commissioner to D.N. Walker, Per Mr. V.H.K. Littlewood, Asst. District Commissioner" (1938).

they did not really engage with the deeper history of Agotime, it was difficult for them to get to the bottom of what *was* in dispute.

In November 1931, Matti Sorkpor died, and the process of seeking a successor began. Predictably, this provided an occasion for Nene Mahumansro to claim that he needed to be consulted over the choice of what he insisted was merely the position of sub-chief in Kpetoe. His insistence on being the headchief was not one that the DC was prepared to countenance, however, and in June the principal sub-chiefs on the British side of the border, including the two *avafiawo* in Kpetoe, gave their backing to a new candidate in the shape of one Lawrence 'Agrona' Dzikpo. The latter was duly enstooled under the title of Nene Noe Keteku II – or as he sometimes preferred to style himself, Nene Keteku XII. However, the new chief quickly made himself unpopular, and in 1937 there were attempts to destool him on the basis that he was a serial adulterer and that he was implicated in the misappropriation of post office funds that he had invested in smuggling activity. The ADC, T.A. Mead, looked into the charges and concluded that whereas Keteku blamed the crisis on unruly youth, the elders and sub-chiefs who had brought him to the stool had turned against him as well. Crucially, he intimated that the destoolment charges concealed deeper motives: "I am informed that the real grievances against him are that he favours the operations of the Village Overseer on [in] Kpetoe and that he is trying to join the Asogli State."[90] Although Mead was unable to verify whether the latter was indeed the basis for the opposition, he concluded that Keteku had become deeply unpopular and that it might be a good thing if he was replaced. The fact that he was being condemned for bending to British pressure did not appear to have struck Mead as in any way ironic.

To further complicate matters, the Agbovi family (from the Agokpome clan) altered its earlier stance and demanded the chieftaincy for itself on the basis that Agbovi I had been the substantive headchief in the past, only for the position to be usurped in recent times.[91] They hoped to kill two birds with one stone by replacing the deceased *avafia* with a new incumbent and then restoring him to his rightful place as Agotime leader. Their subsequent petition went to the heart of the history of power relations since the mid-nineteenth century:

The chief of Agotime is there from ancient days. Now, the late headchief Mati-Sokpo of Kumase [Akumase] – so is his tribe or clan called – [was recognized] two years before the Germans left. The ex-headchief Keteku is also from the same clan. So we have two men only from that family which is now regarded as the ruling tribe for this old

[90] PRAAD (Ho) DA/D288 "Agotime", T.A. Mead, ADC, Ho, to DC, Kpandu (18 March 1937).
[91] PRAAD (Ho) DA/D288 "Agotime", Yawo Akpo and Amatefe Amaglo, Kpetoe, to DC, Ho (8 April 1937).

chiefdom. The question is which tribe was the ruling one from the very beginning? We beg the Government to see into this.[92]

Their power base had been strengthened by virtue of the fact that the late Agbovi I had relocated from his village of Batoumé to Kpetoe rather than come under French rule. Once more a presence in Kpetoe, the head of the Agbovi family could reclaim the right to the chieftaincy. However, there is little evidence to suggest that Lilley and his colleagues fully grasped the historical basis of this claim and even less pointing to a willingness to reconsider the German act of creation. As a consequence, the problem of what to do with Nene Keteku was allowed to drift. At the time Lilley submitted his final Handing Over Report, prior to taking retirement in 1938, the amalgamation issue had become intertwined with intense politicking surrounding the Agotime chieftaincy:

> It is difficult to say whether there is a Headchief of the division or not at the moment as Noe Keteku has been suspended by the people with our approval. The original period was for six months but this has been greatly extended. There is a dispute as to the Headchiefship between the people of Kpetoe and those of Afegame. The latter is very keen on joining Asogli State but the others [are] quite indifferent.[93]

On the outbreak of war, Noe Keteku enlisted – allegedly out of embarrassment at the failure of any of his people to do so – and the affairs of British Agotime were placed in the hands of a regent. It was in November 1941, while Keteku was still in uniform, that amalgamation proceedings with Asogli were finalized. The DC visited Kpetoe and satisfied himself that binding customs had been performed. While Nene Mahumansro refused to attend the final ceremony, it was noted that he had previously performed binding customs with the Ho chief, thereby making the decision to join Asogli supposedly 'unanimous'.[94] In May 1942, Keteku returned to Agotime and sought to make the most of membership in the Asogli State. Balanced against a loss of future claims to a paramouncy of his own was the fact that Keteku was able to operate his own tribunal and to gather a share of the fees. He lost no time in flexing his muscles and went as far as producing a highly interventionist – not to say rather eccentric – set of local by-laws relating to marriage and divorce. This was more than a little ironic in the light of his earlier peccadillos. The by-laws included a stipulation that every marriage had to be reported to the chief with a 4 s fee "to bear evidence", a special clause that adultery with the

---

[92] PRAAD (Ho) DA/D288 "Agotime", Tete Anaglo for the Agokpome family to ADC, Ho (8 June 1937).
[93] See also PRAAD (Ho) "Handing Over Notes", "Handing Over Report by Captain C.C. Lilley".
[94] PRAAD (Ho) ADM 39/1/286 "Amalgamation of Divisions – Asogli State", Provincial Commissioner, Koforidua, to Secretary of Native Affairs, Accra (8 March 1943).

teacher's wife should attract a fine of £5 and a requirement that locally approved Adangbe names had to be given to Agotime children.[95] The attempt to impose these rules elicited a vigorous riposte from Afegame, where Nene Mahumansro demanded recognition of his own tribunal and complained against the headchief's interference in specific marital disputes.

Aside from tribunal fees, membership of Asogli generated additional revenues from the Kpetoe market, which had grown to some size and importance, in part by virtue of its border location. In 1927–8, Captain Lilley had negotiated the acquisition of land to expand the market facilities, and in subsequent years a share of the proceeds had gone to the headchief. When Agotime joined Asogli, control over the marketplace became a matter of contestation, involving the Asogli State, Nene Keteku, a number of sub-chiefs and the putative landlords. In 1945, an agreement was reached with the existing landowners, according to which one-third of the tolls would be transferred to the latter and two-thirds would accrue to Asogli. The demands of the caretaker were considered to be excessive, and Nene Keteku attempted to relocate the market to another site where presumably he would have derived a direct financial benefit. The ostensible rationale was that the existing market was cramped and unsanitary because of the constant threat of flooding from the River Todzie. When the alternative site was judged by a medical officer to be no less unsanitary, there was a reversion to the previous site. A political tug-of-war then ensued in which some sub-chiefs, led by the new head of the Agbovi family, sought to remove the market to a separate location, while others sought to rebuild the market in its original spot. Meanwhile, the landowners took the Asogli State to court over the failure to pay them their one-third share of the revenues – a case that eventually travelled all the way to the West African Court of Appeal.[96] The multi-layered dispute trundled on until 1954, by which time the Native Authority system had already been replaced by institutions of local government. The affair clearly revealed the limits of the authority of the Agotime headchief, as various actors sought to claim a share of what had become the most important local income stream. What finally settled the matter was an objection by the Customs Preventive Service (CPS) to a market site south of the Customs barrier, which would have made it all too easy for uncustomed goods from French Agotime to be traded in the Kpetoe market.[97] The concerns of the Customs men effectively trumped the concerns of the Public Works Department about the unsuitability of the existing site.

---

[95] PRAAD (Ho) DA/D288 "Agotime", "Laws of Reining [sic]".

[96] PRAAD DA/C. 320 "Agotime Kpetoe Market", W.M. Mackay, Government Agent, Ho to Regional Officer, Ho (4 September 1953).

[97] PRAAD DA/C. 320 "Agotime Kpetoe Market", E. Thomas, Collector-in-Charge, Aferingba, to Government Agent, Ho (21 June 1954).

Across the border, the French adopted a cautious approach to start with before introducing far-reaching changes. Although the former Misahöhe District had lost much of its territory to Britain, it continued in the truncated shape of the Cercle de Klouto.[98] Equally, the system of chieftaincy underwent little immediate change. As was the case in the German period, only two tiers of chief were recognized – now dubbed canton and village chiefs.[99] In Agotime, it was the chief of Zukpe who was initially recognized as the *chef de canton*. The Germans had performed the hard work of fixing the boundaries between chiefdoms and identifying broad lines of succession. Unlike in the Casamance, *le commandement indigène* was a system that came to function tolerably well, providing a disincentive for the French authorities to introduce substantial innovations. The one significant exception resided in the creation of *Conseils de Notables*, the first of which became operational in Lomé in 1922 before being extended to the rest of the country in the ensuing years. These councils were elected on a three-year cycle by two electoral colleges: one made up of *chefs de canton* and *chefs de village*, and the other by family and quarter heads in the urban zones.[100] This reform was considerably ahead of its time in that the administration was obliged to formally consult with the Conseils in matters of taxation and in fixing budgets for the *cercle*. By encouraging chiefs to take a wider view than simply that of their particular community, the reform could be presented to the League of Nations as a step towards involving Togolanders in their own governance.

After a long period of continuity, the French introduced more fundamental reforms in 1935–6. On the one hand, the southern half of French Togoland was divided into a Cercle du Sud and a Cercle du Centre, each of which was subdivided into *subdivisions*.[101] The Cercle du Sud embraced Lomé, Anecho and Tsevié *subdivisions*, while the Cercle du Centre was made up of Atakpamé and Klouto. In the process of this reorganization, the Agotimes were divided into discrete segments. Slightly less than half of the towns were included in a separate Canton d'Agotime, one of twenty-six within Tsevié *subdivision*: these were the settlements of Adzakpa, Ando, Agoudouvou, Letsukope, Kodje, Amoussoukope and Batoumé. On the other hand, the northern Agotime towns were enclosed within the Canton d'Agotime Palimé, which formed part of the Cercle de Klouto: namely Kpodjahon, Zukpe, Nyitoe, Wutegble, Atiyi, Egbe, Seva, and Gbekodji, as well as Adame, which was once again treated as an

---

[98] The Cercle de Lomé began south of Agotime.

[99] An additional tier was added in Anecho. Benjamin N. Lawrance, *Locality, Mobility and Nation: Periurban Colonialism in Togo's Eweland 1900–1960* (Rochester: Rochester University Press, 2007), p. 56.

[100] Cornevin, *Histoire*, p. 232.

[101] CAOM, Aix-en-Provence, 1AFFPOL/610 "Affaires Politiques", Arrêté 254 of 4 September 1935.

Agotime settlement. These administrative arrangements were highly controversial because the effect was to elevate the Adzakpa chief to the status of a
chef de canton at the same time as the Zukpe chief was downgraded. Given
that Zukpe had been one of the historical Agotime towns, often rivalling
Kpetoe in importance, this reform was contested. This is implicit in the report
of a *tourneé* by the Commandant de Cercle in June 1935, which commented on
the long discourse on the history of Zukpe to which he had been subjected.[102]
In the mistaken belief that Afegame was the capital of the Agotime people, the
Commandant contrived to meet with the chief on the British side of the border.
He reported that the latter's influence on the French side of the border was
minimal – especially so in Zukpe where the chief was still pressing his own
claims. If he had visited Kpetoe instead, it is doubtful that the picture would
have been so very different. Significantly, there is no suggestion in the archival
record that the administrative changes in French Agotime were a matter of
debate amongst those residing in British Togoland. Equally, the effects of the
amalgamation policy on the headchief in Kpetoe does not seem to have
occasioned much interest on the French Togoland side of the border. This
was the clearest indication of the extent to which Agotime – which had always
been a highly decentralized polity – had been fractured. Given that Agotime
was divided first by the international boundary, and then by internal borders
between the French *cercles*, it had ceased to exist as a discrete political unit.
Although much daily life continued as before, the double partition had the
effect of dissolving some of the political linkages and closing the performative
spaces that helped to reproduce a sense of what it meant to be Agotime. At
the most mundane level, it became difficult to bury one's dead when one's
notional home town was on the other side of the line. The creation of
bureaucratic hurdles is seemingly one reason why the people of Amoussoukope ceased returning to Kpetoe to perform burial rites and resorted to burying
their dead in a local cemetery. What remained of Agotime as an 'imagined'
community turned upon intermarriage, the market and the church, and even
these were unstable. Increasingly, officials and missionaries on both sides of
the border treated the Agotime as a sub-set of the Ewe for the purposes of
convenience. This became more plausible as Ewe became the language of the
church and the market, and increasingly the home as well. The clumsy efforts
of Nene Keteku II to ensure that the Adangbe language was passed on to
the next generation was motivated by a fear that the Agotime were about to be
absorbed by their Ewe neighbours – thereby reversing the hierarchies of the
nineteenth century. This was a particular issue on the British side of the border
where the Agotime were heavily outnumbered.

---

[102] "TNAL 2 APA/31 "Rapports periodiques", Rapport concernant la Tournee effectué par
M. Goujon, 21–30 Juin 1935".

The big difference between the responsibilities of chiefs in French and British Togoland lay in the taxes that the French re-introduced after 1919. The chiefs kept the census rolls updated, mobilized labour and they collected the head tax. Chiefs who failed to perform adequately were punished, sometimes by imprisonment, and could (in extreme cases) be removed from office.[103] The chiefs naturally tended to err on the side of caution lest they be accused of failing to properly discharge their functions. This was a sensitive matter in Agotime because it was not uncommon for people to spend periods of time visiting relatives on the other side of the border – for example, to help out during an illness or the birth of a child. If the visitor spent weeks and months rather than hours or days in a French Togoland village, the chief might feel the need to add him/her to the census roll and demand the payment of the head tax. This became a source of irritation to people from Kpetoe who had close relatives in many villages across the border, especially in Amoussoukope and Batoumé. The following request from Nene Keteku II to the British authorities requesting their intercession could be construed as a means of bolstering his shaky position, but it also reflected the daily complaints he received:

I have the honour to bring to your notice that Agotime comprises of 17 divisions, 13 divisions of which are Zukpe, Nyitoe, Adame, Kpodzaho, Amuzukodzi [Amoussoukope], Adzakpa, Wutegble, Kodze, Lakui, Have, Aguduvu, Letsukofe, and Batume. These divisions were cut by the French Government but are still in harmony with my state, and many of the British subjects frequently visit these. Complaints reach me about troubles met by them about Lempoh [l'impôt]. It is now proposed that if a passport or written authority would [be] furnished by you, empowering me to undersign to every one of my British subjects to be known by the French Government about their short stay in the above towns to return, my British subjects would be save [sic] from troubles about Lempoh.[104]

The other side of the coin was that French Agotimes used the border to escape the burden of taxation. One report covering the village of Wutegble in 1935 observed that the chief had managed to deliver only seven out of the fifteen tax obligations outstanding. The Commandant noted that: "His subjects are hiding in the bush to escape l'impôt. A garde de cercle was placed at his disposal at his request in order to help recover the late ones."[105] In many cases, the people seeking to escape paying tax sought refuge in settlements on the other side of the line. If the evasion of taxes on the French side was one means

---

[103] Lawrance, Locality, p. 58.

[104] DA/D288 "Agotime Native Affairs", Nene Noe Keteku II, Kpetoe, to ADC, Ho (13 June 1936).

[105] "TNAL 2 APA/31 'Rapports periodiques', Rapport concernant la Tournee effectué par M. Goujon, Commandant le Cercle de Klouto dans le region d'Agou du 13 au 18 et du 21 au 35 mai 1935".

by which Agotimes remained connected, the other was through the evasion of Customs duties on the British side. The key to a successful smuggling ring was the maintenance of close networks between participants on two sides of the border. As the CPS imposed a cordon on the eastern border in the 1920s, and increasingly relied on paid informers, kinship ties became fundamental to the exercise of secrecy. As we will see in the Chapter 6, these dynamics had effects that were felt far beyond the borders themselves.

Conclusion: Frontier Zones, Colonial Boundaries and Patchy Governance

In this chapter, I have focused on the vagaries of colonial governance in border spaces during the first decades of colonial rule. I have sought to make two broad arguments of a comparative nature. The first is that it mattered how the colonial border mapped onto an older political topography and how the states in question responded to what they inherited. Historical frontier zones posed particular challenges because they were places where states enjoyed the least traction. At the south-western end of the Gambia/Senegal border, the boundary demarcation brought historical Kombo into the Gambia while leaving a volatile frontier zone to France. The British were able to consolidate their rule around existing institutions once they had reconciled the old ruling lines and those of Muslim reformers. In Narang and Fogny-Jabangkunda, the French were confronted by a much stiffer challenge of building administrative chieftaincies amongst peoples who had actively resisted engagement with centralized polities. The Germans similarly inherited a frontier zone in the trans-Volta, but were helped by the fact that small Ewe chiefdoms already existed, albeit in a highly decentralized form. But in Agotime, where there had been 'big men' rather than chiefs, the Germans needed to convert a fluid system of precedence into the currency of colonial chieftaincy. The Germans imposed a chiefly hierarchy upon the Agotime for the first time, whose legitimacy continued to be contested throughout the first half of the twentieth century. The partition of former German Togoland in 1919 interpolated an entirely new border. The fact that the Ewe *dukɔwo* were mostly small made it easier to avoid splitting them, but the size and geographical location of Agotime always made it likely that it would be cut in two. From the moment of partition, the headchief in Kpetoe was actively discouraged from taking an interest in the affairs of Agotime towns and villages in French territory. Subsequently, divergent chieftaincy policies on the two sides of the line made it very difficult to focus on matters of common interest. For Agotimes on the British side, the contentious issues were the impact of the amalgamation policy on the regional pecking order as well as the (rather notional)powers of the headchief in Kpetoe. For Agotimes in French territory, the greatest bone of contention was the choice of *chef de canton*. The fact that the Agotime were sub-divided by one international border, and then by an internal border within French Togoland, meant that the polity had to all intents and purposes ceased to exist. In addition, the Agotimes lost a space within which they could keep alive a sense of distinction from – and indeed a claim to dominance over – their more numerous Ewe neighbours. The steady decline of the Adangbe language was lamented by an older generation and merely seemed to confirm that the Agotime found themselves on the wrong side of history.

The second argument is that the capacities of the colonial state were severely tested at the border, which often required consenting to arrangements that were not necessarily considered as optimal. In the Gambia, a relatively light-touch European administration functioned through the devolution of responsibilities onto chiefs who were selected from established ruling lines. In the Casamance, the movement of people, cattle and arms across borders contributed to a situation in which French authority was constantly called into question. The re-imposition of military rule during the war years, and the repeated resort to force thereafter, ensured that the colonial state assumed a much more coercive aspect than in the Gambia or central Senegal. The bracketing off of the Casamance had enduring consequences for the politics of that country, as we will see. In French Togoland, the imposition of somewhat lower taxes and a more restrained approach to governance was closely related to the fear of losing population to the Gold Coast. In British Togoland, the Gold Coast model, which had been hammered out in a long negotiation with the chiefs, was brought in alongside the Customs frontier. This meant that the chiefs were defined as lying outside the formal structures of the colonial state. The British could cajole and apply pressure, as Lilley routinely did, but their power of command rested on the willingness of traditional authorities to play ball. In the borderlands, where populations had even greater options, it was necessary to come to an accommodation. While the British sought to impose unpopular border controls, they were responsive to chiefly demands for improved roads. In French Togoland, the chiefs were treated as state functionaries and were charged with maintaining the tax rolls, but the administration was much less intrusive when it came to cross-border trade. In each case, therefore, the colonial state and border populations found their own level, with the chiefs performing a crucial mediating role. The arrangements that emerged were not derived from any handbook of colonial governance: on the contrary, they were the product of cycles of disagreement and compromise. The most important bargaining chip that borderlanders possessed was their intimate knowledge of their environment, a theme which I will now pick up in Chapter 6.

6 Border Regulation and State-Making at the Margins

Taxation, Migration and Contraband during the Interwar Years

Having dealt with the implantation of administrative structures, I turn now to the borderlands as sites of regulation. My aim is, firstly, to reveal in much greater detail the different ways in which the border dynamics became woven into processes of state-making during the interwar period. In the Senegambia, the fundamental issue was the management of mobility, which ultimately proved conducive to the development of relatively open borders. In the trans-Volta, the energies of state officials were concentrated on regulating commodity flows. These contrasting imperatives involved a different range of actors, including traditional authorities whose own relationship to the central state was forged through the daily routines of border control. Secondly, the chapter seeks to account for some of the differences that unfolded on the two sides of the borders in question, resulting not just from divergent government priorities, but also from the fundamental incompatibilities between them. Although there were moments of selfless co-operation – mostly witnessed at times of crisis such as armed rebellion or war – colonial administrations tended to regard each other as competitors. While officials suspected their counterparts of conspiring with border populations to frustrate their own efforts, they also expressed sympathy with populations that were subject to the neighbouring administration.

Demographic Warfare: Settlers, Strange Farmers and Refugees

Within a longer historical time-frame, as we have demonstrated in Chapter 2, the two constants in state-making were control over people and trade routes. For all the imperialist bluster that posited colonialism as a rupture with past configurations, colonial states were markedly similar. In a continent characterized by an abundance of land relative to population, colonial states shared the same concern with sheer numbers. Whereas conservation agendas in Southern and Eastern Africa after the Second World War were often premised on a neo-Malthusian logic, in West Africa the emphasis continued to fall on maximizing access to population. Whereas investments in health infrastructure could be

229

expected to improve reproduction rates and reduce deaths to disease, a demographic shortcut resided in assisted migration. But this had political implications. As Peter Geschiere has noted, there was a profound contradiction at the heart of colonial thinking: "on the one hand, their insistence on fixing and territorializing people – which implied a determined search for autochthons who 'really' belonged – and, on the other, a constant preference for migrants."[1] However, the relationship between these imperatives was susceptible to multiple permutations. Whereas it is a staple of the literature that a premium placed on migration tended to feed a discourse of autochthony – creating a potentially explosive dialectic[2] – in the cases I consider there was actually an inverse correlation between migration and the politics of exclusion. Moreover, this can in large part be attributed to the vested interests of the colonial regimes themselves. My aim is therefore to tease out a more nuanced set of causalities. I begin with an account of the demographic tug-of-war that played itself out across the Senegambia, before turning to a rather different pattern that unfolded east of the Volta. In the second half of the chapter, I play closer attention to the attempt to regulate the flows of consumer goods and livestock across the two sets of borders.

Mobility and State-Making in the Senegambia

At the turn of the century, the authorities in Dakar and Bathurst fretted about the costs of administration and sought a solution in the expansion of agricultural exports and the raising of direct taxes. The rubber boom, which had drawn Aku migrants towards the border, proved short-lived as the production from wild vines was quickly exhausted. Thereafter, the focus turned to the cultivation of groundnuts. As we have already seen, both sets of authorities bemoaned the flight of population during the years of endemic violence and placed great store by efforts to repopulate the borderlands with industrious Jola farmers. The British encouraged refugees living in the Bathurst area, and anyone else who was interested, to relocate to rural Kombo. In 1894, the administrator had written to the Secretary of State along the following lines:

It is hoped that settlers will be dispersed to Combo if the country is annexed and made part of the Colony. Security to life and property is all that is wanted to make this part of the Protectorate a valuable addition to the trade and prosperity of the Colony.[3]

---

[1] Peter Geschiere, *The Perils of Belonging: Autochthony, Citizenship and Exclusion in Africa and Europe* (Chicago and London: University of Chicago Press, 2009), p. 16.

[2] The point has been made, for example, that the language of autochthony was already being deployed in southwestern Cote d'Ivoire in the 1930s in response to the official encouragement given to migration in the cocoa belt. See Ruth Marshall-Fratani, "The war of 'who is who': autochthony, nationalism and citizenship in the Ivorian crisis", *African Studies Review*, 49 (2) 2006, pp. 15–16.

[3] NAGB CSO 1/124 "Despatches from Colonial Office, 1894", Administrator of the Gambia, Bathurst, to Secretary of State, London (19 April 1894).

Equally, the French tried to entice 'their' Jola back across the border. This game of tug-of-war extended well beyond Bathurst because the Gambian authorities also endeavoured to poach people from deep inside the Casamance.[4] Around the time of the partition, Jola from the Casamance had begun selling palm products in Bathurst and purchasing commodities that featured more prominently in household consumption patterns. Moreover, Karoninka migrants established direct relations with Mandinka 'landlords' who permitted them to tap palm-wine in return for their labour and a share of the proceeds of sale. The British administration hoped that favourable reports might filter back so that other Jola and Karoninka would be encouraged to make the move northwards. The inducement was lower tax rates in the Gambia and the promise of relatively easy access to farmland. The French authorities responded to this competitive bidding by actively discouraging people from crossing the border. One British Commissioner complained that:

> Immigrants as far as can be seen must come from French territory and the French have never concealed the fact that they regard emigration to this country with disfavour. Families attempting to move over are usually deprived of everything but the clothes they stand up in; many no doubt would like to come to a country where taxes are low, and where there is neither conscription or forced labour, but they are deterred by the risk they run of losing all their possessions; most who have crossed have come over at night.[5]

At the same time, however, the French made it possible for Jola to relocate from high-density zones in Buluf towards Narang and Fogny-Jabangkunda where there was a perceived population deficit. Faced with what were in effect competing offers, Jola farmers shopped around for the best deal, often crossing the border several times before settling down. The two sets of authorities kept a tally of the score through constant updates of the population rolls in a manner that Gold Coast officers would have found as bizarre as much as it was unnecessary. In the French case, the enumeration included not just the people of a given village, but also horses, cattle, donkeys, sheep, goats and pigs.[6]

The British and the French authorities endeavoured to come to some kind of agreement over seasonal migrant workers. In the nineteenth century, the Gambian groundnut trade had come to depend heavily on so-called strange farmers from French territory, largely from Mali, who worked as seasonal

---

[4] In early 1914, the British were alleged to be engaged in active propaganda along the Casamance border. ANS 1F27 "Delimitation de la Gambie: Incidents de Frontière (1911–1914)", extract from "Rapport Politique du Senegal" (1e trimestre 1914).

[5] NAGB CSO 3/204 "Review of Policy with Regard to the Strange Farmers", E.B. Leese, Commissioner of South Bank Province, to Colonial Secretary, Bathurst (4 February 1932).

[6] For example, see ANS 2G 31/74 "Territoire de la Casamance: Rapport Annuel 1931", "Recensements", p. 42.

sharecroppers in the groundnut fields.[7] There were some variations in the terms that were offered in the early twentieth century, but in most cases strange farmers received free lodging and land to cultivate, as well as a payment that could take the form of a 10 per cent share of the harvest, in cases where the labourer worked for two days a week, or a cash payment of anywhere between £8 and £15 if he worked three days for the landowner. From this, a government tax of 6s was deducted, which meant that the state took a direct cut from migration – and then passed on half of this to the *alkalos*.[8] The only downside from the perspective of the Gambian authorities was that in years when there was a food shortage, such as during the drought of 1913, the strange farmers placed an additional strain on short supplies.[9] The over-riding importance attached to the strange farmers is reflected in a vigorous correspondence in 1923 that began with a circular letter from the Colonial Secretary reporting complaints that they were being "practically treated as slaves" by the chiefs and demanding that firm action be taken in order to avoid scaring migrants away.[10] The various Travelling Commissioners responded by refuting the allegations of abuse, although those of Kombo/Fogni and of North Bank Province did acknowledge the occasional deployment of strange farmers in public works.[11] In March 1925, Governor Armitage issued an explicit directive that strange farmers were not be used in this way or to be required to help the chiefs pay off the debts that had been incurred for advances of rice and groundnut seeds.[12] The context was one of a temporary decline in the number of arrivals, prompting fears that the strange farmers were finding their conditions of work less attractive and voting with their feet. Maintaining a steady flow of migrants was an over-riding priority for the Gambian administration.

Whereas settlers were expected to become an integral part of the Gambian population, the strange farmers were by their nature temporary sojourners. However, the Gambian authorities clearly hoped that many of the migrants

---

[7] Kenneth Swindell and Alieu Jeng, *Migrants, Credit and Climate: The Gambian Groundnut Trade, 1834–1934* (Leiden: Brill, 2006), ch. 2.

[8] Figures relate to 1932. NAGB CSO 3/204 "Review of Policy with Regard to the Strange Farmers", R.W. Macklin, Commissioner North Bank Province to Colonial Secretary (16 February 1932). The tax was increased to 8s 0d in 1932 under the Protectorate Amendment Ordinance. Swindell and Jeng, *Migrants*, p. 206.

[9] Swindell and Jeng, *Migrants*, pp. 150–7, 167–9.

[10] NAGB CSO 2/518 "Strange Farmers", Circular letter from Colonial Secretary, Bathurst, to Travelling Commissioners (12 March 1923).

[11] NAGB CSO 2/518 "Strange Farmers", letter from Travelling Commissioner, Kombo and Fogni, to Colonial Secretary (22 March 1923), and from Commissioner of North Bank Province (21 March 1925).

[12] NAGB CSO 2/518 "Strange Farmers", instructions by Governor Armitage to Travelling Commissioners (25 March 1925).

Table 6.1 *Population increase in the Gambia, 1901–1911*

Area	1911	1901
Bathurst town	9,000	8,807
McCarthy District	19,862	11,997
Upper River	27,604	13,232
North Bank	48,321	27,541
South Bank	18,614	11,747
Kombo and Fogny	22,700	17,087
Total	**146,101**	**90,411**

would eventually decide to stay permanently.[13] In 1932, Governor H.R. Palmer expressed the view that the days when the industry could rely on strange farmers from French territory were numbered, and that the solution was to promote permanent settlement combined with improved production methods, both of which hinged on creating adequate financial incentives for the *alkalos*.[14] While the migrant labour arrangement represented a halfway house for the Gambian authorities, it represented a compromise position for the French. It was better, they considered, for the strange farmers to work in the Gambia and return to French territory to pay *l'impôt* there than lose them altogether.

Although there was much shuttling back and forth across the border, it was already clear before the First World War that the net flow had tilted in favour of the Gambia. In 1912, F. Orcel, the French consular agent and representative of Maurel et Prom in Bathurst, referred to Gambian census figures that revealed a 61.5 per cent increase in the population over a ten-year period. Crucially, this was not accounted for by the expansion of the capital, but rather by immigration into rural districts (see Table 6.1).[15] Orcel ventured three main reasons why the Gambia was experiencing a demographic lift at the expense of French territory. The first was that *l'impôt*, the French head tax of 5 francs, amounted to twice the Gambian yard tax in real terms. The second was the relative ease of access to the Gambia by populations living in the interior, a point that had a particular bearing on the Upper River where the figures

---

[13] "It has always appeared to me that it is as well to encourage Strange Farmers until there is a very definite trend towards settling." NAGB CSO 3/204 "Review of Policy with Regard to the Strange Farmers", Macklin, Commissioner North Bank Province to Colonial Secretary (16 February 1932).

[14] NAGB CSO 3/204 "Review of Policy", memorandum by Governor H.R. Palmer, dated 15 January 1932.

[15] CAOM 1AFFPOL/92 "Affaires Politiques", F. Orcel, Agent Consulaire de France, Bathurst, to Consul General de France, London (16 May 1912).

revealed that the population had more than doubled.[16] And the third was the fear of military conscription, which was a mounting factor in the equation by the time Orcel was writing. The French construed military service as one of the obligations that Africans were required to discharge in return for the manifest benefits of their rule. As with direct taxation, it was construed as a non-negotiable component of the colonial social contract. In the years between the Gambian census and the outbreak of the First World War, the flight of population from the Casamance intensified as the French authorities intensified the trawl for African military recruits with the assistance of the chiefs. Given the fact that the Jola scarcely tolerated their appointed chiefs, recruitment needed to be carried out with a display of force – as we have seen in Chapter 5. The arbitrary methods employed, which amounted to the abduction of young men, must have seemed reminiscent of slave raiding in days not long gone. For that reason, it was extremely difficult for the French authorities to convince Jola populations that they were the harbingers of peace. The practical upshot was that potential conscripts easily escaped across the border when they got wind of a recruitment drive.

The Senegalese authorities exhorted their counterparts in the Gambia to send escapees back. When hostilities commenced in 1914, Britain and France became formal allies and it was difficult for the authorities in Bathurst to turn a deaf ear to emotive entreaties, such as the following penned by Orcel himself:

I have no doubt that everything possible on the part of this [Gambian] Government will be done. In this critical moment when British and French Blood is gushing out so much, our countries will find, even outside the Metropolis, the same will and determination to overcome every difficulty with the only aim to trample down by all means our common enemy, the German evil-doer.[17]

In 1915, Governor-General Marie François Clozel wrote to the Governor of the Gambia to request assistance in reversing the flight of population across the northern border from Sine-Saloum. The Travelling Commissioners were duly instructed not to "assist or connive at the immigration of French subjects liable to military service."[18] All the chiefs in Kombo and Fogny were circulated with a letter in October of that year, accompanied by an Arabic translation,

---

[16] In fact, many of the immigrants in this area had fled what is now Mali on account of famine conditions brought on in part by excessive taxation and in part by natural disasters. See Marie Rodet, *Les Migrantes Ignorées du Haut-Sénégal, 1900–1946* (Paris: Karthala, 2009), pp. 97–100.

[17] NAGB CSO 4/108 "French Subjects Liable to Military Service – Escape to British Territory", Orcel to Governor of Gambia (16 November 1916).

[18] NAGB CSO 4/108 "French Subjects Liable", translated letter from Clozel, Governor-General of l'AOF to Governor of the Gambia, and instructions.

instructing them not to grant permission to settle and requiring them to report any fresh arrivals in their domains.[19]

But while the government in Bathurst promised dutiful co-operation, administrators on the ground expressed sympathy with the refugees. O'Farrell, the Commissioner of Kombo and Fogny, after speaking with some of the people in question, suggested that the Jola were being fleeced by chiefs on top of their formal tax obligations: "They all state they are tired of the French method of taxation. The Jolahs have to pay tax to the Commissioner, the Chief and the Interpreter."[20] How the administrators dealt with particular instances turned on shades of interpretation: if those who crossed the border admitted to trying to escape conscription, they might have to be sent back, but if they claimed that they really wished to settle in the Gambia, then it could be construed as legitimate for the chiefs to allocate them land. In fact, even the central administration was prepared to be more pragmatic than its formal position suggested. In the Kansala District, where a large group was refusing to return, the authorities were faced with a dilemma. The Governor instructed O'Farrell not to attempt to send them back forcibly, and introduced further scope for debate about what might be permissible:

We are not undertaking to drive out these French refugees from our territory 'vi et armis'. What we have done is to give instructions that they are not to be encouraged or invited or assisted in any way to come and settle down on the English side in order to thus avoid their own national obligations, and as far as circumstances will admit, not to be allowed to do so. Mr. O'Farrell should inform the Chiefs at Kansalla and at Brikama that he has received their reports and that in the circumstances the French Jolas can be allowed to remain for the present if they wish to without interference, but that they must behave themselves properly and give no trouble, and that he, the Commissioner, will visit the country as soon as he can and see into the matter himself, and hear the reasons why these people have come across the border.[21]

The tension between the two halves of this statement spoke volumes about the lack of a consistent approach. At Karenai, another large group of refugees gathered. Some of them were Mandinka chiefs and their retainers who had been attacked by their Jola 'subjects', whereas others were the Jola insurgents. The evidence given by one of these chiefs pointed to the manner in which forced conscription had provided the tipping point in a context that was already fraught with tension:

---

[19] NAGB CSO 4/108 "French Subjects Liable", circular from Colonial Secretary to Chiefs of Kombo and Fogni (27 October 1915).

[20] NAGB CSO 4/108 "French Subjects Liable", O'Farrell, Travelling Commissioner, Kombo Foni, to Colonial Secretary (21 January 1916).

[21] NAGB CSO 4/108 "French Subjects Liable", minute by Governor Cameron to Colonial Secretary, 18 December 1915.

About two months ago I received orders from Commissioner Ducapa to obtain five recruits for the army. He gave me five shot guns and eight packets of six cartridges etc. I was told to go to each compound and explain to the young men that the Government wanted them for soldiers. If I saw any suitable recruit I was to tie him with rope and take him to 'Benjiona' [Bignona]. I did not get any recruits, as I heard the Jolas would not agree and had attacked 'Brima Jallow', Chief of Bulliot. I then got orders not to take any recruits but to wait the Commissioner's arrival. I sent a messenger to 'Brima Jallow' and on his return he informed me Brima Jallow had been wounded in the back. I wanted to go to 'Bulliot' but a 'Jola' told me if you go the 'Jolas' will kill you because they are coming to attack your compound.[22]

The chief in question, whose settlement had been burned down, was afraid to return, as were the Jola who were clearly anticipating French reprisals.

The Gambian authorities informed their French counterparts that it was not possible to forcibly eject people who had crossed over. And when the French administrators alleged that Gambian chiefs were actively harbouring 'deserters', the Commissioners insisted that they could find no evidence thereof. Although some were sent back, in order to satisfy the Senegalese authorities that some effort was being made, it would seem that a substantial number of refugees were permitted to stay. In their internal correspondence, French officials observed that the population of the Gambia had grown from 153,933 in 1915 to 186,633 in 1918, which could only be accounted for by a population drain on their own territory.[23] This renewed the debate within French colonial circles about the importance of assuming full control of the Gambia, which seemed to remain on the map only to frustrate France. At the end of the war, the French briefly raised the issue of cession once more but dropped the matter when it became clear that the British had no intention of relinquishing the Gambia. They were therefore left with the option of requesting British co-operation in securing the return of populations that had relocated to the Gambia over the previous six years.[24] However, there was now no incentive for the Gambian authorities to play ball and, in fact, their policy returned to one of seeking to poach population from the other side of the border: quite simply, more people meant higher taxes, a greater volume of groundnut exports and increased consumption of taxable imports. From the French perspective, the demographic loss was embarrassing because it drew

---

[22] NAGB CSO 4/108 "French Subjects Liable", statement of Bakari Turay, Chief Mundan, French Territory, Kansala, 12 January 1916, enclosed in O'Farrell to Colonial Secretary (13 January 1916).

[23] CAOM 1AFFPOL/514/2/3 "Affaires Politiques", "Notes Sur la Gambie Anglaise", December 1918. The doubling of the Gambian population from 1901 was clearly due to something other than a natural demographic increase.

[24] CAOM 1AFFPOL/92 "Affaires Politiques", Ambassadeur de la République à Londres, M. Cambon, to le Ministre des Affaires Etrangeres (30 January 1919).

attention to their weakness whilst making it that bit more difficult to create saturated spaces of colonial governance in the Casamance.

At the same time, the contribution made by strange farmers was highly valued by the Gambia administration. Although this was in some respects a second-best option to permanent settlement, the strange farmers were considered to make a vital contribution to the Gambian colony. One Commissioner attempted to calculate what the gains were in financial terms:

If we estimate that the Strange Farmer produces 1 Ton of Nuts per man (which is a low estimate) we have during the 10 years 1921 to 1930 received £175,733 from export duty from the Strange Farmer making a total of £222,452 or an average of £22,845 from Strange Farmers only. Not only this, the Strange Farmer converts a considerable portion of the money he realizes from the sale of his Nuts into Goods before he returns to his own country. The average price per ton paid at the scale during these 10 years is £9.0.0 per Ton so that estimating that he spends one half of his savings in the Gambia – the Strange Farmer has spent £87.866.10.0 during the 10 years under review or an average of £8786 per annum so that the Strange Farmer helps very considerably to circulate money and to stimulate Trade, besides which they are a considerable asset from an Agricultural point of view.[25]

Although most of the correspondence concerned the strange farmers, immigrant traders were occasionally a focus of internal discussion about the desirability of enforcing border controls. In 1929, an immigration officer at Barra on the north bank observed that the influx of Moor – that is Mauritanian – traders had increased significantly and he suggested that the French consul be advised that they required proper papers if they were to be permitted to stay in the Gambia. In a minute, the Governor advised against excessive zeal on the grounds of the economic utility of these traders who performed an important link role in the trade with Senegal:

It must be recognised that the trade of this country very largely depends on the activities of the buyers from outside and it is in the interests of our revenue and very essential at the present time that the Gambia should remain an open market for the Senegal trader. I am very averse to do anything which might discourage these traders from coming here. Will you please explain the position of [to?] the Commissioner of Police who will I am sure fully appreciate the position.[26]

This exchange provides a neat illustration of the ways in which revenue imperatives trumped concerns over immigration. The latter were real enough because, in other contexts, Mauritanians were thought to be the carriers of dangerous religious beliefs.

---

[25] NAGB CSO 3/204 "Review of Policy", Commissioner, Upper River Province, to Colonial Secretary (26 February 1932).
[26] NAGB CSO 3/136 "Control of Immigrants from French Territories", minute by Governor to Colonial Secretary, 17 July 1929.

The French authorities understood the demographic and financial accounting in their own terms and were determined to compete, although one report
implied that this impulse was rather ill-considered given that French companies dominated the Gambian groundnut trade in any event.[27] In 1909, Orcel
had expressed the hope that once the Thiès-Kayes railway was completed, it
would enable the French to compete with the Gambia River in commercial
terms and thereby shift the centre of economic gravity.[28] Aside from trade
considerations, the thinking was that migrants from the French Soudan (Mali)
would be attracted to the railway, where groundnuts could be produced more
cheaply. This would place the government in the Gambia under pressure and
might eventually lead to it becoming an intolerable burden to Britain. Orcel
himself imagined conditions in which cession would be followed by the
construction of a new railway spur to McCarthy Island that would enable the
opening up of a swathe of territory dedicated to the groundnut. In the 1930s,
the French seemed to enjoy some success in retaining strange farmers from the
Soudan within Senegal.[29] These migrants were not liable to pay the full head
tax, but rather incurred a reduced stranger tax. In 1945, French officials noted
that farmers from the Gambia were quietly moving across the international
border to cultivate. The official policy was that they would either have to settle,
in which case they were liable for *l'impôt*, or they would be treated as migrants
who would pay the reduced *impôt flottant*, but without residence rights. The
attempt to police the border more effectively – the opposite of what was
happening in the Gambia – made subtle subterfuges that little bit more difficult. But the railway strategy did not provide a lasting solution to the loss of
Jola to the Gambia – even if the French were somewhat compensated for by
the drainage of population from Guinea-Bissau, where the taxes were higher,
into the southern Casamance.[30]

As the Senegalese authorities made more of an effort to retain seasonal
migrants, they forced the Gambian authorities to offer additional inducements
of their own. In the Gambia, it had become standard procedure to furnish
groundnut seeds and rice in advance of the growing season, a mechanism that
was used to entice strange farmers.[31] Although these advances were supposed

[27] NAGB CSO 2/518 "Strange Farmers", translation from article in *La Depêche Coloniale* of
7 March 1924, entitled "Soudan Labour Will No Longer Go to Gambia". In 1906, Orcel
estimated that French firms controlled 80 per cent of the Gambian trade. ANS 1F12 "Relations
Avec la Gambie: Questions Générales et de Principe", Orcel to Monsieur le Consul Général de
France, London (April 1909).
[28] ANS 1F12 "Relations Avec la Gambie", Orcel to Consul Général de France (April 1909).
[29] As early as 1926, a 'railway rush' was reported by Commissioner Hopkinson. Swindell and
Jeng, *Migrants*, p. 219.
[30] CAOM 1AFFPOL/517/1 "Affaires Politiques", Consul de France, Bissau, to Ministre des
Affaires Etrangeres (1 July 1931).
[31] For a fuller analysis, see Swindell and Jeng, *Migrants,* especially pp. 217–31.

to be recovered at the end of the season, the system culminated in mounting levels of debt. The system also incurred costs to government and was blamed for the high Gambian export duty on groundnuts. This was, in turn, cited as part of the reason why Senegal was becoming more attractive for groundnut farmers, thereby bringing the issue full circle. The distribution of rice and groundnut seed was brought to an end in 1932, in part because of the abuses to which the system was prone. The alternative was to turn it on its head: that is to require farmers and strange farmers to contribute groundnuts to a collective pool at the end of the growing season that could be drawn upon for the next cycle. Hence, the farmers contributed five bushels at the end of the harvest, which were held over by the Native Authority until the following season when four of them were returned to them for planting. The remainder was kept in a village reserve.[32] The strange farmers became a part of this system, and those who did not return to the same village the next season would in effect lose their contribution. This provided an incentive for migrants to return, but it also presented a potential disincentive to out-migration in its own right.

As early as 1926, the Commissioner for South Bank Province reported not merely a decline in the arrival of strange farmers, but even a reverse flow. His analysis of the reasons had to do with differential pricing and perceived price gouging by the traders:

[In Senegal] there is no screening, they can get a better price for their nuts and they can buy more for their money. They said they could not understand why the French could give them such a higher price for their nuts and yet charge less for the goods in their stores. They could only think that the merchants on this side were 'eating' their money.[33]

In 1938, Sheikh Omar Fye, the de facto spokesmen for the Bathurst Muslim community, petitioned the Colonial Secretary about a series of practices that made life in the Gambia less attractive, including the levying of a quota on strange farmers and locals alike in support of the seed-nut reserve, as well as the high export duties. In his view, something needed to be done to offer relief to Gambian farmers who might themselves be tempted to defect to Senegal. His comment on the strange farmers spoke directly to official concerns:

It has sometimes occurred to me to point out that some change ought to be made in our attitude to the Farmer called 'Strange' – when he is called a 'Strange Farmer' the implication is that he is regarded as a 'bird of passage', with little or no interest in the place where he grows his crop, and he is expected to only grow a crop and return whence he came. It would not be out of place if he were made to feel he can RESIDE

---

[32] J.M. Gray, *A History of the Gambia* (Cambridge: Cambridge University Press, 1940), p. 490.

[33] NAGB CSO 2/518 "Strange Farmers", Extract from a report by South Bank Ag. TC, T.W. Doke (2 May 1926).

and SETTLE and the Gambia and that he need not leave the Gambia after the planting season. To this end some effort should be made to supply the Strange Farmers with Seedlings of Economic Crops, his tenure of the land should be made more abiding than it is at present, and he should be made to feel he has, as it were, a Stake in the land where he has come to farm his crops.[34]

In his sympathetic reply, the Colonial Secretary agreed that the ultimate aim was indeed to turn strange farmers into permanent settlers.[35] He argued, however, that when it came to incentives, it was a case of swings and roundabouts. Fye had conceded verbally that while the head taxes in Senegal amounted to only 5s 6d as opposed to 8s in the Gambia, seed-nut reserves in Senegal required deposits of groundnuts to be made that were twice as high as in the Gambia.[36] He also indicated that the government no longer wished to return to a policy of distributing foodstuffs, which had lent itself to such abuse in the past. The solution, he argued, lay in increasing the share of the groundnut price that was retained by the farmer.

In the long run, the reversal of demographic fortunes was not sustained. The turning point was the outbreak of the Second World War. The renewed push for conscripts made it much less attractive to reside in Senegal once again. In 1939, the French government made an approach at the highest levels to request co-operation in preventing the flight of population across the borders of West Africa. The Secretary of State for the Colonies, Malcolm Macdonald, duly wrote to Governor Thomas Southorn to demand every assistance to prevent the flight of potential conscripts into the Gambia.[37] This led to the drafting of the Aliens (Deportation of Deserters) Regulations No. 19 of 31 October 1939. Once again, however, officials on the ground were reluctant to comply with demands for blanket deportations. As the Commissioner of Upper River Province put it:

The crux of the matter is the production of adequate evidence by them [the French] when asking for deportation and this they do not do. Merely sending over a letter asking for the deportation of certain individuals: if these persons on examination put up a good prima facie defence, I do not feel justified in deporting.[38]

---

[34] NAGB CSO 3/204 "Review of Policy", Sheikh Omar Fye, Bathurst, to Colonial Secretary (1 November 1938). Fye was a trader with political ambitions. In 1932, he was appointed to the Legislative Council. Arnold Hughes and David Perfect, *A Political History of the Gambia, 1816–1994* (Rochester: University of Rochester Press, 2006), pp. 95–6.

[35] NAGB CSO 3/204 "Review of Policy", H.R. Oke, Colonial Secretary, to Honourable Sheikh Omar Fye, J.P. (2 December 1938).

[36] In reality, comparing tax rates was not so easy because Gambian yard tax was levied on an entire compound. In 1932, this was increased from 4s 0d to 5s 0d for a compound of up to four huts, with additional huts charged at 1/6d. Swindell and Jeng, *Migrants*, p. 206

[37] NAGB CSO 4/108 "French Subjects Liable", Malcolm Macdonald, Secretary of State for the Colonies, Downing Street, to Governor Thomas Southorn (August 1939).

[38] NAGB CSO 4/108 "French Subjects", Lorimer, Commissioner Upper River Province, to Colonial Secretary (1 May 1940).

In many cases, those whose return the French demanded could often demonstrate that they had been born in the Gambia, such was the level of cross-border mobility. Moreover, British officials were appalled at the treatment of some of those they did send back. In April 1940, the Commissioner of South Bank Province reported that a group who had been persuaded to return had been roped together and frog-marched to Bignona. One man died in the process and, on their arrival in a thoroughly exhausted state, other members of the group were summarily imprisoned.[39] Such incidents made Gambian officials less than sympathetic to French pleas for co-operation. Once Senegal joined the Vichy camp, the moral dilemmas evaporated and Gambian officials could 'steal' population in good conscience. Strictly speaking, the border was closed, but the Gambian authorities were aware that the Achilles heel of the French administration lay in population control. In the context of the times, the privations suffered under Vichy rule – one Commissioner referred to "brutality reminiscent [of] Boche behaviour" in occupied Europe[40] – could also be presented as a good reason why the Gambian authorities should actively support border transgressions. Certainly, the French believed that much of the smuggling activity at the time enjoyed official sanction. Their reports indicated that the intended target of British poaching was not merely sturdy Jola farmers, but also wage labour that was needed to replace Gambians who had been despatched to Sierra Leone.[41]

The French authorities were tempted to play the same game, but there were a number of reasons why they thought better of it. One was that those who might be tempted to re-settle on the French side of the border were considered undesirable elements – or *mauvais garçons* – who had crossed over to escape Gambian justice.[42] Other reasons given by the Governor of Senegal were that border populations were always inclined to exploit their location to their advantage, and so could not be counted upon as loyal subjects; secondly, that offering special inducements would alienate the local population; thirdly, that spies might be lurking amongst those who came to settle; and finally that the British would get wind of the strategy and presumably act to stem the

---

[39] NAGB CSO 4/108 "French Subjects", Commissioner of South Bank Province to Colonial Secretary, Bathurst (3 April 1940).

[40] NAGB CSO 3/422 "Frontier Incidents", Telegram from Commissioner, MacCarthy Island, dated 2 September 1942. On the Vichy years and the French use of propaganda, see Ruth Ginio, "Vichy rule in French West Africa: prelude to decolonization", *French Colonial History*, 4, 2003, and *French Colonialism Unmasked: The Vichy Years in French West Africa* (Lincoln: University of Nebraska Press, 2006).

[41] ANS 10D 1/33 "Renseignements Confidentiels sur la Gambie Anglaise et la Guinée Portugaise; Fourniture de Carburant etc.", note dated 30 July 1941.

[42] This was the expression used. ANS 10D 1/33 "Renseignements Confidentiels", Capitaine Esquilat, Chef de la Subdivision de Bignona to Commandant de Cercle de Ziguinchor (22 August 1941).

flow.[43] Hence the French did not do very much to lure settlers across the border, although the Chef de Subdivision at Bignona reported that he engaged in active propaganda, channelled through the *chefs de canton*, to discourage smuggling and border crossing in the opposite direction.[44] When the Vichy regime in West Africa fell towards the close of 1942, there was a renewed political accord between Dakar and Bathurst. However, there remained limited enthusiasm in the Gambia for returning refugees. On the other hand, the flow of strange farmers was formally resumed, with some 632 being reported for South Bank Province in 1943 and slightly fewer in 1944.[45] In the period after the ending of the war, the shortage of consumer goods was far more acute in French than in British territory. This provided an incentive for strange farmers to work in the Gambia and to return to their villages with basic commodities. At the same time, many farmers from the Casamance relocated to the Gambia where the cost of living was lower and tax obligations were once again less onerous. What emerges from this account is that the regulation of population flows across the international border was taken extremely seriously by both sets of authorities. Whereas the British authorities had an interest in maintaining an open border, the French were not averse to seasonal migration but did what they could to impede permanent settlement. Managing the flows of people had become an affair of state invested with the utmost significance.

The Senegambian Land Equation

In Chapter 7, I will consider how migratory flows contributed to a reshaping of ideas about belonging. An intermediate step is, however, to address the role of the colonial state in facilitating access to land by those who crossed borders. As I have already indicated in Chapter 1, some productive social contracts were of a kind that facilitated change: in this case, what made the difference was a set of regulations that satisfied those who were notionally the landowners, while conferring a measure of security on those who worked the land. In the Senegambia, this was broadly speaking the final outcome, although it was certainly not all due to the foresight of administrators. The imprint of official policy mattered, but the daily interaction between chiefs, ward heads, 'strange farmers' and settlers – not to mention the micro-politics associated with gender and generation – were no less important.

[43] ANS 10D 1/33 "Renseignements Confidentiels", Governor G. Rey to Commandant de Cercle de Ziguinchor (18 May 1942).
[44] ANS 10D 1/33 "Renseignements Confidentiels", Esquilat to Commandant de Cercle de Ziguinchor (5 September 1941).
[45] These figures are drawn from NAGB ARP 34/1 "Divisional Annual Reports", 1943.

Land policy itself was intimately bound up with the demographic tussle between the governments of the Gambia and Senegal, which created an imperative to make land as freely accessible to settlers and migrants as possible. For their part, chiefs had an interest in performing their allotted role of gatekeepers: allocating land to 'strangers' allowed them to garner additional subjects as well as a share of the additional taxes that they collected. When Mandinka chiefs distributed uncultivated land, they encountered relatively little opposition from their subjects, but much of the land was claimed by the wards (*kabilo*) whose heads also had an interest in attracting clients. Indeed Assane Sarr argues that the *kabilo* heads had gained ground relative to the chiefs during the colonial period.[46] Many settlers approached ward heads directly, rather than going through the *alkalos*, given that land could be accessed through either route. Most of the bargaining took place beneath the radar of the authorities. The British and French archival record reveals many instances of bemused officials discovering immigrant populations whose presence had remained undetected and unreported. Although there are excellent studies of land and labour in Jola agriculture, most of this literature tends to skip over the practical impact of European intervention on land use practices during the colonial period.[47] Rather little has been written about the interface between Jola farmers and the Mandinka system of land allocation.[48]

The overarching land policies of the Gambia and Senegal were not that different in their intended effects, or indeed in practice. In each case, the legal instruments conferred the power to allocate 'vacant' land upon the colonial authorities, while devolving the routine management of lands to legally recognized chiefs. Moreover, they both ended up validating some conception of customary land tenure, which meant that while some land was considered to fall under the purview of the chiefs, the rest was managed by ward heads as before. In l'AOF, a consolidated law of 1904 distinguished between the 'public' domain, that is land that was required for state ends, and the 'private' domain. All vacant lands were vested in the state, and in Senegal the Lieutenant-Governor was empowered to appropriate 'private' lands subject to certain conditions.[49] However, the bulk of the land was considered to fall under native law, which meant that the chiefs exercised custodial powers. However, while certain aspects of customary law were considered ripe for

---

[46] Assan Sarr, *Islam, Power and Dependency in the Gambia River Basin: The Politics of Land Control, 1790–1940* (Rochester: University of Rochester Press, 2016), pp. 29, 181.

[47] Olga F. Linares, *Power, Prayer and Production: The Jola of Casamance, Senegal* (Cambridge: Cambridge University Press, 1992).

[48] A notable exception, which focuses on Kombo, is Pamela Kea, *Land, Labour and Entrustment: West African Female Farmers and the Politics of Difference* (Leiden: Brill, 2010).

[49] Raymond Leslie Buell, *The Native Problem in Africa*, Vol. 1 [1928] (London: Frank Cass reprint edn., 1965), pp. 1022–3.

reform,[50] in the Casamance the French did not introduce fundamental changes to the way land was accessed. Despite the fiction that land was a communal resource and was inalienable, there is every reason to believe that land was loaned, pawned and changed hands in various ways – especially given that Jola rice paddies embodied substantial investments of labour over many years.

In the Gambia, the British formally asserted their control over land in a manner that they singularly failed to do in the Gold Coast. In the Colony, the land had been ceded by the king of Kombo was defined as Crown land. In the 1880s, this became subject to English common law, in which the concept of freehold was entertained.[51] As the Gambia expanded, a formal distinction was created between the Colony and the Protectorate in 1894. A Public Lands Ordinance was passed for the Protectorate in 1896 that placed all public land under the control of the administrator – that is, the Governor – and granted the latter the right to make awards of land under freehold or leasehold.[52] The intention was to create an instrument that would free up land intended for government schemes as well as to attract external investment.[53] The early indications were that the authorities were inclined towards a relatively interventionist land policy. However, the subsequent legislation leaned in the opposite direction. The Protectorate Ordinance (No. 30) of 1913 recognized 'native law and custom' with respect to Protectorate lands, and in 1935 parts of the Colony, including so-called British Kombo, became subject to the 'Protectorate system', which meant that 'native law and custom' applied there as well.[54] These measures were part of a conscious effort to return to communal principles of land management. The clinching legislation was the Protectorate Lands Ordinance (No. 16) of 1945. This entrenched the principle that customary rights were paramount. Its innovation lay in conferring the oversight of public lands on the Native Authorities at the District level – in effect the *seyfos* – who were expected to issue leases to indigenes and non-indigenes on the same terms.[55]

---

[50] Hence, the French sought to discourage matrilineal inheritance in Sine. Dennis C. Galvan, *'The State Must Be Our Master of Fire': How Peasants Craft Culturally Sustainable Development in Senegal* (Berkeley, Los Angeles and London: University of California Press 2004), p. 116.

[51] NAGB SECOM 9/402 "Native Land Tenure", Supreme Court Ordinance No. 4 of 1883.

[52] This was reinforced by the Public Lands (Grants and Dispositions) Ordinance of 1905 as amended in 1909.

[53] Michael J. Watts "Idioms of land and labor: producing politics and rice in Senegambia", in Thomas Bassett and Donald Crummey (eds.), *Land in African Agrarian Systems* (Madison: University of Wisconsin Press, 1993), p. 158.

[54] Protectorate Ordinance No. 2 of 1935.

[55] However, where non-indigenes acquired tenancy that extended beyond three years, this was supposed to be covered by a written agreement and approved by the relevant Commissioner.

By the 1940s, the British administration had come to a fairly settled position on the land question.[56] This recognized two historically rooted claims to land, but tacitly permitted the evolution of a system that was altogether more open-ended and that, crucially, acquired its impetus from the process of migration. The first basis for a claim was through initial settlement, so that the families that founded a town in the distant past became the owners of the land. Under colonial law, management was vested in the *seyfos*, who oversaw the allocation of vacant land to those who needed it through the intercession of the village *alkalos*. The second basis for a claim was through conquest, which meant that all of the rights established by Fodé Sylla in Kombo logically passed to the British. In theory, the second claim trumped the first, but in practice they were thoroughly intertwined because the chief was both the representative of the sovereign authority and the leader of the community. Over time, the authorities came to appreciate that there was a firm belief that when a *kabilo* first cultivated a piece of land, it acquired rights that could not be infringed upon by the village or district chiefs. Whereas taxation underpinned the formal claims to land ownership by the rulers of Kombo, uninterrupted land use signalled where effective control actually resided. According to Swindell and Jeng: ". . . while at the end of the year land was symbolically returned to the alkali, usufruct rights were rarely abrogated."[57] Because these claims were regarded as amounting to a form of ownership, *kabilo* heads allocated land to strangers as they saw fit. The latter, in turn, acquired de facto rights that were almost as secure as those afforded to members of the founding families, precisely because the allocation of land was hardly ever revoked. Over time, those who came as strangers sank local roots and later even apportioned parcels of land to fresh arrivals, becoming in effect patrons in their own right. As long as the overall supply of land was abundant, as it was in Kombo in the first half of the twentieth century, this dynamic of segmentation and relentless expansion was sustainable. It was tolerated by the British authorities because whether the chiefs or the *kabilo* heads allocated land, those who needed access could be satisfied without recourse to excessive bureaucracy or incurring risk. The fact that the state did not have the most acute vision – to invoke Scott's optical metaphor yet again – is reflected in the reality that while there are abundant archival records concerning taxation, there is very little relating to the minutiae of land use. In particular, formal tenancy agreements seem to have been rare outside of the towns. One official report described the position as follows:

[56] NAGB 9/891 "Land Tenure", "Land Rights and Compensation", memorandum from 1950. Also extract from D.P. Gamble's report on Kerewan at SECOM 9/402 "Native Land Tenure".
[57] Within lineage groups, some land was farmed communally, whereas other parcels were worked by individual families. Swindell and Jeng, *Migrants,* p. 84.

Nowadays most farming land is acquired by inheritance of rights to use and by one's ancestors. Those wishing to found a new village may be granted unused land by the District Authority. On the foundation of a village, the headman allocates land to those who settle with him, and thereafter their descendants have the right to use such land. Most of the rights are exercised by the heads of compounds who decide where crops shall be planted, and allocate land to various members of the household. Land which is not required by its owner is freely lent for farming purposes for short periods, permission to use the land normally being renewed annually. No rent is paid, though a small gift is normally presented when the request for land is made. The selling of land is unknown, and the pledging of land rare, and generally disapproved of.[58]

Although the foundation of a new settlement was supposed to involve an application to the District authority, in practice it was *alkalos* who allocated land for the foundation of satellite settlements. In this way, new villages emerged in a largely unregulated fashion, although formal registration would typically follow after some time had elapsed.[59] The perception that a hands-off approach worked best played off very British perceptions of social change as something that was inevitably organic. In the post-war years, there was even a recognition that 'tradition' itself was far from static. In 1950, one Commissioner noted that "the best policy is to permit a gradual evolution of land law", and six years later the Senior Commissioner, Humphrey-Smith, agreed that in the Western Division this was indeed the best policy: "... a land law is evolving to meet the changing circumstances of the Western Division. What we have got to do is to guide it rather than try and put the clock back by insisting on tribal tenure."[60] Officials in Kombo were strengthened in this view by the relative lack of litigation that they had to contend with. Between 1940 and 1945, 112 land cases came before native tribunals across the entire Protectorate, averaging 22.4 cases per year.[61] Out of this total, 69 cases emanated from the South Bank Division at an average of 13.8 cases per year. But in Kombo Central, which is our main area of interest, there were only two land cases during the entire period. Most disputes seemed to be resolved expeditiously at the native court level, whereas in the Gold Coast cases were routinely appealed to the Magistrates Courts and from there many progressed to the West African Court of Appeal – and indeed as far as the Privy Council. In subsequent decades, there was a greater incidence of land disputes in Kombo, and these will be addressed in Chapter 7. Although the evidence from

---

[58] NAGB CSO 9/891 "Land Tenure", memorandum entitled "Utilisation of Agricultural Land".

[59] An annual list of approved villages and their alkalos was required to be published in the government Gazette. NAGB CSO 2/1130A "List of Chiefs and Towns", M. Denham-Smith, Acting Colonial Secretary, Bathurst (13 May 1931).

[60] NAGB CSO 9/891 "Land Tenure", G. Humphrey-Smith, Senior Commissioner, to Commissioner Western Division, Brikama (14 April 1956).

[61] SECOM 9/402 "Native Land Tenure", returns by Commissioner, South Bank Division, Brikama, to Senior Commissioner, Bathurst, 30 October 1946.

the Casamance is more patchy, it would appear that an official desire to encourage settlement similarly converged with the willingness of lineage heads to encourage settlement.

Chieftaincy, Mobility and Land Claims in the Trans-Volta

In the trans-Volta, the dynamics were very different. Here, there was a significant movement of population, but this mostly in the direction of the Gold Coast. Before the First World War, Togolanders had gravitated to Accra in search of work, and the numbers became substantial under French rule. As cocoa planting took off in the Gold Coast around the turn of the century, Togolanders also migrated to the Eastern Province where they worked as sharecroppers – and in the Agotime case they doubled up as kente weavers. But the Gold Coast cocoa industry did not depend to any great extent on southern Togoland for its workforce, given that most labourers hailed from the Northern Territories. Although migratory flows were less pronounced than in the Senegambia, the French authorities remained concerned at the drain of population. They therefore sought to persuade their British counterparts that it was in their mutual interest to restrict movement of population. In 1929, Auguste Bonnecarrère wrote to his Gold Coast counterpart in the following terms:

I am of the opinion that it would be sound policy to ascertain as accurately as possible the movements of the people and to find out the causes of these movements on both sides and to try and establish those natives who appear to be desirous of emigrating permanently. Instructions could be given to Commandants of Frontier Districts to enquire into the matter, to make a census of foreigners who have settled in these areas and to submit reports which would be very useful to us, for example to assist us to combine on measures to be taken in order to check these movements which we should not wish to see on the increase. Your Excellency is aware how regrettable these migrations are from the social outlook. An emigrant, whoever he may be, black or white, remains almost always denationalised (declassé) and here even more so in the case of primitive peoples whose principles are based almost entirely on the family system and who, in consequence, are always more or less opposed to strangers. In addition, from a sanitary point of view, these migrations of people present no mean danger. Togoland has been a home for Sleeping Sickness.[62]

Governor Ransford Slater was not persuaded by the rather contrived logic, arguing that immigration was "the reverse of being undesirable".[63] The

[62] NAK CO 96/691/10, "Control of Migration between Togoland and the Gold Coast", translation of letter from Bonnecarrère, Commissaire of French Togoland, to Governor of Gold Coast (25 June 1929).
[63] NAK CO 96/691/10, "Control of Migration", Governor Ransford Slater, Accra, to Lord Passfield, C.O. (26 October 1929).

Secretary of Native Affairs advised non-co-operation on the basis that the French were struggling to collect tax and were jealous of the prosperity in the Ho District that had come at the expense of Kpalimé. Major F.W.F. Jackson, the Acting CEP, who had some knowledge of the area, was of the same opinion:

It has been a recognised fact for many years, and this prior to the war, for the inhabitants of Togoland, both in the French and British Spheres to come into the Gold Coast for employment during the Cacao seasons, at the end of which many of them are in habit of returning to their homes in Togoland. The cause of this is that they receive more profitable remuneration for their services, and this enables them to meet the French Taxes imposed upon them. Further to this, a great number of artisans, washermen and stewards have emigrated to the Gold Coast where they have found work and eventually settled down with their families. These movements have taken place without molestation and to interfere with them would be a distinct infringement of the rights of the subject. The principal cause of emigration into the Colony can be based on the fact that the French policy is distasteful to the French Togolander. The present system of taxation is a burden and is not met with in the Gold Coast, he therefore seeks more congenial surroundings and for this he cannot be blamed.[64]

Hence the request was politely rebuffed, softened only by a promise to co-operate in sleeping sickness control.[65] Be that as it may, there was never a substantial relocation of population to the British side of the border.[66] The one exception was in Buem, where 'strangers' from French Togoland joined farmers from Gold Coast Eweland and other parts of British Togoland in the search for forest land suitable for cocoa cultivation.[67] There was a parallel development in the vicinity of Kpalimé, but in this case the migration occurred from within the boundaries of French Togoland. In most respects, therefore, the demographic profile of the borderlands was remarkably stable, despite the unpopularity of French taxes. Part of the reason is that the British administration gave no strong encouragement to potential migrants.

As far as state involvement in land tenure is concerned, there were three layers of intervention whose combined influences remain in evidence today. The first of these was the attempt by the German authorities to determine the

---

[64] NAK CO 96/691/10, "Control of Migration", Major F.W.F. Jackson, Acting Provincial Commissioner, Eastern Province (CEP), Koforidua, to Acting Colonial Secretary, Accra (9 August 1929).

[65] NAK CO 96/691/10, "Control of Migration", Slater to Commissioner of the Republic, Lomé (26 October 1929).

[66] The British and the French authorities agreed on a period during which people could relocate to the other side of the line if they so chose, but few seem to have taken up the opportunity. The line itself was not fully demarcated until 1930.

[67] Paul Nugent, *Smugglers, Secessionists and Loyal Citizens on the Ghana–Togo Frontier: The Lie of the Borderlands since 1914* (Oxford and Athens: James Currey and Ohio University Press, 2002), pp. 50–61.

borders between individual *dukɔwo*. As has already been indicated, Dr. Grüner devoted considerable attention to establishing internal boundaries between chiefdoms. In 1904, the German government introduced legislation that required the consent of the Governor, through the intercession of the Commissioner, before lands could be alienated to 'foreigners'. This was a highly restrictive provision because it applied to 'non-natives' of a particular *dukɔ* as well to those who crossed the international border. Peki farmers from the Gold Coast did apparently secure land rights in German Togo through formal channels, but their numbers were small.[68] The second layer consisted of the land policies that became operative after the expulsion of the Germans and the partition of Togoland. In their portion of the divided territory, the French imported legislation from the West African colonies in 1920. This meant that most land remained subject to the principle of 'native law'.[69] The most important precedent for British Togoland was set in the Gold Coast in 1896 when the Lands Bill was defeated by a coalition of chiefs and the coastal intelligentsia. Although the military defeat of Asante in 1900 might have led to the declaration of Crown land there, in fact this was only exercised with respect to land within a mile of the fort in Kumasi – an arrangement that itself ended in 1943.[70] Hence, the default position was that land remained under the control of its original owners and was not controlled by the British administration. In the Gold Coast Colony and Ashanti, this meant that chiefs managed stool land, while lineage groups remained in control of family land. Crucially, the subjects of a stool had the right to access stool land for free. The corollary was that those who did not belong to a given stool were considered 'strangers' and were expected to pay a rent, often in the form of a share of the produce, in return for the right to use the land.[71] As the cocoa boom imparted a commercial value to land, so the question of the boundaries between stools became hotly contested. The courts became the site where the boundaries were fought over and occasionally resolved. Crucially, the courts also provided an arena where Africans set the agenda, not merely because some of them were presided over by chiefs, but also because the evidence in land cases tended to be deeply embedded in claims about history – as Sara Berry has pointed out.[72] The evidence typically turned on who had arrived first, who had allowed whom to

---

[68] PRAAD (Accra) ADM 39/1/190 "Transfer of Native Lands", Captain C.C. Lilley, District Commissioner (DC), Kpandu, to Komla Deh, Kpedze (4 June 1938).

[69] Buell, *Native Problem*, Vol. 1, p. 334.

[70] Gareth Austin, *Labour, Land and Capital in Ghana: From Slavery to Free Labour in Asante, 1807–1956* (Rochester: University of Rochester Press, 2005), p. 254.

[71] Austin, *Labour, Land and Capital*, p. 259.

[72] Sara Berry, *Chiefs Know Their Boundaries: Essays on Property, Power, and the Past in Asante, 1896–1996* (Portsmouth, Oxford and Cape Town: Heinemann, James Currey and David Philip, 2001), pp. xxvii–xxx. The native courts were presided over by chiefs, but appeals lay to the Magistrates Courts.

use which portion of land, and subject to what conditions. In the many cases that were appealed upwards from the native courts, the Magistrates Courts struggled to reconcile the welter of conflicting traditions and to verify whether claims made in the court-room corresponded with physical evidence on the ground. The net result was that considerable valence was attached to the discourse of landowner and stranger. This, in turn, reinforced a particular conception of the political realm: namely a colony, and later an independent state, that was the sum of its constituent 'native states' that themselves assumed different sizes and shapes. When British Togoland was attached to the Gold Coast in 1919, the same understandings were brought to bear: in particular, the notion all land had an owner; that chiefdoms had an interest in defending their boundaries against encroachment from their neighbours; and that the status of a 'stranger' was perpetual. Although a desire to impose order was reflected in the amalgamation policy, the 'native states' that were assembled were not themselves uniform while the centre of political gravity remained at the level of the individual *dukɔwo*. On the French side of the border, by contrast, there was a greater concern with establishing administrative symmetry and tidiness.

The third layer derived from the efforts of the British and the French authorities to satisfy the League of Nations that they were adopting measures designed to protect their wards from land alienation. One question that arose early on was whether populations who were divided by the border had a right to use land on the other side. The administrations agreed early on that existing land rights should not be affected by the existence of the border and that communities should be given a chance to relocate to the other side if they preferred. A greater problem arose when individuals sought to acquire new rights to land across what had become an international border. Where Africans migrated from one part of a Trust Territory to another in search of land, there was less of an issue, provided the regulations were fully complied with. This was the case, say, with farmers from Anecho who acquired land around mount Agu or with Agotimes from the British sector who acquired cocoa land in Buem. But as soon as people crossed a border – between the Gold Coast, British Togoland and French Togoland – legal complications arose. Most of the problems arose in relation to Buem where land transactions became the subject of costly litigation that I have written about elsewhere.[73]

The British Sphere of Togoland Administration Ordinance of 1924, following Article 8 of the Mandate agreement, sought to preserve a less restrictive version of the German framework of land regulation. It stated that: "No native land may be transferred, except between natives of the British

---

[73] Nugent, *Smugglers, Secessionists*, pp. 64–76.

Sphere, without the previous consent of the District Commissioner, and no real rights over native lands in favour of non-natives may be created without the same consent."[74] In 1940, this was amended so that the consent had to be secured from the Governor of the Gold Coast. Crucially, the definition of 'non-native' was anyone who was not a native of British Togoland. This placed restrictions on Gold Coast Ewes from Anlo and Peki as well as on French Togolanders. It also created obvious anomalies in somewhere like Agotime because a farmer from Batoumé formally required permission in order to be able to acquire land from someone in Akpokope, just a few miles across the border. The fact that the parties might even be close relatives did not make any difference in legal terms. Hence, the formal position was that partition did not affect existing land rights across the border, whereas legislation created administrative barriers to staking new claims to land on the other side.

In reality, however, the position was more ambiguous. As I have demonstrated elsewhere, it became difficult to defend pre-existing rights to land on the other side of the border,[75] whereas regulation proved a dead-letter in British Southern Togoland. The latter was especially true of Buem. In 1938, the DC of Kpandu, H.C. Ellershaw, estimated that of all the sales in British Southern Togoland, probably 60 per cent had gone to natives of British Togoland, 20–25 per cent to people from Peki, a small amount to Anlos and Adas, and the rest to natives of French Togoland.[76] In 1932, only six cases of formal approval had been recorded, including one in Agotime, and by the mid-1940s this seems not to have exceeded forty instances in total.[77] Captain Lilley, Ellershaw's predecessor, made it clear in 1935 that there was not much that could be done to comply with international obligations: "With regard to the alienation of land generally, I do not see that the Government can do anything useful now."[78] This state of affairs became a source of some embarrassment when litigation in Buem, which was appealed all the way to the Privy Council, together with petitions to the League of Nations, underlined the failings of administrative oversight.[79] Although the cocoa boom was specific to Buem, there was a more widespread practice in the Ho District of distributing land to 'strangers' in areas where the boundaries between one

---

[74] PRAAD (Accra) ADM 39/1/574 "Alienation of Land in Togoland", Captain E.T. Mansfield, DC, Ho to CEP, Koforidua (12 April 1923).

[75] Nugent, *Smugglers, Secessionists*, ch. 2.

[76] ADM 39/1/574 "Alienation of Land", H.C. Ellershaw, DC, Kpandu to CEP, Koforidua (6 January 1938).

[77] PRAAD (Accra) ADM 39/1/190 "Transfer of Native Lands", DC, Kpandu to CEP, Koforidua (14 September 1932). Also note on "Register of Lands Alienated in Togoland" in same file.

[78] PRAAD (Accra) ADM 39/1/574 "Alienation of Land", Lilley to CEP, Koforidua (2 December 1935).

[79] Nugent, *Smugglers, Secessionists*, pp. 72–6.

community and the next were ill-defined or contested. I will have cause to return to this point.

Given the limitations of administrative control, the reason why there was not more movement across the border came down to a number of related factors. As I have already indicated, the lands that were most coveted were located in the Gold Coast rather than in British Togoland itself. But it was also the case that the validation of a discourse of autochthony rendered migration less attractive because the stigma attached to being a 'stranger' was not so easily expunged. Moreover, given the ways in which 'strangers' were used to demarcate disputed territory, the rights that were secured by 'strangers' in British Togoland were inherently risky. Finally, amongst the Ewe and the Agotime there was no such thing as stool land. In British Togoland, all the land was considered to belong to one lineage group or another, even if the boundaries between them remained unmarked. This meant that the chiefs in British Togoland had no capacity to allocate land, except parcels of their own family land. In French Togoland, the chiefs enjoyed a bit more latitude because they could identify uncultivated land on behalf of the French Commandants. But the fact remained that there was little land that was not already claimed, while British Togolanders were deterred by French taxes.

The substantive differences between the Senegambia and the trans-Volta are most apparent with respect to the contours of traditional authority. In the Senegambia, chiefs were responsible for enumerating highly mobile populations, finding land for settlers and collecting taxes from them. In the Gambia, at least, there were some advantages to the chiefs in performing these functions. In the trans-Volta, where there was much less mobility, the chiefs of French Togoland also counted and taxed, but they were dealing with more stable populations. Reporting the presence of 'strangers' was part of their job, but it was not a very onerous one. In British Togoland, the chiefs did not carry out enumerations, collect tax or allocate land, and they do not seem to have volunteered information concerning the movement of individuals unless it was in their interests to do so. Hence, the border marked markedly different practices of state-making, both in the Senegambia and the trans-Volta as well as between them.

The Regulation of Cross-Border Flows

Aside from the control of populations, the second issue that was of particular concern to the colonial authorities was regulation of the flow of goods. On the one hand, there were cash crops and consumer goods that were the principal source of government revenues for each of the states concerned. Curbing contraband always mattered, but for some states it mattered a great deal more. On the other hand, there were criminal networks that were thought to use the borderlands as both a safe haven and a conduit for the transfer of stolen goods of various descriptions. Theft was a constant irritant in relations between communities living on either side of the international border – as indeed it is today – and required the repeated intervention of government officials. It also exposed the limitations of the colonial state's capacity for surveillance and control.

Smuggling in the Senegambia

> It is clear that our political actions and native [policy] are hampered by the existence of this enclave where our natives pass easily, yesterday to escape recruitment, today to avoid this or that tax burden. What is more, it appears that the Gambia is used for the smuggling of arms and ammunition and spirits. This enclave is too easily open to Senegalese populations not to cause numerous, and endlessly growing, difficulties for our native policy.[80]

In the Senegambia, the manner in which the authorities on either side of the line sought to channel the flow of trade goods mirrored the vigorous competition for population. Following demarcation of the boundary, the Gambian authorities expressed irritation at what they considered heavy-handed French measures to discourage people from selling agricultural produce and buying consumer goods across the border. In addition, numerous complaints were transmitted to the French authorities about harassment and illegal seizures by Senegalese *douaniers*.[81] In subsequent decades, the British generally adopted a more relaxed view of cross-border trade, whereas the French sought to uphold Customs controls. But this equation was always complicated by the fact that the trade of the Gambia was dominated by the French commercial houses that exported their groundnuts to France, but imported most of their manufactures from Britain – even during the 1930s when the franc was heavily overvalued.[82]

---

[80] "CAOM 1AFFPOL/514/2/3 "Affaires Politiques", "Notes Sur la Gambie Anglaise", December 1918.

[81] In some cases, the complaints emanated from Senegalese villages themselves. In one instance from Saloum, the chief of Keur Omar claimed that there had been cordial relations with a French Customs officer, but that the posting of an African officer to the village had been followed by arbitrary seizures of cattle and livestock. The chief noted that he had received numerous complaints. ANS 10D 3/41 Correspondance du Gouverneur du Sénégal Avec l'Administrateur du Cercle de Kaolack (1907–1909), Bakary Guèye, chef du village de Keur Omar to chef Déry Yacine Touré, 11 August 1907.

[82] In 1914, 78 per cent of the exports of the Gambia went to France and only 9.4 per cent to Britain. On the other hand, Britain accounted for 61 per cent and France 21 per cent of imports to the Gambia. "Notes Sur la Gambie Anglaise". In 1937, France accounted for only 3 per cent of imports. A Customs officer observed that "Normally, the depreciation of the franc should have the effect of encouraging the purchase of French goods in sterling, but I am informed that the cost of labour in France has risen so much that British manufacturers are unlikely to suffer as

Hence the revenue imperatives of l'AOF did not always correspond with the interests of those French businesses that operated inside the Gambia.

The French decision to create a string of Customs posts reflected a deep-seated fear that the Gambia would otherwise suck in trade from across Senegal. In subsequent years, a pattern of smuggling activity emerged whose dimensions were well understood. First of all, there was the trade in groundnuts themselves. At one level, it did not make such a difference whether these crops were sold in Senegal or the Gambia because the French did not levy an export duty on groundnuts and because these were destined to be purchased by French firms anyway. But from the perspective of the French authorities, a British duty on groundnut exports of Senegalese provenance represented a hidden subsidy that merely perpetuated the existence of a colony that they sorely wanted to erase from the map. Groundnut smuggling was accompanied by the purchase of imported consumer goods that benefited the Gambian exchequer whilst creating a loss of revenue to lAOF.

An uncompromising approach to border regulation had its critics. In April 1909, Orcel observed that it was doubtful whether the Customs posts even covered costs. His view was that there was little financial incentive for smuggling that could be attributed to differential levels of duty:

Smuggling properly called is not carried out, and cannot be carried out from Gambian territory to the Senegalese territories. The import duties paid in the Gambia on alcohol, tobacco, kola nuts are exactly the same as those that have to be paid to the Customs in Senegal; they are slightly higher on salt and sugar but a bit less on cloth. The bonded warehouse does not exist in the Gambia; everything that leaves the Customs house has to pay import duties.[83]

The practical problem, he maintained, was that much of the Senegalese population was located far from French commercial centres whereas the Gambian wharf towns were close by. In the Gambia, they were able to purchase consumer items like cloth, soap and sugar, which was a reason why they brought groundnuts for sale. In the opinion of Orcel, it was pointless trying to uphold a genuine Customs cordon until the Kayes railway was complete because markets were simply more accessible in the Gambia.

British officials also believed that the French were fighting a losing battle. The following reflections by Dr. Hopkinson – on this occasion following completion of the railway – are worth quoting at length:

a result of the depreciation. The Manager of the C.F.A.O. informed me this morning that he had been investigating the possibility of ordering such commodities as biscuits and sugar from France instead of from England but that for the reason stated above he does not think that it would be to his advantage to do so at present." NAGB CSO 2/284 "Customs Traffic", Memorandum from Customs Officer [illegible], 6 May 1938.

[83] ANS 1F12 "Relations Avec la Gambie", Orcel to Consul Général (April 1909).

They [the French] naturally do all they can to shut us in and in this have been more successful during the last few years with the completion of the railway along our northern boundary, but even now although they try by customs stations and prohibition of the export of nearly everything to prevent their products coming in, they cannot prevent this entirely, so long is the boundary and so few the customs station [sic]. The real evil from our point of view is that under the guise of customs, our people are liable to be seized – and are seized by 'Customs guards', despoiled of all they have and often maltreated, but we can never get any redress. It is done under the law, though generally the way in which it is done cannot possibly be considered justified by any law which has any connection with real justice. Now it is hardly safe for our people to cross the boundary without a passport, and yet there is constant communication and constant leakage of French products across to us for the better price we give . . . According to the French law not a nut should come in; yet we know they still do, mostly by dodging the customs, but some on payment of a small export duty, when towards the end of the season the French find they cannot carry away what is for sale. Cattle come over continually, and in a good year corn and rice as well, yet the export of all is strictly forbidden and the few offenders ever caught dealt with most severely.[84]

As the final sentence indicates, the trade in groundnuts was closely bound up with the cross-border traffic in foodstuffs. In the nineteenth century, the expansion of groundnut cultivation went together with a structural food deficit in the Gambia.[85] In drought years, such as 1897, 1901, 1907 and 1913, there was acute hunger. As Swindell and Jeng demonstrate, the prolific expansion of the 'strange farmer' system in the first decades of the twentieth century placed additional strains on the food supply, given that hosts were responsible for feeding their strangers.[86] There were some attempts by the Gambian authorities to stimulate the production of rice under 'scientific conditions', but these were generally costly failures.[87] This meant that the deficit needed to be covered through increased imports of rice. Although the Casamance might have provided the solution to the problems of the Gambia, it is striking that the French never sought to exploit the potential for a cross-border trade in wetland rice. Instead, the vast majority of the imported rice came from overseas. In 1913, the Gambia imported £62,409 worth of rice and in 1920 this peaked at £329,069. In 1913, these imports represented about 10 per cent of the value of groundnut exports, rising to 14 per cent in 1920.[88] The Gambian state had a clear stake in the rice trade because stabilizing the food supply was crucial to maintaining the flow of 'strange farmers' – creating what Michael Watts justifiably calls a "colonial house of cards".[89] Indeed the Gambian authorities became directly involved in the distribution of rice on credit at the turn of the

---

[84] NAGB CSO 4/10 "Gambia: Development and Relations with Neighbouring Territories of", memorandum by Hopkinson, Commissioner of South Bank, July 1922.
[85] Swindell and Jeng, *Migrants*, pp. 87–93   [86] Swindell and Jeng, *Migrants*, pp. 162–73.
[87] Watts, "Idioms", p. 168.   [88] Swindell and Jeng, *Migrants*, pp. 149, 154.
[89] Watts, "Idioms", p. 168.

century, when the firms became reluctant to commit further.[90] For their part, the merchants profited from the sale of rice through the wharf towns.

Normally, colonial states did not pay much attention to a cross-border trade in foodstuffs, provided supplies were abundant. But in the Senegambia, there was a much greater degree of sensitivity attached to the food trade, especially in drought years. The reality was that, whether due to differential supply or divergent prices, there were often incentives to smuggle rice and millet. Most of the smuggling was in the direction of the Gambia, with the 'Syrians' or Lebanese traders being considered the chief culprits. In March 1938, a United Africa Company (UAC) manager complained about nocturnal smuggling of rice across the northern border which, he claimed, was ruining the local market for the imported product.[91] R.S. Syme, the Commissioner for the North Bank, was more sanguine. He noted that it was the indebtedness of the Gambian farmers to the European firms that was partly to account for their resort to alternative sources; but more importantly he observed that:

Money saved by the purchase, if it is true, of smuggled rice, will find its way into the firms' shops. Moreover, the sellers of this imported rice will almost certainly spend 50% in English territory in shops and stores.[92]

Occasionally, however, imported rice from the Gambia was smuggled across the Senegalese border, especially during the hungry months. Hence in 1937, a British official referred to smuggling into the Casamance:

It is known that a considerable amount of smuggling of rice and kola nuts is carried on from the wharf towns on the south bank of the river in this Province into the Casamance, but it is thought that little activity of this description is prevalent on the north bank of the river.[93]

Whereas agricultural commodities tended to flow in the direction of the Gambia, manufactures exited in the opposite direction. This was especially true of Manchester cotton goods that tended to be cheaper than their French equivalents. These were a major source of Gambian import duties and their availability provided one of the principal attractions of the wharf towns. In the estimation of Orcel, the Manchester textile lobby had been one of the most vocal in arguing the case against cession of the Gambia, regarding it as their special preserve.[94]

---

[90] Swindell and Jeng, *Migrants*, p. 132.

[91] NAGB, CSO 3/340 "Smuggling from Senegal etc", Mr. Martin, General Goods Manager, UAC, to Receiver General (8 March 1938).

[92] NAGB CSO 3/340 "Smuggling", R.G. Syme, Commissioner North Bank Province to Colonial Secretary (22 March 1938).

[93] NAGB CSO 3/308 "Anglo-French Boundary – Incidents", J.F.G. Hopkins, Ag. Commissioner Upper Division, Basse, to Colonial Secretary (15 January 1937).

[94] ANS 1F12 "Relations Avec la Gambie: Questions Générales et de Principe", Orcel to Consul Général (April 1909).

There are two other items of cross-border trade that deserve particular mention. The first is cattle, which were a valuable economic resource in the Senegambia. Cattle were permitted to cross the border for grazing purposes by mutual agreement between the two administrations. However, where the intention was to sell cattle in Gambian markets, an export duty was levied by the French authorities. The latter relied on local intelligence to identify herds that crossed the border without passing through an approved Customs post. A recurrent complaint from the Gambian side was that the Senegalese *douaniers* seized cattle from herders even when they had no intention of making a sale. Another issue of mutual concern was the transmission of cattle diseases, which broke out successively in the first decades of the twentieth century. The second category of trade was firearms and gunpowder. As Sokhna Sané has indicated, while the British and French authorities generally adopted divergent positions on arms control – with the former accepting the right of Africans to possess guns for hunting purposes and the latter aiming at complete disarmament – the Gambian authorities were closer to the French position than was normally the case.[95] However, both guns and gunpowder from the Gambia regularly exited across the border, and there was a lively trade as far south as Guinea-Bissau. Sané quotes an intelligence report from Bandjikaky (Casamance) in 1952, which indicated that the boats carrying ammunition cartridges from the Gambia travelled with fishing pirogues in order to avoid detection.[96] This was almost certainly a long-established practice. In the opinion of the French authorities, firearms and ammunition that entered from British and Portuguese territory contributed to the difficulties of establishing effective control over unsettled border zones. The French Customs men therefore paid particularly close attention to arms smuggling.

Aside from contraband, there was the broader question of crime control. On a day-to-day basis, there was co-operation between the authorities when it came to serious crimes against the person, including murder and assault, and large-scale theft, because uncontrolled criminality was understood to have serious implications for both sides – especially when lawbreakers were able to secrete themselves in the interstices of the borderlands. But there was also a suspicion that neighbouring authorities sought to push some of their undesirable elements across the border. At the same time, it was not uncommon for those accused of criminal behaviour to receive a more sympathetic hearing on the other side where it was felt that charges were trumped up by chiefs and informers or concealed different motives. Immediately following the partition, some of the most complicated cases of theft concerned human property. The

---

[95] Sokhna Sané, *Le côntrole des armes à feu en Afrique occidentale française 1834–1958* (Paris and Dakar: Karthala and CREPOS, 2008), p. 106.
[96] Sané, *Le côntrole des armes*, p. 183.

British reported that there were relatively few slaves in Kombo because Fodé Sylla had sold most of them in return for firearms. However, the efforts by slaves to free themselves created serious problems in other localities. In Saloum the French policy was to encourage slaves to purchase their freedom rather than to liberate them. In 1898, there was a revealing exchange of correspondence between the Travelling Commissioner in Niumi and the administrator in Saloum over the arrest of some individuals from the Gambia. While Ozanne, the British Commissioner, maintained that they were carrying a letter from himself clarifying their reasons for being in Senegal, the chief who intercepted them alleged that they were helping slaves to escape across the border. In the opinion of the French Commissioner, who was inclined to trust his chief, this represented the thin end of a demographic wedge:

> From the time of the internecine wars between the tyeddos of Saloum and the Muslims of Rip, many Diolas [Jolas], Malinkés, Bambaras and other slaves were reduced to captivity. If it is permitted to certain audacious people like Aly Khoudiaby and others to enter the country surreptitiously and to divert these slaves or former captives for the profit of the neighbouring foreign colony the region will suffer as a result. And the audacity of these natives, seeking refuge in the Gambia, would have no limits if they managed to obtain the protection of the English authorities in their irregular actions.[97]

The question of slavery was, of course, intimately bound up with the ownership of other forms of property. This was underscored in 1909 when the Gambian and Senegalese authorities were drawn into the case of some cattle that had allegedly been stolen in Niumi and taken away to Velor in Saloum. Governor Denton reported to the Governor-General of l'AOF that a cattle dispute had been adjudicated by the Commissioner of the North Bank in 1903, and the latter had ruled that one Sarrah Ba had no legitimate claim to the cows because he was a former slave. The latter had subsequently stolen twenty-two head of cattle and driven them into French territory.[98] Whereas Denton regarded this as a straightforward case of theft, the French Commandant reported that 'Sara Bâ' had worked for his master for 25 years and had managed to acquire two cows of his own that were kept in the communal herd.[99] Bâ and four other former slaves (who owned another two cows) had decided to move across the border rather than remain with the daughter of their former master. The Commandant observed that it was the refusal to release the cows on her death that had led Bâ to remove the entire herd, although he and

---

[97] ANS 10D 4/4 "Rapports Politiques à Goudiry et Dans le Sine-Saloum; Réclamation du Gouvernement de Gambie (1898)", H. Alsace, Administrateur du Sine-Saloum to le Directeur des Affaires Indigènes, Saint Louis (9 August 1898).

[98] ANS 1F14 "Relations Avec le Gambie: Reclamations Particulières (1905–1910)", Governor Denton to Governor General l'AOF (18 July 1909).

[99] ANS 1F14 "Relations Avec le Gambie", Brocard, l'Administrateur du Cercle du Sine-Saloum to Monsieur le Lieutenant-Gouverneur du Sénégal, St. Louis (19 Septembre 1909).

the former slaves were only claiming six of the cows as their own property. These two cases reveal the ways in which the border was used by slaves to establish their effective freedom and the complexities that sometimes underpinned stories of theft. In a more general sense, the theft of cattle was a recurrent issue given that rustling rings were known to operate between Guinea-Bissau, the Casamance and the Gambia. The strategy was to move the stolen cows across a border as quickly as possible because Customs officers were not permitted to engage in hot pursuit. By the time information had passed between officials the herds would have been long gone. Waterways provided another conduit for the swift removal of stolen goods, and as we will see, there was a lively trade in British military supplies during the war.

There were similarities and differences in the ways the French and British authorities went about border policing. Both expected their chiefs to carry out everyday surveillance and to report the presence of those they considered suspect. The chiefs had an especially important role to play as an early warning system in the pursuit of stolen cattle. However, when it came to the enforcement of the Customs regulations, the operating cultures were quite different. The French expected dutiful co-operation from the chiefs, as minor state functionaries, but it was the obligation of the uniformed Customs officers to enforce the regulations. The French appear to have invested considerable manpower in regulating the border flows and collecting the relevant duties. In the Gambia, by contrast, the Customs service only really functioned in Bathurst – that is, at the point of exit for groundnuts and of entry for consumer goods. In the Protectorate, there were no regular Customs officers, which meant that it was the chiefs who were formally required to collect duties. In 1932, the Commissioner for the Upper River suggested that the chiefs should receive a 25 per cent commission but following some discussion the proposal was rejected and the point that *alkalos* and *seyfos* were expected to levy duties was underlined.[100] This was repeated in 1938 in response to the UAC complaint above about rice smuggling:

I am directed by the Governor to say that the reported smuggling of rice has been brought to His Excellency's notice, and he desires you to impress on the Seyfolu and Alkalolu in every way possible the necessity for customs duties to be collected. The difficulties of patrolling the international frontier are fully recognized, but it is thought that at Jawara, in close proximity to your Provincial headquarters, it should be feasible for a more rigorous control to be exercised than at other points.[101]

---

[100] NAGB CSO 2/1280 "Commissions to Chiefs, Headmen, Repayment of Customs Dues", Commissioner, Upper River Province, to Acting Colonial Secretary (16 September 1932), and L.A.W. Brooks for Colonial Secretary to Commissioner, Upper River Province (8 February 1933).

[101] NAGB CSO 3/340 "Smuggling", R.H. Gretton for Colonial Secretary, to Commissioner, North Bank Province (18 March 1938).

However, because the chiefs did not receive a commission, there was limited incentive for them to be contentious in the performance of these responsibilities. In theory, the Commissioners possessed the powers of a Customs officer, but nobody really understood what that meant.

This somewhat farcical state of affairs was thrown into sharp relief as late as 1938 when none other than J.M. Gray, the author of *A History of the Gambia*, presided over a complicated smuggling case in his capacity as a judge of the Supreme Court. He reported that he could find no legislation that invested chiefs with the powers to collect duties or any stipulation that the duty had to be paid at the first village of entry.[102] That same year, when it was suggested that people ought to be drafted in to help enforce the Customs regulations, the Colonial Secretary's office replied that:

I am to say that the proposal to supply men for customs duty is not considered practicable and, moreover, that it should be borne in mind that an open frontier is of more value to this Colony than it is to the French.

In other words, the British regarded it as both impractical and unwise to bother unduly about Customs enforcement along the land borders. This remained the position down to the late 1950s when the first significant effort was made to establish a Customs presence in the Protectorate. However, even then the responsibility of the Customs Preventive Officers was largely that of checking the 'duty receipts books' that approved *seyfos* were required to keep.[103]

Throughout, there was a suspicion that Gambian chiefs were complicit with the smugglers. In the case just referred to, the Commissioner of the North Bank noted that the truck that had been used to smuggle coos (millet) and rice had been highly conspicuous, but the chief in question had paid no attention:

The penalty of losing his lorry is severe but considering the amount of rice and coos that the owner has been smuggling, he deserves no sympathy. Unless action such as this is taken, smuggling on a wholesale scale will continue, as the Native Authorities are entirely in favour of it. Lorry loads of smuggled goods have stood openly in villages during the last few weeks, while the owners extolled their goods.[104]

But as unreliable as the chiefs might have been, the Gambian authorities had no better alternative, being reluctant to pay for a substantive Customs

---

[102] NAGB CSO 3/340 "Smuggling from Senegal", case of Receiver-General vs Taim Jobe heard on 28 June 1938.

[103] NAGB CUS 1/4 "Collector of Customs, Border Trade and Smuggling", "List of Duties to be Performed by the Customs Preventive Officer Stationed at Georgetown", from Collector, 25 January 1958 (draft), and Commissioner of Central Division, Mansa Konko, to Collector of Customs (29 December 1957). This provides a list of authorized seyfos.

[104] NAGB CSO 3/340 "Smuggling", Commissioner of North Bank to Colonial Secretary (12 May 1938).

presence. In a nutshell, while fixing people in space – and taxing them – was something that the chiefs were expected to treat as a priority, the authorities were less concerned about their performance in regulating the movement of goods. This level of detachment, in which we can see the emergent roots of the permissive contract, is singular and reflects the reality that the Gambia was really one long border that defied proper policing.

Contrabanding in the Trans-Volta

In my previous work, I have dealt with the specificities of the Customs regime that took shape in the trans-Volta after the First World War.[105] Here, I wish merely to tease out the salient general points, while sketching in some additional local detail for the purposes of the wider comparison. There is a certain similarity between the two cases with respect to the centrality of communications. However, the roles of the British and the French were reversed in the trans-Volta. Much as the port of Bathurst and the Gambia River conferred an advantage on the Gambia as a conduit for trade, the French port at Lomé and the Kpalimé railway created a zone of economic penetration that extended well beyond the border as established in 1920.

The British assumption was not merely that their section of Togoland would be administered from Koforidua in the Eastern Province,[106] but also that it ought to revolve in the commercial orbit of the Gold Coast. For their part, the French, who had battled hard to retain Lomé and the three railways, imagined that this infrastructure would continue to carry goods from the two Togolands and that their neighbours would see the good sense in permitting this arrangement to continue. However, when the French refused to grant a general 'bond-in-transit' for goods destined for British Togoland, the Gold Coast authorities decided to go their own way. They moved the Gold Coast Customs frontier to the boundary between the Togolands in 1920 in the face of complaints that this was against the spirit of the Mandate. The effect upon prices was almost immediate. Towards the end of 1921, it was noted that tobacco could be purchased for 6s to 7s per kilogram in Kpalimé as against 9s to 10s in Ho. Again, cotton goods were reported to be 20 per cent dearer in Ho.[107] The British invested heavily in infrastructure in the 1920s with a view to reducing the cost of trading directly with Accra. Road construction was a priority, although the Senchi ferry remained a significant bottleneck until the 1950s

---

[105] Nugent, *Smugglers, Secessionists*, ch. 2.

[106] This was the headquarters of the Commissioner of the Eastern Province under whom the District Commissioner in Ho was placed.

[107] PRAAD 39/5/80 "Preventive Service", C.L. Trotter, Record Officer, Ho, to CEP, Koforidua (26 September 1921).

when the Volta River was finally bridged. All of this investment meant that it became possible to evacuate cocoa and to import goods from Accra at more realistic cost. Rather than lose the entire cocoa trade and be saddled with an under-utilized railway system, the French made specific concessions for the export of British Togoland cocoa. From 1925, cocoa that was certified as coming from British Togoland could be transported through Lomé and was included in the imperial preference for French Togoland. British and French firms exported part of their cocoa through French territory, and the remainder through Accra – although over time the Accra–Senchi route gained in significance.[108] Some consumer goods were also landed at Lomé and, following payment of French duties, legally imported into British Togoland.

The introduction of the Gold Coast Customs regime in 1920 was defended on the grounds that the colony could not reasonably be expected to subsidize British Togoland. Because the Gold Coast authorities did not levy direct taxes, the administration could only be funded through revenues derived from Customs duties. However, this had the predictable effect of making most consumer goods more expensive in British territory, even once the infrastructural barriers had been dealt with. Imported liquor, and more specifically Dutch gin, was the largest single source of government revenues in the Gold Coast, as we have seen, but it was also the leading item in the contraband trade. Tobacco products, including both cigarettes and raw tobacco, also featured strongly, as did textiles. The British authorities prohibited the importation of firearms and ammunition across the land border as early as 1915,[109] whilst seeking to regulate access to gunpowder for approved purposes. The resulting shortages fuelled demand in their own right. Unlike in the Senegambia, foodstuffs and cash crops (in this case cocoa) hardly featured at all as an issue in the contraband trade, although there certainly was a trade from French Togoland in some staples – as indeed there had been in the German period.

The French authorities displayed a quite specific interest in the dynamics of the border. As we have seen, they did what they could to minimize the loss of population to the Gold Coast. They kept a close watch on criminal activity in the border zone and exchanged information with the Gold Coast authorities with a view to apprehending suspects. They were also alert to what they regarded as seditious political influences infiltrating from British territory. However, unlike in the Senegambia, they paid relatively little attention to cross-border trade. Imported goods were taxed at the point of entry in Lomé,

[108] Nugent, *Smugglers, Secessionists*, p. 47. The principal firms in the early 1920s were G.B. Ollivant, F & A Swanzy, John Holt, CFAO (Compagnie Française de l'Afrique de l'Ouest) and SCOA (Société Commerciale Ouest Africaine).

[109] PRAAD 39/5/80 "Preventive Service", C.L. Trotter, Record Officer, Ho, to Collector, Northern Section (17 September 1921).

but the authorities had no interest in discouraging the flow of contraband goods into British territory – in fact, quite the opposite. On the British side of the border, the picture was more like that in Senegal. The Customs Preventive Service (CPS) was a leading player within the colonial bureaucracy because the Gold Coast state ran on Customs duties. After the CPS was mandated to check smuggling along the border between British territory and French Togoland, it pursued this function with gusto. It established a number of approved crossing points where duties were levied and where proscribed goods were seized. In addition, the CPS patrolled strategic areas along the border, mostly at night when most of the loading and unloading of consignments took place. Unlike in the Gambia, the CPS did not involve the chiefs in its work to any great extent. They had no function in revenue collection and they were not particularly relied upon to supply intelligence, part of the reason being that they were often regarded as being complicit.[110] In fact, chiefs in British Togoland often had a rather fraught relationship with the CPS who were perceived as conferring few benefits whilst fomenting a lot of local irritation. Whereas chiefs in French Togoland were expected to act as instruments of the administration, chiefs in British Togoland saw themselves as representing their communities more than central authority. Given that smuggling was a source of local income, they tended to share a more general distaste for the tactics of the CPS. Typically, it was chiefs who relayed complaints about the arbitrary behaviour of the Customs men to the authorities.

The CPS did what it could to improve its chances of success in challenging terrain. It resorted to the use of paid informers, which helped to narrow down the number of possible points of entry during preventive operations. Along the Togoland hills that made up much of the border north of Ho, there was often a limited number of routes from one point to another, whereas in the grasslands south of Ho the permutations were far more complex. A case in point is Agotime where the landscape was very flat and where new smuggling trails could be opened up relatively quickly. In fact, the population of Agotime was ideally positioned to profit from the contraband trade. Many of the Togolese towns were close to the railway and the main trunk road between Lomé and Kpalimé, which ensured that consumer goods were always freely available.

---

[110] Numerous chiefs were found guilty of smuggling in the 1920s. In 1923, chief Abusuahun of Ahamansu was found guilty of importing and secreting five bottles of trade spirits with intent to deceive a Customs officer. In 1925 Headchief Martin Akototse of Likpe was found guilty of being in possession of gunpowder, percussion caps and ammunition that had probably been smuggled. He was fined £10 or two months in prison. PRAAD ADM 43/4/18 "Criminal Record Book, Kpandu District". And in a remarkable case from 1928, Togbe Sesinu Kuma, the chief of Hoe, was found guilty of being at the centre of a highly organized ring involved in gin smuggling and fined £100 or 6 months in prison. PRAAD ADM 39/4/3 "Civil Record Book, Ho District". For more on this case, see also Nugent, *Smugglers, Secessionists*, pp. 107–12.

There were also a number of Agotime settlements within striking distance of the border where goods could be stored before being headloaded after nightfall.[111] Moreover, given that Kpetoe was located on the main road to Ho, it was possible to relay contraband to other traders who conveyed these goods to towns in British Togoland and in the Gold Coast. The existence of family relationships across the border also meant that relations of trust were more easily constructed.

Under the Customs Ordinance of 1923 (as amended in 1939), breaches of the regulations entitled the Comptroller to initiate a civil suit seeking forfeiture of the goods alongside a sum amounting to three times the value of the goods together with the duty, or a sum of £100 (or in default imprisonment in hard labour).[112] Agotime featured prominently in the cases that came to court before the Second World War. In fact, a very good overall picture can be ascertained simply by considering the cases in Agotime and its immediate environs. To start with, these provide an indication of the range of goods that were smuggled. In 1925, the CPS requested an arrest warrant for one Komla Okunka, a native of Agotime-Afegame, having sued him in absentia for smuggling fifty-two bottles of gin.[113] Tobacco smuggling, like that of gin, featured consistently and was made up both of 'Clipper' cigarettes and unmanufactured tobacco.[114] As we have seen in Chapter 5, Nene Noe Keteku II was suspended from his position of chief in 1937 following accusations that he had colluded with the postal agent in Kpetoe to use the agency's funds to engage in tobacco smuggling.[115] A more typical case was that of Joseph Dandoo who was eventually apprehended and charged for seeking to import "60 lbs Unmanufactured Tobacco having a duty paid value of £11. 5/-", after he had initially made good his escape.[116] In March 1940, George Noshie was apprehended near to Kpetoe for being in possession of unmanufactured tobacco and

---

[111] Some evidence from Wodome and Batoumé is presented in Benjamin N. Lawrance, "'En proie à la fièvre du cacao': land and resource conflict on an Ewe frontier, 1922–1939", *African Economic History* 31, 2003, pp. 158–9.

[112] PRAAD ADM 4/1/52 "Ordinances of the Gold Coast, Ashanti and the Northern Territories, 1923", Customs Ordinance of 1923, section 126 (9).

[113] The unsuccessful arrest had left two Customs officers seriously injured and an arrest warrant was issued. ADM 39/4/2 "Civil Record Book (Ho)", Comptroller of Customs versus Komla Okunka in Supreme Court, Ho, 18 August 1925.

[114] 'Clipper' was a Players brand, but the term was probably used in a more generic sense.

[115] In 1938, Nene Keteku brought a libel case against Ahowotor Legbe and won, after the latter had claimed that Keteku had publicly admitted using Post Office funds for smuggling purposes. The court found that while the alleged embezzlement had taken place in 1934, when the Post Office had to be closed, the allegation did not surface until 1937 when Keteku was under fire for other reasons. The court deemed the allegation as political and unproven, and awarded damages of £10 and costs of £3. ADM 39/4/9 "Civil Record Book – Ho", Nene Noe Keteku versus Ahowotor Legbe, in Magistrate's Court, Ho.

[116] ADM 39/4/5 "Civil Record Book (Ho)", Comptroller vs. Kofi Dandoo in Supreme Court, Ho, 26 October 1933.

matches in respect of which the CPS sued for the more modest sum of £5 8s 9d.[117] Although the flow of goods was generally in one direction, the acute shortage of consumer goods in French Togoland during the Second World War led to a flourishing trade in textiles in the opposite direction. Hence in November 1942, Yesufu Chambra pleaded guilty to the attempted exportation of "378 yrds Grey Baft, 4 yards Velvet and 20lbs Beads having a total value of £22/7/6".[118] The following month, Akua Adjei pleaded guilty to attempting to export "12 yards Khaki Drill, 6 yards White Drill, 3 yards Dyed Cloth, 2 yards White Skirting, 2 tins Pomade, and 1 tin Powder".[119] The latter, together with other cases involving the smuggling of perfumes, was an indication that women upheld a stubborn demand for cosmetic products, even at a time of austerity – bearing out Tim Burke's findings on the ways in which new expressions of selfhood in Zimbabwe were expressed through consumption of products designed for the body.[120]

Secondly, the Agotime cases reveal something about the ways in which the contraband trade was organized.[121] In some cases, rings – or what the CPS preferred to call 'gangs' – operated in a more or less stable fashion, but more commonly smugglers came together on an ad hoc basis. A group would typically consist of three or four people, but occasionally more than a dozen smugglers would cross the border together. This reduced an individual's chances of being caught or being waylaid by robbers on the way. Men and women were more or less equally represented, and groups of smugglers could be either mixed or single sex in composition. Many of the smugglers operating around Agotime were local residents, but there were a number of cases that involved so-called Hausas, probably including Chambra. In another instance, a CPS patrol intercepted five 'strangers' on the road between Kpetoe and Afegame in April 1941 who were found to be carrying headloads consisting of 'Hausa gowns', clothing and blankets and cosmetics of various kinds.[122] This was one of many such cases.

---

[117] ADM 39/4/19 "Civil Record Book (Ho)", Comptroller vs. George Noshie, in Magistrates Court, Ho, 26 March 1940.

[118] ADM 39/4/16 "Civil Record Book (Ho)", Comptroller vs. Yesufu Chambra, in Magistrates Court, Ho, 14 November 1942.

[119] ADM 39/4/16 "Civil Record Book (Ho)", Comptroller vs. Akua Adjei, in Magistrates Court, Ho, 2 December 1942.

[120] Timothy Burke, *Lifebuoy Men, Lux Women: Commodification, Consumption and Cleanliness in Modern Zimbabwe* (London: Leicester University Press, 1996).

[121] This account may be compared with that of gin smuggling in the coastal region. See Dmitri van den Bersselaar, "'Somebody must necessarily go to buy this drink': gin smugglers, chiefs and the state in colonial Ghana", *Cultural and Social History* 11 (2) 2014, pp. 249–54.

[122] ADM 39/4/16 "Civil Record Book (Ho)", Comptroller vs. Sannie (Musa Fulani) and four others, in Magistrates Court, Ho, 18 April 1941. Also the case against Idi Bogobiri on 9 December 1942 involving 67 bottles of perfume.

The market town of Assahun in French Togoland was located relatively close to the border. A direct route led to Batoumé and from there to Kpetoe. Dandoo, who lived at Agotime-Bè, was found guilty largely on the evidence of William Attipoe, who worked for the firm of John Walkden at 'Adzanu', or Assahun.[123] The latter claimed that Dandoo was a regular customer and a smuggler who had purchased tobacco at the store on a number of occasions. The efforts of Attipoe to save his own skin, after his own arrest at Ziope, were unsuccessful, and like Dandoo he was found liable for a penalty of £33 15s as the person who had supplied the contraband goods. What Attipoe did not know is that when Dandoo escaped to Togo, an informer had been sent across the border to gather information in order that a trap could be set. The court noted that Attipoe had one previous offence for smuggling and another for illicit distillation.[124] In the case of Alice Gbedema and Amegavi, which came to court in August 1934, the accused were intercepted on a lorry at Batome Junction and found to be in possession of 60 lbs of tobacco. In evidence they stated that they had bought it on credit at the G.B. Ollivant store in Assahun. Unusually, the accused were acquitted after they claimed that they were on their way to pay the duty when they were apprehended.[125]

The CPS strongly suspected that European firms that operated stores on the French side of the border were fully aware of the activities of smugglers on whose business they ultimately depended. As one self-confessed smuggler confirmed in interview, the firms extended goods on credit to traders who then despatched them across the border.[126] The case of Martin Silas Attipoe was regarded by the CPS as symptomatic of the problem. Attipoe was employed by G.B. Ollivant in Ho and was also doing business as a "general merchant", according to his defence lawyer (a comparative rarity in smuggling cases). But he owned a house in Assahun and was a regular visitor to that town. In 1938, a lorry was intercepted at Koforidua, in the Eastern Province of the Gold Coast, and was found to contain 716 lbs of unmanufactured tobacco and 34,500 cigarettes as well as 10 gallons of prohibited gin packed in cases marked 'Lomé'. Attipoe claimed that the goods had not come from G.B. Ollivant, but from various local sources, but the Collector indicated that they had been entered in the firm's books to conceal the reality that they originated from French territory. Presumably, Attipoe had purchased the goods in Lomé, ferried them across the border and then used Ollivant paperwork to bamboozle the Customs service. In smuggling cases, the burden of proof rested on the

---

[123] A further variant in the spelling was Azanu.

[124] ADM 39/4/5 "Civil Record Book (Ho)", Comptroller vs. William Madjaka Attipoe, in Magistrates Court, Ho, 26 October 1933.

[125] ADM 39/4/5 "Civil Record Book (Ho)", Comptroller vs. Alice Gbedema and Amegavi, in Supreme Court, Ho, 15 August 1934.

[126] Interview with Etu Adabra, Amoussoukope (Togo), 9 September 2003.

defendant. Having failed to satisfy the court of his innocence, Attipoe was fined a massive £709 plus legal costs. Being unable to pay he was sent to prison for a period of one year.[127]

Finally, these cases demonstrate some of the ways in which relationships of trust were built up – and broke down. On the one hand, seasoned smugglers generally sought to establish friendly relations with particular Customs officers who might be prepared to look the other way or to provide them with tipoffs. These relations were underpinned by money and gifts, but their durability also hinged on establishing 'friendships' and a sense of conviviality. During the 1940s, Etu Adabara was a food trader based in Amoussoukope who sent yams, maize, beans, gari and groundnuts for sale in Accra. She recalled that she was in the practice of paying duty on some of the items, but never the whole consignment because that would have rendered her trade unprofitable. The Customs men would let her off the full duty in return for "something small".[128] She also recalled that she concealed smuggled goods like gin bottles between the foodstuffs. On one occasion she was arrested close to Tema. The lorry was seized, and she was placed in Customs cells pending trial. Fortunately for her, one of the Customs officers, who was presumably well known to her already, enabled her to make good her escape. On the other hand, because the CPS could count on little sympathy in the conduct of its work – and often encountered outright hostility in border towns – it was common for the Customs men to forge intimate relations with paid informants. This practice was sanctioned by European officers as A.J. Beckley indicated as early as 1918: "On this Frontier I have no regular detectives, but reliable information has from time to time been offered by outsiders, who have subsequently received a share of the money awarded as laid down in the Customs Ordinance."[129] European officers

---

[127] PRAAD ADM 39/4/8 "Civil Record Book (Ho)", Comptroller vs. Martin John S. Attipoe, in Supreme Court, Ho, 1 December 1938, continued on 15 August 1934, at ADM 39/4/9 "Civil Record Book (Ho)". The CEP later drew special attention to this case and expressed regret that the vehicle had not been forfeited to the state. PRAAD ADM 39/1/570 "Buem Strangers Union", CEP, Koforidua, to Secretary of Native Affairs, Accra (28 January 1938). This was possibly not Attipoe's last brush with the law because in 1944, one M.S. Attipoe, who was said to be a storekeeper and a dealer (with a store at Atikpui that was operated by his brother) was found guilty of smuggling flour into French territory. PRAAD ADM 39/4/10 "Civil Record Book (Ho)", Comptroller of Customs vs. M.S. Attipoe, in Supreme Court, Ho, 20 June. An important test case occurred in 1949 when the driver of a UTC lorry was caught smuggling gin at Dormaa in 1949. The lorry was seized and sold, but the UTC subsequently made representations to the Colonial Office, which recognized the force of the argument that the UTC could not be held liable for the conduct of an employee, especially as the company, as a successor to the Basel Trading Company, did not itself trade in liquor. The Gold Coast government was prevailed upon to repay the cost of the lorry. National Archives (UK) CO 96/817/3 "Miscellaneous Gin-Running Offence".

[128] Interview with Etu Adabra, 9 September 2003.

[129] PRAAD ADM 39/5/79 "Preventive Service", A.J. Beckley, CPS District Supervisor, Aferingba to Holliday, District Political Officer, Misahöhe, 12 June 1918.

sanctioned particular arrangements, but it is evident that the Customs men came to recruit their own informers in the hope that they would be rewarded for their eventual success.

Encounters between Customs men and smugglers were steeped in ambiguity, which became apparent during moments of crisis. Smugglers could never be sure that their 'friends' in the CPS would risk their own position by protecting them, while the Customs men had cause to worry that they might be accused of irregular behaviour. In 1938 a case was brought against Albert Amedzro, the SCOA (Société Commerciale Ouest Africaine) storekeeper in Kpedze. The charge was that he had kept uncustomed Clipper cigarettes in his house and had tried to bribe the Customs officers at the time he was arrested. Amedzro claimed that, at the time, he had admitted bringing the cigarettes from Kpalimé to pay off his debts. The SCOA agent in Hohoe confirmed that Amedzro was indeed in debt to the firm, but reported the latter as saying that the cigarettes were given to him by individuals who owed him money in Kpalimé. When asked about the bribe, the defendant replied: "I did not give the Superintendent the money so that he should not take action against me for smuggling. I gave the Superintendent the money because he used to come to purchase goods from me and we became friends. He used to take credit from me." It appears that while Amedzro was in debt to SCOA, he was competing with his employer by selling contraband cigarettes on credit to his own customers.[130] He clearly knew the Customs men in question, and one of the defence witnesses confirmed that the Superintendent had said something along the lines of "do something for me". The court chose not to dig deeper into the maze of relationships and found Amedzro guilty of smuggling and attempted bribery.

A still more fascinating case unfolded in Kpetoe at the end of the same year. A British Customs officer, C.M. Bayfield, told the court that he witnessed a lorry arriving at Kpetoe and saw someone taking some bottles into the Customs guard room, which turned out to be eight bottles of whisky, gin and schnapps (these were marked as Exhibit B). When he enquired further, Bayfield was told by Conrad Buckle, the Superintendent at the station, that he had ordered the bottles from Keta for Christmas. When a further bottle of whisky (Exhibit A) arrived with another driver later in the day, Bayfield became suspicious because they bore the mark of the CFAO, which had no store in Keta. When asked to make a written report, Buckle explained to Bayfield that the first set of bottles was supposed to have been left at the

---

[130] The SCOA agent said rather limply "I was surprised to hear that the defendant was smuggling cigarettes. The company forbids a storekeeper to sell goods other than the company's goods". PRAAD ADM 39/4/8 "Civil Record Book, Ho", Comptroller vs. Albert Amedzro, in Magistrate's Court, Honuta, 2 September 1938.

French side of the border, at Batoumé, where he intended to celebrate Christmas. In court, the driver of the vehicle confirmed that these bottles had indeed been purchased in Assahun. In court, Buckle explained further:

I had chosen to spend my Xmas at Batome as the Collector had stated we could spend Xmas anywhere as long as he knew where we were. I had a sheep and fowls and everything at Kpetoe. The fowls are at Batome actually – the sheep is at Kpetoe. I was going to have my Xmas party with my informers.

In this case, the court was remarkably lenient. Normally where witnesses gave conflicting evidence, the court credited the one indicating guilt, but in this instance, it accepted that Buckle had not knowingly imported the bottle of whisky. As far as the other bottles were concerned, the magistrate was "satisfied that the spirits were for Xmas consumption". Although Buckle was fined £8, there was no suggestion that he had done anything wrong in spending the holiday season with his informants/friends at Batoumé.[131] These informants appear to have been cultivated by Buckle without any explicit authority to do so, a practice that was apparently quite common. The Customs service tolerated such unofficial arrangements because from time to time they yielded valuable results. Here we are presented a classic instance of the way in which practical governance actually functioned.

Conclusion

The lessons that emerge from a closer analysis of attempts to regulate the movement of people and goods can now be made explicit. First of all, whereas control over migration and settlement was central to the daily actions and long-term strategies of the Senegalese and Gambian colonial regimes, it was much less of an issue on the border between two Togolands where the interpolation of a border reinforced other factors that served as an impediment to mobility. The presumption of mobility in the first case study contrasts sharply with the entrenchment of the distinction between landlord and stranger in the second. Secondly, the regulation of cross-border trade mattered equally in both contexts, but it mattered considerably more on one side of a given border than the other. In the Senegambia, it was the French who sought to impose a stringent Customs regime, whereas in the trans-Volta it was the British who endeavoured to do so. In the Gambia and French Togoland, where there was very little interest in inhibiting the flows, the fiscal reproduction of the state itself was dependent on the facilitation of cross-border trade, much of which was illicit. The context for the latter was the demand of ordinary people for access to

---

[131] PRAAD ADM 39/4/9 "Civil Record Book, Ho", Comptroller vs. Conrad Buckle, in Magistrate's Court, Ho, 15 December 1939.

consumer goods that had once been the exclusive preserve of urban populations.

Thirdly, these differences had an important bearing on the institutional fabric. In Senegal, French Togoland and the Gambia, traditional authorities were absorbed into the state, although in the second two cases some deference was paid to working through chiefly lines. In the Gold Coast and British Togoland, chiefs existed outside the state and enjoyed much greater autonomy as a consequence. The institutional patterns that emerged across the four colonies were different by virtue of the very different roles the traditional authorities were expected to perform. In the Gambia, the chiefs collected yard taxes, managed the settlement of migrant populations and even collected duties in the absence of a functioning Customs service in the Protectorate. As Swindell and Jeng indicate, the intention was to absorb traditional authorities into the colonial state:

> The new arrangements regarding traders licenses were not just intended to raise revenues payable in cash, but to ensure that chiefs were turned into salaried officials ... and make them part of the local bureaucracy who were expected to collaborate with the British Administration ... [The] district chiefs in the Gambia were summoned each June to the capital to receive their share of the license fees, when any matters of dispute or appeal could be resolved by the chief magistrate. Also this was an attempt to keep the chiefs in contact with the Administration and visibly establish the hegemony of British rule.[132]

In Senegal, the chiefs collected taxes, dealt with the settlement of strangers, generated military conscripts and tackled cattle rustling and border crime, but were not actively involved in Customs work. In French Togoland, the chiefs functioned much as in Senegal, but they had a more limited role in the allocation of land and were not involved in the control of contraband. Finally, in the Gold Coast the chiefs did not collect tax or maintain population rolls and they were not involved in Customs work, which was jealously guarded by the CPS. The chiefs were broadly loyal because they were permitted to preside over their respective communities and to oversee the administration of uncultivated land. In a counter-intuitive way, therefore, the Gold Coast state was forged not through the appropriation of traditional authority, but by recognizing a boundary beyond which the state was unwise to transgress. The performative dimension lay in the *durbar* – a hybrid between Asante royal practice and a model imported from India[133] – where state officials and traditional rulers openly recognized the status and jurisdiction of the other

---

[132] Swindell and Jeng, *Migrants*, pp. 112–13.

[133] Fittingly, the Indian durbar itself was a hybrid between a British form of pageantry and what was encountered in situ – but scaled up. Bernard S. Cohn, *Colonialism and Its Forms of Knowledge: The British in India* (Princeton: Princeton University Press, 1996), p. 129.

party. A common understanding of the limits of the state was fundamental to an understanding of the colonial nexus in the Gold Coast and southern Togoland. Indirect Rule purists might have regarded the Gambia as deficient in significant respects, but Lord Lugard would scarcely have recognized the configuration in British Togoland and the Gold Coast. Mapping these various orders of difference does not merely tell us about the border dynamics, therefore, but provides us with a key to understanding the underpinnings of the larger social contracts.

7   Land, Belief and Belonging in the Borderlands

Having highlighted the role of colonial states in either facilitating or inhibiting mobility, I now consider the implications for framings of identity in the two regions concerned. As I have indicated in Chapter 2, the demography of frontier zones in the nineteenth century was often highly fluid, and this was accentuated by the political turbulence around the time when the borders were being demarcated. In that sense, the cherished notion that fixed communities were destabilized by the imposition of colonial borders is somewhat problematic. Whereas flight and displacement had been a feature of the frontier regions in the later nineteenth century, colonial regimes had an interest in fixing populations in productive spaces whilst regulating the flow of migrants. Whether people were at liberty to cross a border and to access land on the other side, or not, had a very practical bearing on the issue of what it meant to claim membership of a community. In the trans-Volta, as we will see, the casting of settlers as strangers entailed a perpetual disability, whereas a more open regime in the Senegambia tended to erode the distinction between indigenes and more recent arrivals. In the first case strangers tended to be sectioned off in distinct residential quarters, whereas in the second the settlement patterns were more interspersed. This, in turn, had a bearing on the practical salience that was attached to ethnicity when projected onto a larger canvas.

Religion was an intervening variable that played a very different mediating role in the two contexts. Christianity and Islam both formally transcended ethnic distinctions, but they interacted very differently with other elements in the equation. In the Senegambia, adherence to Islam was associated with the emergence of new model communities that downplayed the significance of ethnic origins. In the trans-Volta, the competition between multiple Christian denominations added another layer of complexity. But the fundamental point is that the primacy attached to the landlord–stranger distinction trumped adherence to a common religion. However, the underlying differences also have everything to do with the manner in which religion was closely woven into the histories of the two regions at the turn of the century. The process of conversion was not only tied to the process of colonization but was also bound up with the making and reproduction of the international borders. The churches depended on the goodwill of the colonial authorities, and as much as they might have wished to proselytize across borders, they found themselves constrained and moulded by them. Islam, by contrast, was not a part of the colonizing project, at least to start with, and tended to slice through the borders with consummate ease. Moreover, in the first case the churches tended to be built upon the foundations of a notional host community, whereas conversion to Islam was closely associated with the realities of serial mobility.[1] Although both Christian and Muslim converts claimed that the new religion would bring peace and prosperity to a troubled world, the readings of history were also significantly different.

Once more, I begin this comparison in the Senegambia where processes of settlement and Islamic conversion became closely interwoven and together reconfigured 'we-group' distinctions between Mandinka, Jola and Kalorn/ Karoninka. I then return to the trans-Volta and seek to account for the entrenchment of a much less inclusive understanding of what it meant to *be* Agotime, at the same time as the cleavages between the Agotime and their Ewe neighbours were accentuated. Although the trajectories were noticeably different in these two regions, none of this should be viewed as pre-ordained. Indeed, in the light of the nineteenth-century historical processes that were outlined in Chapter 2, one might even have expected the opposite outcome. That this did not come to pass has much to do with the ways in which states interacted with border populations.

Islam and the Reshaping of Community in the Gambia/ Casamance Borderlands

At the start of the colonial era, European officials held pretty rigid ideas about the ways in which Jola and Mandinka populations related to one another. The stereotype of the Jola was one of physically tough and hardworking rice cultivators who had developed an ingrained disdain for authority and who remained deeply attached to their spirit shrines and sacred groves. The Mandinka, on the other hand, were regarded as amenable to hierarchy, but were thought to harbour a deep disdain for agriculture. By the end of the nineteenth century, Mandinka was also synonymous with being Muslim. As we have seen, both sets of authorities used Mandinka chiefs to govern Jola populations, but with variable levels of success. The Mandinka were thought to look down on the Jola as pagans, while it was believed that the Jola

---

[1] The partial exception was so-called Christian villages which were new and mostly populated by former slaves. But these were drawn from the adjoining communities and were not migrants in the same sense.

mistrusted the Mandinka because of their past involvement in slave raiding. The firmly rooted notion that Mandinka and Jola were opposed 'tribal' categories seemed to find confirmation in specific occurrences: at one moment, it was hapless Jola being cheated by wily Mandinka traders; at another, it was Mandinkas being waylaid by Jola bandits as they moved through border spaces. But contrary to European readings of an entrenched and immutable difference, Mandinka and Jola populations became closely intertwined in the early twentieth century. Jola from Buluf, north of the Casamance River, migrated into the border zone, while Mandinka marabouts moved south and eastwards into the Casamance, forging new religious communities that were distinctly, and often explicitly, pan-ethnic in character. Although the underlying distinctions were never erased, ethnic boundaries softened as village communities on both sides of the Gambia–Casamance border became highly mixed entities. Unravelling the threads of this complex story is my concern in what follows. It is a story that begins with the mass conversion of the Jola to Islam.

A Peace Dividend: Cheikh Mahfoudz and Islamic Conversion

In the first thirty years of colonial rule, the conversion of the Jola began incrementally and then gathered momentum. Whereas there remained many non-Muslims south of the Casamance River, conversion was virtually total in the Gambian border region by the end of the 1930s. This raises the question of why it was that the Jola came to embrace the religion they had previously associated with violent enslavement. A minor part of the answer is that the colonial authorities did little to support Christian missionary activity that could have created a viable alternative. In the Gambia, the Methodists, Catholics and Anglican missions had the greatest impact in Bathurst itself, despite some efforts to implant themselves in Kombo and Fogny.[2] In Senegal, a strong tinge of anti-clericalism created a less than supportive environment for the Catholic Church. However, it has to be said that officials were of the view that no encouragement ought to be given to Islam either – indeed quite the contrary. Paul Marty, who became the leading expert on Islam Noir, expressed this view in unequivocal terms in 1915:

Mandinka Islam must remain in Mandinka country and the marabouts of the Middle Casamance who would be tempted to found their stations for prosyletism or to beg or send their propaganda agents into Fogny must be rigorously invited to take their efforts

---

[2] Martha T. Frederiks, *We Have Toiled All Night: Christianity in the Gambia, 1456–2000* (Zoetermeer: Uitgeverij Boekencentrum, 2003).

elsewhere, to not disturb the social condition of the Jola and to let us complete our work of education.[3]

A different answer has been offered by Peter Mark who, in his various writings, brings together socio-economic change, agency and social crisis in a multi-causal explanation for Jola conversion. As far as the first is concerned, Mark observes that the introduction of groundnut cultivation into Buluf villages at the start of the twentieth century is widely attributed to the influence of Mandinka traders – in addition to the pressure to pay French taxes – which could be seen as indicative of new relationships of proximity.[4] Mark maintains that socio-economic change in Buluf led to a receptivity to different ways of thinking about the world, especially amongst young men who travelled further afield in search of employment in the 1930s. This "alternative value system" enabled youth to achieve a degree of autonomy from the elders who had hitherto presided over the Jola religious landscape.[5] Secondly, Mark places considerable importance on the role played by French chiefly intermediaries (see Chapter 5). The French chose their chiefs from amongst those individuals who were the most travelled, and these happened to be the people who were the most likely to have encountered Islam. Mark cites the case of Dianku Diedhiou who was one of the first Muslim converts in Tiobon and who was elevated to the position of village chief.[6] He also refers to Ansoumane Diatta – the first Muslim in Tendouk who served as the *chef de canton* between 1916 and 1925 – who proceeded to select his village notables from amongst the converts.[7] On this view, Muslim chiefs helped to create a receptive environment in which marabouts could assemble their followings. Finally, Mark argues that from the First World War onwards, the Buluf Jola experienced a series of shocks that led people to seek out new remedies that their religious system was not dealing with effectively: in particular, the influenza pandemic, falling groundnut prices at the onset of the Depression, followed by a triple dose of cattle plague, drought and renewed grasshopper invasions. Mark summarizes the crisis of belief in the following terms:

The pharaonic plagues of the early 1930s seem to have induced a general sense of loss of control over their lives and environment among the people of Boulouf. Already during the preceding two decades, rapid economic change together with urban migration and consequent challenges to the authority of the elders, had placed strains on the

---

[3] ANS 13G 67 "Politique Musulmane: activité des marabouts (1906–17)", Paul Marty, "De l'influence religieuse des cheikhs Maures du Senegal", 31 May 1915 (File 5).

[4] Peter Mark, "Urban migration, cash cropping and calamity: the spread of Islam among the Diola of Boulouf (Senegal), 1900–1940", *African Studies Review* 21 (2) 1978, p. 4.

[5] Mark, "Urban migration", p. 10.

[6] Peter Mark, *A Cultural, Economic and Religious History of the Basse Casamance since 1500* (Wiesbaden: Franz Steiner Verlag, 1985), p. 102.

[7] Mark, *Cultural, Economic and Religious*, p. 102.

local social structure. The catastrophes of the 1930s added to this dislocation. Together, these social and economic developments stimulated the rapid spread of Islam among the Diola.[8]

Hence, in Buluf there was an especially rapid conversion in the years immediately after 1933.

One of the familiar problems with sociological explanations for conversion is precisely that they are so logical. That is, they draw conclusions on the basis of historical conjunctures, but without necessarily revealing the process of conversion from within the mindset of the converted. For the latter, the experience is often a spiritual journey that cannot be reduced to something else. However, two further observations were made during interviews that would suggest that the context and the spiritual experience cannot be so easily disentangled. The first is that Muslim clerics offered a coherent explanation for the difficulties that the Jola had experienced, not just in the 1930s but also around the turn of the century when slave raiding and grasshopper invasions similarly created acute hardship and displacement. The contention is that the Jola were being punished for dabbling with the spirit world and that it was only by making a heart-felt conversion to Islam that they would enjoy respite. The second observation is that Islamic reformers offered their own critique of deviant Muslims such as Fodé Sylla and re-inscribed Islam as the religion of peace. To become a devout Muslim meant turning one's back *both* on the old Jola religion *and* the divisive legacies of the warrior marabouts. The synthesis lay in the creation of new communities of believers that were configured in entirely different ways. By associating Islam with the peaceful pursuit of farming and trade, therefore, the historical signs were reversed. In that sense, the critique of Jola religious practice simultaneously embodied statements about the seamlessness of history, cosmology and the practicalities of everyday life.

Although the French authorities insisted that they were the guarantors of peace in a troubled region, the intimidation surrounding tax collection and enlistment must have made that pitch seem rather hollow. Instead, Muslims give most of the credit to particular marabouts who managed to forge new religious communities, while engaging at some level with the French authorities. In the areas where I conducted research, I found little evidence that colonial chiefs played a catlytic role, simply because their legitimacy was so tenuous (see Chapter Five). The colonial social contract in the Casamance, such as it was, was mediated by the actions of religious leaders who were not part of the state in the making. Given the suspicion that would have attached to

---

[8] Peter Mark, "Urban migration", p. 8. This formulation is broadly endorsed by Olga Linares, *Power, Prayer and Production: The Jola of Casamance, Senegal* (Cambridge: Cambridge University Press, 1992), pp. 94–6.

Mandinka marabouts at the turn of the century, a crucial function was performed by Mauritanian holy men. In the borderlands, no figure was more influential than Chérif Mahfoudz – and his son, Chérif Chamesedine.[9] Thanks to Paul Marty and his colleagues in the Bureau des Affaires Musulmanes, who collected intelligence on all marabouts of any note, we have a reasonably complete picture of the history and movements of Mahfoudz. It has also been possible to supplement the archival record with interviews with members of his network today, including his successor, Chérif Mouhidinne Ibnou el-Arabi Aidara.[10] Most villages in Kombo, Narang and Fogny-Jabangkunda harbour rich oral histories of the activities and interventions of Cheikh Mahfoudz. These are kept alive by the large number of people from both sides of the border who make the annual pilgrimage to Daroussalaam on the anniversary of his birth. At this point, it is necessary to embark on a short diversion in order to situate Mahfoudz in his regional context.

Mahfoudz was born in Mauritania, possibly in 1855, and was the grandson of the founder of the Fadeliyya order, Mohamed al-Fadel. Throughout his life, he remained formally attached to his teacher and uncle, Cheikh Saad Bou, who became the trusted intermediary of the French in Mauritania – although the relationship with his mentor reputedly became strained in later life.[11] Mahfoudz was peripatetic, spending long periods of time in what are now Mauritania, Mali, the Gambia, Portuguese Guinea and the Casamance. An intelligence report, which was evidently penned by Marty, claimed that his original ambitions were political rather than religious – that, is he sought to sell his services as an advisor to local rulers. The report recalled that he had once offered his good offices to mediate in the conflict between Samory and the French, but after living in Wasulu and failing to make any headway, he decided to move on in 1895.[12] The tradition that is recounted by Chérif Mouhidinne paints an entirely different picture of a man driven by his inner faith.[13] One episode recounts how one of Samory's aides came to perceive Mahfoudz as a threat and persuaded his master that he should be killed. Mahfoudz was invited to a meeting, at which they intended to cut off his head. But as the assassin was about to strike, both he and Samory were paralysed. When Mahfoudz released them from this state, Samory – who was reputedly a

---

[9] In Kabadio, Chamesedine's intercession in praying for rain is remembered in the same way as in Buluf. Interview with Alkalo Landing Jabang, assistant Alkalo, Seku Jabang and Yusuf Darbo Kabadio (Casamance), 21 July 2005.

[10] Interview with Chérif Cheikh Mouhidinne Ibnou el-Arabi Aidara, Darsilami-Cherifkunda (Daroussalam) (Casamance), 17 February 2004.

[11] David Robinson, *Paths of Accommodation: Muslim Societies and French Colonial Authorities in Senegal and Mauritania, 1880–1920* (Oxford and Athens: James Currey and Ohio University Press, 2000), pp. 161–77. On the strains, see Marty, "De l'influence religieuse".

[12] Marty, "De l'influence religieuse".

[13] Interview with Chérif Cheikh Mouhidinne Ibnou el-Arabi Aidara, 17 February 2004.

formidable magician in his own right – recognized that Mahfoudz was no ordinary marabout. The story goes that he attempted to persuade Mahfoudz to stay on, but when the latter expressed his firm intention to leave, he gave him gifts that included a couple of European captives. Mahfoudz is said to have parted company with Samory, warning him against the folly of continuing to fight the French whose time had come. Mahfoudz returned to Mauritania to present his gifts to Saad Bou, finding time to hand over the French captives to the authorities in Saint-Louis. He then set out again on his travels once more.

The Marty report simply says that Mahfoudz left Mali and proceeded to join Moussa Molo in Fuladu (1895), where he spent a year before proceeding to Sandugu at the moment the Joint Boundary Commission was engaged in its work. After returning to Mauritania, he travelled through Sandugu en route to Voyi in Portuguese Guinea where he ended up becoming the marabout of the chief at Pahane. This was apparently a position of some importance because the latter was brother to the ruler of Kabu, Modi Sellou Kayaba. After yet another visit to Mauritania, he returned to Portuguese Guinea and settled at Pakoua between 1891 and 1901. His next move was to Marsassoum on the borders of Fogny before finally relocating to Narang where Mahfoudz remained between 1901 and 1905. It was during this period that local traditions recall that he was most active in bringing the Jola to Islam. Local traditions even claim that Mahfoudz met Fodé Sylla and warned him that it was senseless resisting the whites and trying to convert people by force.[14] The chronology makes it rather unlikely – although he is reported to have met and taken a wife from Fodé Kaba – but the claim is important as a statement about the contrasting faces of Islam.

It is said today that Mahfoudz did not condemn local religious practices but sought to gently persuade the Jola of the need to give up 'worshipping idols' if they were to be released from the litany of woes that had been visited upon them. His approach consisted of spending enough time in a village to make some converts, at which point he would leave a *talibé* or two behind and move on. Whereas Fodé Sylla stands in the Jola Muslim imagination for a corruption of Islam, in which the supposed quest for conversion concealed a taste for slave raiding and plunder, Mahfoudz is seen as fighting a jihad of the heart.[15] It will be recalled that traditions in Kujube claim that Fodé Sylla singularly failed to defeat the Soninke ruler, Mansa Kalamar. The fulfilment of Sylla's subsequent prophesy of a mass conversion is not credited to himself, but rather to Mahfoudz who visited Kujube and all the other villages in Narang and won

---

[14] Interview with Chérif Cheikh Mouhidinne Ibnou el-Arabi Aidara, 17 February 2004.
[15] This is, of course, similar to the language deployed by other Muslim leaders of a more pacific strain. See, for example, Cheikh Anta Babou, *Fighting the Greater Jihad: Amadu Bamba and the Founding of the Muridiyya of Senegal, 1853–1913* (Athens: Ohio University Press, 2007).

people over by his charisma and the appeal of his message of peace and devotion. The Gambian border town of Darsilami derives its name from the personal intervention of Mahfoudz. In the context of the devastation wrought by Fodé Sylla, the significance of the name – that is, a place of peace – requires little decoding. It is also no coincidence that Mahfoudz founded his own village of Daroussalaam (or Darsilami-Cheriffkunda) in the Narang forest in close proximity to the border. This could be read as a statement to the effect that the spiritual dangers associated with the forest held no dangers for one who was devout. But it was also about laying the foundations of a religious community that would be less susceptible to French surveillance. In his own way, Mahfoudz was evidently using the boundary to good effect.

By 1905, the Portuguese were confronted with an uprising in Voyi, and Mahfoudz crossed back across the border into Guinea-Bissau, apparently offering to play the role of peacemaker. After being engaged by the Portuguese administration for some time – which Marty insinuated brought a lucrative stake in tax collection – he fell out of favour. He therefore returned to the Casamance and settled at Binako, on the upper reaches of the Casamance River in December 1906. He did so with the explicit permission of the French administrator, Paul Brocard.[16] The version that is recounted by Chérif Mouhidinne claims that there was a meeting between Mahfoudz and Brocard, at which the latter greeted the marabout with open arms, to the former's evident surprise. It transpired that Brocard was one of the captives that Mahfoudz had handed over to the French authorities in Saint-Louis a couple of decades earlier.[17] I have not encountered this twist in other sources, but its discursive significance resides in the contention that Mahfoudz always dealt with the French from a position of mutual trust and genuine friendship. French reports, by contrast, present a rather jaundiced picture of Mahfoudz and his followers. Against the backdrop of their travails in Fogny, the French clearly believed that Mahfoudz had been fishing in troubled waters. In the famously recalcitrant village of Kartiak, the authorities had found amulets in the

---

[16] Christian Roche, *Histoire de la Casamance: conquête et résistance, 1850–1920* (Paris: Karthala, 1985), p. 296.

[17] A recent rendition of the history claims that Mahfoudz had been sent by the French to secure the release of a French officer by the name of Borcal, which is presumably a corruption of Brocard. See Dah Dieng, "L'Islam en Casamance: Cheikh Mahfoudh le Cheikh de Binako", viewed at www.facebook.com/notes/dah-dieng/lislam-en-casamance-cheikh-mahfoudh-le-cheikh-de-binako/945662798781846/

Brocard later became the administrator of Sine-Saloum and found himself at the centre of a political storm in 1913 when he summarily imprisoned one Mody M'baye, an African clerk who claimed the rights of a citizen, simply for having criticized the administration in writing. G. Wesley Johnson, "William Ponty (1866–1915) and Republican Paternalism in French West Africa", in Lewis H. Gann and Peter Duignan (eds.), *African Proconsuls: European Governors in Africa* (New York, London and Stanford: Free Press, Collier Macmillan and Hoover Institution Press, 1977), p. 145.

possession of the chief that they linked to Mahfoudz – although they never managed to produce conclusive evidence of anything other than a religious connection.[18] In some respects, the French could not make up their mind whether Mahfoudz was a dangerous religious fanatic, cleverly concealing his real intentions, or a fraudster who lived off the credulity of others. The Marty report goes into considerable detail on his farming and trading activities in Binako, where he allegedly gave up trying to exercise any religious influence over what he described as "thieving Balantas". His trading operations, which relied largely on waterborne transport, were alleged to extend across the Casamance, into British Kombo and down into Portuguese Guinea. Moreover, other reports referred to particular followers who were accused of separating gullible Jola from their cattle through what the French considered to be the provision of dubious religious services.[19] In the context of cattle plague and drought, however, the prayers that were offered to protect livestock and to ensure good crops were entirely explicable in terms of the religious agenda that Mahfoudz and his followers were pursuing.[20] Indeed, it largely explains their success in winning converts.

The one respect in which Marty's report remains useful to us is in mapping the regional network over which Mahfoudz presided. This was impressive in that it straddled three colonies – namely the Gambia, Senegal and Portuguese Guinea. Mahfoudz lived out his last days in Binako where he carried out much of the teaching in a koranic school, along with two or three others. Daroussalaam was left under the control of one of his brothers, Hadrami. It was significantly larger than the Binako settlement and was estimated to contain a hundred houses and several hundred inhabitants. Unlike the settlement in Binako, which was appended to an existing Balanta village, Daroussalaam was an entirely new settlement, at the centre of which was a mosque and the Mahfoudz compound. Although he was resident elsewhere, he remained an influential factor in the settlement histories of the area. Hence, the founder of Donbondir apparently approached Mahfoudz to predict his fortune, with the intention of finding out where he might best establish his

---

[18] "ANS 13G 67 "Politique Musulmane", Marty, "De l'influence religieuse". Mark writes that "Cherif Mahfoudz is said to have dispensed charms among the Diola to protect them against the danger of military attack by the French." It is not clear whether he is basing this statement on fieldwork or this file, which is not referred to in this context. Mark, *Cultural, Economic and Religious*, p. 111.

[19] French reports refer to Jolas being defrauded of their cattle and other goods by unscrupulous marabouts, including members of Mahfoudz's family. His nephew, Mohammed Fadel, was one of those under suspicion around the time of the First World War. ANS 13G 67 "Politique Musulmane", extract du rapport mensuel du Cercle du Kolda by Castel, 20 December 1914.

[20] Mark observes that Chamesedine was asked to bless the rice fields in Mandegane in 1933. *Cultural, Economic and Religious*, p. 111. Chamesedine was also said to have preyed for rain in the Fogny-Jabangkunda. Interview with Alkalo Landing Jabang, 21 July 2005.

own village.[21] Mahfoudz had married his sister and there was therefore a bond of trust between them. Mahfoudz is said to have predicted that his in-law would become the master of his own domain if he left what is now Mahamouda and moved further to the west where there was vacant land. This appears to have occurred during the First World War. Mahfoudz also maintained a smaller outpost in Pakao in the Middle Casamance. The Gambia/ Casamance border evidently did not present a barrier to Mahfoudz, and his influence is openly acknowledged in many Gambian villages to this day. In Portuguese territory, he maintained a sizeable station at Pakoua, on the River Geba, with an estimated population of several hundred disciples. In addition, he retained outstations at Voyi and Brassou.

The Marty report indicates that the *talibés* who played a catalytic role in Daroussalaam were a diverse group. The largest was made up of eight Mandinkas: three from Kabu, and one each from Kiang, Pakao, Niumi, Brassou and 'French Kombo'. The second largest group comprised Tukolor: three from Niani and one from Macina. Finally, there were two Sarakolle and one Wolof. The missing ingredient was, of course, the Jola. They were not amongst the original followers of Mahfoudz, but as the process of conversion advanced, the Jola became the largest constituency in numerical terms. One has to envisage a scenario, therefore, in which Jola villages encountered disciples of diverse ethnic origins. This, in turn, eased the way for other Mandinka marabouts that were not necessarily part of the Mahfoudz network, but nevertheless benefited from his proselytism and that of his successors. In a nutshell, Mahfoudz remains such a commanding figure because he was instrumental in forging a religious community that crossed ethnicities as well as traversing territorial boundaries. That is also how he is venerated today.

There is more research to be done in terms of profiling the first Jola converts. During interviews in Narang and Fogny-Jabangkunda, it was confirmed that only a few individuals converted during the time of Fodé Sylla. The first Muslim in Kujube was apparently the son and successor of Mansa Kalamar, Diatta Kajambona, who converted in order to secure the freedom of his sister who had been taken captive by Fodé Sylla.[22] In Kabadio, Lamine Kending apparently converted, but his people distanced themselves from his example.[23] The real breakthrough seems to have taken place in the first years of the twentieth century at the point when Mahfoudz installed himself in Narang. Mahfoudz travelled widely throughout Narang and Buluf and, as we have

---

[21] Interview with Famara Diatta, Moussa Sonko and Janko Diedhiou, Donbondir (Casamance), 16 February 2004.

[22] Interview with Tombon Ture and others, Kujube (Casamance) 18 February 2004.

[23] The relationship with Sylla is glossed in terms of personal 'friendship'. Interview with Alkalo Landing Jabang, 21 July 2005.

Figure 7.1 Photograph of Mahfoudz mural at Daroussalaam.

seen, is credited with having made the first significant converts. Mosques were established in the villages, and koranic schools followed in short order. Moreover, as Mark indicates, the introduction of a regular cycle of religious festivals, which he associates with the legacy of Mahfoudz, created important linkages between converts in different settlements.[24] In that way, a genuine network was assembled, albeit one that remained highly decentralized. The *talibés* who studied with Mahfoudz or one of the other marabouts, typically established their own koranic schools. They proudly advertised the long line of transmission of Islamic learning, as is customary throughout the Islamic world, whilst becoming functionally autonomous. This segmentary tradition, which was integral to Islamic practice in the Gambia and the Casamance, was rather unlike northern Senegal where the brotherhoods provided a more structured pattern of religiosity.

As an example, one could mention the case of Kemo Diatta in Diouloulou. In 1913, he was described as being one of two marabouts in that town, and the one who commanded the greatest respect. Diatta had been a student of Saad Bou and had spent time in Tivouane and the Gambia before settling down in Diouloulou.[25] Although he belonged to the same religious branch as Mahfoudz, there is no suggestion in the documents that they stood in any direct relationship to one another. The koranic school that Kemo Diatta established in Diouloulou became popular, to such an extent that it posed a direct threat to the

[24] Mark, "Urban migration", p. 11.
[25] Kemo Diatta is mentioned in "De l'influence religieuse".

newly established French school.[26] In September 1913, Diatta was fined 50 francs and sent to prison for eight days for having presumed to mount an evening course in Arabic that was drawing students away from a course in French.[27] The harsh treatment meted out to Diatta underlines that the French authorities remained highly suspicious of the marabouts. Be that as it may, the growth of Islamic education was impressive. Mark notes that within the Bignona *cercle*, there were 84 schools with a total enrolment of 1,419 pupils by 1934 – which was the fifth highest number amongst the sixteen *cercles* in Senegal.[28]

In her own interpretation of Jola conversion, Olga Linares invokes the famous debate between Robin Horton and Humphrey Fisher over the inroads made by the world religions.[29] She rejects Horton's model – in which widening horizons lend credence to macrocosmic religions over microcosmic ones – and suggests that Islam and Jola religious practice could actually co-exist. She writes that "a kind of division of labour persists between the spirit shrines, which stand for social categories and punish transgressions through inflicting disease, and Islam, which regulates the positive relations among individuals and between them and the supreme being."[30] For the same reason, she questions Fisher's observation that a period of mixing is followed by a reformist impulse in which greater orthodoxy – or rather orthopraxy – necessarily ensues. Her position amounts to the proposition that Islam was adopted because it was possible to do so without overturning the cosmological system that was in place and which, as Baum has demonstrated in great detail, had proved itself extremely flexible in the past.[31] Whereas a religious layering almost certainly did occur amongst some Jola sub-groups, it is a somewhat problematic depiction of conversion in Kombo, Narang and the northern part of Fogny-Jabangkunda. Here there seems to have been a cleaner break with older forms of religious practice – and indeed it was the rupture that was integral to its appeal.[32] Typically, the Muslim convert turned his back on the

---

[26] The context was one in which the French were seeking to promote teaching in French. See Kelly M. Duke Bryant, *Education as Politics: Colonial Schooling and Political Debate in Senegal 1850s–1914* (Madison: University of Wisconsin Press, 2015).

[27] ANS 2G 13/57 "Résidence de Diouloulou, Rapports mensuels d'ensemble 1913", report for September 1913.

[28] Mark, *Cultural, Economic and Religious*, p. 113. Elsewhere the figures that are cited are 85 schools and 1,149 students. Mark, "Urban migration".

[29] Robin Horton, "African conversion", *Africa* 41, 1971, Humphrey J. Fisher, "Conversion reconsidered: some historical aspects of religious conversion in Africa", *Africa* 43 (1) 1973, pp. 27–40, and Horton, "On the rationality of conversion. Part I", *Africa* 45 (3) 1975 and "On the rationality of conversion. Part II", *Africa* 45 (4), 1975.

[30] Olga Linares, "Islamic 'conversion' reconsidered", *Cambridge Anthropology* 11, 1986, p. 15

[31] Robert M. Baum, *Shrines of the Slave Trade: Diola Religion and Society in Precolonial Senegambia* (New York and Oxford: Oxford University Press, 1999).

[32] Similarly, Mark notes that conversion was accompanied by the abandonment of the spirit shrines (except for medicinal purposes) and abstention from pork and alcohol. Mark, "Urban

spirit shrines and *jalangs* and abandoned the consumption of alcohol. More-over, new religious spaces were constructed: while the sacred groves were left on one side, new towns were reconfigured around the mosque, the koranic school and public meeting places for co-religionists. Finally, within towns that became ethnically highly mixed, Islam provided a veritable charter for full social equality – at least as between men. This was in itself a radical conceptual break from the notion that settlements were 'owned' by those who could claim to be first settlers.

By the outbreak of the Second World War, the Jola of the Gambia/Casa-mance borderlands had come to share in an aesthetic and ethical code that traversed ethnic boundaries. The British and the French authorities were highly sceptical as to whether the Jola could ever become 'real Muslims', but over time it became evident that they were not so different from their Mandinka neighbours after all. Such an outcome had not been anticipated, and to some extent the Europeans found it threatening to their settled picture of a world inhabited by static and knowable tribes. In this story, the brokerage performed by Cheikh Mahfoudz and other Mauritanian marabouts was of paramount importance.[33]

The Formation of New Model Communities

In Chapter 6, I demonstrated that the relationship between the British and French administrations was heavily coloured by their jostling for demographic advantage. Whereas much of the mobility took place through the international border, this occurred against the backdrop of the northwards drift of Jola from the Casamance, where land was relatively scarce, towards the lightly populated border zone. The Gambian and Senegalese authorities hoped that Jola settlers could be persuaded to take to the cultivation of groundnuts. The settlement histories that were collected in the course of conducting this research (see Table 7.1) suggest that people often relocated several times in the search for land that had the right mix of attributes: the ideal was some combination of wetlands that were suitable for cultivating rice, other plots that could be turned over to vegetables and groundnuts, and finally land that was suitable for grazing cattle.[34] A few examples from the Kombo borderlands will illustrate the ways in which this worked in practice. The first is the village of Dimbaya that presently straddles the international border. The original settlers were

migration", p. 8. Linares distinguishes Islamic codes from a Mandinka style of cultural comportment. Linares, *Power, Prayer and Production*, p. 97.

[33] Mahfoudz has his rivals, most notably Chérif Sidi, a native of Kabu, who claimed his authority directly from Saad Bou and challenged the dominance of Mahfoudz in the Casamance. Marty, "De l'influence religieuse".

[34] The cattle often grazed on the fields after harvest, thereby restoring the fertility of the fields.

Table 7.1 *Types of settlement along the Gambia/Casamance border*

Name of village	Status	Acquired land from	Composition
A. Gambia			
Darsilami	Old town repopulated by strangers, renamed by Mahfoudz	–	Karoninka (Kalorn) Jola Fula Manjago Mandinka
Dimbaya	New settlement	Darsilami	Jola
Jiboro Kuta	Old settlement with Bainunk origins	–	Mixed
Kartong	Old Mandinka town – new settlers from Sindian	–	Mandinka Karoninka Jola and many others
Marakissa	New village	–	Manjago
Nyofelleh	New village located in forest	Brikama District Council	Manjago
Sifoe	Old Mandinka town – new settlers	–	Mandinka Karoninka (Kalorn) Jola
Tranquil	New settlement – from Mlomp via Touba	Darsilami	Jola
B. Casamance		–	–
Abéné	Old Mandinka town	–	Mandinka Karoninka (Kalorn)
Daroussalam (Darsilami-Cheriffkunda)	New village founded by Cheikh Mahfoudz	In forest, on French authority	Moors and many others
Diana	Old town	–	Mandinka Jola (various)
Donbondir	New village (WW1) on site of deserted village	Kujube, with advice from Mahfoudz	Jola Karoninka (Kalorn)
Kabadio	Old Mandinka town		Mandinka Jola (various)
Coubanak	Village founded by settlers from Tiobon, but before colonial era		Jola
Kujube	Old Bainunk/Mandinka village – repopulated		Mandinka Karoninka (Kalorn) Manjago
Mahamouda	New villages founded in 1936 by settlers from Mlomp via Berending	-	Jola (Buluf)
Makuda	Old village, totally repopulated		Jola (various)
Naneeto	First settled by Jola		Jola
Touba	Founded 1954 by settlers via Nyofelleh and Makuda	Chef de canton, Badiana	Jola (Mlomp) Mandinka Balanta

Source: author's interviews.

Colleys from Sindian who passed through Bunto (near to Brikama) and Sifoe in the Gambia before reaching the village of Darsilami. They stayed there for some time before they discovered a fertile area that was not occupied. They approached the *alkalo* of Darsilami and asked to be granted the land on which the new village was eventually constructed.[35] It is not clear exactly when this happened, but it was probably around the 1940s. A second case is that of the Casamance village of Mahamouda that was apparently founded around 1936.[36] Informants recalled that the lack of sufficient paddy fields in Mlomp (Buluf) had led some families to relocate to Berending in the Gambia, which had previously been settled by people from Diatock.[37] Some of this group took to fishing along the Allahein River and, in the process, happened on an area of fertile land on the opposite bank – that is, in the Casamance. They approached the *alkalo* of Kujube who granted them permission to settle. There is no reference to the intervention of the *chef de canton*, and it appears that the historical claims of Kujube, pre-dating Fodé Sylla, were still recognized by people in Narang despite the fact that the French had not elevated its chief to a position of any importance. One of the attractions of Mahamouda, and Narang more generally, was that it was suitable for the planting of fruit trees, especially mangoes and oranges. A third and related case is that of Touba, with whom the people of Mahamouda share close family connections. In this case, another group of kinsmen set off from Mlomp, probably in the 1930s, and settled around what is now Nyofelleh in the Gambia.[38] But because of pressure on land, which brought about disagreements, they decided to move back across the international border. In this instance, they approached the *chef de canton* at Badiana, Landing Jatta, who granted them permission to settle. They first lived at Makuda, and then moved to their present location in 1954 after a temporary period of commuting to their fields. In an interview, the *alkalo* of Touba confirmed that the area possessed the great advantage of combining fertile land for rice cultivation with other places where coos, groundnuts and millet could be grown.[39] It was also the site of relatively dense forest that provided additional resources, including roofing materials and firewood. The villages of Touba in the Casamance and Darsilami in the Gambia, which faced each other across the border, came to an agreement whereby lands could be accessed by farmers on the other side. The deep-water swamps of Darsilami were favoured by the people of Touba because it was similar to what they were familiar with in their original homes, whereas farmers in Darsilami harboured a preference

[35] Interview with Yusupha Colley, Dimbaya (Gambia), 11 February 2004.

[36] Interview with Malem Coly and others, Mahamouda (Casamance), 22 July 2005.

[37] The founder of Donbondir had a brother who settled at Berending. Interview with Famara Diatta (alkalo), Moussa Sonko, Janko Diedhiou, Donbondir (Casamance), 16 February 2004.

[38] Interview with Habib Jatta, *alkalo* of Touba (Casamance), 11 February 2004.

[39] Interview with Habib Jatta, 11 February 2004.

for shallow swamp land.[40] At one point this arrangement was threatened, allegedly because farmers from Darsilami were making excessive demands, but a compromise was brokered by the *seyfo* at Brikama and the *chef de canton* at Badiana, thereby permitting the exchange of fields to resume. This was one instance where the influence of senior chiefs on the two sides of the border manifested itself at the village level. Today, Touba is populated mainly by Jola, but it is also home to a number of Mandinka and Balanta residents.

Two important findings emerge from such settlement histories. The first is that *alkalos* normally (albeit sometimes with the involvement of the *seyfo*) allocated land without the payment of any formal rent. The partial exception is Touba where Landing Jatta originally charged a rent, but this arrangement did not endure. In the other villages, informants repeatedly underscored that it was necessary to request permission to farm from the *alkalo* who was considered the landowner, but that this was invested with symbolic significance. Hence, the people of Donbondir still inform the *alkalo* of Kujube of important events in the village as a matter of courtesy. But informants also insisted that they were never charged a rent. Anyone wanting land to farm was simply told by the landowning chief: "Go and look for a suitable place for yourself and settle down."[41] Again, the villagers who established Dimbaya apparently believed that their prior residence at Darsilami freed them of any obligation to pay for the land.

A second finding is the significance attached to certain rites of settlement. Once the formalities of negotiating access to land had been transacted, settlers set about formally creating a village in which the business of naming was a matter of cardinal significance. In Narang, which had been denuded of population during the time of Fodé Sylla, particular areas already possessed names. Hence the place that came to be known as Touba was previously called Kunkujang, connoting 'a far away place'.[42] Once it became a village, it was considered appropriate to choose a more befitting name. A member of the group, by the name of Yussuf Goudiaby, had recently returned from a stint in the Mouride capital. Hence it was decided to call the village Touba – although none of the villagers actually adhered to the brotherhood in question. Similarly, the village of Donbondir, whose origins are linked to the intercession of Mahfoudz, was founded at a place that had been known by the people of Kujube as 'Bangonolit' after the thorny grass that held a person back as (s)he sought to advance through the forest. The individual who renamed the village

---

[40] NAGB PRM 2/11 "Senegalo-Gambian Relations – Customs", "Senegalo-Gambian Farming Problems", draft of letter from Ministry of External Affairs, dated 19 January 1966.
[41] Interview with Famara Diatta, 16 February 2004.
[42] The name is somewhat generic given there is a Kunkujang and another Kunkujang Manjago in Kombo.

had served with the colonial medical corps during the First World War. The name of Donbondir was an amalgam of two French words, namely 'don' and 'bon'. Combined with 'dir' this yielded the rough meaning of 'a good gift worthy of protection'.[43]

The reason why naming mattered so much was that each new village was conceived of as a moral community, but also because in effect it became the equal of the one it had separated from. The village acquired its own *alkalo*, whom the French styled *chef de village*.[44] Although a formal deference continued to be paid to the original landowners, to all intents and purposes the new village became a distinct entity headed by a chief who occupied an equivalent place in the pecking order. This was as true of the Gambia as it was of the Casamance: hence Gambian Dimbaya was the equal of Darsilami, much as Touba was the equal of Kujube. This pattern of segmentation owed something to government policies that were explicitly encouraging to migrants, but one can also discern traces of a much older discourse about land. That is, some rights were associated with first cultivation, which meant that a settler who opened up a virgin area acquired rights that were co-joined with those of the *alkalo* who formally claimed precedence as landowner. It was for this reason that many settlers actually accessed land without recourse to the *alkalos* (see Chapter 6) – a reality that tends to be conveniently forgotten within the founding charters. Surprisingly perhaps, the privileging of 'native custom' did not lead to the deepening of the discourse of landlord and stranger. Colonial policies tended to place limits on the capacity of the chiefs to play such a game, given that a premium resided in attracting as many settlers as possible. Conversely, the rights of notional strangers were affirmed by the authorities who they regarded as productive assets.

Broadly speaking, there were three categories of settlement in the borderlands. First of all, there were the historical Mandinka towns of the coastal strip that retained their overall shape, but absorbed significant numbers of Jola and Karoninka settlers over time. Examples would be Kartong in the Gambia and Abéné in the Casamance. In Kartong, there was a total of 129 compounds in 1947, of whom 57 were Mandinka, 52 'Jola' (Jola and Karoninka together), 9 Fula, 4 Wolof, 3 each Kusanko and Susu, and 1 Aku. The Mandinka, therefore, found themselves in a numerical minority.[45] At the start of the colonial period, the Karoninka embarked on a cycle of temporary migration during the non-farming season. Typically, they would attach themselves to Mandinka

---

[43] Interview with Famara Diatta (alkalo), 16 February 2004.
[44] Local practice is to refer to the *alkalo* in the same manner as in the Gambia.
[45] NAGB SEC 9/795 "Alkali of Kartong, Kombo South District", Senior Commissioner, Western Division, Protectorate Administration, Bathurst, to Commissioner, Western Division (13 January 1947).

landowners who would permit them to tap palm-wine and extract palm-oil in return for a share of the proceeds, or possibly their labour.[46] Where a particular migrant returned to the same Mandinka town over a number of years, there was a strong likelihood that the relationship with a particular landowner would develop into an affective bond. This might, in turn, lead to the Karoninka client settling permanently with his family. If he converted, he might also adopt the name of his host. This conformed to a wider pattern in which settlement was not necessarily mediated by the *alkalos*.

The second pattern was one in which older settlements were taken over by immigrant populations. The prime example is Makuda, whose original population fled during the violence at the end of the nineteenth century. Today, the village is made up almost entirely of Jola, drawn from different parts of the Casamance, as well as some Karoninka who were apparently the first to settle.[47] Another example would be Darsilami on the Gambian side of the border, where the largest segment of the population is Karoninka, but with significant numbers of Jola, Manjago, Balanta and Fula adding to the mix.[48] The third pattern was one where an entirely new village was founded after seeking permission to settle from the chief who was construed as the landowner. The Narang forest became a particular focus for the Buluf Jola who were conscious of entering a lightly populated zone. Many of these were initially temporary migrants, but in the 1930s they seem to have arrived with a view to long-term settlement. The timing of the formation of the new settlements tallies extremely well with Peter Mark's depiction of the early 1930s as a period when stricken Jola from Buluf resettled in the Gambia.[49] The one qualification is that the settlement in question occurred on both sides of the border. A common pattern was one in which settlers from a single town would subsequently be joined by others from further afield. The result is that villages came to comprise distinct groups of people who shared in membership of a new village community. Regardless of the specific pattern, what is clear is that settlement fundamentally altered the terms of belonging. Although the

[46] As Muslims, the Mandinka landowners were not able to tap palm-wine. The Karoninka clients would often despatch their produce to Bathurst for sale or (in the case of palm-wine) consume it themselves. However, in some places palm-wine was considered as a taboo. One report noted that "wine is forbidden in Gunjur and there are no tappers in East Kombo." NAGB SEC 1/196 "Western Division Conferences", Report of Western Divisional Chiefs' conference, 28 November 1948. The Karoninka–Mandinka relationship today is construed as an intimate one. Interview with Alhaji Demba Jabang, *alkalo* of Kartong (Gambia), 4 June 2004.

[47] A list of places from which people came (which is no doubt incomplete) is Buluf, Essin, Mlomp, Tenduk, Bakaya, Jianki, Djinand, Balingore, Kartiak, Jatang, Hayor and Karone. Interview with Alieu Badji and elders of Makuda (Casamance), 16 February 2004.

[48] Many of the Manjagos and Balantas came from Portuguese Guinea, and some have come in recent decades.

[49] Some seasonal migrancy from Buluf to the Gambia had previously occurred involving, as with the Karoninkas, the sale of palm produce. Peter Mark, "Urban migration", pp. 6–7.

'landowners' would typically insist on their over-riding claims, immigrants acquired local citizenship rights surprisingly quickly on both sides of the international border and regardless of ethnicity. This was eased by the conversion of the Jola to Islam in the first three decades of the twentieth century. Being a devout Muslim was valorized within a conception of the village as a community of believers – or what Muslims worldwide refer to as the *umma*. In the historical Mandinka towns, the 'indigenes' provided the *alkalo* as a matter of course, and often the *imam* as well.[50] In somewhere like Makuda, where everyone was a stranger, the *alkaloship* and the *imamship* were not considered the preserve of any one segment.

In the 1950s, the increased incidence of disputes reflected mounting population pressure in Kombo and the knock-on effect of local government reforms. In the Casamance, there had always been a much greater level of administrative intervention, which was underlined with the abolition of the status of *chef de canton*. Henceforth, the *chef de arrondissement*, who presided over an amalgamation of the former cantons, was a government official and functioned as a kind of prefect. He exercised his authority with the assistance of *chefs de village* who were now the only designated chiefs. In the Gambia, the two-tier system of *alkalos* and *seyfos* was retained, but with local government functions now transferred to District Councils. Land management became a grey area in which different claims to jurisdiction competed. Ironically, it is in the intricate detail of disputes that one can best observe the way in which strangers successfully pressed their case for local citizenship. Three specific cases are indicative of the entanglement of competing claims to land, the jockeying for position by the chiefs and the attempt by local and central government actors to assert their own authority.

In the Gambia, particular chiefly lines retained proprietary rights over traditional offices, but this became increasingly difficult to reconcile with the reality that strangers often comprised the numerical majority. As tax-payers, the latter felt entitled to assert their own claims to local citizenship. The first case, from Kartong, illustrates the nature of the problem, given the numerical preponderance of strangers. In 1947, when the authorities in Bathurst mediated in the choice of a new *alkalo*, they revealed the delicate balancing act in which they were engaged. The chiefs' list revealed a rotation dating from the late nineteenth century: from Ture to Jabang to Manneh, to Ture (1904–11), to Manneh (1914–20), to Jabang (1920–6) and back to Ture (1926–46).[51]

---

[50] In Kartong, the alkaloship and the imamship rotated between three families – Jabang, Ture, Manneh – with the expectation that neither should reside in the same family at any one time. NAGB SEC 9/795 "Alkali of Kartong", Senior Commissioner, Western Division, Protectorate Administration, Bathurst, to Commissioner, Western Division (13 January 1947).

[51] NAGB SEC 9/795 "Alkali of Kartong", Senior Commissioner, Protectorate Administration, Bathurst, to Commissioner, Western Division (13 January 1947).

Because the Manneh occupied the *imamship* they were effectively ruled out of contesting the *alkaloship* at this time. In 1946, when Nianko Ture died, the Jabang expected to provide the next candidate, but the Tures endeavoured to put forward another candidate of their own by the name of Malang Ture.[52] When the opinions of all the compound heads were canvassed, it became clear that a majority of the Mandinka favoured a Ture candidate, whereas a large majority of the Jola and Karoninka were in favour of a Jabang succession. Soliciting the views of Jola compound heads was tantamount to suggesting that they had a voice in proportion to their numbers. After a vote, the administrator eventually decided that the overall majority in favour of the Jabang candidacy was decisive but fell back upon the additional rationale that it was their turn anyway. Sana Jabang was to remain *alkalo* until 1976 when he eventually died.[53] This ostensibly resolved the issue, but there were other settings where the decision was not so straightforward – either because the settlers backed the side that might not otherwise have succeeded, or they were so numerous that they completely outnumbered the indigenes and had a case to install their own *alkalo*.

The second case involved the Brikama District Council, Seyfo J.M. Bojang and the *alkalos* of Kassakunda and Nyofelleh. The land in question was a forested area that had been claimed by Gunjur in the nineteenth century. In the mid-1950s, it was re-allocated from Kombo South to Kombo Central, following the findings of an internal Boundary Commission. Although the land was formally allocated to Brikama town, it was placed beneath the Kassakunda *alkalo* for the reason of convenience.[54] The latter was expected to oversee the forest and to enumerate and collect taxes. Five Manjago yards were affected by the transfer and, logically enough, these were allocated to the *alkalo* of Kassakunda. However, a further influx of Manjago settlers meant that no fewer than sixty compounds emerged in the forest. In recognition of this demographic expansion, a separate village of Nyofelleh, with its own *alkalo*, was formally recognized.[55] Although the *alkalo* of Kassakunda retained a devolved custodianship over the forest, his jurisdiction had been circumscribed in a way that he found distasteful. This led to a disagreement between Seyfo J.M. Bojang and the *alkalo* of Kassakunda, Illo Sabally, in which each accused the other of having extorted money from Manjago land-seekers. This led the District Council to partition the forest between Kassakunda and Nyofelleh.

[52] Interview with Alhaji Demba Jabang, 4 June 2004.
[53] He was succeeded by his son. Interview with Alhaji Demba Jabang, 4 June 2004.
[54] NAGB SEC 1/896 "Complaints and Petitions", Seyfo J.M. Bojang, for Kombo Central District Authority, to Minister for Local Government, Lands and Mines (11 October 1968).
[55] NAGB SEC 1/896 "Complaints and Petitions", Commissioner, Western Division, Brikama, to Acting Permanent Secretary, Ministry for Local Government, Lands and Mines (18 November 1968).

To add further insult to injury, the Council attempted to transfer eighteen compounds from the jurisdiction of Kassakunda to Nyofelleh. Sabally complained to the Commissioner of the Western Division who overturned the Council decision. The Commissioner was of the opinion that Manjago settlers had indeed been fleeced, but in his view the real culprits were the Badge Messengers of the *seyfo* and the District Council officers.[56] His inclination to recommend dividing the Manjago compounds between the two villages, rather than recognizing a new *alkalo*, was a pragmatic attempt to resolve the dispute.[57] In this case, the Manjago were able to use their demographic weight to acquire their own *alkalo*, and enjoyed the backing of Seyfo Bojang once the latter had parted company with the Kassakunda chief. However, the latter was able to appeal upwards to the administration and thus prevented himself from being divested of all his Manjago 'subjects'. Ultimately, neither side gained outright victory.

The final case was more complicated because it spilled across the international border. The Tranquille conundrum points to the problems that could arise when a village was never formally constituted. The settlement was actually given its present name by someone seeking to escape the attentions of the French authorities at Diouloulou. He wanted to live in peace (*reste tranquille*), which was a coded way of saying he wished to avoid being chased for taxes. He was granted land by the *alkalo* of Darsilami, and when he decided to move away, his place was taken by one Kabayor Badjie from Kaniobo (Casamance) in 1956. The elderly Badjie was granted relief from payment of his yard tax on grounds of lacking sufficient means. But when he was subsequently joined by his son, Alieu, the demand for tax was renewed in 1964. At this point, it transpired that he had been paying tax to the Senegalese *chef d'arrondissement*, Keluntang Jatta, for some time. A cross-border meeting was convened in 1968 that was attended by Keluntang Jatta, Landing Bojang (the then *seyfo* of Brikama) and other interested parties, but it broke up amidst mutual recriminations. A document that was later written by *alkalo* of Darsilami claims that the chieftaincy in that town had been usurped for some time by one Kejang Sambou who conspired with the *chef d'arrondissement* to

---

[56] NAGB SEC 1/896 "Complaints and Petitions". Commissioner, Western Division, Brikama, to Acting Permanent Secretary, Ministry for Local Government, Lands and Mines (18 November 1968).

[57] The Ministry of Local Government accepted the logic of such a division, but suggested that nothing precipitous should be done for fear of enflaming the situation. In the interim, it recommended that all the 18 disputed compounds should be placed beneath the revenue collector of Kombo Central rather than any of the chiefs who were party to the dispute. NAGB SEC 1/896 "Complaints and Petitions", Acting Permanent Secretary, Ministry for Local Government, Lands and Mines, Banjul, to Commissioner, Western Division, Brikama (28 November 1968).

recognize Tranquille as Senegalese.[58] The document also alleges that the two conspirators divided the Senegalese tax revenue between them. At this point the boundary pillar was allegedly uprooted and more Casamance settlers were permitted to settle at Tranquille. This particular dispute seemed to go largely unnoticed by the two governments – to the extent that one senior civil servant in the Gambia informed the author that he had not even heard of it – that is, until a standoff over the location of the border in 2007.[59] The border setting imparted some special features to this dispute, but it demonstrates some of the ambiguities surrounding settlement itself. The common opinion in Darsilami was that Tranquille had never been constituted as a separate village – unlike Dimbaya – and should therefore have remitted its yard tax through the *alkalo*. However, the Jola settlers regarded their village as having separated from Darsilami, and they enjoyed the vocal support of the *alkalo* of Touba (Casamance) with whom they are closely connected. Today, the inhabitants of Tranquil do not deny that they originally received the land from Darsilami, but they insist that they are living in the Casamance, which means that Darsilami claims and Gambian land laws are essentially irrelevant.[60]

These wrangles demonstrate that while a discourse of landlord and stranger had not been eradicated, it competed with the principle that those who worked the land acquired rights of local citizenship and that a properly constituted town or village enjoyed parity with every other. This idealized model worked best where the settlers were fellow Muslims, as was the case with most Jola migrants. In the case of the Karoninka, the historical relationship of clientage with Mandinka populations helped to smooth the way. The Manjago and Balanta were typically non-Muslim and were more recent arrivals from Guinea-Bissau. By testing the terms of local citizenship, they played their own part in cementing certain rules of the game. The relative ease of settlement in the Senegambia – despite the disputes I have outlined – could not have been more different to the pattern in the trans-Volta, as we will now see in some detail.

Land and Autochthony in the Agotime Borderlands

Shifting Boundaries of Inclusion

Here I focus primarily on the period after the partition of Togoland in 1919 and, at the risk of chronological untidiness, will pursue the threads of a seminal

---

[58] Ismaila Sambou "Re. Meeting, Historical Fact-Findings – 'Tranquille Settlement Establishment'", undated.

[59] In 2015, representatives of the Gambian and Senegalese governments embarked on negotiations to resolve what threatened to become an international dispute.

[60] A closer inspection of the maps would tend to suggest that Tranquil is located just inside the Gambia.

dispute down to the early 1980s. In Chapter 6, I indicated that there was greater demographic stability within this border zone by comparison with the Senegambia. The British and French authorities interpreted the terms of the League of Nations Mandate to mean that people from across the border were 'strangers' to whom land could not be alienated without express permission. This played a part in the hardening of the boundary between landowners and strangers.

During the eighteenth and nineteenth centuries, as we have seen, Agotime was a polity that had historically incorporated outsiders through enslavement and tributary relationships. At the end of the nineteenth century, the ability to acquire fresh captives was closed off, while the Agotime lost control over some of their 'tributaries' – a trend that was further accelerated during the German period. This bore implications for what it meant to be Agotime, although there is no easy means of reconstructing these processes. But what does emerge clearly is that there was a period of about a generation when it still remained possible for outsiders to become accepted as Agotime. The most clear-cut case is that of Anlo traders who settled in Kpetoe after the Asante withdrawal. Because Agotime was located on the main Volta-coast trade route, which assumed heightened significance after 1874, many Anlo traders passed through Kpetoe. Leading Agotime traders had historically cultivated close relationships with particular Anlo towns – often sealed through marriage ties – which was almost certainly a factor. After some time, a number of these traders decided to settle and requested land from the head of the Dapaah clan. They were granted a portion just behind what was until recently the Kpetoe police station. Nene Keteku II apparently opposed their attempts to select a 'headman' in 1943 for fear that this would become an extension of Anlo influence from the coast.[61] Eventually, it was decided that they should be allowed to appoint their own sub-chief, known as the *Anlofia* (or 'Anlo chief'), who could be formally included in decision-making. He came directly beneath Nene Dapaah, who was one of the principal town chiefs within Kpetoe. Through serial intermarriage, the Anlo became more difficult to distinguish from their Agotime hosts over time, although they still occupied a distinct physical space. One simple indicator of where one's roots lie is where one is finally buried. These days, most of the people from the Anlo quarter are interred in Kpetoe, although a minority still have their bodies sent 'home' for burial.[62]

Because trade was so much bound up with the currency of the Ewe language, substantial differences arose between the Agotime settlements that

---

[61] Alexander Keese, *Ethnicity and the Colonial State: Finding and Representing Group Identifications in a Coastal West African and Global Perspective (1850–1960)* (Leiden: Brill, 2016), p. 263.
[62] Interview with Nene Dapaah VI, Kpetoe (Ghana), 7 September 2007.

were situated closest to the main lines of colonial communication and those that were quite literally off the beaten track. The village of Afegame, which had not absorbed Ewe captives in the nineteenth century, was located too far from the main road to attract Anlo strangers in the twentieth century. This served to reinforce the self-image of Afegame as the guarantor of Adangbe purity. In addition, in an effort to increase their coverage, the churches tended to follow the main lines of communication on either side of the border. Given that Ewe was the language of the Presbyterian and Catholic churches, as well as the classroom, the linguistic effects were unevenly distributed across Agotime. Whereas Ewe became the first language of Kpetoe, and most of the other towns located in proximity to the Ho–Aflao and Kpalimé–Lomé trunk roads, three particular settlements continued to adhere to Adangbe – namely Afegame itself and its immediate neighbours in French Togoland, Kpodjahon and Zukpe. The highly uneven distribution of markets, churches and schools had an important bearing on the ways in which Anlo strangers were received by the Agotime.

The case of the Anlo settlers is different in interesting respects from two others. The first is that of the people inhabiting the small settlement of Bè. The Germans required porters along the Ho–Lomé road, and with that in mind, they resettled a group of coastal Ewes in the no-man's land between Agotime and Adaklu in order to bridge the gap. Although these strangers were deposited there by the German authorities, the Agotime maintain that they agreed to release land to the Bè settlers, thereby establishing a landlord/stranger relationship. The village of Bè was later allowed to appoint a sub-chief who was subsequently slotted into the Agotime chiefly hierarchy. Although Bè people never became accepted as 'true Agotimes', they continue to be invited to participate in communal activities. In that sense, they acquired an intermediate status that was different to that of strangers who arrived subsequently. The second instance is that of the Hausa minority in Kpetoe. The Hausa traders arrived after the Anlo, assumed the same status as strangers, and equally settled on Dapaah land in Kpetoe. Indeed, their *zongo* was directly adjacent to the Anlo quarter. But the Hausa remained classificatory strangers despite their length of residence. To some extent, religion was a mediating factor here. Because the Hausa were Muslims and did not normally marry Agotimes, it was easier for a sense of difference to be reproduced over time. The *zongo* became a special kind of space across the colonial Gold Coast, signalling simultaneously a degree of integration and a measure of social distance. While *zongo* populations were normally permitted a headman, or one for each subcommunity, they would not be granted a chief in the accepted sense. Such was also the case in Kpetoe. But if religion reinforced a sense of difference between the Agotime and the Hausa, adherence to Christianity did not smooth the path for Ewe-speaking strangers who arrived after the First World War.

This was especially true of the Ando whose local presence was acknowledged, but who were always treated as outsiders despite the fact that they were both Ewe and Christian. The Ando came to be regarded in positive terms as hardworking farmers, but they were never considered as candidates for local citizenship.

Extrapolating from these cases, what explains the differential treatment that was extended to strangers in Agotime? First of all, those who settled around the turn of the twentieth century were more likely to be integrated, not merely because they had a longer time to find their groove, but because some Agotime settlements still tended to valorize inclusiveness. By the 1930s it was inconceivable that new arrivals in Agotime would be treated as anything other than perpetual strangers, such was the importance attached to firstcomer status. Even in Kpetoe itself, *being* Agotime came to be seen as something fixed and immutable. One reason for the shift is that whereas there was previously a distinct advantage to absorbing outsiders – in a system in which the size of one's following underpinned claims to leadership – there were fewer advantages under colonial conditions. Claims to chiefly office in the colonial period depended much less on building numbers and much more on manipulating the pecking order that the Germans had installed – and which was modified in various ways by the British and the French. In British Togoland, where chiefs came to be defined outside the structures of the state, the incumbents did not acquire the financial benefits that might have come with a system of direct taxation that could have been extended to strangers. In French Togoland, where head taxes were indeed collected, there was more of an incentive to attract strangers. But because the chiefs did not control the land, they were never in a position to steer the process in the way that they did in the Senegambia. Those who entered from outside therefore tended to be traders whose stranger status was never in question.

A second consideration was whether strangers arrived in sufficient numbers to achieve critical mass. Where this happened, they were far more likely to be invited to nominate their own chiefs or headmen and so to acquire a place in the pecking order – albeit a subordinate one. Thirdly, it mattered where the settlers were located. The closer they lived to a recognized Agotime town, the greater the chance that they would be treated as favoured strangers. Living in one of the quarters in Kpetoe meant that the strangers needed to be taken account of, as the dispute over the relocation of the market (discussed in Chapter 5) demonstrates. The next best option was to live in a village that was considered a recognized settlement, such as Bè or Wodome. Those settlers who lived in scattered farm 'cottages' (or hamlets) were the quintessential strangers whose access to Agotime affairs was mediated through their individual landlords. If the need arose, such as in a personal dispute, the latter spoke on their behalf. In the twentieth century, Ando strangers acquired considerable utility as human boundary markers, but this hinged on them being physically on the land and hence largely invisible to most Agotimes other than on market days.

In a nutshell, the integration of settlers that was taken for granted in the Senegambia became unthinkable in the trans-Volta, and especially so on the British side of the border. What it meant to be Agotime came to be defined through idioms of kinship – coming from a recognized lineage – and an attachment to place. Because the logic was essentially circular – one could only be regarded as truly Agotime if one originated from an Agotime settlement – it was difficult for strangers to stake a claim to local citizenship. There was no chance that they could compete for chiefly offices or even for positions of leadership within the local church community. And in the outlying settlements, it was inconceivable that Ando settlements could become distinct villages with their own chiefs. By stark contrast, strangers repeatedly founded their own villages, installed their own *alkalos*, and provided *imams* in the villages of the Gambia/Casamance borderlands. Nevertheless, what the two cases had in common was a very low centre of affective gravity: in other words, it was membership of the town or village to which the greatest salience was attached. Religious observance tended to be structured at that level, whereas ethnic identities operated at a much greater remove. I now turn to consider the ways in which the land disputes between the Agotime and their neighbours impacted on the latter dynamic.

Firstcomer and Latecomer: Land Litigation and the Boundaries of Community

Elsewhere, I have demonstrated how the value attached to cocoa as a cash crop contributed to a series of protracted land disputes in the forested borderlands roughly north of Kpedze in British Togoland and Klouto in French Togoland, and stretching into Buem and Akposso respectively.[63] It might be considered surprising that land disputes were much more pervasive in the trans-Volta than in the Senegambia, where there was considerably more in-migration. The reason is that litigation was not just about land as a factor of production. It was just as much about territory and its importance for the definition of political community. Cocoa was a relatively minor crop in Agotime, much of which consisted of sandy flatlands, as well as amongst the Ewe *dukɔwo* located to the immediate east, west and south thereof. The partial exception was Adame, which bordered onto Agu where much of the cocoa from French

---

[63] Paul Nugent, *Smugglers, Secessionists and Loyal Citizens on the Ghana–Togo Frontier: The Lie of the Borderlands since 1914* (Oxford, Athens and Legon: James Currey, Ohio University Press and Sub-Saharan Publishers, 2003), ch. 2.

Togoland was produced. At the same time, there was nothing approximating to stool land amongst the Agotime or the Ewe polities of the trans-Volta. All land resided with individual families who claimed ownership on the basis of first cultivation at some point in a more remote past. The sum total of these lands defined what belonged to a town or village, while the territory of Agotime or Adaklu represented a further aggregation based on the totality of the lands that notionally belonged to all the constituent settlements. In reality, the polities had often maintained no-man's lands between themselves, reflecting frontier logics in a region that had witnessed considerable conflict in the nineteenth century. While Agotime chiefs did not control land, they had a vested interest in defending what they regarded as their historical claims to territory. As I have already indicated, there is some reason to believe that the Agotime possessed a clear sense of their boundaries in the nineteenth century, even if they never created a state. The overlay of colonial chieftaincy structures tended, if any-thing, to increase the salience attached to territory.

Crucially, individual disputes over parcels of land became thoroughly intertwined with competing claims about where Agotime, or any other *dukɔ*, began and ended. When a dispute broke out, it was invariably between individuals who claimed to be working on family lands, but they would typically invoke the supposedly historical boundaries of the town/village and, by logical extension, the *dukɔ*. Conversely, headchiefs would enter into litigation on behalf of their *dukɔwo* even when their own farmlands were not directly affected, because this was fundamental to the defence of their political domain. The fact that parcels of land did, in fact, change hands through purchase and lease – despite legal prohibitions – further complicated the picture, because it meant that there was no one-to-one correlation between farm and *dukɔ* boundaries in practice. Litigation, and the claims-making that accompanied it, took place against the backdrop of a discourse of firstcomer and latecomer that was, as we have seen, a defining aspect of the Gold Coast more broadly. But there was also a feedback effect because litigation, as well as physical clashes, placed a premium on tightening the rules of belonging.

The Agotime confronted hostile neighbours in the twentieth century and struggled to formulate a co-ordinated response. On the one hand, the inter-national border, and the further subdivision of the Agotime in French Togo-land, made it practically difficult to make common cause over issues that were confined to one side of the line. Most of the land disputes took place on the British side, and while Agotimes in French territory were broadly supportive of their 'kinsmen', there were issues closer to home that affected them more directly – most notably the redrawing of administrative boundaries that threatened to erode their own territory. On the other, the existence of the border tended to have a bearing on the standing of witnesses within the colonial courts. In the case of the Hodzo–Agotime dispute, which we will come to shortly, many of the interested parties were from Zukpe in French Togoland who had farms on the British side. Although their land rights were in theory unaffected by the border, it was difficult for people to defend themselves against allegations of encroachment when they were perceived as having come from somewhere else. In subtle ways, therefore, the border was naturalized and invoked by litigants when it suited them. The elision of traditional and colonial boundaries was something that colonial officials contributed to, but they were typically guided by informants who invoked the colonial state in defence of their claims.[64]

The courts tended to privilege certain forms of evidence over others. The extensive German colonial documentation was hardly ever consulted because none of the parties could read it and because the documents themselves were located in Lomé. Although the Sprigade map (or Karte Von Togo) of 1905, and some other German sketch-maps, were known about, the courts took little account of them. It was easy enough for litigants to assert that the Germans had drawn their maps in error, and in the absence of supporting written documentation that gave an account of how Dr Grüner came to his conclusions, the cartographic evidence was at best contested. The courts, both before and after independence, were therefore inclined to leapfrog the German period and return to a supposedly more authentic history that could best be recaptured through renditions of oral history. The claim that trumped all others was that of being firstcomers in a given area.[65] The fact that a notional transaction between the two parties might have taken place two centuries previously was, in theory at least, immaterial: in the relationship between firstcomer and latecomer, inequality was deemed inherent and perpetual. This placed the Agotime in an uncomfortable position. They either had to claim to be firstcomers in their own right, which was difficult to sustain when their neighbours ganged up on them, or they could claim to have seized the land by force. The latter was not a line that Agotime litigants were inclined to adopt, although it was actually much closer to the truth. It might work for the Ashanti or the Dagomba, but maybe it was considered risky for the Agotime because they could not point to the existence of a powerful kingdom to back up their assertions. Moreover, it transpired in court that witnesses could only recount the history before the Asante wars with the sketchiest of outlines. This might be considered surprising, but it became apparent during oral interviews that the Asante wars of the early 1870s had become such a lightning rod for collective memories that deeper historical processes had been pushed to the cognitive margins. As it

---

[64] This is parallel to what is described in Dereje Feyissa, *Playing Different Games: The Paradox of Anywaa and Nuer Identification Strategies in the Gambella Region, Ethiopia* (New York: Berghahn Books, 2011).

[65] Only some of the Central Togo minorities could claim to be genuine autochthons.

happened, the world of paper would have supported the Agotime case rather well, but the realm of the spoken word left much greater scope for creativity. A final factor is that the wheels of the judiciary ground extremely slowly, which was exacerbated by successive changes of regime in Ghana after independence. In the context of long periods of stasis, litigants could move more of their own strangers onto the disputed land and claim de facto occupation. This was very difficult for the courts to reverse when they finally got around to making a decision. In principle, this cut both ways, but in reality, the encroachment seems to have been mostly on the land that the Germans had once defined as belonging to Agotime. In what follows, I will examine the Agotime struggles with two of their neighbours, Hozdo and Adaklu, in order to flesh out these broad observations. I begin this account in the 1950s and trace it through to the early 1970s.

In 1958, the Agotime were sued collectively by the Hodzo Division at the Ho District Native Court over ownership of a piece of land that lay somewhere between Zukpe, in French Togoland, and Hodzo in British Togoland (marked Chodjo on the Sprigade map; see Map 7.1).[66] This framing is in itself significant because the suit itself conflated land and territory. Exactly where the disputed land was located was never made very clear, and indeed this was symptomatic of a more general problem: namely that whereas the courts were being asked to pronounce on specific boundaries, the definition of lands that were claimed were often vague and overlapping. As a result, those who presided in judgement were often uncertain as to whether the litigants were even contesting precisely the same piece of land. In this instance, the Hodzo plaintiffs began with a statement of claim that sought to disable the Agotime with a single blow. They recalled that they had historically shared boundaries with Nyive to the north, Kévé to the south, Adaklu to the west, and Agu and Adame to the east. They went on to relate that Le strangers had arrived in the area and had requested land on which to settle (see Chapter 2 for a more extended discussion). Because the Le could not speak Ewe, it was claimed, three individuals were allocated to them to teach them the language, while the Le swore an oath of allegiance to the Hodzo chief. In return, the Hodzo allocated them land to the east and southeast that bordered onto Kévé and Agu. The Hodzo plaintiffs maintained that the two communities had enjoyed friendly relations until the very recent past – the complete absence of any reference to nineteenth-century warfare is striking here – but that this had been disturbed when someone from Zukpe had attempted to sell a piece of their land bordering onto Takla. The latter is located to the south-west of Hodzo and north-east of Ho, and quite some distance from Zukpe. The plaintiffs allegedly objected, but in a spirit of good neighbourliness suggested demarcating the

---

[66] What follows is drawn from the case of "Geze Anku and seven others vs Togbe Mahumansro and nine others in Ho District Native Court 'A' at Ho" (copy in my possession).

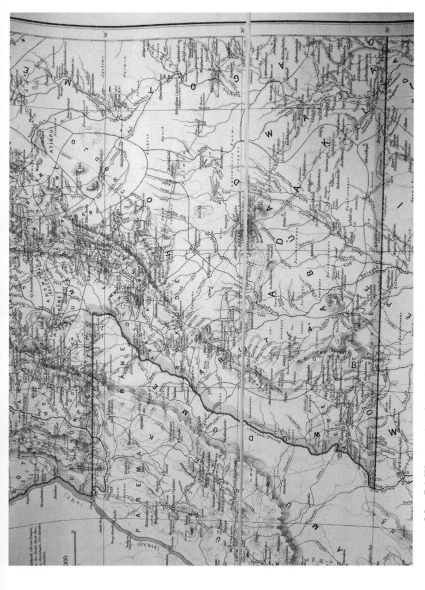

Map 7.1 Western Agotime and its neighbours according to 1905 Sprigade map.

Hodzo/Agotime boundary in order to avoid future misunderstandings. They also claimed to have modified the proposed line to take account of subsequent representations by the Agotime. The plaintiffs went on to note that they had proceeded to physically demarcate the boundary and had invited the Agotime to inspect the work, having notified all the interested chiefs on both sides of the international border. But a year later when Hodzo people were felling palms, the Agotime complained to the Police that the latter had destroyed some coffee trees. At that point, the plaintiffs said, they had decided to remind the Agotime that they were actually living on Hodzo land and had initiated the court action to protect their ownership of the disputed portion that they called 'Agomlanyi'.

The ten defendants represented an Agotime coalition, which was an achievement in itself in view of disagreements surrounding chieftaincy. Clearly, the perceived stakes were high enough to warrant a joint effort by chiefs located on both sides of the international boundary. Nene Mahumansro XII of Afegame was named as the first defendant, and amongst those who joined him were the Zukpe chief, Nene Teh Doku III, and Nene Agbovi IV from Kpetoe. The involvement of the Zukpe chief arose from the fact that farmers from that town were central to the case, but the lands that the Hodzo claimed also encroached on the territory that Afegame and Kpetoe regarded as their own. The defendants entered a counter-claim on the basis that they were the owners of a piece of land they called Agotime-Nyigba. The basis of their case was their ancestors had been the first to arrive in the area, some time before the Adaklu and the Hodzo. Whereas the Agotime had no allies to give supporting testimony, the plaintiffs called on witnesses from many neighbour-ing divisions – notably Akome, Adame, Nyitoe, Ave-Dzalele, Takla and Adaklu. Each of these had a historical reason to dispute Agotime claims. Adame and Nyive had been attached to Agotime, and their witnesses used the opportunity to deny that they were Agotime at all. The Nyitoe witness insisted that his people were Adaklus, while the Adame chief said his people came from a place called Feda and had arrived in the area after some of the other Ewe divisions, but well before the Agotime. The Dzalele witness con-firmed the Hodzo claim to have allocated land to the Agotime, adding that "The Hodzos might [have] sold to them or gave them [land] but they would be regarded as Hodzo people's strangers or tenants." He also took the opportunity to claim that a number of Agotime towns were located on Ave land, citing Batoumé, Letsukope/Wodome, Zomayi and Akpokope as cases in point.

The key witness for the plaintiffs was one Tsadide Kofi, a linguist from Adaklu-Tsrefe, because he provided the most detailed evidence supporting the Hodzo case. He had a vested interest in that some of the alleged encroachment from Zukpe was in the tiny area where Hodzo and Adaklu bordered onto each other. Tsadide asserted that in the distant past hunters from these Ewe *dukɔwo* had arrived at a common boundary along a river – a reference to the Todzie. He recalled that Le strangers had subsequently arrived and asked for land, but because there were too many of them, the chief had referred them to Hodzo. He recalled that the latter had allocated them a place to settle, where Afegame was founded, and after some time they released further land at the place where Zukpe was established. He went on to say that some of the Agotime had subsequently crossed back over the Todzie and settled on Adaklu land without permission. This was evidently a reference to the foundation of Kpetoe. There were some tensions in the evidence presented – such as when Tsadide Kofi claimed that the Dzalele were themselves living on Adaklu land or when he claimed that the Adaklu rather than the Hodzo were the first to have met the Le – but on the whole the witnesses presented a reasonably consistent story centred on the narrative of first- and latecomer. In all these versions, the Agotime brought up the rear and were cast as ungrateful supplicants. The evidential base consisted entirely of oral histories with a very foreshortened timeline. Hence Tsadide Kofi estimated that the Agotime had arrived 100 years previously and that the Adaklu had migrated from Notsie a mere 133 years before. A hundred years of history had been erased in the process. Quite how the Agotime would have mounted their full defence is unclear because the case never came to a full hearing. When the new Local Courts were created, the case was transferred and hearings re-commenced. But as luck would have it, one of the key plaintiffs was detained by the Nkrumah regime under the Preventive Detention Act – presumably as a supporter of the Togoland Congress[67] – and the litigants withdrew from the action in January 1961. Partisan politics and border tensions had come together at this point to complicate the matter. The case was therefore dismissed with costs, and seemingly was not reactivated.[68]

However, by this time, a far more intense land dispute had come to a head in which the Adaklu and the Agotime locked horns directly. Although the Adaklu had a side-interest in the Hodzo case, the real focus of their attention was located slightly further south, in an area that they called *Segbale* and the Agotimes called *Akuete* after the stream by that name (see Map 7.2). In August 1961, Agbovi IV and seven other representatives of the Todze and Atsiati families, from Afegame and Kpetoe respectively, brought a joint action at the local court against the headchief of Adaklu, Togbe Gbogbi, and the sub-chief of Wumenu.[69] Their request was for "a declaration of right, title, interest,

---

[67] Hodzo was one of the places where supporters of the Togoland Congress had allegedly taken up arms to resist incorporation into Ghana in 1957.

[68] Judgement by Magistrate J.K. Aidam in Local Court Division 'I' held at Ho, 9 January 1961. This is not entirely clear because the chief of Kpodjahon in Togo, who noted that most of his lands were in Ghana claimed to have been on the winning side twice against Hodzo. Fieldwork diary entry 4 April 2011.

[69] By this point, the native courts had given way to local courts. What follows is drawn from a dossier, running to 510 pages, that includes all the applications, evidence and judgements given in the case from beginning to end. It was given to me by Solomon Kwami Tetteh from the Agotime legal team. I will cite it hereafter as "Adaklu-Agotime Land Case". All specific references that follow are drawn from this documentation.

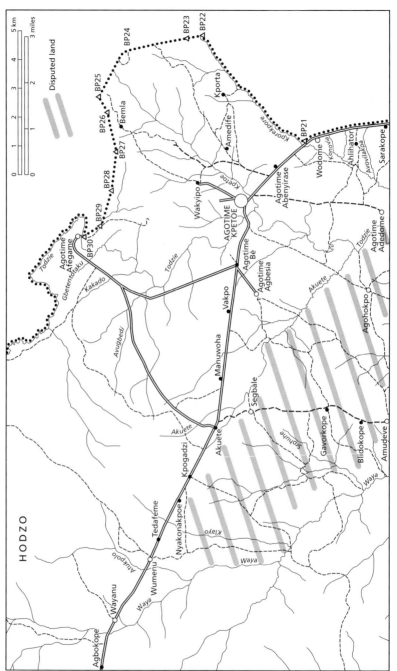

Map 7.2 Lands disputed between Agotime and Adaklu.

ownership, and recovery of possession" of the lands that they alleged had been founded by their 'grandfathers', Nortey Bediako, Alimo Ankrah and Todze. The defendants responded with a counter-claim asserting that Segbale had been founded by their 'great grandfather' – note the temporal one-upmanship – by the name of Tsadide. They were subsequently joined by eight other co-defendants from Adaklu, including Tsadide Kofi himself.

The Sprigade map located the Akuete stream squarely within Agotime and depicted the border with Adaklu-Abuadi as following the Kalajo (or Kalayo) River up to the point where it divided, after which it cut through dense thickets. The Adaklu town of Wumenu was placed just to the west of the border. A version of the Sprigade map, with English annotations, was tabled in evidence before the court.[70] The plaintiffs recalled that as far back as 1938 they had taken a case to the Asogli State Council, when the first Adaklu encroachments had occurred, and had won. Three years later, they noted, the defendants had resumed giving out land to strangers, which led to a second action being brought. The case had reached the Magistrate's Court but had then petered out. This was probably because the parties failed to come up with the money needed to enable the land to be surveyed. Nartey Ankrah of Afegame (also known as Asafoatse Abri), who had initiated the action, complained that the cost of carrying out a survey, that is £300 for each party, was disproportionate to the value of the land, which he made the mistake of describing as "only a barren grassy plain without palm trees nor cocoa trees or any valuable plants on it."[71] This evidently understated the attractions of land that had become a focus of Ando in-migration, mostly from across the border.[72] The Ando, who the Agotime claim to have expelled when they first settled in the area in the eighteenth century, were reputed to be adept at cultivating food crops such as yams. Given that the disputed land was close to the Ho–Aflao trunk road, the opportunity to sell produce to a number of possible markets made its location rather attractive. A further reason given for the fizzling out of the action was that Ankrah himself died, leaving a hiatus in terms of leadership. Meanwhile, both sides continued to allocate land to strangers in the hope of being able to project their claims more effectively. This rendered the next round of disputes inevitable. In 1958, just as the Hodzo case was being brought to court, the Agotime requested an injunction preventing the Adaklu from entering Akuete land and receiving rents from strangers. The legal submission noted that the Agotime had since provided their share of the survey costs, whereas the

---

[70] The map that is cited in the evidence as "Exhibit F" was at the same scale of 1:200,000 and simply added English translations of some of the detail.

[71] This was later used by the Adaklu as evidence of a lack of interest in pursuing the suit. Petition of Plaintiff, for Atsiati family, Afegame, dated 22 August 1945.

[72] This statement later came to haunt the Agotime because it could later be used to argue that they had left the Adaklu in possession of the land, believing it to have limited value.

Adaklu had failed to do so and instead had permitted two further villages to be constructed.[73] The full-blown court action that began in 1960 therefore followed from these early warning shots.

Having taken the initial statements in the Akuete case, the local court requested the two parties to cut tracks through the disputed area in order that a surveyor could make a field visit. It also issued an interim injunction to prevent the litigants from starting new farms or using resources from the disputed area until the matter was resolved. In 1966, the local courts were abolished by the National Liberation Council (NLC) and the case was transferred to the District court (see Chapter 12 for the politics of this period). But, although some evidence was taken, the matter was never satisfactorily concluded, and it was widely believed that the injunction no longer had any legal force. Not surprisingly, therefore, the two parties resumed the practice of inviting strangers onto the land. It later transpired that a well-known road contractor, Kassardjan, had been winning sand from Akuete land and had agreed to pay financial compensation of 400 Cedis to the plaintiffs when they had objected. This elicited bitter complaints from the defendants who pointed to this payment as a blatant violation of the injunction.[74] In 1971, the two parties found themselves back in court, with the Adaklu complaining that Agbovi had authorised a Togolese farmer from Ando to build a hamlet and a coconut plantation, whilst refusing to pay the money that was needed for the survey to proceed. On the basis that the Agotime were apparently "no more interested in the whole matter", they requested that the case be struck out.[75] In reply, Agbovi insisted that the Agotime had repeatedly sought to elicit a judgement but had been thwarted by judicial paralysis. The surveyors, in their own defence, explained that the delay was really due to the ongoing failure of both sets of litigants to pay the money to enable the survey work to proceed.[76]

In August 1972, more than ten years after the case had been initiated, the plan of the disputed lands finally became available. This led the Agotime to seek to extend the area covered by the written statement of claim, on the basis that "It was when the plan was completed it was found that the boundaries as shown on it differed from those shown in the claim."[77] This was contested by the Adaklu who argued that it would be unfair to them since they had planted

---

[73] Petition of Plaintiff, Nartey Ankrah, dated 16 April 1958.

[74] Nene Agbovi subsequently admitted that after the fall of the Nkrumah regime, both parties had moved into the land and had made money from selling the right to exploit its resources, in the belief that the injunction had been voided. Evidence of Nene Agbovi IV, before J.K. Ampiah, District Magistrate, sitting at Ho, 8 November 1974. The sale of charcoal along the Ho–Aflao road had become highly lucrative by this time.

[75] Submission by Tsyami Tsadide in the District Magistrates Court, 7 July 1971.

[76] S.T. Lassey, licensed surveyor, to Registrar of District Court, Ho (28 March 1972).

[77] Hearing before J.K. Ampiah, District Magistrate, sitting at Ho, 23 October 1974.

trees with an economic value. Just as it seemed some headway was being made, the transfer of the Magistrate to Suhum led to the hearings stalling once again. However, the court finally agreed in 1974 that the injunction should cover the wider area indicated on the surveyor's plan. In November, a new District Magistrate began hearing evidence. Nene Agbovi gave an account that was premised on the Agotime being the first occupants.[78] He alleged that the name *Akuete* was derived from the Adangbe language and represented a truncated form of the statement that "You should not stand on a stone to look for water". Agbovi described the land as being bounded by the Waya and Klayo streams and added that it bordered onto Adedome land. This description no doubt compounded the confusion because the Sprigade map clearly indicated that the Klayo stream marked the western boundary of Agotime whereas the Waya stream was part of Adaklu. The land between the Klayo and Waya streams would seem to overlap with what was previously contested with Hodzo, thereby conflating the two disputes. Crucially, Akuete itself was located further to the east, as was Adedome. This makes it difficult to precisely indicate on a map the land that was being contested (the hatching in Map 7.2 depicts the more expansive set of claims). Agbovi went on to state that strangers had been legitimately settled by the Agotime, and he listed a number of small hamlets that had been founded by them. He maintained that the problems had begun during the interwar years when people in the village of Segbale began to assert that they were tenants of Adaklu. It was for this reason that Nartey Ankrah had taken action, on behalf of the Atsiati family, against the chief of Wumenu in 1941. Agbovi further noted that some time after judgement was given against Hodzo in 1961, the Adaklu had allowed two new strangers' villages to be established, called Kpogadzi and Komla Gavor.[79] Agbovi went on to state that these fresh encroachments had led him to initiate the present action. On the other side, the defendants disputed the assertion that the Agotime had settled first, pointing out that most of their settlements bore Ewe names and that their very ethnonym was Ewe in origin. They also identified spirits ('fetishes') associated with particular streams, which they alleged the Agotime were ignorant of. This battle, in which linguistic colonization of the landscape was imbued with deeper meaning, was one that tended to complicate the Agotime case. Nene Agbovi responded by asserting that Mahe was the name of the first town (Afegame), and that because Ewes could not pronounce it, they had called the location Agotime instead. But this must have come across as a rather unlikely explanation. The reality is that the Agotime

---

[78] Evidence of Nene Agbovi IV, before District Magistrate J.K. Ampiah, sitting at Ho, 6 November 1974.

[79] Contemporary maps locate these villages on the Ho–Aflao road and south of Segbale respectively.

had become linguistically closer to their Ewe neighbours as they incorporated slaves and clients and elaborated their trade networks, but this was a subtlety that was difficult to present in court.

Reciprocating the earlier favour, the Adaklu called a witness from Hodzo who stated that the Adaklu boundary with the Agotime lay at the River Todzie. This would have brought it right up to the outskirts of Kpetoe itself, while placing Bè on Adaklu land.[80] Some of the strangers in the disputed villages also testified that they had paid yams, maize or cash to their Adaklu landlords and that they had never been disturbed in their possession by the Agotime. Having heard the evidence, the Magistrate decided to visit the land, and clearly struggled to match the statements made in court with evidence on the ground. His final judgement of January 1975 came down in favour of the Agotime, for two principal reasons: whereas their rendition of the traditional history was consistent, Adaklu witnesses presented divergent versions; and secondly, some of the longstanding settlements mentioned by the defence witnesses turned out to be non-existent. Moreover, whereas the defendants insisted that their tenants had enjoyed uncontested usage, the judge found that the Agotime had repeatedly taken action to defend their claims to Akuete land and could not therefore be said to have assented. The Adaklu launched an immediate appeal on the basis that the Agotime had failed to prove their claim; that the District Magistrate had not taken sufficient cognisance of the defence case; that he had become fixated on minor inconsistencies and that he was a lay Magistrate who made basic mistakes in the hearing of evidence. In February 1982, the Adaklu lawyers added that the Agotime were estopped from re-litigating because they had discontinued an earlier suit without leave; that the Magistrate had failed to take evidence in court after the visit to the field; and that the plaintiffs had failed to prove all the boundaries of their land.[81] The appeal judge agreed that the appellants would have had a good case for pleading estoppel on the grounds that it was not possible to re-enter a case from which the plaintiffs had withdrawn in 1941. However, he accepted the respondents' argument that it should have been pleaded in the original trial. He also found that the Magistrate had indeed erred in not having taken further evidence in court after visiting the field. Moreover, he found discrepancies in the description of the boundaries given by the witnesses for the Agotime. The crux of the matter was that the onus was on the plaintiffs to have proven their exact boundaries because the defendants had withdrawn their counter-claim at an

---

[80] However, his evidence also seemed to weaken the defence by suggesting that when the Hodzo granted the Agotime land, they ceased to share a boundary with the Adaklu in part of the disputed area. Evidence of Defence witness 7, Dzakpa Yao, before District Magistrate, J.K. Ampiah, at Ho, 16 December 1974.

[81] By this time, Ghana was in the throes of the 31 December 'revolution', and it is somewhat surprising that the appeal was heard so quickly.

earlier juncture. Furthermore, in weighing up the historical claims, the appeal judge was impressed by the fact that the village of Segbale was in the middle of the disputed land and that its occupants claimed to be tenants of the Adaklu. On the other hand, the Agotime failed to locate the points in the landscape that bore out their own story. With little to choose between the traditional accounts, the judge felt that the Magistrate should not have found in favour of the plaintiffs. At the end of his 42-page judgement, delivered on 8 November 1983, Justice Apatu-Plange made a ruling in favour of the Adaklu appellants.[82] Significantly, his findings took no account of the German maps. In placing the burden of proof on the plaintiffs, the court conferred a distinct advantage on actors who assumed de facto possession of the land. The Adaklu had made an earlier start and had been more successful in planting Ando settlers on the disputed land. The repeated judicial delays played into the temporal dynamic in very obvious ways.

At this stage, it would be helpful to take stock of what lessons emerge from the Agotime–Adaklu land case. Firstly, it is clear that the historical fuse had been lit in the eighteenth century as a consequence of Agotime involvement in warfare and enslavement. This had pitted the Agotime against their neighbours, and the Ando themselves whose lands the Agotime are said to have forcibly seized. The mutual hostility was also embedded in memories of the different sides that had been taken in the Asante campaign of the 1870s (see Chapter 2). There was certainly no love lost between the Agotime and the Adaklu on this particular score. Secondly, state actors played their own inglorious part in complicating and prolonging the dispute. It was the German authorities in the shape of Grüner who had sought to determine the boundaries between the dukɔwo, and to capture these on the Sprigade map.[83] Although the German administration later excised Adame from northern Agotime, the boundary in the west was more generous. There had previously been a thick buffer zone between Agotime and Adaklu, which explains the need for the settlement of porters at Bè. In drawing a line of demarcation through a lightly populated area, Grüner resorted to natural features such as rivers and streams. But with the construction of the trunk road from Ho, the buffer zone became more attractive and began to assume greater prominence in charcoal production and food crop farming. What started out as a land dispute became a contest over traditional boundaries and history itself, in which the state became the ultimate arbiter. The courts might have chosen to rely entirely on the highly detailed Sprigade map. In choosing to privilege oral evidence, however, they became bogged down in the unrewarding business of validating some historical accounts and discounting others. They opened this veritable Pandora's

---

[82] Judgement delivered in the High Court, Ho, by Justice H.B. Apatu-Plange, 25 July 1983.
[83] Significantly, Grüner's name is littered across the map, signaling where he had been active.

Box in the absence of any systematic tools for weighing up the welter of conflicting evidence.

Thirdly, the process of composing a plausible history was also important in forcing litigants to both reflect on their place in history and to situate themselves in relation to their neighbours. In Adaklu, the challenge was to be able to unite all the towns and villages behind their cause, whilst seeking the support of neighbouring *dukɔwo* who had their own differences with Agotime. However, this was almost never expressed in terms of ethnicity per se. As we will see in subsequent chapters, an Ewe identity mattered much less than mobilization around the individual *dukɔwo*. In Agotime, the insistence on being Adangbe was an ethnic claim of a kind, even if it was undercut by the realities of linguistic absorption. But it counted for rather little in practical terms, given that there were no operative political connections between the Agotime and either the Adangbe minorities in French Togoland or the Adangbe of the Gold Coast. The British and the French treated the Agotime as if they were to all intents and purposes a sub-type of the Ewe. Although this rankled, the Agotime did behave as if they were another *dukɔ* rather than as a distinct 'tribe'. Moreover, the Akuete land case underlined the difficulties of mobilizing the Agotime across international borders. The active engagement of Agotimes from French Togoland in the land case became more attenuated as they were forced to focus on matters closer to home. The context was one in which the border itself hardened in the years after Togolese independence (see Chapter 10). In a nutshell, while it became almost impossible for strangers to become Agotime, what it actually meant to *be* Agotime was a question that increasingly failed to elicit a consistent response.

Conclusion

In this chapter, I have explored the link between mobility and identity, and have pinpointed some strikingly different patterns in the Senegambia and the trans-Volta. In the first case, I demonstrated that the ease with which Jola migrants were able to access land and claim membership within towns and villages owed much to colonial land policies as well as to the role of Islam in creating an alternative vocabulary of community. In the borderlands today, it is Cheikh Mahfoudz and his network that is credited with the forging of new model communities where Mandinka and Jola lived, worshipped together and overcame their historical differences. The Karoninka were much slower to convert, and the Balanta and Manjago slower still, but they also participated in this process of community-making. In the Senegambia, the importance attached to these communities, as well as the particular relationships between them, made for a low centre of affective gravity. There was a residual identification with Kombo as a former kingdom, but the administrative units counted for less. On the Casamance side of the border, Narang and Jogny-Jabangkunda were the stuff of historical imagination, but not an active focus of identity politics in the colonial period.

In the trans-Volta, it was much more difficult for migrants to access land, and because chiefs did not control this resource, strangers needed to attach themselves as clients to individual landowners. Interestingly, there was also a marked shift over time. The Anlo traders who settled in Kpetoe after 1874 became Agotime whereas the Bè and Hausa settlers who arrived later were treated differently. By the time of the First World War, settlers in Agotime were consigned to the status of perpetual stranger. The Ando, who farmed on Agotime land, were the archetypal strangers whose relationship to the external environment was channelled through their landlords – which is deeply ironic because the Agotime freely admitted that they had seized their land two centuries before. The Ando were favoured because they were deemed to be diligent farmers who had no interest in staking claims to ownership or land, or indeed local citizenship. There was no mechanism according to which the Ando could found recognized settlements (Segbale existed to be sure, but it was treated as a mere hamlet) or claim full membership of existing communities. I have also demonstrated in some detail that at the same time as the Agotime category became more restricted, land disputes sharpened the divisions between the Agotime and their Ewe-speaking neighbours. The land case against Adaklu, which was adjudicated on the basis of oral claims, brought the history of the eighteenth and nineteenth centuries back into play. But interestingly, the Agotime and the Adaklu did not frame the dispute in ethnic terms. Moreover, it became increasingly difficult to keep the majority of Agotimes living in French Togoland invested in the case. In both respects, what it meant to be Agotime had shifted in significant ways by the 1930s. I will return in Chapter 13 to the impact of the land case in more recent times. But having taken this analysis well beyond the moment of independence, I now wish to backtrack and consider the period of decolonization itself.

Part III

Decolonization and Boundary Closure, c.1939–1969

In Part III of this book, which is dedicated to the decade on either side of independence, I redirect the focus to more overtly political questions. I also take in more of the 'national' and regional dynamics. Chapter 8 is a shorter contribution that pursues some of the points raised in Chapter 6 in greater depth. It serves as a bridge between Part II and the analysis that follows. Here I am concerned with the ways in which the acute material scarcities and the increased demand for manpower during the war enhanced the perceived importance of border flows. I also underline the importance of the post-war years for the creation of a new discourse of development that was based on particular assumptions about the relationship between the centre and the margins. In Chapters 9 and 10, I address the issue of why efforts to redraw boundaries, or to limit their practical consequences, bore such meagre fruit in the decade after independence. This entails a closer investigation of the role of elite and non-elite actors in promoting or opposing agendas for an alternative to colonial border dispensations. These are also the chapters where I begin to trace the evolution of quite distinct social contracts, all of which were grounded in the material realities of the border.

8   Bringing the Space Back In

Decolonization, Development and Territoriality in West Africa

> The failure to promote the interests of our people was due to the insatiable demands of colonial exploitation. However wise, enlightened and good-hearted certain individual officers may have been, their functions and authority fitted into a pattern of colonial administration which was itself conditioned by the central and over-all need to extract the riches of the colonies and transfer them overseas. If in the process it was necessary to build some roads, to construct a harbour, or to educate some Africans, well and good. The point I want to make is that any welfare activity for the benefit of the people was little more than incidental. It was far from being the underlying purpose of colonial rule.[1]
>
> (Kwame Nkrumah, 1963)

The enduring reputation of Kwame Nkrumah as a pioneer of nationalism rests on two legs: his role in hastening the end of the British empire in West Africa and his vision of a unified African continent unfettered by colonial borders. What is less often recognized is the tension between these agendas. If the Gold Coast was truly to push for an accelerated independence, that made it more or less inevitable that this would incur within the existing borders of the Gold Coast. In principle, the circle could be squared by positing a two-stage process of grasping the offer of independence first and then swiftly embarking on a process of unification. In practice, it was much more difficult to do away with colonial borders once new states had come into existence within their territorial integuments. Many aspects of Nkrumah's record in office have been criticized, and in some respects, it is the twinning of national liberation and continental unity that has spared his image from much worse. But Nkrumah was first and foremost a Gold Coast nationalist who was highly protective of the boundaries that the British had invested in. He instrumentalized borders much in the way that the colonial regimes had done – with the difference that he exhibited a less nuanced understanding of the limits of state power at the margins. And for all his rhetoric about border populations that were cut in two by artificial border-lines, he displayed almost no interest in addressing everyday border realities.

---

[1] Kwame Nkrumah, *Africa Must Unite* (New York: International Publishers, 1963), pp. 30–1.

Although Nkrumah was perhaps an extreme case, many other leaders exhibited similar blind spots. In this chapter, what I wish to highlight is some of the broad continuities between colonial regimes and their African successors, both institutionally and in terms of the ways in which they thought of desirable outcomes.

In an earlier study, I engaged with the debate about the factors driving decolonization and their entanglement with the modern concept of development.[2] It is not necessary to revisit this well-trodden ground here, but it is worth highlighting that the anniversary of half a century of independence across Africa has sparked a renewed bout of revisionism that has yet to run its course. There is a reluctance to revert to writing histories of nationalism, except where it has been deemed necessary to rehabilitate actors who were previously marginalized – most notably women.[3] But what has happened is that historians have begun to investigate some of the paths not taken and to write some of the apparently lost causes back into the larger narrative of decolonization.[4] The alternatives included a different distribution of power between national centres and sub-national units, as well as a reconfiguration of the colonial boundaries themselves. The earliest histories of nationalism, which worked within putative national containers, did not have much to say about alternative spatial imaginings. It is true that some political scientists conducted research on secessionist movements and the demise of colonial

---

[2] Paul Nugent, *Africa Since Independence: A Comparative History*, 2nd edn. (Houndmills and New York: Palgrave Macmillan, 2012), ch. 1. I owe a very obvious debt to the writings of Fred Cooper on this subject, especially in the shape of "Modernizing bureaucrats, backward Africans and the development concept", in Frederick Cooper and Randall Packard (eds.), *International Development and the Social Sciences: Essays on the History and Politics of Knowledge* (Berkeley and London: University of California Press, 1998), and Frederick Cooper, *Decolonization and African Society: The Labor Question in French and British Africa* (Cambridge: Cambridge University Press, 1996).

[3] Susan Geiger, *TANU Women: Gender and Culture in the Making of Tanganyikan Nationalism, 1955–65* (Oxford: James Currey, 1997) and Elizabeth Schmidt, *Mobilizing the Masses: Gender, Ethnicity, and Class in the Nationalist Movement in Guinea* (Portsmouth: Heinemann, 2005).

[4] Derek R. Peterson and Giacomo Macola (eds.), *Recasting the Past: History Writing and Political Work in Modern Africa* (Athens: Ohio University Press, 2009). Revisionism has been taken furthest in recent work on Zambia. See, in particular, Jan-Bart Gewald and Marja Hinfelaar (eds.), *One Zambia, Many Histories: Towards a History of Post-Colonial Zambia* (Leiden: Brill, 2008); Giacomo Macola, *Liberal Nationalism in Central Africa: A Biography of Harry Mwaanga Nkumbula* (Houndmills and New York: Palgrave Macmillan, 2009); and Miles Larmer, *Rethinking African Politics: A History of Opposition in Zambia* (Farnham and Burlington: Ashgate, 2011). For the Tanzanian case, see James R. Brennan, "The short history of political opposition and multi-party democracy in Tangayika, 1958–1964", and other contributions to Gregory H. Maddox and James L. Giblin (eds.), *In Search of a Nation: Histories of Authority and Dissidence in Tanzania* (Oxford: James Currey, 2005). For reflections on Zimbabwe, see Terence Ranger, "Nationalist historiography, patriotic history and the history of the nation: the struggle over the past in Zimbabwe", *Journal of Southern African Studies* 30 (2) 2004.

federations, but this agenda was never really taken up by historians when their time came.[5] However, a new wave of scholarship has directed attention to protagonists who wanted to redefine what the post-colony might actually look like on a map. Some of the dissenters wanted to encompass related peoples from next door – as with Ugandan Bagisu who campaigned for the inclusion of the Babukusu from Kenya – while others articulated a demand for a unique constitutional status or even a separate independence.[6] The counter-visions turned on alternative readings of history as well as insurgent cartographies.[7] In almost all cases, the movements were ignored by the winning side, and in many instances they were actively repressed. And, of course, being the losers, they were generally written out of the official histories of national independence. But fifty years on, the work of historical revisionism seems highly pertinent once more, as earlier demands for recognition are dusted off and refitted with a vocabulary that is more in tune with the times. But the task here is not merely to rehabilitate movements and individuals that came off second best, but also to pay greater attention to thought and action that was not entirely confined by territorial boundaries

In Chapters 9 and 10, I consider the ways in which borders became fundamental to attempts to configure political order and to frame economic alternatives around the moment of independence. I will argue that there was a striking difference in how this played out in the Senegambia and the trans-Volta. Whereas the push for a revision of colonial borders in the Senegambia was essentially top-down – and in that sense was heavily infused with the discourses and practices of state actors – it was more bottom-up in the trans-Volta. But in either instance, the manner in which boundary issues were settled, stifled or fudged was fundamental to the design of larger social contracts that, in turn, helped to fix governance patterns for decades to come. Finally, if we are to situate these trajectories in proper historical relief, we need

---

[5] Saadia Touval, *The Boundary Politics of Independent Africa* (Cambridge: Harvard University Press, 1972), and *Somali Nationalism: International Politics and the Drive for Unity in the Horn of Africa* (Harvard: Center for International Affairs, 1963).

[6] In some respects, the vast corpus of work on Mau Mau that has emerged since the 1990s was precisely about reconstructing the history of a heterodox movement. The irony is, however, that it has tended to drown out the stories of other Kenyans whose loyalty to the colonial state was at best conditional. Some of the latest work has begun to redress the balance. See Justin Willis and George Gona, "Pwani C Kenya? Memory, documents and secessionist politics in coastal Kenya", *African Affairs* 112 (446), 2013. For Tanzania, see Ralph Austen, "Colonial boundaries and African nationalism: the case of the Kagera salient", in Maddox and Giblin (eds.), *In Search of a Nation*. A recent attempt to do something similar for the Togoland unification movement is Kate Skinner, *The Fruits of Freedom in Togoland: Literacy, Politics and Nationalism, 1914–2014* (Cambridge: Cambridge University Press, 2015).

[7] For the Luhyia use of maps in the service of constructing a shared identity, see Julie MacArthur, *Cartography and the Political Imagination: Mapping Community in Colonial Kenya* (Athens: Ohio University Press, 2016), ch. 7.

to begin with the Second World War when the British and French colonial authorities began the process of rethinking colonial states – institutionally, ideationally and materially. Although challenges to European rule were most obvious in the cities – where demonstrations, strikes and mutinies underlined that there could not be a return to business as usual – many of the cracks in the colonial edifice had already become apparent at the margins in the early 1940s. And so it is there that our work of historical reconstruction necessarily begins.

Finessing the Margins to Supply the Cities

During the early 1930s, the retrenchment necessitated by the Great Depression had subjected the foundations of European rule to a stern test. The outbreak of the Second World War posed a more profound threat because larger imperial structures were themselves placed in question. The capitulation of France in 1940 exposed her internal disarray. When the colonies split down the middle between the pro-Vichyites and the Free French – which was replicated in the geographical divide between West and Equatorial Africa – the lack of any imperial consensus was strikingly obvious.[8] Ruth Ginio has rightly pointed out that the need for the competing blocs to appeal to the loyalty of their African subjects – a virtually unprecedented phenomenon – further exposed the frailty of the French grip on their colonies.[9] In the British case, the war had less obviously dramatic consequences. To a surprising degree, educated and traditional elites rallied to the defence of Britain in its hour of need. However, the war did expose the gulf between the rhetoric and the realities of British imperial power – one that became especially evident to those who were enlisted. By their very nature, empires were grandiose abstractions whose sustainability hinged on creating the impression of a common structure and purpose. At times of crisis, when it became more difficult to keep up appearances, the threads holding the fabric together could suddenly appear very flimsy indeed. In the past, there had been bouts of mutual incomprehension between the British and the French authorities in West Africa, but they had generally refrained from actively sabotaging each other. Although the Vichy authorities in West Africa sought to maintain some distance from Germany, relations with the British became antagonistic following the failure of the latter to capture Dakar in September 1940.[10] Once the Vichy authorities were in

---

[8] Nancy Lawler, *Soldiers, Airmen, Spies and Whisperers: The Gold Coast in World War II* (Athens: Ohio University Press, 2002).

[9] Ruth Ginio, *French Colonialism Unmasked: The Vichy Years in French West Africa* (Lincoln: University of Nebraska Press, 2006); Joseph-Roger Benoist, *L'Afrique Occidentale Française de la conférence de Brazzaville (1944) à l'indépendance (1960)* (Dakar: Nouvelles Editions Africaines, 1982); and Catherine Akpo-Vaché, *L'AOF et le seconde guerre mondiale (Septembre 1939–Octobre 1945)* (Paris: Karthala, 1996).

[10] Ginio, *French Colonialism Unmasked*, pp. 47–8.

control of the capital cities, their next priority was typically to secure the boundaries. The borders were closed and the movement of people and goods through 'enemy territory' was expressly prohibited.[11] In the calculations of both sets of authorities, hard borders came to be envisaged as instruments to inflict the maximum discomfort upon the other side. Conversely, they were also conceived of as the first lines of defence against subversion, espionage and economic crime.[12]

In Senegal, the French authorities had counted on British co-operation in enforcing a demand for conscripts. But now the Gambian authorities openly encouraged desertion and recruited from amongst those who crossed the border. In retaliation, the French prevented 'strange farmers' from working in the Gambia. In addition, both sides engaged in routine spying, allegedly making use of smugglers as sources of intelligence, and in the dissemination of propaganda targeted at African populations. For example, French officers left leaflets on the border close to Bwiam, accusing the British of seeking confrontation and expressing sympathy for Gambians living under military occupation.[13] This touched a raw nerve because the deportment of soldiers in the Gambia was already a source of some discontent.[14] In May 1942, the Vichy authorities were seeking to spread the message that there was virtual famine in the Gambia, with rice being reserved solely for the military and most other goods subject to rationing.[15] In their counter-propaganda, the British targeted the evils of fascism and highlighted the material hardships endured under Vichy rule. In the trans-Volta, the verbal sparring and attempts to undermine the standing of the neighbouring regime followed parallel lines. The Gold

[11] These were construed as virtual battle lines even if no actual fighting took place. Tony Chafer, *The End of Empire in French West Africa: France's Successful Decolonization?* (Oxford and New York: Berg, 2002), pp. 39–41.

[12] The French believed that Moor and Lebanese traders, in particular, were recruited as spies. Some of the information that was collected on specific individuals may be found at ANS 10D 1/33 "Renseignements Confidentiels sur la Gambie Anglaise et la Guinée Portugaise; Fourniture de Carburant etc". French concerns about spying led them to refrain from attracting people back across the line once they had entered the Gambia. For a more detailed account of espionage in the Gold Coast, and some connections to smuggling, see Lawler, *Soldiers, Airmen, Spies and Whisperers*, chs. 5–6.

[13] Commissioner Biddulph could not resist a touch of sarcasm about the propaganda that was left behind: "Such leaflets are in great demand locally to relieve the rather sombre tone of the month of Ramadan. The scanty and spasmodic supply is nowhere nearly equal to the demand which is a pity, as there are all too few things to laugh at these days." NAGB CSO 4/242 "Intelligence Reports (South Bank Province)", R.G. Biddulph, Commissioner at Cape St. Mary to Colonial Secretary, Bathurst (17 October 1941).

[14] In Brikama, which hosted the 2nd Gambia Regiment, simmering tensions between soldiers and the town population culminated in some sixty soldiers, mostly of Senegalese origin, burning down the police station in October 1944. The disagreements were largely over access to women. This was one small episode amongst many of a breakdown of military discipline during the war. NAGB ARP 34/2 "Divisional Annual Reports, 1944".

[15] ANS 10D 1/33 "Renseignements Confidentiels", Governor-General of l'AOF to Commandant de Cercle de Ziguinchor (1 May 1942).

Coast authorities expressed satisfaction at their enlistment rates from east of the Volta, which reflected the reality that many of the troops actually originated from French territory. Here too, it was in British interests to encourage flight and desertion from Côte d'Ivoire and from French Togoland.[16] The main difference was that while it was easy for the British to exploit the unpopularity of the French administration in Togoland, they had to be careful about nurturing an expectation of a return to German rule that could rebound upon them in the future.

The war years brought manifold material hardships that strained the moral authority of the incumbent regimes.[17] Shortages, rationing and forced labour were major sources of discontent and a significant cause of cross-border population movements. In the French colonies, the demands actually became more onerous after the Free French displaced the Vichy regimes and joined the war against Germany. For many Africans, European rule seemed overtly predatory in a way that was designed to permit the colonizer to survive at the expense of the colonized.[18] As Fred Cooper and David Killingray have reminded us, grievances over pay, working conditions and unequal treatment led to a rash of strikes and mutinies in both the British and the French colonies in the 1940s.[19] But colonial regimes had reason to feel particularly concerned about their hold over border regions, which appeared to serve as the breeding grounds for dissidence and heterodoxy of various kinds. A particular case in point was the Casamance region of Senegal. Jean Girard notes that the monoculture of groundnuts in Senegal created a situation where the population had become heavily dependent upon imported rice. With the interruption to international shipping caused by the Allied blockade, staples were in short supply.[20] The response of the Vichy authorities was to requisition rice and cattle from the Casamance. According to Girard, the seizure of cattle mostly affected the wealthier members of Jola villages, but when the granaries that were built up for the performance of initiation rites were also emptied, this had wider implications.[21] What is more, requisitioning coincided with the onset of

---

[16] Much of this movement occurred after the fall of the Vichy regimes. In the case of the movement of population from Gyaman in Côte d'Ivoire, see Lawler, *Soldiers, Airmen, Spies and Whisperers*, ch. 7.

[17] In the case of l'AOF, Thompson and Adloff concluded that: "The Second World War brought retrogression to French West Africa in every sphere". Virginia Thompson and Richard Adloff, *French West Africa* (Stanford: Stanford University Press, 1957), p. 29.

[18] For a detailed account in relation to Côte d'Ivoire, see Nancy Lawler, "Reform and repression under the Free French: economic and political transformation in the Cote d'Ivoire, 1942–45", *Africa* 60 (1) 1990, especially pp. 91–7.

[19] Cooper, *Decolonization and African Society*, ch. 4; and David Killingray, *Fighting for Britain: African Soldiers in the Second World War* (Woodbridge: James Currey, 2010), ch. 4.

[20] Jean Girard, *Genèse du pouvoir charismatique en Basse Casamance (Sénégal)* (Dakar: IFAN, 1969), pp. 214–15.

[21] Girard, *Genèse du pouvoir*, pp. 215–16.

drought, mirroring an unhappy conjuncture from the last decade of the nineteenth century. The resort to compulsion and further threats of reprisals in 1942 led to a recurrence of armed resistance that repeated some patterns from the First World War.[22] The greatest concern for the French was the rise to prominence of Aline Sitoe Diatta, a young woman from near Kabrousse, whose spiritual intercession for rain attracted a multi-ethnic following that reached across the borders with the Gambia and Guinea-Bissau.[23] French intelligence reports claimed that she had demanded the sacrifice of large numbers of cattle, banned non-indigenous rice varieties and groundnut cultivation, and had urged non-compliance with French tax and recruitment demands.[24] This appeared to attribute the crisis of subsistence directly to the French presence. Her message was interpreted as a rejection of the civilizing mission and a coded call to arms. In arresting and deporting Aline Sitoe, the French authorities believed they had nipped an insurgency in the bud, but in the short-term Jola dissidents secreted themselves in the border zone with Portuguese Guinea where they continued to represent a real threat.

In the trans-Volta, there was no directly comparable response, but the borderlands were a concern for the French authorities because Lomé lay within a stone's throw of the Gold Coast. As we have seen, the prosperity of French Togoland had depended on the advantages enjoyed by Lomé as a commercial entrepôt. Once the Allied blockade was in place, the number of ships that called at the port plummeted from 329 in 1939 to 29 in 1941, while imports of cotton goods and sugar fell to 10 and 19 per cent respectively of their former levels.[25] This meant that the re-export trade collapsed, affecting many traders in Lomé, at the same time as consumer shortages became the order of the day. The collapse of the external market for cocoa equally had a deleterious impact on the farming community in the vicinity of Kpalimé. Yves Marguerat has noted that while Vichy rule in Côte d'Ivoire weighed very heavily on the African population, it was actually after the takeover by the Free French that the demands became more onerous in Togoland. The reasons included the requisitioning of crops like cotton, palm-oil and maize and a renewed resort to forced labour with attendant penalties for non-compliance. There is some truth to this, although the pattern in Côte d'Ivoire was arguably not that different.

---

[22] Akpo-Vaché, *L'AOF*, p. 137.

[23] Wilmetta J. Tolliver-Diallo, "'The woman who was more than a man': making Aline Sitoe Diatta into a national heroine in Senegal", *Canadian Journal of African Studies* 39 (2) 2005; Robert M. Baum, "Prophetess: Aline Sitoe Diatta as a contested icon in contemporary Senegal", in Toyin Falola and Fallou Ngom (eds.), *Facts, Fiction and African Creative Imaginations* (London: Routledge, 2009).

[24] The claims about resistance to French demands were contested by other officials. Girard, *Genèse du pouvoir*, pp. 218–19.

[25] Yves Marguerat, *Dynamique urbaine, jeunesse et histoire au Togo* (Lomé: Presses de l'UB, 1993), p. 214.

Marguerat is certainly justified in his observation that sympathy for French rule was irreparably damaged after 1942, although the flight of population into British territory before that time also indicates that the problem surfaced rather earlier.

While colonial regimes grappled with the challenge of asserting effective control over border regions, they contributed to their own discomfort in various ways. A degree of transgression at the margins was tolerated in order to alleviate some of the pressures accumulating in the cities. In the trans-Volta, as in the Senegambia, the war coincided with a severe drought – particularly in 1944. Acute shortages of basic foodstuffs, especially maize, were reflected in high prices in border markets.[26] The British authorities, through the good offices of the chiefs, urged the population of their section of Togoland to plant more maize and other crops such as cotton that were needed to support the war effort.[27] However, their concern was that any surplus might simply disappear across the border. Towards the end of 1941, British intelligence reports noted that the French authorities were actively encouraging the smuggling of maize and other consumer goods – most notably salt, flour, cotton goods, kerosene and petrol – despite the formal closure of the border.[28] This trade continued after the installation of a Free French regime for the simple reason that the authorities in Lomé continued to struggle with making basic goods available to a population that already felt hard done by.

Requisitioning after 1942 appears to have had a deleterious impact on food production in French Togoland. In 1945, the Manager of the Ewe Presbyterian Schools in Ho reported to the District Commissioner that:

It is without doubt that the exorbitant demand of Palm Oil and Kernel by the French Government, imposed upon the inhabitants of the French Mandated Togoland, for which the individuals have a very little time to work on their farms, has consequently brought a very great scarcity of food to that part of the country, and the little food we have here is likely to be transported there by one means or the other. On the other hand, during the past years when the inhabitants of the French Mandated Togoland were free to farm on a large scale, sufficient food was brought here from that part

---

[26] In July 1944, 3 d would purchase six tins of gari (grated cassava), four tins of ground maize and nine tomatoes in Ho market. One year later, the corresponding amounts were four tins, two tins and four tomatoes respectively. NAGA ADM 39/1/312 "Food Control", A.K. Dzodzomenyo, Agricultural overseer, Ho, to District Commissioner, Ho (25 July 1945).

[27] The British also experimented with trying to use local cloth to make uniforms and items of clothing. The focus was on Avatime. NAGA ADM 30/1/654 "Awatime Weaving". Curiously, the authorities do not seem to have focused on Agotime whose weaving industry was renowned.

[28] NAGA ADM 39/1/312 "Food Control", Colonial Secretary, Accra, to CEP, Koforidua; and NAGA CSO 6/5/21 "Smuggling and Seizures in the Southern Section, Eastern Frontier Preventive Station", "Report on Patrols, Smuggling and Seizures for the Month September 1941". Ginio also cites evidence to suggest that the British, in other contexts, sought to poach produce from French territory. Ginio, French Colonialism Unmasked, p. 63.

of French Togoland until the French Government restricted the importation of food-stuffs to this part of Togoland.[29]

In August of that year, James Moxon, who briefly served as the District Commissioner (DC) in Kpandu, circulated a letter to the chiefs in British Togoland reminding them that the export of foodstuffs was still prohibited except under licence from the Customs Preventive Service (CPS).[30] This prohibition, which dated to Defence Regulations in 1939, was reiterated under the "Conveyance of Maize (No.2) Order, 1946". Although the British author-ities blamed smuggling for local food shortages, these were partly a conse-quence of the fact that not only maize, but also cassava, yam, pepper and groundnuts were being sent to Accra to alleviate the shortfall in the capital. This had the predictable consequence of driving up the economic rents associ-ated with border trade.

In the Senegambia, a contradictory approach to border flows was, if any-thing, even more apparent. The Vichy regime in Dakar believed that the Gambian authorities were actively encouraging the contraband trade, espe-cially in respect of rice and cattle.[31] The Gambia had to contend with food deficits at the best of times, which meant that poaching supplies was an imperative. The Senegalese authorities did their best to mount patrols, which drew them into confrontation with organized gangs of smugglers operating along the Casamance–Gambia border. In one incident at Makuda in July 1941, for example, the *douaniers* confronted a band of no fewer than sixty smug-glers.[32] While the British authorities were inclined to encourage the trade when it worked in their favour, it was not always so easy to identify which kinds of flows were conducive to some notion of the public good. During the war, there was a lively trade in smuggled foodstuffs from the southern Casamance and Guinea-Bissau. A report from 1944 made it clear that this had relieved some of the pressures in the Gambia:

War conditions have naturally brought shortages of many important commodities, but compared with other countries, the Gambia has been very fortunate and there has

---

[29] NAGA ADM 39/1/312 "Food Control", M.W. Akama, Reverend Manager, Ewe Presbyterian Schools, Ho, to District Commissioner, Ho (27 July 1945).

[30] NAGA ADM 39/1/312 "Food Control", R.J. Moxon, District Commissioner, Kpandu, to all chiefs (28 August 1945). Moxon enjoyed a colourful career, in different postings, and stayed on after independence.

[31] Ginio, *French Colonialism*, pp. 62–3. ANS 10D 1/33 "Renseignements Confidentiels", Gov-ernor of Senegal, Saint-Louis, to Commandants de Cercle (14 August 1941). It was claimed that Moor traders were being encouraged to carry cloth from Bathurst to a village close to the border where it was exchanged against cattle. Governor-General of l'AOF, Dakar, to Governor of Senegal (6 August 1941).

[32] ANS 10D 1/33 "Renseignements Confidentiels", Capitaine Esquilat, Chef de la subdivision de Bignona to Commandant de Cercle de Ziguinchor (5 September 1941).

practically been no real hardship. The supply of cotton goods was excellent and was bartered against groundnuts, coos and rice. The high quality attracted many French farmers in frontier area to bring their produce into the Gambia, although it is believed this was frowned on by the French authority. Articles which were hardest to obtain were hardware (especially kettles), cotton cards, iron bars, gunpowder, percussion caps, and mosquito netting.[33]

While the encouragement given to border trade helped to alleviate food shortages, especially around Brikama, the same report also alluded to the manner in which criminal gangs had managed to exploit the unique circumstances afforded by the war:

In general, there has been a distinct wave of prosperity throughout the division and there is a great deal of money in circulation. However, this has had bad effects as well as good, since the shortages of commodities which can be bought for cash has lead [sic] to a good deal of inflation, and the prices of foodstuffs in the markets have risen, in spite of controls, while the black market has never got out of hand, its existence was very evident and seemed to be accepted quite philosophically by the people, who made only slight efforts to check it. There has been a good deal of trade with Portuguese Guinea from the Kombo area, especially during the rainy season. The principal imports were rice, coos and flour, but it is to be regretted that much of the property for which they were bartered consisted of service stores stolen from the army and the Royal Air Force. Petrol and motor tyres fetch especially high prices and thus present a great temptation.[34]

The link between the cross-border food trade and the trafficking in stolen goods posed a constant headache for the Gambian authorities. While it was easier to keep a check on what passed through the land border in Kombo, British officials recognized that the waterborne traffic was especially difficult to monitor. As the South Bank Division report for 1944 explained: "Police work is very difficult in this area since most of the stolen property is loaded onto canoes on the Atlantic coast and taken to Portuguese Guinea within a short time of the theft occurring."[35] The Colonial Office strongly suspected that the Portuguese authorities were conniving in the smuggling of rice in return for the fuel, tyres and spare parts that they desperately needed.[36] The vaguely comical situation in which the Army and Airforce were forced to buy back some of their stores in Bissau spoke volumes about the difficulties involved in regulating the passage of the pirogues.

The border town of Kartong, located at the edge of the Allahein River, was thought to play a particularly prominent role in the trafficking of stolen goods. The fact that this town attracted a considerable number of Manjago

---

[33] NAGB ARP 34/2 "Divisional Annual Reports, 1944".
[34] NAGB ARP 34/2 "Divisional Annual Reports, 1944".
[35] NAGB ARP 34/2 "Divisional Annual Reports, 1944".
[36] NAGB CSO 3/400 Minute from O.C. RAF, Bathurst, 25/7/1944. This file provides detailed inventories of smuggled military goods.

immigrants from Portuguese Guinea was surely not coincidental. As late as 1952, the Superintendent of Police recommended that special attention be paid to the town:

It is evident that an ilicit [sic] import and export trade of quite a considerable scale is being carried on through Kartung. Apart from the traffic in goods to which there may be no objection from the standpoint of the Customs laws, there is ample evidence that a considerable trade in the exportation of stolen property, much of which has been stolen from the Government, is also being carried on through Kartung. For example, only recently a member of the Criminal Investigation Department staff visited Portuguese Guinea where he recovered a radio receiving set valued at £70, the property of the Information Office, and a typewriter, valued at £30, the property of the United Africa Company, both of which had been stolen in Bathurst only a few weeks previously. In another instance two bales of new twill bags (600 bags in all valued at £225) which had been shipped in H.M.C.S. 'Fuladu' from Carrols Wharf to Bathurst and unloaded on to the Government Wharf on 10th April were subsequently stolen from the wharf. On 22nd April the Police visited Kartung and there seized a canoe loaded with 686 new bags exactly similar to those reported stolen from the Government Wharf.[37]

Around this time, there was a vigorous contraband trade. Substantial quantities of 'Lucky Strike' and 'Clipper' cigarettes entered the Gambia from Portuguese territory and the Casamance, leading the Collector of Customs to speculate that "if this situation should continue unchecked, the revenue on tobacco which is one of our principal items of duty would drop thereby creating a very precarious spectacle on the Colony's revenues."[38]

At the same time a wide range of consumer goods crossed into Senegalese territory from the Gambia. In 1954, for example, goods seized by *douaniers* at Badiara, on the Gambia border, included a variety of cotton goods, knives, batteries, locks and Bata shoes. Towards the end of the decade, transistor radios also featured prominently, which was an indication of shifting patterns of consumer demand in rural areas once the war had come to an end.[39] The larger lesson is that the border regions occupied a fluctuating – but always pivotal – position in the calculations of colonial officials. They understood that the political distemper in the urban centres could only be alleviated by managing border flows: typically by sucking in scarce commodities from the other side, while trying to prevent scarce goods passing the other way. As border populations exploited the opportunities, officials fretted that trade that was technically illegal was breeding a spirit of contempt for European

---

[37] NAGB CUS 1/4 "Collector of Customs, Border Trade and Smuggling", Superintendent of Police, Bathurst, to Collector of Customs (19 July 1952).

[38] NAGB CUS 1/4 "Collector of Customs", letter from Collector to all Commissioners (21 January 1953).

[39] ANS 11D 1/269 "Douanes", "Avis de Ventre, 30/1/1954" and "Brigade mobile de Velingara, Rapport Trimestriel, Ier trimestre, 1959".

authority. Hence, bringing the borderlands under more effective control became a priority in each of the colonies when the war ended.

Development, Modernity and the Margins

Even before the end of the war, British and French politicians were actively deliberating about what would be needed to breathe life back into the colonial project. In very similar ways, they attempted to forge new social contracts based on the promise of a package we now call 'development'. This, in turn, entailed a reconceptualization of the role of states and their points of contact with African societies. The intention was not to prepare for the termination of empire, but rather to place it on a more secure footing. In the case of the French, this was made explicit at the Brazzaville conference of 1944 where the emphasis was upon binding the colonies and the metropole together in their supposedly common interest. This necessitated paying closer attention to the material needs of ordinary Africans, who graduated from the status of subjects to citizens two years later.[40] The institutional mechanism through which transformation was to be achieved was the Fonds d'Investissement pour le Développement Economique et Social (FIDES) which was established in 1946. Through FIDES significant financing was made available to the African colonies for the first time. In the British case, the passage of the Colonial Development and Welfare Act in 1940 (renewed in 1945) can similarly be viewed as a conscious attempt to recast the colonial relationship at a time when Britain was heavily dependent on the dollar earnings of its African colonies. In the short run, there was bound to be a substantial net outflow from the colonies,[41] but the *quid pro quo* was a commitment to promoting the welfare of Africans whilst creating the preconditions for economic growth. But woven into these schemas was a presumption of gradualism. Rather than seeking to retard social change, as before, the goal was ostensibly to create the modern African citizen, and yet it was repeatedly stated that this was a process that needed to be carefully managed.

Three dimensions of the development package are worth singling out briefly for the purposes of this discussion. The first was the belief that the relationship between the imperial centre and the colonies could only truly cut both ways

---

[40] Akpo-Vaché, *L'AOF*, ch. 9; Cooper, *Decolonization and African Society*, pp. 177–82; Chafer, *End of Empire*, pp. 56–61. For an extended treatment of the question of citizenship, see Frederick Cooper, *Citizenship between Empire and Nation: Remaking France and French Africa, 1945–1960* (Cambridge: Cambridge University Press, 2014).

[41] David Fieldhouse estimated that the African colonies received £40.5 million in loans, but the West African Marketing Boards surrendered £93 million, while sterling balances docked in London rose to £920 million. Quoted in David Throup, *Economic and Social Origins of Mau Mau, 1943–53* (London: James Currey, 1987), p. 20.

if transport bottlenecks were tackled. This applied not merely to ports and transport hubs, but also to large swathes of the interior whose productive potential was regarded as untapped. The construction of connective infrastructure was therefore treated as a first-order priority in rendering Africa *utile*. Although the extension of electricity beyond the cities was considered more of a long-term ambition, the Volta River Project in the Gold Coast provides an example of the societal spinoffs that were expected to ensue from the generation of hydroelectric power. The second dimension was an increased interest in matters of welfare provision. This was expected to boost the productivity of labour, but what mattered equally was that it was valorized by Africans. One of the central aims of post-war development interventions was therefore to substantially increase the share of the budget that was earmarked for education and health, and to distribute these more evenly across colonial space.

Thirdly, the new development paradigm involved a re-appraisal of the principles of 'native administration'. During the war, Joyce Cary – who had served as a District Officer in Northern Nigeria in the 1920s and had written *Mister Johnson* as a fictionalized critique of the lack of colonial ambition – published *The Case for African Freedom*. In it, he drew attention to the singular lack of progress in education and health in colonies like Nigeria and Uganda, which he attributed to the inertia instilled by Indirect Rule. Cary insisted that the latter actually had no higher purpose than to perpetuate existing structures. This, he contended, was no longer sufficient to justify the colonial mission:

Indirect rule must be judged, like all governments, by its purpose, and its results. One must ask of it, does it promote advancement of the African in education, and standards of life? Does it prepare him for a share of responsibility in his own government? ... This is the important point, that the government, whatever it calls itself, should know what it really wants and it should be anxious, in all sincerity to prepare the African to take his part as the full citizen of a *modern* state, in a *modern* world.[42]

The last phrase summed up precisely the direction in which official thinking was heading. The critique of traditional rule closely mirrored the critical re-appraisal of colonial priorities carried out by Lord Hailey during the early 1940s.[43] Increasingly, Indirect Rule was construed as a barrier to effective modernization rather than its natural ally.[44] In its place, the British envisaged

---

[42] Joyce Cary, *The Case for African Freedom and Other Writings* (Austin: University of Texas Press, 1962), pp. 59–60. His critique of the timidity of colonial officialdom was the dominant theme in *Mister Johnson* (London: Carfax, 1952).

[43] Robert Pearce, "The Colonial Office and planned decolonization in Africa", *African Affairs* 83 (330) 1984, pp. 80–2.

[44] Robert D. Pearce, *The Turning Point in Africa: British Colonial Policy 1938–48* (London: Frank Cass, 1982), pp. 49–58, 155–6.

an elected local government system that would be charged with delivering basic services. During the war, the process of 'democratizing' Native Authorities in the British West African colonies had already begun in a halting fashion.[45] In 1947, a Local Government Dispatch signalled an intention to move towards a system of elected councils. Although traditional authorities would remain, they would henceforth constitute a minority on local government bodies. In the French colonies, official thinking was moving along broadly comparable lines.[46] In both cases, however, the follow-through took considerably longer.

The development package had potentially far-reaching implications for the ways in which colonial states were configured. Firstly, as we have seen, there was some redefinition of the institutional contours of the state, as the relationship between traditional authorities and the central administration was re-calibrated. Secondly, and most obviously, states were expected to play a proactive role in the delivery of public goods. Here there was a degree of tension between technocratic and political imperatives. Constructing roads, bridges, health posts and other public works was partly about unlocking the economic potential of the colonies, but it was also a means by which the state rendered itself legible to its African subjects. This required that institutions be refitted or created from scratch. In the 1930s, significant retrenchment had led to the withering of certain branches of the bureaucracy. Posts in the field administration continued to be staffed in order to avoid the impression that colonialism was in retreat. Hence the cuts had fallen mostly on the technical branches – such as public works and the veterinary services. In the period after the war, colonial states were patched up, with renewed recruitment into the technical services as well as into the field administration. The dual process of deepening and broadening – or "thickening the thin white line" as Lewis puts it – was part of what has come to be known as the "second colonial occupation" in British Africa.[47] This was reinforced by an enchantment with the application of scientific knowledge as well as with planning, which together made the state's presence seem more invasive. At the same time, hitherto marginal institutions became integral to the attempt to render the state visible throughout the colonies. The construction of rural post offices across

---

[45] Pearce, *Turning Point*, p. 141.

[46] Togoland enjoyed a head start in the sense that the Conseils de Notables dated to before the war.

[47] Although this is often thought to have had the most dramatic impact in the settler colonies, the effects were felt in West Africa as well. For the Kenyan case, see J.E. Lewis, "The ruling compassions of the late colonial state: welfare versus force, c.1945–1952", *Journal of Colonialism and Colonial History* 2, 2, 2001; Bruce Berman, *Control and Crisis in Colonial Kenya* (London: James Currey, 1990) and Throup, *Economic and Social Origins*. For the size of the colonial service, see A.H.M. Kirk Greene, "The thin white line: the size of the British colonial service in Africa," *African Affairs* 79 (314) 1980, pp. 25–44.

both the British and the French colonies is a case in point. Although all of this activity implied the recruitment of greater numbers of European officials, it was considered imperative for Africans to be recruited to fill more responsible positions, especially with the rolling out of local government.[48] However, the possibility for rapid Africanization of the civil service depended greatly on improvements to the existing educational infrastructure.

Thirdly, there was an expectation that states would devote greater attention to generating the resources necessary for the refashioning of the colonial project. While colonial governments would be able to draw on funds from the metropole, they were expected to reach a point where they could rely more upon their own revenue-raising powers. Taxes were a means to an end, in the sense of generating the revenues that enabled recurrent commitments and development priorities to be financed. But modernization of the tax system was also seen as integral to the refashioning of government institutions themselves. At the national level, the ideal was to create a modern tax system – one that would match liability to income, whether that of an individual or a company. The image of a stable urban working class enjoying the facilities of modern living and paying a personal income tax is one that Lugard would certainly have approved of.[49] While head and poll taxes were usually retained, they were devolved to local government bodies and mattered to the central state in a more indirect way. Although subventions were considered a necessary evil, the intention was to equip local councils to raise enough revenue to cover some of the rising spending commitments.[50] Following a familiar logic, collecting taxes was also supposed to make local government bodies more accountable to the populations they notionally represented. In practice, taxation was one of the state practices that proved most resistant to modernization. Where states had a reliable revenue stream, there was a disincentive to look elsewhere, and where revenues were scarce there was often an inclination to play safe.

Finally, this brings us to some of the implications for the ways in which late colonial states related to border regions. Within l'AOF (l'Afrique Occidentale Française), decisions about infrastructural investments inevitably cut across the borders of individual colonies. But where British, French and Portuguese colonies rubbed shoulders, officials tended to think of infrastructural investments, and development more broadly, in zero-sum terms. In most cases, the

---

[48] The first African Assistant District Commissioners in the Gold Coast were appointed during the war, including Kofi Busia who eventually became Prime Minister of the Second Republic (1969–72).

[49] Personal income tax was introduced in the Gambia in 1940 and the Gold Coast in 1943 (albeit first collected in 1944/5).

[50] Leigh A. Gardner, *Taxing Colonial Africa: The Political Economy of British Imperialism* (Oxford: Oxford University Press, 2012), p. 162.

intention was to bind peripheries closer to the centre, which ought to have translated into greater investments at the margins. But there was also a reluctance to finance infrastructure – especially motorable roads and bridges – that might benefit a neighbouring colony. As export duties and associated taxes on cash crops became more crucial for public finances, the authorities also had cause to worry about the prospect of cocoa, coffee and groundnuts being spirited across borders. Practically speaking, the result was that infrastructure was often left in a rudimentary state in border regions. Whereas some roads traversed boundaries, health and educational priorities were viewed through an explicitly territorial lense. When decisions were made about where to locate a health post, these tended to ignore the existence of people across the border for whom a given facility might be considerably closer than the nearest equivalent in their own territory. This created a structural disincentive to locate health posts, schools and even local councils in proximity to borders. Hence the paradoxical situation in which state agents might be highly visible at the border post, but nowhere to be seen a few kilometres from the line. Not surprisingly, a perception of deliberate neglect fed directly into the grievances that border populations often harboured with good reason.

Although the borders of post-colonial states hardened very quickly, there was a period from the mid-1950s to the early 1960s when alternative territorial configurations were conceivable – and indeed were actively touted. The proposals for the creation of a greater Senegambia, and reunification of the Ewe people and/or the two Togolands, were the subject of intense debates in the region as well as in international fora. In the end, they came to nothing, with the net result that four independent states emerged within the same boundaries that had existed since 1919. In accounting for this stasis, there is an understandable inclination to point to elite self-interest: on this view, it may have been less risky for African leaders to work with what was there rather than risking the alternatives. In the two chapters that follow, I do not entirely discount the instrumental role of political elites, but this can only explain so much. Certainly, the idea that African leaders were only too happy to play along cannot be taken at face value. Léopold Senghor had firmly opposed the break-up of l'AOF and had tried to lure the separate colonies back into a territorial union in the late 1950s. The fact that the Mali Union was eventually reduced to the former French Soudan and Senegal, and then quickly fell apart in acrimony, does not alter the fact that Senghor had consistently stood out against 'balkanization'.[51] It must be remembered, of course, that the demise of

[51] For a short discussion of the contradictory uses of the term by African leaders, see Benyamin Neuberger, "The African concept of balkanisation", *Journal of Modern African Studies* 14 (3) 1976, pp. 523–9. See also Joseph-Roger de Benoist, *La balkanization de l'Afrique Occidentale Francaise* (Dakar: Nouvelles Éditions Africaines, 1979).

l'AOF circumscribed the terrain of the budding Senegalese managerial elite and turned Dakar from the capital of a large federation into something altogether more modest.[52] The pursuit of a unified Senegambia was considered highly desirable by Senegalese politicians who bemoaned an artificial line that divided kith and kin. By contrast, there was greater caution in the Gambia. The first government formed by the United Party (UP) under the leadership of P.S. N'Jie entered into preliminary discussions on the issue. Dawda Jawara, who emerged victorious in the 1962 elections, was more insistent on achieving independence first, but envisaged that a closer union with Senegal would follow.[53] Similarly, it was members of the educated elite in the south-eastern Gold Coast and French Togoland who clamoured for reunification of the Ewe people. Although Sylvanus Olympio eventually opted for a separate Togolese independence, this was not what the leadership of the Comité de l'Unité Togolaise (CUT) had campaigned for in their alliance with unificationists in British Togoland.

In order to account for the final outcomes, it is necessary to entertain the possibility that it was the failure of political elites to carry the wider population with them that was the decisive factor rather than the other way around. This insight is already implicit in the comparative study conducted by Claude Welch half a century ago. In it, he wrote that:

The idea of unification was first propounded by a small group of men with greater political sophistication, education and motivation than most of their compatriots. This 'political elite' was characterized by a common desire for independence and by a realization of the economic weakness of West African states.[54]

But Welch was merely echoing what Daniel Chapman, the Oxford-educated founder of the All-Ewe Conference (AEC), had already articulated in 1946:

Let us remember, however, that the unification of Eweland means a great deal of hard work of various kinds. We should be continually instructing our illiterate neighbours in facts about our unification which they must know.[55]

Perhaps the "illiterate neighbours" declined to follow their lead. I wish to argue that this insight has partial relevance for the Senegambia, whereas in

---

[52] More seriously, it downgraded St. Louis from the capital of Senegal to a provincial town devoid of any administrative importance.

[53] Claude Welch, *Dream of Unity: Pan-Africanism and Political Unification in West Africa* (Ithaca: Cornell University Press, 1966), p. 281. The UP was generally more inclined towards links with Senegal, although it later reversed its stance. Arnold Hughes and David Perfect, *A Political History of the Gambia, 1816–1994* (Rochester: University of Rochester Press, 2006), p. 153.

[54] Welch, *Dream of Unity*, pp. 345–6.

[55] *The Ewe News-Letter*, Organ of the All-Ewe Conference, No. 20, December 1946, p. 3.

the trans-Volta a popular movement for the rectification of boundaries did take root but fell foul of the state-building priorities of nationalist leaders. In Chapter 9, I deal with the reasons why the push for unification of the Senegambia failed to bear fruit, following which I return to the case of the trans-Volta in Chapter 10.

9   The Vanishing Horizon of Senegambian Unity

Statist Visions and Border Dynamics

> Our attitude towards the future status of the Gambia is based on our
> understanding that the territories of the Gambia and Senegal are ethnically,
> geographically and historically one unit, and that division was imposed only
> by a hazard of colonization. Thus we feel that it would only be natural if
> the Gambians sought to unite with us after achieving their independence.[1]

A press statement issued by their embassy on the occasion of a visit by
Léopold Senghor to London in October 1961 summed up the official Senegalese position, namely that the Senegambia comprised a 'natural region', in
which there were also many elements of a shared culture[2] – all of which was
at odds with the rigidities associated with colonial boundaries. The border
between Senegal and the Gambia, which comprised a series of straight lines
and arcs of circles, seemed to typify the arbitrary manner in which the
Europeans had imposed boundaries that separated one colonial domain from
the other. The question that arises is why it was that the legacy was not put to
rest, whether by erasing the borders or lessening their practical consequences.
One possible answer is that the Europeans had an interest in perpetuating the
balkanization of the region, but in fact the British and the French came to a
consensus – admittedly rather late in the day – that Senegal and the Gambia
would make a better fist of independence if they joined forces. An alternative interpretation which posits that the status quo was in the interest of
Senegambian political elites is difficult to reconcile with the stance of leaders
like Senghor. The third alternative, which is that most of the population had
come to accept the status quo, is the one that has received the least serious
consideration because it challenges the assumption that they would necessarily
have been opposed to the borders that separated them. But it is the one that
comes closest to capturing the truth. In this chapter, I will seek to account for
the reality that borders became even more deeply entrenched in the decades

---

[1] Claude Welch, *Dream of Unity: Pan-Africanism and Political Unification in West Africa* (Ithaca:
Cornell University Press, 1966), quoted p. 278.
[2] This is close to the position advanced by Boubacar Barry, *Senegambia and the Atlantic Slave*
(Cambridge: Cambridge University Press, 1997), pp. 5, 303.

on either side of independence. At the same time, I also want to advance the proposition that border dynamics were of fundamental importance to the rather different social contracts that took shape in the Senegal and the Gambia.

The Matter of a River: Decolonization and the Infrastructural Deficit

A question mark had long dangled over the Gambia. The colony had always been regarded as the poor relation of the British empire. If anything, this image became even more firmly entrenched in the post-war years when every other colony seemed to be forging ahead.[3] In 1941, the Gambian government responded to passage of the Colonial Development and Welfare (CDW) Act by setting up the Blackburne Committee to carry out the first comprehensive survey of the colony's economic and social needs. It provided the material for a detailed plan, whose premise was that the Gambia would draw substantially on CDW funding.[4] During the war, the government committed itself to implementing aspects of the plan, although Gailey observes that the funds that were allocated for medical and health infrastructure mostly went unspent.[5] With a return to peace, the expectation was that the plan would be rolled out in full. However, the British government initially turned out to be much less forthcoming than the Gambian authorities had anticipated. Gailey recounts an episode in which the government believed that it had secured approval for an ambitious scheme to relocate the administrative centre from Bathurst to the vicinity of Sukuta. In 1945, the authorities duly applied for CDW funding to cover just over half of the million pounds that was required, with the remainder expected to come from a modest Gambian government contribution of £50,000 and a British government loan of £450,000. However, the loan was turned down and the work, which had already begun, had to be abandoned.[6] The reality was that the public finances of the Gambia were in an extremely precarious state (Table 9.1). In 1943 and 1944, there was a significant budgetary shortfall. In 1945, the picture was more favourable, but not overwhelmingly so given that revenues stood at £501,988 and expenditure at £430,729. In subsequent years, the Gambia enjoyed greater success in levering resources from the metropole, but this amounted to an admission that the Gambia was unable to finance all its expenditure commitments, and least of all those

---

[3] See, for example, Berkeley Rice, *Enter Gambia: The Birth of an Improbable Nation* (London: Angus and Robertson, 1968).

[4] The Committee was chaired by K.W. Blackburne whose papers are located in Rhodes House Library, Oxford The product of its work was the *Report on Development and Welfare in the Gambia* (Bathurst, 1943). Harry Gailey, *A History of the Gambia* (London: Routledge and Kegan Paul, 1964), pp. 169–70.

[5] Gailey, *History of the Gambia*, p. 170.   [6] Gailey, *History of the Gambia*, p. 172.

Table 9.1 *Gambia recurrent revenue and expenditure (excluding development funds and funds from West African Produce Control Board)*

Year	Revenue	Expenditure	Balance	UK Treasury
1952	1,431,495	1,424,213	+7,282	–
1953	1,201,068	1,085,693	+115,375	–
1954	1,420,356	1,168,309	+252,047	–
1955	1,533,030	1,279,846	+253,184	–
1956	1,405,006	1,646,899	−241,893	–
1957	2,128,107	1,817,930	+310,177	–
1958	1,895,006	1,961,539	−66,633	–
1959	1,538,440	1,816,449	−278,009	–
1960	1,572,488	1,710,069	−137,581	–
1961	1,973,855	2,154,940	−181,085	£45,666

Source: Gambia. *Financial Report with Appendices for the Year 1961*, Sessional Paper No. 6/64, p. 3.

relating to development. According to Gailey, a sum of £1,058,800 was allocated for development projects between 1947 and 1957, of which no less than £976,340 derived from CDW grants.[7] The prospect that the Gambia might become permanently dependent on British financial support was one that inevitably raised eyebrows in London and contributed to a greater responsiveness to Senegalese overtures there.

In Senegal, access to metropolitan financing through the Fonds d'Investissement pour le Développement Economique et Social (FIDES) led to accelerated expenditure on infrastructure with a view to more effectively exploiting the economic potential of the colony. The Casamance was regarded as a potential bread-basket, but this was only ever likely to be realized if the region could be sutured to the rest of the colony. The problem was that the Gambia scythed Senegal in two. In Dakar, the suspicion – somewhere between a belief and a faint hope – was that the British authorities were growing weary of their commitments in the Gambia and that the time was ripe to reopen negotiations, if not for outright cession, then at the very least for the construction of a fully integrated infrastructural network. In 1948, the French found the British authorities unyielding over what they regarded as discriminatory tariffs, but two years later the Governor-General of l'Afrique Occidentale Française (l'AOF) reported that there was a greater willingness to make concessions on tariffs and the freedom of movement for French vessels on the river. This he attributed to the financial travails of the Gambia, which had been exacerbated by the French Customs cordon:

---

[7] Gailey, *History of the Gambia*, p. 172

The Gambian traffic, which dwindled in a critical manner before the war, to the point where in 1939 certain Englishmen dreamed of ceding us the enclave, is going down again after the artificial 'boom' which it enjoyed during and after the war. Gambian revenues are declining dangerously and don't make up for maintaining a country reduced to a central artery, and its annexes in the hinterland, without population. The Gambia has lived these past years on its traffic, whether or not this is admitted, with l'AOF. But French provisioning of Senegal has improved considerably and our Customs cordon surrounding the enclave has assumed in these recent times a certain efficacy.[8]

In the French imagination, Dakar would serve as the focal point of a road and rail network radiating outwards towards the peripheries. In the case of the Casamance, this meant that north–south communications were a priority for the targeted use of FIDES funding. What the French wanted from Bathurst was agreement on a paved road crossing the Gambia and, if the river could not be bridged, a modernized ferry system that would considerably reduce the bottlenecks. However, official thinking in Bathurst was directed along an east–west axis. The major issue for the Gambian authorities was how towns upriver could be better linked to Bathurst. Up until this point, the Gambia's commerce had depended overwhelmingly on river transport, but in the post-war years attention switched to the construction of better roads. In view of the underlying funding constraints, this raised the question of whether one good trunk road should track the north or the south bank. None of this was of any great concern to the Senegalese authorities, for whom the priority was a motorable road running from Dakar to Ziguinchor.

The Trans-Gambian highway was agreed upon in the early 1950s, but in 1954 the French authorities expressed frustration at the length of time it was taking for the British to fulfill their side of the bargain. There was some recognition of the financial constraints under which they laboured, but there was also a suspicion that the Bathurst authorities were lukewarm about the project. As one memorandum put it: "They considered, in effect, that the useful lines of communication were situated on either side of the river in an east-west direction".[9] Despite the delays, the Trans-Gambian highway was finally opened in 1958. This represented progress of a kind, especially as a decision on the east–west road proved even slower to come to fruition.[10] This was nevertheless a qualified victory, given that the river crossing still created a serious bottleneck. The French had invested in a modern ferry across

[8] ANS 11D1/251 "Affaires Politiques et Administratives (APA): Relations avec la Gambie", Gouverneur-Général de l'AOF, Dakar, to Ministre de la France d'Outre-Mer (3 May 1950).
[9] CAOM, Affaires Politiques: 1AFFPOL/2184/1, "Entretiens Complementaires des Delegations Françaises et Britanniques le 14 aout 1954 à Dakar".
[10] Meanwhile, chiefs on the north bank were quick to point out that traders would be forced to travel through Senegalese territory for lack of a decent road.

the Casamance River and hoped to persuade the authorities in Bathurst to follow suit. A decrepit ferry service was compounded by a British decision to introduce what was regarded as discriminatory fares for Senegalese vehicles in 1954.[11] The French believed that the situation would best be resolved by permitting them to operate their own service. The grounds for broaching the issue lay in Article 5 of the 1904 Convention. This notionally transferred the most easterly town of Yarbutenda to the French, and provided that if the river turned out not to be navigable up to that point, then rights of transit on the river should be settled by agreement between the parties. There were, however, various difficulties with relying on this agreement. The precise location of Yarbutenda had initially been a bone of contention because its disputed location – either on the north or the south bank – affected where the arc of a circle would define the easternmost limits of the Gambia. But by this point in the proceedings, Yarbutenda had ceased to exist, and anyway the British had failed to ratify the original agreement. The basis for staking a French claim to the river bank consequently seemed tenuous and thoughts returned to negotiating a deal whereby the ferries might be co-managed or operated by French firms.[12]

In December 1955, a joint meeting was convened to thrash out the various points in contention. The Gambian delegation, which included J.C. Faye, conceded the importance of modernizing the ferries, but when the French delegation raised the possibility of operating their own service, this was rebuffed on the grounds that it would infringe on Gambian sovereignty.[13] The most the Gambian delegation would concede was modernization of the roads and an improved ferry service to be run entirely by the Gambia, as well as a negotiated agreement on tariffs.[14] The final agreement in March 1956 included "a categorical assurance that the proposed new ferry will give an efficient service" and "that there will be no discrimination in the charges paid by the Gambian and non-Gambian users of the proposed new ferry service."[15] On paper, this met the minimal French demands, and it was confidently

---

[11] By a decree of August 1954, the tariff was raised to £2 10 s for non-Gambian vehicles and £1 10 s for locally registered ones. CAOM, Affaires Politiques: 1AFFPOL/2184/1, A. Chataigner, Consul de France in Bathurst, to Ministre des Affaires Etrangeres, Paris (23 November 1954).

[12] CAOM, Affaires Politiques: 1AFFPOL/2184/1, Ministre de la France d'Outre-Mer to Ministre des Affaires Etrangeres (31 October 1955).

[13] J.C. Faye was Minister of Communications. CAOM, Affaires Politiques: 1AFFPOL/2184/1, Haute Commissaire de la Republique en l'AOF to Ministre des Affaires Etrangeres (24 December 1955).

[14] CAOM, Affaires Politiques: 1AFFPOL/2184/1, Chataigner to Ministre des Affaires Etrangeres (12 December 1955).

[15] CAOM, Affaires Politiques: 1AFFPOL/2184/1, "Agreement Concerning the Construction of the Trans-Gambian Road and Matters Incidental Thereto and Concerning Arrangement for the Ferry Service", signed 10 March 1956.

predicted that the Gambia would be sucked inexorably into the Senegalese orbit.[16] However, in 1964 Gailey was led to conclude that the "ferry service is not only poor, it is dangerous ... The equipment is old and untrustworthy, and if all goes well, the trip across the river takes one hour".[17] In reality, the river crossing continued to represent an irritant in everyday communications between the Casamance and Dakar.

The Case for Union

The fraught negotiations over communications in the 1950s, which took place at a time of relative economic buoyancy, conformed to a familiar pattern in which the Gambian authorities sought to avoid being reduced to a French satellite. But the British authorities began to reconsider their options as the public finances of the Gambia deteriorated significantly at the end of the decade. Part of the reason was that both the world price for groundnuts and the volume of exports fell sharply. The Governor, Sir Edward Windley, indicated that the attempt to raise more income through import duties had backfired because, in the context of a re-valuation of the franc, it "had a crippling effect on trade with neighbouring territories".[18] This was a reference to the decline of the re-export trade that had served the Gambia so well in the past. The recurrent deficit snowballed and Windley reasoned that there was not much the Gambian government could do about it. Part of the problem was that the salaries and pensions of British officials had begun to impose an onerous burden. In 1961, total expenditure came to £2,154,940, of which £1,024,347 (or 48 per cent) was accounted for by emoluments and pensions.[19] In that same year, Medical and Health Services commitments stood at £205,838, of which £140,704 was attributed to emoluments – amounting to no less than 68.4 per cent of expenditure under this head.[20] The other problem was that rising expenditure in areas such as education involved important commitments that could not easily be scaled back – not least because they were so long overdue. Moreover, the Gambian government position was that some of these commitments were "development projects which can contribute to modernizing and diversifying the economy of the Gambia so that it may be better able to meet

---

[16] CAOM, Affaires Politiques: 1AFFPOL/2184/1, Chataigner to Ministre des Affaires Etrangeres (22 March 1956).

[17] Gailey, *History of the Gambia*, p. 174.

[18] Gambia House of Representatives, *The Financial Position: Exchange of Despatches between the Governor and the Secretary of State for the Colonies*, Sessional Paper 11 of 1960 (Bathurst: Government Printer), p. 2.

[19] Gambia, *Financial Report with Appendices for the Year 1961* (Bathurst; Government Printer, 1961), appendix 12, p. 36.

[20] All figures are drawn from Gambia, *Financial Report with Appendices for the Year 1961*, table, p. 35.

its needs on the recurrent account".[21] In other words, it was necessary to invest more to generate income and thereby to fashion a way out of the fiscal blind-alley the colony found itself in. Finally, the government considered it expedient to increase the producer prices for groundnuts because Senegalese producers received a French subsidy that provided a temptation for Gambian producers to sell across the border – with a corresponding loss to the Gambian exchequer. In 1960, the Gambian authorities were reporting a nocturnal 'invasion' of the borderlands of Niumi and Baddibu by French lorries, whose owners sold rice and palm-oil, and purchased groundnuts inside the Gambia. The same report also referred to the widespread Gambian use of donkeys to transport groundnuts into Senegal.[22] In his response to the Gambian government, the Secretary of State, Iain Macleod, acknowledged that a recurrent deficit was inevitable unless there was an exceptional turnaround in the groundnut economy and "a substantial revival of the border trade". The latter was in itself a highly significant admission of the dependence of the Gambian state upon border flows. Macleod committed the British government to the provision of grants-in-aid, but on the understanding that "we cannot contemplate meeting an ever-increasing deficit".[23] In 1961, the grants-in-aid covered about a quarter of recurrent expenditure, which underlined the weakness of the Gambian fiscal position.[24] A key condition was that the budget would have to be approved by the British government in advance, which caused some discomfort because it amounted to a reassertion of metropolitan control at the very moment when the first African government was being ushered into office.

Throughout this exchange over Gambian public finances, the border equation was crucial in framing thinkable solutions. The movement of cash crops and consumer goods had proven to be absolutely integral to the fiscal architecture of the Gambian state. At the same time, it was crucial for the Gambian authorities to do what they could to encourage the free flow of population. As Windley stated with respect to trade with the short-lived Mali Federation:

... I must expect that the present uncomfortable conflict of rival economic systems must continue to operate to the Gambia's detriment for the present. While it does continue, any attempt to increase substantially the revenue by fresh taxation could have the

---

[21] Governor E.H. Windley, to Secretary of State, Iain Macleod, 12 January 1960, *Financial Position*, p. 5

[22] NAGB FIN 1/46 "Groundnut Smuggling (1960)", Assistant Commissioner, Kerewan, to Commissioner for Local Government (22 August 1960).

[23] Macleod to Windley, 17 May 1960, *Financial Position*, p. 8.

[24] J.H. Proctor, "The Gambia's relations with Senegal: the search for partnership", *Journal of Commonwealth Political Studies* 5 (2) 1967, p. 143. The growing funding gap necessitated a rising level of metropolitan contributions, which reached £745,000 in 1965. Tijan Sallah, "Economics and politics in the Gambia", *Journal of Modern African Studies* 28 (4) 1990, p. 624.

opposite effect – either by reduction in the level of commercial activity or even by starting a large-scale emigration of the farming community to neighbouring countries.[25]

In a subsequent letter to London, K.G.S. Smith, the Officer Administering the Government explained:

You will also be aware of the widely held view in the Gambia that price support for our groundnut export should be considered both as a measure to discourage the traffic of produce into neighbouring territories and also to promote production itself – production which could otherwise dwindle from the absence of 'strange farmers' and the migration of Gambian farmers into Senegal.[26]

Continuing to attract 'strange farmers' implied the adoption of a low-tax policy, which existed in tension with the expressed desire to raise the resources needed to maximize development spending. The complex equation worried the Colonial Office, who feared that the colony could become a permanent drain on the British exchequer.

It was an established principle that part of the contribution to the Development Funds should come from internal sources. The colony did receive one significant windfall, which was the return of its share of the balances accumulated by the West African Produce Control Board (WAPB) in 1950. The money was transferred to the Gambia Oilseeds Marketing Board (GOMB) and was later divided into equal halves of £1 million each. One-half was allocated to stabilization of groundnut prices, while the other was reserved for development on the basis of the interest accrued. In 1961, the Farmers' Development Fund paid for development projects costing a total of £60,510. However, this amount remained significantly less than the £527,965 devoted to CDW schemes alongside the additional CDW sums allocated to agricultural research, experimentation and improvement. The latter included significant investments in infrastructure, the most important of which were £112,436 spent on upgrading the Barra ferry terminal and £107,100 on constructing the south bank road between Brikama and Mansakonko. The fact that government contribution was always the lesser again underlined the utter economic dependence on the metropole. On the eve of independence, in 1964, the Governor summed up the picture in these sobering terms:

[O]ur major concern and our major problem on the eve of our independence is that the Government has to pay out more than it earns even to maintain the present level of services. This means that the Government cannot at present provide enough schools, enough hospitals, enough good roads and all those things which go to make for better living: and in turn this means that our people are not so well-informed as they should be and that they must sometimes go ill and hungry because of lack of medical care and

[25] Windley to Macleod, 31 May 1960, *Financial Position*, p.11.
[26] Letter by K.G.S. Smith to Macleod, 9 September 1960, *Financial Position*, p. 13.

because the country is not as productive and as prosperous as it could be. It is true that we receive, and that we have every reason to hope that we will continue to receive, substantial assistance towards development from overseas, at present almost wholly from the United Kingdom, but this in itself does not offer, nor can it offer in the future, a complete solution.[27]

At this point, it is necessary to say something more about what was informing Senegalese government policy, bearing in mind Robert Bates' argument about the ways in which urban interests generally trumped rural ones.[28] The collapse of the Mali Federation had forced Senghor to fall back upon forging a close relationship with France. The bi-lateral agreements included French subsidization of civil service salaries, which was of particular importance because Senegal had been forced to absorb large numbers of civil servants after the winding up of l'AOF.[29] In addition, France offered to maintain staff in key sectors of the bureaucracy under the rubric of technical assistance. At the same time, the economic agreements committed Senegal to the perpetuation of a protected market for French manufactured goods in return for guaranteed prices for agricultural exports. The broad continuity was accentuated by the domination of the import/export trade by a handful of French commercial houses, whose interests in nurturing local industry were initially limited. In a detailed examination of the textile sector, Catherine Boone has detailed how the attempt by local firms to enter into competition with imported textiles, by undercutting the markups charged by the French commercial houses, was initially defeated.[30] She goes on to reveal how this culminated in an alliance between the French commercial houses and aspirant local producers, underwritten by preferential duties and tax breaks granted by the Senegalese state. While the market for Senegalese textiles did expand, French commercial dominance was actually reinforced. The inevitable result was the high costs that were passed on to consumers. Boone concludes that:

Senegal paid a high price for the industrial growth achieved in the 1960s. Tax concessions granted to French firms reduced industry's contribution to government revenues to almost zero ... The government, however, did not come away empty-handed. It shared in the benefits of market protection. Import taxes and duties constituted the

---

[27] The Gambia, *Summary of Proceedings of the Twenty-First Conference of Chiefs and Area Council Members Held at Georgetown, McCarthy Island Division from the 25th to 27th February, 1964.* Sessional Paper No. 14 of 1964, p. 5.

[28] Robert Bates, *Markets and States in Tropical Africa: The Political Basis of Agricultural Policies* (Berkeley: University of California Press, 1981).

[29] Donal B. Cruise O'Brien, *Saints and Politicians: Essays in the Organisation of a Senegalese Peasant Society* (Cambridge: Cambridge University Press, 1975), p. 130.

[30] Catherine Boone, *Merchant Capital and the Roots of State Power in Senegal, 1930–1985* (Cambridge: Cambridge University Press, 1992), pp. 75–7.

government's leading source of fiscal receipts. Consumers bore these costs of taxes and rents generated by 'sell dear' policies.[31]

Given the continued French domination of the import–export trade, and what little industry existed, Senegalese businessmen were squeezed into narrow marketing channels where the returns were relatively high. The most important of these became the distribution of the country's staple, rice. The Casamance was a wetland region, where rice yields were not that far below those of South-East Asia. The raiding of granaries during the war amounted to a back-handed recognition of Jola productivity, but it also underscored that there had been little attempt to actively support peasant production. The failure to resolve the infrastructural bottlenecks in the 1950s provided an additional reason why the Senegalese authorities postponed plans to promote rice culture. After independence, the shortfall of rice led to increasing imports through the port of Dakar. From 1964, rice was imported under a state monopoly and was then distributed through a quota system to a mixture of private (including French) companies, merchants' co-operatives, independent businessmen and smaller traders.[32] The irony was that the staple dish of most Senegalese – *tiep bou dien*, or rice with fish – was based on a commodity that increasingly came from distant lands and that was relatively expensive.[33] All of this was part of an attempt to juggle an alliance with France, the demands of Senegalese entrepreneurs and the strong consumption preferences of the population.

The relatively large bureaucracy continued to proliferate in the decade after independence, with the result that the general services consumed over 40 per cent of current expenditure by 1971/72 – with 18.27 per cent of the total absorbed by the general administration (see Table 9.2). The government sought to maintain a wage freeze, and there are divergent interpretations as to whether it managed to curb an increase in the size of the bureaucracy.[34]

---

[31] Boone, *Merchant Capital*, p. 119.

[32] This was ripe for abuse because quota allocations were often traded on. Edward J. Schumaker, *Politics, Bureaucracy and Rural Development in Senegal* (Berkeley, Los Angeles and London: University of California Press, 1975), pp. 146–7.

[33] In 1968, it was estimated that domestic paddy rice accounted for 100,000 metric tons and imported rice for 185,000 metric tons. Schumaker, *Politics, Bureaucracy and Rural Development*, p. 191. The preferred fish for *tiep bou dien* was *thiof*, which was caught in Senegambian coastal waters.

[34] On one view, the bureaucracy mushroomed from 10,000 functionaries around the time of independence to 34,900 in 1965 and 61,000 in 1973. Donal B. Cruise O'Brien, "Ruling class and peasantry in Senegal, 1960–1976: the politics of a monocrop economy", in Rita Cruise O'Brien (ed.), *Political Economy of Underdevelopment: Dependence in Senegal* (Beverly Hills and London: Sage, 1979), p. 213. But according to a World Bank assessment, "Employment by the Senegalese government has remained roughly stationary since pre-independence times." World Bank, *Current Economic Position and Prospects for Senegal* (Washington DC: World Bank, 1968), p. 3.

Table 9.2 *Share of recurrent government expenditure, Senegal (in billions CFA francs and percentages)*

Item	1962/1963	1967/1968	1971/1972
A. *General services*	11.3 (37.80%)	14.17 (41.42%)	16.45 (40.39%)
General administration	7.10	7.01	7.44
Defence	2.36	4.10	4.96
Foreign affairs	0.63	0.88	1.40
Finance	1.21	2.18	2.65
B. *Social services*	8.57 (28.67%)	10.87 (31.77%)	13.32 (32.70%)
Education	5.4	7.27	9.33
Health	2.73	3.16	3.50
Information	0.44	0.44	0.49
C. *Economic services*	2.66 (8.90%)	3.99 (11.66%)	4.52 (11.10%)
Rural development	1.17	1.78	2.31
Public works	0.92	1.05	1.04
Plan	0.18	0.56	0.49
Industry, trade, handicrafts	0.22	0.56	0.56
Tourism	–	0.04	0.03
Other	0.17	–	0.09
D. Common expenditure	3.01 (10.07%)	2.22 (6.49%)	2.87 (7.05%)
E. Interest on debt	0.41 (1.37%)	0.28 (0.82%)	0.40 (0.98%)
F. Other	3.94 (13.18%)	2.68 (7.83%)	3.17 (7.78%)
Total	100%	100%	100%
	29.89 billion CFA	34.21 billion CFA	40.73 billion CFA

Source: World Bank, *Senegal: Tradition, Diversification and Economic Development*, table 5.3, pp. 316–17.

Be that as it may, given the limitations placed on import substitution industrialization, civil service employment in 1970 (61,000) almost matched the numbers involved in other sectors of formal employment (63,000).[35] It was this lopsided profile that led Donal Cruise O'Brien to conclude that state officials had come to constitute a 'ruling class' that reproduced itself at the cost of rural producers.[36]

Bates looked to Cruise O'Brien for confirmation of his thesis about the dominance of an urban coalition. However, there are elements of the Senegalese story that do not square particularly well with this narrative. The first point is that while one could certainly talk of a dominant urban coalition at a time when it was only the population of the Four Communes that held citizenship rights, this was turned upside down in the 1950s when the rural population was fully enfranchised. The lines of division manifested themselves in the electoral

---

[35] Cruise O'Brien, *Saints and Politicians*, pp. 130–1.
[36] Donal B. Cruise O'Brien, "Ruling class and peasantry in Senegal", pp. 213–14.

contest between Lamine Guèye, whose Section Française de l'International Ouvrière (SFIO) had its main support base in the towns, and Senghor's breakaway Bloc Démocratique Sénégalais (BDS), which sought to mobilize the rural vote.[37] After 1951, the BDS and its successor, l'Union Progressiste Sénégalaise (UPS), established an unassailable position, increasing its share of the vote in successive elections from 68 per cent in 1951 to 94 per cent in 1963.[38] The UPS maintained its political dominance by paying particular attention to its alliance with the Muslim brotherhoods whose orientation at that time was overwhelmingly rural. The terms were dramatically re-inscribed shortly after independence during the power struggle between Senghor and his Prime Minister, Mamadou Dia. The latter had relished the opportunity to make a clean break with the colonial model and regarded it as a state imperative to intervene directly in the structures of rural society – all in the name of modernization and development. This posed a direct threat to the relationship between the *marabouts* and their *talibés*. By yielding to their demand that Dia be removed from the government in 1962, Senghor in effect acknowledged that the post-colonial state had to respect certain limits, and conversely that the *marabouts* had a right to protect the semi-autonomous sphere that they had carved out in colonial times.[39] This was fundamental to the design of the larger social contract in Senegal. Had the power struggle of 1962 turned out differently, it would in all likelihood have resulted in a more interventionist state with an even stronger urban orientation.

Secondly, if we examine the tax structure that took shape after independence, the picture was mixed. In the colonial period, *l'impôt* had represented a significant burden on the rural population. Although the tax remained in place, its relative significance receded over time (see Table 9.3). It was much less attractive for an independent government to chase the population for what had always been an unpopular tax. Henceforth, the reconstituted Regional (later Rural) tax became the preserve of newly established Regional authorities, but it only defrayed part of their running costs. At the same time, the contribution of income taxes, which affected the urban wage-earning populations, increased

---

[37] Senghor split from SFIO in 1948. In 1951, the BDS captured both seats to the French National Assembly. In 1956, a number of smaller parties joined with BDS to form the Bloc Populaire Sénégalais (BPS). In 1958, there was a further regrouping following the split between adherents and opponents of the Rassemblement Démocratique Africain (RDA) in West Africa. Those opposed to the RDA formed the Parti du Regroupement Africain (PRA), which in Senegal was comprised of the UPS, which later absorbed Guèye's party. Gerti Hesseling, *Histoire politique du Sénégal: institutions, droit et société* (Paris: Karthala, 1985), pp. 160, 163, 166.

[38] Schumaker, *Politics, Bureaucracy and Rural Development*, p. 26. For a study of the ruling party, see François Zuccarelli, *Un parti unique Africain: l'Union Progressiste Sénégalaise* (Paris: Pichon et Durand-Auzias, 1970).

[39] On the details of this formative episode, see Hesseling, *Histoire politique du Sénégal*, pp. 230–7.

Table 9.3 *Senegalese government revenue (1965/1966–1971/1972),*
in billions of CFA francs

Category	1965/ 1966	1966/ 1967	1967/ 1968	1968/ 1969	1969/ 1970	1970/ 1971	1971/ 1972
A. Direct	*8.43*	*8.43*	*8.56*	*8.69*	*11.03*	*10.95*	*11.15*
Poll taxes[a]	1.20	1.17	1.21	1.06	1.43	1.50	1.64
Income taxes	5.84	5.75	6.12	6.54	7.99	8.13	8.10
Other direct	1.39	1.51	1.23	1.09	1.61	1.32	1.41
B. Indirect	*24.14*	*24.71*	*25.06*	*24.54*	*25.01*	*27.43*	*31.12*
Import taxes	13.17	14.08	14.54	13.59	14.00	15.49	17.95
Export taxes	3.21	2.86	2.68	2.58	1.84	1.61	1.83
Taxes on production	7.76	7.77	7.84	8.37	9.17	10.33	11.34
C. Registration stamp duties	1.19	1.00	0.97	0.97	1.29	1.40	1.43
Total tax	33.76	34.14	34.59	34.20	37.33	39.78	43.70
D. Non-tax revenue	2.07	1.24	1.25	1.99	1.60	1.59	1.43
Grand total	35.83	35.38	35.84	36.19	38.93	41.37	45.13

[a] Includes livestock tax and regional tax.
Source: World Bank, *Senegal: Tradition, Diversification and Economic Development*
(Washington DC: World Bank, 1974), table 5.1, p. 314.

over time and contributed around 20 per cent of revenue in the 1960s.
However, the revenues derived from import duties were the most important
contributor to public finances by some margin.[40] To a large extent, these
represented taxes on consumption, and hence fell disproportionately on the
urban population. The taxes on exports made a significantly smaller financial
contribution, and essentially amounted to a charge on the groundnut economy.
Admittedly, this does not tell the entire story. The creation of the Office de la
Commercialisation Agricole (OCA), which was granted control over the
marketing of groundnuts, enabled the state to introduce a hidden tax through
the practice of systematically paying farmers at well below the world market
price. A World Bank Report of 1972 observed that the levies on groundnut
farmers increased significantly at the end of the preceding decade when world
prices rose faster than producer prices:

Though these profits are not formally budget revenues, they are deposited by the
Groundnut Stabilization Fund at the Tresor and in fact are used heavily to finance
development outlays. For all practical purposes these profits represent an additional tax
on groundnut producers, who have not received the full amount of the improvement in
export prices. Export taxes and marketing profits together resulted in a very substantial
tax on groundnut farmers in the last few years.[41]

[40] World Bank, *Senegal: Tradition, Diversification and Economic Development* (Washington DC:
World Bank, 1974), p. 184.
[41] World Bank, *Senegal*, p. 194.

The Report indeed estimated that the combined total of taxes on groundnuts amounted to between 30 and 35 per cent of the value of the crop.[42] Bates himself estimated that 20 per cent of the Senegalese budget was derived from the export crop economy.[43]

In Senegal, the overall level of taxation was high by African standards. The same World Bank Report observed that "Senegal has little unused tax capacity left: the country is already heavily taxed."[44] It observed that "a large part of total revenues derives from the well-to-do urban classes who have high incomes and have adopted Western consumption patterns".[45] Moreover, a government policy of wage restraint, which saw real wages decline by 25 per cent between 1960 and 1967, is indicative of a willingness to squeeze those in formal employment.[46] The Report concluded that "low income persons living in the towns are probably the worst off in terms of real income ... as they normally pay more taxes than the rural population." Conversely, it made the point that "incomes from most other crops remain virtually untaxed".[47] Hence the taxation of the groundnut economy has to be weighed in the scales against the heavy tax burden imposed on wage workers and the population of Dakar in particular.

The early years of independence witnessed an attempt to piece together a composite social contract in Senegal in which the productive element was dominant, but with hints of something more permissive to follow. Although the ability of the government to deliver on a developmental agenda was limited, investments in urban infrastructure and irrigated agriculture in the lower reaches of the Senegal River Valley continued to conform to a modernist vision of development. At the same time, the Senghor regime made concessions to the Muslim brotherhoods in a way that turned a blind eye to practices bordering on the illicit. This was reflected in the routine corruption that was tolerated within the Centres Régionaux d'Assistance et Développement (CRAD), which connected the OCA and the village co-operatives, and the usury that arose out of the system of delayed payments for groundnuts.[48] These may be considered an example of the 'side-payments' to which Bates

[42] World Bank, *Senegal*, p. 167.   [43] Bates, *Markets and States*, p. 17.

[44] World Bank, *Senegal*, p. 214. In Senegal, taxes amounted to 18.2 per cent of GNP, as opposed to 10.2 per cent in Togo between 1966 and 1968, p. 210a.

[45] World Bank, *Senegal*, pp. 210–11.

[46] Boone, *Merchant Capital*, p. 170. The decline in real wages is examined in more detail in Guy Pfeffermann, *Industrial Labor in the Republic of Senegal* (New York, Washington and London: Praeger, 1968), pp. 234–5. See also Maureen Macintosh, "The political economy of industrial wages in Senegal", in Rita Cruise O'Brien (ed.), *Political Economy of Underdevelopment.*

[47] World Bank, *Senegal*, p. 211.

[48] Cruise O'Brien, *Saints and Politicians*, p. 129; Schumaker, *Politics, Bureaucracy and Rural Development*, p. 165; Catherine Boone, *Political Topographies of the African State: Territorial Authority and Institutional Choice* (Cambridge: Cambridge University Press, 2003), pp. 81–2.

refers. But contrary to the logic of his thesis, the interests that had the greatest political voice were actually the ones that were the most heavily taxed – which conforms to one variant of the classic tax bargain as I have indicated in Chapter 1. Conversely, the interests that were considered marginal to the long-term politics of the regime – especially the regions that produced rainfed staples and reared cattle – often paid far lower taxes. This is better accounted for in Boone's interpretation, according to which states generally feel impelled to bargain with well-organized interests.[49]

The Senegalese social contract of the 1960s was inherently unstable as all the constituent elements depended on what was unfolding across the border. In the early 1960s, the Gambian government found itself torn between alternative strategies. A low-tax policy would revitalize the re-export trade, stem the outflow of groundnuts to Senegal and conceivably relieve the pressure on public finances. But none of this would be to the liking of the Senegalese authorities. The alternative was to harmonize economic policies and infrastructural decisions with Dakar and strike a bargain on the division of the fiscal receipts. In Bathurst itself, there was some acceptance that the dog-in-the manger approach of days gone by had hobbled the economy of the Gambia. As K.G.S. Smith himself expressed it: "The separation of the Gambia from its hinterland has progressively retarded the economic development of the country."[50] Hence, opening up the Senegambia through infrastructural investments could provide a much-needed boost to the sub-regional economy and lead to greater traffic passing down the Gambia River towards the port at Bathurst. Provided the Senegalese and Gambian authorities could agree on a division of the revenues, there might be much to recommend closer integration.

It was Windley who was the first to actively pursue the case for closer links with Senegal. His encouragement induced the government of P.S. N'jie to agree to an Inter-Ministerial Committee. Welch observes that it only met twice prior to fresh elections in the Gambia in 1962, but it reached agreements on the upgrading of roads, co-operation on the running of telephone services and further measures to minimize the delays on the Trans-Gambian highway.[51] In 1962, the governments of the Gambia and Senegal jointly approached the United Nations (UN) to request a technical mission to assess the prospects for association. The Van Mook report of 1964 framed the choice in terms of two central issues that were being widely debated in the region. The first concerned viability of the Gambia as a separate entity. The Report queried

---

[49] Boone, *Political Topographies*.

[50] K.G.S. Smith, Officer Administering the Government of the Gambia, Bathurst, to Macleod, 9 September 1960, *Financial Position*, p. 14.

[51] Welch, *Dream of Unity*, pp. 279–80. The Committee was supposed to meet quarterly. It only met on one more occasion after the election of Jawara. Proctor, "Gambia's relations", pp. 148–9.

some conventional wisdom about Senegal's 'big brother' role and the Gambia's inherent lack of viability, but it was prepared to entertain a positive case for integration:

In the first place, the question has to be faced whether the Gambia will be able to bear, by itself the cost and responsibility of international statehood. This question is not answered by the mere statement of fact that the Gambia is small and even today needs considerable outside help to pay the current cost of its Government and services. Many larger countries, including Senegal, receive sizeable subsidies for their regular expenditure, although not always in the form of grants-in-aid to cover a budgetary deficit; other independent states exist that are neither larger nor more populous than the Gambia. This fact by itself, however, does not recommend the creation or the isolated continuation of such weak states if forms of mutual support can be found wholly compatible with their right to self-determination.[52]

This led to a second question about the economic disadvantages to both countries of maintaining artificial borders:

For Senegal it means a partial isolation of the Casamance, even though the transgambian road has eased the access to the southern province. It poses the problem of guarding a customs frontier of inordinate length that can easily be crossed at many places. It finally deprives southern Senegal and the adjoining countries of the full use of the splendid waterway and harbor of the Gambia river. For the Gambia, it means that the part of the river basin which forms the main agricultural asset of the country cannot be fully and rationally exploited and that Bathurst cannot become the port of a much wider area, which its natural advantages entitle it to be.[53]

This passage underlined the contention that the Gambia had as much to gain from integration as Senegal did.

The Report weighed the relative merits of three possible alternatives. The first was the outright integration of the Gambia with Senegal, albeit with the possibility of special protections for the identity of the former. The mission considered that this was unlikely to be acceptable in the Gambia at a time when opinion was moving in the direction of a more cautious attitude towards relations with Senegal.[54] The second option was a weaker politico-economic association that would preserve the legal personality of both countries, whilst setting up a central authority to oversee common functions that might be augmented over time. The mission considered that there might already be enough support for a Senegambian federation to proceed provided the terms were clearly set out. Economic and defence agreements and others covering

---

[52] The Gambia, *Report on the Alternatives for Association between the Gambia and Senegal* (By Hubertus J. Van Mook, Max Graessli, Henri Monfrioni and Hendrik Weisfelt, Appointed Under the United Nations Programme of Technical Assistance), Sessional Paper No. 13 of 1964, pp. 5–6.
[53] *Report on the Alternatives*, p. 6.   [54] *Report on the Alternatives*, pp. 19–20, 24–5.

common diplomatic representation, which the Senegalese government tabled as the minimum requirements, could also be written into a constitutional document in a way that would satisfy Gambian opinion. Finally, the mission considered the alternative of a loose 'entente' in which the sovereign countries would agree to co-operate in matters of common interest. Of the three options, the mission considered that federation offered the most advantages in the current circumstances. But the mission was explicit that an immediate priority should be the abolition of the customs frontier regardless of whichever option was chosen:

The frontiers of the Gambia, which is entirely surrounded by Senegal, are artificial and arbitrary ... Strict surveillance of the frontier is impossible, which means that smuggling cannot be controlled effectively. To stamp out the contraband traffic would necessitate a customs apparatus, the costs of which would be out of proportion to the scale of the smuggling and to the foreseeable results; besides which there is a chronic shortage of staff. The abolition of the customs frontier does not involve immediately the disappearance of the political frontier. However, as economic integration proceeds the frontier loses its importance. This fact is likely to make the two Governments intensify their efforts to achieve a rapprochement in constitutional and legislative matters.[55]

This was an explicit acknowledgement of the fact that the realities of the border imposed constraints on what was practically possible.

Following publication of the Van Mook report, negotiations in May 1964 confirmed that the two governments adhered to quite different preferences. While the Gambian team favoured a looser form of confederation, the Senegalese argued for greater powers to be conferred on a central authority.[56] A fundamental sticking point was over a proposed Customs union, which Jawara maintained would drive up the cost of living in the Gambia and have an adverse effect on already tenuous government revenues.[57] In effect, the Gambians had reverted to the view that a combination of low taxes and open borders was the most attractive option, at least in the short run. The Senegalese authorities were deeply concerned that the net effect would be to stimulate smuggling, thereby pulling the rug from underneath their own finely poised economic strategy. The most that could be achieved, therefore, was the agreement to two treaties of co-operation, one covering foreign policy and another covering defence and security – to which a third accord was added later on, covering the integrated management of the Gambia River Basin. The final outcome therefore came closest to the third alternative canvassed by the UN mission, in the sense that the governments only really committed themselves to co-operation at some indeterminate point in the future. With the advent of Gambian independence in February 1965, the best that could be

---

[55] *Report on the Alternatives*, p. 61.   [56] Welch, *Dream of Unity*, pp. 289–90.
[57] Proctor, "Gambia's relations", p. 152.

hoped for was to build mutual trust based on practical results. In subsequent years, there was limited progress in implementing the agreements. Under the first treaty, High Commissioners were exchanged who were empowered to attend Cabinet meetings in the other country when matters of common interest arose. In fact, this never happened. Equally, the Gambia never made use of the Senegalese diplomatic missions abroad.[58] As far as defence and security co-operation are concerned, this was left on ice for the time being. Equally, progress on the Gambia River basin was painfully slow. The one incremental step forward was the creation of an Inter-Ministerial Committee in 1967, following the signature of a Treaty of Association, which provided for regular meetings at the highest level.

The Border As a Lived Space

It is tempting to blame elite intransigence for the failure of integration initiatives to bear fruit. Given that the Senegalese authorities were in favour of erasing the border, or at least of minimizing its economic significance, most of the blame has accrued to the Gambian side. In 1975, an article in *Marchés Tropicaux* blamed the obstructionism of the Creole (Aku) elite in Bathurst whose facility with English and Christian identity made them wary of playing second fiddle to a Francophone, Muslim majority.[59] There is a measure of truth to this claim. Jeggan Senghor, for example, quotes from an editorial in the *Vanguard*, at a time when the Malian Federation was still operational, in which fears were expressed about being turned into "a tiny minority in a sea of French-educated, infinitely more go-ahead Malians (Senegalese)".[60] However, this is only part of the story, as Senghor goes on to indicate. A far more significant reason was that an incipient social contract in the Gambia hinged on the continuation, and indeed the expansion, of the contraband trade. The Van Mook report estimated, on the basis of an earlier French study, that smuggling was worth about £138,000 to the Gambian exchequer in 1958.[61] Given that total Customs revenue for that year amounted to £1.14 million, the report concluded that the loss to the Gambia of economic harmonization was likely to be marginal. However, it conceded that significantly higher estimates for the volume of the trade existed. Moreover, 1958 was an exceptional year. If the base year had been taken as 1960, when Customs revenue had slipped to £819.4 million and the volume of contraband may well have doubled, the

---

[58] Omar A. Touray, *The Gambia and the World: A History of the Foreign Policy of Africa's Smallest State, 1965–1995* (Hamburg: Institute of African Studies, 2000), p. 34.

[59] "Gambie et Sénégambie", *Marchés Tropicaux et Méditerranée*, 9 mai 1975, pp.1354–55.

[60] The quote is from the article. Jeggan C. Senghor, *The Politics of Senegambian Integration, 1958–1994* (New York: Peter Lang, 2008), pp. 36–7.

[61] This was based on a report by De Christen. *Report on the Alternatives*, p. 56.

report could have come to a very different conclusion.[62] It is possible that around a fifth of Gambian Customs revenue was attributable to smuggling – leaving aside the official trade, some of which was also intended for re-export. This was a paramount consideration in view of the fiscal travails of the Gambia in the early 1960s. Indeed, it was the very reason why the Jawara government turned it back on the recommendations of the report.

But more importantly, a very substantial segment of the Gambian population would have been materially worse off if the government had conceded to Senegalese preferences. As I have indicated, the independence deal that was struck by the Senegalese government was one in which, in return for a premium paid on Senegalese groundnuts, French imports were granted a privileged status.[63] Because the Gambia sourced imports from where they were cheapest – typically from Asia – and lowered its import duties in the early 1960s, the cost of living would have risen significantly if the Gambia had signed up to an economic union. In 1963/64, the Van Mook report estimated that Gambians paid £4.5 (CFA 3,200) per capita in taxes, whereas Senegalese paid as much as £14 (CFA 10,000).[64] It also estimated that the cost of living in Dakar was between 30 and 50 per cent higher than in Bathurst, while in the rural areas the French study referred to above came to the higher figure of 50 per cent.[65] For the population of Bathurst and for the rural population alike, there was little to recommend closer integration. This would help to explain why the government negotiating position was so uncontroversial in the Gambia where a grassroots movement for integration was striking only for its absence. In the border regions of Senegal, there was an appreciation that it was access to cheaper goods from the Gambia that made the necessities of life that bit more affordable. In effect, because border populations of Sine-Saloum, the Casamance and eastern Senegal benefited from everyday commerce, we have to regard smuggling as integral to rural livelihoods across much of the countryside. The aggregate figures tend not to capture these spatial nuances, based as they are on the abstractions of national statistics. According to estimates, smuggling accounted for around 60–70 per cent of Senegalese shoe, 50 per cent of textile and 80 per cent of tobacco imports in 1961/62.[66] The estimate that between 50 and 60 per cent of the matches entering Senegal

---

[62] The report concluded that "In Senegal, as in the Gambia, the State, the traders and the businessmen will all benefit in the long run." *Report on the Alternatives*, p. 70. However, things were not so obvious in the short- to medium-run. The argument that there would also be a net savings in Customs administration has to be qualified because this was actually skeletal outside of Bathurst.

[63] Senghor, *Politics of Senegambian Integration*, pp. 41–2.

[64] *Report on the Alternatives*, p. 77.

[65] The Report felt that the De Christen estimate for the rural areas was too high, but without giving reasons. *Report on the Alternatives*, pp. 55–6.

[66] *Report on the Alternatives*, p. 58.

were contraband may seem trivial, but these were the kind of everyday items that featured prominently in the lives of villagers. A match factory had been constructed in Dakar in 1959, with an output of 19,000 cases (133 million boxes). In 1960, the importation of 3,356 cases through Bathurst was far in excess of local consumption – given that the whole of Nigeria only imported 12,000 cases – which pointed strongly to smuggling activity.[67] It was in the nature of things that much of this trade tended to be consumed in close proximity to the international border.

As important is the fact that urban and rural incomes in the Gambia revolved around the workings of cross-border trade. In Banjul, the larger merchants had historically been French, but Lebanese and Mauritanians had made significant inroads after the war – initially in produce buying, but increasingly in the re-export trade as well. In the period just before independence, a handful of Gambians assumed a prominent role, the most celebrated being Alhaji Momodou N'Jie who featured prominently in Berkeley Rice's much unloved profile of the Gambia at independence.[68] For our purposes what is worth noting is that N'Jie's commercial links stretched across the sub-region, while inside the Gambia his lines of credit extended to the far east of the country as well as to the wharf towns on both banks of the river. Larger traders worked in close association with a myriad of small traders who were physically located in the borderlands. In addition, there were the vehicle operators, drivers, donkey cart owners and carriers, to mention only the most obvious players, all of whom made a living from the ebb and flow of the border economy. These people often originated from one side of the border and worked on the other, thus investing in both a literal and a figurative sense in its existence. Although traders and their facilitators would arguably have adjusted to whatever dispensation existed, it is certainly the case that integration would have created more losers than winners – both in the Gambia as well as in the border regions of Senegal.

It could be argued, of course, that this is to place too much emphasis upon commerce and to ignore the many practical impediments and inconveniences experienced by ordinary people who were not immersed in trade. Through the correspondence between the Gambian and Senegalese authorities, it is possible to identify numerous incidents in which accusations about harassment and illegal seizures of cattle and goods were made against state officials. In the 1950s, both sets of authorities become more assiduous in demanding passports

---

[67] "La contrebande à la frontière de la Gambie représente un danger réel pour l'essor des jeunes industries dakaroises", *Marchés Tropicaux et Méditerranée*, No. 747, 5 mars 1960, p. 596.

[68] Rice, *Enter Gambia*, pp. 215–19. See also Mohamed Mbodji, "D'une frontière à l'autre, ou l'histoire de la marginalisation des commerçants Senegambiens sur la longue durée: la Gambie de 1816 à 1979", in Boubacar Barry and Leonhard Harding (eds.), *Commerce et commerçants en Afrique de l'Ouest: le Sénégal* (Paris: l'Harmattan, 1992), pp. 226–30.

and often used the inability to produce a document as an excuse to refuse entry or even to deport people considered undesirables.[69] Many of the misunderstandings arose out of the lack of clarity about where the border ran. Problems usually came to light when one administration or the other attempted to levy taxes, or seized cattle and goods, and met with local opposition. During the 1930s, the French and British authorities had sought to settle some of the problem cases and agreed on the need to demarcate a no-man's land to avoid any further ambiguity. But farmers continued to encroach on the open spaces, leading to renewed difficulties in the 1940s. In the early 1950s, when the British authorities used aerial photography to produce maps on a larger scale, they found that some of the earlier agreements conflicted with the formal boundary agreements.[70] The French authorities were aware of the underlying problem, but like the British they were loathe to reopen the issue for fear that they might lose territory and create yet one more complication in intergovernmental negotiations. A mutual policy of drift perpetuated the uncertainty along many stretches of the common border. This was a source of concern to some traditional authorities but was a boon to other actors who exploited the situation in order to avoid paying taxes. In 1945, the Governor-General of l'AOF had drawn attention to the Gambian village of Nioro (in Kiang) that had relocated twenty metres southwards, apparently bringing it into the Casamance.[71] Because this was notionally a Gambian village, delicate issues over tax collection arose. The Governor-General noted that the lack of boundary pillars created some ambiguity, but he clearly suspected that the relocation was a calculated bid to gain more land while avoiding paying tax.

Some of the daily irritation had the effect of rendering the border more rather than less salient in the eyes of local actors. The reputation of the Senegalese *douaniers* for arbitrariness antagonized border populations in the Gambia. The latter channelled complaints to the authorities who then took them up with their Senegalese counterparts. In fact, the Gambian authorities gained much of their day-to-day information not from surveillance, but from what reached them by way of petitions. The other source of intelligence was the *alkalos* and *chefs de village* in the Gambia and Senegal respectively. On the Senegalese side of the border, the chiefs were expected to assist the *douaniers* in their work. On the Gambian side, despite misgivings, selected *alkalos* and *seyfos* functioned as revenue collectors, on the basis of a 10 per cent commission, because the Customs service insisted that it was not cost

---

[69] The context was concern about the level of criminal activity in border areas.

[70] NAGB CSO 10/302 "Anglo-French Boundary", A.N.W. Waddell to R.G. Miller, Fareham, Sussex (16 December 1952)

[71] CAOM 1 AFFPOL/2148/8 "Affaires Politiques", Gouverneur-Générale de l'AOF to Ministre des Colonies (2 August 1945).

effective to maintain a substantive presence.[72] These makeshift arrangements placed a burden on the shoulders of the *alkalos*, even as it created some opportunities for enrichment. The Trans-Gambian highway posed a particular challenge because the authorities believed that the *alkalos* would be left to cope with the additional trade that was funnelled through the border aperture.[73] However, the performance of these devolved functions also gave chiefs a stake in the border at least as much as it gave the authorities a continuing stake in chieftaincy. In 1952, the Commissioner of the Western Division wrote to the Collector of Customs expressing concern about the degree of latitude being exercised by the *alkalo* of Barra on the northern border:

> May I draw to your attention the fact that George Senghore, the Alkali of Bara and customs collector there, has no copy of the current tariff from which to assess the duty he collects. In consequence he appears to impose whatever charge he feels is appropriate. If you would send to this office copies of the current table of duties for the border trade, I will have a translation made for him and post a copy to the Police Station.[74]

It transpired that the *alkalo* had a schedule of duties dating back to 1943 but had never received the revised list from 1946. This particular chief performed an essential function at a busy border crossing and clearly benefited from the performance of this work. Between 1948 and 1953, the *alkalo* had collected duties to the tune of £5,095 and had received a substantial commission of £511 as his reward.[75]

This brings us to the final factor in the larger equation, which was the influence exercised by the traditional authorities themselves. In Senegal, a law of January 1960 restructured the framework of administration, creating a three-tier hierarchy of *régions*, *cercles* and *arrondissements*. The Casamance survived as a single region (one of seven), which Boone suggests was a political decision, arising out of a fear of feeding Jola particularism.[76] The *chefs d'arrondissement* were henceforth government appointees, while the canton chiefs were abolished altogether as a category of superior chiefs.[77] In the Casamance, where there had been so many re-organizations in the past, the latest innovation was arguably not so consequential. Elected Rural Councils

---

[72] The *seyfos* employed Badge Messengers to carry out much of the work.

[73] ANS 11D1/251 "Affaires Politiques et Administratives (APA): Relations Avec la Gambie", C. Guy for Commissioner Central Division to Collector of Customs (16 November 1955).

[74] NAGB CUS 1/4 "Collector of Customs, Border Trade and Smuggling", R.W. Mansfield, Commissioner Western Division, Brikama, to Collector of Customs, Bathurst (10 March 1952).

[75] NAGB CUS 1/4 "Collector of Customs", Collector to Financial Secretary, Bathurst (11 February 1954).

[76] Boone, *Political Topographies*, pp. 117–18.

[77] In the short-term, some canton chiefs were recruited as *chefs d'arrondissement*. Schumaker, *Politics, Bureaucracy and Rural Development*, pp. 87–9.

were only added to the institutional architecture some years after independence, which meant that it was the *chefs de village* who served as the interface
with the *chefs d'arrondissement*. In the areas that comprise the object of this
study, the village chiefs possessed little inherent legitimacy, except in the
Mandinka towns along the coastal seaboard. There was no formal mechanism
that enabled traditional authorities to meet together or to articulate a common
agenda even if they had taken an active interest in some form of union with
the Gambia. In the Gambia, on the other hand, the British authorities were
reluctant to abandon a system of governance that relied on the intermediary
functions performed by the traditional authorities. Local government structures
were introduced only two years before Gambian independence, that is in 1963,
in the shape of elected Area Councils. Before that point the administration
relied entirely on the established hierarchy of *seyfos* and *alkalos*. The Chiefs'
Conferences, which rotated between the main towns in the Gambia, provided a
regular forum for the government to channel information downwards, while
affording an opportunity for the *seyfos* to make their views known on particular issues. Although they exhibited a keen interest in matters relating to roads
and the level of import duties, there is no evidence to suggest that they openly
supported integration with Senegal.[78] *Seyfos* in the Gambia had to put up with
more administrative interference than their counterparts in the Gold Coast,
but they also enjoyed greater status by comparison with the village chiefs
in Senegal – which, after all, was the only comparison that really mattered.
Looking across the border, the *seyfos* would have been only too conscious of
the fact that chiefs in Senegal were treated as minor functionaries.

Conclusion

In this chapter, I have advanced two main propositions. The first is that while
there there was a predisposition amongst key players to pursue some form of
closer union between the Senegal and the Gambia, there was a distinct lack of
urgency amongst the population of the two countries – and least of all in the
borderlands themselves. The French authorities and incoming Senegalese
politicians were both adamantly in favour of something like a confederation,
whereas the British came to the belated conclusion that if the Gambia was
not viable as an independent country, it made sense for it to seek a closer
relationship. But politicians in the Gambia were less sure, and in part they were

---

[78] For example, at a joint meeting between the chiefs and members of the newly created Area
Councils in 1964, which was addressed by Dawda Jawara and each of his Ministers, *seyfos* from
the north bank expressed their dissatisfaction at the decision to locate the main road on the south
bank, pointing out that traders would be forced to pass through Senegalese territory because of
the poor state of the roads. Gambia, *Proceedings of Twenty-First Conference*, p. 16.

responding to pressure from below. It was very clear that a Customs union, in particular, would have increased the cost of living for Gambians, as well as for many Senegalese who depended on smuggled items, and would have undercut the livelihoods of the many who depended on cross-border trade for work. Given that mobility was never placed in question, there were good reasons for ordinary people to favour the retention of the border. When the Senegalese authorities attempted to ratchet up border controls, in an effort to place pressure on their Gambian counterparts, they merely confirmed a popular view that it was better to remain separate.

The second proposition is that the composite social contracts in the Gambia and Senegal, which were built on very different foundations, were deeply embedded in border dynamics. In Senegal, the efforts of the Senghor regime to reconcile urban, rural and external interests around the expansion of groundnut production and the nurturing of home-grown industries presumed an ability to control what passed through the borders. Rampant smuggling threatened the very viability of the alliance. In the Gambia, by contrast, the Jawara regime lacked the resources to appreciably expand the delivery of public goods or to develop its own industries. But what it could do was to keep taxes low, thus attracting contraband groundnuts from Senegal and nourishing a re-export trade in manufactured goods. This helped to sustain the livelihoods of countless Gambians in Banjul and in the countryside alike. But even more fundamentally, the smuggling trade was what underpinned Gambian public finances. Within a few years of independence, the Gambia was functioning as an archetypal entrepôt state governed according to the logic of a permissive social contract. This made it virtually impossible for the Jawara regime to seriously contemplate the harmonization of economic policies with Senegal. In the next chapter, I consider how far the same was true of the trans-Volta.

10   Forging the Nation, Contesting the Border
Identity Politics and Border Dynamics in the Trans-Volta

In this chapter, I perform a parallel exercise to that of Chapter 9 with a focus on the trans-Volta and the Gold Coast. I revisit the question of why the Ewe/Togoland unification movement, which did enjoy a groundswell of popular support in the 1940s and 1950s, ultimately fell short of fulfilling its objectives and why there was actually a hardening of the boundary in the decade after the independence. This entails a close investigation of local, national and transboundary entanglements. The Ewe/Togoland case is ostensibly different not merely because there was a popular discourse that took aim at existing borders, but also because ethnicity was central to the political debate: that is, the border was initially framed as a specifically Ewe problem, whereas the Senegal–Gambia border was rarely articulated as a matter affecting the Mandinka or Jola as ethnic collectivities. But the difference should not be exaggerated for the reason that the unification movement after 1951 focused on upholding the historic integrity of the two Togolands, which was comparable to the insistence that the Senegambia represented an organic whole. Part of the reason for the discursive shift was that the Ewe ethnic category came to be contested by its notional constituency, while many non-Ewes, including the Agotime and the Central Togo minorities, needed to be brought into the fold. The eventual outcome was that British Togoland was swallowed whole by Ghana, whereas French Togoland entered the world of independent nations as a micro-state with an uncertain future. The rupture between the political leaders in the successor countries was more rancorous than in the Senegambia, which helps to explain why so little effort was devoted towards promoting cross-border co-operation in the decade that followed. However, this also had much to do with the sedimentation of quite distinct social contracts in Ghana and Togo. Much like in the Senegambia, these were contingent on bordering processes that played out differently on the two sides of the line.

Unification Politics in the Trans-Volta

I have just returned from a hurried trip through Togoland where I was struck by how little had been done to develop the Mandated Territory. In the

357

Gold Coast itself the roads are, generally speaking, very good: in Togoland they are very bad. In the Gold Coast, telegraph and telephone communication is provided at every important centre: in Togoland no such facilities exist. In some cases even the work done by the Germans has been allowed to deteriorate. Although nothing is in writing on the subject I understand that [Governor] Hodson, fearing (before the present war) the possibility that the mandated Territory would be given up deliberately discouraged any expenditure on development and refused to approve of some much-needed works.[1]

From the start, the debate concerning the future of boundaries in the trans-Volta took a different turn from that in the Senegambia. First of all, the issue of the viability of a small colony did not arise, at least initially, because the French were intent on absorbing their Trust Territory into the much larger political constellation of the French Union, whereas the British aimed to merge British Togoland into the Gold Coast. Neither side contemplated the reunification of the two halves of former German Togo or the perpetuation of standalone territories. Whereas the British were touted as possible administrators of a unified Togoland, they had no desire to antagonize their French counterparts and did not lend any credence to such scenarios. After the mutual recriminations of the Vichy years, the British and the French closed ranks at the Trusteeship Council and the Fourth Committee of the General Assembly of the United Nations (UN).[2] Unlike in the Senegambia, the demand for unification emanated from populations within border regions. A second difference is that the centrality of the state in delivering 'development' assumed a quite different role in the larger political debate. Because the preferred option of the British and French authorities presumed a relatively hard boundary, they expressed minimal interest in promoting synergies in the routing of roads and the siting of amenities. Although the Volta River loomed as large as the Gambia River did in official thinking, it was never conceived of as a shared resource that might provide the basis for closer co-operation. One consequence was that British Togoland was initially treated as an afterthought, as Governor Burns was surprised to discover. A sense of neglect after the war was a large part of what motivated the initial demands for unification, much like in British Cameroons.

---

[1] National Archives, Kew, CO 96/776/5 "Post-War Development of Mandated Territory – Togoland", Governor Alan Burns to Arthur Dawe, Colonial Office (6 December 1942). At the height of appeasement, the British government had actually given some consideration to the possibility of handing over its section of Togoland to Germany – although whether this was ever communicated to the Governor or openly discussed remains unclear. Minute by O.G.R. Williams dated 29 December 1942.

[2] D.E.K. Amenumey, *The Ewe Unification Movement: A Political History* (Accra: Ghana Universities Press, 1989), ch. 6.

The complex story of the struggle for Ewe/Togoland unification has been told in great detail,[3] and here I will restrict myself to teasing out some of the principal threads that are important for building the larger comparative argument. Chronologically speaking, the demand for Togoland unification was the first to be clearly articulated. In the 1930s, the Bund der Deutsch Togolander (or Togo Bund) had been led by French Togolanders living in the Gold Coast, but it was also supported by so-called German scholars in British Togoland who identified with the demand for a return to the pre-1919 borders.[4] Interestingly, at this point it was the perceived neglect on the part of the French authorities that was at issue. During the war, there were explicit demands for the removal of the borders when peace returned. These did not make a very clear distinction between demands for the unification of all the Ewe people and the reconstitution of the former borders of German Togo.[5] The assumption was that if Britain were to assume responsibility for French Togoland, that would kill two birds with one stone. After 1945, however, the focus shifted to the explicit demand for unification of the Ewe peoples distributed across three territories: that is, the two Togolands and the Gold Coast colony.

In May 1945, the *Ewe Newsletter* was launched by Daniel Chapman, who was at that time a geography teacher at Achimota College.[6] The maiden issue recognized the diversity amongst the Ewe sub-groups as well as the history of discord between them that I have addressed in Chapters 2 and 3. It attributed these to the divisive consequences of the slave trade, which, as we have seen, has a credible basis in the historical record. But Chapman also treated the shared destiny of the Ewe people as axiomatic, whereas it would be very difficult to claim that historically there was a strong sense of unity. The *Newsletter* maintained that any border that ran through Eweland would be as impractical as it would be illegitimate:

Most of our people toil and suffer in silence in face of the difficulties imposed by the frontier . . . No one who knows anything about the Ewe people can pass from the British to the French side without being struck by the absurdity of the frontier arrangement.

---

[3] See Claude Welch, *Dream of Unity: Pan-Africanism and Political Unification in West Africa* (Ithaca: Cornell University Press, 1966), chs. 2–3; Amenumey, *Ewe Unification Movement*; Paul Nugent, *Smugglers, Secessionists and Loyal Citizens on the Ghana–Togo Frontier: The Lie of the Borderlands Since 1914* (Oxford and Athens: James Currey and Ohio University Press, 2002), ch. 6; and Kate Skinner, *The Fruits of Freedom in Togoland: Literacy, Politics and Nationalism, 1914–2014* (Cambridge: Cambridge University Press, 2015).

[4] Nugent, *Smugglers, Secessionists*, p. 194.

[5] In 1944, the chiefs of Asogli petitioned Governor Alan Burns for "the restoration of Ewe unity", by which they apparently meant Ewes in British and French Togoland. United Nations Trusteeship Council, *Official Records*, Annex Volume II, Appendix A, p. 186. Amenumey, *Ewe Unification Movement*, p. 37.

[6] Welch, *Dream of Unity*, pp. 65–6. An incomplete set of the *News-letter* may be found at NAGA ADM 39/1/339 "Unification of the Ewe Speaking Peoples".

The frontier cuts indiscriminately through villages and farms. A man's house may be on the British side while his farm is on the French side, and vice versa. The real truth of the matter is that it is impossible to set up a satisfactory frontier anywhere between the lower Volta in the Gold Coast and the lower Mono on the western border of Dahomey. One village has close family ties with the next village, and so on, all the way from the River Volta to the River Mono.[7]

The *Newsletter* asserted that a desire for unity amongst the Ewe was frustrated by two concrete realities. The first was the divergent policies of the two governments, notably with respect to language, education and chieftaincy.[8] Specifically, the *Newsletter* echoed some of the self-criticism in colonial circles in its assertion that existing chieftaincy structures served as a barrier to progress whereas what was needed was to establish "sound and progressive native administrations".[9] The second impediment arose from the strict Customs controls that stood in the way of the freedom of trade and the unwarranted hardship this visited upon border populations:

Lome is ... for the people of Eweland, a more convenient seaport town for the purpose of trade than is Accra. But since Lome is in the French territory of Eweland and is separated from the greater half of Eweland by strict frontier regulations, trade between Lome and the greater half of Eweland which is British territory is a protracted impossibility. One side of the Anglo-French frontier may be starving for want of food and yet, because of strict frontier regulations, no help whatever is possible from the other side which may be thriving in plenty. We people of Eweland consider this a grave wrong both socially and economically and do persistently ask that this be brought to an end by the unification of Eweland.[10]

In this, Chapman was picking up on the practical consequences of British–French rivalries that were manifest during the war (see Chapter 8).

The appeals to progress and modernity indicate that Chapman and his colleagues were drawing on the same discursive repertoire as the European authorities were. Indeed, unificationists turned their arguments against them in asserting that they had singularly failed to deliver on the promise of development:

In British Eweland as in French Eweland, the administration has not been particularly energetic in the building of roads and the provision of postal and telegraph services as it has been in the Gold Coast Colony west of the River Volta and in Ashanti.[11]

The echo of Burns' personal observations, which preface this section, is certainly striking. The remedy that the authors proposed was the erasure of

---

[7] *Ewe Newsletter*, No. 2, June 1945, p. 4.   [8] *Ewe Newsletter*, No. 1, 21 May 1945, p. 2.
[9] *Ewe Newsletter*, No. 1, 21 May 1945, p. 2.   [10] *Ewe-Newsletter*, No. 20, December 1946, p. 2.
[11] *Ewe-Newsletter*, No. 10, February 1946, p. 2.

borders between the Ewe people, and the creation of common structures through which they could fulfill their material needs and give vent to their political aspirations.[12] The emphasis on institutional change implied a radical reconfiguration of the states in question.

After the replacement of League of Nations Mandates by UN Trusteeship agreements, Ewe unificationists generated a steady stream of petitions to the Trusteeship Council. The signatures appended by chiefs from all three territories enabled the petitioners to counter any insinuation that they simply represented the opinion of a vocal, educated minority in the urban centres.[13] In due course, they were invited to state their case in person, a privilege that had not been granted under the Mandates. A concerted effort to forge a united front culminated in the formation of the All-Ewe Conference (AEC) in Accra in 1946. The prime movers were Gold Coast Ewe intellectuals, most notably Daniel Chapman, C.H. Chapman and Phillip Gbeho. However, prominent chiefs from all three sections of Eweland associated themselves with the AEC platform. Moreover, the Comité de l'Unité Togolaise (CUT) was a highly valued affiliate in French Togoland, given its political following in the south of the territory. Under the leadership of Sylvanus Olympio, the CUT balanced a nationalist appeal to all parts of French Togoland with support for the demand for Ewe unification and outright opposition to involvement in a French Union.

At the UN, the performance of the administering authorities came under intense scrutiny, especially from representatives of countries that had only recently achieved their own independence.[14] International oversight did not substantially infringe on the exercise of sovereignty, but it did force the authorities to account for their stewardship. In 1947, the Trusteeship Council fielded a series of petitions from the AEC and the CUT to which the British and the French reacted in a manner that set the tone of the future debate. Whereas colonial regimes invested heavily in the spurious certainties of 'tribe', there had been a partial push-back in the trans-Volta precisely because the British and French authorities wanted to pre-empt any expectation that an Ewe tribe should have the right to demand self-determination. In a Joint Memorandum, the governments conceded the existence of "an Ewe tribe which possesses marked characteristics clearly distinguishing them from neighbouring peoples and which is becoming increasingly aware of its own identity."[15] But they immediately closed the door by arguing that Eweland was not viable as a

---

[12] On the pamphleteering of G.K. Tsekpo, see Skinner, *Fruits of Freedom*, pp. 124–5.
[13] Amenumey, *Ewe Unification Movement*, p. 42.
[14] On the role of the UN, see Amenuney, *Ewe Unification Movement*, chs. 6–7.
[15] UN Trusteeship Council, *Official Records*, Second Session, First Part, 20 November 1947–16 December 1947, Memorandum of the Governments of the United Kingdom and France on the Petition of the All-Ewe Conference to the United Nations", p. 27.

distinct political entity and by insisting that Gold Coast Eweland (including Anlo and Peki) was not up for discussion because it was an integral part of the British colony. Going further, they reasoned that unification of the two halves of Togoland was not a realistic option either because it would divide peoples in the north – especially the Dagomba who had actually been reunited by the 1919 adjustment. Instead, the memorandum advocated some practical measures to render the border less of an imposition – in effect seizing on some of the specific complaints that had been raised by the *Ewe Newsletter* in 1945. First of all, the two governments pledged to work towards removing:

as far as possible obstacles which at present impede the movement of individuals and the transport of their personal property, as well as commerce in local goods and the carriage of individual loads of locally-produced foodstuffs. In order to give full effect to these measures, permits and formalities restricting movements across the frontier are already being abolished.

Secondly, they promised to look into the possibility of establishing a conventional zone with a common Customs regime, albeit subject to the French insistence on maintaining exchange controls. Thirdly, the memorandum proposed measures to avoid double taxation and to harmonize the per capita tax burden across the two Togolands. Finally, it recommended the teaching of English and French in schools on either side of the border, as well as funding to facilitate student exchanges. In effect, the memorandum committed the two sets of authorities to facilitating ease of interaction, whilst refusing to entertain the feasibility of repositioning the boundary line itself.

The educational proposals were largely symbolic, whereas the promise to free up the movement of people and foodstuffs was potentially more significant. The consideration of a conventional zone went deeper because it would have recreated Togoland as a single economic space, potentially fuelling political expectations. The authorities in Accra and Lomé were quick to spot the trap and found reasons to shoot the proposal down. On the one side, the Gold Coast authorities maintained that a conventional zone was untenable because it would necessitate the erection of a Customs barrier between British Togoland and the Gold Coast. This would also require subsidization of the Trust Territory by the rest of the Gold Coast, which they maintained was unacceptable. The practical alternative would have been to treat British Togoland as a distinct administrative unit, but the authorities wished to avoid this at all costs. Moreover, it was far more convenient to maintain the Customs cordon at the existing boundary where it was possible to establish posts at strategic locations along stretches of the Togo hills. Having to patrol the entire left bank of the Volta River, as had been the case before 1914, was a decidedly unattractive prospect. On the other side, Commissaire Jean Cédile was of the opinion that French Togoland would forfeit valuable revenue if such a zone were to be established.[16] As was so often the case, Customs considerations assumed primacy in official thinking on both sides of the border. Despite an agreement to jettison the proposal, the British and French governments were rather slow to let this decision emerge for fear of alienating international opinion. For the same reason, they went through the motions of consulting opinion in the two halves of Togoland. A Standing Consultative Commission (SCC) was established to look into measures to ameliorate the practical difficulties created by the border. This was subsequently transformed into an Enlarged Consultative Commission (ECC) and eventually a Joint Council for Togoland Affairs, which became mired in controversy over parity of representation. The underlying intention was to generate sufficient inertia to frustrate any movement in the direction of unification, while using the delay to build up a solid wedge of contrary opinion that could be deployed as a counterweight at the UN.[17] Not surprisingly, the Consultative Commissions achieved very little, other than freeing up the cross-border movement of foodstuffs to a limited degree.

While the administering authorities managed to stem the early momentum of the unification movement, the latter underwent a series of internal schisms. The first opposed the early leadership of the AEC and those who coalesced around the Togoland Union (TU). The latter argued for unification of the two Togolands, specifically excluding Gold Coast Eweland. The refusal of northern Ewe leaders to accept that 'Ewe' was a meaningful political category directly contradicted the claims made by Chapman in the pages of the *Ewe Newsletter*. Ironically, it also echoed the contention of the British authorities. Kate Skinner has presented the most detailed account of how school teachers, who provided the backbone of the TU, coupled personal grievances over career progression with an acute sensitivity to the neglect of British Togoland.[18] Whereas the *Ewe Newsletter* had claimed that Eweland as a whole was poorly served, the TU asserted that Gold Coast Ewes stood in a relatively privileged position – especially with respect to secondary education – and should not presume to speak on behalf of Togolanders whose conditions were very different. In French Togoland, the CUT campaigned against French plans to terminate the distinct status of the Trust Territory, while across the border, the TU railed against British efforts to tighten the bonds with the Gold Coast. Following the recommendations of the Coussey Committee on constitutional reform in the Gold Coast, the British stance was that Togolanders should

---

[16] Nugent, *Smugglers, Secessionists*, p. 167.

[17] This emerges strongly from files in the Ghana Archives. GNAA ADM 39/1/676 "Standing Consultative Commission for Togoland", ADM 39/1/171 "Joint Council for Togoland Affairs – Views Expressed", and ADM 39/1/169 "Proceedings of First Session of J.C. for Togoland Affairs". For more discussion, see Nugent, *Smugglers, Secessionists*, pp. 177–80.

[18] Skinner, *Fruits of Freedom*, chs. 3–4.

partake equally in the political structures of the colony. This opened up a secondary division in the ranks of the TU, because some leaders could see the logic of the argument that Togolanders were more likely to receive an equitable share of resources if they exercised a voice within the emerging structures of political representation. However, the majority of the TU leadership advocated a boycott of the 1951 elections and sealed an alliance with traditional authorities in support of their position. This culminated in the removal of TU leaders who agreed to take up seats in parliament, and the launch of the Togoland Congress (TC) under the leadership of S.G. Antor.[19] The TC faced a formidable challenge when a Trans-Volta Togoland (TVT) region was established in 1952, thereby merging British Southern Togoland and Gold Coast Eweland for administrative purposes. This was partly justified on the basis of creating a more coherent framework of local government, given that newly created District boundaries straddled the colony and the Trust Territory.[20] The arrangement also enabled the British to claim that they were responding with good faith to one of the longstanding demands of the Ewe unification movement by erasing one of the offending borders. But by blurring the lines between British Togoland and Gold Coast Eweland, it became more difficult for the leadership of the TC to substantiate their allegations of systematic discrimination in resource allocation.

On opposite sides of the Togoland border, the British and French authorities cultivated constituencies that would line up behind their preferred outcomes. Having conceded the importance of creating representative institutions, the French actively supported two political parties that backed a closer association with France, namely the Parti Togolais du Progrès (PTP) and Union des Chefs et Populations du Nord-Togo (UCPN).[21] After 1951, the corresponding British policy was to concede progressively greater powers to a popularly elected government in Accra led by Kwame Nkrumah and the Convention People's Party (CPP). Aside from a loss of face, the excision of British Togoland would have recreated a boundary with the south-eastern Gold Coast, which, as we have already noted, was bound to complicate Customs control. But additionally, the realization of the Volta River Project was threatened by the prospect of a breakaway. Even if the projected dam was located within the Gold Coast, the left bank of the resulting lake would have constituted foreign soil.[22] Moreover, the displacement of populations as a result of the flooding was

---

[19] The main leaders who parted company with the TU were F.Y. Asare (who was later appointed government Minister), E.O. Kofi Dumoga and G.O. Awuma. The initial meeting that led to the creation of the TC was held at Buem-Borada in November 1950. Nugent, *Smugglers, Secessionists*, pp. 180–1. On the schism, see also Skinner, *Fruits of Freedom*, pp. 118–20.

[20] Skinner, *Fruits of Freedom*, pp. 132–3.

[21] Amenumey, *Ewe Unification Movement*, pp. 156–65.

[22] Nugent, *Smugglers, Secessionists*, pp. 184–5.

bound to have repercussions on both sides of the border. When the TC leadership raised objections to the lack of consultation, the head of the Preparatory Commission advised that advanced planning should await resolution of the political question.[23] Given that the Volta project was crucial to the larger compact between the British and the Nkrumah administration, there was a possibility that the smooth transition would stall unless integration could be effected with minimal delay.

At this point, it is necessary to step back from the detail and to consider the contested nature of the emergent social contract in the Gold Coast. Around the time of the first nationwide elections in 1951, both the CPP and the United Gold Coast Convention (UGCC) held very similar views about the responsibility of the state to deliver public goods.[24] As I have indicated, this was rooted in a historically embedded sense of entitlement that had stayed the hand of the British during the Depression. When the CPP won the elections, it was quick to claim the developmental agenda as its own, at the same time as insinuating that the UGCC was backward looking and beholden to traditional authority. Some of the mud stuck and was later transferred to the National Liberation Movement (NLM). Planning held a particular allure for the CPP because it offered the most direct route from practical means to desirable ends. But the Ten-Year Development Plan, which was inaugurated in 1951, also posed some problems. One of the most delicate issues was the imperative to generate sufficient revenue to sustain the commitments, which was made explicit in the foundational document that was presented to parliament:

> If the men and materials are available, there remains the question of finance. This must be found from existing reserves, future taxation and loans. In planning development account must be taken of the money likely to be available and the cost of the projects involved; and the plan must be drawn up within the limits imposed by these financial considerations.[25]

Whereas import duties had been the primary source of revenues until 1951, buoyant cocoa prices opened up a potentially lucrative alternative in the shape of an export duty on cocoa. In the early 1950s, the latter contributed more than a third of government revenues, in addition to which the CMB made increasing financial contributions (reflected in the final column of Table 10.1) based on the difference between the world price and what was paid to the farmers.

---

[23] NAK CO 554/1035 "Togoland Administration", extract of letter from R.G.A. Jackson to J.A.R. Pimlott, Board of Trade (30 September 1954).

[24] Earlier commentators spotted the fact that both the UGCC and the CPP had very similar manifestoes, based on planned development in the 1951 elections. Dennis Austin, *Politics in Ghana, 1946–1960* (Oxford: Oxford University Press, 1964), p. 138; Roger Genoud, *Nationalism and Economic Development in Ghana* (New York: Praeger, 1969), p. 95.

[25] Gold Coast, *The Development Plan, 1951* (Accra: Government Printing Department, 1951), p. 1.

Table 10.1 *Gold Coast government revenue, 1950–1958 (£000s)*

Year	Total revenue	Indirect (1) import duties	Indirect (2) export duties	Indirect (3) other	Direct (1) income tax	Direct (2) profit tax and mineral duty	Other revenue, including CMB grants
1945	7,172	1,869	1,421	50	1,472	104	2,256
1946	7,568	2,461	975	53	1,819	138	2,122
1947	10,246	3,595	856	67	3,011	47	2,670
1948	11,639	4,295	1,236	85	2,959	11	3,053
1949	18,106	7,516	3,454	99	3,441	186	3,410
1950	20,861	7,222	4,949	112	4,239	214	4,125
1951	38,929	9,732	19,576	128	4,766	412	4,305
1952	42,965	9,545	16,827	106	6,773	1,581	8,133
1953	48,428	12,010	18,570	783	5,685	2,232	9,148
1954	80,587	12,944	49,271	173	5,977	1,207	11,015
1955	64,099	18,280	24,690	307	6,148	1,357	13,317
1956	49,502	16,364	12,586	799	5,221	2,010	12,522
1957	59,922	14,938	22,734	1,999	5,443	2,330	12,478
1958	66,719	16,109	25,757	2,991	6,016	1,759	14,087
1959	70,231	18,900	22,358	3,027	5,643	1,508	18,795
1960	83,413	25,862	16,158	3,165	6,578	2,036	29,614

Source: Geoffrey Kay, The Political Economy of Colonialism in Ghana, pp. 348–57.

Under the Plan, the cocoa export duty contributed £91.5 million out of the £125.4 of projected expenditure, with grants from the CMB accounting for a further £19.7 million.[26]

It was the decision to freeze the producer price in 1954 that brought a storm about the head of the CPP and provided the rationale for the formation of the NLM. The latter and its allies targeted what they regarded as the misuse of state resources, but they also argued for a federal constitution that would properly reflect the pluralism of the Gold Coast/Togoland. The NLM envisaged a federation built on the principle of derivation, meaning in essence that revenues derived from cocoa would be spent overwhelmingly in the producing regions – which would have protected Ashanti interests. Given the importance of the Ashanti chiefly hierarchy to the NLM, the party was also bound to demand that greater respect be paid to traditional authority – although it is doubtful that it would have granted the latter substantive powers if they had been victorious.[27] The Northern People's Party (NPP) envisaged a federal

[26] Gold Coast, *Economic Survey 1955* (Accra: Office of the Government Statistician, 1956), p. 72.
[27] The shifting political terrain occupied by the NLM has received detailed consideration in Jean M. Allman, *Quills of the Porcupine: Asante Nationalism in an Emergent Ghana* (Madison: University of Wisconsin Press, 1993).

formula that would have prioritized need, thereby enabling resources to be channelled northwards. The TC aimed to be outside the constitution altogether, but for the sake of the alliance it endorsed federalism as a second-best option, subject to the proviso that British Togoland would constitute a distinct unit. Hence, each of the opposition parties expected something very different from their shared platform. For its part, the CPP was implacably opposed to federalism on the basis that only a strong central authority could deliver rapid development and address the legacy of regional inequalities. In addition, the CPP's position was that it was not the institutions of the colonial state per se that were deficient, but rather the uses to which they had hitherto been put. A fully Africanized civil service working towards the goal of rapid economic modernization was expected to transform the lives of Ghanaians in a matter of years – such at least was the grandiose promise.

During the 1950s, the CPP government presided over significant improvements in the provision of public goods. Between 1950 and 1960, the number of children in primary and middle schools jumped from 266,850 to 921,910, while the numbers enrolled in secondary education increased even more rapidly from 2,776 to 20,110. The most striking improvements were in Northern Ghana where education had lagged behind in the past due to the relative lack of a missionary presence. The pattern in the health sector was comparable. The number of government hospitals increased from 54 in 1948 to 74 in 1960. Whereas there were 126 doctors and 936 nurses in government hospitals in 1954, the corresponding figures for 1960 were 227 and 1,848 respectively. There was an even more impressive increase in the number of health clinics in the rural areas.

It is in this context that the response of the British and CPP to the unification challenge needs to be viewed. The Gold Coast authorities responded by imparting a novel twist to the nexus between development and decolonization. First of all, they injected greater resources into British Togoland in a manner that was calculated to convince international and local opinion alike that second-class treatment was already a thing of the past. Under the Ten-Year Plan, the territory was scheduled to benefit from expenditure on infrastructure and welfare on an equal footing with the rest of the Gold Coast. The first secondary school, Mawuli, had already been opened in Ho in 1950, and this was followed by Bishop Herman College in Kpandu two years later. Under the Plan, teacher training colleges were established in Jasikan and Hohoe, while a new hospital was opened in Hohoe. A sum of £847,490 was allocated for the construction of roads in TVT, with a further £45,000 dedicated to road improvements.[28] In addition, the government announced an additional

---

[28] Gold Coast, *The Development Plan, 1951: Financial Summaries* (Fifth Edition) (Accra: Government Printer, undated), pp. 27–28.

Table 10.2 *Special allocations to trans-Volta Togoland from £1 million development fund*

Project head	Allocation	Comments
Health	£191,000	Hospitals and dressing stations
Water	£300,000	Boreholes
Education and Social Welfare	£161,000	Including scholarships
Communications	£354,000, of which rural feeder roads £298,500	Posts and telecommunications, rural roads, tarring Ho roads
Total	£1,006,000	

£1 million to support funding priorities identified by the TVT Council (Table 10.2). Out of the total sum, £298,500 was allocated to feeder roads, with the expectation that some communal labour would be mobilized by local government.[29] The demand for rural roads had always outstripped the capacity of the administration to deliver, and any improvement was bound to be well received. Much the same was true of rural water supplies, which consumed the second largest chunk of the additional allocations. All of this supported the claim that Togoland was actually receiving more than its fair share of the national cake.

Secondly, the Gold Coast authorities traded on their claim to be in the vanguard of African decolonization – even if this came at the risk of upstaging the French. At the UN, the British government pointed to political advances in Gold Coast and argued that it would be fully in accord with the terms of the Trusteeship agreement, as well as in the interests of the population, for British Togoland to be part of the historic move to independence. In the territory itself, a concerted effort was made to piece together a political constituency that would articulate the case for integration. Although this was relatively easy to accomplish in Northern Togoland, a successful southern strategy required tackling the TC on its own home turf. The CPP was relatively slow to engage with the Togoland question, but after 1954, Nkrumah displayed a greater appreciation of the fact that there were compelling reasons for doing so. He understood that if negotiations over the Trust Territory became protracted, that might delay the advance of the Gold Coast towards independence. But for Nkrumah the crucial consideration was that any realistic vision of economic development was predicated on the electricity that would be generated by the Volta dam. If British Togoland were hived off, there was a good chance that

---

[29] GNAA ADM 39/1/533 "Standing Finance Committee: Memorandum by the Minister of Communications" (undated, 1954).

the project, which had already run into serious financial difficulties, would stall completely.[30] Nkrumah and the British therefore worked closely together to make sure that the matter was dealt with as expeditiously as possible. Sir George Sinclair, the Regional Officer, later contrasted the reluctance of some officials in Accra to accept the case for a special development allocation for the TVT Region with the political astuteness of the CPP politicians:

This took a good deal of persuasion but we were fortunate in these days in having some political Ministers who could see the political argument – if you wish the people of Togoland to throw in their lot with you, then you've got to prove to them that it is worthwhile belonging to the new Gold Coast Government and to be associated with it.[31]

In a speech before the TVT Council in 1954, Nkrumah was at pains to insist that the CPP government would treat the country as a single unit and "ensure that national interests remain paramount over regional considerations". However, he was also quick to draw attention to the future benefits to TVT of the Tema harbour, the planned Adomi bridge across the Volta and a 'Eastern Highway' running from Senchi to Bawku in the far north-east.[32] The significance of the latter two projects was that they were intended to improve the transport links between British Togoland and the Gold Coast. Noticeably absent was any reference to infrastructure that might have forged synergies with French territory. In 1953, the TC attempted to cause maximum embarrassment by publishing a leaked document, dubbed *Most Secret*, which appeared to advocate bribing the electorate of British Togoland through targeted expenditure. The Gold Coast authorities believed that the document had originated within the CPP and that it was genuine enough.[33] Despite the furore, the CPP actually made no secret at all of the fact that it sought to

---

[30] The travails of the project are dealt with in the remarkable documentary about the Volta Project in the BBC's Pandora's Box series, Episode 5 "Black Power". It includes interviews with many of the key protagonists. One of the key revelations is that the finances were becoming too great for Britain to handle. Bizarrely, it was the racist treatment meted out to Komla Gbedemah, the Minister of Finance, in an American roadside restaurant that led to an invitation to the White House and the recovery of the project with American support and World Bank financing.

[31] Rhodes House Library, Oxford, Mss. Afr. S.1622 "Transcript of Interview with Sir George Sinclair" (undated).

[32] "Address by the Honourable Prime Minister Dr. Kwame Nkrumah to the Trans-Volta/Togoland Council at Ho on the 24th August, 1954", p. 2. The highway never materialized. In the run-up to the 2016 elections what was now dubbed the 'eastern corridor' resurfaced as a campaign pledge by President John Mahama.

[33] The "Most Secret" document, "with its advocacy of bribery and strong arm methods" to achieve control of the trans-Volta apparently originated in the CPP and caused some embarrassment to the British authorities. Minute by M.G. Smith, 1 June 1954, and Smith to M de N. Ensor, c/o Government House, Accra (15 July 1954). NAK CO 554/1034 "Togoland Administration, 1954–56". For an analysis, see Skinner, *Fruits of Freedom*, pp. 125–31.

persuade British Togolanders that it was in their material interests to vote for integration rather than uniting with a much poorer French territory.

Since as early as 1950, unification leaders had been claiming that cocoa farmers in British Togoland were subsidizing development in the colony. In reality, the picture was much more complicated. Most of the cocoa was farmed in the forested hills of Buem, even if many of the farmers were Ewe migrants. However, all but one of the new roads that were budgeted under the Ten-Year Plan were located south of Ve-Golokwati.[34] Indeed, the town marked a dividing line between one half of the region where infrastructure was greatly improved and another where roads were unpaved and prone to erosion and seasonal waterlogging. Indeed, it is largely because of the parlous state of the roads in Buem that significant quantities of cocoa and coffee were headloaded across the border into French territory. In the Ho and Kpandu Districts the picture looked distinctly different. Between 1954 and 1958, official statistics indicated that the volume of vehicular traffic between Accra and Ho had increased by 147 per cent. This was the greatest recorded increase in road traffic in the entire Gold Coast/Togoland over the time-frame.[35] Given that the Adomi bridge was only completed in 1957, it seems likely that road improvements across southern TVT made the crucial difference. And it was precisely in the Ewe and minority areas south of Golokwati that the CPP sought to effect a change of political orientation. Here, it became increasingly difficult for the TC to explain away the reality of better roads, and the construction of schools, post offices and health facilities.[36]

The increase in expenditure brought the state closer to communities in Togoland in both a symbolic and a material sense. However, it also unleashed competition for resources within and between localities. The selection of Local Council capitals was often followed by an upgrade to amenities, but it also created a sense of grievance in the towns that were passed over. In addition, the selection of projects for financing became intricately bound up with party alignments. In many cases, the lines of fracture reinforced those that had been occasioned by the amalgamation of chieftaincies in the 1930s and 1940s.[37] Skinner makes a fair point that unification leaders could not "construct a national identity on behalf of their followers, either by lumping together at a territorial level a series of local disputes, or by presenting a clear-cut case

---

[34] The one exception was the Kadjebi–Papase road. Gold Coast, *The Development Plan, 1951: Financial Summaries*, p. 27.

[35] In Ashanti and the Northern Region it increased at less than 10 per cent per year. Ghana, *Economic Survey 1958* (Accra: Ministry of Finance, 1959), p. 47.

[36] During fieldwork in the mid-1980s, it was striking how many older informants explained their support for the CPP along the lines of the improved amenities that became available in the early 1950s.

[37] I have dealt with this matter in detail in Nugent, *Smugglers, Secessionists*, pp. 129–45.

based on material self-interest."[38] She goes on to explore the political language deployed by unification leaders – expressed in pamphlets, speeches songs and slogans – which appealed to common values and a sense of being rendered dependent on the goodwill of others.[39] While the argument is broadly convincing, two riders need to be entered. The first is that the larger political debate was often interpreted in the light of local circumstances, at both the village and the *dukɔ* level. This did not make the commitment to one political cause or the other any less genuine; on the contrary, local framings brought home the relevance of the larger political debate. And secondly, forging a larger sense of political community cut both ways. To endorse the CPP's version of integration was to embark on a different political imagining, one that highlighted what Togolanders shared with Gold Coasters. It was this consideration that led some of the early leaders of the AEC, like Daniel Chapman and Ephraim Amu, to switch their loyalties to the CPP.[40] But it was not only connections within Eweland that counted. In somewhere like Agotime, the deeper historical associations with Anlo were significant, as was the history of migration to the cocoa-growing areas of the Eastern Province.

In fact, the case of Agotime offers broader insights into the reasons why it is difficult to disentangle local and territorial dynamics. Given that the Agotime constituted the most straightforward case of a people divided by the boundary, one might have predicted robust support for Togoland unification on two sides of the border. In reality the picture was much more mixed. Kpetoe was one of the beneficiaries of the resources that were channelled into the TVT Region in the early 1950s. It was conveniently located on the main trunk road and therefore benefited disproportionately from the knock-on effects of infrastructural spending. The Kpetoe market derived much of its vitality from its intermediate position between the Ho market and the weekly market in Amoussoukope in French Togoland, even if this was not part of government calculations. The Ten-Year Development Plan allocated £13,704 for the construction of a new bridge over the River Todzie and a further £15,000 for a piped water supply in Kpetoe, both of which were completed over 1952/53.[41] By contrast, Afegame, which was located away from the main road, fared less well. Unificationists in that town could plausibly argue that there was little to show for all the pious talk about development. There was no bridge at Afegame that might have facilitated their interactions with neighbouring towns in French Togoland like Kpodjahon and Zukpe. Moreover, the only decent road that connected the two halves of Agotime passed through the border post

---

[38] Skinner, *Fruits of Freedom*, p. 144.   [39] Skinner, *Fruits of Freedom*, pp. 135–52.
[40] Chapman went on to serve Nkrumah as Cabinet secretary.
[41] Gold Coast, *The Development Plan, 1951: Financial Summaries*, pp. 28–9.

at Batome Junction en route to Assahun. Most of the Agotime lived further to the north and saw little of the benefit.

And then there was the intricate matter of chieftaincy politics. On the face of it, Nene Keteku II had been a significant loser in the decision to amalgamate with Asogli in 1943. With most of his people residing in French Togoland, the stool had suffered a double blow to its prestige. But as a result of the ongoing chieftaincy dispute in Ho, Nene Keteku ended up being elected president of the Asogli Native Authority.[42] In 1950, when a Southern Togoland Council (the precursor to the TVT Council) was set up, Nene Keteku was elected as one of the three Asogli representatives. At the first meeting he was voted in as the president of what was then the most important body in the trans-Volta.[43] In the midst of ongoing disputes within Ho-Dome and within Ho more generally, District Commissioner Weatherburn wrote that:

I believe that the key to Asogli lies in the Divisional Chief of Agotime for he is the one man who can hold the Native Authority together. His judgement in Asogli Native Affairs is excellent and now that he has been elected President of the Southern Togoland Council his word is law in the area.[44]

Not surprisingly, this helped Nene Keteku to consolidate his own contested position within Agotime.

Nene Keteku initially attempted to steer a middle course between the unification and integration camps. In January 1951, a meeting was held in Agome-Kpalimé (in French Togoland) that attempted to reconcile the AEC and TU positions. This generated a resolution that was signed by leaders from both sides of the border and a number of chiefs, including Nene Keteku in his capacity as President of Asogli.[45] Thereafter, the Agotime headchief identified strongly with the TC. However, he became a less influential player within Asogli and British Togoland politics more broadly – in part, it would seem, because of growing ill-health. Be that as it may, his successor today recalls that both Nene Keteku and Nene Agbovi were staunch supporters of *Ablode*, because they wanted to reconstitute the two halves of partitioned Agotime. They only switched their allegiance to the CPP after independence when the

---

[42] On Ho chieftaincy affairs, see Benjamin Lawrance, "Bankoe v. Dome: traditions and petitions in the Ho-Asogli amalgamation, British Mandated Togoland, 1919–1939", *Journal of African History*, 46, 2005; and Skinner, *Fruits of Freedom*, pp. 71–4.

[43] GNAA ADM 39/1/689 "Southern Togoland Council – Constitution of".

[44] GNAA ADM 39/1/456 "Handing Over Reports", "Handing Over Notes, Ho Sub-District – From Mr C.M. Weatherburn, Assistant District Commissioner, to Mr A.V. Cameron, Assistant District Commissioner" (September 1952), p. 4.

[45] GNAA ADM 39/1/676 "Standing Consultative Commission for Togoland", "Resolution Adopted by the Joint Congress of the Natural Rulers, the Principal Political and Other Organisations and the Peoples of Togoland Under Kingdom Trusteeship and Togoland under French Trusteeship at Agome Palime on January 7th 1951".

threat of destoolment and detention became very real.[46] It also seems that Nene Keteku's ability to fend off rival claims to the chieftaincy rested on demonstrating his political loyalty to the CPP.[47] In 1946, the Asogli State had referred the protracted dispute between Nene Keteku and Nene Mahumansro XII to the Agotime Divisional Council, which eventually found in favour of the former. However, the backers of the Afegame claim interpreted the judgement as establishing the principle of chiefly rotation between Kpetoe and Afegame.[48] Although Nene Mahumansro appeared to have accepted defeat when an accord was reached in April 1953, at a meeting which was attended by the senior Togolese chiefs, the case had not been definitively settled. After independence, the Nkrumah regime was prepared to lend its weight to pro-CPP candidates in chieftaincy disputes, which meant that chiefs like Nene Keteku needed to assert their loyalty.

Across the border, some of the chiefs continued to focus on issues closer to home. In 1953, the chiefs of Nyitoe and Adame despatched letters to the French authorities associating themselves with PTP opposition to planned elections for a reconstituted Joint Council for Togoland Affairs. Given that both of these towns had disassociated themselves from Agotime in the Hodzo land case (see Chapter 7), it is significant that a third letter emanated from Zukpe, whose chief had been restored to the position of *chef de canton*. At this particular moment, the stool was vacant, and would not be filled until 1955, but the regent and others styling themselves *sous-chefs* and *chefs de quartier* sent a version of the same letter. Their alignment with the main anti-unification party in French Togoland is at first glance surprising, but it is comprehensible if one takes into account that the coveted status of *chef de canton* would probably have been forfeited for good if the two halves of Agotime had been put back together again.[49] The fact that Agotimes adopted divergent positions on the unification question reflected political alignments that were at once local *and* territorial. Crucially, they were also understood differently on the two sides of the border.

The denouement of the unification saga does not need recounting in any detail here. Suffice it to note that in 1955, the British government forced the hand of the UN, pointing out that it was not in a position to administer Togoland once it had withdrawn from the Gold Coast. The Visiting Mission

[46] Interview with Nene Keteku, Ho, 26 March 2001.
[47] Fieldwork diary entry 20 August 2001.
[48] Nene Ahortor Makaku V, *A Brief History of the Lehs Vis-à-Vis the Agotimes* (Accra: the author, 2016), pp. 67–89.
[49] Unfortunately, there is no evidence of how the matter was viewed from the perspective of Batoumé whose origins as an outpost of Kpetoe might have led one to expect greater sympathy for the CUT position. Copies of these letters may be found at CAOM 1AFFPOL/1361 "Affaires Politiques".

Table 10.3 *Voting in Anyigbe local council area in 1956 plebiscite*

Area	Polling stations	Total votes	Union	Separation
Agotime	Kpetoe West	238	153	83
	Kpetoe Central	299	169	130
	Kpetoe East	290	111	178
	Akpokope	315	107	208
	Afegame	137	32	104
Not stated	Dremave	249	229	17
Not stated	Ziope	270	252	18
Not stated	Wudorkpo/Tsrigoni	278	257	21
Not stated	Amule	278	263	15
Not stated	Dzalele	255	25	230
Dakpa	Dzadefe	119	63	56
Dakpa	Dakpa	219	200	16
Dakpa	Have	219	202	15
Total		*3,155*	*2,063*	*1,092*

UN, *Plebiscite Commissioner's Report*, p. 184.

of that year recommended a plebiscite to be held exclusively in British Togoland. The eventual wording of the question did not offer unification as an option, but merely a choice between accepting a union with the Gold Coast or separation pending the ultimate determination of Togoland's future. The vote in favour of separation carried the day in southern Togoland but was outweighed by the vote for union in the north. Elsewhere, I have examined the results in greater detail.[50] Here, it is worth simply underlining that there was no straightforward pattern of block voting in southern Togoland. Although there was a clear majority in favour of union in Buem-Krachi District, and an equally solid majority in favour of separation in the Ho and Kpandu Districts, large numbers of the electorate jumped the other way in either instance. Moreover, proximity to the border was not a good predictor of preferences. While Akpini, which was located towards the Volta River, voted overwhelmingly for separation, the Agotime and Ave populations of Anyigbe, who were closely related to populations in French Togoland, voted for union with the Gold Coast (Table 10.3). In Agotime, Afegame joined Akpokope in voting for separation from the Gold Coast. In Kpetoe itself, the vote was more or less evenly split, with a small overall majority coming down in favour of union with the Gold Coast. This underlines the larger point that it was not the

[50] Nugent, *Smugglers, Secessionists*, pp. 188–92. See also James S. Coleman, *Togoland* (New York: Carnegie Endowment for International Peace, 1956), pp. 70–80.

boundary as a physical barrier that was at issue, but rather competing conceptions of political community.[51]

Interpreting the will of the British Togoland electorate ultimately fell to the UN. If the latter had decided that southern Togoland should be permitted to separate because of the majority vote there, there is a strong possibility it would have united with French Togoland at some point in the future – although this clearly depended on the passage of events across the border. On the other hand, aggregating all the votes meant that British Togoland would be integrated with the colony and would lose its distinct status. That implied the final erasure of the border with the Gold Coast, but the confirmation of a permanent boundary with French Togoland. In the final event, the UN came to the fateful decision that the votes of north and south should indeed be counted together. The result was that the trusteeship status of British Togoland was brought to an end, and the territory formally became a part of independent Ghana on 6 March 1957. The efforts of TC supporters to mount a final act of defiance on independence day, at Alavanyo and Hodzo, backfired and provided the CPP with the excuse to impose a Peace Preservation Order.[52] Following the arrest of many *Ablode* supporters, the first flight of refugees across the border occurred – a pattern that was repeated over successive years. A number of prominent chiefs also went into exile, which typically culminated in destoolment and the installation of pro-CPP candidates. Although the TC lived on until the enforced merger of all the opposition parties in 1958, the moment when an alternative future was conceivable had come to an abrupt halt in 1956.

The CPP had never given serious consideration as to whether the state could have been differently configured. Its consideration of the federal option was as close at it came, and although the CPP was forced to concede Regional Assemblies as the price for independence, they were wound up as soon as was decently possible. When the CPP embraced socialism after 1960, the role of state institutions was significantly augmented and Nkrumah began to talk of the need for a different kind of bureaucratic mentality, one that was "utterly devoted and dedicated to the ideal of reconstructing our country".[53] But even then, there was as much continuity as change. Formally, the party was supreme and vested with the responsibility for making the civil service dutifully serve

---

[51] The 1952 UN Visiting Mission had itself noted that "the frontier problems are of secondary consideration and of no great significance." Quoted in Coleman, *Togoland*, p. 52.

[52] Skinner, *Fruits of Freedom*, pp. 165–7. Nugent, *Smugglers, Secessionists*, pp. 209–10.

[53] Kwame Nkrumah, Africa Must Unite (New York: International Publishers, 1963), pp. 93 and 129. The same sentiments are expressed in the statement of socialist intent, again without clarification as to what a "remodelled" civil service would look like. See Ghana, *Programme of the Convention People's Party for Work and Happiness* (Accra: Ministry of Information and Broadcasting, undated), p. 33.

the ends of socialism. At the same time, the party subsumed the main bodies representing powerful societal interest groups, most notably the Trade Union Congress (TUC) and the United Ghana Farmers' Council (UGFC).[54] In the wake of the February 1966 coup that toppled Nkrumah, there was an understandable tendency to accentuate the gulf between socialist posturing and the realities of everyday corruption, authoritarianism and the cult of the leader.[55] Critics also maintained that statism had singularly failed to deliver the kind of rapid economic growth that would have enabled the regime to fulfill its promises of development for all.[56] Subsequent academic work has tended to offer a rather more nuanced assessment. Tony Killick's analysis of economic policy, in particular, made the important point that planning was informed by current development orthodoxies that stressed the need for a 'big push' to break the cycle of economic dependency in a country such as Ghana.[57] Killick noted, however, that the economic strategy was almost bound to fail because of the unrealistic demands it placed on the administrative structures.[58]

The CPP's actions can best be understood in terms of the relentless pursuit of a productive social contract that sought to straddle urban, rural and distinct regional constituencies. On more than one occasion, Nkrumah observed that the CPP was driven by societal pressures as much as it was shaping popular opinion:

---

[54] On the Farmers' Council, see Bjorn Beckman, *Organising the Farmers: Cocoa Politics and National Development in Ghana* (Uppsala: Nordic Africa Institute, 1976).

[55] For a particularly jaundiced account of Nkrumah's role, see Henry L. Bretton, *The Rise and Fall of Kwame Nkrumah: A Study of Personal Rule in Africa* (New York: Praeger, 1986). Only slightly less critical is Trevor Jones, *Ghana's First Republic, 1960–1966: The Political Kingdom* (London: Methuen, 1976), who also notes that there was a fundamental lack of realism attached to the economic agenda, pp. 143–75. For a more recent, and more sympathetic, appraisal, see Ama Biney, *The Political and Social Thought of Kwame Nkrumah* (New York and Houndmills: Palgrave Macmillan, 2011).

[56] The argument that the pursuit of economic transformation was fundamentally flawed was made in a seminal article by Elliott Berg, "Structural transformation versus gradualism: recent economic development in Ghana", in Phillip Foster and Aristide Zolberg (eds.) *Ghana and the Ivory Coast: Perspectives on Modernization* (Chicago and London: University of Chicago Press, 1971). This contrasts with the distinctly more sympathetic treatment by Reginald H. Green, "Reflections on economic strategy, structure, implementation and necessity: Ghana and the Ivory Coast", in the same volume. Jonathan Frimpong-Ansah, who was with the Bank of Ghana at the time, emphasizes the "uncontrollable desire to modernize" on the part of Nkrumah himself, which was at variance with the resources available. See *The Vampire State in Africa: The Political Economy of Decline in Ghana* (London and Trenton: James Currey and Africa World Press, 1991), pp. 90–1. This echoes a much earlier work, which argued that Nkrumah's socialism was really all about modernization. See Roger Genoud, *Nationalism and Economic Development*.

[57] Tony Killick, *Development Economics in Action: A Study of Economic Policies in Ghana* (London: Heinemann, 1978), pp. 18–24.

[58] Killick, *Development Economics*, p. 353.

Table 10.4 *Basic indicators of social provision, Ghana, 1950–1966*

Item	1950	1955	1960	1966
Primary and middle school attendance (public)	266,850	543,407	696,270	1,404,929
Secondary school attendance (public)	2,776	10,017	20,110	42,628
Doctors in government service	n/a	126	227	296
Nurses in government service	n/a	936	1,848	2,944
Government hospitals	21	32	32	53
Health centres and field units	–	9	31	53

Sources: Ghana, Economic Survey 1958, table 39, p. 55, table 40, p. 58; Ghana, Statistical Yearbook *1961*, tables 161–2, p. 146; tables 26–27, pp. 28–9; Republic of Ghana, Statistical Handbook 1967, table 9, p. 7, tables 14 and 15, pp. 12–13; Republic of Ghana, Statistical Yearbook, 1969–70, tables 21–22, pp. 28–30, table 143, p. 153.

We cannot tell our peoples that material benefits and growth and modern progress are not for them. If we do, they will throw us out and seek other leaders who promise more. And they will abandon us, too, if we do not in reasonable measure respond to their hopes.[59]

Robert Bates' depiction of the CPP and the NLM as representing urban and rural interests respectively is therefore overdrawn.[60] Apart from the fact that the stronghold of the NLM was Kumasi, a substantial city in its own right, the CPP had its political feet planted firmly in the countryside. Unlike in Tanzania, and much more like in Western Nigeria, the rural population in southern Ghana typically lived in towns, which became the primary beneficiaries of the expansion of educational and health infrastructure (Table 4). At the same time, the CPP targeted regions that had fared less well in the past. For example, the regional distribution of public investments in health is of interest: of eleven new hospitals built in the decade before 1958, six were in the North, three in TVT and two in Ashanti.[61] The disappointing performance of the NLM at the polls in 1956 is not adequately explained by the subsidization of inputs and easy terms of credit as a political payoff.[62] The CPP won because the promise to redistribute resources held an appeal for a broad swathe of the rural population who produced little or no cocoa.[63] There is no doubt that cocoa farmers contributed the lion's share of the revenues – through a combination of the export duty, CMB grants and subsequent 'voluntary' contributions (Table 5). Whereas income tax, which had once been regarded as an indicator of successful modernization, remained static, the relative contribution of

[59] Quoted in Killick, *Development Economics*, p. 35.
[60] Bates, *Markets and States*, pp. 106–8.   [61] Ghana, *Economic Survey*, 1958, p. 55.
[62] Bates, *Markets and States*, p. 110.   [63] Austin, *Politics in Ghana*, pp. 351–3.

Table 10.5 *Sources of Ghana government revenues, 1954/1955–1960/1961 (£G million^a)*

Item	1954/ 1955	1955/ 1956	1956/ 1957	1957/ 1958	1958/ 1959	1959/ 1960	1960/ 61
Total revenue	80.5	64.1	52.4	60.1	67.0	70.2	83.4
Income tax	6.0	6.1	5.2	5.4	6.0	5.6	6.6
Import duty	12.9	18.3	16.4	15.0	16.1	18.9	25.9
Cocoa export duty	48.9	24.1	12.1	22.1	25.0	20.9	15.3
CMB grants	3.5	3.2	2.8	3.0	2.3	1.1	1.4
Cocoa farmers' voluntary contribution	–	–	–	–	–	6.1	11.0

^{a} The ghana pound was adopted at independence and replaced by the cedi, a decimalized currency, in 1960.
Sources: Ghana, Economic Survey 1958, table 57, p. 74; Republic of Ghana, Statistical Handbook 1967, table 79, pp. 108–13.

import duties increased significantly – which pointed to the stubborn persistence of colonial patterns. Much of this is attributable to the increasingly variegated nature of urban consumption – much like in Senegal. This posed a tricky problem for a government that regarded consumer spending as a luxury at a time when foreign exchange was in short supply.

Despite the achievements of the 1950s, the slide in world cocoa prices at the end of the decade underlined the vulnerability of public finances to external shocks.[64] Nkrumah became convinced that it was necessary to escape reliance upon a cash crop whose price was inherently unstable when so many countries were pursuing the same agricultural export strategies.[65] After 1960, the focus of planning began to shift away from infrastructure towards directly productive investments, especially in industry, agro-industry and agriculture. The Second Five-Year Plan (1959–64) in fact consisted of two variants, one more ambitious and the other more cautious. Infrastructure received less emphasis, with the singular exception of the Volta project. What was different about the plan was the stated intention to create 600 new industries and to focus on creating youth employment.[66] In 1961, the Plan was abandoned, and work began on drafting what was eventually launched as the Seven-Year Plan in 1963. This Plan, which was based on exhaustive consultation with external development

[64] Killick, *Development Economics*, pp. 1–29.   [65] Nkrumah, *Africa Must Unite*, p. 109.
[66] Jerker Carlsson, *The Limits to Structural Change: A Comparative Study of Foreign Investments in Liberia and Ghana, 1950–1971* (Uppsala: Scandinavian Institute of African Studies, 1981), p. 82.

experts, envisaged the investment of substantially greater state resources.[67] Whereas the optimistic version of the Second Plan allocated a sum of £G 250 million, the Seven-Year Plan anticipated state investment of £G 475.5 million and private investment to the tune of £G 540 million. Of state investments, 23 per cent of allocations were earmarked for industrial development, the priorities being consumer goods; agro- and minerals processing; construction materials; and the machine and electrical industries. Because there was no Ghanaian entrepreneurial class deemed adequate to the task, and because foreign capital was treated with a residual suspicion, the implication was that the state needed to take the lead. By the time of the 1966 coup, Killick estimates that fifty-three state enterprises and twelve joint ventures as well as twenty-three public boards were in existence.[68] Apart from industries, there was the State Farms Corporation (SFC), the State Fishing Corporation and the State Gold Mining Corporation (SGMC). There was also a raft of state enterprises covering distribution – notably the Ghana National Trading Corporation (GNTC) – utilities and the service sector.

The unhappy conjuncture between increased state commitments and a shrinking revenue base led the Nkrumah government to resort to expedients that were distinctly unpopular – in particular, 'voluntary' contributions that were imposed on workers and cocoa farmers. The railway workers' strike of 1961 was a clear indication that while co-opting the TUC leadership might be relatively easy, that did not mean that the rank-and-file would meekly fall into line.[69] But the fact that the CPP was prepared to court unpopularity can only adequately be explained by its belief that Ghanaians would come to appreciate that austerity in the short run was necessary to achieve improved living standards in the future. The CPP's strategy consisted of a balancing act. It was mindful of the need to create employment opportunities to absorb the number of people feeding through the educational system. But it also sought to impose wage restraint on workers, in return for which it pledged to keep the cost of living down. Indeed, full employment and labour discipline were explicitly linked in the CPP's *Work and Happiness* document.[70] If the CPP had genuinely been held hostage to the demands of urban labour, it is very unlikely that it would have opted for austerity measures in the way that it did. Moreover, there is a fallacy in thinking that the expansion of formal employment was a strategy that was confined to the cities. While the factories were

---

[67] Republic of Ghana, *Seven-Year Development Plan, 1963–64 to 1969–70* (Accra: Office of the Planning Commission, 1964).

[68] Killick, *Development Economics*, p. 217. See the list at pp. 320–2.

[69] For an analysis of the strike, see Richard Jeffries, *Class, Power and Ideology: The Railwaymen of Sekondi* (Cambridge: Cambridge University Press, 1978), ch. 5.

[70] Convention People's Party, "Program of the Convention People's Party for Work and Happiness" (1962), pp. 30–2.

Table 10.6 *Relative shares of current expenditure in Ghana, 1957/1958–1966 (%)*

Item	1957/1958	1960/1961	1965
A. *General services*	*22.4*	*25.3*	*29.3*
General administration	12.6	12.4	14.6
Defence	5.7	8.8	9.4
Justice and Police	4.1	4.1	5.3
B. *Community services,* *including roads and water supply*	*11.4*	*8.4*	*7.2*
C. *Social services*	*24.0*	*24.4*	*38.4*
Education	14.3	13.2	25.8
Health	5.2	5.2	8.2
Social security/special welfare	2.7	1.7	2.8
Other	1.9	4.3	1.6
D. *Economic services*	29.5	33.7	16.6
E. *Unallocatable, including debt repayments*	12.7	8.2	8.5
Total expenditure	**100.00**	**100.00**	**100.00**
	£G 63,726.9	**£G 113,653.8**	**NC 219.8**

Source: Ghana, Economic Survey, 1960, table 75, p. 81; 1961, table 90, p. 107; 1969, table 11, p. 29.

mostly located in Accra and the new township of Tema, public investments also created employment in rural towns and villages. In fact, the people who typically supported the CPP at the local level were people who were relatively well educated, but whose roots and everyday interactions were distinctly rural: such as cocoa purchasing officers, school teachers and postal agents.[71]

Perhaps the primary beneficiaries of socialism were those who staffed the bureaucracy, as Cruise O'Brien argued for Senegal. But in Ghana, the central administration consumed fewer resources than its Senegalese counterpart, with general services accounting for less than a third of government expenditure in 1965 (see Table 10.6 and compare with Table 9.2). Much of the latter is attributable to the military rather than the general administration. Conversely, the expenditure on health, education and other social services actually rose in relative terms during the 1960s despite the pressure to prioritize productive investments (Tables 10.4 and 10.6) – leading Douglas Rimmer to conclude that "[E]vidently, strong pressures in favour of non-productive investments were felt during the years of the big push as they had been in the 1950s."[72]

---

[71] The Workers Brigade represented a more direct intervention to create gainful employment for youth, but this was not particularly geared towards the cities.

[72] Douglas Rimmer, *Staying Poor: Ghana's Political Economy, 1950–1990* (Oxford, New York, Seoul and Tokyo: Pergamon Press, 1992), p.88.

There was indeed considerable demand from below, and this can be gauged from one of the more memorable passages in the *Programme for Work and Happiness*:

We would add here a comment upon the pressures brought to bear upon members of parliament by their constituents to force the establishment of projects in their villages or towns, irrespective of the value to the general community or to the wider needs of the nation. This has just as detrimental effects as bribery, and is, in fact, a form of corruption which deflects the national loyalty of parliamentarians to sectional interests.[73]

The fact that MPs continued to pass the demands of their constituents upwards is an indication that an active negotiation continued well into the 1960s. In a nutshell, the dominant element in the social contract conformed to the expectations of a broad spectrum of Ghanaians located in both the urban and the rural areas. The cocoa farmers bore a disproportionate share of the tax burden in the 1950s, but the resources were largely redistributed to other parts of the countryside in the shape of public goods. Moreover, food crop farmers seem to have fared relatively better in the first half of the 1960s, because of relatively high prices and improved communications.[74] What remained to be seen was whether the CPP could deliver on the larger promises it had made.

If one accepts that the commitment to achieving rapid growth through industrialization was genuine enough, one is left with the question of how far elements of the repressive and the permissive were also embedded in the Ghanaian social contract. The authoritarian tendencies of the Nkrumah regime featured prominently in much that was written after 1966. It is fair to say that the CPP, like many nationalist parties, was inclined to set itself up as the embodiment of the nation and to treat opposition as sectarian and as almost by definition unpatriotic. The Avoidance of Discrimination Act of December 1957, which prohibited parties formed along ethnic, regional lines and religious lines, was clearly intended to cast doubt on the very legitimacy of the opposition, as well as to practically disrupt it. The Preventive Detention Act of 1958 was repeatedly invoked in order to detain troublesome opponents, including Members of Parliament from the trans-Volta.[75] In effect, Ghana became a de facto one-party state long before the formal declaration in 1964.[76] But the Nkrumah regime never developed a well-honed surveillance apparatus – certainly by comparison with Guinea under Ahmed Sekou Touré. Although the military consumed significant resources, it was not deployed as an instrument of internal repression, but was more a product of Nkrumah's desire to project Ghana's influence on the world stage. Again, while the primacy of the party over the bureaucracy was outwardly proclaimed, this

---

[73] *Programme for Work and Happiness*, p. 19.   [74] Rimmer, *Staying Poor*, p. 103.
[75] Austin, *Politics in Ghana*, pp. 380–3.   [76] Austin, *Politics in Ghana*, pp. 414–15.

did not necessarily make much practical difference. By maintaining most of the existing administrative boundaries, within which the borders of traditional areas nested, the CPP built upon very solid foundations.[77] In fact, if the NLM had succeeded in turning Ghana into a federation, the consequences would have been far more radical. The administrative hierarchy of Regional Commissioners (RCs) and DCs was a direct carryover from the colonial period, with the major difference that the incumbents were politicians rather than civil servants.[78] In practice the incumbents needed to be mindful of a political landscape in which 'traditional areas' were presumed to represent the building blocks of the nation. It is true that many pro-opposition chiefs were forced to vacate their stools, but this had to proceed through traditional channels. Moreover, there was never any chance that the CPP would seek to abolish chieftaincy as an institution, as happened in Tanzania, or to abolish specific monarchies, as happened in Uganda.[79] Its preference was to have chiefs who endorsed the CPP, or at least did not actively oppose it. But the CPP did elevate particular stools in the hierarchy, and by making the gazetting of chiefs a prerequisite for recognition, it was able to establish a broad margin for manipulation. But the government never selected the chiefs, and officials had no formal powers of command in relation to traditional authorities. Perhaps most telling is the fact that the Nkrumah regime did not feel able to interfere with the principle that chiefs remained the custodians of the land (where stool land existed). One of the passages in *Africa Must Unite* is revealing in this respect:

Certain changes in our land tenure system seems to me inevitable if we are to pursue our development plans, but these will have to be carefully worked out. They must avoid the creation of rifts in the body politic, and will accordingly have to take account of customs and fundamental relations.[80]

During the Nkrumah period, therefore, the broad limits of state power continued to be respected, however much the modernist rhetoric implied something altogether more totalizing. Indeed, the very essence of the Ghanaian social contract was the balance between expectations of state agents to deliver and knowing when to back off.

[77] The former Provinces became Regions, while the configuration of Districts did not change greatly. The most obvious rupture was the separation of Brong-Ahafo from Ashanti Region in 1958 and the separation of the Upper from the Northern Region in 1960.

[78] For a detailed account of the administrative structure, see Benjamin Amonoo, *Ghana 1956–1966: The Politics of Institutional Dualism* (London: Allen and Unwin, 1981).

[79] See Richard Rathbone, *Nkrumah and the Chiefs: Politics of Chieftaincy in Ghana, 1951–60* (Athens: Ohio University Press, 2000).

[80] Nkrumah, *Africa Must Unite*, p. 99.

In the aftermath of the 1966 coup, a great deal was also written about endemic corruption – in part fed by successive commissions of enquiry set up by the National Liberation Council (NLC).[81] The allegations began in the early 1950s in relation to the cocoa industry,[82] but corruption became a much more serious issue after independence as an expanding field of state intervention multiplied the opportunities for rent-seeking. Although corruption became deeply ingrained within particular agencies like the CMB and the GNTC, this is different from the proposition that the CPP struck deals based on endorsing systemic corruption. That there was a problem was openly acknowledged by Nkrumah in his Dawn Broadcasts, but he resorted to this unusual expedient – in effect talking over the head of the party to the people – precisely because a perception of mounting corruption was undermining the legitimacy of his government.[83] Despite the negative publicity, the permissive elements had not reached anything like a tipping point by 1966.

The ability of the CPP to deliver on the promise of a productive social contract depended on three socio-economic considerations: building a raft of domestic industries with linkages to agriculture; channelling consumption patterns; and protecting revenue streams. These were interdependent, in such a way that measures taken to tackle one element inevitably had an impact on the others. But in addition, the fulfillment of all three collectively depended on being able to control what passed through Ghana's borders, and especially the eastern one. Although Nkrumah proudly proclaimed his commitment to pan-Africanism on the continental stage, socialism was pursued from behind the safety of the boundary fence – despite the fact that Nkrumah repeatedly claimed that socialism in one country was self-defeating. If cheap consumer goods flowed across the border from Togoland, and if cocoa exited in the opposite direction, the predictable effect would have been to undermine state industries while placing greater pressure upon foreign exchange and government revenues alike. All of that, in turn, placed the larger social contract in jeopardy. This meant that the Nkrumah regime developed an interest in securing relatively hard borders.

In 1958, a different scenario seemed conceivable. Nkrumah, who hailed from the western borderlands of Nzima, claimed to have a particular interest in addressing the baleful consequences of colonial boundaries. In French Togoland, the victory of the CUT in the 1958 elections brought a pro-unification

---

[81] It is a theme in most of the books cited above. But see also Victor LeVine, *Political Corruption: The Ghana Case* (Stanford: Hoover Institution Press, 1975). The culture of corruption was also immortalized in the classic novel by Ayi Kwei Armah, *The Beautyful Ones Are Not Yet Born* (Oxford: Heinemann Educational, 1968).

[82] Beckman, *Organising the Farmers*, pp. 59–65.

[83] In April 1961, Nkrumah made his Dawn Broadcast in which he addressed the canker of corruption. Austin, *Politics*, pp. 403–5.

party to office for the first time. Olympio had consistently opposed being drawn into the French Union and had been encouraged by Nkrumah in this stance. Existing outside of the French Union meant that foreign exchange restrictions would be removed and that Togo could source cheaper goods from elsewhere. However, the downside was that preferences for Togolese agricultural commodities were likely to be withheld, while there would be limits to French aid. An independent Togo also needed to find a solution to the currency issue if it abandoned the CFA franc, which made a deal with Ghana potentially attractive. There was also much to recommend a Customs union because at this point there was a rather limited re-export trade from Togoland. On the other side, such a union would have enabled Ghana to expand the market for its own commodities, while facilitating co-operation in the area of border policing. The terrain on which closer co-operation could have been pursued was, therefore, at least as favourable as in the Senegambia.

Ultimately, the two sides were unable to reach an agreement on how to proceed. The Ghana government insisted that the solution to a whole host of political and economic issues was for Togo to simply merge with Ghana. This was very difficult for the Olympio regime to swallow because the CUT's legitimacy was rooted in the claim to being the liberator of the Togolese people. But it became virtually impossible once Nkrumah talked openly of Togo becoming Ghana's seventh region.[84] The repeated use of the term 'integrate', a word which came with a lot of baggage in the Togolands, only compounded the misunderstanding. And then there was a series of other irritants. First of all, there was the fact that thousands of refugees and political exiles had crossed into French Togoland. As Skinner has shown, exiled supporters of the TC identified openly with the CUT and expected Olympio to fight their corner.[85] By taking up complaints about the effacement of the separate identity of British Togoland, Olympio raised the hackles of Nkrumah who considered the matter closed. In 1958, the first of many alleged plots against the CPP regime was said to have been hatched from Togoland, which also raised questions about how much the Olympio government knew. Moreover, each side claimed to speak on behalf of border populations, in effect questioning the legitimacy of the other side. In January 1959, the *Accra Evening News* personally targeted Olympio:

[T]he hearts of Ewes everywhere are still burning, yearning for that true unity and freedom which, frankly, Olympio has never yet been clear-cut and outspoken [about] since his assumption of power. Let Olympio speak out for once and shame

---

[84] W. Scott Thompson, *Ghana's Foreign Policy, 1957–1966: Diplomacy, Ideology, and the New State* (Princeton: Princeton University Press, 1969), p. 84.

[85] Skinner, *Fruits of Freedom*, ch. 5.

the devil. Too long have Ewes agitated for the removal of the wicked artificial border dividing them. There are far more serious issues involved than the prestige of being called Prime Minister.[86]

All of this raised suspicions about irredentism on the one side and annexationist ambitions on the other.

As late as October 1959, a Ghanaian deputation was sent to Togo to make a proposal for full 'integration', but this was rebuffed. By this point, the Olympio government had decided that the immediate priority was to achieve independence from France. In April 1959, a British consular despatch confirmed that the Togoland government's interest in dealing with Ghana was "only in the commercial and economic fields leaving any political involvement until the end of next year".[87] With the independence of Nigeria in the offing, the Minister of Commerce expected "much wind to be taken out of the Ghanaian leaders' sails when the great mass of Nigeria draws alongside". The Togolese were starting to think of an alternative economic association, possibly involving other countries in the sub-region. Revealingly, the same despatch referred to an interest in pursuing the Swiss option:

Some Ministers hinted rather optimistically that Togo would like to become a little Switzerland in West Africa, living quietly, without any strings from abroad, subsidised by the French and anyone else who cared to help, exporting little cocoa and some phosphates, and indulging in a modest but lucrative contraband trade across the several frontiers.

After Togo became independent in 1960, the 'Swiss option' receded very quickly. Whereas Ghana's economy was stalling after successive years of rapid growth, that of Togo remained stagnant throughout.[88] It did not help that independence coincided with sliding world prices for cocoa and coffee, while foreign exchange controls retarded a return to a freewheeling trade economy. When an alternative economic union with Benin and Nigeria failed to bear fruit in 1962, the options narrowed still further.[89] On the expenditure side, Togo inherited a bureaucracy that was relatively large for such a small country, accounting for around 55 per cent of government expenditure.[90] This reflected the imperative of absorbing a good number of educated Togolese who were squeezed out of their positions in other Francophone states.[91] Much

---

[86] NAK FO 371/138262 "Internal Political Situation in Togoland", article entitled "Olympio speaks out", *Accra Evening News*, 22 January 1959.

[87] NAK FO 371/138270 "Foreign Policy in Togoland", A.T. Oldham, Consulate-General, Dakar to H.F.T. Smith, Foreign Office, 24 April 1959.

[88] According to Decalo, Togo's economic performance was the weakest of all the Francophone states between 1956 and 1965. Samuel Decalo, *Coups and Army Rule in Africa: Motivations and Constraints*, 2nd edn. (New Haven: Yale University Press, 1990), p. 209.

[89] Thompson, *Ghana's Foreign Policy*, p. 309.   [90] Decalo, *Coups*, p. 210.

[91] Decalo, *Coups*, p. 210.

like across the border, expenditure on education remained a priority because of popular demand.[92] Whereas overall education levels were high by West African standards, schooling was heavily concentrated in the south – especially in areas such as Agu where the missions had historically sunk deep roots. Indeed, the Kpalimé District had the highest schooling levels in the country, which was unlike the common pattern where the capital city dominated.

In this context, it was very difficult for the Olympio regime to fashion a viable social contract based on a bold developmental vision. A widening gap between revenues and expenditure meant that the CUT regime could scarcely promise a rapid transformation of the economy or the delivery of improved social services without incurring large external debts – which Olympio was disinclined to do. Whereas Nkrumah diverted resources northwards, partly in the hope of attracting political support, the Olympio regime did not have an immediate plan for addressing regional disparities. This ensured that its power-base remained firmly rooted in the southern half of the country. But even there, important constituencies quickly became alienated from the regime, including the market women of Lomé whose businesses were struggling, and cocoa farmers who had their own grievances over pricing.[93] Chiefs were treated with minimal respect and had their stipends as minor state functionaries reduced. In addition, in a country that had a very youthful population and significant numbers of school-leavers, there were expectations of an expansion of employment that the regime was unable to satisfy. The youth wing of the CUT had already broken away as JUVENTO in 1959. Drawing inspiration and some support from the CPP in Ghana, JUVENTO sought to mobilize youth in opposition to the CUT before it was banned outright in 1962. Under tight fiscal constraints, the Olympio regime elected to place a moratorium on new recruitments into the civil service and froze wages. The most fateful decision was to hold down military spending, which Olympio justified on the grounds that the country could not afford more.

The political dispute with Ghana escalated at the same time as the regime was haemorrhaging political support. This forced Olympio back into the arms of the French. In 1961, after a failed coup that was thought to have been instigated from Ghana, Olympio invoked a military defence agreement with France that had been signed in May 1960.[94] The attempted assassination of Nkrumah at Kulungugu, near the border with Upper Volta, in 1962 brought relations to their lowest point yet. It was widely believed that Ghana was

[92] Marie-France Lange, *L'école au Togo: processus de scolarisation et institution de l'école en Afrique* (Paris: Karthala, 1998), p. 129.

[93] Decalo, *Coups*, p. 212.

[94] Thompson, *Ghana's Foreign Policy*, p. 233. Saadia Touval, *The Boundary Politics of Independent Africa* (Cambridge: Harvard University Press, 1972), p. 157.

planning to resort to a military solution to the dispute. Given that Olympio had refused to support more than a token army, there was little that he could do other than to fall back upon France and potentially Nigeria for support. Meanwhile, the Nkrumah regime sought to exploit the manifest economic discomfort of the Olympio regime. In October 1960, the government restricted the export of consumer goods across the border, imposed currency restrictions and deprived Togolese vehicles of access. Then in 1962, the Ghanaian authorities closed the border altogether and imposed an economic blockade – ironically restoring the rigidities of the Vichy years and ending the relatively free trade in foodstuffs, which had been the principal achievement of negotiations in the 1950s.[95] The Nkrumah regime appreciated that political consent was closely bound up with expectations of consumption. The Ghana state media was quick to claim that the economic stranglehold was leading to acute food shortages, and even to famine, in Togo.[96] By contrast, one British report observed that:

The Ghanaian near-blockade of Togo merely caused irritation: legitimate trade was affected, but the traditional smuggling of Ghanaian cocoa and manufactured British goods into Togo continued as before.[97]

Whatever the initial rationale, closure of the border provided a convenient pretext for the Nkrumah regime whose own economic strategy was unravelling. In the 1960s, the expansion of the black market manifested itself in two specific locations where populations began to seek each other out in a manner redolent of the war years: namely in the cities and at the borders. The determination of the regime to push ahead with industrialization had implications for the role of the state in managing the expectations surrounding consumption. Many industries were geared to the production of basic consumer goods, which were supposed to make the country less dependent upon foreign imports. But capital investments in machinery and the need for increased supplies of raw materials forced Ghana to increase its import bill. One means to square the circle was to restrict the importation of consumer goods to those that were deemed to be strictly necessary. The introduction of specific import licences with effect from 1962 inevitably resulted in shortages in certain product lines. Despite a government enquiry and attempts to redress the problem, shortages in urban markets had become endemic by 1964.

---

[95] The supply of petrol through the Tema harbour was deliberately interrupted, and Togolese vehicles were prevented from entering Ghana. NAK FO 371/161372 "Togo: International Political Situation", O. Kemp, British Embassy, Lomé, to K.M. Wilford, West and Central African Department, FO (21 April 1962).

[96] "Hunger Strikes Togo: Where is Olympio?", *Evening News* 20 March 1962.

[97] NAK FO 371/161372 "Togo", J.H.A. Watson, British Embassy, Dakar, to E.B. Boothby, African Department, FO (28 October 1960).

A second commission of enquiry in 1965 identified various kinks in the state distribution system. The GNTC both imported essential goods and controlled the channels through which they reached the consumer. The Abraham Commission concluded that the GNTC bore much of the responsibility because its employees often elected not to sell commodities through its own approved outlets, but to favoured private traders, often at a mark-up.[98] Even within GNTC stores, it identified anomalies, citing the specific case of Ho where cartons of milk, sugar and textiles were concealed and sold to customers at well above the control price.[99] It also identified practices of hoarding in stores owned by the United Africa Company and the CFAO (Compagnie Française de l'Afrique de l'Ouest). Because the supply constraints were common knowledge, a premium resided in cornering scarce commodities, hoarding them and then cashing in when the price rose. The second domain was at the border with Togo. The Commission claimed that some of the shortages were attributable to foreign traders who sought to repatriate their profits by despatching goods across borders – citing the specific examples of Honda motorcycles, locally produced shoes and foodstuffs.[100] It also referred to trafficking in Ghanaian currency, which was rife. Curiously, it did not recognize that there was a countervailing incentive to transport consumer goods in the opposite direction. Whereas Togo had been the recipient of consumer goods from Ghana after the war, the flow had begun to reverse in the early 1960s as shortages became routine and the cost of living rose sharply. This is reflected in the pattern of Customs seizures, which were initially weighted towards exports, but increasingly reflected the illegal importation of basic consumer items. In the case of cocoa farmers, it made sense to sell their crops across the border in exchange for hard currency that could then be used to purchase the necessities of life. Traders had an additional incentive to offload scarce commodities in urban markets where the black market was growing. In fact, it is at this time that we begin to witness the emergence of 'worm-holes' that linked urban areas to the borderlands. Much as goods that were intended for sale in the outlying regions had a tendency to find their way back to Accra, smugglers found ways and means to transport commodities from across the border to the capital. The fact that the goods were cheaper than the products of Ghanaian factories, when these were available, underlined the failure of state industrialization.

The Nkrumah regime was fighting a losing battle and, following a common pattern, resorted to institutional tinkering in a way that merely created further

[98] Republic of Ghana, *Report of the Commission of Enquiry into Trade Malpractices in Ghana* (Accra: Office of President, 1965) (Abraham Commission), p. 28. Members of Parliament were apparently amongst the beneficiaries, p. 53.
[99] Abraham Commission, p. 31.   [100] Abraham Commission, p. 12.

dislocation. As we have seen, the Customs Preventive Service (CPS) had carried considerable weight within the colonial state since the turn of the century. Because cocoa was smuggled in considerable quantities in the 1950s, the relationship between the CPS and border communities was often a tense one. In 1954, the year when producer prices were frozen, the scale of cocoa smuggling was such that the government recruited temporary preventive officers, allegedly from amongst the ranks of CPP supporters, to patrol the border.[101] In a further attempt to bolster surveillance, a law of 1959 created a presumption of intent to smuggle when cocoa was being conveyed in the direction of the border. As the trafficking of a wider range of goods increased, the Nkrumah regime concluded that preventive functions needed be accorded greater priority. In 1957, a debate in parliament elicited vocal cross-party criticism of chronic understaffing and poor remuneration and terms of service – and all that despite the fact that Customs and Excise contributed no less than 70 per cent of national revenue. Komla Gbedemah, the Minister of Finance, explained that an attempt was being made to accelerate Africanization, but that this was subject to the availability of trained personnel.[102] Kodzo Ayeke, the Togoland Congress MP for Ho West and a former Customs officer in his own right, pointed to the fact that large numbers of posts were unfilled, thus placing an intolerable strain on existing personnel.[103] The CPP Member for Kpandu South, G.R. Ahia, recommended that the Preventive operations be granted a separate existence because it had come to be treated as the poor relation of the revenue side of the operation.[104] In 1960, the Preventive Service was finally hived off and allocated to the Police, leaving the Customs Service to concentrate on revenue collection. Because the Police service was already constrained, the staff complement was augmented by individuals re-assigned from the Field Agricultural Service. This reform was accompanied by a rise in the number of seizures and convictions (Table 10.7), but the pattern was not sustained. Complaints about corruption and under-performance, which had already raised their head in the 1957 debate, eventually led to the creation of a separate Border Guards unit in 1962, but again this produced patchy results. In light of the failure of successive institutional reforms, the Nkrumah government decided that the simplest solution was to close the border altogether. Because anything that was traded across the border was by definition illegal, that in theory made policing more straightforward. But it hardly simplified the business of tackling actual smuggling. Preventing vehicles from crossing the

---

[101] Ghana. *Parliamentary Debates,*14 June 1957, speeches by Joe Appiah and Mahama Tempurie, pp. 911, 914–15.
[102] *Parliamentary Debates,* 14 June 1957, speech by Komla Gbedemah, p. 893.
[103] *Parliamentary Debates,* 14 June 1957, speech by Kodzo Ayeke, p. 898
[104] *Parliamentary Debates,* 14 June 1957, speech by G.R. Ahia, p. 902.

Table 10.7 *Indices of success in Ghana Preventive Operations, 1959–1966*

Item	1959	1960	1961	1962	1963	1964	1965	1966
Total seizures	1,305	930	2,005	1,871	1,292	1,748	1,277	2,004
Import seizures	486	480	904	934	752	1,003	675	1,046
Export seizures	621	423	1,075	937	540	745	602	958
Other	198	27	26	–	–	–	–	–
Persons convicted	1,439	1,061	2,595	2,132	1,316	1,724	1,117	1,838

Source: Republic of Ghana, Statistical Yearbook, 1969–70, table 163, p. 169.

border notionally addressed large-scale contraband, but it had no impact upon the trade that was carried out through countless unofficial crossings. The Border Guards were left with the unenviable task of trying to monitor the movement of traders across the coastal lagoons, along the innumerable tracks that crossed the flat terrain of somewhere like Agotime, and along the trails that traversed the Togoland hills.

In January 1963, Olympio turned down an appeal, made by one Sergeant Etienne Eyadéma, to absorb veterans who had been demobilized from the French colonial army. Soldiers and veterans reacted by joining forces to remove the regime, killing Olympio in the process. In a gesture of goodwill towards the incoming junta, the Ghana government reopened the border in February, and many of the specific restrictions on the trade on foodstuffs and small quantities of manufactured goods were removed. But the border was sealed again in June, in part because of the unwillingness of the Togolese authorities to increase their duties on spirits. The smuggling of alcohol, which had always featured prominently in the list of contraband items, was related to the fact that Ghana's own factories were producing a more expensive product and in insufficient quantities. The Nkrumah regime manufactured multiple excuses to keep the border closed over the next two years. It was briefly reopened in July 1965, and then closed again at the end of the year, and remained that way until the Nkrumah regime was itself toppled in a coup on 24 February 1966. The coups in Togo and Ghana were both broadly popular and reflected the inability of the regimes to satisfy popular expectations. The Swiss option remained an attractive option in Togo, but it was only some time after the fall of the Olympio that the framework for establishing an entrepôt state was fully operationalized. In the aftermath of the coup, short-term considerations assumed priority. The army was expanded from a mere 250 to 1,200 men, which enabled the army commander to expand the numbers of Kabré soldiers from the north.[105] A corresponding jump in the budgetary

---

[105] Decalo, *Coups*, p. 214.

allocation to defence merely consumed already scarce resources. The election of a power-sharing government under Nicolas Grunitzky, following a brief military interregnum, was followed by political infighting, which provided an excuse for the military to intervene for a second time in 1967. Samuel Decalo has suggested that the decision by Etienne Eyadéma to return to power was partly based on a fear that a 'populist Ewe takeover' would lead to the installation of a regime that might seek retribution for the murder of Olympio.[106]

In Ghana, the social contract had not necessarily lost its salience, but the gulf between what the CPP had promised and what Ghanaians experienced in their daily lives had become unsustainable. After the coup, the NLC was quick to cement two sets of alliances that were crucial for its capacity to govern effectively. The first was with the civil service, where some resentment had accumulated over the growth of the president's office.[107] By making the civil administration partners in government, the NLC was able to avoid becoming embroiled in much of the minutiae of decision-making. The second alliance was with traditional authorities who were openly courted by the junta because of their social embeddedness outside of the state. The CPP's meddling with the chiefly hierarchy was annulled and some 200 Paramount Chiefs were downgraded to their former status.[108] This had repercussions in the Volta Region where many chiefs who had been on the receiving end of British amalgamation policy had successfully lobbied the CPP for their elevation. Because the NLC was only ever intending to pave the way for a return to multi-party rule, there were limits to its capacity to initiate structural change. The immediate priority was stabilization of the economy: this included scaling back on capital investments; renegotiating debt repayments with the assistance of the International Monetary Fund (IMF); increasing cocoa producer prices in order to restore incentives and minimize smuggling; devaluing the currency by as much as 30 per cent; and curbing the operations of many parastatals that were running at a heavy loss.[109] At the same time, it is revealing that the NLC sought to ease some of the pressure on Ghanaian households by allocating more import licences for consumer goods and reducing the burden of taxation.[110] But crucially, the NLC did not tear up the social contract that had been forged in the 1950s. Moreover, by fixating on a series of economic reforms at the centre, the NLC failed to give much consideration to what might be

---

[106] Decalo, *Coups,* pp. 219–20.
[107] Robert Dowse, "Military and police rule", in Dennis Austin and Robin Luckham (eds.), *Politicians and Soldiers in Ghana* (London: Frank Cass, 1975), pp. 18–21.
[108] Dowse, "Military and police rule", p. 22.
[109] J.D. Esseks, "Economic policies", in Dennis Austin and Robin Luckham (eds.), *Politicians and Soldiers in Ghana* (London: Frank Cass, 1975), pp. 43–6.
[110] Killick, *Development Economics,* p. 305.

necessary to effect at the geographical margins where the CPP's own strategies had unravelled so spectacularly.

Conclusion

In this chapter, I have advanced two arguments that can be set alongside those I developed in Chapter 9. The first is that the constellation of forces was different to that in the Senegambia. In this case, the British and the French authorities set their faces against any possibility of unification of Togoland or Eweland, and they explicitly avoided developing infrastructural synergies between the two sides of the border. In principle, nationalist politicians saw the world very differently. Olympio was the pre-eminent leader of the unification movement, whereas Nkrumah was a vocal advocate of pan-African unity. Both were explicitly opposed to any perpetuation of colonial boundaries. In theory, their interests were closely aligned, but in practice they ended up pursuing incompatible objectives. Moreover, the unification movement itself grew out of a grassroots demand for rectification of the border. In the mid-1950s, the balance tilted in the direction of those who favoured the territorial status quo. One reason was that Nkrumah did not wish the unification conundrum to derail or delay Gold Coast independence. When the TC made common cause with the NLM that put them on a collision course with the CPP. In addition, once Ghana had achieved its own independence, the Nkrumah regime found other priorities. The promotion of state industrialization created an imperative to manage the flow of cocoa and consumer goods, which translated into a preference for hard, and in due course closed, borders. Although the absorption of French Togoland would have provided a convenient solution, it could never have been conceded by Olympio whose own claim to legitimacy rested on having delivered Togoland from the French. An important difference with the Gambia is that the Olympio regime and its military-cum-civilian successors struggled to actualize their own version of the entrepôt state, the so-called Swiss option.

This brings me to my second argument which is that the emergent social contracts conformed broadly to the patterns in the Senegambia, albeit with some important nuances. The CPP regime in Ghana borrowed from a post-war developmental script and sought to position the state at the centre of economic life. Ghanaians were enjoined to embrace austerity on the basis that the socialist programme would deliver greater societal benefits in the long run. The CPP's vision was high-modernist, and there is good evidence to believe that many rural and urban Ghanaians bought into it – at least to start with. In Ghana, roads and schools had long been regarded as the key indicators of progress, and it was pressure from below that led to so much emphasis being placed on delivery of these public goods. But it was also the images that swirled around the promise of private and collective consumption that held persuasive value. Across the border in Togo, there was no realistic possibility that the state could drive development, and nor could it provide that much in the way of basic social services. Although the smuggling trade had begun to open up fresh possibilities, the permissive social contract had not yet come to fruition by 1967 when Eyadéma seized power for a second time. Hence, the political malaise in Togo was as palpable as it was in Ghana. As we will see in Part IV, the trajectories diverged markedly over subsequent decades.

States, Social Contracts and Respacing from Below, c.1970–2010

In the final section of this study, I elaborate upon two themes that were central to the analysis in Part III: namely, efforts to reconfigure political boundaries or to modify their practical effects and the piecing together of social contracts that were mediated by border dynamics. During the 1970s and 1980s, the territorial configurations that had emerged at the point of independence remained broadly stable, although they were framed within a much less favourable external environment. While there were renewed efforts at resurrecting the goal of Senegambian unity, the border remained a source of perennial tension between Ghana and Togo and was closed for extended periods of time. In the 1990s, there was a partial reversal of these patterns, as reflected in the outbreak of a secessionist insurgency in the Casamance and the relative normalization of relations between Ghana and Togo. All of this was bound up with modifications to the larger social contracts. Whereas a failure to deliver in Ghana and Senegal was accompanied by the surfacing of permissive elements, these became dominant in Togo and the Gambia. As quintessential micro-states, the latter achieved a modicum of success by feeding off their larger neighbours. The contraband trade, and the livelihoods that spun off it, was what enabled these states to reach an accommodation with large swathes of the population who would otherwise have derived little benefit from their existence. Although there was considerable continuity, a qualitative shift was the emergence of a new manifestation of urbanism in which the fortunes – both literally and figuratively – of the cities and the geographical margins were bound together in manifold ways.

In composing the final clutch of chapters, I was tempted to begin with an account of trade, mobility and urbanism and only then to allocate the states a role in the unfolding plot. This would have been faithful to the reality that many of the outcomes were the cumulative effect of the daily strategies enacted by borderlanders to fashion a living and to maintain their consumption preferences. Although the account that I offer might appear to be politically over-determined and state-centred, the aim is actually to underline the profound limits to state power. When governments intervened, they did so on the mostly unspoken assumption that it was the responsibility of state institutions to manage economic processes and to channel social change in the name of development and national unity. The reality is that intervention often had entirely different consequences to those that were intended. As populations variously sought to live with, appropriate, evade and subvert the notional rules of the game, they effectively forced governments to re-evaluate their own ways of working – thereby bringing about a recalibration of the relationship between institutions and the population at large. This cycle of bargaining and repeated re-negotiation was especially striking within border regions where the mismatch between official declarations of intent and concrete outcomes was particularly stark. By switching the focus back and forth from the centre to the geographical margins, I hope to convey some of the dynamics according to which real-time governance was constituted. As before, I begin this comparison in the Senegambia before turning to the trans-Volta in Chapter 12.

11   Barnacle States and Boundary Lines
States, Trade and Urbanism in the Senegambia

As a recent comparative history of a very different topic nicely demonstrates, points of crisis tend to prompt a re-negotiation of the terms of engagement between the state and societal actors.[1] Such was the case in the Senegambia in the decades after 1970 when the crisis was situated within an unhappy conjuncture between the great Sahelian drought of 1968–73 and the OPEC oil price hikes of 1973–4. Declining global prices for agricultural exports, including groundnuts, further compounded an already dire economic picture during the 1980s. The initial response of government was to attempt a rescaling of state institutions as well as a respacing of economic activity in a manner that was intended to draw the geographical margins deeper into state planning objectives. Given that the starting points in Senegal and the Gambia were so different, and given the disparities of size, it is not surprising that the responses varied. Precisely because what *was* attempted had a knock-on effect on the other side of the border, governments in the two countries often found themselves locked in active competition, which belied a professed commitment to good neighbourliness. The difficulty of managing a complex web of relationships helps to account for a renewed Senegalese interest in the pursuit of cross-border co-operation that culminated in the short-lived Senegambian Confederation (1982–9). At the same time, the outbreak of the Casamance insurgency and the emergence of new modes of peripheral urbanism may be counted amongst the unintended consequences of state intervention.

---

[1] The study deals with the Aude and Guadaloupe during the French Third Republic. In this case, Elizabeth Heath demonstrates how social contracts were renegotiated in the context of the global economic crisis and the outbreak of phylloxera in the last decades of the nineteenth century. Elizabeth Heath, *Wine, Sugar and the Making of Modern France: Global Economic Crisis and the Racialization of French Citizenship, 1870–1910* (Cambridge: Cambridge University Press, 2014).

Reconfiguring Social Contracts: State Planning and Border Flows

In Senegal, the first decade of independence culminated in a crisis that was profoundly social and political as much as it was purely economic.[2] In the drylands, acute food shortages arising from drought conditions threatened to force many peasants and pastoralists off the land. In addition, farmers in the groundnut basin suffered the consequences of the withdrawal of French subsidies in 1968, the increasing bureaucratic costs associated with state marketing, and declining yields resulting from soil exhaustion. The net result was that the real income of groundnut farmers halved in a matter of years.[3] During the so-called *malaise paysan*, farmers refused to honour their debts to the co-operatives or to sell their groundnuts through the approved marketing channels. The *grand marabouts* took their cue from these rumblings of peasant dissent by assuming a less accommodating stance towards the ruling party, especially following the accession of Abdou Lahatte M'Backe to leadership of the Mourides.[4] In 1974, in response to expressions of concern by the Mouride leadership, producer prices were doubled.[5] But the damage had been done, and many farmers began to turn their backs on the groundnut altogether.

The rural crisis accelerated the drift to urban centres, which inevitably placed greater pressure upon an already burdened infrastructure. Dakar was the primary magnet, but Senegal also experienced a distinctive form of urbanism in the groundnut basin. The Mouride capital of Touba was a very modest town of 5,000 *talibés* in 1964, but by 1976 it had grown to a settlement of 30,000 inhabitants and by 1980 it was home to no fewer than 50,000 people. Although the really prolific growth came still later, it was already clear that the

---

[2] The crisis and attempted restructuring have already been dealt with by a number of authors, which means that the overview offered here can be somewhat abbreviated. Edward J. Schumaker, *Politics, Bureaucracy and Rural Development in Senegal* (Berkeley, Los Angeles and London: University of California Press, 1975), pp. 171–85; Robert Fatton Jnr., *The Making of a Liberal Democracy: Senegal's Passive Revolution, 1975–1985* (Boulder and London: Lynne Rienner, 1987), pp. 53–75; Donal B. Cruise O'Brien, "Senegal", in John Dunn (ed.), *West African States: Failure and Promise – A Study in Comparative Politics* (Cambridge: Cambridge University Press, 1978), pp. 173–88; and Catherine Boone, *Merchant Capital and the Roots of State Power in Senegal, 1930–1985* (Cambridge: Cambridge University Press, 1992), pp. 165–206.

[3] Boone, *Merchant Capital*, pp. 110–11.

[4] Boone, *Merchant Capital*, pp. 199–201; Cruise O'Brien, *Saints and Politicians*, p. 140. Abdou Lahatte even appeared to endorse the abandonment of groundnuts in favour of foodstuffs. Donal B. Cruise O'Brien, "Ruling class and peasantry in Senegal, 1960–1976: the politics of a monocrop economy", in Rita Cruise O'Brien (ed.), *Political Economy of Underdevelopment: Dependence in Senegal* (Beverly Hills and London: Sage, 1979), p. 222; Robert Fatton, *The Making of a Liberal Democracy: Senegal's Passive Revolution, 1975–1985* (Boulder and London: Lynne Rienner, 1987), p. 100.

[5] Cruise O'Brien, "Ruling class and peasantry", p. 225.

Mouride order was beginning to actively embrace urbanism and associated modes of making a living – most notably in the shape of trade.[6] What is remarkable is not just Touba's meteoric rise to the status of Senegal's second city, but the fact that the state authorities had so little to do with it. Hence Eric Ross writes that:

It is the [Mouride] order that has managed the entire urbanization process, including such fundamentals as the laying out of streets and thoroughfares, the creation of housing allotments, the distribution of water, the management of markets, schools, and hospitals, and so forth.[7]

In subsequent years, Touba established its position as a unique politico-religious space – dubbed 'Senegal's Vatican' – where state institutions such as the Police were symbolically absent from the scene – if actually hovering at the urban margins.[8] This meant that state agencies were not in a position to monitor the activity that radiated out of this emerging commercial hub – much of which was illicit, as we will see. Moreover, Touba was treated as a tax-free zone until 1997, which conferred a particular advantage on its Marché Ocass.[9] The respect for Mouride autonomy may have gone against the instincts of Senegalese bureaucrats, but it was a necessary concession at a time when the ruling party's support was at a low ebb. Although Touba was an extreme case, the institutional limits of the state were set in a process of constant bargaining with religious authorities in emergent urban centres across Senegal, with profound consequences.[10]

Meanwhile, the Senghor regime struggled to cope with the mounting problem of unemployment and its attendant social effects. Dakar mushroomed from a city of around 315,703 people in 1960 to 967,051 in 1980.[11] Although much of this increase was attributable to natural growth, inward migration accounted

---

[6] Eric Ross, *Sufi City: Urban Design and Archetypes in Touba* (Rochester and Woodbridge: University of Rochester Press, 2006), p. 2. As head of the Mourides between 1968 and 1989, Abdou Lahatte presided over the institutional adaptations needed for the successful management of the growth of Touba. Cheikh Guèye, *Touba: la capitale des Mourides* (Dakar and Paris: Enda, Karthala and IRD, 2002), pp. 231–2.

[7] Ross, *Sufi City*, p. 2.

[8] Donal B. Cruise O'Brien, *Symbolic Confrontations: Muslims Imagining the State in Africa* (New York: Palgrave Macmillan, 2003), p. 67.

[9] Cruise O'Brien, *Symbolic Confrontations*, p. 65

[10] Fatick was a smaller urban centre, where the Mourides were not dominant, and here the tensions between state actors and the local population were more obvious. But the process of negotiation with religious authority was present here as well. See Leonardo Villalón, *Islamic Society and State Power in Senegal: Disciples and Citizens in Fatick* (Cambridge: Cambridge University Press, 2006).

[11] K.C. Zachariah and Julien Condé, *Migration in West Africa: Demographic Aspects* (Washington DC: World Bank and OECD, 1981), p. 88. Cruise O'Brien cites a higher estimate of 374,000 for Dakar in 1960/1, *Saints and Politicians*, p. 163.

for as much as 40 per cent of urban expansion as a whole between 1960 and 1970.[12] There were long-established patterns of seasonal migration towards Dakar, not least from the Casamance. With the declining returns to rice culture in the Casamance, and the near collapse of agrarian economies in northern Senegal, there was a tendency for both men – and increasingly Jola women as well – to remain in the city in the hope of finding permanent employment.[13] For the majority of these incomers, many of whom lacked formal education, the aim was to secure manual work or employment in the informal sector – in small-scale craft production (e.g. tailoring), services (e.g. hairdressing), or buying and selling in formal markets and on the streets.[14] Given its limited capacity to create jobs for the masses, the Senegalese authorities had little option than to permit an enlarged space for the so-called informal sector. The Senghor regime had more of a problem when it came to an increasingly disaffected stratum of educated youth whose prospects for formal employment after leaving school and university looked distinctly bleak. This came to a head in the student unrest of 1968 – at a time of global ferment – when specific grievances were linked to a wider critique of the dictatorial tendencies of the regime and the baleful effects of French neo-colonialism.[15] National strikes of public sector workers over 1968–9, which were led by the Union Nationale des Travailleurs Sénégalais (UNTS), equally signalled worker discontent with a government policy of maintaining downward pressure on wages. Finally, the government faced more strident demands for better treatment from aspirant businessmen, who formed the Union des Groupements Economiques du Sénégal (UNIGES) in 1968 to lobby for curbs on French and Lebanese commercial dominance and greater state backing for Senegalese business.[16]

The government reflex was, first of all, to deflect and channel the emerging sources of opposition. Following a crackdown on student protests in 1968, the regime proceeded to co-opt the leadership of the student movement through the selective offer of official positions. At the same time, the UNTS was disbanded in favour of a new union, the Confédération Nationale des Travailleurs du Sénégal (CNTS), which was formally integrated into the structures of the UPS, a pill that was sweetened by the offer of party sinecures.[17] Much

---

[12] Dakar itself accounted for around 60 per cent of net migration. Zachariah and Condé, *Migration in West Africa*, pp. 82–3, 88–9.

[13] On the importance of the migration to the city of Jola, and especially women, see Michael C. Lambert, *Longing for Exile: Migration and Making of a Translocal Community in Senegal, West Africa* (Portsmouth: Heinemann, 2002). See especially ch. 6 for a discussion of women's migratory patterns.

[14] For an analysis, see Chris Gerry, "The crisis of the self-employed: petty production and capitalist production in Dakar", in Rita Cruise O'Brien (ed.), *Political Economy of Underdevelopment: Dependence in Senegal* (Beverly Hills and London: Sage, 1979).

[15] Boone, *Merchant Capital*, p. 171.   [16] Fatton, *The Making*, p. 60.

[17] Boone, *Merchant Capital*, p. 171.

the same strategy was adopted in handling critics within the business sector: a rival business association to UNIGES was established and then they were merged to form the much more biddable Groupements Economiques du Sénégal (GES).[18] An altogether different strategy is reflected in the decision to re-admit the possibility of organized political opposition, which Robert Fatton argues was designed to fragment the forces of the left.[19] The Casamance played its own part in prising open this political opportunity. In 1970, an avowedly left-wing party calling itself Sunu Gaal was formed with a view to securing better representation for the Casamance, but was denied formal recognition.[20] In 1974, its leaders joined forces with Abdoulaye Wade to establish a new political party, the Parti Démocratique Sénégalais (PDS). On this occasion, the government agreed to recognize the party, creating the first legal opposition since 1966.[21] The Senegalese political system henceforth operated as a controlled quasi-democracy with three political parties occupying fixed points on the ideological spectrum: the Parti Africain de l'Indépendance (PAI) representing Marxism; the UPS, now recast as the Parti Socialiste (PS) standing for socialism; and the PDS notionally representing liberalism, despite its ideological roots in Sunu Gaal.[22]

Whereas these reactions were intended to buy time, a more profound response was the attempt to reconfigure the role of the Senegalese state. Hitherto, state intervention had been constrained by French economic interests, on the one hand, and the influence of the Muslim brotherhoods, on the other. Although these still needed to be taken into account, there was a perceived need to break with some of the established patterns by virtue of the disappointing record of Senegal's development strategy up until this point. One measured step was the decision to scale back the French presence, which created openings in relatively senior positions in the bureaucracy and deflected some of the criticism of neo-colonialism.[23] At the same time, the creation of a series of new ministries enabled the regime to fashion fresh openings for university graduates.[24] These changes were introduced despite the fact that government salaries already consumed more than half of government expenditure at the end of the 1960s.[25] Catherine Boone observes that decentralization reforms in

[18] Boone, *Merchant Capital*, p. 184.   [19] Fatton, *The Making*, p. 12.

[20] Vincent Foucher, "The Mouvement des Forces Démocratiques de Casamance: The illusion of separatism?", unpublished paper, p. 10.

[21] Cruise O'Brien suggests that it was the very difficulties the PDS experienced in establishing itself as a credible alternative that also led to the Senghor re-legalizing the PAI. Cruise O'Brien, "Senegal", p. 176.

[22] In 1979, a fourth party was admitted, the Mouvement Républicain Sénégalais. Fatton, *The Making*, p. 74.

[23] Boone, *Merchant Capital*, p. 178.   [24] Boone, *Merchant Capital*, p. 179.

[25] In 1962/3, revenue amounted to 34,548 million CFA francs, while expenditure stood at 29,888 million CFA. In 1968/9, revenue had increased to 36,750 million CFA, which matched

1972 deflected some of the bureaucratic expansion downwards and outwards to the regional and local levels.[26] This attempt at rescaling the state bureaucracy was of course deeply ironic because it was conducted in the name of decentralization. In the same vein, state institutions were expected to assume a much greater role with respect to the economy. The Third Development Plan (1960–73) placed considerable emphasis on the promotion of industry as the engine of Senegalese economic development.[27] Although there were efforts to attract foreign investment, for example through the establishment of an industrial zone, the state was expected to take the lead role. Between 1970 and 1975 no fewer than seventy parastatals were established, which translated into the creation of many substantive jobs.[28] Given the underlying budgetary constraints, all this additional investment meant drawing heavily on external loans for the start-up costs. In some respects, Senegal was following in the footsteps of Ghana, albeit a decade later. The difference is that the Senegalese state entered into many more joint ventures: for example, in the textile sector the state took an 80 per cent stake in the French cotton firm, the Compagnie Française de Développement des Fibres Textiles (CFDT), leading to the creation of another parastatal, the Société de Développement des Fibres Textiles (SODEFITEX).[29]

The agrarian crisis simultaneously led to a renewed interest in interventions to address the issue of food security and to promote national self-sufficiency. This involved parastatals, often in association with private capital, and was part of a more sustained effort to reconfigure national economic space. Whereas the middle and upper Senegal had hitherto been neglected, priority was now attached to the development of irrigated rice farming along the riverain border with Mauritania.[30] At the same time, the historical centre of irrigated agriculture in the Senegal River delta was turned over to the production of sugar cane.[31] Greater deference was also paid to the potential to significantly increase agricultural output in the Casamance, in part through the dissemination of improved seeds. The projected increases in production

expenditure. République du Sénégal, *Projet de IIIe Plan Quadriennal de Developpement et Social, 1969–1973*, Tome I (Dakar: Ministère du Plan et de l'Industrie, 1969), pp. 22–4.

[26] Boone, *Merchant Capital*, p. 180.

[27] The Plan estimated that 5,270 jobs would have been created between 1967 and 1973. République du Sénégal, *Projet de IIIe Plan*, Tome II, pp. 30–1. The first steps were taken with the creation of the Société Nationale d'Etudes et de Promotion Industrielle (SONEPI) which was mandated to nurture Senegalese entrepreneurship through "training, financial guarantees, project preparation and the establishment of industrial estates." World Bank, *Senegal: Tradition, Diversification and Economic Development* (Washington DC: World Bank, 1974), pp. 161–3.

[28] Fatton, *The Making*, p. 73.

[29] CFDT continued to run the company. Boone, *Merchant Capital*, p. 175. The Plan projected a significant expansion of cloth production from 12 to 20 million metres by 1973, *Projet de IIIe Plan*, Tome I, p. 195.

[30] Boone, *Political Topographies*, pp. 304–14.   [31] World Bank, *Senegal*, p. 143.

were accompanied by plans for developing associated agro-industries: notably the production of groundnut oil and feed cakes, sugar, fertilizer (from phosphates) and fish-meal.[32] Amongst its priorities, the Third Development Plan identified the production of refined and raw sugar at a new refinery in Richard Toll; rice mills and tomato canneries along the Senegal River and in the Casamance; and milk treatment factories.[33] The rationale was that these investments would reduce Senegalese dependency on consumer imports and thereby save vital foreign exchange. But in crucial respects, the Senegalese government was also stating its intention to revive the colonial model of *mise en valeur*, in which different parts of the national territory would play their centrally allotted roles. Crucial for our purposes, most of this investment was located in border regions, which became fully integrated into state planning objectives for the first time. In that sense, an agenda for rescaling state institutions had profound spatial consequences as well.

Nurturing indigenous capitalism was an integral part of the package, but Senegalese entrepreneurs typically made their inroads into commerce rather than industry. In 1973, a list of consumer products was released that required industries to sell a fixed proportion of their output to one hundred approved *hommes d'affaires*, who also qualified for preferential bank credit.[34] In addition, the lucrative rice trade was opened up, so that in the words of Boone: "[s]ix or seven Senegalese trading companies imported and handled the wholesale distribution of all Senegal's rice in 1971–72."[35] The parasitic character of the business stratum, which prospered on the basis of mark-ups made from selling on, was mercilessly parodied by Sembène Ousmane in his classic novel, and extremely graphic film, *Xala*.[36] State regulation conferred economic rents on those who enjoyed access to the inside track, and as the Mourides shifted their own interests into commerce, it is not surprising that they were amongst the principal beneficiaries.[37] And herein resided a contradiction that became strikingly apparent over time: namely, that while the Mourides were located at the heart of the ruling coalition, their interests ran directly counter to the government strategy of nurturing national (agro-) industries. In particular, Mouride traders became deeply embedded in the re-export

---

[32] Mark Gersovitz and John Waterbury, "Introduction", in Mark Gersovitz and John Waterbury (eds.), *The Political Economy of Risk and Choice in Senegal* (London: Frank Cass, 1987), p. 5.
[33] *Projet de IIIe Plan*, Tome II, pp. 24–5.   [34] Boone, *Merchant Capital*, pp. 194–5.
[35] Boone, *Merchant Capital*, p. 194.
[36] The film begins with the Senegalization of the Chamber of Commerce – an actual event – and addresses the dubious practices surrounding the distribution of rice.
[37] But the political logic of regulation was also apparent at lower levels as well. For example, Cruise O'Brien cites the specific example of the retail bread trade in Dakar in which a school-leaving certificate became a requirement for the allocation of a kiosk. Cruise O'Brien, "Senegal", p. 181.

trade from the Gambia – which included the systematic trafficking of contraband textiles, sugar and rice, the three commodities that assumed pride of place in Senegalese development plans. The World Bank estimated Senegalese fiscal losses arising from the trafficking of goods at 30 per cent of total import levies at the close of the 1960s. The same report observed that:

The wide-stretching frontiers of Senegal, not easily policed, tempt smugglers. Through the Gambian enclave, which has considerably lower tariffs on imports easily transportable commodities such as cigarettes, transistors, and toilet soaps were illegally imported into Senegal.[38]

In the Gambia, the government response was both similar and different. In the first ten years of independence, the authorities did not even come up with a substantive development plan, despite the fact that revenues had plotted a modest upward trajectory. The government of Dawda Jawara did generate three capital expenditure programmes geared towards infrastructural improvements, but these were essentially ad hoc. As an official report later explained:

... in particular neither private investment nor macroeconomic targets were included. Rather, they sought to implement readily identifiable public sector projects in a way that reflected broad development opportunities within the constraints of finance and execution capacity.[39]

If the money could be found for a particular project, and the latter seemed likely to have some positive spinoffs, it was generally adopted. This pragmatic logic tended to reinforce a bias in favour of infrastructural spending for which external funding tended to be more readily available. The lack of any larger vision was apparent from Jawara's speech to mark ten years of independence: it offered a general overview of the record in agriculture and listed projects that were anticipated in the coming years, but without laying out a coherent plan for a more prosperous future.[40]

As in Senegal, the Sahelian drought forced the Gambian government to reconsider its priorities, culminating in the adoption of the first Five-Year Plan, which was operative from 1975/6 to 1979/80. The Plan, which was couched in the borrowed language of "popular participation and self-reliance", aimed at achieving self-sufficiency in cereals production and a diversification of agriculture away from an exclusive focus on groundnuts.[41] The emphasis on agriculture and livestock was reflected in the allocation of a greater share of

[38] World Bank, *Senegal*, p. 192.

[39] Republic of the Gambia, *Country Economic Memorandum for the Donors' Conference on the Gambia, 1984, Vol I, Main Report* (Banjul: Ministry of Economic Planning and Industrial Development, 1984), p. I-5.

[40] Republic of the Gambia, *Presidential Address Delivered by His Excellency Sir Dawda Kairaba Jawara, President of the Republic of the Gambia at the State Opening of Parliament on Thursday 5th June, 1975* (Banjul: Government Printer, 1975).

[41] Gambia, *Country Economic Memorandum*, p. I-6.

Table 11.1 *Gambian budgetary outlays, 1963/1964–1976/1977 (000s Dalasis at 1976/1977 prices)[a]*

Heading	1963/ 1964	1966/ 1967	1968/ 1969	1970/ 1971	1972/ 1973	1974/ 1975	1976/ 1977
1. General							
Presidency	594	1,084	1,019	1,602	1,878	2,746	2,454
Foreign affairs	111	766	1,402	2,262	3,183	4,728	5,350
Finance	239	944	1,042	1,151	1,368	1,844	1,363
Police, fire	2,516	2,612	2,540	3,051	2,758	2,338	3,273
Sundry	1,248	1,218	1,420	1,780	1,807	1,878	2,285
Sub-total	*4,708*	*6,624*	*7,423*	*9,846*	*10,994*	*13,534*	*14,725*
	17.99%	*21.89%*	*22.29%*	*25.72%*	*28.71%*	*31.81%*	*25.61%*
2. Devt. admin.							
Local govt	1,628	1,411	1,425	1,500	1,848	1,793	2,488
Agriculture	1,461	2,226	2,836	3,848	4,144	4,424	7,975
Works, comm	5,895	7,683	8,028	7,996	6,809	9,851	13,223
Education	3,097	3,708	4,593	5,238	5,090	4,866	7,281
Health	3,177	3,205	3,220	3,832	3,837	3,780	6,272
Sub-total	*15,258*	*18,233*	*20,102*	*22,414*	*21,728*	*24,714*	*37,239*
	58.30%	*60.34%*	*60.36%*	*58.56%*	*56.73%*	*58.09%*	*64.78%*
3. General accounts							
Pensions	3,810	4,228	3,843	3,685	3,144	2,097	2,433
Public debt	267	383	376	1,373	1,500	1,129	1,939
Misc.	2,129	800	1,561	959	963	1,070	1,153
Sub-total	6,206	5,411	5,780	6,017	5,577	4,296	5,525
	23.71%	17.82%	17.36%	15.72%	14.56%	10.10%	9.61%
Grand Total	**26,172**	**30,368**	**33,305**	**38,277**	**38,299**	**42,544**	**57,489**
	100.00%	**100.00%**	**100.00%**	**100.00%**	**100.00%**	**100.00%**	**100.00%**

[a] Prices deflated by average of import retail price index and retail price index.
Source: World Bank, The Gambia: Basic Needs in the Gambia (1981), table 6, p. 117.

the budget to this sector (see Table 11.1). But unlike in Senegal, the Gambian market was simply too minuscule to make autonomous industrial development a viable option. The industry, such as it was, was largely confined to agricultural processing, most notably the production of groundnut oil for export. It also included the manufacture of beer and soft drinks, the two consumer items where preferences tended to mould themselves to international borders.[42] Only

---

[42] In that sense, they were unlike cigarettes where consumers tended to be influenced most heavily by price. In the 1980s, just over half of the harvest was crushed for oil before exportation. Hazel R. Barrett, *The Marketing of Foodstuffs in the Gambia, 1400–1980: A Geographical Analysis* (Aldershot: Avebury, 1988), p. 89.

three enterprises employed in excess of 100 workers, which is a telling indicator of the size of Gambian industry.[43] Nevertheless, there were certain parallels with the Senegalese response, most notably in the proliferation of parastatals in the agro-industrial and service sectors. And, as in Senegal, this led to an expansion in size of the public sector payroll. In 1977/8 alone, the civil service is alleged to have grown by as much as 70 per cent.[44]

The continuity resided in the lack of attention to the delivery of social amenities. Hence public expenditure on works and communications accounted for as much as health and education together. In 1981, a World Bank study painted a bleak picture of the provision of basic needs in the Gambia. At 35 years, life expectancy was ten years below the continental average.[45] The report noted that there were two hospitals, one in Banjul and another in Bansang, alongside ten health centres and some sixty dispensaries.[46] However, salaries consumed most of the health budget (67.2 per cent of the total in 1974/5), leaving scant resources for the purchase of equipment and drugs. But these aggregate figures also obscure marked regional variations. In Banjul, child mortality was half that in the countryside. In the sphere of education, the same report noted that there were only eighty primary schools outside the capital: while national enrolment was 35 per cent, this climbed to 90 per cent in Banjul and Kombo St. Mary, but fell to as low as 20 per cent in most of the countryside.[47] In 1973, there were only 6,994 children in secondary school, and of these, 3,240 were located in the Banjul, 1,353 in Kombo St. Mary and 1,083 in the Brikama Local Government Areas respectively.[48] The report, which observed that spending was more skewed in education than health, concluded that "It can be estimated that about 50 percent of the funds for education are spent on the 16 percent of the population that live in the area of the capital city."[49] Although the First Five-Year Plan was supposed to rectify the imbalances, this had manifestly not happened by the end of the decade.

As in Senegal, it was innovations in the sphere of distribution that created some of the easiest pickings for Gambian entrepreneurs. Most of the European commercial firms had wound down their trading operations at independence.

---

[43] Gambia, *Country Economic Memorandum*, p. I-4. In 1974/5, out of a total GDP of 296.6 million Dalasis, manufacturing accounted for only 8 million, by comparison with 107 million for agriculture, 36.8 million for transport and communications and 36.8 million for trade, including the groundnut trade (table 3.3, pp. 3–27).

[44] Malcolm F. McPherson and Steven C. Radelet, "The Economic Recovery Programme: background and formulation", in Malcolm F. McPherson and Steven C. Radelet (eds.), *Economic Recovery in the Gambia: Insights for Structural Adjustment in Sub-Saharan Africa* (Cambridge: Harvard University Press, 1995), p. 22.

[45] World Bank, *The Gambia: Basic Needs in the Gambia* (Washington DC: World Bank, 1981), p. iii.

[46] World Bank, *The Gambia*, p. 20   [47] World Bank, *The Gambia*, p. 18.

[48] World Bank, *The Gambia*, table 11, p. 19.   [49] World Bank, *The Gambia*, p. 18.

Lebanese merchants, many of whom relocated from Dakar, secured their niche by sourcing cheaper Asian goods.[50] But after 1973, the Lebanese were themselves subject to competition from the National Trading Corporation (NTC). The latter imported consumer goods in its own right and was one of the internal distributors of rice imported by the Gambia Produce Marketing Board (GPMB).[51] Although the NTC occupied a prominent position in commerce, its items were mostly distributed through the channels of private traders. At the top of the distribution chain, a handful of Gambian merchants engaged in the import trade and competed with the Lebanese in the purchasing of groundnuts when the European firms withdrew from the scene.[52] But these urban merchants depended on a dense network of smaller traders on both sides of the border, to whom they were often connected by the extension of lines of credit. Hazel Barrett refers to a system of formal markets in the Gambia, where dues were collected and basic facilities like market stalls were provided, but these existed alongside a proliferation of informal markets. If the latter grew sufficiently large, they might become absorbed into the formal structure, but at any given time, much of the trading activity was 'uncaptured' and untaxed.[53] Cross-border trade became integral to the livelihoods of a large segment of the rural population, and most of it – from imported rice to a lengthening list of consumer items – entered through the port at Banjul. Traders were supported by a host of other actors, including the owners of vehicles and donkey carts, porters, canoemen and scouts, all of whom exploited their specialist knowledge of the border.

The greatest contributor to Gambian public finances was import duties. The latter were the principal component of indirect taxes, which accounted for 66 per cent of all revenue in 1976/7.[54] Because the duties were generally set rather low, it could be argued that the urban population gained disproportionately because it consumed more. This was accentuated by state subsidies on imported rice that were consumed primarily in Banjul and its environs.[55] However, a very large proportion of what was imported was taxed and then re-exported to Senegal through unofficial channels – including, of course, the most important staple of all, namely rice. To that extent, the population of Banjul benefited indirectly from consumption in Senegal. Moreover, while

---

[50] Mohamed Mbodji, "D'une frontière à l'autre, ou l'histoire de la marginalisation des commerçants Senegambiens sur la longue durée: la Gambie de 1816 à 1979", in Boubacar Barry and Leonhard Harding (eds.), *Commerce et commerçants en Afrique de l'Ouest: le Sénégal* (Paris: l'Harmattan, 1992), pp. 229–30.

[51] Barrett, *Marketing*, p. 80.

[52] The principal Gambian traders were Alhaji Momodou N'jie, S. Bojang and Korr Joor Jeng. Mbodji, "D'une frontière à l'autre", p. 224.

[53] Barrett, *Marketing*, pp. 108–41.   [54] World Bank, *The Gambia*, table 4, p. 115.

[55] Barrett estimated that Banjul and Kombo St. Mary consumed over 70 per cent of the imported rice, despite containing only 16 per cent of the population in 1978/9. Barrett, *Marketing*, p. 150.

taxes on groundnuts were a significant contributor to the public coffers, there were limits on how far the producers could be squeezed in a country that represented one long border. Memories of the 1950s, when Gambian ground-nuts had been traded into Senegal, were still fresh. Hence the Gambian authorities sought to maintain a sufficiently high producer price to placate their own farmers, whilst sucking in as many groundnuts from the Senegalese side of the border as possible. In the early 1960s, the maintenance of French subsidies on Senegalese groundnuts ensured that producer prices were com-petitive with those in the Gambia. However, the withdrawal of the French groundnut subsidy, combined with a decision to reduce the producer price by 15 per cent in 1967/8, meant that a significant gap opened up with prices in the Gambia.[56] In 1969, an article in *Le Monde* noted that while farmers in Senegal received 17 CFA francs per kilogramme for their crop, the equivalent in the Gambia was 24 CFA francs, in addition to which smugglers could return home with consumer items that cost half as much.[57] As with import duties, the revenues derived from smuggled groundnuts helped to alleviate the burden that might otherwise have been placed on Gambian farmers. As the 1970s wore on, it became increasingly evident that the Gambian government had a vested interest in facilitating the contraband trade. By 1980, it is estimated that re-exports to Senegal accounted for around 38 per cent of the Gambia's GDP, and most of this trade was illegal.[58] Contraband had quite literally become an affair of state as well as the daily business of the multitude.

This was closely related to the consolidation of a political system that was relatively open and free of repression – as manifested in the legal operation of opposition parties, the holding of regular elections, the absence of political prisoners and a minimalist security apparatus. The People's Progressive Party (PPP) was initially perceived as a party of the Protectorate whereas the United Party (UP) was construed as a party of the capital. In successive elections, the PPP was able to assert its dominance in most parts of the country, faring best in areas with a preponderance of Mandinka voters.[59] The opposition continued to capture the majority of votes in Banjul proper, despite the fact that the government channelled a disproportionate share of public goods there. Signifi-cantly, though, the PPP was also able to establish a commanding position in the Kombos, including Serekunda and Brikama, whose flourishing as centres of regional commerce hinged on the maintenance of open borders. Although

---

[56] Schumaker, *Politics, Bureaucracy and Rural Development*, p. 182.

[57] NAGB EXA 1/8 "Senegalo-Gambian Co-operation Customs (1967–1975)", *Le Monde* 11 Sep-tember 1969, translated copy in file.

[58] Stephen Golub and Ahmadou Aly Mbaye, "National trade policies and smuggling in Africa: the case of the Gambia and Senegal", *World Development* 37 (3) 2008, figure 3, p. 601.

[59] Arnold Hughes and David A. Perfect, *A Political History of the Gambia, 1816–1994* (Roches-ter: University of Rochester Press, 2006), pp. 166–70.

the Jawara regime could not create many jobs,[60] it was able to secure a broad measure of acceptance in the urban areas by permitting commercial networks to flourish relatively unhindered.

The divergent approaches of the Senegalese and Gambian governments had institutional consequences. The Gambian Customs service remained a skeletal operation for the simple reason that it was uneconomic to invest in anything more than the most desultory operations upriver. A Customs report from 1968 followed a familiar colonial script:

> As the Gambia is surrounded by the Republic of Senegal, there is much scope for the smuggling of goods across the boundary between the two countries. The Customs outposts established at Barra, Jawara, Farafenni, Georgetown and Basse might not be considered effective against smuggling, but serve as useful checking posts; for it will not be economical to have outposts established along the whole boundary because the revenue that will accrue will not compensate for the heavy cost of collection. There are village revenue collectors in all the divisions that are appointed on a 10 per cent commission basis. They pay their collections to the Customs Preventive Officers in each of the divisions.[61]

If collecting revenue outside Banjul was characterized by a distinct lethargy, tackling smuggling was even less of a priority. Despite the reference to Preventive Officers, there is no evidence that they mounted patrols. By contrast, the Police had their hands full dealing with the rustling of cattle and the trafficking of stolen goods.

On the Senegalese side of the border, the challenge was very different. Whereas Customs had hitherto patrolled within a few miles of the line, the effective borderlands now extended well into the groundnut basin. Kaolack, a longstanding commercial centre, remained deeply embedded in the trade with the Gambia. The surrounding rural areas of Sine-Saloum also became fully implicated in the smuggling of groundnuts. The most important shift was the emergence of Touba as a second commercial hub – one that was located far from the border and yet profoundly implicated in its dynamics. In the other direction, trading networks extended from Serekunda and Brikama deep into the Casamance, where they connected up with parallel networks reaching down into Guinea-Bissau. Hence the ground that the *douaniers* were expected to cover grew progressively larger. While it was relatively easy to set up barriers along the main roads, along which the larger trucks travelled, much of the contraband was transported by donkey carts that moved through a

---

[60] A particular challenge was to accommodate those who had acquired a higher level of education. One of the features of the Gambia was that it became an exporter of international civil servants, given the limited career trajectories for senior personnel. Creating jobs lower down posed more of a problem.

[61] The Gambia, *Customs Department Report for the Period January 1965 to June 1966, Sessional Paper 1 of 1968* (Bathurst, Government Printer, 1968), p. 112.

labyrinth of bush paths slicing across an unrelentingly flat landscape. In the Casamance, the challenge of tracking these carts – some of which allegedly relied on homing donkeys – was compounded by the difficulty of keeping track of the pirogues that ranged from the Gambia border down to Guinea-Bissau. Senegalese *douaniers* had previously relied on informants to keep them abreast of cross-border movements, but relations with villagers soured as the former resorted to more forceful tactics. In an attempt to take matters in hand, the Senegalese authorities made some adjustments. Penalties for corruption were increased, some import duties were reduced and the Customs service was overhauled to give it more the aspect of a paramilitary force.[62] But this tinkering had a limited effect.

Inevitably, relations between the two governments became strained. In 1969, the (French) Minister of Finance in Senegal, Jean Collin, complained bitterly that it was

... incontestable that an important and increasing proportion of goods entering the Gambia officially is in fact destined for Senegal. To that extent, the smuggling from the Gambia can be said to assume the character of an economic aggression, and ought to be, it appears to me, to be resisted as such.[63]

The Senegalese government was divided between hawks who wished to apply greater pressure to the Gambia and doves, including Senghor himself, who still preferred a negotiated settlement.[64] The result was that interventions tended to swing between heavy-handed interventions and diplomatic overtures. In 1969, the Senegalese authorities introduced a regulation that anyone found in possession of matches or cigarettes that were not stamped "for sale in Senegal" was liable to arrest. No exception was made for Gambians in transit, and the inevitable result was a series of unseemly incidents and formal complaints.[65] The following year, however, the two governments managed to sign a one-year interim agreement, which was renewed in subsequent years, that committed the two Customs authorities to working together. And in 1974 they agreed to the removal of many of the restrictions on the movement of goods in non-commercial quantities. In addition, the Senegalese consented to goods being transported by pirogue from Guinea-Bissau to the Gambian town of Kartong

---

[62] World Bank, *Senegal,* p.192.
[63] Omar A. Touray, *The Gambia and the World: A History of the Foreign Policy of Africa's Smallest State, 1965–1995* (Hamburg: Institute of African Studies, 2000), pp. 38–9.
[64] NAGB EXA 1/8 "Senegalo-Gambian Co-operation Customs (1967–1975)," *Le Monde* 11 September 1969.
[65] NAGB EXA 1/8 "Senegalo-Gambian Co-operation", B. Semega-Janneh, Gambian High Commissioner, Dakar, to Minister of External Affairs (24 July 1969). Gambian demonstrators retaliated at one point, forcing Senghor to change his route back into Senegal after a meeting in Banjul. *Le Monde* 11 September 1969.

via the Casamance, albeit subject to Customs control.[66] But at the very same time, there were several incidents in which Senegalese *douaniers* were accused of making arrests on the Gambian side of the border. In 1971, Senegalese soldiers attacked and abducted a number of villagers from Bullock in Foni Berefet, following an incident in which a *douanier* and a policeman were arrested after having crossed the border in hot pursuit. And in 1974, the Senegalese allegedly arrested twenty people on Gambian soil.[67]

Some of these incidents were an indirect consequence of the postponement of negotiations to iron out the remaining border anomalies. One of the problems with straight-line boundaries was that where the pillars were placed at some distance apart, it was not always clear where the border actually ran – which was further compounded when the pillars were removed by those who had an interest in uncertainty. Where the border was supposed to track the contours of the Gambia River, a lack of pillars multiplied the confusion. The colonial holding action of provisionally allocating villages according to where they paid their taxes did not resolve the issue, especially when settlements were being newly established. This was precisely the problem on the southern fringes of Darsilami where there was a lack of agreement as to whether the village of Tranquille was located in the Gambia or in Senegal. In January 1967, a Lebanese trader complained that his vehicle had been seized, while it was loading groundnuts near to Darsilami, and taken off to Diouloulou.[68] The Gambian authorities were unsure whether the trader was operating inside the Casamance or whether he was legitimately purchasing groundnuts on Gambian soil. During the 1970s, the picture remained confused. The accumulation of daily irritations ensured that border populations did not feel greatly invested in the limited co-operation initiatives that were announced by the authorities in Dakar and Banjul.

The Oddity of Adjustment in One Country

Across Africa, the decade of the 1980s is associated with a paradigm shift that was as profound as the discovery of 'development' after the war. Indeed, Structural Adjustment was conceived of as the nemesis of a statist conception of development.[69] As most African countries struggled with mounting debt and tenuous public finances, governments were forced to turn to the Bretton

---

[66] NAGB EXA 1/8 "Senegalo-Gambian Co-operation", Report of the meeting of Customs Officials from the Gambia and Senegal by I.B.M. Jobe, for Comptroller (5 December 1974).

[67] Touray, *The Gambia*, pp. 42–3.

[68] NAGB EXA 1/8 "Senegalo-Gambian Co-operation," Raffie Tabbel, Gunjur, to Minister of External Affairs, Bathurst (22 January 1967).

[69] Paul Nugent, *Africa Since Independence: A Comparative History*, 2nd edn. (London and New York: Palgrave Macmillan, 2012), chs. 8–9.

Woods institutions for relief in return for signing up to a package of reforms. Under adjustment, the state was supposed to be scaled back and to retreat from making productive investments, thereby creating a breathing space for the private sector and external investors. The mantra of 'getting the prices right' implied restoring incentives, most notably to the producers of cash crops. Given that state intervention had been advanced with a view to uniting different interest groups around the renewed promise of development, the package of reforms was bound to have troubling political implications. Not surprisingly, canny politicians sought ways and means of stalling and blunting the impact of policy prescriptions.[70] But in addition, it was genuinely far from evident what 'getting the prices right' actually meant when there was an alternative set of prices, recorded in another currency, right next door. Much like the statist approach it was supposed to replace, Structural Adjustment was based on the false premise of a bounded national space.

In Senegal, fresh hopes were placed on the production of phosphates and the promotion of tourism in the Casamance, but this could not disguise the reality that there had been limited diversification during the 1970s.[71] Although groundnuts had lost much of their allure for producers, they remained the most important export commodity in their raw or processed form. Adverse weather conditions after 1978 continued to play their part in diminishing returns. In 1981, purchases plummeted to a low of 189,256 tonnes from an average of nearly 900,000 tonnes in the 1970s.[72] But there was no disguising the fact that rampant smuggling lay behind these sobering statistics. Indeed it is estimated that the actual groundnut crop may actually have been twice the size of what passed through official Senegalese marketing channels.[73] Whereas rural producers were able to somewhat cushion themselves against falling prices, the impact on state revenues was disastrous. As important were the

---

[70] However, it has been pointed out that African governments typically sought to give way on certain issues while seeking to protect their core interests. Nicolas van de Walle, *African Economies and the Politics of Permanent Crisis, 1979–1999* (Cambridge: Cambridge University Press, 2001).

[71] Phosphates accounted for 15.6 per cent of total exports by value between 1976 and 1980, slightly ahead of fish. However, a sharp decline in prices in 1975 reduced much of the optimism surrounding this commodity. Mark Gersovitz and John Waterbury, "Some sources and implications of uncertainty in the Senegalese economy", p. 39; John P. Lewis, "Aid, structural adjustment, and Senegalese agriculture", p. 297, both in Gersovitz and Waterbury (eds.), *Political Economy*. Plantings declined by just under 300,00 hectares between 1975 and 1981, but with the real drop coming after 1983. John Waterbury, "The Senegalese peasant: how good is our conventional wisdom?", table 2, p. 53, in the same volume.

[72] The substitution of soy for groundnuts in European markets exercised a further depressing effect on prices. Mark Gersovitz and John Waterbury, "Introduction" and John Waterbury, "Dimensions of state intervention in the groundnut basin", p. 192, both in Gersovitz and Waterbury (eds.), *Political Economy*, pp. 10, 12.

[73] Sheldon Gellar, "Circulaire 32 revisited: prospects for revitalizing the Senegalese co-operative movement in the 1980s", in Gersovitz and Waterbury (eds.), *Political Economy*, p. 137.

inefficiencies associated with state marketing. The greatest offender was the Office National de Coopération et d'Assistance Pour le Développement (ONCAD), which both marketed the crop and supplied inputs to farmers on credit. It performed the former function in a cumbersome manner, and it continued to extend credit well beyond the capacity of the farmers to repay.[74] In 1980, ONCAD collapsed under the weight of unpaid debts, leaving a hefty deficit of 75 billion CFA francs.[75] The record of state intervention in staple crop production was simply unspectacular. Because rice was produced at three times the cost of the Asian alternative, the smuggled product continued to be traded through the Gambian border.[76] Whereas the country was producing 61 per cent of its cereal needs in 1974/6, this had declined to 39 per cent in 1983/5. Part of the gap was bridged through food aid, which accounted for 14 per cent of total supply in the latter period. Meanwhile, food imports increased by as much as 75 per cent between the same years, which has to be added to the large volume of trafficked rice.[77] The imports came on top of a mounting fuel import bill, following the second OPEC price hike, which alone offset 31 per cent of export revenues in 1981.[78]

Equally, the attempt to pursue a more ambitious strategy of import substitution had produced disappointing results. Of the seventy parastatals, no fewer than thirty operated at a loss, which represented a drain on the public purse without necessarily contributing much to national self-sufficiency.[79] In the case of the textile industry, the government came under pressure to protect private enterprise by imposing special licences for imported goods.[80] However, as with rice, the local product was considerably more expensive, which meant that there was an incentive for traders to source their supplies through the Gambia. Threatened with bankruptcy, the textile firms lobbied for even tougher border controls and for financial relief.[81] The economic downturn at

---

[74] In the context of declining yields, the application of increasing quantities of fertilizer was necessary merely in order to stand still.

[75] Gellar, "Circulaire 32", p. 137.

[76] Frederic Martin and Eric Crawford, "The new agricultural policy: its feasibility and implications for the future", in Christopher L. Delgado and Sidi Jammeh (eds.), *The Political Economy of Senegal under Structural Adjustment* (New York, Westport and London: Praeger, 1991), p. 91.

[77] Martin and Crawford, "New agricultural policy", p. 86. Rice imports rose from 102,126 tons in 1975/6 to 321,800 in 1981/2. Waterbury, "Senegalese peasant", table 6, p. 64

[78] Carolyn Somerville, "The impact of reforms on the urban population: how the Dakarois view the crisis", in Delgado and Jammeh (eds.), *Political Economy*, p. 154.

[79] Somerville, "Impact", p. 154. In the three years between 1974 and 1977, government outlays increased to the tune of 78 per cent. Prosper Youm, "The economy since independence", in Delgado and Jammeh (eds.), *Political Economy*, p. 26.

[80] Catherine Boone, "Politics under the specter of deindustrialization: 'structural adjustment' in practice", in Delgado and Jammeh (eds.), *Political Economy*, p. 142.

[81] Boone refers to the case of ICOTAF (Industrie Cottonière Africaine), for example, which received a series of state-guaranteed loans, tax breaks and bailouts in the 1970s. In addition, the state "suspended the totality of ICOTAF's fiscal obligations to the state, provided new

the end of the decade left the regime over-committed across a wide front. The difficulty of raising additional revenues forced the government to resort to increased borrowing from commercial banks and to an escalation of the national debt.[82] The resort to ad hoc measures to buy off dissent tended to exacerbate the problem. The government increased wages by an average of 36 per cent in 1979, and increased subsidies on rice and sugar imports, in an attempt to head off urban discontent.[83] Writing off the debts of rural producers was similarly designed to maintain longstanding alliances in the groundnut belt. But such measures were ultimately unsustainable. In 1980, renewed student protests and strikes by teachers were an indication of mounting dissent and signalled that a change of leadership was essential for the long-term survival of the regime.[84]

Senghor dutifully went into retirement, paving the way for the succession of Abdou Diouf to the Presidency in 1981. Diouf was a young technocrat rather than a machine politician, who many thought would be more inclined to take the difficult decisions.[85] In fact, Diouf embraced reform rather gingerly. The first Structural Adjustment agreement with the International Monetary Fund (IMF) and World Bank, which came into effect in 1980, was scrapped by mutual consent within a year.[86] The demand for far-reaching reforms in agriculture and the rolling back of the public sector were not politically acceptable at that time. Indeed, it was not until 1984 that an agreement with the donors was reached. The eventual adjustment package contained a standard list of policy prescriptions, in return for which the government of Senegal was permitted to draw down loans from the IMF and World Bank. The centre-piece of the government's modified agenda was the New Agricultural Policy (NAP), which was launched in 1984. Without really accounting for what had gone awry, the NAP proposed the achievement of national self-sufficiency in cereals through improved yields in areas of rainfed and irrigated agriculture alike.[87] The anticipated stimulus would lie in a combination of higher producer prices and efficiency gains associated with the withdrawal of parastatals from the delivery of inputs and credit. In the latter part of the 1980s, the NAP did not in fact let market forces prevail because subsidies were retained for rice and cotton and even groundnut production. At the same time, the government

---

government subsidies on domestic inputs (cotton, water electricity), and exempted the firm from duties on imported capital goods and inputs." Catherine Boone, "Politics", pp. 142–3.

[82] Somerville, "Impact", table 11.3, p. 154.   [83] Lewis, "Aid", p. 298.

[84] Delgado and Jammeh, "Introduction", p. 14.

[85] But as Mbodji puts it, Diouf had inherited "a disastrous situation on many fronts." Mohamed Mbodji, "The politics of independence: 1960–1986", in Delgado and Jammeh (eds.), *Political Economy*, p. 122.

[86] Pierre Landell-Mills and Brian Ngo, "Creating the basis for long-term growth", in Delgado and Jammeh (eds.), *Political Economy*, p. 48.

[87] See Martin and Crawford, "The new agricultural policy", *passim*.

increased taxes on imported rice in an effort to restore incentives to producers.[88] Agricultural policy had notionally been turned on its head, but without
effecting liberalization in the manner that critics of adjustment have sometimes
imagined.

Meanwhile, the Diouf regime continued the process of political liberalization that had begun somewhat tentatively under Senghor. The remaining
restrictions on the formation of political parties were abandoned, which meant
that Senegal's democratic opening began a good decade ahead of most of the
continent. This served to fragment the opposition when no fewer than fifteen
political parties entered the arena. While seeking to renovate the internal
structures of the PS, Diouf also weeded out those who had opposed his
succession.[89] As many of the so-called Barons were marginalized or removed,
a new cohort of educated technocrats who owed their positions to Diouf were
parachuted into government positions. In addition, there were some concessions towards greater press freedom. As recently as 1979, the Press Code had
prescribed prison sentences for defamation, weakening the morale of the
Armed Forces and bringing the reputation of the president into disrepute.[90]
Diouf sought to engage in a dialogue with the press and decreed an amnesty
for press offences committed prior to 1981.[91] Given that the independent press
was closely tied to the opposition, this implied an enlarged space for critical
debate.

For our purposes, what is more significant was the pledge of the Diouf
regime to resuscitate co-operation agreements with neighbouring countries,
and especially with the Gambia. An indication that the time was right came
with the agreement in 1978 to set up a common structure to manage the
resources of the Gambia River basin, in the shape of the l'Organisation Pour
La Mise en Valeur du Fleuve Gambie (OMVG).[92] As part of the initiative,
the two sides agreed to finally settle the unresolved question of the eastern
limits of the Gambia – the Yarbutenda puzzle that dated back to the unrati-
fied agreement of 1904.[93] The OMVG accord also included an agreement
in principle to construct a bridge across the Gambia River with financial

---

[88] Valerie Kelly and Christopher L. Delgado, "Agricultural performance under Structural Adjustment", in Delgado and Jammeh (eds.), *Political Economy*, p. 107.
[89] Mamadou Diouf, "Beyond patronage and 'technocracy'", in Momar Coumba Diop (ed.),
Senegal: Essays in Statecraft (Dakar: CODESRIA, 1993), pp. 250–1.
[90] Moussa Paye, "The regime and the press", in Diop (ed.), *Senegal*, p. 354.
[91] Paye, "The regime", p. 355.
[92] This followed the creation of the Senegal River Development Project (OMVS) in 1972.
[93] Although the OMVG agreement was only signed in 1978, there were understandings as early as
1971. Ieuan Griffiths, "Maps, boundaries, ambiguity and change in the Gambia", in Jeffrey
Stone (ed.), *Maps and Africa: Proceedings of a Colloquium at the University of Aberdeen, April
1993* (Aberdeen: Aberdeen University African Studies Group, 1994), pp. 71–2.

assistance from the European Development Fund.[94] This project provided a means to satisfy a longstanding Senegalese ambition to integrate the two halves of their territory and to terminate the enclave status of the Casamance. However, the Gambian government held out for a bridge-cum-barrage that would permit irrigated rice cultivation along the river by blocking the flow of saline water. In effect, the bridge project stalled as the two governments continued to debate what it might look like in practice.[95]

The context for re-engagement inside the Gambia was the internal distemper that confronted the Jawara government. The formula of minimal state interference, married to the limited delivery of public goods, seemed to work tolerably well until the mid-1970s. The country had managed to resolve doubts about its viability by chalking up reasonable levels of economic growth and modest improvements in some social indicators, while generating sufficient domestic resources to avoid external indebtedness.[96] But towards the end of the decade, the Gambia succumbed to the same external shocks as Senegal, including the increase in the oil price and a falling price for groundnuts. And, much like in Senegal, some governmental responses merely compounded the situation. Maintaining producer prices for groundnuts at around 30 per cent above those prevailing in Senegal made sense at a time of buoyant world prices, but for much of the time it placed a financial strain on the GPMB, which was forced to run up large debts as a consequence. This was compounded by the creeping overvaluation of the Dalasi, which further squeezed its operating margins.[97] Moreover, because the GPMB set its operating allowances at a level that made groundnut purchasing unprofitable for private traders, the Gambia Co-operative Union (GCU) was able to increase its market share, but in a way that multiplied the underlying inefficiencies. The GCU operated at a loss, but was awarded soft loans by the Gambia Commercial and Development Bank, thereby enabling a veritable house of cards to be propped up for some years.[98] At a time when poor rainfall impacted negatively on agricultural production, overvaluation tended to cheapen the price of food imports. All of this meant that the Gambia's foreign exchange reserves were depleted and the country quickly accumulated a significant external debt. In addition, a familiar Gambian problem made its reappearance after 1977 in the shape of a worrying

---

[94] Touray, *The Gambia*, pp. 80–1.   [95] Touray, *The Gambia*, pp. 80–1.

[96] Malcolm F. McPherson and Steven C. Radelet, "The politics of economic reform", in Malcolm F. McPherson and Steven C. Radelet (eds.), Economic Recovery in the Gambia: Insights for Structural Adjustment in Sub-Saharan Africa (Cambridge: Harvard University Press, 1995), p. 34.

[97] Malcolm McPherson, "Macroeconomic reform and agriculture", in McPherson and Radelet, *Economic Recovery*, p. 194.

[98] Christine Jones and Steven C. Radelet, "The groundnut sector", in McPherson and Radelet, *Economic Recovery*, p. 212.

gulf between government revenues and state expenditure. This was caused in part by dwindling returns from import duties and in part by the costs associated with sustaining an enlarged public sector. The result was that many Ministerial budgets were simply overwhelmed by salary commitments.[99] As with Senegal, it seemed inevitable that the Gambia would have to seek assistance from the donors who, in turn, were bound to insist upon unpalatable reforms. Strident opposition came less from the official opposition than from an emerging constellation of left-wing groupings, such as the Movement for Justice in Africa–the Gambia (MOJA-G).[100] An attempted coup in July 1981, which implicated members of the Field Force as well as civilian conspirators, under-lined the fragile base of the Jawara regime. In fact, it took Senegalese military intervention, under the provisions of the mutual defence agreement, to restore Jawara to office. This meant that the Senegalese government was finally in a position to insist on concrete steps to move towards closer integration. The Treaty of the Senegambian Confederation, which was hastily signed in 1981, went considerably further than the union that had been mooted prior to Gambian independence. What it had in common was that it was an initiative imposed from above and with almost no public consultation. Over the following decade, the challenge for the Gambian government lay in steering a steady course between the Scylla of Structural Adjustment and the Charybdis of Confederation.

Meanwhile, the Bretton Woods institutions sought to return the Gambia to the paths of economic righteousness. In 1985, following two years of acute economic distress, the Gambia signed up to its own Economic Recovery Programme (ERP). The Dalasi had already been devalued by 25 per cent in 1984. Under the ERP, a special effort was made to improve incentives to groundnut producers. The problem was that Senegal was being encouraged to proceed down exactly the same route, which meant that agricultural policies remained acutely competitive despite the existence of the Confederation.[101] In 1984, the Gambian producer price was 50 per cent higher than in Senegal, but

---

[99] A World Bank study in 1981 estimated that salaries consumed 70 per cent of the health budget, but given that there were only 20 doctors, 300 nurses and 100 health inspectors in government employment, administrative salaries must have accounted for much of the outlay. The report also observed that while there was an "impressive" network of health centres and dispensaries outside Banjul, there was a chronic lack of medical supplies, equipment and qualified medical staff. The expenditure under Medical and Health Services in 1976/7 was 3,195,900 Dalasis, of which salaries accounted for 2,193,300 Dalasis and drugs a mere 288,700 Dalasis. World Bank, *The Gambia*, pp. v, 20 and table 8, p. 119.

[100] MOJA-G engaged in a sustained critique of the PPP from outside Parliament. When it was banned in 1980, the PPP demonstrated the limits to its willingness to tolerate extra-parliamentary opposition.

[101] Jeggan Senghor observes that the Gambia and Senegal embarked on Structural Adjustment reforms without reference to plans for their economic integration. See *The Politics of Senegambian Integration, 1958–1994* (New York: Peter Lang, 2008), pp. 263–4.

when Senegalese prices were hiked by a third over the following two years, the Gambia began to lose groundnuts across the border.[102] In a remarkable inversion of roles, the IMF actually persuaded a reluctant Gambian government to triple the producer price in 1986/7 in order to tap groundnuts from the Senegalese side of the border.[103] This required a heavy public subsidy but had some of the intended effect.[104] When the subsidy was eliminated in 1988/9 – this time under pressure from the World Bank – there was a slump of GPMB purchases by as much as 60 per cent as the pendulum swung back the other way.[105]

In theory, the sensitivity of agrarian adjustment to border flows strengthened the case for closer co-operation between the states. However, the Senegambian Confederation was marred by misunderstandings from the start. The treaty provided for progress towards an economic and monetary union; the creation of a confederal Armed Forces drawn from the two sides; and the co-ordination of external relations. These concessions to the Senegalese position were softened by the formal respect for the sovereignty of the two states.[106] Despite some early optimism in Dakar, the next decade failed to witness any deepening of the relationship. In the Gambia itself, there was frustration at what was regarded as a highly asymmetrical relationship.[107] But the main sticking point was the perception that Senegal was likely to be the primary beneficiary of closer union. The Senegalese planned to extend the market for their own products, whereas the vitality of the Gambian economy continued to depend on the possibility of re-exporting cheaper consumer goods that accounted for around 30 per cent of GDP in the late 1980s.[108] Moreover, closer integration would have made ordinary citizens, who had benefited from rather stable consumer prices, considerably worse off.[109] Lucie Phillips's comparison of retail prices for a range of commodities in 1986 reveals a consistent disparity: the people of Banjul paid 37.5 per cent less for their rice, 56 per cent less for

---

[102] Phillips, "Senegambia Confederation", in Delgado and Jammeh (ed.), *Political Economy*, pp. 182–3.

[103] The rationale was that this would maximize the foreign exchange that would allow the Gambia to cover its arrears to the IMF. Jones and Radelet, "The groundnut sector", p. 208.

[104] In 1986/87, both countries made a 30 per cent loss on the marketing of groundnuts due to the price subsidies. Phillips, "Senegambia Confederation", p. 182.

[105] Subsequent reforms sought to resolve these issues by reducing marketing inefficiencies. The GPMB henceforth set a price for delivery at the depot and permitted traders to compete with the GCU, whose soft loans were also cut off, with respect to the farmgate price. Jones and Radelet, "The groundnut sector", pp. 210–11.

[106] Arnold Hughes, "L'effondrement de la Confédération de la Sénégambie", in Momar-Coumba Diop (ed.), *Le Sénégal et ses voisins* (Dakar: Sociétés-Espaces-Temps, 1994), p. 37.

[107] The Presidency of the Confederation rested perpetually with Senegal while the Confederal Parliament was weighted two-thirds in favour of the latter.

[108] Golub and Mbaye, "National trade policies", figure 3, p. 41.

[109] World Bank, *The Gambia*, table 3, p. 114.

Table 11.2 *Price differentials in Dakar and Banjul for consumer goods in CFA francs, 1986 and 2006 (percentages in favour of Banjul)*

Items	Difference 1986	Difference 2006
Sugar	37.5	90.5
Flour	55.6	33.2
Rice	37.5	13.1
Matches	37.5	70.5
Tomato paste	73.7	62.6
Soap	68.5	24.9

Note: these are rough orders of magnitude because the units of measurement in these surveys differed. Both involved field data collected by researchers. See Lucie Colvin Phillips, "The Senegambia Confederation", in Delgado and Jammeh (ed.), *Political Economy*, table 12.1, p.181; and Stephen Golub and Ahmadou Aly Mbaye, "National trade policies and smuggling in Africa: the case of the Gambia and Senegal", *World Development* 37 (3) 2008, table 2, p. 602.

millet, 33.3 per cent less for sugar cubes and 73.7 per cent less for tomato paste than their counterparts in Dakar (see Table 11.2).[110] This reflected high levels of Senegalese duty and the continuing protection afforded to its nascent industries. A Customs union would, in effect, have brought Senegalese prices to the doorsteps of Gambians, which explains the distinct lack of popular support for continuation of the Confederation. Indeed, Arnold Hughes observes that the lack of enthusiasm was shared amongst the trading community in both countries. In his words:

There had not been, either in Senegal or the Gambia, any influential pressure groups at the heart of the elite groups in commerce or the public sector or the powerful and more popular organizations that were determined to maintain the Confederation. In fact, as far as the Gambia is concerned the people as a whole shared with the government the same dubious attitude concerning the Senegambia.[111]

Frustrated at Gambian foot-dragging, and disconcerted at talk of a possible withdrawal, the Senegalese authorities unilaterally renounced the Confederation in October 1989. This was followed by the immediate re-introduction of the Customs cordon. The implosion of the Confederation happened to coincide with the eruption of a serious crisis on Senegal's northern border. The construction of a Mauritanian deep-water port in 1986 had threated to open a second point of entry for contraband goods. This was compounded by tensions

---

[110] Phillips, "Senegambia Confederation", table 12.1, p. 181.
[111] Hughes, "L'effondrement", p. 55.

over access to land along the banks of the Senegal River, which was an unintended consequence of the l'Organisation Pour La Mise en Valeur du Fleuve Sénégal (OMVS).[112] A border incident with Mauritania in April 1989 escalated into violence and the expulsion of each other's nationals. In the matter of a few months, the Diouf regime's strategy for promoting closer co-operation with its immediate neighbours lay in tatters.

In the decade and a half that followed, relations between the Gambia and Senegal governments remained distinctly cool, and this (as ever) reflected differing opinions on cross-border trade. In 1992, a report by the IMF found that while there had been some backsliding, the Gambian government had adhered pretty faithfully to its own reform package.[113] Although structural weaknesses remained, there had been a return to economic growth. This averaged 3.4 per cent between 1985/6 and 1991/2, despite poor weather and the falling world price for groundnuts.[114] But the most striking finding of the report was that it was the re-export trade that had fuelled the Gambian recovery:

The traditionally liberal trade regime maintained by the Gambia, combined with the lifting of exchange controls and the introduction of a market-determined exchange rate, boosted the expansion of re-exports to the region. Regional political developments have, on balance, also enhanced the importance of the Gambia as an entry point for regional trade. A broad range of basic consumer goods (such as rice, green tea, sugar, tomato paste, tobacco, footwear and textiles) are usually imported into the Gambia where they are sold wholesale to visiting traders from several neighboring countries. While the development of the re-export sector has had limited employment and income linkages to the rest of the economy, with the exception perhaps of the transport and communications and in part the banking sector, it has had a major impact on foreign exchange earnings.[115]

For obvious reasons, this modest recovery came at the expense of relations with Senegal. In 1994, when there was a second coup attempt in the Gambia, the Senegalese army did not intervene to save the Jawara regime.[116] But if the Senegalese authorities imagined that the incoming government of Yahya Jammeh would be more amenable to their vision of Senegambian unity, the

---

[112] Andrea Nicolaj, "The Senegal Mauritanian Conflict", *Africa* (Rome) 45 (3) 1990, pp. 470–3.
[113] Michael T. Hadjimichael, Thomas Rumbaugh and Eric Verreydt, *The Gambia; Economic Adjustment in a Small Open Economy* (Washington: IMF, 1999), pp. 5–9.
[114] Hadjimichael, Rumbaugh and Verreydt, *The Gambia*, p. 7.
[115] Hadjimichael, Rumbaugh and Verreydt, *The Gambia*, p. 13.
[116] Writing shortly after the coup, Radelet and McPherson maintained that it was unlikely that Structural Adjustment was a cause of the coup, but that it partly helped to explain the way it was received by the public without much protest. Steven C. Radelet and Malcolm F. McPherson, "Epilogue: The July 1994 coup d'etat", in McPherson and Radelet, *Economic Recovery*, pp. 314–15. On the coup, see also Abodoulaye Saine, "The coup d'etat in the Gambia, 1994: the end of the First Republic", *Armed Forces and Society* 23 (1) 1996.

reality was that very little changed. At the end of the 1990s, the re-export trade tapered off, but after 2002 there was a renewed spike in smuggling. And as before, it was the differentials on the two sides of the border that were decisive. Table 11.2, which compares Phillips' price data from 1986 with comparable data from Golub and Mbaye in 2006, points to significant continuities. The price differentials for rice were lower (down from a 37.5 per cent to a 13.1 per cent gap), but those for sugar were substantially higher (up from 33.3 per cent to 90.5 per cent). After 2002, re-exports climbed back to something in the region of 25 per cent of Gambian GDP. Although tourism gave the economy a second leg to stand on, contraband remained fundamental to the finances of the regime as well as to the livelihoods of ordinary Gambians.

The Jammeh regime, which donned the outward trappings of civilian rule, remained in power by virtue of its control of the military, which recruited heavily from amongst the Jola minority on both sides of the border. Jammeh was reputedly obsessive about internal security, having survived a series of plots, and worried at the prospect of a rebel invasion mounted from Senegalese territory.[117] But surveillance along the border concentrated on the movement of people much more than the flow of goods. Indeed, the regime was able to mitigate its unpopularity by giving licence to the contraband trade. The composite social contract in the Gambia blended elements of the permissive and the repressive, in a manner that bore similarities with Togo. Along the Casamance border, the regime was even less inclined to interfere with trade flows because its main support base lay with Jola populations living on either side of the line. Jammeh's own home town of Karenai was said to feature prominently in the smuggling business, but the trade was also conducted in countless unremarkable villages on either side of the border. In 2004, the Gambian town of Kartong remained an important point of exit for a wide range of commodities such as bags of rice, cooking oil, sugar and tomatoes, which were exported by canoe to Guinea-Bissau or by truck towards Kafountine. At the time, the *alkalo* of the town observed that while the Senegalese sought to tax the trade and handed down stiff penalties for smuggling, the Gambian authorities displayed little interest in what crossed the border. The only revenue that was collected was a road tax on the lorries, which was levied on behalf of the area council.[118] At the time, there was abundant evidence for a trade in foodstuffs and other consumer items into the

---

[117] Abdoulaye Saine, *The Paradox of Third-Wave Democratization in Africa: The Gambia under AFPRC-APRC Rule, 1994–2008* (Lanham and Plymouth: Lexington Books, 2009), pp. 75–82; Maggie Dwyer, "Fragmented forces: the development of the Gambian military", *African Security Review* 26 (4) 2017, pp. 8–11. See also Ebrima Jogomai Ceesay, *The Military and 'Democratisation' in the Gambia: 1994–2003* (Victoria BC: Trafford Publishing, 2006).

[118] According to the *alkalo*, the trade to Kafountine was generally by truck because in the event of being intercepted, the Senegalese Customs authorities would only seize the goods whereas

Gambia – whether by truck or by bicycle – and a reverse flow of fruit such as mangoes, which the Gambian authorities did not apparently seek to regulate. Although this pointed to broad continuities, I will now consider two respects in which there was a qualitative break with the past.

Border Dialectics and Territorial Respacing: Secessionism and Urbanism

On 20 April 1990, several decades of peace along the Gambia/Casamance border ended abruptly when secessionist rebels of the Mouvement des Forces Démocratiques de Casamance (MFDC) launched a surprise attack upon the Séléty border post, at the main point of entry for vehicles travelling between Banjul and Ziguinchor. The assault left two Senegalese Customs officers dead. Because the Customs service was typically composed of personnel from northern Senegal who often had a fraught relationship with local populations, the choice of target was surely not accidental. The state-owned newspaper, *Le Soleil*, immediately invoked the dramatic events of 1917 when the dissident marabout, El-Hadj Haidara, had attacked the same border post and beheaded the French Customs officer in charge.[119] In the years after the second Séléty incident, a low-intensity insurgency spread across the Casamance. Although there were no pitched battles, the MFDC rebels successfully deployed hit-and-run tactics and proved extremely difficult to dislodge as they inserted themselves into border spaces and tapped into established trading networks. Along the Gambian border, the rebels became closely implicated in the smuggling of wood from hitherto protected forests. The withdrawal of the forest guards, whose regulatory powers had been augmented in spite of the rhetoric of decentralization,[120] exemplified a more general retreat of the state from the rural Casamance – and further confirmed the abject failure of efforts to rescale governmental institutions.

There have been numerous attempts to account for the outbreak of the secessionist insurgency, some of which I build on here.[121] The notion that

---

they would generally seize the canoe as well as the goods. Interview with Alhaji Demba Jabang, *alkalo* of Kartong, 4 June 2004.

[119] "Attaque du poste du douane de Selety: de la barbarie premeditée", *Le Soleil* 25 April 1990.

[120] Giorgio Blundo, "Seeing like a state agent: the ethnography of reform in Senegal's forestry services", in Thomas Bierschenk and Jean-Pierre Olivier de Sardan (eds.), *States at Work: Dynamics of African Bureaucracies* (Leiden: Brill, 2014). The Senegalese Forestry Service, which was vested with considerable powers of enforcement, dates from 1936. Jesse Ribot, "Forestry policy and charcoal production in Senegal", *Energy Policy* 21 (5) 1993, pp. 563–4.

[121] On the history of the Casamance insurgency, see Jean-Claude Marut, *Le conflit du Casamance: ce qui disent les armes* (Paris: Karthala, 2010); and also his articles, "Le dessous des cartes casamançaises: une approche géopolitique du conflit casamançais", in François George Barbier-Wiesser (ed.), *Comprendre la Casamance: chronique d'une intégration contrastée*

the rebellion was a Christian backlash against Muslim capture of the Senegalese state is problematic for the reason that the vast majority in the Casamance were actually Muslims. But it is true that most Casamançais were not members of the Mouride and Tijani brotherhoods that held sway in Dakar and the other main towns of northern Senegal. Again, the claim that the MFDC was ethnically inspired fails to take full account of the fact that the MFDC counted Mandinka and Jola amongst its leaders – although there was a perception in the northern Casamance that the latter were the dominant element.[122] Much like the Ewe/Togoland unification movement in the 1950s, the MFDC needed to appeal to a much broader constituency if it was to have any chance of success. Nevertheless, the fact that Jola ethnicity was invoked at all was significant. The Senegalese government's own interpretation was that enforced isolation of the Casamance, resulting from the physical obstacle created by the Gambia, was the determining factor. In some respects, this could be seen as the flip-side of the MFDC's own discourse of systematic marginalization. The Senegalese government reproached its Gambian counterpart for its failure either to proceed with the construction of a bridge across the Gambia River, for which external funding was available, or to upgrade the antiquated ferry system. As relations deteriorated, the Senegalese authorities accused the Jammeh regime of covertly supporting the MFDC insurgency. Even if direct complicity was difficult to prove, there was some evidence of firearms trafficking across the Gambian border.[123] What is clear is that the Jammeh regime deployed the MFDC as a bargaining counter, allowing greater or lesser latitude to the rebels depending on the state of relations with Dakar – whilst always being careful to prevent rebel activity from generating instability inside the Gambia.[124] In this there were some parallels with the Togolese government's manipulation of the Ewe/Togoland unification movement in the early 1970s.

(Paris, 1994) and "Le problème casamançais: est-il soluble dans l'état-nation?", in Momar-Coumba Diop (ed.) *Le Sénégal contemporain* (Paris: L'Harmattan, 2002); Geneviève Gasser, "'Manger ou s'en aller': que veulent les opposants armés casamançais?', in the same volume; and Martin Evans, *Senegal: Mouvement des Forces Démocratiques de la Casamance*, Chatham House, Briefing Paper 04/02, November 2004.

[122] Jean-Claude Marut, "Le particularisme au risque de l'Islam dans le conflit casamançais", *L'Afrique Politique* 2002, pp. 147–9, and Vincent Foucher, "La guerre des dieux? religions et séparatisme en Basse Casamance", *Canadian Journal of African Studies* 39 (2) 2005, pp. 361–88.

[123] An article in 1990 claimed that Kalashnikovs were freely available for purchase in Fatoto in the eastern Gambia. These guns allegedly came in from Guinea-Bissau. At this time, the tensions along the Mauritanian border apparently led to a trade northwards. "Traffic d'armes à Tambacounda", *Le Soleil* 30 May 1990.

[124] Here, I am in agreement with the interpretation offered in Martin Evans and Charlotte Ray, "Uncertain ground: the Gambia and the Casamance conflict", in Abdoulaye Saine, Ebrima Ceesay and Ebrima Sall (eds.), *State and Society in the Gambia Since Independence 1965–2012* (Trenton: Africa World Press, 2013), pp. 265–9.

The problem with the marginalization thesis is not that it is wrong, but that it misses important subtleties. It would be difficult to sustain the claim that the economic region was a historically a backwater in relation to the rest of Senegal. In 1962, the region accounted for 120,100 tonnes out of a total groundnut crop of 893,800 tonnes, which meant that it made a broadly proportionate contribution to exports. In the same year, it accounted for 66,900 tonnes of rice out of a total national production of 76,900 tonnes, and it produced 68,300 tonnes out of a total of 424,000 tonnes of millet.[125] Given its higher than average rainfall, the region was repeatedly talked about as the future bread-basket of Senegal. The potential was not exploited to start with, partly because significant vested interests were tied up with the importation of Asian rice through the port of Dakar. But, as have seen, the Casamance was foregrounded in plans for the expansion of rice production and related agro-industries during the 1970s. Demographically, the Casamance was home to 676,800 people out of a population of 3.9 million inhabitants in 1969, which also gave it some demographic clout.[126] Moreover, as Vincent Foucher maintains, it is not true that the Casamance was the poor relation with respect to education.[127] The Catholic presence south of the Casamance River ensured that it was well-served by schools, placing it far ahead of any other region – even if the number of children in attendance was significantly lower than in Cap-Vert (which included Dakar) (see Table 11.3).

However, it is certainly the case that the Casamance had become locked into a different kind of relationship with the Senegalese state. In the decades before the war, the Casamance had been treated as a perennial problem as the authorities struggled to single out willing allies. Again, the Casamance did not feature prominently in the strategic thinking of the Senghor regime in the 1960s. Boone attributes this to the lack of powerful interlocuteurs who could engage directly with the Senegalese state.[128] Subsequently, the Casamance did not produce many influential figures within the ruling party, partly because of the tendency of its leading politicians to move in and out of the latter's embrace. This merely served to entrench the impression that the region was

---

[125] République du Sénégal, Ministère du Plan et du Développement, *Situation Economique du Sénégal (1963)* (Dakar: Service de la Statistique, 1964), table 7, p. 29.

[126] Whereas the average yield for groundnuts in Sine-Saloum was 864 kg per hectare, it was 1,090 in the Casamance. République du Sénégal, Service de la Statistique, *Situation Economique du Sénégal (1963)*, pp. 29–30. The Casamance came third out of seven regions, just behind Cap-Vert, which included Dakar. République du Sénégal, *Projet de IIIe Plan*, p.2.

[127] Vincent Foucher, "Les 'évolués', la migration, l'école: pour une nouvelle interprétation de la naissance du nationalisme casmançais", in Momar-Coumba Diop (ed.), *Le Sénégal contemporain* (Paris: Karthala, 2002).

[128] Catherine Boone, *Political Topographies of the African State: Territorial Authority and Institutional Choice* (Cambridge: Cambridge University Press, 2003), p. 99.

Table 11.3 *Regional distribution of public goods, 1963*

Region	Population	Schools	No. of pupils	No. of doctors	No. of hospital and health centre beds
Cap-Vert (includes Dakar)	444,000	146	54,872	71	1,674
Casamance	530,000	250	28,207	10	429
Diourbel	345,000	97	12,756	10	337
Fleuve (includes St. Louis)	503,000	171	22,204	16	790
Senegal-Oriental	151,000	66	5,945	2	110
Sine-Saloum	727,000	195	25,194	12	518
Thiès	410,000	125	23,573	11	434
Total	3,110,000	1,050	172,751	132	4,292

Source: République du Sénégal, *Service de la Statistique,* Situation Economique du Sénégal (1963), pp. 16, 23–4.

out of step with the rest of Senegal.[129] The specificity of the Casamance was reflected in the reality that the governor was typically a military officer, thereby signalling a striking continuity with French rule.[130] In general, senior administrators in the Casamance were drawn from other parts of Senegal, which cemented the impression that the region was under a kind of occupation. Despite the decentralization reforms, which were intended to bring the state closer to the ground, the Senegalese state seemed very distant indeed. Indeed, people in the Casamance famously talked of 'going to Senegal' when they were making a trip to Dakar. Clearly, therefore, there were deeper structural causes that lay behind the demand for secession.

But this is merely the starting point for an explanation for why Casamance separatism gained traction and when it did so. What also needs to be factored in is the combined effects of mobility and trans-boundary commerce, which offered a counterpoint to the developmental vision of the Senegalese state. In the years immediately after independence, there was broad continuity in the official attitude towards immigration in both countries. Although an attempt by the Senegalese to insist on passport and visa controls initially created some ill-feeling,[131] in practice the authorities were prepared to maintain an open door. In the Gambia, the independence conference in 1964 had agreed that a clause be inserted into the constitution which stipulated that any person born in the

---

[129] The PRA won 12.5 per cent of the total number of registered votes in 1960. Schumaker, *Politics, Bureaucracy and Rural Development*, p. 28; Boone, *Political Topographies*, p. 115.

[130] Boone, *Political Topographies*, pp. 118–19.

[131] J.H. Proctor, "The Gambia's relations with Senegal: the search for partnership", *Journal of Commonwealth Political Studies* 5 (2) 1967, p. 155.

Gambia after independence, or whose father was a citizen by birth, registration or naturalization, would automatically acquire citizenship rights.[132] Equally, any woman who married a Gambian citizen could seek registration as a citizen.

In 1975, there were estimated to be 355,000 foreign nationals living in Senegal, nearly half of whom originated from Guinea.[133] In this case, the line between migrants and refugees was blurred. The flight from the Sékou Touré dictatorship included much of the urban trading community who found the conditions in Senegal more conducive to business. In the case of Guinea-Bissau, the migration was mostly from rural areas. The PAIGC war against the Portuguese created some displacement, but there was a longer history of people moving back and forth across the borders between Guinea-Bissau, the Casamance and the Gambia. This may help to explain why refugees from Guinea-Bissau were permitted to settle in the Casamance without being forced into refugee camps. Hence a Gambian report noted that:

Of the 35,000 Guinean refugees in Casamance at the end of February 1965 over two-thirds (some 25,000) will, after the 1965 harvest, have been absorbed into the indigenous communities and will be self-supporting.[134]

These arrivals sought access to land in the customary manner and, in line with older patterns of migration, often moved from place to place in search of the optimal arrangement. But the peculiarity of the Senegalese migration pattern is that international and internal migration patterns diverged. Senegal was home to some 222,342 immigrants in 1971, of whom only 37,977 resided in Cap-Vert, including Dakar. The latter paled into significance with the 101,402 immigrants who resided in the Casamance – representing half of total lifetime immigration into Senegal.[135] But if the Casamance sucked in population from neighbouring countries, it also lost 122,000 people to internal migration – chiefly in the direction of Dakar in the period from 1960 to 1971.[136]

It was precisely the Casamançais who had some direct experience of Dakar who came to perceive themselves as the victims of an insidious form of cultural domination.[137] Wolofization – a reference to the currency of Wolof as the lingua franca, but also a particular register in which politics

---

[132] *The Gambia Independence Conference 1964* (London: Her Majesty's Stationary Office, 1964), Annex B, clause on Citizenship, pp. 7–8.

[133] Zachariah and Condé, *Migration*, tables 20 and 21, pp. 34–5.

[134] NAGB PRM 3/1 "Joint Senegalo-Gambian Project: Settlement of Refugees from Portuguese Guinea", J.D. Miller to C.W. Squire, Foreign Office (8 April 1965).

[135] Zachariah and Condé, *Migration*, table 25, p. 40.

[136] Zachariah and Condé, *Migration*, p. 40.

[137] Foucher observes that the Jola were actually over-represented in public employment. See "Les 'évolués'", pp. 386–7.

was conducted – was in some respects a rather successful strategy of nation-building, but it produced a sense of exclusion amongst migrants from the Casamance.[138] Hence a politicized Jola ethnicity crystallized not in opposition to the Mandinka, who were closest to home, but to the Wolof who dominated the life of the capital. The initial response assumed the form of a cultural nationalism that expressed pride in Jola culture and sporting prowess.[139] There was subsequently a backlash against a Senegalese discourse that exoticized the Casamance as a region and the Jola as the people most closely associated with it. The latter was closely bound up with official efforts to promote the attractions of the Casamance as a destination for French and other European tourists. Some of the tourism in question was of the enclave variety, as with the Club Med resort that was constructed at Cap Skirring in 1974, but the Senegalese authorities also banked on lower budget tourism in the shape of village *campements* where Europeans could find the 'authentic African experience'. The belated application of the 1964 National Domain law was interpreted as an attempt by northern Senegalese to expropriate land in the Casamance and to profit from the expansion of tourism at the expense of the 'indigenes'.[140] Ironically, therefore, the backlash was an unanticipated consequence of a state-driven project to bring about the *desenclavement*, or opening up, of the Casamance to the rest of Senegal. In some respects, as scholars like Foucher have recognized, it was integration rather than marginalization that posed the fundamental problem.

The manner in which the Senegalese authorities reacted to expressions of Casamance nationalism also had its part to play. In 1982, a revived MFDC began organizing protests in Ziguinchor in support of a demand for independence. This elicited a violent crackdown, following which the use of torture over a number of years was documented by Amnesty International.[141] A heightened sense of grievance provided a ready justification for the resort to armed struggle. The MFDC had one factor working in its favour, namely the relative porosity of the borders and ease of access to safe havens. The southern

---

[138] On Wolofization, and especially the linguistic dimension, see Donal Cruise O'Brien, "The shadow-politics of Wolofisation", *Journal of Modern African Studies* 36 (1) 1998, pp. 25–46. Mamadou Diouf emphasizes the hegemony of the Wolof political model from which the Jola were excluded. Mamadou Diouf, *Histoire du Sénégal: le modèle islamo-wolof et ses périphéries* (Paris: Maisonneuve and Larose, 2001).

[139] Sport often provided a focal point for identity. In the late 1970s, Donal Cruise O'Brien pointed to a heightened sense of Casamance identity, which was crystallized in the emotions surrounding an epic wrestling contest. Cruise O'Brien, "Senegal", p. 186. Later, it was to be football that ignited regionalist passions.

[140] Boone, *Political Topographies*, pp. 132–7; Jacques Faye, *Land and Decentralization in Senegal*, IIED Issue Paper No. 149 (London: International Institute for Environment and Development, 2008).

[141] Amnesty International, *Sénégal: La terreur en Casamance* (Paris: Amnesty International, 1998).

border with Guinea-Bissau had historically been a zone of endemic instability, most recently related to the PAIGC military campaigns in the late 1960s and early 1970s, but also linked to organized cattle rustling.[142] The MFDC was able to import arms across the border and to use Guinea-Bissau as a rear base from which to conduct its hit-and-run campaigns. Conversely, Casamance exceptionalism made it easier for the Senegalese government to quarantine an insurgency that did not materially impinge on the lives of most northern Senegalese. At the same time, rebel disunity made it possible to imagine that a military victory was achievable. Although the Senegalese authorities agreed to a ceasefire with the Front Nord in 1991/2, there was no conclusive peace agreement or ceasefire with the Front Sud. The ongoing pattern was one in which rebels planted landmines, cut the main roads and occasionally attacked government installations. Although the insurgency underwent extended lulls, these were always followed by a resurgence of rebel activity. Following victory over the PS at the polls in 2000, Abdoulaye Wade embarked upon an apparently successful drive to reassert central government control over the entirety of the Casamance. The new regime sought to bring about a wider peace accord in 2004, but when this stalled, it reverted to the military option two years later. Along the Gambia border, the rebels were effectively flushed out, but the situation remained volatile, and at the time of writing, it seems unlikely that the insurgency is finished business.

In the Gambia, meanwhile, the authorities continued to welcome migrants from beyond its borders – and increasingly refugees as well. In 1975, there were some 52,300 foreign nationals residing in the Gambia, amounting to 10.6 per cent of the total population, while between 1963 and 1973 immigration accounted for 55 per cent of its increase.[143] Over the same time period, Senegal received 355,000 foreign nationals, but these accounted for only 8 per cent of its own increase. Immigration was, therefore, proportionately far more important to the Gambia than it was to Senegal. The 45,600 Gambians living in Senegal in 1975 was also significantly greater than the 25,300 Senegalese living in the Gambia. However, this is clearly to privilege a national unit of analysis, whereas a focus on the border reveals a much more intriguing pattern. The striking aspect is that Gambians were not attracted to Dakar, but generally settled in the borderlands. Hence the 15,881 Gambians who moved to the Casamance, and the 8,657 who resided in Sine-Saloum, far outnumbered the 1,680 who relocated to Dakar.[144] Conversely, Banjul proper was not the primary magnet for migrants given that the population of

---

[142] The following file is instructive: ANS 11D1/239 "Sedhiou: Vols de Boeufs sur la Frontière Sénégal-Guinée Portugaise (1949–58)".

[143] Zachariah and Condé, *Migration*, tables 20–21, pp. 34–5, and table 8, p. 45.

[144] Zachariah and Condé, *Migration*, table 25, p. 40.

Table 11.4 *Population growth in Gambia by selected local government area and town, 1963–1973*

Local govt. area and town	Population 1963	Population 1973	Percentage change, 1963–1973	Average annual growth 1963–1973
1. Banjul	27,809	39,179	40.9	3.4
2. Kombo St. Mary	5,644	34,842	517.3	18.2
Bakau	3,563	9,337	162.1	9.6
Serekunda	2,081	25,505	1,125.6	25.1
3. Brikama	18,342	28,804	57.0	4.5
Sukuta	2,504	3,844	53.5	4.3
Brufut	1,901	2,765	45.5	3.7
Gunjur	3,561	4,677	31.3	2.7
Sifoe	1,332	2,080	56.2	4.5
Sanyang	1,282	2,136	66.6	5.1
Kartong	1,184	1,320	11.5	1.1
Tujering	1,282	1,313	2.4	0.2
Brikama	4,195	9,483	126.1	8.2
Faraba	1,101	1,186	7.7	0.7
4. Mansakonko	7,516	9,058	20.5	1.9
5. Kerewan	14,971	17,666	18.0	1.7
6. Kuntaur	2,539	3,467	36.5	3.1
7. Georgetown	4,099	6,075	48.2	3.9
8. Basse	13,689	23,481	71.5	5.4
Total	94,609	162,572	71.8	5.4

Source: Zachariah and Condé, Migration in West Africa: Demographic Aspects, table SA34, pp. 121–2.

the capital actually declined over time. It was settlements in the Kombos – especially Serekunda (Kombo St. Mary) and Brikama (Kombo Central) – that witnessed the most rapid expansion from the 1970s onwards (see Tables 11.4 and 11.5). These were the emergent trading hubs that were closely connected to Kaolack, Touba and Tambacounda in Senegal. Given that the latter were heavily oriented towards the contraband trade, the demographic surge reflects the restructuring of commerce on a truly regional scale. Most border towns tended to grow more slowly, the one exception being Basse in the eastern Gambia, which functioned much like a mini-hub in its own right. Although other border towns experienced more modest increases in population, this does not mean that they were any less wired into cross-border trade.

What the figures point to is a pattern of commerce that was relatively decentralized, as goods passed through the hands of merchants in Serekunda and then entered the trading circuits of small traders operating in border

Table 11.5 *Urban growth in cities, hubs and border towns of Senegal and the Gambia, 1970–2010*

Country	City/Town	1970	1980	1990	2000	2010
Senegal	Dakar	557,256	957,051	1,586,138	1,964,179	2,562,152
	Kaolack	85,142	118,475	153,531	166,382	198,565
	Tambacounda	16,438	30,475	44,899	62,506	84,574
	Touba	9,429	50,623	161,245	331,428	692,136
	Velingara	4,862	10,322	14,933	19,840	25,227
Gambia	Banjul	35,850	42,839	42,889	36,766	30,195
	Basse	2,478	4,533	7,975	16,557	20,458
	Brikama	7,578	16,067	33,929	56,433	84,202
	Farrafeni	2,922	7,844	17,260	19,943	22,626
	Gunjur	4,339	6,285	9,065	12,737	16,361
	Serekunda	-	84,322	206,399	395,969	603,066

Source: Africapolis/e-Geopolis, SWAC/OECD, http://stats.oecd.org/Index.aspx?DataSetCode=
SAH_URBA_LATLON_V3%20.

locations. Rotating border markets, or *lumos,* were an important vector for the transfer of goods – especially along the northern border with Sine-Saloum. In fact, there is some evidence to suggest that these markets also provided a stimulus to local horticulture that brought higher returns in the context of the border than other food crops.[145] Another pattern was one in which villagers participated directly in organized smuggling. An article in *Le Soleil,* for example, provided a detailed exposé of the trade between Bolibana in the eastern Gambia and the Senegalese town of Tambacounda.[146] It asserted that much of the contraband was carried out by women from the latter town who used the proceeds from smuggling to support their families. The article went on to note that they minimized the risk by cultivating special relationships with particular customs officers. Many of the goods were purchased from Mauritanian traders who had relocated to Bolibana after the violent upheavals of the early 1990s. Having presented a somewhat sympathetic view of small-scale smuggling, the article went on to assert that in the early hours of the morning large-scale operators took over, with carts being used to ferry goods from town to vehicles parked in the bush. The co-existence of *lumos* by day and organized trafficking by night was commonplace along the entire Senegal/Gambia border. The Gambian authorities pretended not to notice because such

---

[145] Richard Schroeder, *Shady Practices: Agroforestry and Gender Politics in the Gambia* (Berkeley, Los Angeles and London: University of California Press, 1999), p. 37.
[146] Doudou Sarr Niang et Pape Demba Sidibe, "Boribana, dernier refuge des contrebandières", *Le Soleil* 11–12 September 1999.

trade provided work for people in the urban centres as well as for populations in border areas. And finally, there was the small-scale trade that was commonplace within border regions. In 2004, for example, there was a well-stocked Mauritanian store at the southern tip of the Gambian town of Darsilami, leading to the disputed village of Tranquille. Traders using bicycles or donkey carts would purchase items like mosquito coils, tinned tomatoes, rice, flour and macaroni and transport them back across the border for sale.[147] One such trader explained that he would break the goods into smaller units and then hawk them around villages on the Casamance side of the border, making roughly 20 per cent on the deal. At the same location, a bicycle trader explained how he bought fish from as far away as Gunjur, which he sold around Touba.[148] This kind of small-scale trade tended to be compatible with a relatively dispersed settlement pattern.

On either side of the millennium, Senegalese newspaper articles served up homilies about the need for its people to change their mentality or wrote in praise of the *dounaiers* who risked their lives in the interests of the nation. But some contributions conceded that contraband guaranteed rural livelihoods and access to cheap goods at a time of acute hardship. It was also widely claimed that such trade was fundamental for the functioning of cross-border religious networks. But it was not always so easy to distinguish the trade that was essential to religious sociability from organized trafficking. In 1999, Moustapha Tall, the Director-General of Senegalese Customs, remarked that *daaras* – or communities of the faithful clustered around a marabout – and religious festivals provided a convenient cover for smuggling activity.[149] Another article commented on the fact that there was a surge in the smuggling of sugar just before the end of Ramadan when the commodity was in the most demand. It went on to cite the observations of the officer in charge of the Central zone (covering Louga, Diourbel and Thiès) and Kaloack-Fatick:

According to the lieutenant-colonel of the central zone, the region of Diourbel, although it is not situated towards the border, is a hub of fraud due to difficult areas of access (Touba and the existence of the daaras). The city of Touba, dubbed in the jargon of the agents of the economy 'the Vatican', is an area where the Customs agents cannot carry out policing. This is deplored by the Customs men who maintain that Touba, by virtue of its religious character, is an area inundated by fraud. The daaras are also risk areas because the talibés are often the accomplices of the smugglers.[150]

---

[147] The shop also contained a wider range of items like bicycle tyres, beauty products, insecticides and soft drinks.
[148] Fieldwork diary, 26 July 2004.
[149] "La douane tire la sonette d'alarme", *L'Info*, No. 351, 6/12/1999.
[150] "Fraude dans les daaras et cités religieuses: les douaniers appellent à la collaboration des chefs religieux", *L'Info*, 30 November 1999.

The identification of Touba as the epicentre of the contraband trade touched a raw nerve because it was commonplace but could hardly be spoken of in public. Although Customs officials pleaded for co-operation from the religious authorities, it was common knowledge that the maraboutic networks were deeply implicated in the supply of contraband goods to urban markets across Senegal. This included Dakar's famous Sandaga market, which was closely associated with the Mourides. As Boone notes:

> The Mouride confrérie also used its influence to protect the two-way contraband trade from government intervention. In Dakar, the role of the Mouride hierarchy in organizing and protecting parallel markets has been overt and conspicuous. Unregulated markets provide a source of employment and income for thousands of adherents.[151]

Other contraband goods transited through Touba, including pharmaceuticals whose terms of sale were formally controlled by the state, but which were openly traded on the street, in transport yards and other public places in Dakar.[152] In addition, the marabouts routinely interceded to protect their followers in the event that they were apprehended. The authorities were, in practice, forced to turn a blind eye despite repeated complaints from regulatory bodies and the managers of Senegalese enterprises whose products were undercut by cheaper merchandise entering from the Gambia – and increasingly from Mauritania as well.[153]

Whereas the daily life of Banjul had long been bound up with border flows, the deeper immersion of Dakar in the world of contraband underlined an increasingly intimate relationship between the city and the territorial margins. This, in turn, reflected the extent to which commerce within the Senegambia region had been respaced by the turn of the millennium – and in an entirely different manner to what had been envisaged in Senegalese planning documents. All of this had radical implications for social contracts in Senegal and the Gambia. The Diouf and the Wade regimes continued to adhere to the mantra that it was the business of the state to protect national economic

---

[151] Boone, *Merchant Capital*, pp. 214–15. In the early 1980s, Momar Coumba Diop drew attention to the overlap between membership of the Mouride *daaras* and urban trading networks. See his article "Les affaires mourides à Dakar", *Politique Africaine* 1 (4) 1981.

[152] See Didier Fassin, "La vente illicite des médicaments au Sénégal: économies 'paralleles', état et société", *Politique Africaine* 13, 1986; and "Du clandestin à les officieux: les réseaux de vente illicite des médicaments au Sénégal", *Cahiers d'Etudes Africaines* XXV (2) 1985. Tellingly, the official price of pharmaceuticals in Senegal was considerably in excess of that in France itself. See Jérome Dumoulin and Miloud Kaddar, "Le prix de médicaments dans certains pays d'Afrique: comparaison avec le prix français", *Sciences Sociales et Santé* 8 (1) 1990.

[153] The smuggling of sugar, which was landed at the Mauritanian coast and then spirited into Senegal, was a case in point.

interests at the same time as they routinely ignored infractions of the law.[154] State functionaries, most notably those working for Customs, were left to manage the daily contradictions as best they could. In Senegal, the *douaniers* engaged in anti-smuggling operations in the knowledge that some of the largest players were essentially untouchable. When these operations were intensified, it tended to be the smaller traders who were targeted for seizures and fines. But on a day-to-day basis they were often prepared to let things go, often in return for some consideration paid by the traders with whom they established some familiarity. In the Gambia, the Jawara regime created a credible role for the state as a facilitator of economic activity that plugged its own urban centres into regional trade networks. The Jammeh regime, whose legitimacy was tenuous at the best of times, had no interest in tampering with these arrangements on which most of the population depended at some level.

Conclusion

In this chapter, I have addressed the different reactions of the Senegalese and Gambian governments to the perfect storm of the early 1970s. Whereas the Senegalese response was to substantially enlarge the responsibilities of state agencies and to include the border regions in economic planning, the Gambian response hinged more on maximizing the export of groundnuts and the re-export of consumer goods. This, in effect, meant that governments were pursuing policies that were in direct competition with one another. The Senegalese were fully cognisant of the barnacle-like existence of their smaller neighbour and continued to press for an economic union that would have supported the development of their own agro-industries. Although the Senegalese briefly had their way when an embattled Jawara regime was forced to sign up to a Confederation, it was clear from the start that there was a distinct lack of enthusiasm in Banjul.

Part of the reason why the Senegalese and Gambian authorities failed to reach an accord was that larger social contracts were at stake. In Senegal, state intervention was supposed to drive renewed economic growth, but it was also intended to create opportunities for salaried employment within the bureaucracy, to carve out niches for Senegalese merchants, to keep the Muslim brotherhoods on side and to satisfy consumer demand. What was not planned for was the expansion of urban hubs located within regional trade networks, of which Touba came to be the most important. While Senegalese officials lamented the consequences of organized contraband for the viability of national industries, it was politically impossible to take on the Mourides.

---

[154] In 2000, the incoming government of Abdoulaye Wade pinned its banner to the mast of the Mourides and thereafter struggled to reconcile the very same bundle of contradictions.

Hence, permissive elements crept into the social contract and began to be taken for granted. The other problem was that when the regime struck a deal with key interest groups, it heightened a perception that the government was a predominantly Wolof cabal. The fact that it was Casamançais with direct experience of Dakar who were most affronted by 'Wolofization' is paradoxical in its own way. Be that as it may, the sustained insurgency was an indicator of the limits of a social contract that continued to leave out large swathes of the country. In the Gambia, where state revenues and livelihoods alike depended on the workings of the contraband trade, the social contract was heavily permissive. The Jammeh regime, which ruled with the backing of the military, was much less tolerant of political opposition than its predecessor. However, it shared the same keen appreciation of how Gambians related to the state: that is, above all else, they expected it to guarantee the preconditions for profitable cross-border trade. The consolidation of Serekunda and Brikama as trading hubs in their own right, which was equally unplanned, served to reinforce a vocal urban constituency that had a vested interest in the maintenance of conditions that were conducive to commerce. This included large merchants, with close links to their Senegalese counterparts, as well as a plethora of smaller traders and transporters. In countless communities along the border, the number of people who made a living from contraband was at least as great. As ever, the Gambian state took its cut and pretended not to see.

This account ends at the point when the Senegambia entered a new phase in its history, that is towards the end of the first decade of the new millennium. This is beyond the scope of the present study and can only be hinted at in outline. Having been subjected to the rigours of Structural Adjustment, in which the state was forced to withdraw from direct economic engagement and was subjected to a process of internal restructuring, Senegal embraced the possibilities associated with regional integration, the opening up to global markets and renewed external interest in financing infrastructure. The process of reform involved treading a fine line in which the numbers of perceived losers would potentially far outweigh those who benefited from structural change. The most significant departure under the presidency of Abdoulaye Wade was the decision to pursue closer economic ties with China, following the restoration of diplomatic ties in 2005. The consequence was an influx of Chinese goods through the port of Dakar, and in particular cheap textiles and construction materials.[155] The arrival of Chinese traders along with these imported goods posed a direct threat to Senegalese traders, in whose name the Union Nationale des Commerçants et Industriels du Sénégal (UNACOIS)

---

[155] Trade between China and Senegal grew twentyfold between 1994 and 2009, primarily on the basis of imports from China. Stefan Gehrold and Lena Tietze, "Far from altruistic: China's presence in Senegal", Konrad Adenauer Stiftung, *KAS International Reports* 11/2011, p. 92.

lobbied furiously against what it claimed was unfair competition.[156] But what this also meant is that the Gambia lost the overwhelming advantage that came with control of the re-export trade through the port of Banjul. The Gambia eventually came to its own deal with China and imported the same range of goods, but there was no particular advantage to channelling these through the port of Banjul. The slowdown of commercial activity in the Gambia placed a renewed strain on the relationship between the government and the urban population that left the Jammeh regime more isolated than ever. The eventual downfall of the regime in January 2017, as a consequence of an election result that the president tried to annul and which the Senegalese government was determined to uphold, marked the end of an era. The authorities in Dakar and Banjul talked with renewed enthusiasm about cementing closer ties between the two countries, but it remained an open question whether their interests were congruent. The planned investments in road, rail and port infrastructure in Dakar and Banjul heralded a fresh bout of competition to control the direction of commercial flows within the sub-region. This was different from the competition that has been the focus of this chapter – and it remains to be seen what kinds of social contracts could be erected on such inherently unstable foundations.

---

[156] Laurence Marfaing and Alena Thiel, *Chinese Commodity Imports in Ghana and Senegal: Demystifying Chinese Business Strength in Urban West Africa*, GIGA Working Papers No. 80, 2011, p. 7; and Suzanne Scheld, "Racism, 'free-trade' and consumer 'protection': the controversy of Chinese 'petty traders' in Dakar, Senegal", in Palvi Hoikkala and Dorothy D. Wills (eds.), *Dimensions of International Migration* (Newcastle: Cambridge Scholars, 2011), pp. 54–7.

12 The Remaking of Ghana and Togo at Their Common Border

Alhaji Kalabule Meets Nana Benz

In Chapter 11, I pointed to the very different – and indeed fundamentally incompatible – manner in which incumbent regimes in Senegal and the Gambia responded to the crisis of the early 1970s. I also highlighted the ways in which the enhanced mobility of Senegambians and the accelerated flow of contraband goods together brought about a spatial reordering that was neither in any official plan nor the outcome of any formal cross-border co-operation agreement. In this chapter, I will perform a similar exercise for the trans-Volta with a view to establishing how far comparable dynamics were at play. There are, however, some underlying differences, which it is worth pointing out at the start because they account for some of the variations of emphasis in the text that follows. First of all, as we have seen, Ghana had pioneered a statist vision of development well before the crisis of the end of the 1960s, whereas Togo had yet to find its feet as an entrepôt state by 1967. The points of departure were therefore significantly different from those in the Senegambia. Secondly, a succession of military interventions in Togo (1963 and 1967) and in Ghana (1966, 1972, 1978/9 and 1981) brought another set of forces into the equation. The prolongation of military rule had institutional consequences of its own because the pressure to increase the numbers of armed personnel typically led to greater demands on the budget. In addition, there was a leakage of military norms into other areas of governance, including not only much routine administration, but also border policing. Furthermore, there were more or less explicit demands that the military be considered as partners to the wider social contract. It was only in the Gambia after 1994 that something comparable seemed conceivable.

And thirdly, much less effort was invested in cross-border co-operation initiatives in the trans-Volta than in the Senegambia. From the Nkrumah era onwards, political leaders in Ghana displayed minimal interest in working with their Togolese counterparts and fashioned economic policies almost as if their neighbour did not really exist. In Togo itself, the regime looked to the Francophone world for its formal alliances, whilst seeking to carve out an independent role on the continental stage. But the port of Lomé and the

436

commercial life of the capital came to depend heavily on a web of relationships with Ghana. On the face of things, the economic tribulations that Ghana experienced coincided with at least a decade of relative boom in Togo – in a way which the authorities in Accra found more than coincidental. From their perspective, Togo eked out a parasitical existence – that is, as a barnacle state feeding off the travails of its larger neighbour. Far from wanting to come to a negotiated solution, the inclination in Accra was to try to seal the border more comprehensively. This ultimately proved an impossible task, and in reality, a form of 'integration from below' took shape – driven more by contraband than by mobility. The Alhaji K and Nana Benz of the sub-title stand for key social actors in the story of contraband: the former as an individual who was reputedly Ghana's most prolific smuggler and the latter as the purveyors of cloth in Lomé that were part of his stock in trade. I will begin this account by considering the pursuit of divergent economic paths in Ghana and Togo as a prelude to a discussion of the composite social contracts. In the second section, I will pay closer attention to the organization of contraband trade around the border itself, making use of hitherto-unused Public Tribunal records from Ghana that date to the 1980s and 1990s. Finally, in the third section I will address some of the respects in which border trade and urbanism spun off one another in a manner that bore some resemblances to the Senegambia.

Statist Visions and Social Contracts

In Chapter 10, I dealt in some detail with the efforts of the regime of Kwame Nkrumah to position the state at the centre of Ghanaian economic and political life. The 1966 coup formally ended Ghana's experiment with socialism, but there was to be no abandonment of the statist model. The election of the Progress Party (PP) government in 1969, at a time when the Convention People's Party (CPP) remained proscribed, brought the opposition to power for the first time. Harking back to the great schism in the nationalist movement of the late 1940s, the PP projected itself as the champion of political pluralism, civil liberties and economic liberalism – which formally differentiated it from the CPP in every respect. Deeply rooted in a history of political contestation, the natural constituency of the PP was thought to reside with the cocoa farmers of southern Ghana, the urban business community and traditional authorities across the country. The party manifesto also committed a future government to a more equitable pattern of development, compensating for the neglect of the northern and eastern peripheries, including the trans-Volta:

A Government in power is responsible for the welfare of the whole nation not only its supporters. Particular attention will be paid to those regions of Ghana especially the Northern, Upper and Volta Regions and those parts of the other regions which have been neglected by previous governments. Every effort will be made to correct the wide and unjust gap which exists between the development of some parts of the country and others.[1]

Given the substantial backing for the former United Party (UP) east of the Volta, amongst erstwhile supporters of the Togoland unification movement, the promise to make the Volta Region properly a part of Ghana addressed some of the unfinished business of decolonization. The emphatic victory of the PP in the 1969 elections suggested that it had managed to weld together a broad coalition that cut across regions and spanned the north–south divide. Ironically, however, it fell well short in the Volta Region where older political allegiances failed to transfer to the new political landscape.[2]

The Busia government did surprisingly little to chart a separate course. It pocketed the windfall deriving from high world cocoa prices rather than passing it on in the shape of higher producer prices – repeating the choices made by the CPP in 1954.[3] It also embarked on a resumption of public spending in order to fund many of the same commitments that the CPP had prioritized, despite the fact that government finances remained decidedly fragile. Moreover, there was to be no great cull of the parastatals, even when these had manifestly failed to deliver. Although the State Farms Corporation (SFC) was scaled back, for example, it was not actually abolished. In fact, only four state enterprises were privatized in the aftermath of the 1966 coup. As Killick succinctly puts it:

Out of a total of 53 public enterprises and corporations existing at the end of 1965, 43 remained wholly state-owned at the end of 1971 to which should be added the five new ones. The implication, of course, is that there was little change in the degree of state participation in economic activities after 1966.[4]

Summing up the tenure of the National Liberation Council (NLC) and PP together, Killick concludes that "[e]xchange, price, rent and wage controls retained intact throughout almost the entire period, and in some areas the powers of the state were further augmented."[5]

---

[1] *The Progress Party Manifesto*, issued on 2 August 1969, p. 4.

[2] On the elections, see Yaw Twumasi, "The 1969 elections", in Dennis Austin and Robin Luckham (eds.), *Politicians and Soldiers in Ghana, 1966–1972* (London: Frank Cass, 1972).

[3] Above a certain price, the windfall accrued to the state in the shape of the cocoa export duty rather than to the farmers. Tony Killick, *Development Economics in Action: A Study of Economic Policies in Ghana* (London: Heinemann, 1978), p. 306.

[4] Killick, *Development Economics*, p. 313. Only the United Ghana Farmers' Co-operative Council (UGFCC) was actually abolished. In 1967, the NLC added the Ghana Industrial Holding Corporation (GIHOC) to the list of state enterprises, albeit with more of a co-ordinating function.

[5] Killick, *Development Economics*, p. 315.

Jonathan Frimpong-Ansah, who served as Governor of the Bank of Ghana, later recalled that the Busia government remained committed to state-led industrialization and the 'big push' and speculated that this had something to do with the fact that the Minister of Finance, J.H. Mensah, had been the principal architect of the CPP's Seven-Year Plan.[6] In fact, the PP introduced a plan of its own, albeit on a foreshortened timescale. In practice, the Busia administration continued to believe in the necessity for state enterprises to generate the accelerated economic growth that would furnish the revenues needed for the increased provision of public goods and the commodities destined for mass consumption.[7] The government remained under considerable pressure to deliver and was not insulated by its healthy parliamentary majority. Hence, the injection of significant resources into road construction may have been justifiable in terms of the facilitation of cocoa exports, but it was also a response to persistent demands from rural constituents. Similarly, in the urban areas, the pressure to increase employment opportunities partly explains the ongoing commitment to the public sector as the motor of development.

The principal innovations lay in the sphere of distribution where the Busia government attempted to carve out a protected niche for Ghanaian businessmen and smaller traders. It liberalized import controls with the introduction of an Open General Licence, which covered 75 per cent of goods by 1971. Moreover, importers no longer needed to be licensed by the Ministry of Trade, thus removing a bureaucratic hurdle.[8] Although British import/export companies had mostly turned their hand to other activities in the 1950s, Lebanese traders controlled some of the most lucrative lines of trade by this point. In a manner that prefigured indigenization policies elsewhere in Africa, the Busia regime sought to drive 'aliens' out of the commercial sector. Even the Lebanese who had assumed Ghanaian nationality felt the sharp end of the politics of indigeneity.[9] The NLC had set the ball rolling with the Ghanaian Enterprises Decree of 1968, which required the closure or sale to Ghanaians of small-scale enterprises that were owned by foreigners. The Busia regime went much further with the passage of the Aliens Compliance Order of October 1969.[10] A measure that was ostensibly designed to ensure that foreign nationals

---

[6] Jonathan Frimpong-Ansah, *The Vampire State in Africa: The Political Economy of Decline in Ghana* (London and Trenton: James Currey and Africa World Press, 1991), p. 101.

[7] Killick, *Development Economics*, p. 315.

[8] Importers merely needed to pay a fee into any commercial bank. Republic of Ghana, *Economic Survey 1969–1971* (Accra: Central Bureau Statistics, 1976), p. 23.

[9] On the vulnerability of the Lebanese to exclusivist practices of citizenship, see Xerxes Malki, "The Alienated Stranger: A Political and Economic History of the Lebanese in Ghana, c.1925–1992", unpublished PhD thesis, University of Oxford, 2008.

[10] Killick, *Development Economics*, p. 312.

regularized their immigration status, led to the panicked departure of some 155,000 people in the first four months of 1970.[11] Those who left were predominantly other West Africans. Not surprisingly, many Togolese were caught in the net, despite the ability of many Ewes to pass as Ghanaian.[12] Most of the Sahelian sharecroppers and seasonal labourers never returned but relocated to Côte d'Ivoire where they played a seminal role in the expansion of the cocoa industry there. By closing its doors to foreign migrants, Ghana went down a path that would have been inconceivable in the Senegambia where mobility tended to be construed in much more positive terms. Finally, the government went a step further and passed the 1970 Market Trading Act, which reserved businesses with a turnover of less than ¢500,000, and specific named occupations, for Ghanaian nationals.[13] Although indigenization policies did not have the same immediately disastrous consequences as in Uganda or Congo/Zaire, the loss of labour was serious while the benefits to the trading community were at best transient.

Trade liberalization led to an influx of imported goods through Ghana's ports, and hence to a galloping trade deficit by the end of 1971.[14] A subsequent government report outlined the rationale and the attendant consequences as follows:

Imports were allowed by the Government to expand significantly during the period under review, primarily with a view to avoiding shortages of consumer goods by flooding the market with imported goods, in their efforts to curb the price rises. It was also to enable the expansion of the economy at a much faster rate than had been possible up to 1968, a period considered as the stabilisation period by the government of the National Liberation Council. The Government seems to have achieved these objectives but at a colossal cost of foreign resources and a precarious position in the Balance of Payments.[15]

Appeasing impatient consumers, who had blamed the CPP for earlier shortages, and courting the trading community were closely aligned political objectives. But increasing the imports of raw materials was also justified as

---

[11] John Esseks, "Economic policies", in Dennis Austin and Robin Luckham (eds.), Politicians and Soldiers in Ghana (London: Frank Cass, 1975), p. 50.

[12] The Togolese authorities estimated that 10,000 nationals had returned. Africa Contemporary Record, 1969–70 (London: Rex Collins, 1970), p. B.473. This was a relatively small proportion of the Togolese in Ghana, given that some 280,000 were estimated to be in Ghana in 1960. K.C. Zachariah and Julien Condé, Migration in West Africa: Demographic Aspects (Washington DC: World Bank and OECD, 1981), p. 34.

[13] Robin Luckham, "The Constitutional Commission", in Austin and Luckham, Politicians and Soldiers, footnote 51, p. 88.

[14] Economic Survey, 1969–1971, p. 23.

[15] Economic Survey, 1969–1971, p. 37. The report, which was completed under the NRC, concluded that government policies drove the country to "the brink of economic bankruptcy" (p. 37).

essential in placing state industries back on a viable footing. Consistent with the rationale of planning under Nkrumah, the contention was that while the recovery of state industries would eventually reduce the need for large volumes of imports, higher levels of imports were a practical necessity in the short run. At the same time, the commitments to state-led industrialization and the extension of rural infrastructure placed pressure on state finances. It is significant that over 45 per cent of government expenditure was devoted to Community Services and Social Services in 1971. The fact that no less than 24 per cent of recurrent expenditure was accounted for by the education sector reflects how highly this was valorized by Ghanaians.[16] Predictably, revenues were bolstered by virtue of higher takings from import duties and an import surcharge, and much higher earnings from the cocoa export duty at a time of relatively buoyant international prices. All of this was based on the presumption that the government could plan ahead on the basis of regulating and taxing what flowed through the ports. However, the doubling of cocoa smuggling in the three years after 1969, most of it across the Togo border, provided a clear indication that curbing producer prices and maintaining an overvalued currency would require greater attention to border management.[17] This was not a dimension of reform that the regime had given much thought to, and it quickly came face to face with the realities of the contraband economy.

As the overall gap between revenue and expenditure increased, the Busia government resorted to greater domestic and international borrowing.[18] It attempted to lever bi-lateral support from friendly countries such as Britain, in order to make both the budget and trade deficits sustainable, but these overtures were firmly rebuffed.[19] The government was therefore forced to make a renewed approach to the International Monetary Fund (IMF). In a taste of much more to come, the latter insisted on a series of conditions that proved highly unpopular when they were unveiled in the budget statement of July 1971. This included the imposition of a national development levy and

---

[16] The main difference was that capital expenditure rose considerably, which reflected the importance attached to road construction. *Economic Survey, 1969–1971*, p. 18.

[17] In 1968/9, it is estimated that 17,000 metric tons were smuggled. In 1971/2, this had increased to 37,000 metric tons. G. Robert Franco, "The optimal producer price of cocoa in Ghana", *Journal of Development Economics* 8 (1)1981, table 2, p. 86. The CMB blamed the fact that whereas the official exchange rate was 272 CFA francs to the cedi, the black market exchange oscillated between 170 to 180 CFA francs. Staff writer, "Cocoa smuggling: some reasons", *CMB Newsletter* 45, August 1970, p. 16. In 1970, it is estimated that around half of Togolese cocoa exports came from Ghana. World Bank, *Report and Recommendation of the President of the International Development Association to the Executive Directors on a Proposed Credit of SDR 36.9 Million to the Republic of Togo for a Structural Adjustment Project* (Washington DC: World Bank, 1983), p. 2.

[18] *Economic Survey, 1969–1971*, p. 13.

[19] Frimpong-Ansah, *Vampire State*, pp. 106–8; also Kwaku Danso-Boafo, *The Political Biography of Dr. Kofi Abrefa Busia* (Accra: Ghana Universities Press, 1996), pp. 102–3.

wage restraint on public employees – both of which echoed CPP austerity measures – but also military cutbacks and a devaluation of the currency to the tune of 42 per cent (which was announced at the end of the year).[20] Although austerity was certain to be unpopular, the regime compounded matters by alienating important interest groups. The selective dismissal of 568 employees from the civil service had led to accusations of a calculated witch-hunt against Ewes, in effect punishing them for the political disloyalty of their 'home region'. Busia's tart response to judicial independence in the affair further underlined the distance between rhetoric and practice. Moreover, the government clashed with the recently untethered Trade Union Congress (TUC) as it sought to face down a series of strikes that grew in number over 1969/70.[21] The regime's decidedly illiberal response was to disband the TUC and the National Union of Ghanaian Students (NUGS). When the Armed Forces intervened for a second time on 13 January 1972, there was therefore a broad swathe of opinion that was prepared to countenance a return to military rule, at least in the short run.

Under the leadership of Lt.-Col. I.K. Acheampong, the National Redemption Council (NRC) was primarily made up of officers who had been bypassed or sidelined during the tenure of the NLC and the PP alike – thus constituting "a coalition of the outs", in the words of Valerie Bennett.[22] The fact that officers from the Volta Region were well represented amongst the core group of conspirators, and the subsequent membership of the NRC itself, is hardly surprising.[23] The coup was justified on the grounds that the Busia regime had infringed on the interests of the Armed Forces, that it had introduced ethnic divisiveness into the military, the civil service and public life, and that it had meekly capitulated to IMF conditions. The NRC may have come to power without a clear vision, but it was quick to disabuse Ghanaians of the notion that it was just another caretaker government. It maintained that the priority was winning the 'economic war', which would take years to accomplish. The junta was careful to position itself as the protector of the interests of the nation, in

---

[20] The military budget was slashed, but in addition officers lost many of their allowances, which had made up a significant amount of their take-home salaries. Valerie Plave Bennett, "Epilogue: malcontents in uniform", in Austin and Luckham, *Politicians and Soldiers*, pp. 300–3. The 1971 devaluation came on top of an earlier devaluation under the NLC.

[21] Naomi Chazan, *An Anatomy of Ghanaian Politics: Managing Political Recession, 1969–1982* (Boulder: Westview, 1983), p. 226. The charge of ethnic particularism in the military related to a reshuffle of the military hierarchy.

[22] Bennett, "Epilogue", p. 308.

[23] Only one Ewe remained in a senior role by the time of the coup. Bennett, "Epilogue", p. 304. Brigadier Ashley-Lassen, who had been removed from his position as head of the Airforce, was one of those who joined the NRC. On the marginalization of Ewe officers, see Simon Baynham, "Divide et impera: civilian control of the military in Ghana's Second and Third Republics", *Journal of Modern African Studies* 23 (4) 1985, pp. 630–1. Amongst Ewe officers the placing of Alphonse Kattah on trial for theft rankled.

which borders were construed as a vital line of economic defence. One of its first acts was to revalue the currency and to repudiate some of the country's debts, whilst promising tougher measures to tackle smuggling.[24] The NRC openly identified itself with the CPP legacy and made a point of enlisting the support of some key figures associated with Nkrumah.[25] However, such alliances of convenience were never likely to last very long: after all, it was a central contention of the junta that the politicians had proven themselves collectively incapable of managing the affairs of the nation. Like the NLC before it, the NRC turned to the civil service and the chiefs for support – representing the beating heart of the state and one of the most powerful societal interests respectively. By stark contrast with the NLC, military officers were placed at the head of parastatals and state corporations, as well as Ministries and Regional administrations. This translated into an unprecedented level of involvement by military personnel in decision-making at all levels of the state. Although most of the bureaucracy continued to tick over as before, this blurring of the institutional lines arguably represented a far more radical innovation than anything attempted by Nkrumah.

Although the mid-1970s were as formative in Ghana as they were in Senegal, this period remains relatively under-researched.[26] Here, I merely wish to concentrate on the attempt to re-fashion state institutions and to respace economic activity. Partly in an effort to expose the shortcomings of the Busia regime, which had singularly failed to tackle the realities of cocoa smuggling, the NRC placed a much greater emphasis on securing the borders. Much of the blame was placed at the door of the Border Guards who were thought to be poorly motivated and actively complicit in smuggling. In 1972, the Border Guards were converted into one of the constituent units of the Armed Forces under the leadership of Brigadier E.K. Utuka – an army officer who hailed from the border town of Likpe-Mate in the Volta Region. This completed the separation of border policing from revenue collection. In addition, the regime passed a Subversion Decree that stipulated the death sentence for trafficking in gold, diamonds and timber, and a prison sentence of up to thirty years for cocoa smuggling. Moreover, these cases were henceforth to be tried by Special Military Tribunals rather than by the civil courts. Going further, the Regional

---

[24] "Lt. Col. Acheampong's statement on Ghana's external debts, 5 January 1972", in Eboe Hutchful (ed.), *The IMF and Ghana: The Confidential Record* (London: Zed Press, 1987), pp. 281–6.

[25] This included Komla Gbedemah and Joe Appiah, both of whom had parted on acrimonious terms with Nkrumah. Martin Appiah-Danquah of the UGFCC was a more obvious CPP stalwart. On the attempt to tap into the Nkrumah legacy, see Bennett, "Epilogue", pp. 309–11.

[26] There are only two book-length studies of this period and both have significant blindspots. These are Chazan, *An Anatomy of Ghanaian Politics* and Mike Oquaye, *Politics in Ghana, 1972–1979* (Accra: Tornado, 1980).

Commissioners of Brong-Ahafo and Volta Regions even threatened to expel entire border villages unless there was a change in their orientation.[27] These measures, and the bluster that surrounded them, were intended to signal that the NRC meant business. By contrast, very little thought was paid to the co-ordination of economic policy or border management with the authorities in Togo.

The Five-Year Development Plan that was launched in 1975 offered a structuralist diagnosis of Ghana's economic predicament, identifying over-dependency on a single export crop and the "high marginal propensity to import", which, it pointed out, had been exacerbated by the import substitution strategies of the past.[28] The solution was held to reside in more judicious state intervention, backed up by closer monitoring of performance. The striking difference with the CPP's programme was that the NRC placed a much heavier accent on agriculture. As the Plan stated: "The pre-eminence that agriculture enjoys in the economy make it mandatory that its development should receive the highest attention in the planning strategy."[29] Operation Feed Yourself (OFY), which became the central plank of the NRC, was proclaimed as early as February 1972. The stated objective was to achieve self-sufficiency in staple foods, and to this end the years from 1972 to 1974 were declared "the agricultural war years". In an effort to secure enough raw materials to feed the factories, "Operation Feed Your Industries" was unveiled as a distinct strand within OFY in 1975. Agricultural production targets were set for each region, and these were evaluated on a weekly basis by a National Operations Committee in Accra. By contrast, the Five-Year Plan did not reveal much fresh thinking about the role of industry other than to stress the need to improve capacity, to move beyond the production of consumer goods and to relocate more of the enterprises from Accra-Tema to the regions.[30] The textile industry was deemed of particular strategic importance because of its centrality to popular consumption and the possibility of creating backward linkages. Hence the emphasis was placed upon the production of cotton to feed the factories, often involving joint ventures with foreign companies such as the Dutch firm, Vlisco. At the peak of production in the 1970s, sixteen textile companies

---

[27] Paul Nugent, *Smugglers, Secessionists and Loyal Citizens on the Ghana–Togo Frontier: The Lie of the Borderlands Since 1914* (Oxford and Athens: James Currey and Ohio University Press, 2002), p. 250.

[28] Republic of Ghana, *Five-Year Development Plan, 1975/76–1979/80, Part I* (Accra: Ministry of Economic Planning, 1977), pp. 15–16.

[29] *Five-Year Development Plan, 1975/76–1979/80, Part II* (Accra: Ministry of Economic Planning, 1977), p. 1.

[30] *Five-Year Development Plan, Part II*, pp. 189–90.

accounted for 15 per cent of GDP and 27 per cent of manufacturing employment.[31] From 1968, Juapong Textiles Limited (JTL) supplied grey baft to the industry using cotton from the north, but also from the Volta Region. In an effort to protect the nascent textile industry, the military government imposed restrictions on imports, which made effective surveillance of the eastern border even more of an imperative.

In popular memory, the first three years of the NRC are still construed as a period of relative optimism, when school pupils, civil servants and ordinary citizens eagerly devoted part of their working week to farming activity.[32] However, alongside state-sanctioned voluntarism, the NRC placed its money on the transformative potential of large-scale agriculture. In the first instance, it was state corporations that received the lion's share of the funds – and this is where the project of respacing actively began. A re-invigorated SFC announced its intention to establish large-scale plantations in every region, while the Food Production Corporation (FPC) proclaimed its own plans to increase its number of farms from 75 to 110 in the space of a year.[33] In addition, Regional Development Corporations were established with a remit to set up their own agricultural ventures. Whereas loans to private farmers accounted for 25.9 per cent of the allocations under the first phase of OFY, the FPC received 25.2 per cent, the SFC 8.1 per cent and the Food Distribution Corporation 29.2 per cent.[34] The most radical innovation was the focus on the north as Ghana's own potential bread-basket. Although the various parastatals targeted the Northern and Upper Regions, the real takeoff came with what the Commissioner for Agriculture, Colonel Frank Bernasko, described as a "frenzied" shift into rice by commercial farmers.[35] The latter were attracted to the river basins of the Northern and Upper Regions by the promise of concessionary credit for the purchase of tractors and by the subsidization of inputs. A study of the Fumbisi valley by Konings found that 27 per cent of the rice farmers were actually civil servants, soldiers, policemen and prison officers – and many of these hailed from the south of the country.[36] Amongst these new farmers were prominent members of the NRC itself. In the Volta Region,

[31] The two leading companies were the Ghana Textile Printing Company (GTP) founded in 1964 and Akosombo Textiles Limited (ATL) in 1967. Linn Axelsson, "Making Borders: Engaging the Threat of Chinese Textiles in Ghana", PhD thesis, Department of Human Geography, Stockholm University, 2012, pp. 41–2.

[32] In 1973, civil servants and military personnel were permitted to enter commercial farming without relinquishing their jobs.

[33] The analysis here draws on Paul Nugent, "Rural Producers and the State in Ghana, 1972–1979", unpublished M.A. dissertation, School of Oriental and African Studies, 1984.

[34] Reported in *Daily Graphic* 21 June 1972.   [35] Quoted in *West Africa* 27 April 1974.

[36] Piet Konings, *The State and Rural Class Formation in Ghana: A Comparative Analysis* (London: KPI, 1986), pp. 186–7. See also A.W. Sheperd, "The Development of Capitalist Rice Farming in Northern Ghana", unpublished PhD thesis, University of Cambridge, 1979.

the operations of the SFC were marginal. The FPC maintained eight farms in 1973/4, including one at Agotime-Kpetoe, producing mostly maize and cassava. An attempt to incorporate peasant farmers through Agricultural Settlement Farms was carried out in another six locations, albeit on a limited scale.[37] Much of the effort of the Ministry of Agriculture was funnelled into the Afife Rice project in which selected 'settlers' were recruited to learn about rice culture under the guidance of Chinese experts before being set to work under project management. The Aveyime Irrigation Project was based on a very similar model. By contrast, very little support was extended to the producers of upland (brown or *glaberrima*) rice that is indigenous to the Togo hills. Small farmers were enjoined to form co-operatives that would be eligible to apply for bank loans, but they were at the back of the queue when it came to the provision of credit and inputs.

The statistical record indicates that there was a significant increase in national rice production between 1972 and 1974, although the manner in which the figures were collated raises some questions about their accuracy.[38] In 1974, Acheampong was able to declare the country self-sufficient in rice, and imports in fact ceased for the next two years. Ironically, while the junta displayed little interest in actively supporting peasant production, many small farmers had taken to rice farming of their own accord, renting tractor services from their wealthier neighbours. For the same reason, there was also an appreciable increase in maize production over the period. From 1975 onwards, however, production began to stall. Acheampong blamed factors beyond the government's control: "In 1972 and 1973 we were doing fine. Then came the oil crisis, followed by three years of drought or bad rains. This meant that we had to divert a lot of money to bring in maize and rice."[39] However, this assessment glossed over structural shortcomings. Fundamentally, the SFC and the FPC consumed vast resources, but produced relatively little food. In a damning indictment of the FPC, a commission of enquiry revealed that of the 43,769 hectares it had been allocated it had managed to develop only 9,721 and to plant crops on even less. It concluded that:

---

[37] The FPC farm in Kpetoe farmed 303 acres of maize in 1973/4. Volta Region, Ministry of Agriculture, "Operation Feed Yourself" file CHC 5.

[38] Especially revealing is a minute within the files of the Ministry of Agriculture in the Volta Region (dated 14 April 1975) in which an official enquired as to whether progress against the season's targets had been sent to Accra. In the event that they had not, he suggested merely adding 2–3 per cent to the previous return. Given that the estimates of actual crops typically claimed to be meeting the targets, the implication is that many of the statistics were based on rising estimates based on what looked good rather than hard evidence. "Operation Feed Yourself" file CHC 5. On some other data blindspots, see Alice Wiemers, "A 'time of 'Agric': rethinking the 'failure' of agricultural programs in 1970s Ghana", *World Development* 66, 2015.

[39] Quoted in *West Africa* 5 June 1978.

The performance of the Food Production Corporation has been so poor that the question arises as to whether it is at all possible to carry out food production on a large scale profitably in the country.[40]

As the government lost faith in state corporations, it turned unequivocally to supporting commercial farmers through generous government subsidies and easy access to credit. There was also some effort to engage with small-scale farmers, but subject to the realities of funding constraints. The Upper Region Agricultural Development Project (URADEP) was launched with the support of the World Bank in 1977, and the Northern Region Integrated Project (NORRIP) and the Volta Region Agricultural Development Project (VORADEP) followed.[41] These were part of the new wave of integrated rural development projects across the continent, in which small producers were accorded greater weight. But this did not really have any meaningful effect before the mid-1980s.

The economic programme of the Acheampong regime unravelled in a spectacular fashion in the second half of the 1970s, and this was reflected in shifting dynamics in border regions. Having promised a succession of wage increases for public sector workers, as well as subsidies for agriculture, the junta committed itself to a series of expansionary budgets. This necessitated a return to borrowing from the banks. As the fiscal position deteriorated, the regime was able to dedicate fewer resources to the maintenance of the road network that Busia had prioritized, with the inevitable result that farmers could not deliver their crops to market. In addition, the regime was unable to import the spare parts to maintain the tractors and other machinery upon which OFY depended. Towards the end of 1975, the NRC was facing complaints from commercial rice farmers that the guaranteed minimum price did not take enough account of rising production costs. Whereas the state-owned Rice Mills Unit was offering ¢15.50 per bag in September/October 1976, the real market price was somewhere around ¢100 a bag – which pointed to a widening gap between the official and black-market prices. Many farmers in the north pointedly refused to sell to the Rice Mills, despite having taken state-sanctioned loans, and either offloaded their crops on the urban black market or smuggled them into neighbouring countries. Government seizures of hoarded rice merely increased the incentive to send the crop across the border with the greatest despatch. On the settlement projects in the southern Volta

[40] State Enterprises Commission, *Report on Survey into the Operations of the Food Production Corporation* (Accra: SEC, 1979), pp. 8–9.
[41] NORRIP was funded with Canadian support while VORADEP was supported by the World Bank and only commenced operations in 1981. *Volta Region Agricultural Development Project (VORADEP): Project Review, 1982–1986, and Proposals for a One Year Extension* (Ho: Ministry of Agriculture, Monitoring and Evaluation Unit, 1986).

Region, farmers also refused to work to project rules or to sell the rice to the Rice Mills Unit. The rice in question tended to enter alternative channels where the prevailing prices were considerably more attractive.

A similar story unfolded in the cocoa sector. The NRC inherited the many and varied problems of the Cocoa Marketing Board (CMB) and tried to address these through internal restructuring. This had a temporary effect, and by the mid-1970s chronic inefficiency and corruption within the CMB had reached unprecedented levels. After 1975, the disarray was reflected in the failure of the CMB to even publish its annual accounts. In 1976/7, it was believed that millions of cedis that were supposed to be released to the co-operatives had been embezzled, with the consequence that the farmers could not be paid. Moreover, as the economic crisis deepened, shortages of spare parts, fuel and vehicles meant that much of the cocoa crop was locked up in the interior – requiring the army to resort to transporting cocoa to the ports in 1976. Although the government did increase nominal producer prices year on year, the farmers were worse off because of hyper-inflation and the increasing overvaluation of the currency. The government claimed that it subsidized inputs in a way that neighbouring countries did not, but even when this is factored in, there is no doubt that cocoa farmers in Ghana received a substantially worse deal over time. Farmers in Ashanti neglected their cocoa farms and turned to staple crops for domestic consumption, whereas those in Brong-Ahafo and the Volta Region resorted to smuggling on a massive scale.[42] Farmers who sold their cocoa in Togo were rewarded twice over: they received more money for their crop, and they could use the CFA francs to purchase goods that were fast disappearing from Ghanaian markets. The Togolese authorities did nothing to discourage the contraband trade and were only too happy to perpetuate the convenient fiction that their own production was increasing.

In Togo itself, the 'Swiss option' that had been talked about in the 1950s began to seem more attainable two decades later. While Togo remained a poor country, it negotiated a turbulent decade with considerably greater success than its larger neighbour. Samuel Decalo points out that in 1967 Eyadéma "probably had few political ambitions, and no particular developmental preferences."[43] Like the NLC in Ghana, the junta proclaimed its intention to carry out caretaking functions before leading the country back to constitutional rule. But within relatively short order, the regime began to articulate its own case for

---

[42] In this book, I have focused on the border with Togo, but for smuggling on Ghana's western border see Bianca Murillo, *Market Encounters: Consumer Cultures in Twentieth-Century Ghana* (Athens: Ohio University Press, 2017), ch. 5.

[43] Samuel Decalo, *Coups and Army Rule in Africa: Motivations and Constraints*, 2nd edn. (New Haven: Yale University Press, 1990), pp. 219–20.

a longer term in office, ostensibly in order to heal national divisions. The remarkable longevity of the Eyadéma regime owes something to fortuitous timing, but in many ways, it was the architect of its good fortune. The first is reflected in the timely emergence of phosphates as the most significant export earner and the source of much-needed government revenues. This made it possible for the state to assume a more proactive role in the provision of public goods. It also enabled the regime to lower import duties on consumer items – initially beginning with luxury commodities, but later extended to cover many other goods of mass consumption. The artistry lay in the laying of the foundations for a viable entrepôt state. In the Economic Plan of 1966–70 as much as 58 per cent of expenditure was devoted to infrastructure.[44] The single most important initiative was the improvement to the port facilities of Lomé, beginning with an extension in 1968 and successive upgrades to the deepwater port through the 1970s. The official rationale was that the modernized facilities at the Free Port would service the landlocked states of the Sahel.[45] But in reality, a sizeable percentage of what passed through the port was always intended for the Ghanaian market. Much like in the Gambia, the Eyadéma regime contrived to win both ways. On the one hand, by setting its cocoa producer prices above those in Ghana, it was assured of attracting cash crops from areas relatively close to the border. This meant that the government could tax its own farmers somewhat heavily and still be assured of gathering cocoa from Ghana.[46] On the other hand, consumer goods that were taxed at the port of entry, which were notionally intended for local consumption, were despatched across the border in an increasingly systematic fashion. Unlike Senegal, Togo adopted an 'open-door policy' and sourced more than half of its imports from countries other than France – which meant that they tended to be considerably cheaper.[47] Whereas development planners in Ghana had their backs turned to the border, the Togolese strategy was one that took full advantage of the close proximity.

This brings me to a comparison of the larger social contracts and their rootedness in the realities of the border. In 1969, the Eyadéma's regime began the process of abandoning its military fatigues when the Rassemblement du Peuple Togolaise (RPT) was formally inaugurated as a political party. When

[44] William C. Ladd and James C. McClelland, *Francophone Africa: A Report on Business Opportunities in Togo* (Washington DC: Overseas Private Investment Corporation, 1975) p. 17.

[45] François Bost, "Entre global et local: le cas de la zone franche de Lomé", in Philippe Gervais-Lambony (ed.), *Lomé: dynamiques d'une ville africaine* (Paris: Karthala, 2007).

[46] Between 1967 and 1976, farmers in Togo received only about half of the world price. David Bovet and Laurian Unnevehr, *Agricultural Pricing in Togo, World Bank Staffing Paper No. 47* (Washington DC: World Bank, July 1981), p. 35.

[47] J. Marc Chittum (ed.), *Marketing in Togo, Overseas Business Report 77–70* (US Department of Commerce, Industry and Trade Administration, 1977), p. 2.

the creation of a one-party state was put to a referendum in 1972, Togo was treading a familiar African path. At this point, the RPT seemed to enjoy even "a groundswell of support", although the voting figures in support of the new dispensation were scarcely credible.[48] The one-party state was modelled on formations such as the CPP in Ghana, which had created integral wings for different interest groups such as women and youth. The RPT was careful to weave traditional authorities, who were organized through their own Association des Chefs Traditionnels du Togo (ANCT) after 1968, into the fabric of the one-party state in a manner that had never been attempted in Ghana.[49] Although the Armed Forces retained their institutional distinctiveness, they remained an essential component of the ruling coalition. Throughout his four decades in office, Eyadéma never ceased to remind the Togolese public that he was all that stood between them and chaos. In a more benign guise, especially when seeking to make an impact as a statesman on the international stage, Eyadéma presented himself as the 'man of peace' and as the builder of the nation.[50] But in the final analysis, the regime depended on the perpetuation of an undercurrent of intimidation – sustained by salutary punishments meted out to those who dared to articulate their opposition to the regime in overt forms.[51] The presumption was that any challenge to the regime would most likely emanate from the south. Ewes, who were never very numerous in the military, were eased out of positions of command as the army and the gendarmerie became the de facto preserve of northerners – and Eyadéma's Kabré home area more particularly. At the same time, however, care was always taken to ensure that a reasonable number of ministerial portfolios were filled by southerners.

In place of the bickering of the past, the RPT promised to forge a social consensus around its own vision of accelerated development. The pledge to deliver amenities to all corners of the country was the Togolese variant of respacing through development. The most striking manifestation of the change was the refashioning of Lama-Kara from a provincial outpost into a modern city with the infrastructure to match. Not surprisingly, Eyadéma's home village of Pya was also the beneficiary of infrastructural investments

[48] Decalo, *Coups*, p. 228.
[49] E. Adriaan B. Van Rouveroy Van Nieuwaal, *L'état en Afrique face à la chefferie: le cas du Togo* (Paris: Karthala, 2000), ch. 5.
[50] On the theme of peace, see Georges Ayache, *"Si la maison de votre voisin brûle"*: *Eyadéma et la politique extérieure du Togo* (Paris: Editions ABC, 1983).
[51] Comi M. Toulabor, *Le Togo sous Eyadéma* (Paris: Karthala, 1986), pp. 182–92; Kofi Nutefé Tsigbe, "Cinquante ans de discours sur l'unité national au Togo (1960–2010): les leçons d'une politique toujours de l'actualité", in Theodore Nicoué Gayibor (ed.), *Cinquante ans d'independance an Afrique subsaharienne et au Togo* (Paris: L'Harmattan, 2012), p. 86. Amnesty International kept up a dossier and much more was revealed during the hearings of the National Conference. Amnesty International, *Togo: Il est temps de rendre des comptes* (Paris: Amnesty International, 1999).

and numerous prestige projects. This was counter-balanced by a significant expansion of government employment. Between 1975 and 1978, government employment increased from 23,000 to 38,000 while salaries were increased by 20 per cent in 1975 and a further 15 per cent in 1977 – and all this at a time when the salaries of Ghanaian public servants were falling precipitously.[52] Because southerners held an educational advantage by some margin, they were certain to be well represented in the enlarged bureaucracy. In addition, significant improvements were made to the physical infrastructure of Lomé, rendered in the shape of improved roads, markets and gleaming new hotels. Although many northerners relocated to the capital, these investments were intended to reassure the population of the south that they too had a stake in the new dispensation.

Most importantly, the expansion of the contraband trade was crucial in enabling the RPT to win over merchants and small traders across the south, and especially the powerful market women of Lomé. At the centre of the commercial web lay the *Grand Marché*, the seat of the cloth market in Lomé, where Mina women from south-eastern Togo held sway.[53] With government assistance, the so-called *Nana Benz*[54] succeeded in turning Lomé into a highly successful regional centre for the re-export of textiles. The market women were the arbiters of fashion in the sense that they mediated between the consumers and the manufacturers based in Europe – and especially the Netherlands where factories produced wax prints specifically for the West African market. The established firms continued to import the cloth, which they sold to the Nana Benz who, in turn, distributed it to traders lower down the supply chain. A very high percentage of the textiles were destined for Ghana, especially once the latter's own efforts at import substitution imploded in the face of shortages of raw materials, spare parts and serviceable cotton. The cloth sellers of Lomé placed the full weight of their association behind the RPT, while the government created the optimal conditions for the pursuit of profitable trade by keeping taxes and duties to a manageable level. The Nana Benz were enriched by their privileged relationship to the power structure, but the system also guaranteed a living for large numbers of ordinary traders who hawked the cloth

[52] World Bank, *Report and Recommendation,* p. 6.

[53] Rita Cordonnier found that 55 per cent of her sample of the cloth-sellers were Mina, and most of these were from Anécho. *Femmes Africaines et commerce: les revendeuses de tissu de la ville de Lomé* (Paris: L'Harmattan, 1987), p. 47. See also Nina Sylvanus, *Patterns in Circulation: Cloth, Gender and Materiality in West Africa* (Chicago and London: University of Chicago Press, 2016), ch. 3.

[54] The etymology of the term is itself intriguing. *Nana* is the term of respect used in Akan languages, and hence mostly in Ghana, for men. Given that the Mina originated from Elmina in what is now Ghana, the term presumably originates from here. The Benz is an allusion to the wealth of these cloth traders who could afford to ride Mercedes Benz cars. As a term, it perfectly encapsulates the trans-nationality of the cloth trade.

in Togo and/or traded it across the border into Ghana. The RPT was never likely to be popular, but by facilitating the commercial links that connected the capital with countless smaller towns, it enabled ordinary southerners, especially women, to carve out their own livelihoods. The textile trade also provided an income for male transporters and drivers who plied the routes, and the countless head porters and currency changers who made a living from the border. The Togolese model ran into some difficulty in the late 1970s, mostly because the regime over-committed itself on the basis of overly optimistic projections of earnings from phosphates. There was a proliferation of new parastatals and infrastructural projects that included a number of white elephants.[55] The mounting problem of debt servicing that ensued ultimately forced the government to approach the World Bank for assistance in 1983. But both the perceived need to rein in state expenditure, and the limited returns from phosphate mining, merely underlined the strategic importance of the contraband economy for state revenues and popular livelihoods alike. In Togo, therefore, the composite social contract was an intriguing hybrid: it was underpinned by the threat of force, but this was partially offset by the pronounced permissive and productive elements.

Not surprisingly, the emergent dispensation in Togo had an impact in Ghana where the Acheampong regime found itself divided over its future direction. This culminated in a purge and the reconstitution of the junta in the shape of a Supreme Military Council (SMC I) in 1975.[56] Subsequently, the regime faced increasingly vocal demands for a return to the barracks voiced by University students and professional associations who openly proclaimed that military rule had failed.[57] The Acheampong regime sought to deflect some of the criticism by pointing to the need for strong leadership in the face of an external threat. The government accused the Togolese authorities of undermining its economic recovery effort by actively encouraging smuggling to the detriment of cocoa export earnings and the viability of state industries. It linked this claim to what it alleged were Togolese irredentist ambitions. David Brown has suggested that the crackdown on smuggling in the early 1970s was partly what lay behind renewed unificationist rumblings east of the Volta.[58] This is difficult to verify, and certainly the 'Livre Blanc' that was published in 1976 by the Movement for the Liberation of Western Togoland (TOLIMO) made no

---

[55] A striking case in point was the vast Hotel 2 Février, which was never close to being filled.

[56] The primary casualties were Ewe members of the regime who had instigated the initial coup, thereby reintroducing an ethnic calculus that the NRC had set out to transcend. This was the prelude to a succession of supposed Ewe plots against the SMC.

[57] Chazan, *An Anatomy of Ghanaian Politics*, pp. 242–4.

[58] David Brown, "Borderline politics in Ghana: The National Liberation Movement of Western Togoland", *Journal of Modern African Studies* 18 (4) 1980, pp. 587–8.

reference to such considerations.[59] Brown's speculation that reunification might also have reduced the cost of importing electricity from the Volta Lake is less plausible for the simple reason that the Volta River had never been part of German or French territory. In all probability, the Togolese government chose to resurrect the issue of former British Togoland as part of its wider effort to curry favour with populations in the south.[60] For whatever reason, the Eyadéma regime permitted TOLIMO, which had been formed in 1972, to operate under its protective wing while it openly questioned the legitimacy of the 1956 plebiscite. Predictably this elicited a belligerent response from the Ghanaian authorities who insisted that the issue of unification was definitively closed. Although much of the anger was no doubt real, the spat also afforded the Acheampong regime the perfect opportunity to wrap itself in the flag of patriotism and to claim a special role for the military in the preservation of the country's territorial integrity.[61] Operation Counterpoint, a propaganda exercise launched with some fanfare in 1975, asserted a direct link between smuggling and secessionism/irredentism and promised to tackle the double threat with military force if necessary. The sabre-rattling was sufficient to deter the Eyadéma regime from further raising the stakes, and the latter even offered to co-operate in introducing measures to curb end currency trafficking and smuggling.[62] However, given that there was no incentive for the Togolese government to follow-through, the border remained a source of tension for the duration of the decade.

The Acheampong regime went one stage further in its attempt to recapture the initiative, by attempting to write the military into the social contract. According to Maxwell Owusu, the case for a no-party system had enjoyed strong support in debate leading up to the adoption of the Constitution of the Second Republic in 1969.[63] In some respects, therefore, Union Government (Unigov) was drawing on a stock of ideas that had enjoyed currency for some time. The inclusion of the military as a permanent partner was justified on the basis that the attempt to bracket it off from politics derived from a western

---

[59] The document dealt primarily with perceived unfairness of the plebiscite of 1956. "Livre Blanc sur la réunification du Togo", *Revue Française d'Etudes Politiques Africaines*, 121, 1976, pp. 20–57.

[60] Brown, "Borderline politics", pp. 588–90. The Togolese government may have been acting under some pressure from Ghanaian exiles who had previously been active in the unification movement. Kate Skinner, *The Fruits of Freedom in Togoland: Literacy, Politics and Nationalism, 1914–2014* (Cambridge: Cambridge University Press, 2015), pp. 232–7.

[61] David Brown, "Who are the tribalists? Social pluralism and political ideology in Ghana", *African Affairs* 81 (322) 1982, pp. 62–3; see also David Brown, "Sieges and scapegoats: the politics of pluralism in Ghana and Togo", *Journal of Modern African Studies* 21 (3) 1983.

[62] *Africa Contemporary Record 1977/78*, p. B793.

[63] Maxwell Owusu, "Politics without parties: reflections on the Union Government proposals in Ghana", *African Studies Review* 22 (1) 1979, pp. 99–100.

model of politics – whereas, it was asserted, pre-colonial Akan polities had always reserved a role for the *asafos* in decision-making. Given that one-party and multi-party models had both failed, so the argument continued, it was time to seek a better alignment with Ghanaian cultural norms. In some respects, this was Ghana's variant on the drive for 'authenticity' that swept the continent, including Togo, in the 1970s. The Ad Hoc Committee on Union Government, which was set up to canvass public opinion, actually stopped short of proposing institutional representation for the military. But it did find support for a form of non-party government in which the military and police officers could serve.[64] If Unigov had been adopted, the result might have been a corporatist system of government. As it transpired, a resurgent civilian coalition, including the student movement, professional associations and representatives of both the Nkrumahist and Busia-Danquah political traditions, joined forces behind a demand for an unqualified return to civilian rule. A botched referendum in 1978 ensured that the Unigov proposals were thoroughly discredited, and in an internal putsch Acheampong was swiftly replaced by Major-General Fred Akuffo. The latter promised that there would be an unconditional return to the barracks after fresh elections in 1979. The subsequent passage of events is too well known to bear repetition here. On 4 June, a junior officers and ranks' coup overthrew SMC II and installed an Armed Forces Revolutionary Council (AFRC). Under the leadership of Flt.-Lt. Jerry Rawlings, the AFRC announced a period of 'house-cleaning' prior to the resumption of constitutional rule. The avowed objective was to hold senior officers and their associates to account before the handover to a duly elected government.

On the face of it, the 1979 intervention took the country full circle, but in reality these events had exposed serious fault-lines within the Ghanaian polity that could not be resolved merely by holding fresh elections. At a basic level, the coup highlighted the imminent collapse of the social contract that had been forged in the moment of independence and that had been patched up with varying degrees of success over the following decade. The systemic crisis came to fruition precisely at the moment when a new term entered the Ghanaian vocabulary: namely *kalabule*. The latter apparently derived from Hausa and its meaning – something like 'keep it quiet' – pointed to the key element of secrecy. *Kalabule* served as a polyvalent term that connected the economic, social and political manifestations of the malaise. It also related the realities of everyday life to deep structures. Although the etymological progression of the term arguably still warrants closer investigation, it is clear that its historical roots reside in the knock-on effects of accumulating consumer shortages. As we have seen, these became frequent in the early 1960s, but this

---

[64] Owusu "Politics", footnote 4, p. 107. The Ad Hoc Committee included Togbe Adja Tekpor VI from Avatime in the Volta Region.

was nothing compared to a decade later when the most basic necessities of life had become virtually unobtainable. The country's factories were operating at a fraction of their capacity, while the dearth of foreign exchange meant that fewer consumer goods entered the ports. Shortages, which were felt acutely in the cities, spiralled in a dialectical relationship with the black market. Ghanaians hoarded goods because they were not sure when next they would become available, and traders withheld stocks in the expectation of a price rise. The NRC had imposed minimum pricing for consumer goods under the Price Control Decree of 1972,[65] but in the second half of the decade this merely ratcheted up the economic rents and made it less likely that the traders would release their goods onto the open market. The vicious circle was directly related to corruption because those who could acquire import licences, or commodities at the approved price, could sell them on at a premium. By all accounts, senior members of the military administration, including Acheampong himself, were deeply implicated in this secretive world in which favours were dispensed, and deals were done, behind closed doors. But the cancer also crept into all branches and levels of the state bureaucracy. Ordinary government officials, whose salaries were shrinking in real terms, attempted to make up some of the shortfall through corruption, moonlighting and dabbling in the black market.

A profound sense that *kalabule* had seeped into all walks of life partially explains the behaviour of the AFRC in 1979. The regime was determined to impose exemplary punishments upon those who were accused of having caused the rot and then profited directly from it. The placing of eight senior officers, including three former heads of state, in front of a firing squad was a dramatic manifestation of the upheaval within the Armed Forces.[66] The ranks and junior officers also unleashed violence and humiliation upon senior officers signalling a complete breakdown of the command structure. Within a matter of months, the Armed Forces had gone from being a potential partner in government to the brink of implosion. Aside from the barracks, the most dramatic events unfolded in urban spaces, and especially in the markets. The flogging of market women who were accused of hoarding, or selling commodities at above control price and the destruction of a section of Makola market in Accra were intended as both symbolic and exemplary acts.[67] Although the regime did not have sufficient time to address smuggling at the borders, it is clear that the latter was counted as amongst the most pernicious manifestations of *kalabule*.

[65] Murillo, *Market Encounters*, p. 143.
[66] The three former heads of state were Acheampong, Akuffo and Akwasi Afrifa. Utuka was also amongst the victims.
[67] Claire Robertson, "The death of Makola and other tragedies: male strategies against a female-dominated system", *Canadian Journal of African Studies*, 17 (3) 1983.

In the past, it had been considered axiomatic that a solution to the country's problems lay in a reconfiguration of state institutions. For Nkrumah the colonial state needed to be Africanized and converted to productive ends, while for Acheampong it needed to be infused with military discipline. But by 1979, state institutions were widely seen as part of the problem. And yet there could be no easy return to the private sector because merchants and traders were considered to be up to their necks in *kalabule* as well. Again, previous regimes had assumed that, other things being equal, the interests of consumers and traders were broadly congruent. By contrast, the discourse surrounding *kalabule* posited that traders inevitably profiteered at the expense of ordinary Ghanaians who could neither acquire, nor afford, their most basic needs as a consequence. That represented a fundamental breach in the underlying terms of the social contract. At a very mundane level, it was no longer clear what could be counted as a reasonable margin of profit. At the same time, there was a further discursive shift in which the acquisition of private wealth was transformed from a positive into something altogether more ambivalent.[68] The AFRC did not have an answer to any of the big questions, and its insistence on the need for a moral regeneration rang hollow. However, the seeds of an idea were sown that were to germinate during the next phase in Ghana's history: namely the need for political cadres to serve as the guarantor of moral rectitude. Necessarily, these cadres would sit half outside the structures of the state. Herein lay the origins of the June 4 Movement (JFM), which sought to promote a revolutionary agenda following the return to civilian rule in September 1979.

During the ill-fated Third Republic (1979–81), Ghana remained locked in the grip of an economic crisis in which a crumbling road network, dormant factories and endemic consumer shortages came together to produce an experience of collective misery. As is often the case in such circumstances, Ghanaians took some solace in gallows humour. One apocryphal story told of a woman who went to market to find some tinned sardines to prepare food for her family. The woman was delighted at her good fortune in laying her hands on a product that had become all too scarce. But when she proceeded to open one of the tins, she discovered that the contents had gone bad. Running back to the market she confronted the trader with having sold her rotten fish, to which the latter retorted: "Why did you open the tin? The point was to sell it to the

---

[68] This positive imagery was, in turn, rooted in much older ideas about accumulation. See T.C. McCaskie, "Accumulation, wealth and belief in Asante history, I: to the close of the nineteenth century", *Africa* 53 (1) 1983; "Accumulation, wealth and belief in Asante history, Part II: the twentieth century", *Africa* 56 (1) 1986.

next person." During the CPP years, the availability of fish at an affordable price had become a barometer of the government's ability to satisfy the everyday needs of the urban population. The inadequacies of the State Fishing Corporation, which were emblematic of the parastatal sector as a whole, meant that fresh fish became decidedly scarce despite its obvious abundance offshore. By the end of the 1970s, tinned sardines from North Africa had become central to urban consumption. Because they were often in short supply, they were routinely smuggled, transported to the urban areas and offloaded on the black market.

During the short-lived Limann interregnum, high-bulk commodities like maize became difficult to transport to market and were often left to rot in villages in the interior. At the same time, relatively high-value goods that were smuggled from Togo, like textiles or cosmetics, were transported over considerable distances. The population of the Volta Region came to depend on Togolese supplies, but many of the contraband goods were destined for urban markets well inside Ghana. While cloth and tinned fish were transported by roads, bush paths and waterways, other commodities passed in the opposite direction. Robert Franco has suggested that between a quarter and a fifth of the entire cocoa crop was smuggled at the end of the 1970s, amounting to some 50,000 metric tonnes.[69] In the early 1980s, far more cocoa from the Volta Region was being sold in Togo than to the CMB – even if production was also falling on account of the spread of black pod disease.[70] Given that Togo did not have gold or diamond deposits to speak of, it can safely be assumed that all of these official exports from Togo were contraband. The returns from cocoa provided part of the resources that sustained other forms of cross-border trade. Ernesto May estimated that cocoa smuggling alone afforded the foreign exchange needed to sustain a black-market economy amounting to 32.4 per cent of GDP in 1982.[71] The overall dimensions of the 'real economy' were clearly much greater, although probably not of the order of Zaire where one 'guesstimate' is that the second economy was three times greater than the official GDP.[72]

---

[69] Franco, "Optimal producer price", table 2, p. 86.

[70] The figure of 82 per cent has been invoked for 1982. In 1985/6, only 876 tonnes were bought by the CMB whereas probably something in the order of 4,280 tonnes was probably sold in Togo, representing around half of the latter's exports. Nugent, *Smugglers, Secessionists*, table 7.2, p. 248.

[71] Ernesto May, *Exchange Controls and Parallel Market Economies in Sub-Saharan Africa: Focus on Ghana*, World Bank Staff Working Paper No. 711 (Washington DC: World Bank, 1985) table 11, p. 89.

[72] Janet MacGaffey, *The Real Economy of Zaire: The Contribution of Smuggling and Other Unofficial Activities to National Wealth* (London and Philadelphia: James Currey and University of Pennsylvania Press, 1991), p. 11.

The next round of military intervention, which Limann seems to have anticipated,[73] ensued on 31 December 1981. When Rawlings announced the formation of a Provisional National Defence Council (PNDC), it was in the name of a revolution that would cut across the military–civilian divide. Whereas Unigov was premised on a quasi-corporatist model, the PNDC promised a radical reordering of the military, the bureaucracy and society at large. In the name of 'people's power', existing hierarchies were to be democratized from the bottom up. The new regime enjoined workers to establish Workers' Defence Committees (WDCs), which bypassed the unions and specifically excluded management, while communities across the country were encouraged to set up People's Defence Committees (PDCs) that left out undesirable elements, including traditional authorities. The new regime drew much of its early support from radical intellectuals, including those of the JFM, who maintained that the AFRC had exposed the roots of the crisis but had merely dealt with the symptoms. Although military regimes have often invoked the language of revolution, in the case of Ghana there was a genuine attempt to instil a different way of transacting politics.[74] By contrast with 1979, when the main events played themselves out in Accra and Kumasi, the revolution manifested itself in the outpouring of social tensions across the Regions – and nowhere more so than in the border areas.[75] However, the fundamental reality was that the economic crisis – which was greatly compounded by the drought and the forced return of more than a million Ghanaians from Nigeria in 1983 – was so acute that the PNDC could not postpone making a choice between unpalatable alternatives. The internal power struggles that surrounded a possible approach to the IMF has been discussed at length elsewhere.[76] Equally, the subsequent deepening of donor-led reforms under Structural Adjustment is a story that does not need to be repeated here.[77] What it all added up to was a decade during which Ghana passed from the prospect of revolutionary upheaval to the dismantling of economic controls and the restructuring of both the civil service and the military. After 1983, the

---

[73] In an interview with the author shortly before he died, Limann indicated that he had called Rawlings in on at least one occasion and confronted him with evidence of plotting a coup. He also hinted that the coup did not come as a complete surprise.

[74] After the election of the Kufuor regime in 2000, there was a conscious attempt to deny the historicity of the revolution. Although the Truth and Reconciliation Commission revealed a high incidence of score-settling, the attempt to gloss the revolution as an exercise of violence for its own sake, coupled with manipulation of the populace from above, does not square with detailed evidence I have presented in *Big Men, Small Boys and Politics in Ghana: Power, Ideology and the Burden of History, 1982–1994* (London and New York: Frances Pinter, 1995), ch. 2.

[75] Nugent, *Big Men, Small Boys*, chs. 2–3.

[76] Nugent, *Big Men, Small Boys*, ch. 3. Eboe Hutchful, *Ghana's Adjustment Experience: The Paradox of Reform* (Geneva and Oxford: UNRISD and James Currey, 2002), pp. 43–52.

[77] Hutchful, *Ghana's Adjustment Experience*, chs. 4–7.

PNDC continued to speak in the language of revolutionary change but steered the process of reform in an increasingly technocratic fashion. In the process, the role of the state was redefined from that of the motor of economic change and social transformation to that of a facilitator. Loss-making parastatals were privatized, the currency was floated and the government sought to create an environment that was more conducive to foreign investment. The PNDC managed to sell the reform package to its core constituencies by rehabilitating the national road network, increasing cocoa producer prices, removing price controls and presiding over a modest increase in salaries. At the same time, it astutely deflected some of the donor demands by maintaining control of core utilities and maintaining selective subsidies on strategic items like petrol. By the time Ghana returned to constitutional rule in 1992, there was a broad consensus amongst the newly formed political parties that there was no going back to the Nkrumahist model. At the same time, elected politicians were sensitive to the expectation of voters that they would deliver essential public goods. Hence, in practice the 'neo-liberal state' remained something of a hybrid, retaining some of the older assumptions about the responsibility of the state to deliver social amenities whilst leaving most economic activity to the private sector. The key to keeping the two sides in balance was tax reform, to which I return briefly below.

Inevitably, developments in Ghana created reverberations inside Togo where the location of Lomé created some concerns about political contagion spreading from Ghana. In the early days of the revolution, members of the ousted government escaped across the border and were afforded sanctuary. The Eyadéma government had its own reasons to worry that the PNDC would seek to spread the message of revolution and upset the delicate political consensus that it had cobbled together. In reality, the Rawlings regime was too absorbed with its own litany of problems, but cadres would certainly have been well disposed to any challenge to the power structure in Togo. In September 1982, the PNDC resorted to a familiar Ghanaian expedient when it closed its side of the border as part of a campaign to combat smuggling. Two substantive coup plots in October and November of that year were followed by the infiltration of opposition elements from Togo in June 1983, in an attempted putsch that came close to success.[78] After restoring control, the PNDC closed the border for most of that year. Over 1984 and 1985, there was an abatement of tensions, to the extent that the two governments felt able to convene a joint committee to resolve some outstanding issues of boundary demarcation. But a series of bomb blasts in Lomé and complaints of Togolese encroachments on Ghanaian territory led to a renewed breakdown of relations. As the decade

---

[78] Nugent, *Big Men, Small Boys*, pp. 108–9.

wore on, the Eyadéma regime became convinced that the PNDC was lending support to dissidents, and in particular the Olympio family who resided in Accra. A coup attempt, which the Eyadéma regime traced to Ghana, ensured that the border remained closed once more between September 1986 and October 1987.

Although allegations of plots and counter-plots ensured that the border remained tense for the best part of a decade, Structural Adjustment also had a role to play in reshaping the dynamics of the border. In Togo, austerity measures began to be felt in Lomé just as Ghana embarked on its slow path to economic recovery. Higher producer prices for cocoa, the disappearance of consumer shortages and the shrinkage of the currency black market in Ghana all had an impact on the commercial life of Lomé. This placed significant strain on the social contract at a time when the comparison with conditions across the border no longer seemed so favourable. Matters came to a head as Togo was drawn into the drive for democratization that swept across the continent in the early 1990s. Whereas the transition was relatively smooth in Ghana, Togo endured three years of crisis between 1990 and 1994 that un-did much that the regime had accomplished over the previous decade. In 1990, the first street demonstrations began in Lomé, and these became a recurrent feature over the next couple of years. Workers and students struck, and as part of a concerted effort to bring the economic lie of the capital to a standstill, taxi drivers and traders withdrew their services. The government responded with repression and then, responding to a change in the international climate, conceded a National Conference that was supposed to hammer out a consensus on a new political dispensation.[79] When this process threatened to effectively strip Eyadéma of his powers, the army responded with a violent crackdown which, in one particularly violent incident, culminated in twenty-two bodies washing up in the Bè lagoon.[80] Although Eyadéma regained the initiative through a mixture of brute force, concessions and selective co-optation, the knock-on effects were momentous. Human rights organizations reported numerous deaths and incidents of violence in the years that followed.[81] Large numbers

[79] On these events, see Jean Yaovi Degli, *Togo: la tragédie africaine* (Ivry-sur-Seine: Editions Nouvelles du Sud, 1996); Mathurin Houngnikpo, *Determinants of Democratization in Africa: A Comparative Study of Benin and Togo* (Lanham: University Press of America, 2001), pp. 96–100; and Jennifer C. Seely, *The Legacies of Transition Governments in Africa: The Cases of Benin and Togo* (New York: Palgrave Macmillan, 2009), pp. 49–57 and ch. 4.

[80] Amnesty International, *Togo*, p. 10. On the impact on a quarter closest to the border, see Amandie Spire "Kodjoviakopé à Lomé: le temps et la constitution d'un territoire urbain", in Philippe Gervais-Lambony and Gabriel Kwami Nyassogbo (eds.), *Lomé: dynamiques d'une ville africaine* (Paris: Karthala, 2007), pp. 200–10.

[81] This included seven deaths in Amoussoukope and Assahoun in May 1995 after an armed attack on the Togolese security forces. See http://hrlibrary.umn.edu/commission/country52/89-tgo.htm

of refugees fled across the border into Ghana, while many of the cloth traders transferred their operations to Cotonou.[82] In the process, the commercial centre of Lomé was transformed from a bustling hub to a virtual ghost-town. Ghanaians who had once travelled to shop and to enjoy the good life in the Togolese capital were particularly struck by this reversal of fortunes during the 1990s.

At this point, I will pause and drill deeper to expose the dynamics of the contraband trade and the fate of successive attempts at reforming border policing during the 1980s and early 1990s. I have chosen to concentrate on the Ghana side of the border where there was a far-reaching attempt at reconfiguring the institutional map in the 1980s. It is also the side of the border for which I have managed to collect the richest data. This analysis will also entail scaling down to consider much more local processes.

An Anatomy of Border Control: Public Tribunals and Popular Policing at the Border

A unique source is the voluminous documentation left by the Volta Region Public Tribunal (VRPT) in Ho. The Tribunals were established by the PNDC to try a range of economic crimes, subsumed under the broad rubric of *kalabule*: from corruption and theft of state property to contraband. The smuggling cases predominate in the hefty ledgers which, at the time of initial fieldwork around 2004, were located in the building that used to house the Tribunal itself. As I have indicated, *kalabule* was understood to hinge on relationships of extreme secrecy. This was akin to the logic of the occult, and sometimes they were explicitly linked. Hence early in 1982, when revolutionary fervour was at its height, supporters of the revolution marched on the lodge houses in Ho where they claimed to have discovered human skulls that had been used for nefarious nocturnal activities. But for the most part, the discourse surrounding *kalabule* turned on a common-sense understanding of how profiteering worked. Being one step ahead of the game was seen to depend on gaining privileged access – whether to information or to goods – and cashing in one's chips when the time was right. Within the discourse of the revolution, dubious trading practices were inseparable from the manner in which power was routinely manipulated by the 'big men' for personal gain at the expense of the virtuous majority. The opposite of secrecy was, therefore, the public spectacle in which truth was brought to light in the full public gaze. Cases involving *kalabule,* which were investigated by the National Investigation Committee (NIC) and a range of other bodies, were referred to the

---

[82] Nina Sylvanus, "Chinese devils, the global market and the declining power of Togo's Nana-Benzes", *African Studies Review* 56 (1) 2013, pp. 69–70. See also, *Patterns in Circulation*, chs. 4–5.

Tribunals rather than to the regular courts. This was largely for the reason that the judiciary itself was thought to be compromised. However, the legal system had also become a byword for gross inefficiency, as the serial delays in the Agotime-Adaklu land case amply demonstrate. There was an insistence that most hearings be held in public, although the Tribunals were empowered to take evidence in camera. The VRPT was centrally located in the building adjoining the Regional administration offices in Ho, and by all accounts, its sessions were well attended by local residents and workers from adjoining buildings.

A case would typically commence with a declaration of the charge, following which those who had made the arrest – usually some combination of the Police, Border Guards, PDCs, Committees for the Defence of the Revolution (CDRs) and the People's Militia – would make a statement and would then be cross-examined by the Tribunal. The defendant was then asked to respond and was similarly questioned. Although the Ghana Bar Association (GBA) decided to boycott the process, many of the accused did benefit from legal counsel. Sensitive cases were typically referred to the National Public Tribunal in Accra, to which cases could also be sent on appeal.[83] Occasionally, the Tribunal also heard appeals from District Tribunals.[84] The VRPT dealt with everyday cases of smuggling, theft and corruption, but the sums of money and the quantities of goods were often very substantial indeed. Moreover, the Tribunal frequently unravelled intricate webs of intrigue that extended well beyond the border. A good example would be a smuggling case from the Kete-Krachi area in 1983. Abandoning her initial story that she was one of the returnees forced to leave Nigeria, the defendant revealed that she was actually a 'chop-bar' keeper in Kumasi where she had been approached by a Border Guard to assist his son with the smuggling of cigarettes and cloth. After the deed was done, a number of other Border Guards got wind of the operation and demanded a share of the proceeds. When she and the son were subsequently arrested by the Police, their senior officers demanded a further cut in return for helping her to get off the charge. Finally, when she was unable to pay off a member of the PDC who sought to jump on the bandwagon, she told the Tribunal that she had handed over her daughter, exchanging the latter's sexual

---

[83] The National Public Tribunal was empowered to take over a case, under Sections 4 and 5 of "Public Tribunals Law (PNDC Law 78)".

[84] For example, in 1991 a case was appealed from the Ketu District Tribunal in which two men in Dzodze were convicted on a charge of smuggling ten kente cloths to Togo. The appellants pointed out that they were kente weavers, and although it was night time when they were apprehended, it was not reasonable to infer that they were smuggling. The Tribunal agreed and regretted that the District Tribunal had "failed woefully" to consider the defence. The case was therefore set aside. VRPT, Volume and Case unspecified, "People vs Doe Agbeke and another", 15 October 1991.

services in lieu of the money that had been demanded. The Tribunal ordered the arrest of the Chief Inspector of Police, eleven other officials, the chief and the PDC member. In fact, the case was deemed so serious that it was subsequently transferred to the National Public Tribunal in Accra.[85]

The burden of proof fell on the accused, as had been true of smuggling cases since colonial times. At the same time, the Tribunal was permitted to place weight on circumstantial evidence. Where the incident took place after dark, the Tribunal was generally inclined to convict. In one such case where a vehicle was stopped at Agotime-Kpetoe, this was made explicit: "The time of the night during which the accd [accused] was travelling also lends credence to the view of the prosecution that the accd was doing something illegal."[86] In another case from Kpetoe, a man with a bicycle was caught retrieving two jerry cans from the bush in broad daylight. His explanation was that his uncle was the owner of a corn mill at the border village of Bemla and that he had been sent to buy diesel oil some time before. He had failed to complete the task and had secreted the fuel in the bush until he had time to retrieve it. His legal counsel referred to the time of day as evidence that he could *not* have been smuggling:

The fact that the road leads to Togo is neither here nor there. There are many paths to Togo. When he was seen he was riding an empty bicycle – if he wanted to smuggle the bicycle would have been loaded. It was also in broad day light. Nobody in his right senses would smuggle in broad day light.[87]

In this instance, the Tribunal discounted the clock and the fact that Bemla was located in the direction of the border. The act of having secreted the cans was deemed sufficient to warrant a guilty verdict. In yet another case, a vehicle travelling between Kpetoe and Ho was found to be carrying six cartons of Geisha and two cartons of 'foreign' sardines. The counsel for the defence maintained that there were no documents because the fish had been purchased in Kpetoe, adding that "It is common practice that goods are brought from towns close to the border." The Tribunal concluded that according to the balance of probabilities, the goods were smuggled, but took account of the fact that the accused was a nursing mother and permitted her to pay the fine by installments.[88]

---

[85] VRPT Volume unspecified, Case No. 9/83 "The People vs Felicia Cobbina Serwaah", 14 September 1983. According to a former employee of the Tribunal in Ho, the officials in question were eventually found guilty.

[86] VRPT Volume 8, Case 47/87, "The People vs Prosper Agbelengor", 26 June 1987.

[87] VRPT Volume 7, Case 1/87, "The People vs Ben Komla Agbozo", 14 January 1987.

[88] VRPT, Volume 7, Case No. 41/87, "The People vs Gladys Zormelo", 13 May 1987.

The Tribunal was empowered to deliver the death penalty but was also given a wide degree of discretion.[89] In one case, a Customs official at the Ave-Have border post was placed on trial for having misappropriated revenues and having falsified the records to cover his trail. The Tribunal confirmed the institutional corrosion within Customs, pointing to the fact that the anomalies had begun in 1980 and yet had gone undetected by officials responsible for checking the books. The Tribunal noted that the death sentence was applicable in such a case, but chose to impose a 25-year prison sentence with hard labour on the basis that many of the offences pre-dated the enabling PNDC legislation.[90] That same year, two women pleaded guilty to having paid a driver a substantial sum of money to transport fifty-four packets of St. Louis sugar cubes and eight sachets of granulated sugar, which they had originally purchased in Kpalimé, from Nyive and then on to Ho. The Tribunal refrained from delivering the verdict of death by firing squad and settled instead for a prison sentence of nine years with hard labour and either a fine of ¢100,000 or an additional 15 years in prison. The Tribunal also flexed its muscles in insisting that the Border Guards and Police at Nyive border post, whom it considered must have been in league with the driver, should be forced to appear to explain themselves.[91] The Tribunal was not always so lenient. In a case where two Malian nationals were accused of smuggling brass and copper stripped from cables, the VRPT declaimed that it could not condone aliens indulging in "acts that will tend to sabotage our economy" and recommended death by firing squad.[92] Even in the delivery of revolutionary justice, the status of stranger was a fatal impediment.

In the early years of the revolution, that is roughly up until 1986, the main items that were illegally exported from Ghana were cocoa, petroleum products (petrol and kerosene), precious minerals and timber – all of which exited into Togo by headload or by truck. In the case of cocoa, a combination of unattractive producer prices and the overvalued cedi remained the fundamental incentive to smuggle. Petrol and kerosene were smuggled out despite being in very short supply. For this reason, the government attempted to restrict the number of filling stations located in close proximity to the border. This conferred a particular advantage on those who were granted the right to operate one, especially when they were selling to smugglers. The PDC/CDRs served as the gatekeepers, advising the authorities as to how many stations were

---

[89] Kwadwo Afari-Gyan, *Public Tribunals and Justice in Ghana* (Accra: Asempa, 1988), pp. 10–11.
[90] VRPT, Volume and Case unspecified, "The People vs Henry Hagan", 14 September 1983.
[91] VRPT, Volume unspecified, Case 12/1983, "The People vs Simon Kofi Webu", 22 September 1983.
[92] VRPT Volume unspecified, Case No. 21/83 "The People vs Maige Seidu and Tamboura Belmo Belko", 4 October 1983. Whether this was carried out is not clear.

needed and who could be trusted to operate them. Because there was a temptation for vehicles to fill their tanks in Ghana and then to empty them in Togo, the PDC/CDRs stopped vehicles at the border and gauged how much petrol they had in the tank by means of a dipping stick with which they could compare the reading on the return journey. The reason for rampant smuggling is that petroleum products were subsidized and could be exchanged for hard currency in Togo at well above the official price in Ghana – that is, when they were to be found. From time to time other goods were also smuggled. In May 1984, for example, an anti-smuggling team made up of JFM activists followed a vehicle near Dzodze and came across around 100 carriers loading lemon, kola nuts, cutlasses, odum boards and iron rods that were apparently destined for Togo.[93]

The main items that were imported from Togo were textiles, clothing materials, sugar, tinned sardines and cosmetics – all of which were considered to be amongst the necessities of life. Over 1982/83, the Ghanaian textile industry continued to labour under the difficulties associated with a shortage of raw materials, but in addition a struggle over the direction of the revolution was fought out in the factories.[94] Although the attempt at asserting workers' control at the Ghana Textile Printing Company (GTP) and Juapong Textiles (JTP) was not without some success, there remained a chronic shortage of cloth. Alcohol featured less prominently than in the interwar years because Ghanaians had become adept at turning agricultural produce into *akpeteshie*, a distilled product normally made from palm-wine or sugar cane. However, some sugar was itself smuggled for the purposes of distillation, and beer occasionally featured amongst the list of seizures.

After 1986, cocoa and petroleum products continued to find their way across the border. Indeed, the overall level of smuggling may even have increased. Certainly, many cases involving these products were heard by the VRPT, and CDR reports referred specifically to the buoyancy of the contraband economy.[95] Increasingly, manufactured goods like cutlasses were despatched in the direction of Togo, either because the black-market exchange rate continued to be attractive or because they were subsidized. Natural products also featured prominently, and in particular wood, which was in high demand in Togo as fuel. In one case, a government vehicle was seized at Atikpui just as 150 bags

---

[93] VRPT Volume 6, Case No. 44/86, "The People vs Kofi Atidefe", 2 July 1986.

[94] Nugent, *Big Men, Small Boys*, pp. 67, 120–1, 172–3.

[95] In 2000, a gallon of petrol cost ¢6,400 in Ghana, but the equivalent of ¢12,000 in Togo. Such returns to petty smuggling continued to be attractive given the relative lack of other alternatives. Data from fieldwork diary 18 September 2000. In 2002, the differential remained more or less of the same order despite the sustained pressure on the Ghanaian authorities to remove the remaining subsidies. The price of 10 litres in Togo was the equivalent of ¢39,000, as opposed to ¢23,300 in Ghana.

of salt, which had been transported from the saltworks in Ada, were being offloaded.[96] Late at night in 1991, CDRs and Militiamen who were acting on a tipoff, apprehended a vehicle near Dzodze, which was transporting chemicals used for the spraying of cocoa. The smugglers in this case had gone to the trouble of producing a fake waybill from the CMB in Accra that purported to prove that they were transporting the chemicals to a plantation in Dzodze. The latter was not located in the cocoa belt, and not surprisingly the plantation turned out to be a fabrication.[97] In the latter half of the 1980s, basic commodities returned to the markets in Ghana, but this did not bring about an end to the re-export trade from Togo. Cigarettes continued to enter Ghana illegally, as the following haul that was intercepted en route from Ho to Accra demonstrates: "303 cases of Sukisa Medicated Soap, 53 cartons of Foreign Rothman's King Size cigarettes and 15 cartons of Marlboro King Size cigarettes".[98] Because the price differentials for cloth remained so high, the trafficking in wax prints remained as important as ever. What emerges from the Tribunal records is, therefore, a picture of broad continuity in the patterns of cross-border trade. Some items ceased to be traded when they were no longer profitable and some were traded in either direction depending on price fluctuations – as was the case with cigarettes. But there were many commodities that were consistently smuggled into Togo (notably petroleum products) or into Ghana (textiles).

I turn now to consider the centrality of border policing to the agenda of the PNDC and its constitutional successors. Whereas the June 4 Revolution had been primarily an urban affair, the border regions were very much in the vanguard in the turbulent early 1980s. In 1982, the PNDC sought to shake up established institutional patterns. It explicitly encouraged the formation of anti-smuggling teams by the PDCs, not just to lend additional hands to the fight against smuggling, but also to serve as an independent check on the Border Guards and Police. This was a remarkable inversion, in that private citizens were being invited to assume some of the functions of public officials. The predictable consequence was a clash between rival normative orders: one drawing its inspiration from the prerogatives attached to officials acting in the name of the state and another invoking the higher ideals of the revolution. Inevitably, the PNDC's injunction to Ghanaians to take power into their own hands resulted in confrontation and some physical casualties. In February 1983, following a meeting of PDC Regional Co-ordinators, a letter was addressed to Rawlings pointing to systematic harassment of activists in border regions, and citing concrete examples:

[96] VRPT Volume 7, Case 11/87, "The People vs Vicentia Aza and one other", 28 January 1987.
[97] VRPT, Volume and Case unspecified, "The People vs Francis Owusu Ansah and Joseph Kofi Tetteh", 5 February 1992.
[98] VRT Volume and Case unspecified, "The People vs Fred Akubia", 10 May 1991.

1. The current reign of terror meted out to PDCs and other militant cadres by Border Guards in the Western region which resulted in the mysterious disappearance (Death) of a cadre, Kwesi-Kojo for helping to break up a cocoa smuggling syndicate.
2. At the moment, eight (8) PDC executives from Sefwi Wiawso are languishing in cell at Takorade [sic], they were arrested as far back as November, last year for preventing smuggling. All efforts to release them have failed.
3. In Volta Region the Akatsi PDC Chairman has been picked up and detained since January 15 by the Police at Nima Police Station.
4. The Ketu District co-ordinator also arrested at the early part of January by the military has since been detained at the Field Engineers Guardroom at Teshie.[99]

As this list indicates, the PDCs found themselves variously at odds with the Border Guards, Police and Army. These complaints came on the back of a series of incidents in the Volta Region in 1982. The Deputy Regional Secretary, Kwasi Kamasa, and a group of students were physically manhandled while engaged in anti-smuggling operations. Following a further assault on PDC members, the Regional Co-ordinating Committee of PDCs demonstrated in the streets of Ho to demand the resignation of senior members of the Police, Border Guards and the Regional administration. They accused the latter of being in collusion with smugglers, and in particular with Alhaji K who was reputed to be the biggest smuggler in the Region and quite conceivably the entire country.[100] These events coincided with a power struggle within the PNDC towards the end of the year, in which notional moderates and radicals attempted to dictate the direction of the revolution.[101] The victory of the Rawlings faction over the so-called ultra-leftists of the JFM had profound consequences for many ordinary cadres. In the Volta Region, a number of the militants were purged or were sent to study in Bulgaria and Cuba with the intention of forcing them to cool their heels. At the end of 1984, the PDCs were replaced by the CDRs, which had a tighter command structure presided over by a Political Counsellor who also happened to be a retired military officer. In Ho, the Regional secretariat was given oversight for the Districts, Zones (of which there were twelve in Ho District), Areas and the Unit level. Although the CDRs were expected to work closely with the Regional and District authorities, the relationship remained a prickly one. The cadres were often school teachers[102] – the sort of people who had provided the local backbone of the CPP in the early 1950s and who regarded themselves as the

---

[99] "Memorandum to the Chairman of the PNDC by the Regional Co-ordinators Meeting at Kumasi, 24–27 Feb 1983", personal files of Harry Asimah.
[100] I have chosen to use a pseudonym, but to anyone familiar with the history of contraband in the Volta Region his identity will be very obvious.
[101] Nugent, *Big Men, Small Boys*, pp. 83–97.
[102] A case in point would be the Zonal Organizing Assistant (ZOA) in Agotime-Kpetoe who was one of the teachers who had opted for greener pastures in Nigeria and then had returned after the expulsion of foreign nationals in 1983.

embodiment of the moral order that the revolution spoke for. The Regional and District Secretaries expected the CDRs to acknowledge their own right of command. However, some cadres continued to act in the name of the revolution and, on more than one occasion, questioned the personal integrity of their superiors.

In Ho, for example, the CDRs were frequently at loggerheads with the District Secretary who they accused, at one point, of monopolizing vehicles for his own personal use at a time when they themselves were often grounded for want of transport.[103] The Regional Secretary, Air Commodore (rtd.) Klutse, had his own differences with the CDRs at the Regional level as well as in the Ho District. A particular flashpoint arose over the handling of the influx of Fulani herders, along with some 600 cattle, from the Togo side of the border. This had initially caused some tension in the Nkwanta District in 1984, but the issue recurred in Agotime-Afegame in April 1986. The herders explained that they had suffered harassment in Togo and sought permission to relocate to Ghana. Members of the Ho District CDR secretariat, the Zonal secretariat in Agotime and a self-styled 'Burkina Faso CDR in Ghana' convened a meeting in Afegame. The chief, Nene Mahumansro XIII, expressed his opposition to the presence of the Fulani on the grounds that their cattle had been known to destroy food crops in Togo. Eventually, however, a deal was struck, and it was agreed that the cattle would be 'quarantined' at Afegame.[104] However, the Regional administration appears to have taken a dim view of the agreement. Klutse accused the leader of the 'Burkina Faso CDR' of taking the side of the herders and insisted that, as a foreigner, he should not be permitted to play any role within the CDR structure. Further layers of complexity emerged in a letter penned by the individual concerned in which he claimed to have been dismissed from the Ghana Army for having participated in the assault of senior officers during the upheaval of June 1979.[105] Whilst asserting his rights to be treated as a Ghanaian, he was clearly also establishing his revolutionary credentials. When the herders complained that they had been forced to pay a bribe in return for the right to remain, a CDR executive at the District level and the Zonal Organizing Assistant (ZOA) from Kpetoe were suspended from duties for allegedly accepting a payoff.[106] The CDRs at the

---

[103] "Report of the Ho District Secretariat for CDRs, January–April 1986", 6 May 1986, private papers of Harry Asimah.

[104] Comrade Moumouni Gantara, Volta Regional Bureau of Burkina Faso CDR in Ghana to Ambassador, Burkina Faso Embassy, Accra, 28 April 1986, private papers of Harry Asimah.

[105] Gantara Ghana to Ambassador, 28 April 1986, private papers of Harry Asimah.

[106] The chiefs in Kpetoe attempted to dissolve the secretariat and to appoint an interim management committee. The ZOA was later reinstated, whereas his colleague in Ho was dismissed. In a private discussion he recalled that they were outnumbered at the time and accepted the money in order to diffuse tension.

Regional and District level continued to support their colleagues and were openly critical of the conduct of the Regional and District Secretaries. When the latter were re-assigned some time later, the CDRs in Ho took this as a vindication of their principled stance. Moreover, the cadres continued to criticize the new dispensation in Accra for having taken the wind out of the sails of the structures of popular power. They asserted that whereas workplace CDRs cadres in Ho had become demoralized, their counterparts in the border areas remained committed to the revolutionary cause. In the Volta Region, therefore, the question of who was in control remained a live one long after the revolution was definitively over in the rest of the country.

Those who opposed the CDRs alleged that they were themselves implicated in smuggling. In fact, a number of cases did come before the VRPT in which the CDRs were accused of taking bribes. This typically happened at the moment when a consignment of goods was intercepted and the accused tried to strike a deal. However, it was also inevitable in border towns and villages where the CDRs were dealing with kinsmen or powerful local interests, that there was an incentive to look the other way. The town of Kpedze was a singular case because this was where Alhaji K centred his operations. Alhaji was a stranger to the town but had become locally embedded. He was construed as a local benefactor, both for the work he created and for the projects he endowed. In a town such as this, it was very risky for CDRs to take on someone who wielded such influence. As we have seen, Alhaji K was well connected with the Police and Border Guards, and despite his run-in with the CDRs he actually made financial donations to the CDR Regional Secretariat.[107] At one point, a CDR official in Kpedze was approached by Alhaji K to be allowed to open a petrol station. There were already two of these in town and because he himself had a stake in one of them he would have lost some personal business as a result. When the cadre made a positive evaluation to the District Secretary, the implication is that he did so under some duress.[108] Where the evidence seemed to confirm that cadres had taken bribes or had looked the other way, the Tribunal was prepared to exercise leniency, especially where there was evidence that the CDR members had acted dutifully in the past. Moreover, there was at least one instance where the VRPT exposed a Police attempt to frame the CDRs.[109] To further complicate the picture, whereas the CDRs often portrayed themselves as hapless victims, the Secretary

---

[107] From the documents in the possession of Harry Asimah it transpires that Alhaji K made a donation of ¢20,000 in 1986.

[108] "Report on the Alleged Mismanagement of the Kpedze Zonal Secretariat by the Zonal Organizing Assistant", papers of Harry Asimah, May 1986.

[109] In this case, an individual from around New Ayoma was accused by the Police of smuggling cocoa and was apparently manhandled by them. The counsel for the accused alleged that he had been framed because of his closeness to the PDCs, with whom the Police were at odds.

of Foreign Affairs, Dr. Obed Asamoah, who hailed from the border town of Likpe-Bala, condemned both the Police and the CDRs for mounting unnecessary roadblocks in order to extort money. He also highlighted the harassment of people carrying very small quantities of goods and insisted on the importance of focusing on "eliminating the big-time smugglers and on checking the infiltration into the country of dissidents."[110]

The ongoing controversy over the conduct of the CDRs was one reason why the PNDC decided to establish a People's Militia – with its own command structure and headed by another retired military officer. Because the CDRs continued to take an interest in border issues, the Militia in effect duplicated some of structures that were already in place. In 1984, the Border Guards were formally dissolved and the army assumed directed control of border policing. In practice, the Militia tended to enjoy the same fraught relationship with the Police and army as the CDRs did. What was different about the Militia was the attempt to recruit from amongst the youth and to impart a modicum of military training. Whereas the CDRs were often reasonably well-educated down to the Zonal level, the Militia tended to draw from those who had only completed basic schooling and whose prospects for employment were otherwise limited. Enrolment in the Militia provided a source of income because they received half of the value of any smuggled goods that they seized. In the Volta Region, the Militia became deeply unpopular towards the end of the decade. Militiamen were accused of extorting money from smugglers rather than arresting them. In 1988, the VRPT delivered a searing indictment in a case where currency smugglers had run away and left their haul behind. The Militiamen at the Zonal level had divvyed up the bulk of the haul and then passed a smaller sum to the District Commander. The Tribunal felt impelled to add an "Observation" prior to delivering its guilty verdict:

It is our observation that the sorry and sordid deed was committed due to the lack of proper control that the C.D.O. hierarchy has over the men on the ground. The wrong impression has been created everything that the Militia seizes or impounds should go to them. The leadership at least in the region has not been able to firmly take control of the operations of the Militia and has in most cases contributed to the wrong notion that their boys have that the C.D.O. is an organ which 'Creates [Takes?] and Shares'. The evidence which came out during the trial is that the Militia seize items and only take it to the District Commanders who distribute them without recourse to either the Court of Tribunal or any other appropriate authority. This is wrong and cannot be accepted.[111]

The Tribunal accepted the plea and acquitted the accused. VRPT, Volume 2 and 3, Case 27/84, "The Peoples vs Nelson Zatey and another".

[110] Dr. Obed Asamoah, PNDC Secretary for Foreign Affairs, "CDRs and the Image of Ghana – Speech to CDRs at Hohoe on 3rd May 1985" (copy in my possession).

[111] VRPT, Volume and Case unspecified, "The People vs Bukari Haruna and 9 others", 18 August 1988.

In addition, the wounding and killing of alleged smugglers by Militiamen all along the border,[112] including one such incident in Agotime-Afegame, provoked outrage and heightened tensions with local youth.

By the early 1990s, the PNDC's experiment with popular power had outlived its usefulness. Under Structural Adjustment, part of the objective had been to reduce the incentives that sustained the black market, by making goods freely available and by removing pricing and currency controls. To a large extent, the incentive to smuggle was successfully reduced. At the same time, the feeling in official circles was that a combination of the army, CDRs and Militia had not provided a satisfactory solution to border policing and had merely blurred the lines of jurisdiction. As part of the package that went under the broad rubric of 'good governance', the PNDC regime tackled civil service reform head on. The intention was to improve administrative efficiency, but also to increase the revenue-earning capacity of the state. Given that the latter had historically depended on import and export duties for its fiscal reproduction, it was inevitable that Customs reform should assume pride of place. The preventive functions were taken away from the military and reunified with Customs under an integrated Customs Excise and Preventive Service (CEPS) with effect from 1986.[113] And in 1993, the many enactments were consolidated within a single Customs management law.[114] With the return to constitutional rule in 1992, the CDRs and the Militia were formally wound up.[115] Finally, CEPS was brought under the umbrella of the Ghana Revenue Authority (GRA) in 2009 as a division carrying equal weight with the Domestic Tax Division.[116] As a consequence, Customs was once again located at the very core of the state, an exalted position that it had not enjoyed since the late colonial era.[117] Although restructuring was part of a larger attempt to rationalize and diversify the tax base, for example through the introduction of Value-Added Tax (VAT), Customs revenues remained of paramount importance to Ghanaian public finances.

As regional integration initiatives accelerated in the new millennium, and Ghana increasingly aligned itself with international norms, the nature of Customs work itself underwent a transformation.[118] Brenda Chalfin has pointed

---

[112] Nugent, *Smugglers, Secessionists and Loyal Citizens*, pp. 268–9.

[113] This was enacted under the Customs and Excise Preventive Service Law (PNDC Law 144) of 1986.

[114] Customs Excise and Preventive Service (Management) Law, 1993.

[115] Many of the CDRs were moved sideways into the National Commission on Civil Education (NCCE).

[116] Axelsson, *Making Borders*, p. 108. The semi-autonomous Revenue Authority was a travelling model that, at the time of writing, has been adopted by no fewer than 20 countries in Africa.

[117] However, the Commissioner of CEPS after 2009 came beneath the Commissioner of GRA.

[118] Brenda Chalfin, *Neoliberal Frontiers: An Ethnography of Sovereignty in West Africa* (Chicago and London: University of Chicago Press, 2010).

out that when Ghana became a signatory to the World Trade Organization (WTO) and the World Customs Organization (WCO), it abandoned its own valuations and adopted global Customs values. This narrowed the scope for the kind of protectionism that had been openly championed during the 1960s and 1970s. At the same time, some functions of Customs were outsourced to private companies and to agencies that represented public–private partnerships.[119] At the same time, Togo was forced to abandon its own independent economic strategy and to bring its own practices into alignment. This similarly emerged out of the conjuncture between bureaucratic reforms and the drive towards the creation of a single market undertaken in the context of West African integration. Governance reforms in Customs followed a parallel trajectory to those in Ghana, culminating in the creation of a Togolese revenue authority, the Office Togolais des Recettes (OTR), in 2014.[120] However, these initiatives took time to have any practical effect. In the interim there was actually a revival of the contraband trade. Much of the preventive work of CEPS focused on two particular imported commodities, namely second-hand cars and textiles, whereas fuel continued to be smuggled in the other direction.[121] After 2001, the government of Ghana was particularly exercised by the mass importation of Chinese textiles based on pirated designs. The China trade weakened the position of the Nana Benz,[122] but it also threatened to obliterate Ghana's own textile industry, which was struggling to remain viable in the face of foreign competition. According to Linn Axelsson, Chinese wax prints could be sold in Ghana at half of the price of the products of the country's own textile factories in 2010 and at a fraction of the price of Dutch wax prints.[123] Illegal imports were estimated to account for as much as 48 per cent of the entire market for African prints in Ghana in 2005.[124] That year, in an attempt to tackle smuggling over the Togo border, the government of John Kufuor restricted the importation of approved textiles to the port of Takoradi in the west. However, this merely had the effect of bumping up the economic rents associated with smuggling, and so the illicit trade continued. The intervention

---

[119] Chalfin, *Neoliberal Frontiers*, pp. 229–34. On the fusion of public and private bodies, Chalfin cites the case of Gateway Services Limited (GSL), which was responsible for operating the new cargo scanner in Tema. GSL was owned 70 per cent by COTECNA, 10 per cent by CEPS, 5 per cent Ports and Harbours Authority and the remainder by Ghanaian businessmen (p. 172).

[120] Carpophore Ntagungire, "Togo Revenue Authority: a model for good tax governance" (2 July 2015), www.afdb.org/en/blogs/measuring-the-pulse-of-economic-transformation-in-west-africa/post/togo-revenue-authority-a-model-for-good-tax-governance-14486/

[121] On cars, see Chalfin, *Neoliberal Frontiers*, ch. 5; and on textiles, see Axelsson, *Making Borders*.

[122] Sylvanus, "Chinese devils", p. 71. In the 1990s, some traders who lacked the clout of the Nana Benz began developing independent links with suppliers in India and Pakistan.

[123] Axelsson, *Making Borders*, p. 93. Sylvanus notes that the first Chinese wax print sold in Ghana at one-tenth of the price of Vlisco's Dutch wax print. "Chinese devils", p. 73.

[124] Axelsson, *Making Borders*, p. 110.

ultimately failed and was abandoned in November 2008.[125] Thereafter the Ghana government reverted to a policy of ensuring that the relevant duty on cloth imports was paid and that the goods conformed to quality standards. In some respects, this might be seen as the last stand of economic nationalism pursued at Ghana's borders.

Trade Networks and Peripheral Urbanism in the Trans-Volta

Having considered the shifting dynamics of cross-border trade over time, I turn now to the demographic implications at the border itself.[126] I begin with the organization of the contraband trade which has a close bearing on urbanism. Cross-border trading conformed to one of three modes that broadly correlated with the size of the operation. The first was one in which traders acquired goods in Lomé (or in Ghana), and transported them through designated border crossing points. The illegality resided in the non-payment of duty or in the under-invoicing of the consignments. For the owners of large quantities of contraband goods, the danger was that they would lose the entire consignment, as well as the vehicle, if they were arrested. One means to reduce the risks was to establish a close working relationship with border officials who would typically be paid to look the other way. The problem is that checkpoints tended to spring up at short notice along the main roads inside Ghana – manned by state agents, the CDRs and/or the Militia. Having bribed one set of officials, there was no guarantee that the others would allow the vehicle to pass unhindered without more money passing hands. There were actually risks on both sides because when a vehicle was impounded for smuggling, the VRPT would often demand to know how it had passed through the initial checkpoint. In 1992, for example, a vehicle travelling on the Ho–Nyive road was stopped by the Police and was found to be carrying loudspeakers and other musical equipment. It was ascertained that the vehicle had cleared Customs at the Shia border crossing. The Tribunal summoned the officers to explain why there was a mismatch between the paperwork and what was found in the vehicle. It concluded that "The inevitable inference that could safely be made is that either the customs officials were negligent – or that there was a collusion between them and the owner of the goods."[127]

---

[125] Axelsson, *Making Borders*, pp. 123–4.
[126] For a more detailed comparison, see Isabella Soi and Paul Nugent, "Peripheral urbanism: border towns and twin towns in Africa", *Journal of Borderlands Studies*, 32 (4) 2017.
[127] VRPT, Volume and Case unspecified, "The People vs William Ola and another", 30/4/1992. Surprisingly, because the Customs men adhered to their story that everything had been done according to Customs procedures, the Tribunal merely required the owner of the goods to pay the duty and a penalty without inflicting a much harsher punishment

An alternative was to build secret compartments into the vehicles that might go undetected at the border checkpoints. Hence a heavy-goods vehicle purportedly carrying bulky items like yams or plantain might actually be concealing other items bearing a much higher value. In 1984, a vehicle that was travelling from Batome Junction was stopped by the Police at Kpetoe. The load was ostensibly made up of charcoal, but a closer search revealed "2 cartons of Campari, 56 cartons of assorted sardine and other items".[128] In 1990, another vehicle that entered at Batome Junction was inspected by CEPS officers and was initially thought to be empty. However, a closer inspection found a veritable Alladin's cave concealed in a separate compartment:

282 pieces of foreign imitation Wax print; 31 full pieces of Foreign Real Dutch Wax prints; 21 full pieces of English Wax prints, 9 full pieces of foreign Real Dutch Java; 23 Rolls of suiting material; 4 Rolls of suiting materials; 2 rolls material; 1 roll check material; 1 roll check material; 1 roll cotton Polyester shirting material, 1 roll Cotton Polyester shirting material; 1 roll cotton Polyester shirting materials; 22 rolls Cotton Polyester shirting material; 3 rolls Cotton Polyester Shirting materials; 29 rolls Cotton Polyester shirting material; 25 dozen Ladies Nylon Under-Skirt; 35 dozens Brassier [sic]; 14 pieces of Men Dungaree Jeans; 2 dozens of Ladies Blouses; 42 dozens and 11 pieces of Ladies Pants; 162 dozens of Men's Pants; 7 dozens and 5 pieces of Men's 'T' shirts; One dozen Children's dress; 4 Cartons and 68 pieces of Penlight batteries; 2 Cartons of Canned Beer; 3 Packets of Tubed Top; 10 Cartons + 18 pieces of TCV Hair Relaxer; 6 pieces of Vi Trasheen [sic] Hair Relaxer; one carton Revlon Hair Relaxer; One Carton Super Curl Gel Activator; one piece Phillip '20' Colour T.V. and One piece Samsung '14' B/W.[129]

In this case, the Commissioner of CEPS imposed a fine of a million cedis as was permitted under the Customs legislation. Because the accused could not afford to pay the massive fine, the case was referred to the Tribunal, which reduced the fine to ¢200,000. The Tribunal ruled that the owner of the vehicle had probably been unaware of the intention to smuggle and permitted it to be released with the imposition of a modest penalty. Exercising his authority under the new Customs laws, the Commissioner appealed to the National Appeals/Review Tribunal, highlighted the inconsistency contained within the initial judgement, and demanded that the vehicle be forfeited to the state.[130] A variant on the same strategy was the addition of extra tanks to vehicles involved in the smuggling of petrol.[131] Some of the smuggling through official crossing points was on a modest scale. Women from Ghana often purchased wax prints in Lomé that they tied around their midriff before returning home

[128] VRPT Volume 8, Case 47/87 "The People vs Prosper Agbelengor" 26/6/1987.
[129] VRPT, Volume unspecified, Case No. 38/90, "The People vs Joseph Adu Afful", 9 May 1990.
[130] It is not clear what the final outcome of this case was.
[131] In one case, a vehicle that had an additional tank was found to be carrying 55 gallons of diesel. VRPT Volume 6, Case No. 81/86, "The People vs Anthony Togbe", 12 August 1986.

on passenger vehicles. In one case, two buses were stopped at a checkpoint outside Ho heading in the direction of Accra. Nine of the women – who were "unusually large in size" – were found to have a total of twenty-five pieces wrapped around their bodies, with a further twenty-nine pieces lying on the floor.[132] This clandestine trade continued well into the new millennium. One young woman who the author met in Kpetoe recounted how she made a weekly roundtrip to Lomé. She typically bought a number of pieces of cloth and then returned through a particular border crossing where she had established 'friendly' relations with border officials. She sold the cloth in Ho or Accra before returning to Kpetoe and repeated the trip some days later. The decent returns on relatively small numbers of cloths made this trade worthwhile.

The second broad pattern involved a system of relays. The owner of the consignment would typically acquire the goods and hire a driver to take them to the border. They would then be headloaded into Ghana late at night – avoiding the official entry point – before being loaded onto other vehicles. Kpedze, was reputed to be heavily implicated in the relay trade. The system was also used by traders who were much less financially endowed than Alhaji K and who could therefore afford to make fewer payoffs. They would typically reach an agreement with people in border towns to assist in the headloading of the contraband goods. The village of Agotime-Afegame achieved some notoriety for engaging in this kind of smuggling – especially in the dry season when it was relatively easy to wade across the Todzie. In this case, goods were transported to the nearby Togolese towns of Zukpe and Kpodjahon and were then carried across the border to Afegame, which was in striking distance of the Aflao–Ho road, but was also located beyond the main Police and Border Guard checkpoints in Kpetoe.

The third pattern was one in which contraband items were woven into the pattern of regular weekly transactions between populations living within the borderlands. As in the case of the Senegambia, there were a number of rotating markets that had existed since colonial times at least. A good example is Kpetoe whose market has historically been patronized by traders from Togo. The market was located in the centre of the town after earlier attempts to relocate it had failed. During the 1980s, when the border was closed for long periods of time, the market was much less busy because there was little to buy in Ghana and crossing the border was not always very easy. However, many people from Kpetoe and other towns went to Togo to buy goods for their personal use and for trade – sometimes spending time with family members before returning. Often, a group of between half a dozen and a dozen men or

---

[132] VRPT Volume and Case unspecified, "The People vs Akuvi Mawuko and 8 others", 21 February 1991.

women would walk together across the border, usually with each carrying their own goods. But it was not uncommon for individuals, or couples, to work alone or to carry goods on their bicycles.

Not surprisingly, sites of local exchange could develop over time into something altogether more elaborate. The classic instance is Agotime-Wodome, which is actually a single settlement visibly divided by the border. In the late 1970s, Togolese Wodome was propelled from being a tiny village with a few dwellings into a bustling boom-village. Its advantage arose from being located on either side of the main trunk road between Ho and Aflao. On this section, it is the road that separates Ghana from Togo. The surface itself is part of Ghana, and all the vehicles plying the route Ho pass along it without formally entering Togo. Gabriel, a trader from northern Togo who had initially opened a shop in Assahun, perceived an opportunity and opened a bar and a well-stocked kiosk on the Togolese side of the road.[133] It was virtually impossible to prevent people on the Ghana side of the road from buying their necessities at his store, but his clientele – and his reputation – extended well beyond Agotime. During the years of acute scarcity in Ghana, thirsty customers would reputedly travel from as far away as Kumasi to have a drink of whisky or beer and to buy scarce commodities at Gabriel's shop.

During 1982, the road itself became a marker of radical difference. There was a curfew in Ghana, which meant that there was darkness on one side of the road, but nightly revelry on the other side. When the border was formally closed over 1982/3, PDC/CDRs and Border Guards were stationed along the Ghana side of the road to prevent vehicles and passengers alighting to buy goods.[134] But Gabriel continued to transact a roaring trade – to the extent that he even constructed his own dirt road between Wodome and Batoumé, thereby avoiding having to pass through Batome Junction where he would have encountered the Border Guards.[135] The success of Wodome was such that it eventually began to attract pickpockets and petty criminals, and Gabriel was instrumental in persuading the Togolese authorities to build a Police station in the town to address the problem. In the early 2000s, the Police station remained open and flew the Togolese flag (see Figure 12.1). Once the economic crisis in Ghana passed, however, the vehicles ceased stopping and trade in Wodome fell off. After suffering some setbacks, Gabriel closed up shop and took to farming and rearing cattle on the 240 hectares of land that he managed

---

[133] Interview with Gabriel Basalbi, near Agotime-Wodome, 20 August 2002.

[134] During the border closure of 1982/3, the PDCs who needed cigarettes would roll up money in a piece of paper and then throw it across the road. A few cigarettes would then be returned by the Togolese sellers.

[135] He recalled that he had some difficulties with the Border Guards, but that when he was eventually forced to pass through Batome Junction they let him through in return for a "thank you" (presumably some money or goods). Fieldwork diary 20 August 2002.

Figure 12.1 Wodome, including the road that constitutes the border
and the Togolese Police Station, 2001.
Photograph by the author.

to purchase with his trading profits. Since the mid-1980s, Wodome has
reverted to its humble (and divided) self. Nobody pauses to shop or drink
anymore, and most vehicles pass through in a rush to reach Ho or Aflao. The
Police station has since been closed and the building has now all but collapsed,
which neatly encapsulates the shifting fortunes of Wodome itself.

In the 1990s, the importance of the regular market cycle was re-established.
Following the creation of an Adaklu-Anyigbe District, a decision was taken to
construct a new market for Kpetoe slightly out of town where there was greater
potential for expansion (see Figure 12.2).[136] The Kpetoe market today per-
forms an important mediating function within a network of markets straddling
the two countries. The market in Ho is held on a four-day cycle and is followed
a day later by the Kpetoe market. Reproducing a French colonial diktat, the
market in the Togolese town of Amoussoukope takes place every Thursday.
Given that Ho is closely connected to Accra, and that Amoussoukope lies on
the main trunk road between Lomé and Kpalimé, the Agotime markets are
effectively located at the centre of a commercial web. The complementarity
between the markets in Kpetoe and Amoussoukope means that when commodities like shallots, tomatoes or yams are more abundant or cheaper on one
side of the border, traders can shift their goods accordingly. The approved

---

[136] The construction of market buildings was a significant outlay for the local council. Simon
Amegashie-Viglo, Stephen Komla Bokor and Francis Komla Ganyaglo, "Decentralisation and
the challenge of revenue mobilisation for development: the case of Adaklu-Anyigbe District
Assembly in the Volta Region of Ghana", *Journal of Economics and Sustainable Development*
5 (14) 2014, p. 41.

Figure 12.2 The new Kpetoe market.
Photograph by the author.

crossing point for traders travelling between Kpetoe and Amoussoukope is Batome Junction, but most vehicles follow one of the unofficial tracks. These routes are more direct and minimize the chances of being shaken down by Customs and Immigration officials. Discussions with CEPS officers over successive years revealed that most are not even aware of the existence of the Amoussoukope market or the fact that traders from Kpetoe frequent it on a weekly basis.

The three underlying patterns that I have outlined have a direct bearing on the question of peripheral urbanism. In the previous chapter, I established that while hub towns within regional trading networks in the Senegambia experienced substantial and sustained demographic growth – notably Serekunda and Touba – most border towns did not. A comparable pattern can be identified for the trans-Volta (Table 12.1). Lomé is a singular case in that it was a capital, a border city *and* a hub within a regional trade network.[137] In that sense, its demographic profile was shaped by the confluence between the three sets of forces working in unison. Certainly, Lomé expanded very rapidly from the 1970s onwards when the re-export trade really took off. A modest city of 228,000 people in 1970 was home to 1.5 million people by 2010 as the city crept northwards and enveloped the surrounding countryside. This growth was shaped in profound ways by the dynamics of cross-border trade. Lomé tended to suck in population from other parts of Togo and beyond. By contrast, Kpalimé is an important administrative and commercial centre located in the

[137] See Philippe Gervais-Lambony and Gabriel Kwami Nyassogbo (eds.), *Lomé: dynamiques d'une ville africaine* (Paris: Karthala, 2007).

Table 12.1 *Patterns of urban growth on the Ghana–Togo border*

Town	1950	1960	1970	1980	1990	2000	2010
Accra	158,196	337,800	624,091	854,659	1,185,614	2,015,649	3,269,813
Aflao	2,996	7,400	11,397	17,578	26,393	38,927	50,699
Dzodze	4,144	5,800	10,390	12,970	15,807	18,957	31,727
Ho	6,768	14,500	24,199	33,263	45,396	61,658	80,304
Hohoe	6,148	9,500	14,775	18,989	25,505	35,277	45,945
Kpetoe	n/a	n/a	4,251	4,473	5,445	7,339	9,178
Kpedze	n/a	4,600	5,062	5,180	5,247	5,279	6,875
Lomé	38,904	80,187	228,179	405,512	609,223	917,378	1,499,284
Adéta	n/a	1,551	2,389	3,899	5,085	6,541	8,414
Badou	5,480	5,969	6,501	7,392	8,651	10,158	11,926
Kpalimé	6,756	12,765	23,780	27,128	37,202	52,489	74,057
Noepé	n/a	3,240	3,708	4,433	4,982	5,589	9,414

Source: OECD, Africapolis List and Population of West African Urban Agglomerations 1950–2010, http://stats.oecd.org/Index.aspx?DataSetCode=SAH_URBA_LATLON_V3%20.

prosperous cocoa belt. It is not situated on the border, but it is certainly close enough to tap into its flows. But whereas Lomé was only ten times larger than Kpalimé in 1970, it was almost twenty times larger in 2010. Interestingly, the growth of border towns like Badou and Noepé was modest despite the vitality of cross-border trade. On the Ghana side of the border, the pattern was similar. The growth of Aflao shadowed that of its more illustrious neighbour in Togo. Although the pace of its expansion was slower than Accra, it was considerably more rapid than other towns of a once-comparable size. Elmina, for example, was roughly the same size as Aflao in 1970, but now it is just over half its size. Dzodze expanded somewhat faster than average, possibly reflecting its own increasing proximity to the Togolese capital as it sprawled northwards. However, other border towns that have been renowned for their involvement in cross-border trade – including Kpedze and Kpetoe – grew in a decidedly incremental fashion.

This pattern is explicable in terms of the ways in which trade was organized. The trade that passed through the official crossing points did not have any particular demographic implications because it was essentially transitory. Hence the towns that hosted official crossing points were typically indistinguishable from their neighbours. Batome Junction was especially unprepossessing, but the same was true of towns like Honuta, Shia and Nyive, which do not even make it into most urban rankings. Secondly, the towns that were involved in the relay trade were potentially magnets for people seeking employment as carriers. But for the most part, border work was monopolized by local populations. During the years when smuggling was at its height, there was a constant hum of nocturnal activity in towns and villages along the Ghana/Togo border. But because this tended to be inscribed within the wider logic of landlord–stranger relations, there was an effort to prevent outsiders from muscling in on profitable business. Kpedze is an exception in that Alhaji K had managed to buy his way into the community, thereby creating the possibility for employing other strangers. But generally, there was a perception that strangers were also potential informers, and in a town like Afegame, which was renowned for keeping its secrets to itself, they were decidedly unwelcome. In Kpetoe, the Hausa community was well established and integral to the trade, but its members had their own incentive to discourage new entrants. Conforming to the third pattern, there were other settlements in Togo that experienced periods of boom in the manner of Wodome, but generally the effects were transitory. The trade associated with interlocking border markets sustained incomes for substantial numbers of people who traded, loaded goods, exchanged and drove the vehicles. But because it was local populations who controlled the business, it was not particularly conducive to the demographic expansion of these settlements through in-migration. Given that the migratory flows were more limited than in the Senegambia, the factors favouring demographic expansion tended to be even more circumscribed.

Conclusion

In this chapter, I have revealed how the shifting economic environment towards the end of the 1960s elicited very different responses in Ghana and Togo. In the first case, the Busia regime retained the essential elements of state interventionism, which were modified only slightly under military rule in the 1970s. The presumption was that the state would serve as the engine of economic growth and the purveyor of public goods, especially roads, schools and health facilities. There was also the promise of uplifting the standards of living for the mass of the population, in which access to consumption goods became the litmus test of success. Much of the package presumed the maintenance of relatively hard borders in order both to protect national industries from competition and to preserve the revenue base of the state. What was never really questioned was why the public goods themselves should grind to a halt at the border. It is significant, for example, that the Ghanaian authorities never exhibited any interest in constructing infrastructure that might better connect the country with its neighbours. On the contrary, the feeling was that transversal roads, and connecting bridges, might act as a further spur to smuggling. Hence there was a close correlation between an economic policy that was driven by a centralizing logic and a spatial ordering of fundamental infrastructure. This also embodied a curious tension, in that smuggling offered the one means by which Ghanaians were able to acquire access to consumer goods that had come to be regarded as the necessities of life. In Togo, the emphasis was placed on maximizing commercial flows through Lomé, which was facilitated by improvements to the port and the road network. Although this was justified with reference to the requirements of the landlocked Sahelian states, there was an expectation that much of what entered Togo would be offloaded in Ghana. In the case of textiles the pretence was largely dispensed with because it was an accepted fact that much of the wax print was bound for long-suffering consumers in Ghana. Although the phosphates boom led the Eyadéma government to permit a proliferation of parastatals in the 1970s, it was the re-export trade that sustained the Togolese economy. In that sense, Togo was very much like the Gambia.

Secondly, I have argued that it was not just a matter of two countries pursuing divergent economic models because the latter also underpinned distinct social contracts. In Ghana, the productive elements remained dominant despite the growing gulf between the lofty promises and the gritty realities of everyday life. Planning objectives were shaped by popular conceptions of the responsibility of the state towards its citizens which, in turn, had its deeper roots in colonial bargains. On this point, Eboe Hutchful is surely correct:

Ironically the colonial experience also pointed Ghanaians to two rather contradictory lessons: first a belief in the virtual omnipotence of the state, particularly as an instrument for reshaping social and economic realities; and second a belief in the malleability of the state itself as an institution. Constitutional engineering imparted an architectonic view of the state, and the assumption that the state could ultimately be made workable.[138]

In that sense the *idea* of the state was remarkably stable over time. In the 1970s, the Acheampong regime attempted a respacing of economic activity through the modernization of agriculture, which was premised on hitching the northern and south-eastern peripheries to the quest for national self-sufficiency. Despite the incidence of unprecedented levels of corruption during the second half of the decade, it is noteworthy that this never came to be regarded either as inevitable or politically acceptable in the manner of Zaire under Mobutu. The execution of Acheampong and other members of the military junta was a turning point in a country that had hitherto been marked by rather low levels of political violence. It put paid to the prospect that the military might become a permanent partner in government. But it also underlined a certain societal consensus about the bounds of acceptable behaviour – the very existence of which is very difficult to account for within the closed

---

[138] Eboe Hutchful, "The fall and rise of the state in Ghana", in Abdi Ismail Samatar and Ahmed I. Samatar (eds.), *The African State: Reconsiderations* (Portsmouth: Heinemann, 2002), p. 104.

logic of 'neo-patrimonialism.'[139] But increasingly the *materiality* of the state was placed in question. Revenues declined precipitously and institutions ceased to be capable of carrying out routine functions. The paralysis within the judiciary, which meant that land litigation continued ad infinitum, was symptomatic of the wider problem. During 1982, the perception that the rot had seeped into the inner sanctums of state institutions – including the civil service, the judiciary, the military and border agencies – was part of what informed the heated debates about the need for revolutionary transformation based on mass participation. Although Ghana after Structural Adjustment came to assume a very different aspect from the restructuring that the cadres had in mind, expectations concerning the responsibility of the state proved remarkably resistant to technocratic reforms. In Togo, the phosphate boom enabled the Eyadéma regime to engage in its own rescaling of institutions and respacing of economic activity. Although the objective was to reward the support base of the regime in the north, through the rolling out of infrastructure and the creation of positions within the army and gendarmerie, much of the funding was directed towards Lomé. More fundamental still was the care that was taken to facilitate the re-export trade, which enabled ordinary Togolese to carve out a living through commerce, transport and related occupations. The contraband trade was never incidental to the pursuit of politics in Togo: it enabled the regime to win the active support of the powerful Nana Benz in Lomé and the de facto consent of large numbers of Ewes who made their living from the border. But in Togo, the centrality of productive and permissive elements barely concealed the reality that the regime governed through the threat of force in the final resort. Even traditional authorities, who were bound into the structures of the RPT, were careful not to assert too much independence for fear of the consequences. It was only in the early 1990s, when Togo experienced a perfect storm – conjured up by a shrinking re-export trade, enforced austerity and demands for a return to multi-partyism – that the package threatened to unravel. Although the regime survived the immediate challenge, and even managed to engineer a dynastic succession to Faure Gnassingbé in 2005, the social contract remained very much in the balance in Togo – and remains so.[140]

---

[139] Patrick Chabal and Jean-Pascal Daloz, *Africa Works: Disorder as Political Instrument* (London, Oxford and Bloomington: International Africa Institute, James Currey and Indiana University Press, 1999).

[140] In 2005, after the death of Eyadéma senior, the military attempted to impose his son, Faure, but was later forced to agree to elections, which were won by the latter in controversial circumstances.

Faure's mother was a southerner and he had studied in the United States. The fact that he was not associated with the military, together with his comparative youth, made him seem more suited to the era of electoral politics than his siblings. But there was no doubting that it was the military that had an interest in his perpetuating family rule. In August 2017, opposition demonstrations against 50 years of dynastic rule were repressed with numerous fatalities.

Thirdly, I have sought to reconstruct a detailed account of efforts to tackle smuggling in Ghana during the 1980s and 1990s through a close reading of specific cases that came before the Public Tribunal in Ho. The latter was established at a time when the judicial system in Ghana was at its lowest ebb. This focus on the inner workings of the Tribunal has enabled me to tease out the patterns of smuggling and to document the struggle to redefine the terms of border policing. In the Volta Region, the ongoing power struggle between the Regional administration and the PDC/CDRs, which turned on the issue of popular participation in border management, underlines the extent to which the border continued to loom large within the politics of the Rawlings regime – even when the revolution was formally concluded and Structural Adjustment was in full swing. Although I have not been able to address the reconfiguration of Customs and regional trade in any detail (this is reserved for a different research project), I have pointed to an institutional break with the pattern that had been established in the 1960s.

Finally, in addressing the broad demographic patterns, I have demonstrated that there was no one-to-one correlation between high volumes of smuggling and demographic growth on either side of the border. The expansion of Lomé owed a great deal to its position as a hub within the regional trading economy, but clearly it was also favoured by its status as the capital city. By contrast, most other border towns did not grow faster than the national average. I have accounted for these patterns with reference to the underlying structures of trade. Lomé, and to some extent Aflao, served as a magnet for people drawn from much further afield who were attracted by the possibilities for engaging in trade. But border populations elsewhere tended to assert a monopoly over the right to engage in trading and porterage. Keeping outsiders at arms-length, which was rooted in the very same discourse of indigene and stranger, was partly about maintaining secrecy and partly about protecting the financial returns. I have cited Kpetoe as the prime example of a town that enjoyed close commercial links to towns in Togo – especially by virtue of the weekly market cycle – and yet exhibited a rather unspectacular pattern of demographic growth. In this, we can discern some similarities as well as differences with the Senegambian patterns that were identified in Chapter 11.

13   Boundaries, Communities and 'Re-Membering'

Festivals and the Negotiation of Difference

In this final chapter, I round off the extended comparison by returning to the borderlands as spaces where claims to place and expressions of identity played off one another. In particular, I consider how far the dynamics of international boundaries affected the ways in which 'community' was imagined and acted upon: in a nutshell, the question is whether borders were internalized in such a manner that they became part of the building blocks of community, or conversely community was defined in opposition to the existence of the borders. As indicated in Chapter 1, I deploy 'community' in a deliberately broad sense, connoting a shared feeling of belonging, but manifested in an organized form and arranged spatially – whether that be membership of a village or a religious grouping. I will also address ethnicity as a mode of 'we-group' identification that builds on conceptions of community but operates at a broader and more discursive level. Defining what it means to belong to a community or an ethnic group is typically about the here-and-now, but it inevitably involves a direct engagement with the contours of history. In the cases I am concerned with, what is striking is the frequency with which elements of an apparently long-forgotten past have resurfaced unexpectedly. Clearly much of the history in question does not derive from individual memory because it relates to what happened well before the twentieth century. Although the notion of 'collective memory' is counter-intuitive, there are clearly ways in which traces of the past are encoded. Along with Paul Connerton and Maurice Halbwachs, we can agree that while memory resides in individual experience, it only becomes comprehensible once embedded in a set of social relations.[1] Memories are often invested in things that are spatially embedded – such as shrines, buildings, monuments and indeed border pillars – but they are also harboured in oral forms and reproduced through performative acts. In West Africa, alternatives to the dominant narratives often reside deep within lineages and family lines rather than at the level of the community as a whole – which means that they

---

[1] Paul Connerton, *How Societies Remember* (Cambridge: Cambridge University Press, 1989), pp. 36–40.

484

can remain obscured from view before their sudden reappearance catches everybody by surprise.

Festivals are of particular interest because they involve behaviour that is very conscious – even to the point of being contrived – but they also have a habit of throwing up the unexpected. Because they are an exercise in codifying collective memories, festivals can trigger a plethora of alternative constructions of reality.[2] Cross-border festivals also tend to draw in the authorities from either side of the line who have to reconcile their own interest in the business of representation with the perspectives of local actors.[3] In this chapter, I approach festivals as an exercise in (re)building a sense of community that transcends the international border, and account for some of the reasons why this has turned out to be less straightforward than might have appeared likely. I will begin the analysis in the Senegambia before returning to the trans-Volta.

Constructing Community in the Senegambia

In the Senegambia, the formal commitment by governments to reduce the practical consequences of borders has continued to be undercut by disputes over their daily management.[4] But for all the recriminations, states have not interfered greatly in everyday interactions. Reference has already been made to the rotating markets, or *lumos*, that provide spaces for cross-border trade, and to the exchange of farm land. But there were also many other bonds linking particular settlements. The Mandinka towns that share histories of migration remain connected through regular life-cycle events such as marriages, naming and initiation ceremonies. The latter consists of two sub-types: the circumcision rites (*sunandiro*) that are conducted for adolescents at the age of seventeen or eighteen years, and the major initiation (*kaseba*) for men entering marriage that takes place every twenty to thirty years. It is common practice for related villages and towns to participate in each other's events. The *alkalo* of Sifoe explained that rising costs had led to the fading importance of the *kaseba* and the incorporation of elements thereof into *sunandiro*. Although

---

[2] On the history of festivals and celebrations in Lomé, see Kodjo Koffi, "Réjouissances privées et cérémonies officielles: une histoire socio-politique de la fête à Lomé", in Odile Goerg (ed.), *Fêtes urbaines en Afrique: espaces, identités et pouvoirs* (Paris: Karthala, 1999).

[3] For a fascinating parallel example from the US–Mexico border, see Elaine A. Peña. "Paso Libre: border enactment, infrastructure, and crisis resolution at the port of Laredo 1954–1957", *TDR: The Drama Review* 61 (2) 2017.

[4] In 2016, Senegalese transporters blockaded the border for three months in protest against a massive hike in the Gambia fees paid by trucks crossing to the Casamance, as well as the failure to advance the Gambia bridge project. This was the sixth such closure since 2000. On each occasion, the action by transporters has forced governments to the negotiating table. www.africanews.com/2016/05/16/gambia-senegal-border-remains-closed-as-diplomatic-row-continues/

he felt that this may have reduced some of the interaction, it was still commonplace for towns and villages to exchange visits during the *sunandiro*. The second means by which Mandinka communties remain connected has been through religious festivals, which are again sub-divided into two types. The first is the celebration of the Prophet's birthday – *Mawlud* – which is known in Mandinka as *gammo* and is held in December. Although this should logically take place on a single day, in practice it is staggered in order to enable people to attend events in other towns.[5] The second, *al-Koran Karamo*, is a koranic recitation festival organized annually by each settlement. The *alkalo* of Sifoe observed that when a clash of dates occurred, it was common for towns to delegate a certain number of people to attend the other event.[6] The *al-Koran Karamo* can take place at any time and provides an opportunity for people to renew the bonds between them. In the Casamance borderlands, Daroussalaam occupies a particularly important position in the religious calendar. In April, *talibés* from the many communities where Cheikh Mahfoudz founded religious schools – including those in Guinea-Bissau, Mali, the Gambia and Mauritania – converge on Daroussalaam to pray at his tomb. Although it is clear that Mahfoudz occupies a very special place in the religious understanding of the Jola, his religious network evidently transcends ethnicity. Many goods are transported across the border during these religious events, both as gifts and for entertainment.

The relatively relaxed attitude to cross-border relations in the Senegambia was threatened by the outbreak of the Casamance insurgency in the early 1990s. Rebels of the Mouvement des Forces Démocratiques de Casamance (MFDC) secreted themselves in the forests and exhibited a penchant for border locations where they could establish safe havens. The Guinea-Bissau border offered the ideal location because of the weak control exercised by the authorities there, but the Gambia border was important in its own right. In Senegal, it was widely believed that the Jammeh regime permitted safe passage to the MFDC subject to the latter agreeing to refrain from attacking villages on the Gambian side of the line. On one occasion when the looting of stores in Senegalese Dimbaya strayed into the section of the divided town that was located in the Gambia, a local informant recalled that the rebel commanders realized their mistake and swiftly returned the goods.[7] This was a clear indication that the insurgency had territorial limits.

The MFDC rebels seem to have enjoyed some local support to start with, especially in the settlements that had been newly populated by Jola migrants

---

[5] Interview with Alhaji Malanding Demba, Alkalo of Sifoe (Gambia), 6 April 2004.
[6] Interview with Alhaji Malanding Demba, 6 April 2004.
[7] Interview with Yousupha Colley, Dimbaya (Gambia), 11 February 2004.

from Buluf. Their material demands were modest, consisting of a cup of rice per compound from time to time. Indeed, by scaring off the forest guards they opened up a source of income for farmers who increasingly needed cash to purchase rice as their own paddies dried up.[8] Moreover, the Senegalese authorities ceased collecting the taxes that had previously been levied through the *chefs de village*.[9] But over time rebel demands became more onerous and their behaviour more arbitrary. Mounting insecurity on the roads led to a falling off of attendance at the regular round of religious and social activities. At the height of the insurgency, many people from the Casamance sought refuge across the border. Not surprisingly, they headed for the towns and villages where the connections were strongest. Indeed it is striking that many relocated to the towns that had served as places of refugee in the nineteenth century, such as Bakau.[10] Others joined friends and relations living just across the borderline. Hence Darsilami provided a temporary home for many refugees whose villages were but a short distance from the border. They were taken in by families there rather than being placed in refugee camps – which also made it easier for them to return as tensions subsided. Elsewhere, including in Sifoe, formal refugee camps were established by the United Nations High Commission for Refugees (UNHCR). After the Front Nord reached a modus vivendi with the Senegalese authorities, the military attacks subsided, but the rebels increasingly lived off local populations. According to Martin Evans, the Front's leaders agreed to stop fighting "in exchange for which they were allowed to remain in informal control of much of the northwest of Bignona department".[11] Within the fieldwork area, rebels installed themselves in two camps close to the border: one at Kujube and the other at Mahamouda, between which the personnel were apparently rotated. By 2004, the Wade government had forcibly ejected the rebels, but memories of the hardships associated with the MFDC occupation were still raw. One elderly informant in Kujube recalled being beaten severely.[12] Women in Mahamouda were required to turn up to parties and to dispense sexual favours. In one instance, the youth of Touba were caught partying to the music of Youssou N'Dour and were forced at gunpoint to dance to the same track until the break of dawn – all

---

[8] Although farmers turned increasingly to upland rice varietals, families increasingly contended with a deficit. Fieldwork diary entry 26 July 2004.

[9] Interview with Alkalo Landing Jabang, assistant Alkalo, Seku Jabang and Yusuf Darbo Kabadio (Casamance), 21 July 2005.

[10] Interview with Tombon Ture and others, Kujube (Casamance), 18 February 2004.

[11] Martin Evans, *Sénégal: Mouvement des Forces Démocratiques de la Casamance*, Chatham House, Briefing Paper 04/02, November 2004, p. 5.

[12] Interview with Sidi Jabang and others, Kujube (Casamance), 18 February 2004.

in order to impart the lesson that it was forbidden to listen to 'Senegalese music'.[13] Given that Youssou N'Dour was by far the dominant cultural icon in Senegal, the rebels selected a symbolic target that everyone understood. Ironically, because there was no musician of remotely equivalent stature from the Casamance, they were led to propose Congolese music as a suitable alternative.

In Kujube and surrounding villages, the violence associated with the MFDC occupation invited a historical comparison. In the opinion of one informant, it was as if a much longer cycle of history was repeating itself in an area that had experienced a litany of misfortune:

If you look at the history of Kujube, the people here were really very tired. They were not having peace all the time from the history of Mansa Kalamar up till today. The only time the people of Kujube had peace was during the reign of Mansa Dambeld who was then having his palace in Kabadio. That was the only time the people of Kujube enjoyed peace. But apart from that all these other ones including from Mangone Seye the people of Kujube didn't have any peace ... and this [Fodé] Sylla and the influence of Alhaji [Haidara] and the [MFDC] rebel attack on their efforts ... That is the reason people cannot stay in this area. People will come, fights happen, people will flee and never come back. Another time, people will come back again and the place is settled; another event will happen, people will flee and never come back. That is why the place still cannot develop. It was an old village; it has been in existence [since] a long time ago. Because of the conflicts which are seriously affecting the area, that is why it cannot develop.[14]

This is in many respects a deeply revealing historical reflection, in that it bundles deep history (the legend of Mansa Dambeld), the colonial encounter and the sufferings of the present into a coherent whole. One MFDC camp was established at Bandjikaky, close to Fodé Sylla's former military base – another resonance of the past that did not go unnoticed.[15] Some informants observed a certain similarity in the calculated manner in which Fodé Sylla had waited until the crops were harvested before launching his raids. The difference was that Sylla had met his match in Narang, whereas the forest now provided a safe haven for the rebels. The one village that the rebels dared not interfere with was Daroussalaam. The rebels were apparently warned that an attack on such an important religious centre would surely result in their own defeat.[16] By maintaining a safe, and possibly respectful distance, the rebels seemed to admit

---

[13] During subsequent football matches between Darsilami (Gambia) and Touba (Casamance), the youth from the former town used this episode as an excuse to taunt the opposition. I am grateful to Yusupha Jassey for this anecdote.

[14] Interview with Tombon Ture and others, 18 February 2004.

[15] In September 2004, the centrality of Bandjikaky was underlined when it was chosen as the site for a peace conference between government mediators and most of the rebel factions. Interview with Alkalo Baboucar Jabang, Diana (Casamance), 20 July 2005.

[16] Interview with Marabi Moise Haidara, Darsilami Cheriffkunda (Casamance), 17 February 2004.

the limits of their own capacity to coerce in this part of the Narang forest. In Kujube, on the other hand, there was bemusement over what seemed like collusion between the rebels and the army. At one point, following a series of physical assaults, the villagers sent an appeal to the soldiers based in Diouloulou to remove the rebels from their midst. The response from the local command was that they would speak to them, but there was no follow-up.[17] This merely served to heighten a sense of alienation from the Senegalese state on the part of a population whose relationship with the centre had never been a warm one. At the time of fieldwork in 2004, there was no visible MFDC presence in the area. But the assassination of the *sous-préfet* of Diouloulou and one of the regime's principal interlocuteurs, Samsedine Dino Néma Aidara, at Mahamouda Chérife (near to Djinaki) in December 2007 – followed by attacks upon the same settlement three years later – underlined a residual volatility.[18]

I turn now to consider how these developments affected interactions between Mandinka, Karoninka and Jola populations in the border zone. Villages that had tired of the MFDC presence, and given up on the Senegalese army, eventually turned to forms of self-defence. This culminated in the creation of an association that drew on a conception of the historicity of Fogny-Jabangkunda. Although it is doubtful that the latter had ever been more than a loose collection of related settlements, the idea that the people of the region had once belonged to a unified 'kingdom' served as a charter for revival. This was in part a cultural reference, but it had the practical intent of protecting villages against rebel predation. However, the flip-side was that the association had much less relevance for villages in the Gambia. Fogny-Jabangkunda evoked a historic space in the Casamance, but the Gambians were more inclined to identify with the historical entity of Kombo. In 2004, the *alkalo* of Sifoe intimated that while the association had once enjoyed some support in the Gambia, it had come to be confined to the Casamance:

This Fogny Jabangkunda association is most active in the Casamance area, but it is not active in this area now. The people here don't actively take part in this organization. They have other different organizations: we have the Islamic Kafo, that is consisting of Islamic-educated people, and other kafos, different kafos. But they don't actively take part in this Fogny Jabangkunda kafo association. Its dormant around this area.[19]

---

[17] Interview with Sidi Jabang and others, Kujube (Casamance), 18 February 2004.

[18] Martin Evans and Charlotte Ray, "Uncertain ground: the Gambia and the Casamance conflict", in Abdoulaye Saine, Ebrima Ceesay and Ebrima Sall (eds.), *State and Society in the Gambia Since Independence 1965–2012* (Trenton: Africa World Press, 2013), p. 253. This was one of the villages within the Mahfoudz network, but is not to be confused with the village of Mahamouda located near to Kujube.

[19] Interview with Alhaji Malanding Demba, Sifoe, 6 April 2004.

The framing also posed some difficulties for the villages located closest to the rebels because Narang, which was distinct from Fogny-Jabangkunda, was home to a higher percentage of Jola and Karoninka. In practice, therefore, the association enjoyed the greatest support in the historically Mandinka settlements of the Casamance where support for traditional authority was also strongest.

Amongst Mandinka populations, there was an understandable temptation to attribute the disruptions to the increased local presence of Jola migrants from Buluf – although to my knowledge this was never stated in a public forum. But the underlying reality was that Jola settlers were targeted to a much greater extent than the Mandinka of the coastal strip. As a consequence, their tacit support for the rebels had certainly ended by the time the regime of Abdoulaye Wade set out to restore control. The promotion of a peace festival in Kafountine, alongside the attempt by external donors and the Economic Community of West African States (ECOWAS) to develop a cultural festival in the borderlands between Diouloulou and Brikama in 2006, represented official efforts to emphasize the common bonds linking all the people of the Casamance regardless of ethnicity.[20] By and large, these initiatives were well received, although the presence of the Senegalese state remained distinctly patchy beyond the town of Diouloulou.

Indirectly, the insurgency intensified a rift between the Karoninka and the rest of the Jola. As I have already indicated in Chapter 2, there were versions of Mandinka history that posited a close affinity with the Karoninka in the remote past. When migrants from Bliss and Karone travelled seasonally to Mandinka settlements, and established 'stranger' relationships with their hosts, this could easily be glossed as the renewal of ancient affinities. One of the peculiarities of this relationship is that it became normal for Karoninka to switch their ethnicity to that of being Mandinka when they converted to Islam. This is attributed to the claim that Islam is incompatible with key elements of Karoninka culture – notably the keeping of pigs, the drinking of palm-wine and the "worshipping of idols".[21] Converts physically relocated their compounds to live with their co-religionists. In the process, Karoninka adopted Muslim names, redefined themselves as Mandinka, and even stopped speaking their own language.[22] The process of forgetting was a very conscious process, as one leading activist explained:

---

[20] "ECOWAS Cross-Border Initiatives Programme: Southern Senegambia Pilot Operation", 2007 (copy in my possession).
[21] Interview with Alhaji Malanding Demba, 6 April 2004.
[22] However, most Karoninkas retained their surnames whereas the Manjago converts lost those as well.

The first thing they do is to not to speak the language, and they speak another language. That is, mostly here in the Gambia it is Mandingo they speak. In Senegal it is Wolof. So you find out that there are many Karoninkas here who are Karoninkas that retain their surnames but they don't speak the language anymore. Because they don't want to be known as Karoninkas and that is why even their families also they avoid them.[23]

In fact, physical relocation might be symbolic – such as moving one's compound from one side of the road to the other. The point, however, was that the convert was expected to be reborn as a Muslim and to leave the old ways behind. The fact that this often required turning away from one's family meant that conversion was considered a traumatic event. As the same informant observed:

That is why the first time when a Karoninka converts to Islam it is like a funeral. People cry because they know that now you are not going to be part of them anymore. And for that reason, even their funerals are affected. If a Karoninka Muslim dies a Karoninka non-Muslim is now allowed to go and witness the burial ... Where it is written in the Bible or even in the Koran?"[24]

As Steven Thomson indicates, acculturation operated in one direction only: in other words, it was unheard of for Mandinkas to alter their ethnicity if they were, say, to convert to Christianity.[25]

The flip-side to asserting that the Karoninka had much in common with the Mandinka was the implication that they were fundamentally distinct from the Jola proper. In the 1990s, Karoninka activists attempted to insist on the existence of a distinct *Kalorn* ethnic group – eschewing the very name of Karoninka, which was of Mandinka origin. The Kalorn category was conceived of as distinct from both Mandinka and Jola. On the one hand, there was a categorical insistence on sharp cultural differences with the Jola based on language and culture. In the words of Paul Jarjue, the Secretary of Kayong Kalorn:

We have good reason to distance ourselves from being Jola. We are a different total ethnic group ... because we are constituted by ten different Kalorn villages, settlements or tribes, you may call it. We come from Kombeleul, Kouba, Hilol, Caseel, Mantar, Kayor, Mbouro, Mbovo, Essalolou, Bankassouk. So these are all Kalorn villages or different types of Kalorn. But then [when] meets a Jola and speaks to him or her in Karoninka, or in thus our language Kalorn, she or he will tell you "don't speak Kalorn to me. I can't speak Kalorn. You can speak to me in Jola". So there, before we even

---

[23] Interview with Paul Jarjue, Secretary of Kayong Kalorn, Kartong (Gambia), 3 April 2004.

[24] Interview with Paul Jarjue, 3 April 2004.

[25] Steven K. Thomson, "Children of the Village: Peace and Local Citizenship in a Multiethnic Gambian Community", PhD thesis, Boston University, 2006, pp. 48–9.

think we are not Jola they are already saying "you are not Jola, you are Karoninka so please speak to me in Jola" ... So obviously they are saying we don't belong to them.[26]

He went on to make the point that the very term 'Jola' was derived from Mandinka rather than having any internal integrity. On the other hand, the relationship with the Mandinka was understood to rest on a history of proximity and cultural resemblance. Even Mandinka informants observed closer similarities in initiation rites and dance between Karoninka and Mandinka than with the rest of the Jola.[27] However, the point that the Kalorn leaders insisted upon was that there was no need to equate being a Muslim with being Mandinka, and that the Kalorn ethnic category ought to be flexible enough to accommodate Christians, Muslims and practitioners of traditional religion.

The first Kalorn association was actually founded by youth leaders in Ziguinchor in 1974, who invited selected elders, deemed to be knowledgable about their culture, to join them.[28] The intention was to provide a platform for Kalorn on both sides of the border. In the early years, the format was an annual cultural festival that would rotate between towns that were home to significant Kalorn populations. But within a few years, tensions surfaced between the leadership on the two sides of the border. A leading figure in the Casamance, who had been instrumental in starting the association, recalls feeling marginalized when the events were increasingly held on Gambian soil.[29] He withdrew and the association itself fell into abeyance – although it retained a bank account and continued to make donations to later events. In 1993, there was a renewed attempt at fomenting unity with the creation of an association called Kayong Kalorn ('association of the Kalorn people'). The association had a similar mandate to unify the Karlorn across the international border. It had three objectives: to cement unity amongst scattered Kalorn populations; to recover a shared cultural heritage including the language; and to promote access to education, particularly amongst girls.[30] The association had a distinctly didactic purpose, which distinguished it from the earlier association. In the words of Jarjue again:

But the only difference here is the Kayong Kalorn today do organize an annual general meeting which lasts for three days, but basically the second day is the day that we show our cultural activities that we need to retain – because some of the cultural values are harmful and so we don't think they should be encouraged. But the ones that we think should be retained for the next generation, so we call elders to see how we do it. Where

---

[26] Interview with Paul Jarjue, 3 April 2004.
[27] Interview with Alhaji Demba Jabang, Alkalo of Kartong (Gambia), 4 June 2004.
[28] Interview with Sonkal Jasseh, Abéné (Casamance), 14 February 2004.
[29] Interview with Sonkal Jasseh, 14 February 2004. He was still in possession of the official stamp as President of the 'Bloc des Iles Bliss et Karone'.
[30] Interview with Paul Jarjue, 3 April 2004.

we go wrong, they will put us right. And then the third day is meeting, the day where we give them all the things that we did for the whole year, our finances, and the programmes or projects we have in the pipeline. That's where it differs from the previous Kalorn association. That one was just like people gathered together and then dance ...[31]

The Kayong Kalorn website does not merely highlight the regular round of shared activities but enables users to listen to radio programmes on such edifying topics as the proper use of alcohol and how to maintain a successful 'Alorn marriage'.

The other major difference is that the festival moulded itself to the international border. The first meeting was held in the Gambian village of Brufut in 1994, followed by Darsilami, Kartong, Gunjur, Sanyang, Lamin, Latrikunda, Marakissa, Kitty, Sifoe and Berending in the years that followed. It is striking that all these towns are in the Gambia. The organizers insisted that they sent invitations to all the towns where there were significant numbers of Kalorn, including those in Bliss and Karone. Moreover, arrangements have been made to host those who came from the other side. But the festival was clearly oriented towards those living on the Gambian side, whereas the towns in Bliss and Karone tended to stage their own events. This is suggestive of some similarities with the Agotime case that I will consider below. One crucial difference is that the project of cultural renewal that was advanced by Kayong Kalorn took place against the backdrop of high levels of mobility. Here the threat is cast in terms of an insidious process of de-culturation taking place in the diaspora. It is those living in Kombo who have had the highest propensity to convert to Islam and to lose their language – followed by those in Fogny-Jabangkunda in the Casamance. It is symptomatic that the initiator of Kayong Kalorn was himself a Gambian Karoninka who could not speak the language. The Kalorn who have remained in Bliss and Karone have scarcely been affected by Islam, while the impact of Christianity has been partial. Nor have the latter been in any danger of losing their facility with the language. Although there is some interest in highlighting Kalorn culture amongst these communities, there is much less interest in the process of weeding out the 'backward' elements that Kayong Kalorn advocates.

The second point is that while the Casamance insurgency sharpened the distinction between the Kalorn and Jola categories in the 1990s, the politics of ethnicity in the Gambia also played a formative role. Yahya Jammeh sought to maintain his grip on power through stacking the army with Jola recruits, somewhat like the Eyadéma regime in Togo. Encouraging more Kalorn to migrate to the Gambia was widely interpreted as an effort to lend demography

---

[31] Interview with Paul Jarjue, 3 April 2004. Much the same point is made in *Kayong Kalorn Perspective* (place and date of publication unknown), p. 12.

a helping hand. The expectation was that if the Gambian authorities were welcoming towards the Kalorn project, they would repay the regime with their political loyalty. Conversely, it became a conscious strategy of Kayong Kalorn to cement the status of the Kalorn people as bona fide Gambians. The irony is that the cultural project sought to distance the Kalorn from the Jola. However, this was more of an issue in the Casamance where the MFDC insurgency provided the operative context. In the Gambia, it was absorption into the Mandinka population that was considered to present the greatest threat. Hence Kayong Kalorn endeavoured to speak to different audiences in the Gambia and the Casamance, positioning itself in relation to the Mandinka in one setting and the Jola in the other. The association had to tread somewhat carefully in the Gambia: that is, highlighting common elements of a Kalorn culture but without coming across as anti-Jola. Indeed, staying on the right side of the Jammeh regime was a precondition for being able to operate at all. Hence, it is no accident that a Kayong Kalorn pamphlet was framed by a photograph of Jammeh on the frontispiece while the Gambian national anthem was translated into Kalorn at the back.[32] In 2000, Jammeh attended the festival in person, and later invited the Kayong Kalorn dance troupe to accompany him on an upcountry tour.[33] The Gambian government also permitted a Friday pro- gramme and a monthly Kalorn-language slot on national radio. This was regarded as central to the process of educating the Kalorn population in their own language and counteracting a stubborn tendency towards individualism. Jarjue explained the rationale as follows:

We are very scared of bureaucracy and bureaucrats. So you don't call us to meetings which we attend. You say that "oh I am busy", you go to the bush and say whatever you decide is okay for me. But then have seen that because of that also that we are lagging behind, are behind, when it comes to development. Then again we don't even listen to programmes or listen to radios, and who will bring the messages to us? So what do we do? We say we should be current, we should know what is happening. Then how do we do that? Let us also go on the media like the radio. Let us find a slot and ask government to give us a programme, so that once a week that will be it. Then will be speaking in our language, we will communicate to our people and tell them whatever information comes which will be useful to people.[34]

But inevitably, a programme on national radio spoke more to Gambian issues and had less appeal to the Kalorn in the Casamance proper where the Senegal- ese were trying to promote their own version of local radio.[35]

---

[32] *Kayong Kalorn Perspective.*   [33] Thomson, "Children of the Village", pp. 194–5.
[34] Interview with Paul Jarjue, 3 April 2004.
[35] However, Thomson came across some people in Bliss and Karone who did make a point of tuning in. "Children of the Village", p. 192.

It remains to say something about the structures of traditional authority. For Kalorn activists, the promotion of a shared culture is about developing a network for the diaspora rather than building on structures that were imposed by the French and perpetuated by the Senegalese state. Amongst Mandinka populations, the legitimacy attached to chieftaincy is greater, but also highly variable. On the Gambian side of the border, where the British constructed two tiers of *seyfos* and *alkalos*, there has been considerable continuity in the structures and lines of succession. However, the interference of the Jammeh regime in the selection of the *seyfos* is widely considered to have diminished the autonomy of traditional rulers. In the Casamance, the abolition of every-thing above the level of *chef de village* created a lower centre of gravity. Despite the formal imposition of decentralization policies in the 1990s, it remained the case that the *chefs de village* allocated land, subject to notional oversight from the local councils. When the Senegalese state bureaucracy retreated in the face of the MFDC insurgency, the chiefs were able to assert a leadership role within their communities. Ironically, this was also manifest in communities that had a Jola/Karoninka majority and for whom chieftaincy was not highly valued in the past. In the mid-2000s, there remained close contact between traditional authorities on the two sides of the border. This arose not only out of the regular cycle of events that I have outlined above, but also from the reality that they compensated for the lack of co-operation between state actors at the local level. When cattle were stolen and smuggled across the border – a rather regular occurrence – it was typically the *alkalos* rather than the police who took matters in hand. To some extent, this could be seen as compatible with their role as quasi-state actors, but it also underlined the reality that local actors had their own ideas about what good governance in the borderlands entailed.

In short, belonging is held to reside in active membership of a given town or village, which in many cases is a community of believers. But because there is mobility between settlements, and because historical connections between the Mandinka towns are highly valued, communities are never sharply bounded. To some extent, conceptions of ethnicity are grounded in an appeal to the very same everyday interaction. The Mandinka towns in particular valorize shared stories of migrations in the recent past, and trade and intermarriage in the present. But Mandinka towns of Kombo, on the one hand, and of Narang and Fogny-Jabangkunda, on the other, relate to history rather differently. The fact that the border is superimposed upon a much older frontier region means that the border also underlines and reinforces a sense of difference between Man-dinka settlements. Amongst the Jola, migrants have retained close links to their home towns to the south. They have also responded in quite different ways to the effort to mobilize support along ethnic lines. In the Gambia, welcoming Jola immigrants was part of the political strategy of the Jammeh regime, whereas appeals to Jola values in the Casamance have been advanced in opposition to Wolofization in Senegal. Equally, as Kayong Kalorn pursued a strategy for ethnic autonomy, it needed the imprimatur of the Jammeh regime in the Gambia whilst distancing itself from the MFDC in the Casamance. In the Senegambia, therefore, the border has been woven into emergent understandings of community and ethnicity amongst the various peoples who populate the borderlands. States have played their part either in facilitating ethnic mobilization or in creating a context in which ethnic appeals make a certain sense. In general, it would be difficult to claim that ethnicity trumps other modes of thinking about social relations.

Piecing Together a Fractured Polity

Kpetoe is Not Agotime![36]

As I have already indicated, Agotime had first been divided by the international boundary and then split between administrative units within French Togoland – a reality that has continued down to the present in a modified form. Although almost all Agotimes formally respected the primacy of the Konor in Kpetoe, it is widely repeated that this is a chieftaincy that was created by the Germans. As many informants continued to insist, the Agotime had hitherto been led by 'big men' who were never kings or chiefs in the contemporary sense. After the partition, chiefs in French Togoland had been incorporated into an alternative hierarchy, in which one of the Agotime chiefs usually occupied the position of *chef de canton*, but with an authority that extended to only a section of French Agotime. The remaining settlements were placed under non-Agotime *chefs de canton*. On the Ghana side of the border, the enduring legacy of British amalgamation policy was such that the Konor was treated as a sub-chief under the umbrella of Asogli – and hence inferior in status to the Ho paramount chief.

As we have seen, partition and administrative subdivision meant that Agotime had ceased to function as a political community after 1919. As relations between Ghana and Togo became decidedly fractious in the years after independence, it was difficult to rebuild formal relations. Conditions were no more forgiving in the 1980s, when the Rawlings and Eyadéma regimes regarded one another with thinly veiled suspicion. As Nene Keteku explained:

So things influence the people and they fear coming down for a lot of things. But [for] funerals and other things they still come ... When we are installing a chief we invite them, they come. But when they are installing a chief there, I don't go myself.

---

[36] These are the words of a Togolese chief at a charged moment. Fieldwork diary, 3 September 2001.

Sometimes I send people there. Because they fear when I go there any of my enemies can go and tell Togolese that this man is a spy for Rawlings and before you are aware you are arrested.[37]

Much like in the Senegambia, Agotime people visited relatives on the other side of the border, and attended life-cycle events such as marriages, funerals and the outdooring of new-born children. They also attended each other's markets, even during periods of tension. But there was no space where it was possible to engage in a discussion, far less a celebration, of what it meant to be Agotime. A residual sense of 'Agotime-ness' was reproduced through the enduring relationship between specific towns and families – as indicated in the quotation from Nene Keteku – but the work of shared reflection had more or less ceased. The disappearance of Agotime from official maps, both in Ghana and Togo, was also revealing in its own way. The fact that the Adangbe language only survived in Afegame in Ghana, and Zukpe and Kpodjahon in Togo, facilitated a process of erasure by states in search of administrative simplicity.

During the 1980s and 1990s, a number of developments, which did not necessarily pull in the same direction, provided a context in which Agotime leaders could envisage reassembling the pieces of their fractured polity. The first arose from the ongoing land dispute with Adaklu, which I addressed in detail in Chapter 7. It is worth underlining that the litigation was greatly complicated by the conjuncture of two parallel developments. One, as I have noted, was the increasing paralysis of Ghanaian state institutions during the 1970s, which was reflected in the failure of the courts to deal expeditiously with outstanding litigation. The other was the increasingly tense relationship between the two governments who frowned on the maintenance of contacts across the border. In 1983, the dispute took an ugly turn when H.B. Ankrah – one of the principal litigants from Afegame – was abducted, secretly murdered and his corpse burned. He was only later identified from some of his personal effects.[38] Ankrah had been a somewhat controversial figure, even in Afegame. His family had made money in the cocoa trade and he had allegedly been attempting to found a large village on the disputed land – ostensibly to protect it from further encroachment, but conceivably also to have himself recognized as a chief.[39] As a consequence, he was not universally trusted in Afegame, where it was thought he might be cutting a private deal with Nene Keteku. But because Ankrah had the resources to create a permanent settlement on the disputed land, he posed an even greater threat to his Adaklu opponents. At the

---

[37] Interview with Nene Nuer Keteku III, Ho, 26 March 2001.
[38] Interview with Nene Todze Agbovi V, Kpetoe, 7 September 2007.
[39] Interview with Nene Agbovi V, 7 September 2007, and with Nene Akoto Sah VII, Kpetoe, 5 September 2007.

time, there were some Adaklu soldiers serving with the Mortar Regiment in Ho, and it was they who allegedly conspired to liquidate Ankrah. He was murdered alongside the killing of a number of fetish priests who had been suspected of carrying out ritual murders and trading body parts across the region.[40] This may have been an attempt to establish guilt by association and to disguise a killing that was carried out to advance the Adaklu land claim. The case was one of countless acts of score-settling from the early days of the revolution, at a time when core institutions were in disarray, that have yet to be examined in a systematic fashion. It only resurfaced when the National Reconciliation Commission took evidence of human rights abuses from that period and someone from Afegame came forward to testify.[41] The unhappy fate of Ankrah lurks behind all debates about the land dispute today and partly explains an Agotime sense of grievance. Significantly, however, Ando tenants do not appear to have been targeted by either set of litigants. The assumption is that they could not be blamed for being in occupation, since they were being manipulated by those who claimed to be their landlords. Nor was the fact that the tenants had crossed from the Togo side of the border a point at issue. All of this was thoroughly consistent with the conception of strangers as an extension of the will of their patrons, to whom the real opprobrium attached.[42]

Although many Togolese regarded the ongoing litigation as essentially a Ghanaian affair, it did affect villages closest to the border, which often had more of their farms in Ghana than in Togo itself. Moreover, because the case had turned into a dispute about first settlement and the historical contours of Agotime, this concerned the population of Togolese towns whose own relationships with their Ewe neighbours was contentious. The murder of Ankrah also increased the stakes appreciably. But it was difficult for the Togolese to take an active part in proceedings at a time when the border itself was frequently closed. The Ankrah affair nevertheless caused Agotime activists to lament the fact that their Ewe neighbours had apparently forgotten who the overlords in the past had been. But when the call to arms came, it was not directed against the Adaklu, but rather against Fulani herders who had become a source of worry in the mid-1980s. In 1986, Nene Mahumansro XIII of Afegame had been in close touch with his counterparts in Togo who reported on some of the problems they were encountering with Fulani cattle. Although

---

[40] I owe the inside information on the other killings to Harry Asimah who was serving with the PDCs at that time.

[41] The Commission was created in 2002 and reported in October 2004. For an evaluation, see Nahla Valji, *Ghana's National Reconciliation Commission: A Comparative Assessment* (New York: International Center for Transitional Justice, 2006).

[42] At the time of writing, the case remains in abeyance. There is a belief that while Agotimes have been focused on other matters, the Adaklu have moved more Ando strangers onto the land and created a form of effective occupation.

the Fulani could be located within the established category of strangers, they also seemed to defy convention because they were perceived as being perpetually on the move and therefore outside of any commonly understood sense of community. After the matter was peacefully resolved in Afegame (see Chapter 12), the tensions receded. However, in January 1991 the distraught population of an outlying village marched to the *chef de canton* in Adzakpa, Togbe Nyamago Pattah II, to complain that their entire harvest had been destroyed by Fulani cattle. The chief proposed that they should go to the land to see for themselves. When they reached the spot, some of the herders opened fire, leading the villagers to flee the scene. The *chef de canton* and some of the elders who were left behind were set upon with cutlasses, and the former was killed. After one of the party managed to raise the alarm, a call to arms was taken up by Agotimes on both sides of the border.[43] Although it is not entirely clear how many fatalities there were,[44] most of the cattle were seized and the Fulani were expelled from Agotime lands on the two sides. This was a defining moment because it was the first time that Agotimes had acted in a concerted fashion and in a way that took no account of the border. It is also striking that, in the heat of the moment, they did not defer to the authorities in either country. In Togo, there had been a mounting sense of exasperation after a string of complaints to the *préfet* in Agou had failed to elicit any response, giving rise to a strong suspicion that the latter had been paid off.

The Fulani clash re-focused attention on the lament that the Agotime had forgotten how to work in unison. An important step towards redressing this deficit was, therefore, to begin rebuilding the bonds between the different sections of partitioned Agotime. Given that resurrection of the idea of a greater Agotime would potentially enhance the status of the Kpetoe stool, it is perhaps not surprising that Nene Keteku was in the vanguard. The business of historical reconstruction was hardly straightforward, given that nobody in Agotime had access to the Danish records or could have read them even if they had been readily available. Although the German administrative records were located in the archives in Lomé, almost none of the Agotime who could have read the old script were still alive. But a modest attempt to reconstruct a history of Agotime did proceed on the basis of the published material that was available in English, such as the work of Carl Reindorf, as well as oral traditions drawn from various sections of Agotime.[45] This was inevitably complicated by the

---

[43] Interview with Togbe Nyagamago Pattah IV, Agotime-Adzakpa (Togo), 15 August 2002.

[44] An obituary for the late Nene Adzah Narte Wletu V of Kpetoe implies that there was substantial fighting. http://spynewsagency.com/nene-adzah-narte-wletu-v-to-go-home-this-weekend/?upm_export=print

[45] Reindorf was specifically mentioned by Nene Keteku as a source. Fieldwork diary 27 March 2001. The only published history of Agotime, which was written by one of the Kpetoe chiefs,

fact that the versions of history in Kpetoe, Afegame and Zukpe harboured quite distinct emphases.

Meanwhile the Agotime-Adaklu land case continued to grind on at a glacial pace. In 1987, the Agotime appealed once more, with their legal team now arguing that the case should properly have been referred to the Stool Lands Boundaries Settlement Commission. They received short shrift from the Court of Appeal, which handed down its judgement in July 1988.[46] The appeal judges made it clear that they considered the historical evidence, which was pretty much all of it, pretty worthless: "Turning then to the traditional history of this land in dispute called Akuete land by the Plaintiffs and Segbale by the Defendants it is obvious no reliance can be placed on any of the rival versions to found a claim thereon." However, the court reiterated that the burden of proof lay with the plaintiffs in the original case. The judges accepted the argument that Adaklu tenants had been in possession of the land for around 30 years before the original suit and commented that the "lethargy [of the plaintiffs] does not inspire any confidence in the plaintiff's claims". Once again, no reference was made to the German map that would have clarified the Agotime insistence on the Waya and Klayo streams as forming their boundary with the Adaklu. More bizarrely, the judges picked up on the statement of Agbovi that "The Klayo stream is nearer to Adaklu land than Kpetoe" and concluded that this contradicted the claim that the Klayo consti-tuted the boundary. In fact, the statement was an entirely logical one.[47] Crucially, the judges sprung the trap that had been set for the Agotime in the debate about naming, landscape and first settlement. To quote:

Obviously the Adangbe community settled in an Ewe enclave. If they had originally founded the land they would not have rejected an Adangbe name in preference for the Ewe name, especially as the evidence disclosed that they knew no Ewe when they arrived on the land. A grant by another party rather than an original acquisition by them seems to be indicated by the entire circumstances.

This reasoning was highly questionable, but the underlying problem was that the Agotime had not offered a coherent account of how it was that they had come to embrace elements of Ewe usage. A crucial factor was that it had become difficult for Agotime witnesses from the Togo side to establish their credibility as witnesses before the Ghanaian courts. To all intents and

---

was released during Agbamevoza in 2016. See Nene Ahortor Makaku V, *A Brief History of the Lehs vis-à-vis the Agotimes* (Accra: the author, 2016).

[46] Judgement delivered in the Superior Court of Judicature, in the Court of Appeal, Accra, before J.S.C. Francois, J.A. Ampiah and J.A. Lamptey, 15 July 1988 (Adaklu-Agotime land case records).

[47] The judges reasoned that "Either the stream is a boundary or it is not. There can be no halfway house." Simple logic would have suggested that precisely because the Klayo stream provided the boundary, it would have been closer to Adaklu land than to Kpetoe.

purposes, Agotime lawyers were forced to rely on witnesses from Ghana whose own historical narrative contained significant gaps. In that sense, the Agotimes were left fighting with one hand tied behind their backs. Finally, the judges regarded the invocation of the Stool Lands Boundary Settlement Decree as a tactic of last resort. Having lost their case, the Agotime made their final pitch in appealing to the Supreme Court. At the time of writing, the case has still to be settled despite the fact that some ten years have passed since the declaration of the intention to appeal. The feeling in Agotime today is that the failure to actively pursue the matter has led to a situation in which the Adaklu have managed to physically occupy the land with strangers. In a practical sense, the battle is probably lost.

Throughout these protracted legal battles, the parties evinced a particular concern with fixing their territorial boundaries, and in a manner that was most advantageous to themselves. The use of strangers to claim physical occupation was a strategy that was resorted to by all sides. Ando strangers were considered ideal in the sense that they created physical evidence of occupation and land use without staking any troublesome claims of their own. This was very different to what transpired when Jola from Buluf settled on Gambian land. As perpetual strangers, there was never any question of the Ando becoming either Agotime or Adaklu. But by helping the litigants to stake out their preferred boundaries, they also contributed to a game of territorial politics that not only pitted particular land claimants against each other, but also reinforced the mutual antagonism between the Agotime and their neighbours – especially the Adaklu, Hodzo and Nyive. Whereas potential witnesses from Togolese Agotime ran up against a barrier, that was mental as well as physical, the Ando slipped through the border with consummate ease.

Turning to the second set of developments, just when it seemed that the Agotime were locked into a dynamic that seemed destined to frustrate attempts at cementing unity, the landscape of power was suddenly transformed in the early 1990s. In Ghana, the return to constitutional government in 1992 was accompanied by a freeing up of public debate, such that very little was considered off-limits. For the first time in decades, it was possible to talk openly about how the border came to be, why the two halves of former German Togo remained divided and what might be done to redress the various problems caused by partition.[48] In Togo, the democratic momentum ultimately stalled, and yet the grip of the regime had weakened sufficiently in the south to

---

[48] This has been noted by Kate Skinner, *The Fruits of Freedom in Togoland: Literacy, Politics and Nationalism, 1914–2014* (Cambridge: Cambridge University Press, 2015), pp. 249–53. The advocacy of the respected Member of Parliament for Hohoe South, Kosi Kedem, was especially significant in this regard. See, for example, his book entitled *How Britain Subverted and Betrayed British Togoland* (Accra: Government and Electoral Systems Agency, 2007).

alter the political dynamic. The toppling of the statue of Eyadéma near the market in Kpalimé was one public manifestation of opposition to the regime. The sudden willingness of the traditional authorities to speak openly on the matters that concerned them was also indicative of a shift in the balance of power.[49] In the case of Agotime, the sense of fresh possibilities manifested itself in an ostensibly innocuous attempt to establish a cross-border festival that would speak to the concerns of people on both sides of the line.

In fact, the attempt to create a single festival for the Agotime people had a longer lineage. In 1978, at a moment when there was a brief easing of tensions between Ghana and Togo, chiefs had seized the opportunity to launch a festival called *Avakeza*, which translates roughly as 'the festival for the ending of war'. According to one informant, this was a reworking of the principle that there needed to be a ritual cleansing after a period of conflict.[50] The invocation of peace was likely to resonate positively with the regime in Togo, which deployed the same language in its own rhetoric. It also appealed to a Christian aesthetic that was shared by Agotimes on two sides of the border. Although Togolese chiefs took the lead, Nene Keteku claimed to have been actively supportive of the initiative.[51] Zukpe hosted the inaugural festival and a second followed in Amoussoukope in 1981. The expectation was that the third iteration would take place in Kpetoe itself. But at this point the momentum stalled. A recurrence of the dispute between Kpetoe and Afegame was one factor. Another was the closure of the border at the end of 1982, which meant that it was practically impossible to proceed as planned. This remained the case even when tensions eased somewhat after 1984.

It was Nene Keteku who eventually decided to re-activate the idea of a cross-border festival in 1995, but with two significant modifications. Firstly, the festival was to centre on Kpetoe as the notional capital of the Agotime people. This was contentious because while some of the Togolese towns like Amoussoukope traced their origins to Kpetoe, Zukpe regarded itself as the historical equal of Kpetoe. Needless to say, the decision rankled in Afegame, which considered itself to be the original home of the Agotime people. Moreover, the fact that the planning committee was mostly drawn from Kpetoe created its own misunderstandings. Invitations were sent to Agotime towns in Togo, and families in Kpetoe looked forward to hosting their kinsmen, but inevitably the latter were treated as if they were guests rather than co-organizers. This rankled, especially when the Togolese were making financial contributions to support the festival.[52] In an attempt to address these

[49] E. Adriaan B. Van Rouveroy Van Nieuwaal, *L'état en Afrique face à la chefferie: le cas du Togo* (Paris: Karthala, 2000), pp. 132–41.

[50] Interview with Emmanuel Tetteh Kpeglo, Agotime-Akpokope (Ghana), 2 September 2003.

[51] Fieldwork diary entry 18 September 2001.

[52] Interview with Togbe Nyagamago Pattah IV, 15 August 2002.

sensitivities, it was decided to hold one of the set-piece events – the 'firing of musketry' – in the Togolese village of Batoumé. Given that the latter was a hamlet founded by Nene Agbovi I in the late nineteenth century, this was a highly symbolic gesture. However, even this concession ran foul of the Togolese authorities. In 1996, they abruptly closed the border as people were preparing to make the crossing after someone reported that the festival concealed a subversive agenda.[53] Although the Togolese government later softened its stance, the firing of musketry – however antiquated the guns – risked provoking a rather jumpy military. For that reason, it was considered wise to hold this part of the festival in Ghana until things eased up in Togo.

Secondly, the festival was reframed as *Agbamevoza*, or the 'kente weaving festival'. The reason for the change is that *Avakeza* had also been construed as a coded celebration of Agotime militarism. For many, memories of warfare, and in particular resistance to the Asante invasion of the early 1870s, remained a matter of pride. The 'Adzakpa war' against the Fulani herdsmen had brought these memories back into relief. But, as we have seen in Chapter 2, the Agotime had absorbed many Ewe captives into their own lineages. The issue of servile origins is more contentious in Agotime than almost anywhere in the Volta Region, with the possible exception of Anlo. Batoumé was the place where Agbovi I had chosen to settle his personal captives after the Asante war, and for that reason the matter was acutely sensitive there. But in towns like Kpetoe and Akpokope there were also sections that were made up of former war captives. And then there were the people whose relationship to Agotime assumed the form of clientage. The status of Nyitoe vis-à-vis the rest of Agotime was one that remained contentious. Nene Keteku recalled that great offence had been caused at *Avakeza* in Amoussoukope when someone had performed a dance that alluded to standing on one's enemies.[54]

An early chairman of the *Agbamevoza* committee, who hailed from Akpokope, maintained that the change of name was specifically intended to draw a line under the past – a past that was all the more troublesome precisely because it was held in common.[55] Whereas appeals to military prowess were contentious, a celebration of Agotime mastery in weaving the highest-quality kente cloth seemed to offer a focus for collective pride that neither national governments nor local constituencies could find fault with.[56] It also enabled the Agotime to distinguish themselves from their Ewe neighbours who were

---

[53] Fieldwork diary entry, 21 March 2001.
[54] Fieldwork diary entry on discussion with Nene Keteku, 18 September 2000.
[55] Interview with Emmanuel Tetteh Kpeglo, Akpokope, 2 September 2003.
[56] On Agotime and Ewe kente weaving, see Malika Kraamer, "Colourful Changes: Two Hundred Years of Social and Design History in the Hand-Woven Textiles of the Ewe-Speaking Regions of Ghana and Togo (1800–2000)", unpublished PhD thesis, School of Oriental and African Studies, 2005.

known for farming rather than weaving. Finally, given that kente was considered a prestige product across Ghana and in the diaspora, the focus on weaving held out the prospect of developing a profitable local industry – thereby generating gainful employment for the youth, while at the same time banking cultural capital within Ghana. Kente enabled Agotime to become a player on the national stage, trading in part on invitations to exhibit its product overseas.[57] Nene Keteku even courted national controversy by publicly asserting that it was the Agotime, and not the Ashanti, who were the originators of kente cloth.[58] To the surprise of many, these claims were publicly vindicated by none other than Nana Agyeman Rawlings, the wife of Flt.-Lt. Jerry Rawlings, who hails from a prominent Ashanti family.

Although there was a broad consensus that it was necessary to work together, *Agbamevoza* brought forth fresh disagreements about which elements of a shared history and culture deserved to be highlighted. This manifested itself in three specific areas of contention. The first was over who the festival really belonged to. The success with which the organizers in Kpetoe drew in sponsors, such as Star Lager in the early years, as well as attracting national media coverage, was impressive. However, the downside was that it seemed to reinforce a perception that the festival had been hijacked by Kpetoe. The greater number of Agotime towns were located in Togo, and in most years it was only the settlements closest to Kpetoe, both spatially and in terms of kinship relations, that attended. The second bone of contention was over the selection of the theme itself. 'Festivalization' as a means by which traditional areas have jostled for a place in the national spotlight has become a defining feature of the politics of recognition in Ghana. *Agbamevoza* is the festival that has attracted the most attention in the Volta Region, with the possible exception of *Hogbetsotso* in Anlo, primarily because of its close association with kente weaving. During one of the festivals, I happened to be staying in the same motel as some Togolese guests and asked them why so few of their people were in attendance. Their response was that the wearing of kente was something that Ghanaians took pleasure in and was not really part of their sartorial repertoire as Togolese. The latter preferred suits or wax prints as formal attire. Togbe Nyagamago Pattah IV of Adzakpa confirmed that there

---

[57] In 1998, the IMF/World Bank Africa Group invited Agotime to exhibit its kente in Washington DC, and the following year UNESCO extended an invitation to mount an exhibition in Paris. This external recognition receives prominence in the publicity for *Agbamevoza* and is given prominence in interactions with the Ghana media.

[58] His contention was that the Asante had hitherto worn calico cloths with adinkra designs, and it was the Agotimes, who were taken back to Asante as captives and settled at Bonwire, who brought the skill of weaving with them. He also made the point, which I encountered on several occasions, that kente has no meaningful etymology in Twi whereas in Ewe, *ke-te* (translating as 'open and press') refers to the act of weaving. Fieldwork diary 29 March 2001.

was little weaving in his area and added that because the soil was especially fertile, the population tended to concentrate on farming food crops and cotton.[59] Successive trips to Togolese villages revealed much less evidence of weaving – even in those settlements that were located close to the border. By contrast, on the Ghana side of the line even Ando and Avenor strangers in towns like Sarakope and Wodome had taken up the pursuit.[60] In that sense, the boundary served to inscribe quite different practices, even when there was almost no physical evidence of a border. In fact, the organizers of *Agbamevoza* implicitly recognized that kente weaving was a Ghanaian pursuit in their own publicity materials. In the tenth-anniversary brochure of 2005, a key section entitled "Kente Festival, Epitome of Ghanaian Culture" managed to make no reference to Togo at all and, without a hint of irony, concluded that:

Consequently, it must be noted that the Kente festival, which has become in recent times the perfect example of Ghanaian culture depicts the salient aspects of our way of life and to a larger extent gives the Ghanaian that singular identical symbol in the maze of varying and conflicting socio-cultural values in Africa and the larger world.[61]

It is hardly surprising, therefore, that some Togolese Agotimes felt offended by the manner in which the anniversary was pitched.

And thirdly, the staging of the festival heightened sensitivities over rank and precedence. As has been indicated, Nene Keteku was considered a sub-chief in Ghana. The chiefs of Zukpe and Adzakpa enjoyed the status of *chefs de canton*, and in the early 1990s they were joined by the chief of Amoussoukope who was permitted to hive off from Adzakpa.[62] Ironically, Nene Keteku had actually been asked for his opinion by the Togolese authorities before the decision was taken to split the canton.[63] It was evidently very difficult for the three canton chiefs to be seen to occupy a lesser position within the Agotime traditional hierarchy.[64] The picture was further complicated because in Kpetoe

---

[59] Interview with Togbe Nyagamago Pattah IV, 15 August 2002.

[60] This was true, for example, of Avenor people who lived in Sarakope, which was located on the Ho–Aflao road. At the remote Ando village of Agohome, I encountered children from Lomé who had been sent there to learn weaving. Fieldwork diary entry 11 September 2003.

[61] Agotime Traditional Area, *Kente Festival, Agbamevoza 2005 – 10th Celebration from Monday 29th August to Monday 5th Sept. 2005*, pp. 18–20.

[62] At the time of writing, Nene Teh Doku is the *chef de canton* in Agotimé-Nord, while Togbe Nyagamago and Togbe Nipa are both *chefs de canton* in Agotimé-Sud. Both of these are located in Agou *préfecture*, whereas Batoumé and some of the nearby villages like Wodome and Sarakope are located in the *préfecture* of Kévé.

[63] The question of which villages ought to come under which chief remained a matter of contention for some years. This internal boundary issue was finally resolved with the 56 settlements being divided: 39 were allocated to Adzakpa and 17 to Amoussoukope. This involved the exchange of a handful of settlements. https://ucasinitiative.wordpress.com/category/realisations/

[64] The same was true of the chief of Afegame who continued to insist that he was the rightful head of all the Agotime.

itself there was an insistence that it was necessary to uphold the status of the heads of the Agbovi and Akoto families, being the recognized war chiefs (or *avafiawo*) of the whole of Agotime. During festivals, when seating arrangements make powerful statements about who is who, there was always a danger that the Togolese chiefs would feel slighted. Nene Teh Doku III from Zukpe and Togbe Nyagamago IV from Adzakpa both participated on at least one occasion, but then stayed away because of dissatisfaction with the way the protocol had been handled. The chief of Batoumé, Togbe Apaloo IV, took part on several occasions, but that is in large part attributable to his close family links to Kpetoe. In 2001 matters came to a head when a new chief was enstooled in Akpokope and was permitted by Nene Keteku to ride in a palanquin of his own. This precipitated an uproar amongst the Agbovi and Akoto quarters of Kpetoe. But the senior chiefs in Togo also agreed that it was not in the power of Nene Keteku to grant such privileges, and they refused to take any further part in *Agbamevoza* until the latter rescinded his decision. At this point, a messy convergence of chieftaincy disputes threatened to bring about the complete suspension of co-operation amongst the Agotime towns. On the one hand, there was the ongoing tussle between Nene Keteku and Nene Mahumansro XIII, which entered a fresh round of recriminations after an attempt to trick the former into permitting the installation of a chief bearing a title that could have been used as a vindication of Afegame claims. On the other hand, there was a renewed attempt to launch a destoolment action against Nene Keteku on the basis that he had been improperly enstooled in 1969, at a time when Nene Noe Keteku II was still alive.[65] Some of the town chiefs in Kpetoe supported this action, which naturally enjoyed the sympathy of the Afegame chief. The latter's contention was that under the principle of rotation, which was supposedly laid down in 1946, the headchiefship would pass to Afegame after the death of Keteku II. By installing a new chief before the old one was dead, the argument went, the objective had been to prevent events from taking their natural course. In an incendiary history, Nene Makaku V appears to vindicate this position and further alleges that Nene Keketu III actually abdicated in 1993 before changing his mind under pressure from the youth in Kpetoe.[66] Nene Keteku was clearly embattled on all fronts, and the manner in which the Akpokope chief was elevated was seen by many as the last straw.

---

[65] Apparently Nene Keteku II had become incapacitated and there was an attempt to destool him on these grounds. Whether this was properly done is a matter of ongoing dispute. Nene Keteku III was enstooled as his successor. In fact, the former Konor survived until 1981. This sensitive matter is raised by Nene Makaku in his book, *A Brief History of the Lehs*, pp. 83–90, 101–2.

[66] Makaku, *A Brief History of the Lehs*, pp. 84–8.

At this point, intermediaries in Ghana and the canton chiefs of Adzakpa and Amoussoukope brokered the establishment of a committee to effect a reconciliation between Nene Keteku and the rest of the chiefs. Nene Keteku was required to pay a traditional fine and to accept the 'downgrading' of the Akpokope chief whose palanquin was taken away. In addition, there was agreement on the establishment of a standing committee to avoid such mishaps in future. The Togo chiefs also agreed to participate once more in *Agbamevoza* provided the safeguards for their status were guaranteed. In 2002, a public reconciliation ceremony was held in full view of the Ghanaian national media, in which the principal Agotime chiefs from the two sides of the border, with the exception of the Afegame chief, participated.[67] However, optimistic predictions of a new dawn turned out to be decidedly premature. In 2003, Nene Keteku caused fresh offence when *Agbamevoza* was cancelled in order to enable him to join a delegation to Canada to promote the virtues of kente. On the very days when *Agbamevoza* should have been celebrated, the Togolese chiefs met to discuss the reactivation of *Avakeza*.[68] The festival of 2005 was counted as a modest success, as reflected in a full schedule of events, but there was minimal Togolese participation. In 2007, *Agbamevoza* was scaled back because of a renewed disagreement between Nene Keteku and the other chiefs. In that same year, Nene Teh Doku III of Zukpe tellingly elected to celebrate a yam festival instead – a decision that was pregnant with meaning because it is normally associated with neighbouring Ewe peoples rather than the Agotime.

We can see, therefore, that *Agbamevoza* has served as a barometer for relations between the constituent sections of Agotime. When there has been discord, participation in the festival has been confined mostly to Kpetoe. But when relations have been more harmonious, the festival has been well patronized. But *Agbamevoza* has also functioned as a lightning conductor by virtue of the fact that much of the discord has turned on the performance of the festival itself. During the course of research over a 15-year period, I have managed to attend *Agbamevoza* on several occasions and to witness its successive transformations. While there are a number of constants, no iteration of the festival is entirely like any other because new elements are introduced to take account of current concerns. Very often, it is the intersection of national and local politics in Ghana that affects the dynamic. For a number of years, *Agbamevoza* took place against the backdrop of the ongoing tussle between Agotime and Adaklu. In the run up to the 2004 elections the separation of Adaklu-Anyigbe District from Ho District led to a heated dispute. Adaklu leaders insisted that because they were the 'landowners', they should be

---

[67] A copy of the video is in my possession.   [68] Fieldwork diary, 3 September 2003.

granted the capital – a claim that continued to be contested by the Agotime. Adaklu-Waya was initially chosen by the Kufuor government, but the decision was subsequently overturned and Kpetoe was selected in its place. This set in motion an acrimonious dispute in which both sides sought to call in favours from regional and national politicians. In 2005, the Regional Minister, Kofi Dzamesi, warned the audience at the closing durbar that Agotimes should not interpret the decision as a victory over the Adaklu and that the latter should equally not take it as a sign of their defeat. In 2006, a decision to suspend the festival was informed in part by a feeling that tensions were running high and that it might be considered provocative. At this time, there was speculation that the dispute might even escalate into full-blown armed conflict. While the Adaklu boasted of their greater numbers in the event of a confrontation, the expectation in Kpetoe was that the Togolese towns would come to the defence of their kinsmen. Over the course of the year that followed, Nene Keteku and his Adaklu counterpart, Togbe Gbogbi Atsa V, sought to broker a comprom- ise, and in 2007 the latter even attended Agbamevoza as an invited guest.[69] But it was only when a separate Agotime-Ziope district was established in 2012, with Kpetoe as the capital, that the issue was finally put to rest.

Over time, *Agbamevoza* has become a closely choreographed series of events that seeks to balance – and accord recognition to – the various segments of Agotime. The fact that the festival has recently won much greater accept- ance would suggest that some important lessons have been learned. In 2013, a new chief was enstooled in Afegame with the stool title of Nene Mahumansro XIV, and in a gesture of reconciliation he took part in the *Agbamevoza* of that year. In 2014, however, he reactivated the claim that the Agotime chieftaincy should rotate and that Nene Keteku was not rightfully enstooled. This brought about a suspension of relations. However, after a further effort to mend fences, the Afegame chief participated in 2016 and hosted *Godigbe* (see below) for a second time. It probably helped that a woman from Afegame was included on the planning committee. Even more noteworthy has been the involvement of the principal chiefs from Togo. In 2012, there was a breakthrough when the firing of musketry took place in Adzakpa. The same event was staged in Zukpe in 2013, which acknowledged the importance of this town in Agotime history – as well as the status of its chief who also happened to be the longest occupant of any Agotime stool. In 2016, a symbolic statement was made when the firing of musketry was staged in Adame on the northern frontier of Agotime with Agu. Adame had been clearly marked as belonging to Agotime on the Spri- gade map but had then been hived off. It is often claimed that the Adame

---

[69] These efforts at reconcilation rebounded upon the Adaklu chief against whom a destoolment action was brought. It was only in 2010 that this was rescinded. www.modernghana.com/news/ 271417/adaklu-paramount-chief-regains-recognition.html

people are more like the Nyitoe in the sense that they were originally Ewes, with links to Adaklu, who had been incorporated into Agotime.[70] In fact, Adame leaders had pointedly disassociated themselves from Agotime in the Hodzo land case (see Chapter 7). In 2016, there was no doubt in anyone's mind that Adame was an integral part of Agotime. But almost nobody in Kpetoe, including the chiefs, had ever been to this distant town and there was a palpable excitement about making the journey.

If one compares *Agbamevoza* with Kayong Kalorn, the similarities and differences point to the quite different contexts in which festivalization has been pursued. In each case, the planning committee consists of private citizens who are considered amongst the high achievers of the community.[71] And in each instance, the planning committee is effectively confined to one side of the border – Gambia in one case and Ghana in the other. They both showcase elements of cultural practice that are considered to be under threat. In the case of Agotime, this includes *dipo* initiation rites for pubescent girls. And there is a similar, rather utilitarian, emphasis on making culture work in the service of local development. But the chiefs play a crucial role in the shaping and performance of *Agbamevoza,* which has no equivalent in the case of Kayong Kalorn. At the same time, the didactic element is much less pronounced. Strikingly, the question of the revival of the Adangbe language, which is now spoken by the minority of Agotimes, has not been taken up – even if it is considered to be a marker of identity in Afegame. There are two further differences that are suggestive of the rather different dynamics in the two settings. The first is that Kayong Kalorn has very little to say about history – other than that the Kalorn had been migrating to and from Kombo well before the colonial borders were drawn – whereas *Agbamevoza* is as much about positioning the Agotimes within history as defining the elements of a common culture. And secondly, while the manner in which the Kayong Kalorn festival travels from town to town clearly reflects the underlying patterns of Karoninka migration, *Agbamevoza* pivots around Kpetoe because of the emphasis that is placed on traditional hierarchies and place-making in the trans-Volta. Although migration is never absent from the context – given the presence of Ando settlers and the Agotime's own movements to and from the Eastern Region of Ghana – it is incorporated into *Agbamevoza* only as deep history.

---

[70] Interview with Nene Keteku, 26 March 2001, and observations by Togbe Apaloo IV of Batomé. Fieldwork diary, 15 August 2001. Also interview with Togbe Kudiabor III, Agotime-Nyitoe (Togo), 19 August 2002. In 2002, the latter gave me a government publication with his own name inside it. It referred to himself as *Avafiaga*, which would indicate he had been making the claim to being a war chief for quite some time.

[71] For example, the chair of the planning committee in 2015 was Gabriel Katamani, the Commissioner of CEPS in charge of Support Services.

In *Agbamevoza*, the constituent elements are carefully threaded through the programme of activities that unfolds across five days, culminating in the final durbar in Kpetoe. In most years, the festival begins with a church service, which provides a Christian framing. In 2013 and 2016, the festival proper began with the staging in Afegame of *Godigbe*, a stylized re-enactment of the history of the Le people (see Chapter 2). This is a conscious attempt to heal the divisions of the past by acknowledging Afegame's foundational status for the Agotimes as a whole. At first sight, the enactment of history is rather confusing, because while it might appear that the performance of discovering a place to settle is referring to the founding of Agotime – it depicts a scouting party followed up by a group of settlers disembarking from canoes along the River Todzie – the background narration clearly signals that it is intended to represent the arrival of the Le people in Lekpo on the Atlantic coastline. Hence Lekpo is not discursively anchored as the ultimate place of origin but is identified as a transit point in an even longer history of migration. The reason is that the organizers have chosen to trace their origins to Sudan and Ethiopia – a variant perhaps on the familiar West African claim to Middle East origins.[72] Surprisingly perhaps, in the light of the dispute with Adaklu, the organizers have not chosen to make a statement about their settlement in Agotime itself – although the allusion to settling an *empty* place could perhaps be considered a coded reference.

Godigbe is usually followed by a day dedicated to keep-fit activities, in which a route march by Customs trainees assumes pride of place. There is also a football competition, which in 2016 included an entry from an Adame team. Communal labour is also mobilized to clean (and cleanse) the Agotime towns, especially those where activities are programmed. The next day is generally designated as Women and Children's Day and is held in the Agotime towns in rotation. In 2015 and 2016, this took place in Wodome and Adzakpa respectively. Usually, this entails extended speeches that highlight the continuing relevance of cultural practices such as the *dipo* initiation rites that the Agotimes share with the Krobo,[73] and which again distinguish them from their Ewe neighbours. Although it took place on a different day in 2016, a highlight is *Adziawofetormedede*, in which the older women in Kpetoe draw water from the Todzie River and process, with pots on their heads, to where the chiefs are assembled.[74] This is really the only occasion on which any significance is attributed to the Todzie River, and even then it is not ritualized in any obvious sense. At least half a day is dedicated to the open-air kente-weaving

---

[72] This is the version that also appears in Makaku, *A Brief History of the Lehs*, p. 1.

[73] Since 2003, there has been an attempt to build closer links, with people from Agotime and Krobo Odumasi attending each other's festivals.

[74] For more than a decade, this involved Julia Azuma-Mensah, the MP for the area.

Figure 13.1 Kente-weaving competition, 2016. Photograph by author.

competition in Kpetoe (Figure 13.1), with the winner being presented to the audience and carried on a kind of a plinth at the final durbar. The competition is sometimes followed by a fashion show and a beauty pageant that culminates in the crowning of "Miss Kente". All of these activities, the latter of which are now ticketed events, are intended to appeal to the youth. The fact that so many Agotimes return from Accra and further afield to take part is an indicator of considerable success in this regard in recent years.

In early iterations of the festival, the 'firing of musketry' took place towards the beginning of the festival, but this has tended to be shifted backwards in the programme. On this day, which is second only to the closing durbar in its importance, everyone dresses in red – the colour of mourning – and converges on the town that has been designated to host the event. The entire performance is steeped in ambiguity, in that through the dances, and re-enactment of mock battles, the *avafiawo* revel in references to their prowess as warriors. But the performance always ends with a symbolic laying down of arms and an acceptance of the message of peace. In crucial respects, therefore, the 'firing of musketry' represents a scaled-down version of *Avakeza*. As with much else, the event has become more formalized and less spontaneous in its performance. In Adedome in 2005, the event was dominated by the two *avafiawo* and their followers – with equal weight accorded to Akoto and Agbovi – while Nene Keteku and other chiefs were present as spectators (see Figure 13.2). In 2016 the programme in Adame was far more elaborate. Unlike in the past, the *prefét* from Agou and the District Chief Executive (DCE) from Agotime-Ziope District participated and delivered speeches. Nene Keteku did not attend in person, but a speech was read on his behalf. In the absence of an Agbovi chief, the incumbent having died in 2014, the field was ostensibly open for Nene

Figure 13.2 Firing of musketry, Adedome, 2005. Photograph by author.

Akoto Sah to occupy the limelight. However, a standoff ensued when the chief of Nyitoe unexpectedly entered the grounds in a palanquin of his own. Although the latter was forced to withdraw, this incident underlined that the maintenance of status hierarchies remains a sensitive issue during public events.[75]

The Adame proceedings also highlighted the differential ways in which national politics makes its presence felt. In 2015, primary elections for the choice of a National Democratic Congress (NDC) parliamentary candidate had been held in advance of the 2016 national elections. The sitting MP, Juliana Azumah-Mensah from Kpetoe was standing down after three terms, and the expectation was that someone from Ziope would succeed her. In Agotime, some were of the opinion that this would be acceptable provided the position of DCE changed hands in the opposite direction. When the candidate from Ziope duly won the party nomination, one of the losing candidates from Agotime announced his intention to stand as an independent. The complication was that the latter was a member of one of the planning sub-committees for *Agbamevoza*. Amidst allegations that the constituency NDC was seeking to sabotage the festival,[76] Nene Keteku made a pointed and public declaration that *Agbamevoza* was not the creation of the political parties and that no

---

[75] By 2016, the number of palanquin chiefs had been expanded to four, to include the Akpokope chief and Nene Korsorku from Kpetoe. The fact that the status of Nyitoe as a 'real' Agotime town is in question made this intervention especially contentious.

[76] The organizers, for example, introduced a levy on motorcycle taxis, *okada*, which the DCE claimed was illegal. The proliferation of *okada* at the expense of the taxi was a new development and a potential source of revenue that the organizers sought to tap.

Figure 13.3 Nene Akoto Sah riding on a palanquin to final durbar, 2005.

politician, other than the invited dignitaries, would be permitted to speak. During the 'firing of musketry' in Adame, the DCE in fact delivered a speech that introduced the NDC candidate to the assembled audience – precipitating a demand that the New Patriotic Party (NPP) and independent candidates should be accorded the same recognition. The altercation was remarkable because the event in question was being hosted in Togo. The notion that a Togolese political dispute might be publicly aired in Kpetoe would have been unthinkable – underlining the extent to which *Agbamevoza* has continued to be treated as a Ghanaian affair even when it travels across the border.

The festival always reaches its climax with the closing durbar at the grounds of the Customs, Excise and Preventive Service (CEPS) Training Academy, which is the national training school. At the durbar, every man and woman dons his or her finest kente, including most of the invited guests. A conscious effort is made to publicly acknowledge the rank and role of all the key participants. While the stars of the show are the *avafiawo*, riding on their palanquins in battle dress (see Figure 13.3), Nene Keteku presides from a raised dais in the full splendour of his kente cloth (see Figure 13.4). His importance is also reflected in the fact that he is the only Agotime chief who makes a substantive speech to the assembled guests. Understandably, much is made by Nene Keteku, and the invited speakers alike, of kente as a cultural product that the Agotimes can claim as their own unique contribution to the cultural pantheon of Ghana. Another recurring theme is the importance of weaving in creating employment and of the festival itself in boosting tourism in the Region. In 2016, *Agbamevoza* received extensive media coverage as well as external sponsorship. Indeed, by common consensus the festival, from which only the Akpokope chief was conspicuously absent, was the best

Figure 13.4 Nene Keteku III at final durbar, 2005, with Nene Agbovi
seated to his right with cap. Photograph by author.

patronized and most successful to date. The participation of chiefly delegations
from the Volta Region and Central Regions was taken as a matter of particular
pride because it signalled recognition on a national stage.[77]

This raises the question of the role played by state actors. Festivals such
as this are of fundamental importance because they enable states to render
themselves visible and to participate in performative rituals that both convey
the idea of the state and its material embodiments. State actors are in a strong
bargaining position. For *Agbamevoza* to take place at all, it is necessary for the
authorities to be flexible in their management of border crossings. For some
years now, they have suspended routine checks during the days when it is
anticipated that people – including tourists – will cross the border to take part
in proceedings. These days of exception enable Agotimes to imagine themselves living in a borderless world, but always in the knowledge that the
concessions are strictly time-limited. In Kpetoe, security is provided by the
Police and to some extent by CEPS, which gives the Ghanaian state a formal
stake in the proceedings. A different culture of policing in Togo was on display
in 2016 when the audience in Adame was informed that it was in the presence
of the military and paramilitaries who would arrest anyone who failed to
respect the rules. During the actual firing of musketry, a security cordon was
placed around the field. All of this was intended to underline that the Togolese
state was very much present and taking an active interest. At the final durbar,
the Volta Regional Minister and other government representatives are usually

---

[77] The Avatime paramount chief, Osie Adza Tekpor VII, was amongst those in attendance.

counted amongst the invited guests. In 2016, President John Mahama was supposed to attend, but withdrew at the last minute to general disappointment. The Togolese do not appear to have sent a Minister to any of the durbars, but the Ambassador has attended on occasion.

Where states rub up against each other, it is important to maintain the appearance of parity. In 2016, there was simultaneous translation between English and French for those who did not speak Ewe. There was probably nobody present who spoke only French, but it was necessary to be seen to respect the official language of the Togolese state. Interestingly, the translation was more cursory during *Godigbe*, where the alternation was between Ewe and Adangbe, thus highlighting the special status of the latter language in Afegame. The attendance of state officials is highly valued because it is a marker of the importance which the authorities ascribe to the traditional area, but on a more mundane level it is what ensures that the media are present and engaged. Not surprisingly, there is an occasional clash between competing status hierarchies. At the close of the final durbar in 2016, for example, the exit of one of the *avafiawo* on his palanquin blocked the vehicle of the Regional Minister who, according to state protocol, ought to have been permitted to leave first. By giving way only grudgingly the chief and his retinue were reiterating the point made earlier in the week by Nene Keteku, namely that the festival is the work of the Agotime people and not the Ghanaian state. In Ghana, even government officials are treated as guests entering onto the terrain that is owned by traditional authority. In Togo, by contrast, state authorities assert their own co-ownership of the performative space that a festival such as this affords. The differences may appear subtle, but they reflect fundamental differences arising out of the divergent manner in which state institutions have been assembled over more than a century.

What this extended discussion of *Agbamevoza* points to is a conscious effort to (re)build a sense of Agotime community *in spite of* the border. This was also manifested in other moments of engagement with agents of the state. On one occasion in 2001, when I returned to Kpetoe after an absence, I was regaled by a story that was doing the rounds in town. A native of Kpetoe had died in Lomé, and his family had arranged for the body to be claimed from the mortuary and transported home for the funeral. When the vehicle carrying the corpse reached the road barrier on the outskirts of Kpetoe, CEPS officers asked the occupants where they were coming from. When it transpired that they had entered from Togo, the officers asked to see the appropriate paper-work. When they were unable to produce any documents, the occupants were instructed to return to Togo to carry out the necessary formalities. The vehicle headed back in the direction of Batome Junction, but then took a diversion along one of the unofficial dirt tracks, circumvented the Customs barrier and entered Kpetoe further to the north. That evening a wake was held and the following morning, after the church service, the funeral cortege processed towards the cemetery. When it reached the same Customs barrier, but from the opposite direction, the officers on duty thought they recognized some of the mourners from the day before and enquired whether they were indeed the same people. The latter responded that they were surely confusing them with another group of people and proceeded on their way. The encounter was a source of great merriment, not least to Nene Keteku, but there was also a serious point behind the encounter: that is, while government officials felt in their rights to demand compliance with the laws of Ghana, mourners believed they had every right to transport a body across the border for burial. For some years, they had been prising open every chink in the armoury of the state in order to cement connections between the two halves of Agotime.

But Agotimes are constantly reminded that the same border has become inscribed in their daily lives. Hence it is not just the distinct configuration of state institutions that matters: as important are those differences arising from the lived experiences of Agotimes on the two sides of the line. A border effect is reflected in the mutual stereotypes that Ghanaian and Togolese Agotimes hold on to. A common perception of the Ghanaian Agotimes is that they "know how to enjoy",[78] but that they are also litigious and disrespectful of authority. The first observation was captured in a reflection by a female informant in Togo who sought to explain why Ghanaians embraced kente-wearing on the basis of their willingness to embrace life. The second is clearly informed by the repetitive cycle of chieftaincy disputes in Ghana, but it also derives from the experience of land litigation of which many Togolese have had some experience. It is symptomatic that when the CEPS Training School was being constructed, there was fierce disagreement over who the land belonged to. The Togolese generally consider that there is a clear procedure for handling disputes that are referred to the chiefs' courts in the first instance, but with a right of appeal upwards to the civil courts.[79] It is widely believed on both sides of the border that cases are settled more expeditiously in Togo, whereas in Ghana they tended to drag on indefinitely, thereby unleashing a kind of snowball effect.

The third observation is based on a perception of the scant respect with which chiefs in Ghana are supposedly treated by their subjects. The sense of a moral decline was made explicit in a speech given by Nene Keteku after the church service that kick-started Agbamevoza in 2007:

---

[78] Fieldwork diary, 5 September 2003.

[79] In 2001, the Kpodjahon chief said that the chef de village would normally hear the case first, with an appeal to the chef de canton and from there the case was referred to Kpalime and eventually Lome. Fieldwork diary, 4 April 2001.

At the end of the mass, Nene Nuer Keteku III spoke. He expressed disappointment that so few people had come to the church service and commented that people from Togo had come very early, but many Kpetoe people were missing. He noted that the weavers were missing despite the fact that this was a kente festival. He then chided the people of Kpetoe for not respecting their chiefs and elders, which included gossiping about them and refusing to attend meetings when called. He said that many people had put up storey-buildings in Kpetoe in the past, but they were now crumbling and their owners were poor. The reason, he suggested, is that Kpetoe was cursed because of the fact that its people did not respect the chiefs and elders. He also noted that the chiefs were now working closely together and it was up to the people to come together in unity.[80]

During fieldwork, chiefs on both sides freely reflected on the distinct patterns on the two sides of the border. In an extended comment, Nene Keteku observed that in Togo the chiefs had real powers of enforcement, unlike in Ghana where he claimed that successive governments had weakened the institution:

When they take a case to the chief of Batoume now, he is not a canton [chief], but woe betides you if you don't attend. But here they will bring a land case: the person will just come and tell you the person should take it to High Court. Because the governments didn't give us any recognition! ... Right now, if two people fight in this house now, or somebody come and take somebody's things here now and there is a scuffle over it and they bring it to me as the chief of the town, one person can come and look at you and say he is sorry, it isn't that he didn't respect you but the person should take him to High Court. And that's the end! When you go to Togo, they respect. You can't just do any foolish thing there! The chief can just give orders and they flog you there severely: you will see ... But here in Kpetoe town right ... there is a boy he used to come from London, when he comes the moment he gets to the town he becomes a lunatic. He goes about beating people indiscriminately. When they take him to the Police, the Police just say "We are fed up with this man. You take him away." That's all. But you can't do that in Togo ... If we are not giving the proper discipline in the various villages, you don't expect discipline in the country.[81]

In 2001, Nene Makaku V claimed to have been shoved by a young man (probably the same individual) when he remonstrated with him for dangerous driving and asserted that such a thing would have been unthinkable in Togo.[82] Chiefs there generally agreed, but then Kpetoe had more of the unruly dynamics associated with a large town. Some Togolese chiefs considered that a proliferation of chiefs in Kpetoe made it difficult to uphold respect for the institution. Although there had been an increase in the number of Togolese canton chiefs, the situation had stabilized, and the feeling was that the traditional authorities continued to command greater respect as a consequence. The underlying reason for the difference is that chieftaincy is not regulated by

[80] Fieldnotes on *Agbamevoza*, 2–9 September 2007.
[81] Interview with Nene Keteku, 26 March 2001.
[82] Observations by Nene Makaku V; fieldwork diary, 3 April 2001.

the state in Ghana, whereas chiefs remain part and parcel of the state apparatus in Togo. The difference was brought home to me some months after Nene Makaku shared his grievance. On a particular day I travelled to Batoumé with a view to meeting with Togbe Apaloo IV. I quickly realized that I had chosen the wrong day to pay a surprise visit because there was already a queue of people waiting patiently outside the home of the chief. The latter, it turned out, was hearing cases that day and did so on a regular basis. I learned that Togbe Apaloo did not merely settle personal disputes, but also assumed some responsibility for criminal cases such as common assault or theft. He had the power to detain offenders, and if the cases were serious enough, his responsibility was to send them to the police in Kévé. In this case, the state was effectively working through the office of the chief who derived a large part of his right of command from the Togolese administration. Ironically, however, while the Togolese chiefs might appear to be creatures of the state, they have also set themselves up as the defenders of Agotime tradition. When the Asogli paramount chief, Togbe Afede Asor II, passed away in 2001, Agotime chiefs from the two sides of the border met to consider their response. Nene Keteku appeared willing to head an official delegation despite having distanced himself from Asogli in the past. It was the Togolese chiefs who insisted that if Nene Keteku wished to attend the funeral events he should only do so as a private citizen because they did not consider themselves related to Asogli.[83] The manner in which the Togolese chiefs applied pressure to revoke the elevation of the Akpokope chief to the status of a palanquin chief similarly illustrates the attempt to maintain respect for tradition that they thought was being eroded in Ghana.

The Ghanaian stereotype of the Togolese mirrors the stock images attached to themselves in reverse. The Togolese are seen as embodying a certain style that is decidedly un-Ghanaian – manifested for young men in closely cropped hair and for women in the wearing of fashionable wax print. The fact that Lomé is relatively close to towns in Togo, whereas Accra is much further away, means that a certain urban chic rubs off. But the Togolese are generally regarded as being more reserved than their Ghanaian counterparts and as being excessively beholden to authority. One informant jokingly claimed that you could always tell the Togolese because they walked very fast, as if they were being chased by a policeman.[84] Such light-hearted observations reflect a keen appreciation of the fact that for five decades the Togolese had lived in fear of the state, whereas Ghanaians had managed to maintain a margin for manoeuvre even when times were hard. Even today, Ghanaians regard an

---

[83] They asked whether the Ho chiefs had sent a delegation when Nene Keteku I had died. Since they had not done so, they took this as proof of the lack of a relationship. Interview with Togbe Nyagamago Pattah IV, 15 August 2002.

[84] Fieldwork diary, 29 March 2001.

encounter with Togolese officials as something to be avoided. By contrast, the Police and CEPS in Kpetoe have been assimilated to the category of 'stranger'. The main Police station and the CEPS Academy were built on land that has an owner. In the former case, the chief of the Dapaah clan treated the Police as his paying tenants until very recently when a new District headquarters was constructed on the road to Ho.[85] In such an instance, it is state officials who are expected to act with deference in their dealings with the landowner, even if this is generally transacted with good humour on both sides. The somewhat distant and inscrutable Togolese state contrasts with the everyday familiarity associated with functionaries in Kpetoe. The Togolese policemen who used to occupy the post at Wodome enjoyed good relations with the community that hosted them, but they construed themselves as agents of the central state and never as tenants. In these apparently small details, we can observe the ways in which the larger social contracts and local understandings of community have become intertwined in very different ways.

The paradox is the fact that while the border as a physical obstacle scarcely exists – except as a road surface or as an imaginary line linking border pillars – it has remained important as a field of social action. In the sense conveyed by Donna Flynn, borderlanders imagine that they 'own' the border[86] and yet are also moulded by it in profound ways.[87] The complexities are especially apparent if one scales down to the level where settlements are located hard against the international border. During fieldwork, it was clear that many Togolese Agotimes routinely made use of the health clinic in Kpetoe rather than the more distant facilities in Kévé. In addition, many children attended schools on the Ghana side of the border, crossing back and forth on a daily basis. None of this was regarded as controversial, but other aspects of strad-dling raised more delicate issues. Sarakope is a village that appears to be divided in two by the Ho–Aflao road – although strictly speaking it would not have existed were it not for the existence thereof. Most of the people residing in Togolese Sarakope are Avenors who identify strongly with their home towns in Ghana. They vote in Togolese elections on the basis that they are resident in Togo, but they also vote in Ghana on the principle that Avenors are by definition Ghanaian. By contrast, those living in Sarakope-Ghana would not deign to cast their ballot in elections in Togo, which they regard as a foreign country. Here, we can see that the border remains important to the manner in which local populations construe the relationship between nationality and local

---

[85] However, many of the Policemen and women continued to lodge in the old building that was built alongside Nene Dapaah's compound.

[86] The new Police headquarters were located in the new District Assembly buildings. These observations are based on informal discussions with Nene Dapaah.

[87] Donna Flynn, "'We are the border': identity, exchange and the state along the Benin-Nigeria border", *American Ethnologist* 24 (2), 1997, pp. 311–30.

belonging. Chieftaincy draws on both registers. In Sarakope, the substantive chief lives on the Togolese side of the road, and it would appear that he exercises traditional authority on the Ghana side with the consent of Nene Keteku.[88] In Wodome, the chief is also located in Togo and he nominates a 'headman', or *odikro*, to carry out his duties on the Ghanaian side of the road.[89] These local arrangements are not formally recognized by either state. In Ghana a chief has no right of command anyway, while a Togolese chief clearly has no authority in Ghana. As far as the Togolese authorities are concerned, the Sarakope and Wodome chiefs derive their authority from the *préfet*. Now that the police station in Wodome has closed, the chief of that village is the sole local embodiment of the Togolese state.[90] But it is highly significant that the chiefs of Wodome and Sarakope openly acknowledge their own stranger status within Agotime by deferring to Nene Keteku in Kpetoe.

Further north, if one draws an imaginary line between pillars number 24 and 25, the small village of Agohome, which comprises a mixture of Andos and Agotimes, is cut in two by the border. Those living on the Togolese side of the line regard themselves as Ghanaian and claim that the Togolese authorities more or less acknowledge this reality by not entering the village. They vote in Ghanaian elections and send their children to school inside Ghana.[91] During fieldwork, an even more fascinating arrangement was apparent at Ibenyeme, which sits at the fork in the road at Batome Junction. In 2003, the chief of the Togolese settlement was proud to proclaim his unique status as an 'international chief'. He hailed from the Ghanaian side of the road, where he was enstooled as *odikro* of Wusikope in 1966, bearing the stool name of Nene Odikro Todze II. But in order to protect his lands from encroachment he relocated to the Togolese side of the road.[92] The authorities there finally recognized him as a substantive chief in January 2002 without his having relinquished his position in Ghana.[93] Even more surprisingly, his son, who also lived on the Togolese side of the road, was elected District Assemblyman in Ghana. Both spoke excellent English and considered themselves to be as much Ghanaian as Togolese. Such straddling is not officially accepted and almost certainly would not be condoned if it came to light. But at the border a degree of fuzziness is accepted provided nobody chooses to make an issue of

---

[88] Interview with Kodjo Sadja, Agotime-Sarakope, 3 September 2003.

[89] Interview with Togbe Drafor and others, Agotime-Wodome, 3 September 2003.

[90] Interestingly, in 2014 the National Election Commission of Ghana plastered voter registration information to the walls of the building, apparently in ignorance of the fact that they were in Togo. In 2016, these had been removed.

[91] Fieldwork diary, 11 September 2003.

[92] His own house faced the Ghanaian border post at Batome Junction, which was a statement of his dual status.

[93] Interview with Nene Odikro II, Agotime-Ibenyeme (Togo), 2 September 2003.

it. But even here where state norms are warped, it is significant that some people on the Ghana side of the line complained that since the chief lived inside Togo – if only by a matter of metres – he ought to be replaced.[94] The idea that chieftaincy should rest within national containers has therefore been internalized at some level.

In Agotime, there is a very strong identification with home towns, especially those that have a very deep history such as Afegame and Zukpe. This localized sense of community co-exists with a strong sense of national identity. It is the level in between – a sense of belonging to an entity called *Agotime* – that is in some respects the most problematic. By comparison with Kayong Kalorn, the attempt to assert a distinct ethnic identity is rather muted in Agotime. In Afegame, there is an interest in playing up the links with the Adangbe of coastal Ghana. There is also a parallel attempt to insist on close cultural links with the Krobo of the Eastern Region. But the Adangbe category is not really ethnic in anything other than a rough cultural sense. More surprisingly per-haps, the feeling of being at loggerheads with neighbouring Ewe peoples is rarely expressed in ethnic terms. At some level, Agotimes accept that they are closely connected with their neighbours, whose people they have absorbed and whose language they have adopted as their own. This is reflected in the inconsistent use of chieftaincy titles. The Afegame chief designates himself as the Le Mantse, echoing Adangbe usage. The other chiefs in Ghana tend to call themselves 'Nene', as does the Zukpe chief, but Togolese chiefs such as that of Adzakpa prefer the Ewe title of 'Togbe'. In Ghana, where the salience attached to the traditional area counts for more than ethnicity, the real issue is one of advancing the status of Agotime within a pecking order. Although it is entirely conceivable that appeals to ethnicity could be instrumentalized in the future, this seems a long way off. It is even less likely to find favour in Togo where the Adangbe settlements scattered across the south have weaker links to the Ga and Krobo of Ghana than to their Ewe neighbours. There is really no entirely satisfactory answer to what it means to be Agotime in the present – except, paradoxically enough, as part of a loose collection of people forged through a notionally timeless history of migration and admixture.

Conclusion

In this chapter, I have shown how attempts to define community have been mediated by the existence of the international border in often unexpected and counter-intuitive ways. In the Senegambian case, the fact that historical Kombo was located in the Gambia whereas Narang and Fogny-Jabangkunda

---

[94] The fact that he has adopted the title of *Odikro* as a family surname caused some irritation.

were placed in the Casamance meant that the border was much less contentious. Nevertheless, the Mandinka towns have maintained a strong sense of their interconnectedness based on histories of migration. Moreover, there has never been the same restrictions on maintaining active relations across the border as in the trans-Volta. The MFDC insurgency played a catalytic role in that it disrupted everyday relations across the border and placed a premium on self-defence. The attempt to unite under the umbrella of a Fogny-Jabangkunda association represented an attempt to invoke the memory of a polity that had once existed. This history was not elaborated upon in great detail, but it did provide a charter of a kind for the Mandinka and some of the Jola settlements. It had much less appeal to the more recent Jola migrants, most of whom hailed from further south in the Casamance. Whereas the Mandinka straddled the border, the Karoninka/Kalorn had migrated towards it from Bliss and Karone to the south. They had a long history of seasonal migration to Kombo, and it is often claimed that they were there before the Mandinka arrived. In recent decades the Karoninka have settled in substantial numbers on both sides and have converted to Islam. It is amongst the migrants that the effort to mobilize a sense of Kalorn identity has held the greatest salience. History has not figured greatly, except with reference to the issue of first settlement. Kayong Kalorn in fact pursued a highly presentist agenda, partly in response to the ethnic politics of the Jammeh regime. It sought to disseminate a codified version of Kalorn culture, to promote the language, and to resist the tendency for Muslim converts to merge into the Mandinka population. Kayong Kalorn has been most active on the Gambia side of the border and has struggled to win the active adherence of those in Bliss and Karone for whom language loss and cultural assimilation are less of a pressing issue. In the Gambia itself, the Kalorn agenda was promoted with the support of the Jammeh government, which was keen to boost the number of Jola within the population. Because Kayong Kalorn was actively distancing itself from the Jola category, it had to tread carefully. In Narang and Fogny-Jabangkunda, where this framing has potentially greater resonance, Kalorn from the area have played a limited role in the association. As in Agotime, therefore, the border has provided a spur to unity, but at the same time it has inscribed the differences between otherwise related peoples.

In Agotime, the changing political context of the 1990s opened a space within which it was possible to envisage recreating a sense of belonging to a trans-boundary community by means of a cross-border festival. The work of recapturing a 'lost' history was integral to this project, but created problems of its own because while the preference of Nene Keteku was for a version that placed Kpetoe at the centre, the rest of Agotime adhered to a much more de-centred conception of their history. Moreover, in Kpetoe itself the *avafiawo* were amongst those who claimed that it was their forebearers who had provided leadership in the nineteenth century. As I have also indicated, the emphasis on the martial prowess of the Agotime also turned out to be highly divisive. The shift to an emphasis on kente weaving as an ostensibly more innocuous focus for *Agbamevoza*, proved problematic because Agotimes in Togo felt much less affinity with the product. In a curious way, therefore, the border assumed a double aspect: it both provided something against which to mobilize and yet also reinforced a sense of difference between the Agotime on either side of what is in many respects an imaginary line. This underlines the manner in which different national imaginaries have taken hold, but it is also indicative of the variant ways in which state institutions have become embedded within the borderlands. This is most obvious with respect to traditional authority, which is formally integrated into the structures of the state in Togo, but not in Ghana.

Conclusion

Boundaries and State-Making – Comparisons through Time and Space

One of the most persistent tropes relating to African borders, which is much beloved by travel writers and bloggers, is the remote and dusty crossing that appears to have been all but forgotten by national governments: the roads are rough, there is no electricity and formalities are adhered to, but in a scarcely recognizable bureaucratic form. Of course, it is easy to point to such representations as, at best, partial truths. Many of Africa's capitals and many of its largest cities are actually located on international boundaries, while border towns are often bustling zones of engagement where substantial volumes of trade and large numbers of people enter and exit on a daily basis. Viewed from the margins, it is the multiple levels of connectivity – between settlements on two sides of the border but also much further afield – that stands out. Finally, with so many resources currently being invested in cross-border infrastructure, the stock images of remoteness and neglect seem more misplaced than ever. In this book, I have repeatedly underlined the vitality of African borderlands, but I have also sought to advance a much larger claim, namely that the geographical margins have shaped states at least as much as the other way around.

I have argued for the centrality of the margins in three specific respects: *temporally*, in that colonial states were forged in a protracted process of converting frontier zones into boundaries; *institutionally*, in that the bureaucratic fabric and fiscal structure of colonial and post-colonial states were shaped by the management of border flows; and *politically*, in the sense that the larger social contracts have been mediated by border dynamics. At the same time, I have examined some of the ways in which states have moulded a context in which it has been possible to re-fashion notions of community. The book has taken the form of an extended reciprocal comparison with a view to distilling insights that would not necessarily have emerged from a single-case study.[1] I have drawn on these insights to make larger statements about both

---

[1] Gareth Austin, "Reciprocal comparison and African history: tackling conceptual Eurocentrism in the study of Africa's economic past", *African Studies Review* 50 (3) 2007.

state formation and space-making that have a bearing on debates about the spatial factor in African history and its role in politics today.[2]

The nature of the enquiry has required me to repeatedly shift the spatial focus and to grapple with processes unfolding at multiple scales. As a consequence, the text has dealt with disparate materials and has been written in contrasting registers. For example, I have addressed taxation at a rather abstract level, drawing on administrative records, whereas my treatment of trade and land has concentrated on individual strategies and is grounded in a combination of interviews and legal documentation. Equally, I have ranged from the grand abstractions of Five-Year planning documents to the mundane circulation of bottles of gin, bags of rice and tins of sardines. All of these are central to the patterns I have identified, and they speak in equal measure to the relationship between states and their populations. It is not possible to repeat all of the particular arguments I have advanced, which are mostly summarized at the end of each chapter. However, I do need to recapitulate the principal claims and to bring to the fore a number of transversal themes that emerge out of the text. These are violence (and peace-making), territoriality (including land), taxation, mobility, trade (including smuggling) and consumption. The shifting permutations between them underpin my larger story of change over time.

Temporalities

In this book, I argued for extended temporal connections between state- and space-making processes in the Senegambia and the trans-Volta. In a nutshell, it did not all begin with the Scramble for Africa in the 1880s and 1890s when colonial states and their boundaries were supposedly conjured into existence. But that raises the question of where it makes sense to begin. Methodologically speaking, a useful point of departure is to think about what larger comparisons might prompt one to ask about West African trajectories. When it comes to the history of state formation in Europe, there is a broad consensus that protracted cycles of warfare over territory led to the elaboration of new tax systems and the eventual fixing of territorial boundaries, and that these outcomes in turn shaped the emergence of systems of political representation. It is worth considering how far comparable patterns were evident in West Africa where organized violence was foundational in its own right. It seems clear that the slave trade did not lead to the consolidation of states and the sedimentation of

---

[2] Allen M. Howard and Richard M. Shain, *The Spatial Factor in African History: The Relationship of the Social, Material and the Perceptual* (Leiden and Boston: Brill, 2005); Jeffrey Herbst, *States and Power in Africa: Comparative Lessons in Authority and Control* (Princeton: Princeton University Press, 2000); Catherine Boone, *Political Topographies of the African State: Territorial Authority and Institutional Choice* (Cambridge: Cambridge University Press, 2003).

territorial borders in a uniform manner. It is true that states such as Asante were built on revenues derived from trade taxes and tribute (largely in human form), both of which presumed a sense of territoriality. Slave raiding constituted a mode of theft, as Claude Meillassoux and others have argued.[3] The most obvious beneficiaries were states such as Dahomey and Asante that traded and absorbed large numbers of slaves, but the case of Agotime also exemplifies the manner in which other kinds of polities were constituted through the absorption of captives. At the start of the nineteenth century, a map of West Africa – one that is more detailed than what we actually have at our disposal – would have revealed a scattering of states with identifiable borders, no-man's lands between polities, and extensive frontier regions existing outside the control of any state.[4] These spatial arrangements were closely related in that states systematically raided the frontier zones for slaves. Violence heightened a tendency towards segmentation, and indeed resistance to state formation, broadly along the lines that James C. Scott has posited for South-East Asia.[5] This was true, for example, of the Jola and the Balanta of what is now Guinea-Bissau and the Casamance, who were able to sustain high population densities on the basis of rice culture in areas that were less susceptible to raiding.[6] At the same time, the history of Agotime exemplifies how polities that actively participated in the slave trade found ways of channelling violence, managing indebtedness and maintaining physical security in the absence of states. In the nineteenth century, the weakening of the largest entities, which was in part a consequence of the steady decline of the Atlantic slave trade, led to a geographical contraction of states and a further expansion of frontier zones. It is certainly plausible to attribute the African frontier phenomenon to low land-to-population ratios, and to link this to a deeply rooted discourse of landlord and stranger that is so familiar from oral traditions.[7] But the spatial configurations

[3] Meillassoux, Claude, *The Anthropology of Slavery: The Womb of Iron and Gold* (London: Athlone Press, 1991).

[4] For a discussion, see Paul Nugent, "Arbitrary lines and the people's minds: a dissenting view on colonial boundaries in West Africa", in Paul Nugent and A.I. Asiwaju (eds.), *African Boundaries: Barriers, Conduits and Opportunities* (London: Frances Pinter, 1996).

[5] James C. Scott, *The Art of Not Being Governed: An Anarchist History of Upland Southeast Asia* (New Haven and London: Yale University Press, 2009).

[6] Walter Hawthorne, *Planting Rice and Harvesting Slaves: Transformations along the Guinea-Bissau Coast, 1400–1900* (Portsmouth: Heinemann, 2003).

[7] Igor Kopytoff, "The internal African frontier: the making of African political culture", in Igor Kopytoff (ed.), *The African Frontier: The Reproduction of Traditional African Societies* (Bloomington and Indianapolis: Indiana University Press, 1987). See also Benedikt Korf, Tobias Hagmann and Martin Doevenspeck, "Geographies of violence and sovereignty: the African Frontier revisited", in Benedikt Korf and Timothy Raeymaekers (eds.), *Violence on the Margins: States, Conflicts and Borderlands* (New York and Houndmills, 2013); and Herbst, *States and Power in Africa*, ch. 2.

were clearly rooted in the dynamics of the slave trade, which played off the underlying demographic realities and indeed magnified their effects.

The no-man's land between Agotime and Adaklu provides an excellent example of the ways in which even decentralized polities exhibited a sense of territoriality. The Agotime conformed to a common pattern of using settlements to peg the margins of the polity. Narang and Fogny-Jabangkunda conformed to a classic slaving frontier, but even here there remained a sense of the southern limits of Kombo. In both the trans-Volta and the Senegambia, a premium was attached to land that lay in close proximity to rivers and forests that were rich in resources. But in the context of an economy of pillage much of the optimal land was left uncultivated. Aside from defensible positions, there was a premium attached to securing corridors for safe passage along the principal trading routes. Historians have yet to address the various permutations in a sustained way, and what is offered in this book is intended as a first cut. But what clearly emerges is that the diverse spatial configurations provided the unstable foundations upon which colonial states came to rest.

As I have indicated in Chapter 1, there is a very well-worn debate about whether the European push into Africa at the end of the nineteenth century was driven by crises at the periphery or the will to empire in Europe.[8] I have leaned towards the former with respect to the 1880s, but I have pointed to a much longer gestation period and a different constellation of political forces. During the height of the Atlantic trade, changing patterns of consumption became closely linked to a shifting landscape of alliances. European merchants purchased slaves and sold goods that were imported from Europe and the Americas – a list that was not confined to firearms. These circulated in the interior and helped to fuel cycles of indebtedness. The pre-history of colonial states lies in European mediation in commercial disputes and seizures for debt (*panyarring*), which became pressing concerns for European traders at the coast as well as for African traders in the interior. The main concern was to protect property rights – remembering, of course, that property included human chattel and that it could be social as much as private in nature. The mercantile and legal origin of colonial states is something that left an enduring legacy that deserves a more detailed treatment. A second driver lay in novel expressions of political community. Over the course of the nineteenth century, African populations in the coastal ports began to make their own, often very vocal, demands for what we now call 'public goods': going beyond dispute settlement to include the basics of life such as space for housing and potable water. The ways in which Africans in towns articulated these demands helped

---

[8] Ronald Robinson and John Gallagher, *Africa and the Victorians: The Official Mind of Imperialism* (London: Macmillan, 1961); P.J. Cain and A.G. Hopkins, *British Imperialism 1688–2000*, 2nd edn. (Harlow and London: Pearson Education, 2002), pp. 26–30.

to shape a discourse of entitlement that subsequently influenced colonial politics in profound ways.

The accumulating demands upon fledgling administrations posed a challenge because governments in Europe were reluctant to commit public funds to serve the interests of the small trading community in Africa. The means of squaring the circle was for those who ran the coastal settlements, who also tended to be drawn from the ranks of the merchant community, to re-adjust the terms of trade. They increasingly refused the payment of taxes to African rulers, whilst endeavouring to suck more of the trade towards their own ports. It was this effort to restructure and respace trade that led to a more active engagement with what I have dubbed the proximate and further frontiers. The objective was not to control territory, which would have been disavowed by the metropolitan authorities, but to increase the volume of trade that was captured. This, in turn, provided the key to maximizing revenues under an overall regime of low taxation. At the same time, revenue from import duties – which were essentially a tax on African consumption – deflected some of the burden back onto urban populations. The further frontier regions developed a particularly close relationship with the port cities, which was reflected in the forging of marital alliances, the extension of relationships of credit and in the emerging practice of conflict mediation. These fluid zones of engagement at the frontiers eventually solidified in the shape of colonial boundaries as European competition escalated in the context of the first Great Depression. The cherished notion that Europeans partitioned Africa at the Berlin Conference has been debunked,[9] although it remains surprisingly resilient. The process of turning frontiers into borders in West Africa began decades before 1884, and it continued some decades thereafter. The institutional practices of emerging states were, however, elaborated through concrete practices such as treaty-signing, surveying, map-making, and intelligence-gathering – and of course, the regulation and taxation of trade. It was only after a period of bureaucratic consolidation in the twentieth century that colonial regimes were in a position to convert border regions into peripheries.

Institutions

In this study, I have placed considerable emphasis on taxation for the reason that it speaks to issues of institutional capacity, but also reveals a great deal about the ways in which states engaged with their populations. Fred Cooper's shorthand of the 'gatekeeper state' points to the ways in which colonial states

---

[9] Simon Katzenellenbogen, "'It didn't happen at Berlin': politics, economics and ignorance in the setting of Africa's colonial boundaries", in Nugent and Asiwaju (eds.), *African Boundaries*.

depended on regulating and taxing commercial flows.[10] In this, we can see broad continuities with the patterns that were established in the nineteenth century. But I have sought to offer a more nuanced rendering of the colonial record based on a comparison of the ways in which different states taxed and prioritized heads of expenditure. In every case, the outcome reflected the jockeying for advantage by European vested interests, including commercial firms and mining companies, as well as the demands levelled by urban populations – but also by rural constituencies. In the Gold Coast, where British attempts to introduce personal taxation were decisively rebuffed in the nineteenth century, the authorities faced sustained pressure to deliver public goods, most notably roads in rural areas. These demands were couched in the language of citizenship despite the fact that Gold Coasters were legally colonial subjects. This culminated in a fiscal structure that relied overwhelmingly on import duties – and hence on taxing the increased consumption that came with the expansion of earnings from cocoa.[11] Personal taxation was eventually introduced to the Northern Territories but was never attempted again in the Gold Coast proper. Nevertheless, the state managed to tax its population relatively heavily through recourse to high levels of import duty, and it was also successful in diversifying its revenue streams over time to include export duties.

In the Gambia, which was a very different kind of British colony, the authorities successfully imposed a yard tax, but continued to rely overwhelmingly upon Customs duties. The state imposed a significantly lower burden on the population than in the Gold Coast, but the flip-side was that it delivered much less in the way of amenities outside of Bathurst. In Senegal, there was a much greater incentive to raise head taxes, given that the Customs duties accrued to the Federal administration, while expenditure was heavily concentrated on the Four Communes. The administration in French Mandated Togoland taxed Africans less heavily than in Senegal because, lying outside of the Federation, it was able to draw on its own Customs receipts. The state also facilitated wider access to social amenities than in Senegal, although it did preside over a pronounced north–south divide. The significance of these colonial variations became strikingly obvious during the Great Depression when administrative retrenchment and increased taxation in French Togoland contrasted with an ongoing commitment to social expenditure in the Gold Coast. The paradox is that whereas the state in the Gold Coast was the most extraverted of all, it was also the most assiduous in taxing and spending – in

---

[10] Frederick Cooper, *Africa Since 1940: The Past of the Present* (Cambridge: Cambridge University Press, 2002), p. 5.

[11] For a history of consumption in Ghana, see Bianca Murillo, *Market Encounters: Consumer Cultures in Twentieth-Century Ghana* (Athens: Ohio University Press, 2017).

large part because it was responding to sustained pressure from below. Once again, we can point to some continuity from the later nineteenth century when bargains between the British and Gold Coasters were hammered out through repeated cycles of contestation over the terms of the relationship.

The manner in which the local governance structures were consolidated was strikingly divergent across the four cases. In most colonies, the perceived need to collect personal taxes from Africans placed a premium on finding chiefly intermediaries to maintain the population rolls and to physically oversee the collection. Chiefs were normally regarded as an integral part of the state, which meant that they were expected to follow directives and were often punished and or/replaced when they failed to do so. In the early years, European administrators felt it necessary to make regular tours of their districts in order to monitor compliance and to deploy force where necessary, but the intention was to make the appointed chiefs assume greater responsibility. Colonial administrators faced a particular challenge within historical frontier regions where a deep-rooted suspicion of authority was reinforced by a disinclination to deliver taxes – especially those that were levied in kind. The travails of the French administration in the Casamance, where Jola and Karoninka populations repeatedly took up arms to resist demands for *l'impôt*, is illustrative. By constantly reshuffling the pack in a desperate effort to find credible intermediaries, the French authorities compounded their discomfort. The military re-occupation of the Casamance during the First World War signalled that the colonial relationship remained a highly abrasive one long after the French were nominally in control. Across the border, the Gambian authorities benefited from the fact that the Mandinka of Kombo were no strangers to chiefly authority or to systems of direct taxation. By reconciling the old ruling lines with those associated with Fodé Sylla, the authorities eventually found relatively willing collaborators.

In the trans-Volta, the Germans imposed new chiefly intermediaries amongst Ewe populations who had recognized some form of supra-village authority in the past. In Agotime, where there had only been 'big men' and war leaders, or *avafiawo*, the Germans created a headchief from scratch. During the German period, head taxes and forced labour imposed an onerous burden and precipitated a withdrawal of population into the Gold Coast. Across the border, the British had dispensed with direct taxes and had been forced to recognize the de facto autonomy of the chiefs. After the partition of Togoland at the end of the First World War, the French authorities re-introduced head taxes and re-confirmed the chiefly lines. However, the taxes needed to be modulated, for fear of losing population to British territory – which underscores how mindful the authorities needed to be of border dynamics. In British Togoland itself, the chiefs remained in place, but they were no longer required to collect taxes and they now lay outside the structures of the colonial state. This parting of the ways contributed to the emergence of a very different pattern of governance on the two sides of the Togoland border, the legacy of which remains obvious to this day.

Aside from highlighting the variant forms of taxation, my contention is that colonial state practices were shaped in fundamental ways by the imperative of managing border flows. The credibility of the colonial project hinged on asserting effective control at the margins. The French in the Casamance constantly fretted about a possible contagion arising out of the failure of the Portuguese to get a grip on their side of the border, as reflected in constant cattle rustling and periodic rebellions. Even within the Casamance, there was a perception that defiance that went unpunished would lead to increasing disregard for European rule. Secondly, the possibility of achieving colonial *mise en valeur* often depended on tapping labour from well beyond the border. And thirdly, the fiscal base of colonial states hinged on being able to tax and regulate what passed through. At particular moments, colonial regimes found it expedient to share information and to deal with perceived threats in a co-ordinated fashion. But for much of the time, border management assumed the logic of a zero-sum game in which the authorities on either side of the line actively undermined each other's position.

In the Senegambia, there was vigorous competition to control the flow of migrants who were considered essential to the successful promotion of groundnut production and the maximization of yard and head taxes. No sooner had the border been demarcated than the British and the French authorities attempted to repopulate an area that had been ravaged by the violence of the later nineteenth century. Over subsequent decades, the Gambian administration actively solicited seasonal migrants, or 'strange farmers', from French territory. Whereas these were typically drawn from the French Soudan, the British were also interested in poaching Jola populations from the Casamance. The French consented to the migration of 'strange farmers', in part because they could tax them on their return, but they opposed efforts to inveigle the Jola. In the context of a struggle for the demographic upper hand, the Gambian administration set lower taxes and guaranteed access to a wide range of consumer goods that were imported from Britain. But an even greater inducement in the long run was the minimization of barriers of access to farm land. In the Gambia, the *seyfos* and *alkalos* were instructed to make land available to settlers coming from Buluf and Portuguese Guinea with the minimum of fuss. In practice, *kabilo* heads also released land under their own authority. In the Casamance, the French similarly encouraged the relocation of Jola populations from high-density areas to the lightly populated borderlands. The competition between them created a buyer's market, in such a way that migrants frequently crossed the border several times over in search of the right mix of grazing and farm land. The chiefs were generally found welcoming because they had a direct stake in increasing the number of people paying the yard and head taxes. Hence demographic imperatives tended to align with the ambitions of traditional rulers.

Whereas both sets of authorities displayed a keen interest in channelling populations, their approach to cross-border trade was markedly different. The French were concerned about the loss of groundnuts and the importation of British consumer goods from the Gambia. Because the Gambia struggled with a perennial food deficit, which was exacerbated by the presence of the 'strange farmers', there was a lively trade in rice, maize and other foodstuffs that the French authorities were keen to restrict. They did permit the movement of cattle through the border, but subject to the payment of duties. The French authorities imposed a Customs cordon and demanded the active co-operation of the *chefs de village* in monitoring the various flows. By contrast, because the Gambian authorities had an interest in facilitating much of the trade, minimal resources were invested in patrolling the border. Indeed, the Gambian Customs service scarcely operated outside of Bathurst, which meant that basic revenue collection was devolved onto the traditional authorities and the field administration.

In the trans-Volta, the underlying patterns were strikingly different. Although many French Togolanders did migrate to Accra and the Eastern Province, there was relatively little migration in and around the border itself. The exception was in the forested hills of Buem and Akposso to the north where migrants from both sides of the border acquired land for the production of cocoa. Otherwise, mobility was confined to small-scale movements of people seeking to join relatives or to be closer to their farms. In the case of Agotime, for example, a number of villages on the French side were populated by people from Kpetoe who, for some time, continued to send their dead home for burial. The French were mostly concerned about collection of *l'impôt*. But because so much Agotime land was in French Togoland, there was never likely to be a mass exodus into British territory. The really contentious issues turned on the circulation of consumer goods that were rapidly becoming viewed as house-hold necessities. The French authorities persuaded their British counterparts to permit cocoa from British Togoland to be exported along the Kpalimé–Lomé railway. The same British firms who handled the crop also maintained stores in Lomé and in towns across British Togoland, catering to the demand for items like tobacco and sugar. The public finances of the Gold Coast depended overwhelmingly on import duties levied on a single item, namely Dutch gin, which accounted for around a quarter of all revenues during the interwar years. The CPS sought to ensure that spirits entered through Gold Coast ports where it could be taxed at the point of entry. However, British firms like John Holt and G.B. Ollivant also imported Dutch gin and manufactured goods through the port of Lomé. Because these commodities were usually cheaper on the

French side, a lively contraband trade ensued in the 1920s, in which the CPS accused the British firms of being at least tacitly complicit. Unlike in the Gambia, the CPS represented an elite arm of the administration and was able to insist on the imposition of a tight Customs cordon as a deterrent to smugglers. The chiefs were not dragooned into service and tended to express sympathy with their own people in their frequent brushes with the Customs men. By contrast, the French authorities exhibited very little interest in interfering with the commercial flows from which they indirectly benefited. In this, there were some similarities with the insouciant stance of the authorities in the Gambia.

Contracts

My third argument is that the larger social contracts within each of the countries were mediated by border dynamics. Although I have paid some attention to colonial social contracts, the greater part of the analysis concerns the decades after independence when states notionally operated in the service of their populations. I have been conscious of the need to avoid a conflation of states and regimes. In the context of the one-party state and of military rule, these are often difficult to differentiate. In their quest for legitimacy, governments invoked a dynamic role for the state institutions, but the configurations that were assembled usually outlived the regimes in question. In Part III, I dealt with the territorial aspects of post-colonial state-making, whereas in Part IV I concentrated on the recalibration of social contracts over successive decades.

In Chapter 8, which serves as a bridge between the two halves of the book, I identified the Second World War as a pivotal moment when borders were instrumentalized in the struggle for advantage between pro-Vichy regimes in the French colonies and their British rivals. At a time of scarcity, securing access to foodstuffs was considered essential to maintaining the compliance of restless urban populations. The smuggling of consumer goods was actively encouraged by the governments of the Gambia and of French Togoland, whereas the regimes on the other side of the border attempted to impede the flows and to divert surpluses to feed the cities. In both of the sub-regions, the conclusion of hostilities was accompanied by pledges to invest substantial resources in promoting economic development and social improvement. This was part of a very conscious effort by colonial regimes to restore their credibility after the hardships experienced during the 1930s and the war years.

Inevitably, this raised the question of whether development ought to take place within the framework of existing borders or in the context of a territorial reconfiguration. In both the Senegambia and the trans-Volta, there were requests for practical measures to alleviate the impediments that borders brought with them as well demands for their complete erasure. I have proceeded in Chapters 9 and 10 to detail the reasons why these initiatives came to nothing, culminating in borders that were more deeply entrenched than ever after independence. In Senegal, and to some extent the Gambia, sections of the political elite were seduced by the vision of a greater Senegambia that would unify closely related populations. The French had historically framed the issue in terms of the incorporation of the Gambia into Senegal, which would also have resolved the Casamance anomaly once and for all. The British had resisted such overtures in the past and had steadfastly refused to invest in improvements to the Gambia River crossing. But as decolonization gathered pace, they sought to divest themselves of their smallest colony in Africa. Given that the Gambia depended on metropolitan subventions, the British authorities belatedly came round to the position that the colony needed to embrace some form of association with Senegal. The Van Mook mission of 1964, which was mandated to weigh up the options, eventually came down in favour of a federal arrangement that, it maintained, would enable optimal use to be made of the Gambia waterway and would confer significant benefits on both parties. In the event, Gambian politicians demurred because of the implications of entering into a Customs union. The cost of living in the Gambia would have soared, while many ordinary people who had constructed their livelihoods around the existence of the border would have lost out. In the final analysis, the vision of a greater Senegambia foundered for want of popular support on both sides of the border.

During the 1960s, social contracts became encrusted around the distinct bordering practices of the micro-states and their larger neighbours. In its own version of the productive social contract, Senegal sought to balance a range of interests by retaining close economic ties with France, expanding groundnut production in alliance with the Mourides, and nurturing domestic industries in which Senegalese entrepreneurs held a stake. This involved multiple trade-offs that are not so easily accounted for within the model of urban bias that Robert Bates has advanced.[12] Although the intention was to expand urban employment, wages were restrained, and taxes levels were maintained at a rather high level. And while groundnut producers were highly taxed in their own right, this was part of the price to pay for the preferential treatment extended to the Mourides by the Senegalese state. Conversely, the truly voiceless regions of the country, located at the northern, eastern and to some extent the southern peripheries, were the least heavily taxed. In the Gambia, there was never any realistic chance of pursuing an autonomous path to industrial development. The Jawara regime instead sought to maximize its groundnut purchases, whilst increasing the re-export of manufactured goods that entered through the port of

---

[12] Robert Bates, *Markets and States in Tropical Africa: The Political Basis of Agricultural Policies* (Berkeley: University of California Press, 1981).

Banjul. These were considerably cheaper by virtue of being sourced from Asia, which ensured that there would be a ready market for them in Senegal. I have demonstrated that the composite social contract in the Gambia was premised on active complicity between the state and its population in the development of the contraband trade. The state received its cut by taxing the goods at the port, while traders of various kinds were able to profit by despatching them across the border into Senegal. In the 1960s, the Senegalese government complained that the Gambian strategy was explicitly designed to undercut their own economic policy. As the Senegalese authorities imposed tougher controls at the border, the scope for closer co-operation in border management narrowed further.

In the trans-Volta, a popular movement emerged in the post-war years that supported some variant of Ewe and/or Togoland unification. Although I have written on this subject elsewhere, I have returned to the topic for purposes of the larger comparison.[13] The substantive difference with the Senegambia is that the British and French authorities were both firmly opposed to any modification of the existing borders. Although they committed themselves publicly to alleviating the many practical inconveniences, in reality the British were determined to bind their section of Togoland more tightly to the Gold Coast, whereas the French wanted a free hand to absorb their territory into the French Union. Symptomatically, the increased levels of infrastructural spending of the 1950s took the border as an immutable given. Hence, the Volta River Project was approached as if it concerned the Gold Coast exclusively. And while substantial funding was channelled into road building, none of the projects treated the borderlands as an integrated space. The Convention People's Party (CPP) in the Gold Coast came to regard the Togoland unification question as a potential drag on the path to independence. It therefore attacked the political strongholds of the Togoland Congress (TC), deploying the promise of increased development spending as an enticement to the electorate. This strategy was broadly successful as the CPP managed to win over waverers with the additional promise to broker unification with French Togoland after the achievement of Ghanaian independence. The 1956 election and plebiscite effectively sealed the fate of the unification movement, and once Sylvanus Olympio opted for a separate independence for Togo in 1960, the possibility of the two sides coming to a deal on unification evaporated.

---

[13] Paul Nugent, *Smugglers, Secessionists and Loyal Citizens on the Ghana–Togo Frontier: The Lie of the Borderlands Since 1914* (Oxford and Athens: James Currey and Ohio University Press, 2002), ch. 6. The most noteworthy addition to recent scholarship is Kate Skinner, *The Fruits of Freedom in Togoland: Literacy, Politics and Nationalism, 1914–2014* (Cambridge: Cambridge University Press, 2015).

Although Kwame Nkrumah is widely regarded a champion of pan-Africanism, as well as a staunch critic of the artificiality of colonial boundaries, this is difficult to square with the reality that he pushed for a hard border with Togo. In the 1960s, as numerous studies have shown, Ghana's economic strategy shifted from a narrow focus on infrastructural investments to maximizing investments in state industries.[14] The composite social contract foregrounded the productive element, based on the premise that accelerated economic growth would lead to improved living standards and a more equitable distribution of amenities. The resulting balancing act was broadly comparable to that of Senegal. State-led development was expected to create more jobs, but in the short-term workers were expected to accept the necessity of wage restraint. The chiefs continued to enjoy considerable autonomy, but they were expected to support the taxation of cocoa in order to generate the resources to pay for the 'big push' – much as the Mourides were implicated in groundnut pricing in Senegal. The differences lay, firstly, in the manner in which the CPP locked the Trade Union Congress (TUC) and the United Ghana Farmers Council (UGFC) into the structures of the one-party state and used them to drum up support for enforced austerity. And secondly, the CPP was not inclined to offer any assistance to Ghanaian entrepreneurs whose political loyalties were considered doubtful. In Togo, by contrast, the ambition of Olympio was to create a successful entrepôt state, in what was described in the early 1960s as the 'Swiss option'. Although this took some years more to bear fruit, it was already clear in the 1960s that the livelihoods of many Togolese depended on the workings of the contraband economy. As Ghanaian parastatals ran into difficulties, and shortages became endemic, there was an increased incidence of smuggling of cocoa in one direction and of consumer goods in the other. The Nkrumah regime identified the textile industry as the motor of industrial development: it would consolidate a consumer culture based on the products of state enterprise and would shape a modern working class around the planned city of Tema. For these reasons, the regime could scarcely afford to permit a much cheaper product to be smuggled across the border from Togo. Hence Nkrumah repeatedly closed the border, ostensibly in order to impart a political lesson to the Togolese leadership, but also to tackle the realities of smuggling. The rather crude measures that were adopted, much like in Senegal, contrast with the technocratic language deployed in official planning documents.

---

[14] For example, see Tony Killick, *Development Economics in Action: A Study of Economic Policies in Ghana* (London: Heinemann, 1978); Jonathan Frimpong-Ansah, *The Vampire State in Africa: The Political Economy of Decline in Ghana* (London and Trenton: James Currey and Africa World Press, 1991), chs. 5–6.

In Chapters 11 and 12, I have dealt with the recalibration of the social contracts over a period of roughly three decades from the end of the 1960s, and the manner in which this was bound up with processes of respacing from the margins. Some elements of this story have their parallel in other parts of the continent, most notably in Eastern and Central Africa where the sclerosis of state institutions, the proliferation of cross-border trade and new forms of peripheral urbanism spun off one another in comparable ways.[15] At the close of the first decade of independence a series of economic shocks, associated with the great Sahelian drought of 1968–73 and the OPEC oil price hikes of 1973–4, took a heavy toll on government budgets and adversely affected the terms of trade across West African states. The response in Senegal was to throw caution to the wind and to create a raft of new parastatals that were charged with accelerating industrial and agro-industrial development. Although French capital remained deeply embedded within the Senegalese economy, greater emphasis was placed on channelling state investments into directly productive activity. As part of an exercise in respacing, the margins were inserted into planning objectives for the first time. The northern drylands and wetlands of the Casamance were to be rendered productive through irrigation projects, well-construction and agro-industrial investments. These measures were accompanied by renewed efforts to co-opt elements within the student and labour movements whilst offering greater support to the Senegalese business community. However, contradictions abounded because the businessmen in question relied heavily on the profits made from trading in imported consumer goods. This put paid to the prospects for promoting rice culture in the Casamance, whilst maintaining urban food prices at an artificially high level. Moreover, as the Mourides began to embrace urbanism and developed their own cross-border trading networks, they threatened to pull the rug from the government's economic strategy.

In Ghana, the statist model of development had already run into trouble in the early 1960s when the international price for cocoa declined steeply. With the overthrow of the Nkrumah regime in 1966, the one-party state was wound up, and the mantle of leadership passed those who had hitherto been on the losing side. But while steps were taken to liberalize external trade under the Busia regime, and to support Ghanaian entrepreneurs against 'alien' competition, the fundamental assumptions about the role of the state in promoting economic development went unchallenged. Under military rule in the early 1970s, parastatals even came back into favour, with the difference that much

---

[15] Janet MacGaffey, *The Real Economy of Zaire: The Contribution of Smuggling and Other Unofficial Activities to National Wealth* (London and Philadelphia: James Currey and University of Pennsylvania Press, 1991); Nelson Kasfir, "State, magendo and class formation in Uganda", *Journal of Commonwealth and Comparative Politics* 21 (3) 1983.

more importance was attached to promoting agriculture and agro-industry. Under Operation Feed Yourself, a version of respacing was pursued by the Acheampong regime with the focus on mechanized rice farming in the river valleys of the north and on irrigation schemes in the lower reaches of the Volta. When OFY faltered in the mid-1970s, the junta attempted to recapture some of its fading moral authority by foregrounding its role in guaranteeing the territorial integrity of the country in the face of an irredentist threat from Togo. The regime subsequently went further by introducing plans for Union Government that sought to make the military a permanent partner in government. I have devoted considerable space to teasing out the ways in which the relationship between the state and its citizens was coloured by the escalating economic crisis. On the one hand, government institutions ceased to be capable of performing core functions effectively – as was reflected in the deteriorating road network and paralysis in the courts. On the other hand, the modernist vision of a nation of consumers clashed with the everyday reality of shortages of the most basic commodities. The attempt to enforce price controls in the context of endemic scarcity turned urban markets into sites of heated contestation, as exemplified in the events of 1979 when the Armed Forces Revolutionary Council (AFRC) targeted the urban market women. A new term entered the national political vocabulary at this time, namely *kalabule*, which had connotations much like those attached to *magendo* in Uganda.[16] By the time of the declaration of a revolution on 31 December 1981, state institutions had come to be seen as an integral part of the larger problem rather than the self-evident solution to it. The invocation of 'people's power' may be considered as an attempt to square the circle by taking the battle to those who profited from *kalabule*, but also by subjecting bureaucratic norms to the logic of mass participation. In border regions, there were experiments with popular power that directly challenged the monopoly of the Border Guards and the Police and hence the institutional limits of the state.

In the Gambia and Togo, the response to external shocks was very different. In the latter case, high prices for phosphates somewhat compensated for the costs incurred by higher fuel prices. This meant that the Eyadéma regime was in a position to channel significant resources into infrastructural spending in the north at the same time as affording the capital a facelift. In the Gambia, there were fewer options, but the Jawara regime did look to the modernization of agriculture through irrigation projects. But what was more important in either country was the effort to actively nurture an entrepôt economy. These were not so much vampire states as barnacle states, feeding off their larger and increasingly embattled neighbours. In the Gambia, the strategy involved

---

[16] Kasfir, "State, magendo"; Murillo, *Market Encounters*, pp. 143–4.

setting groundnut prices higher than those in Senegal, in order to draw part of the crop from across the border, whilst promoting the re-export of manufactured goods in the other direction. In Togo, improvements to the port enabled traders in Lomé to re-export a wide range of commodities to Ghana: including tinned fish, cosmetics and textiles. In the Gambia and Togo alike, the contraband trade underwrote the fiscal foundations of the state. But it also came to sustain the livelihoods of large swathes of the urban and rural populations who made a living out of trade, transport, currency-changing and porterage. In Togo, the permissive elements leavened the realities of repression in a country where the power base of the Eyadéma regime was centred on the military and the north of the country. However, the visible support offered by the Nana Benz in Lomé was indicative of the bargain that had been struck with commercial interests in the capital. In the Gambia, the permissive elements had been cemented rather earlier and initially went together with a rather forgiving political environment. However, after the military takeover by Yahya Jammeh in 1994, the Gambia came to resemble Togo in significant respects. Recruitment into the Armed Forces gave preference to Jola recruits, many of whom actually originated from the Casamance. Despite a veneer of civilian normality, the Jammeh regime governed with the veiled threat of force. But much like in Togo, it gave full licence to the wider population to carve out a living from the border.

Although official attempts at remaking space in Senegal and Ghana ultimately unravelled, a form of respacing from the margins produced some remarkable outcomes. One was the efflorescence of commercial hubs that were not necessarily located on the border but were very much integral to its various flows. In the Gambia, Serekunda outstripped Banjul proper as the urban centre of the Gambia, while the Mouride capital of Touba mushroomed to become Senegal's second city. These two urban hubs were closely connected to each other as well as to Dakar, which is where many of the contraband goods were ultimately consumed. Then there were the conurbations that grew up around the border itself. Lomé is a special case because it was also a capital city, but there can be no doubt that its pivotal position within regional trade was what sustained much of its dynamism. Just across the line, Aflao grew steadily as a border town that was deeply embedded in the trade with Lomé. And finally there were ordinary towns and villages along the land border through which much of the contraband passed, such as Kpetoe in Ghana or Darsilami in the Gambia. These settlements did not grow especially rapidly, in part because the goods often passed through rotating border markets. But many towns were implicated in smuggling in a more direct way, typically involving the carriage of goods by night – either on foot or by bicycle. Unlike in the Senegambia, the salience attached to being the landowners in the trans-Volta made it relatively difficult for 'strangers' to gain a foothold in cross-border trade there.

Although much has been written about African urbanism,[17] the focus on capital cities has tended to locate them at the centre of national life and at the interface with the global economy. Given the importance I have attributed to the Atlantic world in the nineteenth century, and to the China trade in more recent times, I am clearly not in disagreement here. But I have pointed to the fact that African cities were shaped by their close relationship with the margins. In times of hardship, consumers in the urban areas depended on supplies – including tins of sardines and bags of Asian rice – that crossed borders. Equally, urban merchants were closely connected to traders located within border towns where markets provided a vital connective function in their own right. As Olivier Walther has indicated, the networks of trade remained as adaptive as ever during the years of Structural Adjustment.[18] Across Africa, some of the most rapid urban growth has been witnessed in border regions– most notably in the case of the twin-city pairings of Kinshasa and Brazzaville and Goma and Gisenyi.[19] Some of the contours of peripheral urbanism are now beginning to emerge more clearly,[20] and this monograph has sought to make a contribution to an emerging research agenda based on a detailed account of the making of particular towns and cities over time.

Community

The greater part of this book has been devoted to establishing the ways in which the margins have shaped institutions and practices. But I have also been concerned with some of the consequences of state engagement for framings of community at the border. Whereas social contracts involved arrangements that were notionally bounded by national territory, questions of affinity and

---

[17] Bill Freund, *The African City: A History* (Cambridge: Cambridge University Press, 2007); Abdoumaliq Simone, *For the City Yet to Come: Changing African Life in Four Cities* (Durham: Duke University Press, 2004); Garth Myers, *African Cities: Alternative Visions of Urban Theory and Practice* (London: Zed Press, 2011); Simon Bekker and Goran Therborn (eds.), *Capital Cities in Africa: Power and Powerlessness* (Cape Town: HSRC Press, 2012).

[18] Olivier Walther, "Trade networks in West Africa: a social network approach", *Journal of Modern African Studies* 52 (2) 2014, pp. 194–5.

[19] Isabella Soi and Paul Nugent, "Peripheral urbanism: border towns and twin towns in Africa", *Journal of Borderlands Studies*, 32 (4) 2017, pp. 537–8; Martin Doevenspeck and Nene Morisho Mwanabiningo, "Navigating uncertainty: observations from the Congo-Rwanda border", in Bettina Bruns and Judith Miggelbrink (eds.), *Subverting Borders: Doing Research on Smuggling and Small-Scale Trade* (Wiesbaden: VS Verlag, 2012). For a discussion of twin towns, see Paul Nugent, "Border towns and cities in comparative perspective", in Thomas M. Wilson and Hastings Donnan (eds.), *A Companion to Border Studies* (Chichester: Wiley-Blackwell, 2012).

[20] In particular, see Walther, "Trade networks in West Africa" in Marie Trémolières and Oliver J. Walther (eds.), *Cross-Border Co-operation and Policy Networks in West Africa* (Paris: OECD/Sahel and West Africa Club, 2017), ch. 5.

belonging inevitably traversed physical borders and posed an implicit challenge to official ways of seeing.

In Chapter 7, I indicated that the conversion of the Jola to Islam in the first decades of the twentieth century served to reduce their social distance from Mandinka populations. Much of the appeal of Islam lay in a message of peace, which has to be understood in the light of the sustained violence that characterized the late nineteenth century. In popular memory today, it is the Mauritanian marabout and consummate borderlander, Cheikh Mahfoudz, who is credited with attracting the Jola to Islam. Whereas the memory of Fodé Sylla is associated with slave raiding carried out in the name of religion, Mahfoudz is venerated as a holy man who genuinely convinced the Jola that their misfortunes were attributable to their heathenism. Conversion was closely bound up with resettlement as multi-ethnic communities came into existence on both sides of the border, often through the mediation of Mahfoudz and his associates. Jola migrants joined existing Mandinka towns along the coastal seaboard, but in many cases entirely new villages were founded by settlers drawn from across the region. Within new model communities, rather little valence was attached to place of origin and to ethnicity. Instead, they were constituted on the basis of the shared religious adherence of their members – even if significant numbers of non-Muslim Karoninka, Manjago and Balanta were present as well. The pursuit of peaceful co-existence was somewhat complicated by demands for colonial taxes backed up by the implicit threat of force. From the standpoint of the populations in question, colonial taxes came at the expense of consumption, and at times of hardship threatened subsistence itself. Hence, the consolidation of these communities also involved a degree of negotiation with the colonial authorities over the terms of their existence.

In the trans-Volta, conversion to Christianity was equally infused with a message of peace at a time when the traumas associated with the Asante invasion and the imposition of German rule were relatively recent memories. But conversion did not have the same catalytic effects upon framings of community, except in those places where former slaves established so-called Christian villages. The reason is that this played out in the context of a deepening of the distinction between landlord and stranger. Migration was not incentivized by the authorities, while the chiefs – at least in British Togoland – had nothing to gain from attracting settlers who were not subject to direct taxation. At the same time, the administrative practices of the Germans and the French served to entrench distinctions at the level of the *dukɔwo*. The Germans recognized a strong sense of territoriality amongst the peoples of the trans-Volta and sought to stake out their boundaries – the cartographic fruits of which are reflected on the Karte Von Togo. Meanwhile, the Gold Coast had come to be constituted as a federation of 'native states', of unequal size and significance, to which British Togoland became a party after the 1919.[21] In the context of the cocoa revolution, there was a proliferation of land litigation in the Gold Coast as chiefs sought to defend their claims to territory. In the 1930s, the British embarked on a renewed effort to bring chiefs into direct engagement with the state through native administration reforms. In British Togoland, this was linked to amalgamation policies that were designed to replace a multiplicity of small chiefdoms with a handful of 'states' notionally based on past relationships of precedence. The net effect was to stoke up old antagonisms and to create fresh sources of rivalry between the *dukɔwo*.

In the case of Agotime, Anlo settlers who arrived in the last decades of the nineteenth century became fully integrated into Kpetoe. But later arrivals were treated as strangers even when they belonged to the same Christian denominations and traced their origin to towns with which the Agotime had cultivated close links in the past. It is not so surprising that the Hausa in Kpetoe, who were Muslims, were treated as quintessential strangers – because this was the case in *zongo* communities across the Gold Coast. Ando migrants, who moved across the border to British Togoland to farm on Agotime land, provide a more interesting test-case because they were both Ewe and Christian. The Ando became crucial to staking out disputed land boundaries from the late 1950s in the areas that had once constituted no-man's lands. But the Ando were treated as perpetual strangers, and to this day they remain virtually invisible in local affairs. Land litigation became more prevalent in the Gambia from the 1960s onwards, in part because of increasing population densities, but this was nothing compared to the Gold Coast/British Togoland, and later Ghana, where the courts were inundated with cases that often went through multiple levels of appeal. The protracted Agotime-Adaklu dispute is of particular interest because it illustrates that even when it was farm land that was contested, the arguments turned on much older framings of territoriality. This case, and many others like it, underline the ways in which decades of contestation entrenched the divisions between neighbouring *dukɔwo*. On the French Togoland/Togo side of the border, there was much less land litigation and the discourse of autochthony seems to have been more muted as a consequence.

There was nothing inevitable about the distinct trajectories that unfolded in the Senegambia and the trans-Volta. Indeed, one might have expected precisely the opposite outcome. Given the mutual antipathy between Mandinka and Jola populations in the nineteenth century, one might well have predicted an ongoing pattern of mutual avoidance. Equally, because the Agotime had

---

[21] Carola Lentz and Paul Nugent, "Ethnicity in Ghana: a comparative perspective", in Carola Lentz and Paul Nugent (eds.), *Ethnicity in Ghana: The Limits of Invention* (Houndmills: Macmillan, 2000), p. 15.

historically boosted their numbers by absorbing Ewe people, and then found this route closed off with the ending of slavery, one might have expected them to embrace settlement from further afield. The fact that the opposite transpired is a consequence of the ways in which states encouraged certain types of border flows and inhibited others.

In Chapter 13, I turned to the ways in which understandings of community, and expressions of ethnicity, have been revisited since the 1990s. The Casamance separatist movement may be considered, at least in part, as an unintended consequence of efforts to shore up political alliances through a respacing of Senegalese national territory. It was typically Casamance migrants to Dakar who felt the greatest sense of exclusion from a political project summed up as 'Wolofization'. Within the Casamance itself, armed insurgency posed a serious threat to the peace and religious unity that had been so integral to the foundation of new model communities earlier in the century. In the trans-Volta, the issue of secession was not explicitly revived, but there were acute tensions arising from the violent repression of opposition to the regime in Lomé in the early 1990s. I have compared the very different efforts to mobilize a sense of shared identity in the two border settings. In each case, readings of deeper historical processes combined with new forms of association that notionally transcended borders.

In the Casamance, there was a perception that an older cycle of violence and flight was repeating itself.[22] One response was to promote a system of self-defence by appealing to Fogny-Jabangkunda as a historical entity that had notionally unified Mandinka towns in a more remote past. A quite different reaction was the creation of an association that sought to redefine the boundaries of Karoninka/Kalorn ethnicity. In their own ways, each sought to create a distance from the Casamance secessionist project, which was, not entirely accurately, perceived as a Jola initiative. The first was necessarily confined to the Casamance because Fogny-Jabangkunda was considered distinct from Kombo. The second initiative involved the dissemination of separate ethnic messages in the Gambia and the Casamance – distinguishing the Kalorn from the Mandinka in the one case and from the Jola in the other. Symptomatically, the annual festivals and regular cultural activities of Kayong Kalorn ended up being confined to the Gambian side of the line.

In Agotime, it had generally been possible to participate in funerals, weddings and outdoorings of new-born children, but formal interactions had ceased because of the tense relations that existed between the governments of Ghana and Togo. When tensions eased in the mid-1990s, a window of opportunity emerged to re-activate a cross-border festival that the organizers

---

[22] Paul Nugent, "Cyclical history in the Gambia/Casamance borderlands: refuge, settlement and Islam from c.1880 to the present", *Journal of African History* 48 (2) 2007.

hoped would unite the Agotime around a sense of their place in history and pride in elements of a shared culture. Celebrating the martial prowess of the Agotime touched a raw nerve because many settlements included people who were descended from war captives or had previously occupied a client status. Because revelling in militarism raised sensitive issues, kente weaving was substituted as the focal point of *Agbamevoza*. Kente was the one item of conspicuous consumption that, quite unlike wax prints, was almost entirely home-grown. The small problem was that the Togolese Agotime do not by and large practice weaving. Ironically, the Agotime seem to have been renowned as traders of cotton rather than as weavers of cloth at the start of the colonial period. The tradition of kente weaving was taken up by Agotime migrants to the Eastern Province during the colonial period, and it is tempting to conclude that it has its roots there as much as in Agotime itself. The upshot is that the border has continued to frustrate efforts to prove that the Agotime are after all one and the same people – even if *Agbamevoza* does now straddle the boundary line. Much like in the Senegambia, the border is woven into everyday economic activities, understandings of community and collective memories. It is the persistent itch that cannot be scratched.

Agbamevoza is an appropriate point on which to bring this account to a close, for the reason that it bundles all the traversal themes together in a single performative moment. The history of Agotime settlement, warfare and peace-making are all explicitly referenced during the week's staged events. The importance attributed to physically crossing the international border and staking out the boundaries of Agotime are rooted in a keen sense of territoriality – one that derives in part from an appreciation of historical relations and in part from very practical concerns about land encroachment. And yet one would be hard pressed to find a physical map anywhere during the proceedings. *Agbamevoza* is also a celebration of conspicuous consumption as participants show off their finest kente cloth and most expensive wax prints, while indulging in a cycle of feasting and imbibing of beer, schnapps, whisky and soft drinks – items which have all been smuggled in substantial quantities over the years. Fittingly perhaps, the climax unfolds in the physical premises of the Revenue Authority. Every year at *Agbamevoza*, and at countless festivals like it, the idea of the state and a sense of being a border community are co-instantiated in a public spectacle that brings them together in a single imaginative space.

Bibliography

PRIMARY SOURCES

SELECTED ARCHIVAL SOURCES

National Archives, Kew (NAK)
CO 96/691/10 "Control of Migration".
CO 96/693/14 "Customs Queries and Protests".
CO 96/776/5 "Post-War Development of Mandated Territory – Togoland".
CO 96/817/3 "Miscellaneous Gin-Running Offence".
CO 554/1034 "Togoland Administration, 1954–56".
CO 554/1035 "Togoland Administration".
CO 724/1 "Division of Togoland".
FO 371/138262 "Internal Political Situation in Togoland".
FO 371/138270 "Foreign Policy in Togoland".
FO 371/161372 "Togo: International Political Situation".

Rhodes House Library, Oxford
Mss. Afr. S.1622 "Transcript of Interview with Sir George Sinclair"
(undated).

Centre des Archives Nationales de l'Outre-Mer,
Aix-en-Provence (CAOM)
Series: Affaires Politiques (AFFPOL)
1AFFPOL/1361.
1AFFPOL/92.
1AFFPOL/610.
1AFFPOL/517/1.
1AFFPOL/514/2/3.
1AFFPOL/2184/1.
1 AFFPOL/2148/8.

Archives Nationales du Sénégal (ANS)
Series D
10D 1/33 "Renseignements Confidentiels sur la Gambie Anglaise et la
Guinée Portugaise; Fourniture de Carburant etc.".

10D 3/41 "Correspondance du Gouverneur du Sénégal Avec l'Administrateur du Cercle de Kaolack (1907–1909)".

10D 4/4 "Rapports Politiques à Goudiry et Dans le Sine-Saloum; Réclamation du Gouvernement de Gambie (1898)".

11D 1/151 "Casamance, Bignona: Renseignements Politiques et Militaires (1927–1954)".

11D 1/224 "Casamance: Dossiers Divers".

11D 1/226 "Ossouye: Affaires Politiques et Administratives".

11D 1/239 "Sedhiou: Vols de Boeufs sur la Frontière Sénégal-Guinée Portugaise (1949–58).

11D 1/251 "Affaires Politiques et Administratives (APA): Relations avec la Gambie".

11D 1/259 "Velingara: Gendarmerie, P.V. de Vol aux Frontières".

11D 1/269 "Velingara: Douanes".

11D 1/977 "Correspondence Entre le Gouverneur du Sénegal et l'Administrateur de la Haute-Gambie".

Series F

1F8 "Relations du Gouvernement du Sénégal avec le Gouvernement de la Gambie (1891–1894)".

1F12 "Relations Avec la Gambie: Questions Générales et de Principe".

1F14 "Relations Avec le Gambie: Reclamations Particulières (1905–1910)".

1F16 "Délimitation de la Gambie".

1F18 "Délimitation de la Gambie".

1F19 "Delimitation de le Gambie: Mission Fargues (1895–96)".

1F25 "Delimitation de la Gambie: Incidents de Frontière (1906–1908)".

1F27 "Delimitation de la Gambie: Incidents de Frontière (1911–1914)".

1F30 "Application de la Convention Franco-Anglaise du 8 avril 1904 en ce qui Concerne la Gambie".

2F7 "Reclamations Particulières".

2F13 "Incidents d'ordre".

Series G

1G 355 "Monographies des cercles du Togo: Anécho, Atakpamé, Klouto et Lomé (1921)".

2G 13/57 "Résidence de Diouloulou, rapports mensuels d'ensemble 1913".

2G 14/51 "Casamance, rapports mensuels d'ensemble 1914".

2G 16/37 "Casamance, rapports mensuels d'ensemble 1916".

2G 17/37 "Territoire de la Casamance, rapport politique, Juillet 1917".

2G 22/33 "Cercle de Bignona: rapports d'ensemble trimestriels (1922)".

2G 23/70 "Territoires de la Casamance, Administrateur Supérieur: rapports d'ensemble semestriels 1923".

2G 24/50 "Territoire de la Casamance: rapport politique annuel (1924)".

2G 26/66 "Territoire de la Casamance: rapport politiques général annuel (1926)".

2G 28/61 "Territoire de la Casamance: rapport général annuel 1928".

2G 29/83 "Cercle de Bignona: rapport général annuel 1929".

2G 29/91 "Territoire de la Casamance: rapport politique annuel 1929".
2G 31/74 "Territoire de la Casamance: rapport annuel 1931".
13G 67 "Politique Musulmane: activité des marabouts (1906–17)".
13G 372 "Casamance: Correspondance du Résident 1892–1894".
13G 382 "Casamance Affaires Politiques".
13G 384 "Casamance Affaires Politiques".
13G 385 "Casamance Affaires Politiques (1918–1919)".

National Archives of the Gambia, Banjul (NAGB)
Series ARP (Annual Reports)
ARP 27/1 "Customs Department Report for the Period 1965–66".
ARP 27/2 "Customs Department Report for the Period 1966–67".
ARP 33/1 "Reports on Kombo, Foni and Kiang (1894–1899)".
ARP 33/2 "Reports on Kombo, Foni and Kiang (1900–01 and 1906–07)".
ARP 33/3 "Travelling Commissioner's Report on the Kombo and Foni
    Province, 1902–06 and 1908–1921".
ARP 33/4 "Annual Report Kombo, 1908".
ARP 33/5 "Annual Report Kombo/Fogny".
ARP 34/1–2 "Divisional Annual Reports" (1943, 1944).

Series CSO (Colonial Secretary's Office)
CSO 1/120 "Draft Despatches to Secretary of State".
CSO 1/124 "Despatches from Colonial Office 1894".
CSO 1/171 "Despatches to Secretary of State".
CSO 2/284 "Customs Traffic".
CSO 2/518 "Strange Farmers".
CSO 2/1068 "Rice – Regarding Cultivation by the Djougoutes of Cercle de
    Bignona".
CSO 2/1130A "List of Chiefs and Towns".
CSO 2/1230 "N'Dong, J.N. and Others, Detention of, with Lorries and
    Personal Effects at Ziguinchor".
CSO 2/1280 "Commissions to Chiefs, Headmen, Repayment of Customs
    Dues".
CSO 3/26 "Immigration of Natives from French Territories to Escape
    Military Service".
CSO 3/136 "Control of Immigrants from French Territories".
CSO 3/159 "Annual Confidential Reports on Seyfolu - South Bank".
CSO 3/172 "French Casamance: Report on a Visit Paid".
CSO 3/204 "Review of Policy with Regard to the Strange Farmers".
CSO 3/214 "Sefo Jammi".
CSO 3/299 "South Bank Province – Administration of".
CSO 3/308 "Anglo-French Boundary – Incidents".
CSO 3/340 "Smuggling from Senegal".
CSO 3/422 "Frontier Incidents".
CSO 3/400 "Illicit Trade in British Service Property".
CSO 4/10 "Gambia: Development and Relations with Neighbouring
    Territories of".

CSO 4/108 "French Subjects Liable to Military Service – Escape to British Territory".
CSO 4/132 "Anglo-French Colonial Relation Since Capitulation".
CSO 4/242 "Intelligence Reports (South Bank Province)".
CSO 9/891 "Land Tenure".
CSO 10/302 "Anglo-French Boundary".
CSO 23/4 "Expedition against Foday Sillah (1893–94)".
CSO 54/9 "Correspondence Relating to Territories on the Gambia River".

Series CUS (Customs Department)
CUS 1/4 "Collector of Customs, Border Trade and Smuggling".

Series EXA (Ministry of External Affairs)
EXA 1/8 "Senegalo-Gambian Co-operation Customs (1967–1975)".

Series FIN (Ministry of Finance)
FIN 1/46 "Groundnut Smuggling (1960)".

Series MP (Maps and Plans)
MP 1/1 "Correspondence Relating to the Territories of the River Gambia" (Colonial Office, section of Confidential Print Africa 248).
MP1/1 "Papers Relating to the Gambia Colony and Protectorates".

Series PRM (Chief Minister/Prime Minister's Office)
PRM 2/11 "Senegalo-Gambian Relations - Customs".

Series SEC (Senior Commissioner)
SEC 1/45 "Anglo-French Boundary – Western Division".
SEC 1/196 "Western Division Conferences".
SEC 1/896 "Complaints and Petitions".
SEC 9/795 "Alkali of Kartong, Kombo South District".

Series SECOM (Senior Commissioner)
SECOM 9/402 "Native Land Tenure".

Gambia, National Centre for Arts and Culture,
Oral Archives (NCAC)
Transcripts of oral traditions, collected in 1970s and 1980s.

Public Records and Archives Division, Ghana (PRAAD)
Accra
Series ADM
ADM 4/1/52 "Ordinances of the Gold Coast, Ashanti and the Northern Territories, 1923".
ADM 11/1620 "Togoland Secret and Confidential Papers" (1918–1924).
ADM 39/1/312 "Food Control".

ADM 39/1/169 "Proceedings of First Session of J.C. for Togoland Affairs".
ADM 39/1/171 "Joint Council for Togoland Affairs – Views Expressed".
ADM 39/1/190 "Transfer of Native Lands".
ADM 39/1/286, "Amalgamation of Divisions – Asogli State".
ADM 39/1/339 "Unification of the Ewe Speaking Peoples".
ADM 39/1/456 "Handing Over Reports".
ADM 39/1/533 "Standing Finance Committee: Memorandum by the Minister of Communications".
ADM 39/1/545 "Amalgamation of Divisions in Togoland under British Mandate".
ADM 39/1/570 "Buem Strangers Union".
ADM 39/1/574 "Alienation of Land".
ADM 30/1/654 "Awatime Weaving".
ADM 39/1/676 "Standing Consultative Commission for Togoland".
ADM 39/1/689 "Southern Togoland Council – Constitution of".
ADM 39/4/2 "Civil Record Book (Ho)".
ADM 39/4/3 "Civil Record Book, Ho District".
ADM 39/4/5 "Civil Record Book (Ho)".
ADM 39/4/8 "Civil Record Book, Ho".
ADM 39/4/9 "Civil Record Book, Ho".
ADM 39/4/10 "Civil Record Book (Ho)".
ADM 39/4/16 "Civil Record Book (Ho)"
ADM 39/4/19 "Civil Record Book (Ho)".
ADM 39/5/73 "District Record Book".
ADM 39/5/79 "Preventive Service".
ADM 39/5/80 "Preventive Service".
ADM 39/5/81 "Customs Dues on Boundary between British and French Zone".
ADM 43/4/18 "Criminal Record Book, Kpandu District".

Series CSO
CSO 21/22/30 "Agotime History".
CSO 6/5/21 "Smuggling and Seizures in the Southern Section, Eastern Frontier Preventive Station".

Ho
RAO C.273 "Togoland: A History of the Tribal Divisions of the District of Misahuhe and of the Sub-Districts of Ho and Kpandu".
DA/D288 "Agotime Native Affairs".
DA/C.320 "Agotime Kpetoe Market".
DA/D78, "Handing Over Notes", "Handing Over Report by Captain C.C. Lilley, O.B.E., District Commissioner to D.N. Walker, Per Mr. V.H.K. Littlewood, Asst. District Commissioner" (1938).

Ghana, Ministry of Agriculture, Volta Region (Ho)
CHC 5 "Operation Feed Yourself".
Ministry of Agriculture. *Volta Region Agricultural Development Project (VORADEP): Project Review, 1982–1986, and Proposals for a One Year*

Extension (Ho: Ministry of Agriculture, Monitoring and Evaluation Unit, 1986).

Ghana, Volta Region Public Tribunal, Ho (VRPT)

Volume unspecified, Case No. 9/83, "The People vs Felicia Cobbina Serwaah", 14 September 1983.

Volume and Case unspecified, "The People vs Henry Hagan", 14 September 1983.

Volume unspecified, Case 12/1983, "The People vs Simon Kofi Webu", 22 September 1983.

Volume unspecified, Case No. 21/83, "The People vs Maige Seidu and Tamboura Belmo Belko", 4 October 1983.

Volume 2 and 3, Case 27/84, "The Peoples vs Nelson Zatey and Another".

Volume 6, Case No. 44/86, "The People vs Kofi Atidefe", 2 July 1986.

Volume 6, Case No. 81/86, "The People vs Anthony Togbe", 12 August 1986.

Volume 7, Case 1/87, "The People vs Ben Komla Agbozo", 14 January 1987.

Volume 7, Case 11/87, "The People vs Vicentia Aza and One Other", 28 January 1987.

Volume 7, Case No. 41/87, "The People vs Gladys Zormelo", 13 May 1987.

Volume 8, Case 47/87, "The People vs Prosper Agbelengor", 26 June 1987.

Volume and Case unspecified, "The People vs Bukari Haruna and 9 Others", 18 August 1988.

Volume unspecified, Case No. 38/90, "The People vs Joseph Adu Afful", 9 May 1990.

Volume and Case unspecified, "The People vs Akuvi Mawuko and 8 Others", 21 February 1991.

Volume and Case unspecified, "The People vs Fred Akubia", 10 May 1991.

Volume and Case unspecified, "People vs Doe Agbeke and Another", 15 October 1991.

Volume and Case unspecified, "The People vs Francis Owusu Ansah and Joseph Kofi Tetteh", 5 February 1992.

Volume and Case unspecified, "The People vs William Ola and Another", 30 April 1992.

Archives Nationales du Togo, (Lomé) (TNAL)

Series: Affaires Politiques

2 APA/2 "Klouto".

2APA/31 "Rapports Periodiques des Cercles: Cercle de Klouto".

2APA/325 "Cercle de Klouto: Service de Demographie" (1956).

2APA/361 "Klouto: Affaires Politiques (1943–1965)".

2APA/3 "Rapports Trimestriel 1927–1931".

2 APA/5 "Rapport de Tournée 1928 dans le Cercle".

2APA/134 "Service de Douanes 1938–1954".

2APA/355 "Canton d'Agotime Sud (1941–56)".
2APA/361 "Commandement Indigène: Petitions de la Population du Canton d'Agotime Nord (1943–65)".

OFFICIAL REPORTS

The Gambia, *Blue Books* (Bathurst), various years.
The Gambia, *Report on Development and Welfare in the Gambia (a Report by K.W. Blackburne)* (Bathurst, 1943).
The Gambia, *The Financial Position: Exchange of Despatches between the Governor and the Secretary of State for the Colonies*, Sessional Paper 11 of 1960 (Bathurst: Government Printer, 1960).
The Gambia, *Financial Report with Appendices for the Year 1961* (Bathurst: Government Printer, 1961).
The Gambia, *Financial Report with Appendices for the Year 1961*, Sessional Paper No. 6/64 (Bathurst: Government Printer, 1964).
The Gambia, *Report on the Alternatives for Association between the Gambia and Senegal* (By Hubertus J. Van Mook, Max Graessli, Henri Monfrioni and Hendrik Weisfelt, Appointed under the United Nations Programme of Technical Assistance), Sessional Paper No. 13 of 1964.
The Gambia, *Summary of Proceedings of the Twenty-First Conference of Chiefs and Area Council Members Held at Georgetown, McCarthy Island Division from the 25th to 27th February, 1964.* Sessional Paper No. 14 of 1964.
The Gambia, *Customs Department Report for the Period January 1965 to June 1966, Sessional Paper 1 of 1968* (Bathurst, Government Printer, 1968).
Republic of the Gambia, *Presidential Address Delivered by His Excellency Sir Dawda Kairaba Jawara, President of the Republic of the Gambia at the State Opening of Parliament on Thursday 5th June, 1975* (Banjul: Government Printer, 1975).
Republic of the Gambia, *Country Economic Memorandum for the Donors' Conference on the Gambia, 1984, Vol I, Main Report* (Banjul: Ministry of Economic Planning and Industrial Development, 1984).
Republic of the Gambia, *Presidential Address Delivered by His Excellency Sir Dawda Kairaba Jawara, President of the Republic of the Gambia at the State Opening of Parliament on Thursday 5th June, 1975* (Banjul: Government Printer, 1975).
Gold Coast, *Blue Books*, various years.
Gold Coast, *The Development Plan, 1951* (Accra: Government Printing Department, 1951).
Gold Coast, *The Development Plan, 1951: Financial* Summaries (5th edn.) (Accra: Government Printer, undated).
Gold Coast, *Economic Survey 1955* (Accra: Office of the Government Statistician, 1956).

Ghana, *Programme of the Convention People's Party for Work and Happiness* (Accra: Ministry of Information and Broadcasting, 1962).

Ghana, *Economic Survey 1958* (Accra: Ministry of Finance, 1959).

Ghana, Economic Survey, 1960 (Accra: Ministry of Finance, 1961).

Ghana, Economic Survey, 1961 (Accra: Ministry of Finance, 1962).

Ghana, *Statistical Yearbook 1961* (Accra: Central Bureau of Statistics, undated).

Republic of Ghana, *Statistical Handbook 1967* (Accra: Central Bureau of Statistics, undated).

Republic of Ghana, *Statistical Yearbook, 1969–70* (Accra: Central Bureau of Statistics, undated).

Republic of Ghana, *Seven-Year Development Plan, 1963–64 to 1969–70* (Accra: Office of the Planning Commission, 1964).

Republic of Ghana, *Report of the Commission of Enquiry into Trade Malpractices in Ghana* (Accra: Office of President, 1965) (Abraham Commission).

Republic of Ghana, *Economic Survey 1969–1971* (Accra: Central Bureau of Statistics, 1976).

Republic of Ghana, *Five-Year Development Plan, 1975/76–1979/80, Part I and II* (Accra: Ministry of Economic Planning, 1977).

Republic of Ghana. State Enterprises Commission, *Report on Survey into the Operations of the Food Production Corporation* (Accra: SEC, 1979).

Ghana/Republic of Ghana, *Parliamentary Debates*, various years.

Gouvernement Général de l'Afrique Occidentale Française, *Bulletin Mensuel de l'Agence Economique de l'Afrique Occidentale Française*, No. 77, May 1927.

République du Sénégal, Ministère du Plan et du Développement, *Situation Economique du Sénégal (1963)* (Dakar: Service de la Statistique, 1964).

République du Sénégal, *Projet de IIIe Plan Quadriennal de Developpement et Social, 1969–1973* (Dakar: Ministère du Plan et de l'Industrie, 1969), p. 2.

Great Britain, *Correspondence Relating to Territories on the Gambia River* (Colonial Office, 1887).

Great Britain, *Further Correspondence Relating to Territories on the Gambia River* (Colonial Office, 1892).

Great Britain, *The Gambia Independence Conference 1964* (London: Her Majesty's Stationary Office, 1964).

United Nations Trusteeship Council, *Official Records*, 1957–1956.

United Nations Trusteeship Council. *Report of the United Nations Plebiscite Commissioner for the Trust Territory of Togoland under British Administration* (T/1258, 19 June 1956).

United Nations, *Plebiscite Commissioner's Report*, p. 184.

NEWSPAPERS, JOURNALS AND YEARBOOKS

Africa Contemporary Record (London: Rex Collins): various years.

The Ewe Newsletter, Organ of the All-Ewe Conference.

[People's] Daily Graphic (Accra): various years.

West Africa (London): various years.

EPHEMERA

The Progress Party Manifesto [Ghana] issued on 2 August 1969.
Dr. Obed Asamoah, PNDC Secretary for Foreign Affairs, "CDRs and the Image of Ghana – Speech to CDRs at Hohoe on 3rd May 1985" (copy in my possession).
Agotime Traditional Area, Kente Festival, Agbamevoza 2005 – 10th Celebration from Monday 29th August to Monday 5th September 2005.
"ECOWAS Cross-Border Initiatives Programme: Southern Senegambia Pilot Operation", 2007 (copy in my possession).
Ismaila Sambou "Re. Meeting, Historical Fact-Findings – 'Tranquille Settlement Establishment'", undated.
Kayong Kalorn Perspective (place and date of publication unknown).

UNPUBLISHED MANUSCRIPTS AND LEGAL RECORDS

Nene Nuer Keteku III, "Short History of the Agotimes" (undated), copy in my possession.
"Lekpos or Lenden-kera Locality History in T.V.T.", Ewe manuscript in my possession, dated 11 November 1954 (translation by Setri Dzivenu).
"Geze Anku and 7 others versus Togbe Mahumansro and nine others", in Ho District Native Court, 15 July 1959 (copy of court record in my possession), pp. 40–7.
"Adaklu-Agotime Land Case" (dossier of legal documents), private papers of Harry Asimah, Ho.

INTERVIEWS

Gambia
Ismaila Sambou, Alkalo of Darsilami, 3 February 2004.
Salifu Saidy, Darsilami, 4 February 2004.
Saano Sambo and Abdoulai Jasseh, Darsilami, 6 February 2004.
Yousoupha Colley, Dimbaya, 11 February 2004.
Habiba Jatta, Alkalo of Touba, 11 February 2004.
Paul Jarjue, Secretary of Kayong Kalorn, Kartong, (Gambia), 3 April 2004.
Alhaji Malanding Demba, Alkalo of Sifoe, 6 April 2004.
Alhaji Demba Jabang, Alkalo of Kartong, 4 June 2004.
Yousoupha Colley, Dimbaya, 11 February 2004.
Bakary Diatta, Assistant Alkalo, Jiboro-Kuta, 17 July 2005.
Fabakary Badjie, Alkalo, and Matar Badjie, Naneeto, 30 July 2005.

Casamance
Alkalo Sasau Badji and elders, Tranquille (Gambia/Casamance), 2 February 2004.
Braimah Jasseh (elder), Malang Jabang (elder), Amadou Jabang (*alkalo*), Abéné, 14 February 2004.
Sonkal Jasseh, Abéné, 14 February 2004.

Famara Diatta (*alkalo*), Moussa Sonko, Janko Diedhiou, Donbondir, 16 February 2004.
Alieu Badji and others, Makuda, 16 February 2004.
Chamsedin Diedhiou, Alkalo, and Sidi Diedhiou, of Darsilami-Cherifkunda (Daroussalam), 17 February 2004.
Marabi Moise Haidara, Darsilami Cheriffkunda (Casamance), 17 February 2004.
Chérif Cheikh Mouhidinne Ibnou el-Arabi Aidara, Darsilami-Cherifkunda (Daroussalam), 17 February 2004.
Tombon Ture, Umar Diatta (assistant Alkalo), Ousmane Badji, Lamin Badji and Sidi Jabang Kujube, 18 February 2004.
Alkalo Jerreh Dembeh and others, Kabadio, 19 February 2004.
Alkalo Landing Jabang, Jerreh Dembeh, Landing Saikou Ba Jabang, Ibrahim Sow, Mamadou Lamin Bojang, Kabadio, 19 February 2004.
Alkalo Baboucar Jabang, Diana, 20 July 2005.
Alkalo Malang Diatta and others, Kujube, 20 July 2005.
Alkalo Landing Jabang, assistant Alkalo, Seku Jabang and Yusuf Darbo, Kabadio, 21 July 2005.
Malem Coly, Djibril Diatta, Ousmane Diatta, Lamine Sanyang and Alioune Gueye, Mahamouda, 22 July 2005.
Alieu Badji, Ansoumane Diatta, Akoba Sambou, Baboucar Badji, Moussa Sambou, Makuda, 22 July 2005.
Ibraima Dogolo Koli, Coubanac, 23 July 2005.
Cherif Marabi and others, Darsilami-Cherifkunda (Daroussalam), 23 July 2005.
Cheikh Umar Atab, Tranquille, 28 July 2005.

Ghana
Nene Nuer Keteku III, Ho, 26 March 2001.
Nene Ahortor Makaku V, Kpetoe, 28 March 2001.
Nene Waku Waku V, Afegame, 20 August 2001.
Augustin Kwadzose, Kpetoe, 28 March 2001.
Nene Dapaah VI, Kpetoe, 19 August 2002.
Nene Adela Tachie II, Adedome, 20 August 2002.
Nene Nuer Keteku III, Kpetoe, 23 August 2002.
Emmanuel Tetteh Kpeglo, Akpokope, 2 September 2003.
Togbe Drafor, Wodome, 3 September 2003.
Nene Gagli III, Kpetoe, 10 September 2003.
Togbe Addo IV, Mama Ozakula and others, Adaklu-Waya 14 September 2003.
Nene Todze Agbovi V, Kpetoe, 7 September 2007.
Nene Todje-Agbo IV, Kpetoe, 7 September 2007.
Nene Akoto Sah VII, Kpetoe, 5 September 2007.
Nene Dapaah VI, Kpetoe, 7 September 2007

Togo
Nene Tetteh Wusu IV, Kpodjahon, 4 April 2001.
Broni Kwesi Soglo, Kpodjahon, 20 August 2001.

Togbe Nipa Soglo IV, Chef de Canton, and others, Amoussoukope,
   16 August 2001.
Catholic priest, Amoussoukope, 16 August 2001.
Togbe Apaloo IV, Batoumé, 16 August 2001.
Samuel Kwesi Broni Soglo, 20 August 2001.
Baba Adzadi Nah, Kpodjahon, 20 August 2001.
Togbe Apaloo IV, Batoumé, 23 August 2001.
Lucia Elo Agbovi, Batoumé, 23 August 2001.
Togbui Gidi V and others, Wodome, 23 August 2001.
Togbui Ati Akli II, Lakwi, 25 August 2001.
Nene Teh-Doku III, Chef de Canton, Zukpe, 27 August 2001.
Togbe Apaloo IV, Batoumé, 15 August 2002
Togbe Nyagamago Pattah IV, Chef de Canton, Adzakpa, 15 August 2002.
Togbe Kudiabor III, Nyitoe, 19 August 2002.
Gabriel Basalbi, near Wodome, 20 August 2002.
Nene Odikro II, Ibenyeme, 2 September 2003.
Kodjo Sadja, Sarakope, 3 September 2003.
Etu Adabra, Amoussoukope, 9 September 2003.

SECONDARY SOURCES

Abrams, Philip, "Notes on the difficulty of studying the state (1977)", *Journal of Historical Sociology* 1 (1) March 1988.

Afari-Gyan, Kwadwo, *Public Tribunals and Justice in Ghana* (Accra: Asempa, 1988).

Aggarwal, Ravina, *Beyond Lines of Control: Performance and Politics on the Disputed Borders of Ladakh, India* (Durham: Duke University Press, 2004).

Ahadji, Ametépé Yawovi, "Le rôle de la station de Misahöhe dans l'integration de l'hinterland a la colonie allemande du Togo (1890–1914)", in Badjow Tcham and Thiou K. Tchamie (eds.), *L'integration de l'hinterland a la colonie du Togo: actes du colloque de Lomé (22–25 mars 1999)* (Lomé: Presses de l'UB, 2000).

Akerman, James R. (ed.), *Decolonizing the Map: Cartography from Colony to Nation* (Chicago and London: Chicago University Press, 2017).

Akpo-Vaché, Catherine, *L'AOF et le seconde guerre mondiale (Septembre 1939–Octobre 1945)* (Paris: Karthala, 1996).

Akyeampong, Emmanuel, *Between the Sea and the Lagoon: An Eco-Social History of the Anlo of Southeastern Ghana, c.1850 to Recent Times* (Oxford: James Currey, 2002).

Allen, John and Cochrane, Allan, "Assemblages of state power: topographical shifts in the organization of government and politics", *Antipode* 42 (5) 2010.

Allman, Jean M., *Quills of the Porcupine: Asante Nationalism in an Emergent Ghana* (Madison: University of Wisconsin Press, 1993).

Amate, C. O. C., *The Making of Ada* (Accra: Woeli, 1999).

Amegan, M., "Les administrateurs allemands de la circonscription d'Atakpame (1898–1914)", in T. Gbeasor, *Espace, culture et developpement dans la region d'Atakpame* (Lomé: Presses de l'UB, 1999).

Amegashie-Viglo, Simon, Bokor, Stephen Komla and Ganyaglo, Francis Komla, "Decentralisation and the challenge of revenue mobilisation for development:

the case of Adaklu-Anyigbe District Assembly in the Volta Region of Ghana",
    Journal of Economics and Sustainable Development 5 (14) 2014.
Amenumey, D. E. K., "The extension of British rule to Anlo (south-east Ghana),
    1850–1890", *Journal of African History* IX (1) 1968.
    The Ewe in Pre-Colonial Times (Accra: Sedco, 1986).
    The Ewe Unification Movement: A Political History (Accra: Ghana Universities
    Press, 1989).
Amnesty International, *Sénégal: La terreur en Casamance* (Paris: Amnesty
    International, 1998).
    Togo: Il est temps de rendre des comptes (Paris: Amnesty International, 1999).
Amonoo, Benjamin, *Ghana 1956–1966: The Politics of Institutional Dualism* (London:
    Allen and Unwin, 1981).
Anene, J. C., *The International Boundaries of Nigeria, 1885–1960* (London: Longman,
    1970).
Anon, "La contrebande à la frontière de la Gambie représente un danger réel pour
    l'essor des jeunes industries dakaroises", *Marchés Tropicaux et Méditerranée*,
    No. 747, 5 mars 1960.
    "Hunger strikes Togo: where is Olympio?", *Evening News*, 20 March 1962.
    "Gambie et Sénégambie", *Marchés Tropicaux et Méditerranée*, 9 mai 1975.
    "Livre Blanc sur la réunification du Togo", *Revue Française d'Etudes Politiques
    Africaines*, 121, 1976.
    "Attaque du poste du douane de Selety: de la barbarie premeditée", *Le Soleil*, 25 avril
    1990.
    "Traffic d'armes à Tambacounda", *Le Soleil*, 30 mai 1990.
    "La douane tire la sonette d'alarme", *L'Info*, No. 351, 6 decembre 1999.
    "Fraude dans les daaras et cités religieuses: les douaniers appellent à la collaboration
    des chefs religieux", *L'Info*, 30 novembre 1999.
Apter, Andrew, *Pan-African Nation: Oil and the Spectacle of Culture in Nigeria*
    (Chicago and London: Chicago University Press, 2005).
Archer, Francis Bisset, *The Gambia Colony and Protectorate: An Official Handbook*
    (London: Frank Cass, 1967, new impression of 1906 1st edn.).
Armah, Ayi Kwei, *The Beautyful Ones Are Not Yet Born* (Oxford: Heinemann
    Educational, 1968).
Asiwaju, A. I., "Migrations as revolt: the example of the Ivory Coast and the Upper
    Volta before 1945", *Journal of African History* 17 (4) 1976.
    *Western Yorubaland under European Rule, 1889–1945: A Comparative Analysis
    of French and British Colonialism* (London: Longman, 1976).
    *Partitioned Africans: Ethnic Relations across Africa's International Boundaries
    1884–1984* (London and Lagos: C. Hurst and University of Lagos Press, 1984).
Austen, Ralph, "Colonial boundaries and African nationalism: the case of the
    Kagera salient", in Gregory H. Maddox and James L. Giblin (eds.), *In Search
    of a Nation: Histories of Authority and Dissidence in Tanzania* (Oxford: James
    Currey, 2005).
Austin, Dennis, *Politics in Ghana, 1946–1960* (Oxford: Oxford University Press,
    1964).
Austin, Gareth, *Labour, Land and Capital in Ghana: From Slavery to Free Labour
    in Asante, 1807–1956* (Rochester: University of Rochester Press, 2005).
    "Reciprocal comparison and African history: tackling conceptual Eurocentrism in
    the study of Africa's economic past", *African Studies Review* 50 (3) 2007.

Axelsson, Linn, "Making borders: engaging the threat of Chinese textiles in Ghana", Ph.D. thesis, Department of Human Geography, Stockholm University (2012).

Ayache, Georges, *"Si la maison de votre voisin brûle": Eyadéma et la politique extérieure du Togo* (Paris: Editions ABC, 1983).

Ayandele, E. A., *The Educated Elite in the Nigerian Society* (Ibadan: Ibadan University Press, 1974).

Babou, Cheikh Anta, *Fighting the Greater Jihad: Amadu Bamba and the Founding of the Muridiyya of Senegal, 1853–1913* (Athens: Ohio University Press, 2007).

Bach, Daniel, "Patrimonialism and neopatrimonialism: comparative receptions and transcriptions", in Daniel C. Bach and Mamadou Gazibo (eds.), *Neopatrimonialism in Africa and Beyond* (Abingdon and New York: Routledge, 2012).

Barrett, Hazel R., *The Marketing of Foodstuffs in the Gambia, 1400–1980: A Geographical Analysis* (Aldershot: Avebury, 1988).

Barry, Boubacar, *Senegambia and the Atlantic Slave* (Cambridge: Cambridge University Press, 1997).

Bates, Robert, *Markets and States in Tropical Africa: The Political Basis of Agricultural Policies* (Berkeley and London: University of California Press, 1981).

Essays on the Political Economy of Rural Africa (Cambridge: Cambridge University Press, 1983).

Baum, Robert M., *Shrines of the Slave Trade: Diola Religion and Society in Precolonial Senegambia* (New York and Oxford: Oxford University Press, 1999).

"Prophetess: Aline Sitoe Diatta as a contested icon in contemporary Senegal", in Toyin Falola and Fallou Ngom (eds.), *Facts, Fiction and African Creative Imaginations* (London: Routledge, 2009).

Bayart, Jean-François, *The State in Africa: The Politics of the Belly* (London: Longman, 1993).

"Africa in the world: a history of extraversion", *African Affairs* 99, 2000.

Baynham, Simon, "Divide et impera: civilian control of the military in Ghana's Second and Third Republics", *Journal of Modern African Studies* 23 (4) 1985.

Beckman, Bjorn, *Organising the Farmers: Cocoa Politics and National Development in Ghana* (Uppsala: Nordic Africa Institute, 1976).

Bekker, Simon and Therborn, Goran (eds.), *Capital Cities in Africa: Power and Powerlessness* (Cape Town: HSRC Press, 2012).

Bellagamba, Alice, Greene, Sandra and Klein, Martin A. (eds.), *The Bitter Legacy: African Slavery Past and Present* (Princeton: Markus Wiener, 2013).

Bennafla, Karine, *Le commerce frontalier en Afrique centrale: acteurs, espaces, pratiques* (Paris: Karthala, 2002).

Bennett, Valerie Plave, "Epilogue: malcontents in uniform", in Dennis Austin and Robin Luckham (eds.), *Politicians and Soldiers in Ghana, 1966–1972* (London: Frank Cass, 1972).

Berg, Elliott, "Structural transformation versus gradualism: recent economic development in Ghana", in Phillip Foster and Aristide Zolberg (eds.), *Ghana and the Ivory Coast: Perspectives on Modernization* (Chicago and London: University of Chicago Press, 1971).

Berman, Bruce, *Control and Crisis in Colonial Kenya: The Dialectic of Domination* (London, Nairobi and Athens: James Currey, Heinemann Kenya and Ohio University Press, 1990).

Berry, Sara, *Chiefs Know Their Boundaries: Essays on Property, Power, and the Past in Asante, 1896–1996* (Portsmouth, Oxford and Cape Town: Heinemann, James Currey and David Philip, 2001).

Bierschenk, Thomas and Olivier de Sardan, Jean-Pierre, "Studying the dynamics of African bureaucracies: an introduction to states at work", in Thomas Bierschenk and Jean-Pierre Olivier de Sardan (eds.), *States at Work: Dynamics of African Bureaucracies* (Leiden and Boston: Brill, 2007).

Biney, Ama, *The Political and Social Thought of Kwame Nkrumah* (New York and Houndmills: Palgrave Macmillan, 2011).

Blundo, Giorgio, "Seeing like a state agent: the ethnography of reform in Senegal's forestry services", in Thomas Bierschenk and Jean-Pierre Olivier de Sardan (eds.), *States at Work: Dynamics of African Bureaucracies* (Leiden: Brill, 2014).

Blundo, Giorgio and Le Meur, Pierre-Yves (eds.), *The Governance of Daily Life in Africa: Ethnographic Explorations of Public and Collective Services* (Leiden and Boston: Brill, 2009).

Blundo, Giorgio and Olivier de Sardan, Jean-Pierre (eds.), *Everyday Corruption and the State: Citizens and Public Officials in Africa* (London: Zed Press, 2006).

Bonney, Richard (ed.), *The Rise of the Fiscal State in Europe, c.1200–1815* (Oxford: Oxford University Press, 1999).

Boone, Catherine, *Merchant Capital and the Roots of State Power in Senegal, 1930–1985* (Cambridge: Cambridge University Press, 1992).

"Politics under the specter of deindustrialization: 'structural adjustment' in practice", in Christopher L. Delgado and Sidi Jammeh (eds.), *The Political Economy of Senegal under Structural Adjustment* (New York, Westport and London: Praeger, 1991).

Political Topographies of the African State: Territorial Authority and Institutional Choice (Cambridge: Cambridge University Press, 2003).

Property and Political Order in Africa: Land Rights and the Structure of Politics (Cambridge: Cambridge University Press, 2013).

Bosa, Miguel Suárez (ed.), *Atlantic Ports and the First Globalisation c.1850–1930* (Houndmills and New York: Palgrave Macmillan, 2014).

Bosman, William, *A New and Accurate Description of Guinea, Divided into the Gold, the Slave and the Ivory Coasts* (new edition by J.R. Willis) (London: Frank Cass, 1967 (original edition 1704)).

Bost, François, "Entre global et local: le cas de la zone franche de Lomé", in Philippe Gervais-Lambony and Gabriel Kwami Nyassogbo (eds.), *Lomé: dynamiques d'une ville africaine* (Paris: Karthala, 2007).

Bovet, David and Unnevehr, Laurian, *Agricultural Pricing in Togo, World Bank Staffing Paper No. 47* (Washington DC: World Bank, July 1981).

Bratton, Michael and Van de Walle, Nicolas, *Democratic Experiments in Africa: Regime Transitions in Comparative Perspective* (Cambridge: Cambridge University Press, 1997).

Brennan, James R., "The short history of political opposition and multi-party democracy in Tangayika, 1958–1964", in Gregory H. Maddox and James L. Giblin (eds.), *In Search of a Nation: Histories of Authority and Dissidence in Tanzania* (Oxford: James Currey, 2005).

Brenner, Neil, "The limits to scale? Methodological reflections on scalar structuration", *Progress in Human Geography* 24 (4) 2001.

New State Space: Urban Governance and the Rescaling of Statehood (Oxford: Oxford University Press, 2004).

Bretton, Henry L., *The Rise and Fall of Kwame Nkrumah: A Study of Personal Rule in Africa* (New York: Praeger, 1986).

Brewer, John, *The Sinews of Power: War, Money and the English State, 1688–1783* (London: Unwin Hyman, 1989).

Brivio, Alessandra, "Evoking the past through material culture: the Mami Tchamba shrine", in Alice Bellagamba, Sandra Greene and Martin A. Klein (eds.), *The Bitter Legacy: African Slavery Past and Present* (Princeton: Markus Wiener, 2013).

Brooks, George E., *Landlords and Strangers: Ecology, Society and Trade in Western Africa 1000–1630* (Boulder: Westview Press, 1994).

Eurafricans in West Africa: Commerce, Social Status, Gender and Religious Observance from the Sixteenth to the Eighteenth Century (Oxford and Athens: James Currey and Ohio University Press, 2003).

Brown, David, "Anglo-German rivalry and Krepi politics, 1886–1894", *Transactions of the Historical Society of Ghana* XV (ii) 1974.

"Borderline politics in Ghana: The National Liberation Movement of Western Togoland", *Journal of Modern African Studies* 18 (4) 1980.

Who are the tribalists? Social pluralism and political ideology in Ghana", *African Affairs*, 81 (322) 1982.

"Sieges and scapegoats: the politics of pluralism in Ghana and Togo", *Journal of Modern African Studies* 21 (3) 1983.

Brownlie, Ian (ed.), *African Boundaries: A Legal and Diplomatic Encyclopaedia* (London and Berkeley: C. Hurst and University of California Press, 1979).

Bryant, Kelly M. Duke, *Education as Politics: Colonial Schooling and Political Debate in Senegal 1850s–1914* (Madison: University of Wisconsin Press, 2015).

Bryars, William Hudson, "The Evolution of British Imperial Policy on the Volta, 1857–1897: From Informal Opportunism to Formal Occupation", unpublished PhD thesis, University of Birmingham, 1994.

Brydon, Lynne, "Constructing Avatime: questions of history and identity in a West African polity, c.1690s to the twentieth century", *Journal of African History* 49 (1) 2008.

Buell, Raymond Leslie, *The Native Problem in Africa,* Vol. 1 and 2 (London: Frank Cass, 1965 reprint of 1928 edition).

Buhler, Peter, "The Volta Region of Ghana: Economic Change in Togoland, 1850–1914", PhD thesis, University of California, 1975.

Burbank, Jane and Cooper, Frederick, *Empires in World History: Power and the Politics of Difference* (Princeton: Princeton University Press, 2001).

Burke, Timothy, *Lifebuoy Men, Lux Women: Commodification, Consumption and Cleanliness in Modern Zimbabwe* (London: Leicester University Press, 1996).

Cain, P.J. and Hopkins, A.G., *British Imperialism 1688–2000*, 2nd edn. (Harlow and London: Pearson Education, 2002).

Carlsson, Jerker, *The Limits to Structural Change: A Comparative Study of Foreign Investments in Liberia and Ghana, 1950–1971* (Uppsala: Scandinavian Institute of African Studies, 1981).

Cary, Joyce, *Mister Johnson* (London: Carfax, 1952).

The Case for African Freedom and Other Writings (Austin: University of Texas Press, 1962).

Casely Hayford, J.E. *Gold Coast Native Institutions with Thoughts on a Healthy Imperial Policy for the Gold Coast and Ashanti* (London: Frank Cass, reprint edn., 1970, original 1903).

Ceesay, Ebrima Jogomai, *The Military and 'Democratisation' in the Gambia: 1994–2003* (Victoria BC: Trafford Publishing, 2006).

Chabal, Patrick, *Africa: The Politics of Suffering and Smiling* (London: Zed Press, 2008).

Chabal, Patrick and Daloz, Jean-Pascal, *Africa Works: Disorder as Political Instrument* (London, Oxford and Bloomington: International Africa Institute, James Currey and Indiana University Press, 1999).

Chafer, Tony, *The End of Empire in French West Africa: France's Successful Decolonization?* (Oxford and New York: Berg, 2002).

Chalfin, Brenda, *Neoliberal Frontiers: An Ethnography of Sovereignty in West Africa* (Chicago and London: University of Chicago Press, 2010).

Chazan, Naomi, *An Anatomy of Ghanaian Politics: Managing Political Recession, 1969–1982* (Boulder: Westview, 1983).

Chittum, J. Marc (ed.), *Marketing in Togo, Overseas Business Report 77–70* (Washington DC: US Department of Commerce, Industry and Trade Administration, 1977).

Clancy-Smith, Julia, *Mediterraneans: North Africa and Europe in an Age of Migration c.1800–1900* (Berkeley, Los Angeles and London: University of California Press, 2011).

Connerton, Paul, *How Societies Remember* (Cambridge: Cambridge University Press, 1989).

Cogneau, Denis, Mesplé-Somps, Sandrine and Spielvogel, Gilles, "Development at the border: policies and national integration in Cote d'Ivoire and its neighbours", *World Bank Economic Review* 29 (1) 2015.

Cohn, Bernard S., *Colonialism and Its Forms of Knowledge: The British in India* (Princeton: Princeton University Press, 1996).

Coleman, James S., *Togoland* (New York: Carnegie Endowment for International Peace, 1956).

Conklin, Alice, *A Mission to Civilize: The Republican Idea of Empire in France and West Africa 1895–1930* (Stanford: Stanford University Press, 1997).

Cooper, Frederick *Decolonization and African Society: The Labor Question in French and British Africa* (Cambridge: Cambridge University Press, 1996).
    "Modernizing bureaucrats, backward Africans and the development concept", in Frederick Cooper and Randall Packard (eds.), *International Development and the Social Sciences: Essays on the History and Politics of Knowledge* (Berkeley and London: University of California Press, 1998).
    Africa Since 1940: The Past of the Present (Cambridge: Cambridge University Press, 2002).
    Colonialism in Question: Theory, Knowledge, History (Cambridge: Cambridge University Press, 2005).
    Citizenship between Empire and Nation: Remaking France and French Africa, 1945–1960 (Cambridge: Cambridge University Press, 2014).

Coquery-Vidrovitch, Catherine "The colonial economy of the former French, Belgian and Portuguese zones 1914–35", in A. Adu Boahen (ed.), *General History of Africa VII: Africa under Colonial Domination 1880–1935* (Paris and London: UNESCO and Heinemann, 1985).

Cordonnier, Rita, *Femmes Africaines et commerce: les revendeuses de tissu de la ville de Lomé* (Paris: L'Harmattan, 1987).

Cornevin, Robert, *Histoire du Togo* (Paris: Editions Berger-Levrault, 1962).

Co-Trung, Marina Diallo, *La Compagnie générale des oléagineux tropicaux en Casamance: autopsie d'une opération de mise en valeur coloniale (1948–1962)* (Paris: Karthala, 2000).

Craib, Raymond B., *Cartographic Mexico: A History of State Fixations and Fugitive Landscapes* (Durham and London: Duke University Press, 2004).

Crisp, Jeff, *The Story of an African Working Class: Ghanaian Miners' Struggles, 1870–1980* (London: James Currey, 1980).

Crowder, Michael, *West Africa under Colonial Rule* (London: Hutchinson, 1968).

"The white chiefs of tropical Africa", in L.H. Gann and Peter Duignan (eds.), *Colonialism in Africa, 1870–1960, II: The History and Politics of Colonialism, 1914–1960* (Cambridge, New York and London: Cambridge University Press, 1970).

Cruise O'Brien, Donal B. *Saints and Politicians: Essays in the Organisation of a Senegalese Peasant Society* (Cambridge: Cambridge University Press, 1975).

"Senegal" in John Dunn (ed.), *West African States: Failure and Promise – A Study in Comparative Politics* (Cambridge: Cambridge University Press, 1978).

"Ruling class and peasantry in Senegal, 1960–1976: the politics of a monocrop economy", in Rita Cruise O'Brien (ed.), *Political Economy of Underdevelopment: Dependence in Senegal* (Beverly Hills and London: Sage, 1979).

"The shadow-politics of Wolofisation", *Journal of Modern African Studies* 36 (1) 1998.

Symbolic Confrontations: Muslims Imagining the State in Africa (New York: Palgrave Macmillan, 2003).

d'Almeida-Ekué, Silivi, *La révolte des Loméennes 24–25 January 1933* (Lomé: Les Nouvelles Editions Africaines du Togo, 1992).

Dalakoglou, Dimitris, *The Road: An Ethnography of (Im)mobility, Space and Cross-Border Infrastructure in the Balkans* (Manchester: Manchester University Press, 2017).

Danso-Boafo, Kwaku, *The Political Biography of Dr. Kofi Abrefa Busia* (Accra: Ghana Universities Press, 1996).

Darwin, John, *Unfinished Empire: The Global Expansion of Britain* (London: Penguin, 2013).

Das, Veena and Poole, Deborah, "State and its margins: comparative ethnographies", in Veena Das and Deborah Pool (eds.), *Anthropology in the Margins of the State* (Santa Fe and Oxford: School of American Research Press and James Currey, 2004).

Daunton, Martin, *Trusting Leviathan: The Politics of Taxation in Britain, 1799–1914* (Cambridge: Cambridge University Press, 2001).

Just Taxes: The Politics of Taxation in Britain, 1914–1979 (Cambridge: Cambridge University Press, 2002).

De Benoist, Joseph-Roger, *La balkanization de l'Afrique Occidentale Francaise* (Dakar: Nouvelles Editions Africaines, 1979).

L'Afrique Occidentale Française de la conférence de Brazzaville (1944) à l'indépendance (1960) (Dakar: Nouvelles Editions Africaines, 1982).

Decalo, Samuel, *Coups and Army Rule in Africa: Motivations and Constraints*, 2nd edn. (New Haven: Yale University Press, 1990).

De Jong, Ferdinand, *Masquerades of Modernity: Power and Secrecy in Casamance, Senegal* (Edinburgh: Edinburgh University Press for the International Africa Institute, 2007).

Debrunner, Hans, *A Church between Colonial Powers: A Study of the Church in Togo* (London: Lutterworth Press, 1965).

Degli, Jean Yaovi, *Togo: la tragédie africaine* (Ivry-sur-Seine: Editions Nouvelles du Sud, 1996).

Dereje, Feyissa, "More than the state? The Anywaa's call for rigidification of the Ethio-Sudanese border", in Dereje Feyissa and Markus Virgil Hoehne (eds.), *Borders and Borderlands in the Horn of Africa* (Woodbridge and Rochester: James Currey, 2010).

Playing Different Games: The Paradox of Anywaa and Nuer Identification Strategies in the Gambella Region, Ethiopia (New York and Oxford: Berghahn, 2011).

Dereje, Feyissa and Hoehne, Markus Virgil (eds.), *Borders and Borderlands in the Horn of Africa* (Woodbridge and Rochester: James Currey, 2010).

Dincecco, Mark, Federico, Giovanni and Vindigni, Andrea, "Warfare, taxation and political change: evidence from the Italian Risorgimento", *Journal of Economic History* 71 (4) 2011.

Diop, Momar Coumba, "Les affaires mourides à Dakar", *Politique Africaine* 1 (4) 1981.

Diouf, Mamadou, "Beyond patronage and 'technocracy'", in Momar Coumba Diop (ed.), *Senegal: Essays in Statecraft* (Dakar: CODESRIA, 1993).

Histoire du Sénégal: le modèle islamo-wolof et ses périphéries (Paris: Maisonneuve and Larose, 2001).

Dobler, Gregor, "Oshikango: the dynamics of growth and regulation in a Namibian boom town", *Journal of Southern African Studies* 35 (1) 2009.

Doevenspeck, Martin and Mwanabiningo, Nene Morisho, "Navigating uncertainty: observations from the Congo-Rwanda border", in Bettina Bruns and Judith Miggelbrink (eds.), *Subverting Borders: Doing Research on Smuggling and Small-Scale Trade* (Wiesbaden: VS Verlag, 2012).

Donham, Donald, "Old Abysinnia and the new Ethiopian empire", in Donald Donham and Wendy James (eds.), *The Southern Marches of Imperial Ethiopia* (Oxford: James Currey, 2002).

Dowse, Robert, "Military and police rule", in Dennis Austin and Robin Luckham (eds.), *Politicians and Soldiers in Ghana* (London: Frank Cass, 1975).

Dumoulin, Jérome and Kaddar, Miloud, "Le prix de médicaments dans certains pays d'Afrique: comparaison avec le prix français", *Sciences Sociales et Santé* 8 (1) 1990.

Dwyer, Maggie, "Fragmented forces: the development of the Gambian military", *African Security Review* 26 (4) 2017.

Edney, Matthew H., *Mapping an Empire: The Geographical Construction of British India, 1765–1843* (Chicago and London: Chicago University Press, 1997).

Ellis, Stephen and Ter Haar, Gerrie, *Worlds of Power: Religious Thought and Political Practice in Africa* (London: C. Hurst, 2004).

Englebert, Pierre, *State Legitimacy and Development in Africa* (Boulder: Lynne Rienner, 2000).

Englund, Harri, *From War to Peace on the Mozambique–Malawi Borderland* (London and Edinburgh: International Africa Institute and Edinburgh University Press, 2002).

Erdmann, Gero and Engel, Ulf. *Neopatrimonialism Revisited – Beyond a Catch-All Concept*, GIGA Working Papers, 16 February 2006.

Esseks, J.D., "Economic policies", in Dennis Austin and Robin Luckham (eds.), *Politicians and Soldiers in Ghana* (London: Frank Cass, 1975).

Evans, Martin, *Senegal: Mouvement des Forces Démocratiques de la Casamance*, Chatham House, Briefing Paper 04/02, November 2004.

Evans, Martin and Ray, Charlotte, "Uncertain ground: the Gambia and the Casamance conflict", in Abdoulaye Saine, Ebrima Ceesay and Ebrima Sall (eds.), *State and Society in the Gambia Since Independence 1965–2012* (Trenton: Africa World Press, 2013).

Fassin, Didier, "Du clandestin à les officieux: les réseaux de vente illicite des médicaments au Sénégal", *Cahiers d'Etudes Africaines* XXV (2) 1985.

"La vente illicite des médicaments au Sénégal: économies 'parallèles', état et société", *Politique Africaine* 13, 1986.

Fatton Jnr., Robert, *The Making of a Liberal Democracy: Senegal's Passive Revolution, 1975–1985* (Boulder and London: Lynne Rienner, 1987).

Faye, Jacques, *Land and Decentralization in Senegal*, IIED Issue Paper no. 149 (London: International Institute for Environment and Development, 2008).

Fisher, Humphrey J., "Conversion reconsidered: some historical aspects of religious conversion in Africa", *Africa* 43 (1) 1973.

Flynn, Donna, "'We are the border': identity, exchange and the state along the Benin–Nigeria border", *American Ethnologist* 24 (2) 1997.

Foucher, Vincent, "Les 'évolués', la migration, l'école: pour une nouvelle interprétation de la naissance du nationalisme casamançais", in Momar-Coumba Diop (ed.), *Le Sénégal contemporain* (Paris: Karthala, 2002).

"La guerre des dieux? religions et séparatisme en Basse Casamance", *Canadian Journal of African Studies* 39 (2) 2005.

"The Mouvement des Forces Democratiques de Casamance: The illusion of separatism?", unpublished paper.

Franco, G. Robert, "The optimal producer price of cocoa in Ghana", *Journal of Development Economics* 8 (1) 1981.

Frankema, Ewout, "Colonial taxation and government spending in British Africa, 1880–1940: maximizing revenue or minimizing effort?", *Explorations in Economic History*, 48 (1) 2011.

Frederiks, Martha T. *We Have Toiled All Night: Christianity in the Gambia, 1456–2000* (Zoetermeer: Uitgeverij Boekencentrum, 2003).

Freund, Bill, *The African City: A History* (Cambridge: Cambridge University Press, 2007).

Frimpong-Ansah, Jonathan, *The Vampire State in Africa: The Political Economy of Decline in Ghana* (London and Trenton: James Currey and Africa World Press, 1991).

Fuller, C.J. and Harriss, John, "For an anthropology of the modern Indian state", in C.J. Fuller and Véronique Bénéï (eds.), *The Everyday State and Society in Modern India* (London: C. Hurst and Company, 2001).

Gailey, Harry A., *A History of the Gambia* (London: Routledge and Kegan Paul, 1964).

Gallagher, John and Robinson, Ronald, "The imperialism of free trade", *Economic History Review*, 2nd series, VI (1) 1953.

Galloway, Winifred, "A Listing of Some Kaabu States and Associated Areas: Signposts towards State-by-State Research in Kaabu", paper delivered at International Kaabu Colloquium, Dakar, 19–24 May 1980.

Galvan, Dennis C., *'The State Must Be Our Master of Fire': How Peasants Craft Culturally Sustainable Development in Senegal* (Berkeley, Los Angeles and London: University of California Press, 2004).

Gardner, Leigh A., *Taxing Colonial Africa: The Political Economy of British Imperialism* (Oxford: Oxford University Press, 2012).

"The curious incident of the franc in the Gambia: exchange rate instability and imperial monetary systems in the 1920s", *Financial History Review* 22 (3) 2015.

Gasser, Geneviève, "'Manger ou s'en aller': que veulent les opposants armés casamançais?", in Momar-Coumba Diop (ed.), *Le Sénégal contemporain* (Paris: Karthala, 2002).

Gayibor, Nicoué Lodjou (ed.), *Le Togo sous domination coloniale (1884–1960)* (Lomé: Presses de l'UB, 1997).

Gehrold, Stefan and Tietze, Lena, "Far from altruistic: China's presence in Senegal", Konrad Adenauer Stiftung, *KAS International Reports* 11/2011.

Geiger, Susan, *TANU Women: Gender and Culture in the Making of Tanganyikan Nationalism, 1955–65* (Oxford: James Currey, 1997).

Gellar, Sheldon, "Circulaire 32 revisited: prospects for revitalizing the Senegalese co-operative movement in the 1980s", in Mark Gersovitz and John Waterbury (eds.), *The Political Economy of Risk and Choice in Senegal* (London: Frank Cass, 1987).

The Making of a Liberal Democracy: Senegal's Passive Revolution, 1975–1985 (Boulder and London: Lynne Rienner, 1987).

Genoud, Roger, *Nationalism and Economic Development in Ghana* (New York: Praeger, 1969).

Gerry, Chris, "The crisis of the self-employed: petty production and capitalist production in Dakar", in Rita Cruise O'Brien (ed.), *Political Economy of Underdevelopment: Dependence in Senegal* (Beverly Hills and London: Sage, 1979).

Gersovitz, Mark and Waterbury, John, "Introduction", in Mark Gersovitz and John Waterbury (eds.), *The Political Economy of Risk and Choice in Senegal* (London: Frank Cass, 1987).

"Some sources and implications of uncertainty in the Senegalese economy", in Mark Gersovitz and John Waterbury (eds.), *The Political Economy of Risk and Choice in Senegal* (London: Frank Cass, 1987).

Gervais-Lambony, Philippe and Nyassogbo, Gabriel Kwami (eds.), *Lomé: dynamiques d'une ville africaine* (Paris: Karthala, 2007).

Gervais-Lambony, Philippe "Lomé", in Simon Bekker and Goran Therborn (eds.), *Capital Cities in Africa: Power and Powerlessness* (Cape Town: HSRC Press, 2012).

Geschiere, Peter, *The Perils of Belonging: Autochthony, Citizenship and Exclusion in Africa and Europe* (Chicago and London: University of Chicago Press, 2009).

Gewald, Jan-Bart and Hinfelaar, Marja (eds.), *One Zambia, Many Histories: Towards a History of Post-Colonial Zambia* (Leiden: Brill, 2008).

Ginio, Ruth, "Vichy rule in French West Africa: prelude to decolonization", *French Colonial History*, 4, 2003.

French Colonialism Unmasked: The Vichy Years in French West Africa (Lincoln: University of Nebraska Press, 2006).

Girard, Jean, *Genèse du pouvoir charismatique en Basse Casamance (Sénégal)* (Dakar: IFAN, 1969).

Goeh-Akue, N'Buéké Adovi, "Finances Publiques et Dynamique Sociale en Afrique Noire Sous Influence Française: Le Cas du Togo (1920–1980)", thèse pour le Doctorat d'Histoire et Civilisations, Université Paris VII-Jussieu, December 1992.

"Atakpame, un carrefour seculaire d'echange multi-sectorel du XVIIIe au XXe siecle", in T. Gbeasor (ed.), *Espace, culture et developpement dans la region d'Atakpame* (Lomé: Presses de l'UB, 1999).

Goerg, Odile, *Pouvoir colonial, municipalités et espaces urbains: Conakry-Freetown des années 1880 a 1914*, Vol. 1 and 2 (Paris and Montreal: l'Harmattan, 1997).

Golub, Stephen and Mbaye, Ahmadou Aly, "National trade policies and smuggling in Africa: the case of the Gambia and Senegal", *World Development* 37 (3) 2008.

Gray, J.M., *A History of the Gambia* (Cambridge: Cambridge University Press, 1940).

Green, Reginald H., "Reflections on economic strategy, structure, implementation and necessity: Ghana and the Ivory Coast", in Phillip Foster and Aristide Zolberg (eds.), *Ghana and the Ivory Coast: Perspectives on Modernization* (Chicago and London: University of Chicago Press, 1971).

Greene, Sandra, *Gender, Ethnicity and Social Change on the Upper Slave Coast: A History of the Anlo Ewe* (Portsmouth and London: Heinemann and James Currey, 1996).

Sacred Sites and the Colonial Encounter: A History of Meaning and Memory in Ghana (Bloomington: Indiana University Press, 2002).

Griffiths, Ieuan, "Maps, boundaries, ambiguity and change in the Gambia", in Jeffrey Stone (ed.), *Maps and Africa: Proceedings of a Colloquium at the University of Aberdeen, April 1993* (Aberdeen: Aberdeen University African Studies Group, 1994).

Guèye, Cheikh, *Touba: la capitale des Mourides* (Dakar and Paris: Enda, Karthala and IRD, 2002).

Guyer, Jane I., "Wealth in people, wealth in things – introduction", *Journal of African History*, 36 (1) 1995.

Hadjimichael, Michael T., Rumbaugh, Thomas and Verreydt, Eric, *The Gambia; Economic Adjustment in a Small Open Economy* (Washington DC: IMF, 1999).

Hailey, Lord, *An African Survey, Revised 1956* (London, New York and Toronto: Oxford University Press, 1957).

Hanretta, Sean, *Islam and Social Change in French West Africa: History of an Emancipatory Community* (Cambridge: Cambridge University Press, 2010).

Hansen, Thomas Blom, "Governance and myths of the state in Mumbai", in C.J. Fuller and Véronique Bénéï (eds.), *The Everyday State and Society in Modern India* (London: C. Hurst and Company, 2001).

Hansen, Thomas Blom and Stepputat, Finn, "Introduction: state of imagination", in Thomas Blom Hansen and Finn Stepputat (eds.), *States of Imagination: Ethnographic Explorations of the Postcolonial State* (Durham and London: Duke University Press, 2001).

Hargreaves, John D., *Prelude to the Partition of West Africa* (London: Macmillan, 1963).

Hawthorne, Walter, *Planting Rice and Harvesting Slaves: Transformations along the Guinea-Bissau Coast, 1400–1900* (Portsmouth: Heinemann, 2003).

Heath, Elizabeth, *Wine, Sugar and the Making of Modern France: Global Economic Crisis and the Racialization of French Citizenship, 1870–1910* (Cambridge: Cambridge University Press, 2014).

Herbst, Jeffrey, *States and Power in Africa: Comparative Lessons in Authority and Control* (Princeton: Princeton University Press, 2000).

Hernaes, Per, *Slaves, Danes and African Coast Society: The Danish Slave Trade from West Africa and Afro-Danish Relations on the Eighteenth-Century Gold Coast* (Trondheim: University of Trondheim, Department of History, 1998).

Herslet, E., *The Map of Africa by Treaty*, Vol. 1 and 2, reprint edn. (London: Frank Cass, 1967).

Hesseling, Gerti, *Histoire politique du Sénégal: institutions, droit et société* (Paris: Karthala, 1985).

Hiribarren, Vincent, *A History of Borno: Trans-Saharan African Empire to Failing Nigerian State* (London: C. Hurst, 2017).

Hopkins, A.G., "Economic imperialism in West Africa: Lagos, 1880–92", *Economic History Review* 21 (3) 1968.

  "The 'New International Economic Order' in the nineteenth century", in Robin Law (ed.), *From Slave Trade to 'Legitimate Commerce': The Commercial Transition in Nineteenth-Century West Africa* (Cambridge: Cambridge University Press, 1995).

Hopkins, Peter, *Peter Thonning and Denmark's Guinea Commission: A Study in Nineteenth Century Colonial Geography* (Leiden: Brill, 2013).

Horton, Robin, "African conversion", *Africa* 41 (2) 1971.

  "On the rationality of conversion. Part I", *Africa* 45 (3) 1975.

  "On the rationality of conversion. Part II", *Africa* 45 (4) 1975.

Houngnikpo, Mathurin, *Determinants of Democratization in Africa: A Comparative Study of Benin and Togo* (Lanham: University Press of America, 2001).

Howard, Allen M. and Shain, Richard M (eds.), *The Spatial Factor in African History: The Relationship of the Social, Material and the Perceptual* (Leiden and Boston: Brill, 2005).

Howard, Rhoda, *Colonialism and Underdevelopment in Ghana* (London: Croom Helm, 1978).

Howland, Douglas and White, Luise, "Introduction: Sovereignty and the Study of States", in Douglas Howland and Luise S. White (eds.), *The State of Sovereignty: Territories, Laws, Populations* (Bloomington: Indiana University Press, 2009).

Hughes, Arnold, "L'effondrement de la Confédération de la Sénégambie", in Momar-Coumba Diop (ed.), *Le Sénégal et ses voisins* (Dakar: Sociétés-Espaces-Temps, 1994).

Hughes, Arnold and Perfect, David, *A Political History of the Gambia, 1816–1994* (Rochester: University of Rochester Press, 2006).

Hughes, David McDermott, *From Enslavement to Environmentalism: Politics on a Southern African Frontier* (Seattle and London: University of Washington Press, 2006).

Hutchful, Eboe, (ed.), *The IMF and Ghana: The Confidential Record* (London: Zed Press, 1987).

Hutchful, Eboe, *Ghana's Adjustment Experience: The Paradox of Reform* (Geneva and Oxford: UNRISD and James Currey, 2002).

"The fall and rise of the state in Ghana", in Abdi Ismail Samatar and Ahmed I. Samatar (eds.), *The African State: Reconsiderations* (Portsmouth: Heinemann, 2002).

Jeffries, Richard, *Class, Power and Ideology: The Railwaymen of Sekondi* (Cambridge: Cambridge University Press, 1978).

Jerven, Morten, *Poor Numbers: How We Are Misled by African Development Statistics and What to Do About It* (Ithaca: Cornell University Press, 2013).

Africa: Why Economists Get It Wrong (London: Zed, 2015).

Jobson, Richard, *The Golden Trade; Or, a Discovery of the River Gambra and the Golden Trade of the Aethiopians* (1st edn. 1623, revised edition by Walter Rodney) (London: Dawsons, 1968).

Johnson, G. Wesley, *The Emergence of Black Politics in Senegal: The Struggle for Power in the Four Communes 1900–1920* (Stanford: Stanford University Press, 1971).

"William Ponty (1866–1915) and Republican paternalism in French West Africa", in Lewis H. Gann and Peter Duignan (eds.), *African Proconsuls: European Governors in Africa* (New York, London and Stanford: Free Press, Collier Macmillan and Hoover Institution Press, 1977).

Johnson, Marion, "Ashanti east of the Volta", *Transactions of the Historical Society of Ghana* VIII, 1965.

Jones, Christine and Radelet, Steven C., "The groundnut sector", in Malcolm F. McPherson and Steven C. Radelet (eds.), *Economic Recovery in the Gambia: Insights for Structural Adjustment in Sub-Saharan Africa* (Cambridge: Harvard University Press, 1995).

Jones, Trevor, *Ghana's First Republic, 1960–1966: The Pursuit of the Political Kingdom* (London: Methuen, 1976).

Joseph, Gilbert M. and Nugent, Daniel, "Popular culture and state formation in revolutionary Mexico", in Gilbert M. Joseph and Daniel Nugent (eds.), *Everyday Forms of State Formation: Revolution and the Negotiation of Rule in Modern Mexico* (Durham and London: Duke University Press, 1994).

Justesen, Ole (ed.), *Danish Sources for the History of Ghana, 1657–1754*, Vol. 1 and 2 (Copenhagen: Royal Danish Academy of Sciences, 2005).

Kanya-Forstner, A.S. *The Conquest of the Western Sudan: A Study in French Military Imperialism* (Cambridge: Cambridge University Press, 1969).

Kasfir, Nelson, "State, magendo and class formation in Uganda", *Journal of Commonwealth and Comparative Politics* 21 (3) 1983.

Katzenellenbogen, Simon, "'It didn't happen at Berlin': politics, economics and ignorance in the setting of Africa's colonial boundaries", in Paul Nugent and

A.I. Asiwaju (eds.), *African Boundaries: Barriers, Conduits and Opportunities* (London: Frances Pinter, 1996).

Kay, Geoffrey (ed.), *The Political Economy of Colonialism in Ghana: Documents and Statistics, 1900–1960* (Cambridge: Cambridge University Press, 1972).

Kea, Pamela, *Land, Labour and Entrustment: West African Female Farmers and the Politics of Difference* (Leiden: Brill, 2010).

Kea, Ray, "Akwamu-Anlo relations c.1750–1813", *Transactions of the Historical Society of Ghana* X, 1969.

"Administration and trade in the Akwamu empire, 1681–1730", in B.K. Swartz and Raymond E. Dumett (eds.), *West African Culture Dynamics* (Berlin: De Gruyter Mouton, 1980).

Kedem, Kosi, *How Britain Subverted and Betrayed British Togoland* (Accra: Government and Electoral Systems Agency, 2007).

Keese, Alexander, *Ethnicity and the Colonial State: Finding and Representing Group Identifications in a Coastal West African and Global Perspective (1850–1960)* (Leiden: Brill, 2016).

Kelly, Valerie and Delgado, Christopher L., "Agricultural performance under Structural Adjustment", in Christopher L. Delgado and Sidi Jammeh (eds.), *The Political Economy of Senegal under Structural Adjustment* (New York, Westport and London: Praeger, 1991).

Killick, Tony, *Development Economics in Action: A Study of Economic Policies in Ghana* (London: Heinemann, 1978).

Killingray, David, *Fighting for Britain: African Soldiers in the Second World War* (Woodbridge: James Currey, 2010).

Kimble, David, *A Political History of Ghana, 1850–1928* (Oxford: Clarendon Press, 1963).

Kirk-Greene, A.H.M., "The thin white line: the size of the British colonial service in Africa", *African Affairs* 79 (314) 1980.

Klein, Martin, *Islam and Imperialism in Senegal: Sine-Saloum, 1847–1914* (Edinburgh: Edinburgh University Press, 1968).

Knoll, Arthur, *Togo under Imperial Germany, 1884–1914: A Case-Study in Colonial Rule* (Stanford: Hoover Institution Press, 1978).

Koelle, Sigismund Wilhelm, *Polyglotta Africana* (Paul Hair and David Dalby, eds.), (Graz: Akademische Druk – U. Verlagsanstalt, 1963 (original edition 1854)).

Koffi, Kodjo, "Réjouissances privées et cérémonies officielles: une histoire socio-politique de la fête à Lomé", in Odile Goerg (ed.), *Fêtes urbaines en Afrique: espaces, identités et pouvoirs* (Paris: Karthala, 1999).

Konings, Piet, *The State and Rural Class Formation in Ghana: A Comparative Analysis* (London: KPI, 1986).

Kopytoff, Igor, "The internal African frontier: the making of African political culture", in Igor Kopytoff (ed.), *The African Frontier: The Reproduction of Traditional African Societies* (Bloomington and Indianapolis: Indiana University Press, 1987).

Korf, Benedikt, Hagmann, Tobias and Doevenspeck, Martin, "Geographies of violence and sovereignty: the African Frontier revisited", in Benedikt Korf and Timothy Raeymaekers (eds.), *Violence on the Margins: States, Conflicts and Borderlands* (New York and Houndmills: Palgrave Macmillan, 2013).

Kraamer, Malika "Colourful Changes: Two Hundred Years of Social and Design History in the Hand-Woven Textiles of the Ewe-Speaking Regions of Ghana and Togo (1800–2000)", unpublished PhD thesis, School of Oriental and African Studies, 2005.

Ladd, William C. and McClelland, James C., *Francophone Africa: A Report on Business Opportunities in Togo* (Washington DC: Overseas Private Investment Corporation, 1975).

Lambert, Michael C., *Longing for Exile: Migration and Making of a Translocal Community in Senegal, West Africa* (Portsmouth: Heinemann, 2002).

Landell-Mills, Pierre and Ngo, Brian, "Creating the basis for long-term growth", in Christopher L. Delgado and Sidi Jammeh (eds.), *The Political Economy of Senegal under Structural Adjustment* (New York, Westport and London: Praeger, 1991).

Lange, Marie-France, *L'école au Togo: processus de scolarisation et institution de l'école en Afrique* (Paris: Karthala, 1998).

Larmer, Miles, *Rethinking African Politics: A History of Opposition in Zambia* (Farnham and Burlington: Ashgate, 2011).

Last, Murray, *The Sokoto Caliphate* (London: Longman, 1967).

Laumann, Dennis, *Remembering the Germans in Ghana* (Berne: Peter Lang, 2016).

Law, Robin, "Dahomey and the slave trade: reflections on the historiography of the rise of Dahomey", *Journal of African History* 27, 1986.

The Slave Coast of West Africa, 1550–1750: The Impact of the Atlantic Slave Trade on an African Society (Oxford: Oxford University Press, 1991).

Ouidah: The Social History of a West African Slaving Port 1727–1892 (Oxford and Athens: James Currey and Ohio University Press, 2004).

Lawler, Nancy, "Reform and repression under the Free French: economic and political transformation in the Cote d'Ivoire, 1942–45", *Africa* 60 (1) 1990.

Soldiers, Airmen, Spies and Whisperers: The Gold Coast in World War II (Athens: Ohio University Press, 2002).

Lawrance, Benjamin N., "'En proie à la fièvre du cacao': land and resource conflict on an Ewe frontier, 1922–1939", *African Economic History* 31, 2003.

"Bankoe v. Dome: traditions and petitions in the Ho-Asogli amalgamation, British Mandated Togoland, 1919–1939", *Journal of African History* 46 (2) 2005.

Locality, Mobility and Nation: Periurban Colonialism in Togo's Eweland, 1900–1960 (Rochester: Rochester University Press, 2007).

Leary, Fay, "Islam, politics and colonialism: a political history of Islam in the Casamance region of Senegal (1850–1914)", unpublished PhD thesis, Northwestern University, 1970.

Lefebvre, Camille, *Frontières de sable, frontières de papier: Histoire de territoires et de frontières, du jihad de Sokoto à la colonisation française du Niger, XIXe-XXe siècles* (Paris: Publications de la Sorbonne, 2015).

Lentz, Carola, *Land, Mobility and Belonging in West Africa* (Bloomington and Indianapolis: Indiana University Press, 2013).

Lentz, Carola and Nugent, Paul, "Ethnicity in Ghana: a comparative perspective", in Carola Lentz and Paul Nugent (eds.), *Ethnicity in Ghana: The Limits of Invention* (Houndmills: Macmillan, 2000).

Levi, Margaret, *Of Rule and Revenue* (Berkeley and London: University of California Press, 1988).

LeVine, Victor, *Political Corruption: The Ghana Case* (Stanford: Hoover Institution Press, 1975).

Lewis, J.E., "The ruling compassions of the late colonial state: welfare versus force, c.1945–1952", *Journal of Colonialism and Colonial History* 2 (2) 2001.

Lewis, John P. "Aid, structural adjustment, and Senegalese agriculture", in Mark Gersovitz and John Waterbury (eds.), *The Political Economy of Risk and Choice in Senegal* (London: Frank Cass, 1987).

Linares, Olga, "Islamic 'conversion' reconsidered", *Cambridge Anthropology* 11, 1986.
    Power, Prayer and Production: The Jola of Casamance, Senegal (Cambridge: Cambridge University Press, 1992).

Lonsdale, John and Berman, Bruce, "Coping with contradictions: the development of the colonial state in Kenya, 1895–1914", *Journal of African History* 20 (4) 1979.

Lovejoy, Paul E. and Hogendorn, Jan S., *Slow Death for Slavery: The Course of Abolition in Northern Nigeria, 1897–1936* (Cambridge: Cambridge University Press, 1993).

Luckham, Robin, "The Constitutional Commission", in Dennis Austin and Robin Luckham (eds.), *Politicians and Soldiers in Ghana, 1966–1972* (London: Frank Cass, 1972).

Lugard, F.D., "Memo No 5: Taxation", in *Instructions to Political and Other Officers on Subjects Chiefly Political Administrative* (London: Waterlow and Sons, 1906).
    The Dual Mandate in British Tropical Africa (Edinburgh and London: Blackwood, 1926).

MacArthur, Julie, *Cartography and the Political Imagination: Mapping Community in Colonial Kenya* (Athens: Ohio University Press, 2016).

MacGaffey, Janet, *The Real Economy of Zaire: The Contribution of Smuggling and Other Unofficial Activities to National Wealth* (London and Philadelphia: James Currey and University of Pennsylvania Press, 1991).

Macintosh, Maureen, "The political economy of industrial wages in Senegal", in Rita Cruise O'Brien (ed.), *Political Economy of Underdevelopment: Dependence in Senegal* (Beverly Hills and London: Sage, 1979).

Mackenzie, John M., *Propaganda and Empire: The Manipulation of British Public Opinion, 1880–1960* (Manchester: Manchester University Press, 1986).

MacGaffey, Janet, *The Real Economy of Zaire: The Contribution of Smuggling and Other Unofficial Activities to National Wealth* (London and Philadelphia: James Currey and University of Pennsylvania Press, 1991).

MacLean, Lauren M., *Informal Institutions and Citizenship in Rural Africa: Risk and Reciprocity in Ghana and Cote d'Ivoire* (Cambridge: Cambridge University Press, 2010).

Macola, Giacomo, *Liberal Nationalism in Central Africa: A Biography of Harry Mwaanga Nkumbula* (Houndmills and New York: Palgrave Macmillan, 2009).

Mahoney, Florence K. Olamara, "Government and Opinion in the Gambia, 1816–1901", unpublished PhD thesis, London University, 1963.

Maier, D.J.E., "The bird and tortoise syndrome: limitations imposed by populace and produce of the Asante-Ewe war of 1869–1871", paper presented at the African Studies Association conference, Bloomington, 1981.

"Military acquisition of slaves in Asante", in David Henige and T.C. McCaskie (eds.), *West African Economic and Social History: Studies in Memory of Marion Johnson* (Madison: Wisconsin University African Studies Programme, 1990).

Makaku, Nene Ahortor V, *A Brief History of the Lehs Vis-à-Vis the Agotimes* (Accra: the author, 2016).

Malki, Xerxes, "The Alienated Stranger: A Political and Economic History of the Lebanese in Ghana, c.1925–1992". Unpublished PhD thesis, University of Oxford, 2008.

Mamdani, Mahmood, *Citizen and Subject: Contemporary Africa and the Legacy of Late Colonialism* (Princeton: Princeton University Press, 1996).

Manchuelle, François, *Willing Migrants: Soninke Labor Diasporas, 1848–1960* (Oxford and Athens: James Currey and Ohio University Press, 1997).

Mann, Kristin, *Slavery and the Birth of an African City: Lagos 1760–1900* (Bloomington: Indiana University Press, 2007).

Marfaing, Laurence and Thiel, Alena, *Chinese Commodity Imports in Ghana and Senegal: Demystifying Chinese Business Strength in Urban West Africa*, GIGA Working Papers No. 80, 2011.

Marguerat, Yves, *Lomé: une brève histoire de la capitale du Togo* (Lomé and Paris: Haho and Karthala, 1992).

Dynamique urbaine, jeunesse et histoire au Togo (Lomé: Presses de l'UB, 1993).

Mark, Peter, "Urban migration, cash cropping and calamity: the spread of Islam among the Diola of Boulouf (Senegal), 1900–1940", *African Studies Review* 21 (2) 1978.

A Cultural, Economic and Religious History of the Basse Casamance Since 1500 (Stuttgart: Franz Steiner Verlag, 1985).

"Portuguese" Style and Luso-African Identity: Precolonial Senegambia, Sixteenth–Nineteenth Centuries (Bloomington: Indiana University Press, 2002).

Markakis, John, *Ethiopia: The Last Two Frontiers* (London: James Currey, 2011).

Marshall-Fratani, Ruth, "The war of 'who is who': autochthony, nationalism and citizenship in the Ivorian crisis", *African Studies Review*, 49 (2) 2006.

Martin, Frederic and Crawford, Eric, "The new agricultural policy: its feasibility and implications for the future", in Christopher L. Delgado and Sidi Jammeh (eds.), *The Political Economy of Senegal under Structural Adjustment* (New York, Westport and London: Praeger, 1991).

Martínez, Oscar J. *Border People: Life and Society in the U.S.–Mexico Borderlands* (Tucson: University of Arizona Press, 1994).

Marut, Jean-Claude, "Le dessous des cartes casamançaises: une approche géopolitique du conflit casamançais", in François George Barbier-Wiesser (ed.), *Comprendre la Casamance: chronique d'une intégration contrastée* (Paris, 1994).

"Le particularisme au risque de l'Islam dans le conflit casamançais", *L'Afrique Politique* (2002).

"Le problème casamançais: est-il soluble dans l'état-nation?"in Momar-Coumba Diop (ed.), *Le Sénégal contemporain* (Paris: Karthala, 2002).

Le conflit du Casamance: ce qui disent les armes (Paris: Karthala, 2010).

Mathys, Gillian, *People on the Move: Frontiers, Borders, Mobility and History in the Lake Kivu Region 19th–20th Century*, PhD thesis, University of Ghent, 2014.

May, Ernesto, *Exchange Controls and Parallel Market Economies in Sub-Saharan Africa: Focus on Ghana*, World Bank Staff Working Paper No. 711 (Washington DC: World Bank, 1985).

Mbembe, Achille, *On the Postcolony* (Berkeley, Los Angeles and London: University of California Press, 2001).

Mbodji, Mohamed, "The politics of independence: 1960–1986", in Christopher L. Delgado and Sidi Jammeh (eds.), *The Political Economy of Senegal under Structural Adjustment* (New York, Westport and London: Praeger, 1991).

"D'une frontière à l'autre, ou l'histoire de la marginalisation des commerçants Senegambiens sur la longue durée: la Gambie de 1816 à 1979", in Boubacar Barry and Leonhard Harding (eds.), *Commerce et commerçants en Afrique de l'Ouest: le Sénégal* (Paris: l'Harmattan, 1992).

McCaskie, T.C., "Accumulation, wealth and belief in Asante history, I: to the close of the nineteenth century", *Africa* 53 (1) 1983.

"Accumulation, wealth and belief in Asante history, Part II: the twentieth century", *Africa* 56 (1) 1986.

State and Society in Pre-Colonial Asante (Cambridge: Cambridge University Press, 1995).

McDougall, James and Scheele, Judith (eds.), *Saharan Frontiers: Space and Mobility in Northwest Africa* (Bloomington and Indianapolis: Indiana University Press, 2012).

McEwan, A.C., *The International Boundaries of East Africa* (Oxford: Clarendon Press, 1971).

McGowan, Jamie, "Uncovering the roles of African surveyors and draftsmen in mapping the Gold Coast", in James R. Akerman (ed.), *Decolonizing the Map: Cartography from Colony to Nation* (Chicago and London: Chicago University Press, 2017).

McGregor, JoAnn, *Crossing the Zambezi: The Politics of Landscape on a Central African Frontier* (Oxford: James Currey, 2009).

McPherson, Malcolm, "Macroeconomic reform and agriculture", in Malcolm F. McPherson and Steven C. Radelet (eds.), *Economic Recovery in the Gambia: Insights for Structural Adjustment in Sub-Saharan Africa* (Cambridge: Harvard University Press, 1995).

McPherson, Malcolm F. and Radelet, Steven C., "The Economic Recovery Programme: background and formulation", in Malcolm F. McPherson and Steven C. Radelet (eds.), *Economic Recovery in the Gambia: Insights for Structural Adjustment in Sub-Saharan Africa* (Cambridge: Harvard University Press, 1995).

Médard, Jean-François, "Patrimonialism, neo-patrimonialism and the study of the post-colonial state in Subsaharan Africa", in Henrik Secher Marcussen (ed.), *Improved Natural Resource Management – The Role of Formal Organisations and Informal Networks and Institutions* (Roskilde: IDS, 1996).

Méguelle, Phillippe, *Chefferie coloniale et égalitarianisme diola: les difficultés de la politique indigène de la France en Basse-Casamance (Sénégal), 1828–1923* (Paris: L'Harmattan, 2012).

Meillassoux, Claude, *The Anthropology of Slavery: The Womb of Iron and Gold* (London: Athlone Press, 1991).

Miliband, Ralph, *The State in Capitalist Society* (London: Weidenfeld and Nicolson, 1969).

Miles, William F.S., *Hausaland Divided: Colonialism and Independence in Nigeria and Niger* (Ithaca: Cornell University Press, 1994).

Miller, Joseph, *Way of Death: Merchant Capitalism and the Angolan Slave Trade, 1730–1830* (London: James Currey, 1988).

Mitchell, Timothy, *Colonising Egypt* (Cambridge: Cambridge University Press, 1988).
  "The limits of the state: beyond statist approaches and their critics", *American Political Science Review* 85 (1)1991.
  "Society, economy and the state effect" in G. Steinmetz (ed.), *State/Culture: State-Formation after the Cultural Turn* (Ithaca: Cornell University Press, 1999).

Monroe, J. Cameron, *The Precolonial State in West Africa: Building Power in Dahomey* (Cambridge: Cambridge University Press, 2014).

Moore, Francis, *Travels into the Inland Parts of Africa* (London: E. Cave, 1738).

Murillo, Bianca, *Market Encounters: Consumer Cultures in Twentieth-Century Ghana* (Athens: Ohio University Press, 2017).

Myers, Garth, *African Cities: Alternative Visions of Urban Theory and Practice* (London: Zed Press, 2011).

Napo, Pierre Ali, *Togo, Land of Tuskegee Institute's International Technical Assistance Experimentation: 1900–1909* (Accra: Onyase Press, 2002).

Neuberger, Benyamin, "The African concept of balkanisation", *Journal of Modern African Studies* 14 (3) 1976.

Newbury, C.W., "The protectionist revival in French colonial trade: the case of Senegal", *Economic History Review* 21 (2) 1968.

Niane, Djibril Tamsir, *Histoire des Mandingues de l'ouest: le royaume du Gabou* (Paris: Karthala, 1989).

Niang, Doudou Sarr and Sidibe Pape Demba, "Boribana, dernier refuge des contrebandières", *Le Soleil* 11–12 September 1999.

Nicolaj, Andrea, "The Senegal Mauritanian Conflict", *Africa* (Rome) 45 (3) 1990.

Nkrumah, Kwame, *Africa Must Unite* (New York: International Publishers, 1963).

Nouhou, Alhadji-Bouba, *Islam et politique au Nigeria: Genèse et évolution de la chari'a* (Paris: Karthala, 2005).

Ntagungire, Carpophore, "Togo Revenue Authority: a model for good tax governance" (2 July 2015), www.afdb.org/en/blogs/measuring-the-pulse-of-economic-transformation-in-west-africa/post/togo-revenue-authority-a-model-for-good-tax-governance-14486/

Nugent, Paul, "Rural Producers and the State in Ghana, 1972–1979", unpublished MA dissertation, School of Oriental and African Studies, London, 1984.
  Big Men, Small Boys and Politics in Ghana: Power, Ideology and the Burden of History, 1982–1994 (London and New York: Frances Pinter, 1995).
  "An abandoned project? The nuances of chieftaincy, development and history in Ghana's Volta Region", *Journal of Legal Pluralism and Unofficial Law* 37–28, 1996.
  "Arbitrary lines and the people's minds: a dissenting view on colonial boundaries in West Africa", in Paul Nugent and A.I. Asiwaju (eds.), *African Boundaries: Barriers, Conduits and Opportunities* (London: Frances Pinter, 1996).
  Smugglers, Secessionists and Loyal Citizens on the Ghana–Togo Frontier: The Lie of the Borderlands Since 1914 (Oxford and Athens: James Currey and Ohio University Press, 2002).

"African Studies in Britain", in David Dabydeen, John Gilmore and Cecily Jones (eds.), *The Oxford Companion to Black British History* (Oxford: Oxford University Press, 2007).

"Cyclical history in the Gambia/Casamance borderlands: refuge, settlement and Islam from c.1880 to the present", *Journal of African History* 48 (2) 2007.

"Putting the history back into ethnicity: enslavement, religion and cultural brokerage in the construction of Mandinka/Jola and Ewe/Agotime identities in West Africa", *Comparative Studies in Society and History* 50 (4) 2008.

"States and social contracts in Africa", *New Left Review* 63, May–June 2010.

"Border towns and cities in comparative perspective", in Thomas M. Wilson and Hastings Donnan (eds.), *A Companion to Border Studies* (Chichester: Wiley-Blackwell, 2012).

Africa Since Independence: A Comparative History, 2nd edn. (London and New York: Palgrave Macmillan, 2012).

Nugent, Paul and Asiwaju, A.I., "Introduction: the paradox of African boundaries", in Paul Nugent and A.I. Asiwaju (eds.), *African Boundaries: Barriers, Conduits and Opportunities* (London: Frances Pinter, 1996).

O'Brien, Patrick K., "Fiscal exceptionalism: Great Britain and its European rivals from Civil War to triumph at Trafalgar and Waterloo", in Donald Winch and Patrick K. O'Brien, *The Political Economy of British Historical Experience, 1688–1914* (Oxford: Oxford University Press for British Academy, 2002).

Ochonu, Moses, *Colonial Meltdown: Northern Nigeria in the Great Depression* (Athens: Ohio University Press, 2009).

Olivier de Sardan, Jean-Pierre, "Practical norms: informal regulations within public bureaucracies (in Africa and beyond)", in Tom de Herdt and Jean-Pierre Olivier de Sardan (eds.), *Real Governance and Practical Norms in Sub-Saharan Africa: The Game of the Rules* (Abingdon and New York: Routledge, 2015).

Oquaye, Mike, *Politics in Ghana, 1972–1979* (Accra: Tornado, 1980).

Owusu, Maxwell, "Politics without parties: reflections on the Union Government proposals in Ghana", *African Studies Review* 22 (1) 1979.

Parker, John, *Making the Town: Ga State and Society in Early Colonial Accra* (Portsmouth, Oxford and Cape Town: Heinemann, James Currey and David Philip, 2000).

Paye, Moussa, "The regime and the press", in Momar Coumba Diop (ed.), *Senegal: Essays in Statecraft* (Dakar: CODESRIA, 1993).

Pearce, Robert D., *The Turning Point in Africa: British Colonial Policy 1938–48* (London: Frank Cass, 1982).

"The Colonial Office and planned decolonization in Africa", *African Affairs* 83 (330) 1984.

Pélissier, Paul, *Les paysans du Sénégal: les civilisations agraires de Cayor à la Casamance* (Saint-Yrieix: author, 1966).

Peña, Elaine A., "Paso Libre: border enactment, infrastructure, and crisis resolution at the port of Laredo 1954–1957", *TDR: The Drama Review* 61 (2) 2017.

Peterson, Derek, *Ethnic Patriotism and the East African Revival: A History of Dissent, c.1935–1972* (Cambridge: Cambridge University Press, 2012).

Peterson, Derek R. and Giacomo Macola (eds.), *Recasting the Past: History Writing and Political Work in Modern Africa* (Athens: Ohio University Press, 2009).

Pfeffermann, Guy, *Industrial Labor in the Republic of Senegal* (New York, Washington and London: Praeger, 1968).

Phillips, Anne, *The Enigma of Colonialism: British Policy in West Africa* (London, Bloomington and Indianapolis: Indiana University Press, 1989).

Phillips, Lucie Colvin, "The Senegambia Confederation", in Christopher L. Delgado and Sidi Jammeh (eds.), *The Political Economy of Senegal under Structural Adjustment* (New York, Westport and London: Praeger, 1991).

Prior, Christopher, *Exporting Empire: Africa, Colonial Officials and the Construction of the British Imperial State* (Manchester: Manchester University Press, 2015).

Proctor, J.H., "The Gambia's relations with Senegal: the search for partnership", *Journal of Commonwealth Political Studies* 5 (2) 1967.

Quinn, Charlotte A. *Mandingo Kingdoms of the Senegambia: Traditionalism, Islam and European Expansion* (London and Evanston: Longman, 1972).

Radelet, Steven C. and McPherson, Malcolm F., "Epilogue: the July 1994 coup d'etat", in Malcolm F. McPherson and Steven C. Radelet (eds.), *Economic Recovery in the Gambia: Insights for Structural Adjustment in Sub-Saharan Africa* (Cambridge: Harvard University Press, 1995).

Raeymaekers, Tim, *Violent Capitalism and Hybrid Identity in Eastern Congo: Power to the Margins* (Cambridge: Cambridge University Press, 2014).

Ramseyer, F.A. and Kühne, J., *Four Years in Ashantee by the Missionaries Ramseyer and Kühne* (London: C. Nisbet, 1975).

Ranger, Terence, "Nationalist historiography, patriotic history and the history of the nation: the struggle over the past in Zimbabwe", *Journal of Southern African Studies* 30 (2) 2004.

Rathbone, Richard, *Nkrumah and the Chiefs: Politics of Chieftaincy in Ghana, 1951–60* (Athens: Ohio University Press, 2000).

Reeve, Henry Fenwick, *The Gambia, Its History Ancient, Medieval and Modern Together with Its Geographical, Geological and Ethnographic Condition and a Description of the Birds, Beasts and Fishes Found Therein* (New York: Negro Universities Press, 1969, reprint of 1912 original).

Reindorf, Carl, *The History of the Gold Coast and Asante, Based on Traditions and Historical Facts Comprising a Period of More than Three Centuries from About 1500 to 1860* (Accra: Ghana Universities Press, 1966 (1st edn. 1889)).

Ribot, Jesse, "Forestry policy and charcoal production in Senegal", *Energy Policy* 21 (5) 1993.

Rice, Berkeley, *Enter Gambia: The Birth of an Improbable Nation* (London: Angus and Robertson, 1968).

Rimmer, Douglas, *Staying Poor: Ghana's Political Economy, 1950–1990* (Oxford, New York, Seoul and Tokyo: Pergamon Press, 1992).

Robertson, Claire, "The death of Makola and other tragedies: male strategies against a female-dominated system", *Canadian Journal of African Studies*, 17 (3) 1983.

Robinson, David, *The Holy War of Umar Tal: The Western Sudan in the Mid-Nineteenth Century* (Oxford: Clarendon Press, 1985).

Paths of Accommodation: Muslim Societies and French Colonial Authorities in Senegal and Mauritania, 1880–1920 (Oxford and Athens: James Currey and Ohio University Press, 2000).

Robinson, Ronald and Gallagher, John (with Alice Denny), *Africa and the Victorians: The Official Mind of Imperialism*, 2nd edn. (London: Macmillan, 1981).

Roche, Christian, *Histoire de la Casamance: conquête et résistance, 1850–1920* (Paris: Karthala, 1985).

Rodet, Marie, *Les migrantes ignorées du Haut-Sénégal, 1900–1946* (Paris: Karthala, 2009).

Rosenthal, Judy, *Possession, Ecstasy and Law in Ewe Voodoo* (Charlottesville: University of Virginia Press, 1998).

Ross, Eric, *Sufi City: Urban Design and Archetypes in Touba* (Rochester and Woodbridge: University of Rochester Press, 2006).

Sahlins, Peter, "The nation in the village: state-building and communal struggles in the Catalan borderland during the eighteenth and nineteenth centuries", *The Journal of Modern History*, 60 (2) 1988.

Boundaries: The Making of France and Spain in the Pyrenees (Berkeley and London: California Press, 1989).

Saine, Abdoulaye, "The coup d'etat in the Gambia, 1994: the end of the First Republic", *Armed Forces and Society* 23 (1) 1996.

The Paradox of Third-Wave Democratization in Africa: The Gambia Under AFPRC-APRC Rule, 1994–2008 (Lanham and Plymouth: Lexington Books, 2009).

Sallah, Tjan, "Economics and politics in the Gambia", *Journal of Modern African Studies* 28 (4) 1990.

Sané, Sokhna, *Le côntrole des armes à feu en Afrique occidentale française 1834–1958* (Paris and Dakar: Karthala and CREPOS, 2008).

Sarr, Assan, *Islam, Power and Dependency in the Gambia River Basin: The Politics of Land Control, 1790–1940* (Rochester: University of Rochester Press, 2016).

Sassen, Saskia, *Territory: Authority, Rights: From Medieval to Global Assemblages* (Princeton: Princeton University Press, 2006).

Schatzberg, Michael, *Political Legitimacy in Middle Africa: Father, Family, Food* (Bloomington: Indiana University Press, 2001).

Scheele, Judith, *Smugglers and Saints of the Sahara: Regional Connectivity in the Twentieth Century* (Cambridge: Cambridge University Press, 2012).

Scheld, Suzanne "Racism, 'free-trade' and consumer 'protection': the controversy of Chinese 'petty traders' in Dakar, Senegal", in Palvi Hoikkala and Dorothy D. Wills (eds.), *Dimensions of International Migration* (Newcastle: Cambridge Scholars, 2011).

Schmidt, Elizabeth, *Mobilizing the Masses: Gender, Ethnicity, and Class in the Nationalist Movement in Guinea* (Portsmouth: Heinemann, 2005).

Schroeder, Richard, *Shady Practices: Agroforestry and Gender Politics in the Gambia* (Berkeley, Los Angeles and London: University of California Press, 1999).

Schumacher, Edward J., *Politics, Bureaucracy and Rural Development in Senegal* (Berkeley, Los Angeles and London: University of California Press, 1975).

Scott, James C., *Domination and the Arts of Resistance: Hidden Transcripts* (New Haven: Yale University Press, 1992).

Seeing Like a State: How Certain Schemes to Improve the Human Condition Have Failed (New Haven: Yale University Press, 1999).

The Art of Not Being Governed: An Anarchist History of Upland Southeast Asia (New Haven and London: Yale University Press, 2009).

Searing, James F., *West African Slavery and Atlantic Commerce: The Senegal River Valley, 1700–1860* (Cambridge: Cambridge University Press, 1993).

'*God Alone is King': Islam and Emancipation in Senegal – The Wolof Kingdoms of Kajoor and Bawol, 1859–1914* (Portsmouth, Oxford and Cape Town: Heinemann, James Currey and David Philip, 2002).

Sebald, Peter, *Togo 1884–1914: Eine Geschichte der deutschen 'Musterkolonie' auf der Grundlage amtlicher Quellen* (Berlin: Akademie-Verlag, 1988).

Seely, Jennifer C., *The Legacies of Transition Governments in Africa: The Cases of Benin and Togo* (New York: Palgrave Macmillan, 2009).

Senghor, Jeggan C. *The Politics of Senegambian Integration, 1958–1994* (New York: Peter Lang, 2008).

Shaw, Rosalind, *Memories of the Slave Trade: Ritual and the Historical Imagination in Sierra Leone* (Chicago and London: University of Chicago Press, 2002).

Sheperd, A.W., "The Development of Capitalist Rice Farming in Northern Ghana", unpublished PhD thesis, University of Cambridge, 1979.

Sherman, Taylor C., Gould, William and Ansari, Sarah (eds.), *From Subjects to Citizens: Society and the State in India and Pakistan, 1947–1970* (Delhi and New York: Cambridge University Press, 2014).

Sidibé, Al Haji Bakary, *A Brief History of Kaabu and Fuladu (1300–1930): A Narrative Based on Some Oral Traditions of the Senegambia (West Africa)* (Torino: L'Harmattan Italia, 2004).

Simone, Abdoumaliq, *For the City Yet to Come: Changing African Life in Four Cities* (Durham: Duke University Press, 2004).

Simpson, James, *Creating Wine: The Emergence of a World Industry, 1840–1914* (Princeton and Oxford: Princeton University Press, 2011).

Sinou, Alain, *Comptoirs et villes coloniales du Sénégal: Saint-Louis, Gorée, Dakar* (Paris: Karthala, 1993).

Skinner, David E., "The incorporation of Muslim elites into the colonial administrative systems of Sierra Leone, the Gambia and the Gold Coast", *Journal of Muslim Minority Affairs* 29 (1) March 2009.

"Islam in Kombo: the spiritual and militant jihad of Fode Ibrahim Ture", *Islamic Africa* 3 (1) 2012.

Skinner, Kate, *The Fruits of Freedom in Togoland: Literacy, Politics and Nationalism, 1914–2014* (Cambridge: Cambridge University Press, 2015).

Smith, Jonathan Vaughan, "The Jolas of Senegambia, West Africa: Ethnolinguistic Identity and Change Across an International Border", PhD thesis, University of Oregon, 1993 (Ann Arbor: UMI Dissertation Services, 1993).

Soi, Isabella and Nugent, Paul, "Peripheral urbanism: border towns and twin towns in Africa", *Journal of Borderlands Studies*, 32 (4) 2017.

Somerville, Carolyn, "The impact of reforms on the urban population: how the Dakarois view the crisis", in Christopher L. Delgado and Sidi Jammeh (eds.), *The Political Economy of Senegal under Structural Adjustment* (New York, Westport and London: Praeger, 1991).

Spear, Thomas, "Neo-traditionalism and the limits of invention in British colonial Africa", *Journal of African History* 44 (1) 2003.

Spire, Amandine, "Kodjoviakopé à Lomé: le temps et la constitution d'un territoire urbain", in Philippe Gervais-Lambony and Gabriel Kwami Nyassogbo (eds.), *Lomé: dynamiques d'une ville africaine* (Paris: Karthala, 2007).

Sprigge, R.G.S. "Ewelands's Adangbe: an enquiry into an oral tradition", *Transactions of the Historical Society of Ghana* X, 1969.

Staff writer, "Cocoa smuggling: some reasons", *CMB Newsletter* 45, August 1970.

Steinberger, Peter J., *The Idea of the State* (Cambridge: Cambridge University Press, 2009).

Stoller, Paul, *Money Has No Smell: The Africanization of New York* (Chicago and London: Chicago University Press, 2002).

Stone, Jeffrey C. (ed.), *Maps and Africa: Proceedings of a Colloquium at the University of Aberdeen, April 1993* (Aberdeen: Aberdeen University African Studies Group, 1994).

Storsveen, Tove (ed.), *Closing the Books: Governor Edward Carstensen on Danish Guinea 1842–50* (Accra: Sub-Saharan Publishers, 2010).

Strickrodt, Silke, *Afro-European Trade in the Atlantic World: The Western Slave Coast, c.1550–1885* (Woodbridge and Rochester: James Currey, 2015).

Swindell, Kenneth and Jeng, Alieu, *Migrants, Credit and Climate: The Gambian Groundnut Trade, 1834–1934* (Leiden: Brill, 2007).

Sylvanus, Nina, "Chinese devils, the global market and the declining power of Togo's Nana-Benzes", *African Studies Review* 56 (1) 2013.

Patterns in Circulation: Cloth, Gender and Materiality in West Africa (Chicago and London: University of Chicago Press, 2016).

Tagliacozzo, Eric, *Secret Trades, Porous Borders: Smuggling and States along a Southeast Asian Frontier, 1865–1915* (New Haven and London: Yale University Press, 2005).

Thom, D.J., *The Nigeria–Niger Boundary, 1890–1906: A Study of Ethnic Frontiers and a Colonial Boundary*, Africa Series, 23 (Athens: Ohio University, Center for International Studies, 2005).

Thomas, Louis-Vincent, *Les Diola; essai d'analyse fonctionnelle sur une population de Basse-Casamance, Mémoires de l'Institut Français d'Afrique Noire* (Dakar: IFAN, 1958).

Thomas, Martin (ed.), *The French Colonial Mind, Volume 1: Mental Maps of Empire and Colonial Encounters* (Lincoln: University of Nebraska Press, 2012).

Thomas, Martin *The French Colonial Mind, Volume 2: Violence, Military Encounters and Colonialism* (Lincoln: University of Nebraska Press, 2012).

Thompson, Virginia and Adloff, Richard, *French West Africa* (Stanford: Stanford University Press, 1957).

"French economic policy in tropical Africa", in Peter Duignan and L.H. Gann (eds.), *Colonialism in Africa, 1870–1960 – Volume 4: The Economics of Colonialism* (Cambridge: Cambridge University Press, 1975).

Thompson, W. Scott, *Ghana's Foreign Policy, 1957–1966: Diplomacy, Ideology, and the New State* (Princeton: Princeton University Press, 1969).

Thomson, Steven K., "Children of the Village: Peace and Local Citizenship in a Multiethnic Gambian Community", PhD thesis, Boston University, 2006.

Throup, David, *Economic and Social Origins of Mau Mau, 1943–53* (London: James Currey, 1987).

Tilly, Charles, *Coercion, Capital and European States AD 990–1992* (Oxford: Blackwell, 1990).

Tolliver-Diallo, Wilmetta J., "'The woman who was more than a man': making Aline Sitoe Diatta into a national heroine in Senegal", *Canadian Journal of African Studies* 39 (2) 2005.

Toulabor, Comi M., *Le Togo sous Eyadéma* (Paris: Karthala, 1986).

Touray, Omar A., *The Gambia and the World: A History of the Foreign Policy of Africa's Smallest State, 1965–1995* (Hamburg: Institute of African Studies, 2000).

Touval, Saadia, *Somali Nationalism: International Politics and the Drive for Unity in the Horn of Africa* (Harvard: Center for International Affairs, 1963).

The Boundary Politics of Independent Africa (Cambridge: Harvard University Press, 1972).

Trémolières, Marie and Walther, Oliver J. (eds.), *Cross-Border Co-operation and Policy Networks in West Africa* (Paris: OECD/Sahel and West Africa Club, 2017).

Tsigbe, Kofi Nutefé, "Cinquante ans de discours sur l'unité national au Togo (1960–2010): les leçons d'une politique toujours de l'actualité", in Theodore Nicoué Gayibor (ed.), *Cinquante ans d'independance an Afrique subsaharienne et au Togo* (Paris: L'Harmattan, 2012).

Tsing, Anna, *Friction: An Ethnography of Global Connection* (Princeton: Princeton University Press, 2004).

Turner, Frederick Jackson, *The Frontier in American History* (New York: Henry Holt and Co., 1921).

Twumasi, Yaw, "The 1969 elections", in Dennis Austin and Robin Luckham (eds.), *Politicians and Soldiers in Ghana, 1966–1972* (London: Frank Cass, 1972).

Ustorf, Werner, *Bremen Missionaries in Togo and Ghana: 1847–1900* (Legon: Legon Theological Studies and Asempa, 2002).

Valji, Nahla, *Ghana's National Reconciliation Commission: A Comparative Assessment* (New York: International Center for Transitional Justice, 2006).

Van de Walle, Nicolas, *African Economies and the Politics of Permanent Crisis, 1979–1999* (Cambridge: Cambridge University Press, 2001).

Van den Bersselaar, Dmitri, "'Somebody must necessarily go to buy this drink': gin smugglers, chiefs and the state in colonial Ghana", *Cultural and Social History* 11 (2) 2014.

Van Rouveroy Van Nieuwaal, E. Adriaan B., *L'état en Afrique face à la chefferie: le cas du Togo* (Paris: Karthala, 2000).

Venkatachalam, Meera, *Slavery, Memory and Religion in Southeastern Ghana, c.1850 to the Present* (Cambridge: Cambridge University Press, 2015).

Verdon, Michel, *The Abutia of West Africa: A Chiefdom That Never Was* (Berlin, New York and Amsterdam: Mouton, 1983).

Villalón, Leonardo, *Islamic Society and State Power in Senegal: Disciples and Citizens in Fatick* (Cambridge: Cambridge University Press, 2006).

Von Trotha, Trutz, *Koloniale Herrschaft: zur sociologischen Theorie der Staatsentstehung am Beispiel des 'Schutzgebietes Togo'* (Tübingen: Mohr, 1994).

Wai, Zubairu, "Neo-patrimonialism and the discourse of state failure in Africa", *Review of African Political Economy* 39 (131) 2012.

Walther, Olivier, *Affaires des patrons: villes et commerce transfrontalier au Sahel* (Berne and Oxford: Peter Lang, 2008).

"Trade networks in West Africa: a social network approach", *Journal of Modern African Studies* 52 (2), 2014.

Waterbury, John, "Dimensions of state intervention in the groundnut basin", in Mark Gersovitz and John Waterbury (eds.), *The Political Economy of Risk and Choice in Senegal* (London: Frank Cass, 1987).

"The Senegalese peasant: how good is our conventional wisdom?", in Mark Gersovitz and John Waterbury (eds.), *The Political Economy of Risk and Choice in Senegal* (London: Frank Cass, 1987).

Watts, Michael J., "Idioms of land and labor: producing politics and rice in Senegambia", in Thomas Bassett and Donald Crummey (eds.), *Land in African Agrarian Systems* (Madison: University of Wisconsin Press, 1993).

Welch, Claude, *Dream of Unity: Pan-Africanism and Political Unification in West Africa* (Ithaca: Cornell University Press, 1966).

Welman, C.W., *The Native States of the Gold Coast: History and Constitution* (London: Dawsons of Pall Mall, 1969) (part I on Peki first published in 1925).

Wesseling, H.L., *Divide and Rule: The Partition of Africa 1880–1914* (Westport: Praeger, 1996).

White, Benjamin Thomas, *The Emergence of Minorities in the Middle East: The Politics of Community in French Mandate Syria* (Edinburgh: Edinburgh University Press, 2011).

Wiemers, Alice, "A 'time of Agric': rethinking the 'failure' of agricultural programs in 1970s Ghana", *World Development* 66, 2015

Wilks, Ivor, *Asante in the Nineteenth Century: The Structure and Evolution of a Political Order* (Cambridge: Cambridge University Press, 1975).

Akwamu, 1640–1750: A Study of the Rise and Fall of a West African Empire (Trondheim: Norwegian University of Science and Technology, 2001).

"'Mallams don't fight with the heathen': a note on Suwarian attitudes to jihad", *Ghana Studies* 5, 2002.

Willis, Justin, "Tradition, tribe and state in Kenya: The Mijikenda Union, 1945–1980, *Comparative Studies in Society and History* 55 (2) 2013.

Willis, Justin and Gona, George, "Pwani C Kenya? Memory, documents and secessionist politics in coastal Kenya", *African Affairs* 112 (446) 2013.

Wilson, Louis, *The Krobo People of Ghana to 1892: A Political and Social History* (Athens: Ohio University, 1991).

Wilson, Thomas and Donnan, Hastings (eds.), *The Blackwell Companion to Border Studies* (Chichester: Wiley-Blackwell, 2012).

Winsnes, Selena Axelrod (ed.), *Letters on West Africa and the Slave Trade: Paul Erdman Isert's 'Journey to Guinea and the Caribbean Islands in Columbia' (1788)* (Accra: Sub-Saharan Publishers, 2007).

Winsnes, Selena Axelrod *Two Views from Christiansborg Castle: Volume I – A Brief and Truthful Description of a Journey To and From Guinea by Johannes Rask* (Accra: Sub-Saharan Publishers, 2008).

Two Views from Christiansborg Castle: Volume II – A Description of the Guinea Coast and Its Inhabitants by H.C. Monrad (Accra: Sub-Saharan Publishers, 2008).

World Bank, *Current Economic Position and Prospects for Senegal* (Washington DC: World Bank, 1968).

Senegal: Tradition, Diversification and Economic Development (Washington DC: World Bank, 1974).

The Gambia: Basic Needs in the Gambia (Washington DC: World Bank, 1981).

Report and Recommendation of the President of the International Development Association to the Executive Directors on a Proposed Credit of SDR 36.9 Million to the Republic of Togo for a Structural Adjustment Project (Washington DC: World Bank, 1983)

Wright, Donald, *The Early History of Niumi: Settlement and Foundation of a Mandinka State on the Gambia River* (Athens: Ohio University Center for International Studies, 1977).

"Beyond migration and conquest: oral traditions and Mandinka ethnicity in Senegambia", *History in Africa* 12, 1985.

The World and a Very Small Place: A History of Globalization in Niumi, the Gambia (New York and London: M.E. Sharpe, 2004).

Wyse, Akintola, *The Krio of Sierra Leone: An Interpretive History* (London: C. Hurst, 1989).

Yarak, Larry, *Asante and the Dutch, 1744–1873* (Oxford: Clarendon Press, 1990).

Youm, Prosper, "The economy since independence", in Christopher L. Delgado and Sidi Jammeh (eds.), *The Political Economy of Senegal under Structural Adjustment* (New York, Westport and London: Praeger, 1991).

Young, Crawford, *The African Colonial State in Comparative Perspective* (New Haven and London: Yale University Press, 1994).

Zachariah, K.C. and Condé, Julien, *Migration in West Africa: Demographic Aspects* (Washington DC: World Bank and OECD, 1981).

Zimmerman, Andrew, *Alabama in Africa: Booker T. Washington, the German Empire and the Globalization of the New South* (Princeton: Princeton University Press, 2010).

Zuccarelli, François, *Un parti unique Africain: l'Union Progressiste Sénégalaise* (Paris: Pichon et Durand-Auzias, 1970).

Index

African Studies Series